SAMUEL D. KASSOW

Who Will Write Our History?

Samuel D. Kassow is the Charles Northam Professor of
History at Trinity College. He is author of *Students, Professors, and the State in Tsarist Russia, 1884–1917* and editor
(with Edith W. Clowes and James L. West) of *Between Tsar
and People: The Search for a Public Identity in Tsarist Russia*. He has lectured on Russian and Jewish history in many
countries, including Israel, Russia, and Poland.

ALSO BY SAMUEL D. KASSOW

Students, Professors, and the State in Tsarist Russia, 1884–1917

Between Tsar and People:
The Search for a Public Identity in Tsarist Russia
(As Editor, with Edith W. Clowes and James L. West)

Who Will Write Our History?

Who Will Write Our History?

REDISCOVERING A HIDDEN ARCHIVE
FROM THE WARSAW GHETTO

SAMUEL D. KASSOW

VINTAGE BOOKS
A Division of Random House, Inc.
New York

FIRST VINTAGE BOOKS EDITION, JANUARY 2009

Copyright © 2007 by Samuel D. Kassow

All rights reserved. Published in the United States by Vintage Books, a division of
Random House, Inc., New York, and in Canada by Random House of
Canada Limited, Toronto. Originally published in hardcover
in the United States by Indiana University Press,
Bloomington, in 2007.

Vintage and colophon are registered trademarks of Random House, Inc.

Published with the generous support of the Helen and Martin Schwartz Endowment.

Library of Congress Cataloging-in-Publication Data
Kassow, Samuel D.
Who will write our history? : rediscovering a hidden archive from the Warsaw Ghetto /
Samuel D. Kassow.
p. cm.
ISBN: 978-0-307-45586-4
Originally published: Indiana University Press, Bloomington and Indianapolis, in 2007.
Includes bibliographical references and index.
1. Jews—Persecutions—Poland—Warsaw. 2. Oyneg Shabes (Group). 3. Holocaust,
Jewish (1939–1945)—Poland—Warsaw—History. 4. Warsaw (Poland)—History—Warsaw
Ghetto Uprising, 1943. 5. Ringelblum, Emanuel, 1900–1944. I. Title.
DS134.64.K37 2008
940.53'1853841—dc22
2008035499

www.vintagebooks.com

Printed in the United States of America
10 9 8 7 6 5 4 3 2 1

Dedicated to my wife Lisa,
my daughters Miri and Serena,
and to the loving memory
of my parents
Jacob Kassow and Celia Kassow

Efsher veln oykh di verter
Dervartn zikh ven oyf dem likht—
Veln in sho in basherter
Tseblien zikh umgerikht?

Un vi der uralter kern
Vos hot zikh farvandlt in zang—
Veln di verter oykh nern,
Veln di verter gehern
Dem folk, in zayn eybikn gang.

[Perhaps these words will endure
And live to see the light loom—
And in the destined hour
Will unexpectedly bloom?

And like the primeval grain
That turned into a stalk—
The words will nourish,
The words will belong
To the people, in its eternal walk.]

—Avrom Sutzkever,
"Grains of Wheat,"
Vilna Ghetto, March 1943.

Translated by
Barbara and Benjamin Harshav

CONTENTS

Acknowledgments xi
Note on Language Use xiii

Introduction 1

1 **From "Bichuch" to Warsaw** 17

2 **Borochov's Disciple** 27

3 **History for the People** 49

4 **Organizing the Community** SELF-HELP AND RELIEF 90

5 **A Band of Comrades** 145

6 **The Different Voices of Polish Jewry** 209

7 **Traces of Life and Death** TEXTS FROM THE ARCHIVE 225

8 **The Tidings of Job** 285

9 **A Historian's Final Mission** 333

Appendix A. Guidelines for a Study of Polish-Jewish Relations 389
Appendix B. Guidelines for a Study of the Warsaw Ghetto 393
Appendix C. Guidelines for a Study of the Jewish Shtetl 396
Notes 401
Selected Bibliography 481
Index 495

Photographs appear after pages 144 and 284.

ACKNOWLEDGMENTS

Many people helped me in this daunting and difficult project. David Roskies encouraged me to begin this book and I learned a lot from many conversations we had and from comments on earlier versions of the manuscript. Havi Ben Sasson graciously took the time to share her enormous knowledge of the subject and read an earlier version of the manuscript. I am deeply grateful to Josephine Woll, Robert Shapiro, Justin Cammy, Berel Lang, Greta Slobin, Mark Slobin, Lisa Kassow, Lisa Grant, May Pleskow, Susan Pennybacker, Natalia Aleksiun, Ronald Spencer, and Kathleen Kete for their careful readings of this work and for their important suggestions, and to Raya Cohen, Joanna Michlic, Ben Nathans, Michael Steinlauf, Nancy Sherman, Aaron Lansky, and Ronald Kiener for their comments on earlier articles and chapter drafts. I appreciate the productive conversations I had with Gunnar Stephen Paulsson about the Ringelblum-Berman correspondence and fruitful discussions with Israel Gutman, Dani Blatman, and Alvin Rosenfeld.

I would like to thank Deans Miller Brown and Steve Peterson for the financial support I received from Trinity College and for the dedicated work of Gigi St. Peter, the history department administrative associate at Trinity, and Mary Curry, the interlibrary loan librarian. Ewa Wolynska of Central Connecticut State University helped me decipher many Polish handwritten documents. I am very grateful to Michlean Amir, archivist at the United States Memorial Holocaust Museum, to the entire staff of the Yad Vashem Archives in Jerusalem, and to the staff of the Ghetto Fighters' Museum at Beit Lohamei Ha-getaot. I am indebted to Eleonora Bergman of the Jewish Historical Institute of Warsaw who helped in my research there, and who read my work and gave me invaluable suggestions. I also thank Jan Jagielski of the Jewish Historical Institute and Elana Weiser of Yad Vashem for their help in making photographic reproductions available to me from their collections. My work in Poland benefited greatly from the kindness of Dr. Feliks Tych, the director of the Jewish Historical Institute, and from Professor Monika Garbowska of the Marie Curie University in Lublin. Alan Schiffman endowed a Trinity research fund which aided my research significantly. I am also grateful to the staff of the YIVO archives and library, including Fruma Mohrer, Marek Webb, Leo Greenbaum, Aviva Astrinsky, and Yeihaya Metal.

I warmly acknowledge the financial support I received from the International Research and Exchanges Board (IREX).

I thankfully appreciate and acknowledge the magisterial scholarship of Ruta Sakowska, whose work on Ringelblum taught me much. I owe a large debt of gratitude to my editor Janet Rabinowitch of Indiana University Press for her patience and encouragement, and to Miki Bird, Jen Maceyko, and Rita Bernhard.

Finally, a heartfelt thank you to my loving wife Lisa, and to my special daughters Miri and Serena, who will always remind me of what is most important in life.

NOTE ON LANGUAGE USE

How to spell the names of cities like Warsaw, Lodz, Lwów, Vilna, or Krakow is not an easy matter to decide. In the multinational spaces of Eastern Europe, which saw frequent changes in political sovereignty until the end of World War II, cities were often known under different names. The Polish Lwów was the Austrian-German Lemberg and the Ukrainian L'viv. Jews, who made up a sizable proportion of the city's inhabitants often used the Yiddish Lemberik or Lemberg, especially when the city was part of the Austro-Hungarian Empire. Vilna presents even greater problems. Claimed by Poles (Wilno), Lithuanians (Vilnius), and Belorussians (Vil'na), Vilna changed hands seven times just between the years 1915 and 1922! Vilna Jews, who modestly believed that they were living in Yerushalyim d'Lite, the Jerusalem of Lithuania, called Vilna by its Yiddish name, Vilne.

The proper Polish spellings of Warsaw and Lodz are Warszawa and Łódź. Poznan, Posen in German, is spelled Poznań. The proper spelling of Krakow or Cracow is Kraków.

To simplify matters this book will use common English spellings for large cities like Warsaw, Lodz, and Krakow. Lwów will remain Lwów while Wilno will be called Vilna. Smaller cities will receive proper Polish spellings with diacritics.

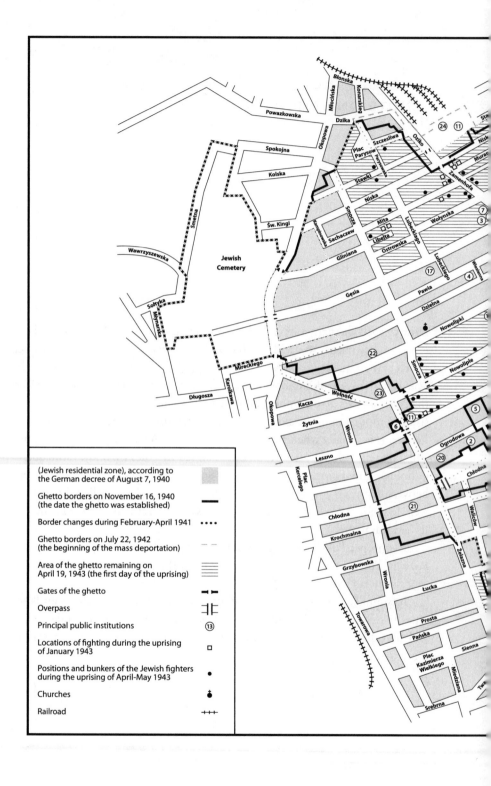

(Jewish residential zone), according to
the German decree of August 7, 1940

Ghetto borders on November 16, 1940
(the date the ghetto was established)

Border changes during February-April 1941

Ghetto borders on July 22, 1942
(the beginning of the mass deportation)

Area of the ghetto remaining on
April 19, 1943 (the first day of the uprising)

Gates of the ghetto

Overpass

Principal public institutions

Locations of fighting during the uprising
of January 1943

Positions and bunkers of the Jewish fighters
during the uprising of April-May 1943

Churches

Railroad

The Warsaw Ghetto
1940 - 1943

0   500

meters

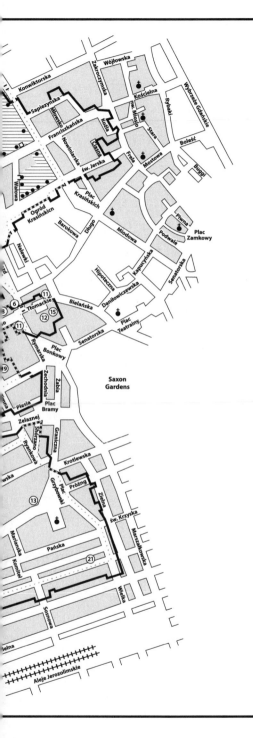

Principal Public Institutions

1. *Judenrat*
2. Order Authority (Jewish Police)
3. Jewish Prison (Gęsiowka)
4. Pawiak Prison
5. Courts
6. Labor Department (*Arbeitsamt*)
7. Post Office
8. Supply Authority
9. Office to Combat Usury and Profiteering
10. Berson and Bauman Hospital
11. Czyste Hospital
12. The Great Synagogue
13. Nozyk Synagogue
14. Moriah Synagogue
15. Ż.T.O.S.
16. Centos
17. TOZ
18. ORT
19. Toporol
20. Center for Professional Studies
21. Orphanage (Janusz Korczak, director)
22. Oyneg Shabes Archive
23. Deportation Center
24. *Umschlagplatz*

Who Will Write Our History?

Introduction

September 18, 1946. After weeks of preparation and planning, searchers had finally begun to dig under the rubble of Nowolipki 68 in the ruins of the former Warsaw Ghetto. They were looking for the buried Oyneg Shabes Archive. It was not an easy job. In the Warsaw Ghetto, the Oyneg Shabes—led by the historian Emanuel Ringelblum—had included dozens of men and women who documented and recorded Jewish life under the Nazi Occupation.[1] But this secret "sacred society," as Ringelblum called the Oyneg Shabes, shared the grim fate of Warsaw Jewry.

Only very few of Ringelblum's coworkers in the Oyneg Shabes survived the war. The journalist and writer Rachel Auerbach was one. Another was Hersh Wasser, who had been its secretary, and his wife, Bluma. Wasser himself had stayed alive by the slimmest of margins. In 1943 he jumped from a Treblinka-bound train. In 1944 Germans discovered his hideout in north Warsaw and killed three of his friends in a short, intense gunfight. But, once again, Wasser and his wife survived. Without Wasser directing the search, it is unlikely that the archive would have surfaced.

The diggers moved carefully. It was slow and dangerous work. Where the Warsaw Ghetto had once stood was now a scene of total destruction. Auerbach compared the painstaking efforts to locate the street and the building to an "archeological expedition."[2] Jews and Poles worked side by side. They dug deep tunnels under the debris, built ventilation shafts, and pushed long metal probes through the rocks and bricks. And then a probe hit something solid: a tin box covered in clay and tightly bound in string—and then nine more.

That September day Rachel Auerbach was in Lodz. For many weeks she worried over the fate of the archive. In one of her last meetings with Emanuel Ringelblum in the Warsaw Ghetto, the historian told her, with quiet confidence, that his comrades had hidden the "legend," as he called it,[3] and that it was safe "from fire and water." No matter what happened to them, the world would know about the final chapter of Polish Jewry and German crimes.

But Ringelblum's greatest fear was that no one would survive to tell the story and the world would never know about the archive. It was just six days before the Germans discovered his hideout when Ringelblum sent a letter to his close friend, Adolf Berman, asking him to make sure that news of the archive's location somehow reached the YIVO—the Yiddish Scientific Institute—in New York City.[4] "If none of us survives, at least let that remain."[5]

Now Auerbach wondered if it had all been in vain. Was the archive really there? Perhaps it burned down during the ghetto uprising. Maybe looters, looking for money or gold, had stumbled upon the precious documents and destroyed them.

But a sudden instinct told her that today would be the day. She hopped on a train to Warsaw and, upon arriving, rushed from the train station to the Jewish Historical Institute on Sienna Street. The moment she arrived she saw the excited staff—they had found the archive!

But initial euphoria, Auerbach recalled, quickly gave way to anxiety and depression. They could hear water in the boxes, and the boxes themselves were covered with a thick greenish mold. Would anything be readable? Experts from Polish libraries and museums stepped in to show the staff of the Jewish Historical Institute how to unpack the materials and how to dry the paper. Finally, they opened the first box. Auerbach and Wasser exchanged looks. The box contained the telltale notebooks that Eliyahu Gutkowski, one of the secretaries of the Oyneg Shabes, had distributed in the Warsaw Ghetto for essay assignments and reports.[6]

Another box contained a poignant message—the last wills and testaments of those who buried the precious cache of documents in the basement of Nowolipki 68. Before the war, the building had housed a Ber Borochov school, a secular Yiddish elementary school named after the hero of the Left Poalei Zion (LPZ), Ringelblum's political party. After the mass deportations to Treblinka began on July 22, 1942, Ringelblum and Wasser told the director of the school, Israel Lichtenstein, to bury the archive.[7]

Lichtenstein had been in charge of the "technical section" of the Oyneg Shabes. Since the start of the organization, only he knew the physical location of the essays and documents. Ringelblum had taken great care to ensure that, if he himself or other leaders of the archive fell into German hands, the secret would be safe.

Lichtenstein recruited two young members of the movement—David Graber and Nahum Grzywacz—to help him. As they worked against time to bury the archive—who knew when the killers would appear?—they wrote down their last messages for future generations. Here is what Graber, nineteen years old, wanted the world to remember:

> What we were unable to cry and shriek out to the world we buried in the ground. . . . I would love to see the moment in which the great treasure will be dug up and scream the truth at the world. So the world may know all. So the ones who did not live through it may be glad, and we may feel like veterans with medals on our chest. We would be the fathers, the teachers and educators of the future. . . . But no, we shall certainly not live to see it, and therefore I write my last will. May the treasure fall into good hands, may it last into better times, may it alarm and alert the world to what happened . . . in the twentieth century. . . . We may now die in peace. We fulfilled our mission. May history attest for us.[8]

The next day, August 3, 1942, Graber hastily penned a postscript:

> Neighboring street besieged. We are all feverish. Mood tense, we prepare for worst. We hurry. Probably soon we will do our last burying. Comrade Lichtenstein nervous. Grzywacz somewhat afraid. Myself indifferent. In my subconscious, a feeling I shall get out of all trouble. Good day. We must only manage to bury [the boxes]. Yes, even now we don't forget it. At work until the last moment.
>
> Monday, August 3rd, 4 PM

Israel Lichtenstein's testament recorded pride in a job well done. He was sure he had hidden the archive well; only Wasser would know where to find it. "I do not ask for any thanks, for any memorial, for any praise," wrote Lichtenstein. "I only wish to be remembered." And Lichtenstein's thoughts then turned to his wife, the gifted artist Gele Sekstein,[9] and his beloved twenty-month-old daughter, Margalit.

> I wish my wife to be remembered, Gele Sekstein. She has worked during the war years with children as an educator and teacher, has prepared stage sets, costumes for the children's theater . . . both of us get ready to meet and receive death.
>
> I wish my little daughter to be remembered. Margalit is 20 months old today. She has fully mastered the Yiddish language and speaks it perfectly. At nine months she began to speak Yiddish clearly. In intelligence she equals children of 3 or 4 years. I don't boast. People who witness it and tell me so are the staff teaching at the school at 68 Nowolipki

Street—Dr. Pola Follman, Mrs. Blit Herzlich, Mrs. Zagan and others. I don't lament my own life or that of my wife. I pity only this little nice and talented girl. She too deserves to be remembered.

All these testimonies also contained short autobiographical sketches. On the brink of death, as they buried the tin boxes on that hot summer night, Israel Lichtenstein, his wife, Gele Sekstein, and the two young men who helped them left their individual markers, touching reminders of personal lives and concerns. Gele Sekstein wrote: "My father was a shoemaker. His children from his first wife are not respectable, they are underworld people. My mother, on the other hand, came from a prestigious line—the Landau family. Because of a deformity—one of her hands was paralyzed—she had to marry my father. She did not have a good life and died young." Eighteen-year-old Nahum Grzywacz wanted to remind whoever found the archive that, because his family was poor, he was not able to finish his education. As he was writing his last testament, he suddenly heard that the Germans had blockaded his parents' building. "I am going to run to my parents and see if they are all right. I don't know what's going to happen to me. *Remember, my name is Nahum Grzywacz*"[10] (emphasis in original).

These last-minute testaments—with their poignant combination of personal and collective concerns—offer important insights into the entire Oyneg Shabes project. Clearly Lichtenstein, Grzywacz, and Graber drew comfort and meaning from the conviction that they were fulfilling a national mission of the highest importance. But part of that mission was to remind future generations that they were individuals. Understanding and memory had to focus not only on the collective catastrophe but also on the individual lives that the Germans were about to destroy. Similarly these were people who, like many other Polish Jews, had a deep sense of political commitment and intellectual engagement. Grzywacz, Graber, and Lichtenstein had been members of the same left-wing political party; Gele Sekstein had devoted her artistic talents to the struggle for secular Yiddish education and a better life for poor Jewish children. To understand and appreciate the Oyneg Shabes Archive, one must not forget that it grew out of this culture of dedication and concern.

Gele Sekstein, Israel Lichtenstein, and their little daughter did not die that week. Thanks to a well-constructed hideout in the same building where Lichtenstein hid the archive, they got a nine-month reprieve. One letter that survived in the archive shows how Sekstein doggedly fought to stay alive. On September 22, 1942, she sent a letter to "Hershel," one of the Jewish directors of Bernhard Hallman, a German woodworking enterprise in the ghetto. Sekstein was asking for a precious "number," a piece of paper that proved that she worked in a shop. Perhaps it might save her and her beloved child from the next roundup. Sekstein reminded Hershel that before the war she had been a noted artist whose work had even won financial support from the Polish Ministry of Education. And just one year ago her work with the ghetto's children had been recognized by Adam Czerniakow, the president of the Warsaw Judenrat, or Jewish Council, the administrative body that the Germans required Jews to form in each ghetto.

> I think I am now the last surviving Jewish painter . . . and perhaps one of the very few Jewish creative artists [writers, painters] who are left.
>
> In the future, I think, the Jewish people should not consist only of tailors, carpenters and shoemakers. There should also be creative artists and cultural figures. Therefore it is important to save the Jewish artist so that (after the war) he'll be able to help rebuild the Jewish people with the help of the pen and the brush. . . . I ask for little. Just give me a chance to live so that I can keep Jewish art alive."

At the bottom of the letter Sekstein noted that nothing came of her request.[11]

Still Sekstein and her husband somehow managed to hold on. In the fall of 1942 the news of German defeats at El Alamein and Stalingrad even gave them fleeting moments of hope. They lived to see the first armed Jewish resistance to the Germans in January 1943.[12] Then, in April 1943, time ran out. The night before the ghetto uprising began on April 19, a Monday, Emanuel Ringelblum had seen Lichtenstein in Brauer's Shop on Nalewki Street. When the battle began, Lichtenstein and his friend, Natan Smolar, another well-known figure in the LPZ, tried to make it back to their hideout on Nowolipki 68. They were never seen again.[13] Gele Sekstein and Margalit probably perished at the same time.

Sometime in February 1943 Lichtenstein buried a second part of the archive in two large aluminum milk cans.[14] He hid them under the same building, Nowolipki 68. Polish construction workers found them in December 1950. There was yet a third part of the archive, with valuable materials on the Jewish resistance, that was buried under Świętojerska 34 on April 4, 1943.[15] Intense searches under the building yielded nothing but a few charred pages of a diary kept by Shmuel Winter, a wealthy businessman who had helped raise money for the Oyneg Shabes in the ghetto.[16] Everything else had vanished.

STONE UNDER HISTORY'S WHEEL

The milk cans found in 1950 contained an essay written in Polish that tried to explain the place of the written word in the Warsaw Ghetto. The writer,

Gustawa Jarecka, had been a leftist author before the war with little interest in Jewish matters. Incarcerated in the ghetto with her two small children, Jarecka found a job working for the Judenrat. The Oyneg Shabes then recruited her to copy Judenrat documents for the secret archive.[17]

Like most of the other documents in this second part of the archive, this one, titled "The Last Stage of Resettlement Is Death," was written sometime after September 1942, when a lull in the deportations had begun. There were no illusions now about German plans for the Jews; the Jews remaining in the Warsaw Ghetto knew that they were living on borrowed time.

But Ringelblum continued the work of the Oyneg Shabes. As the dazed survivors asked themselves how long their reprieve would last, Ringelblum, Gutkowski, and Wasser fanned out through the shrunken ghetto to seek out essays and documents. They asked Jarecka to write about what she had seen. She began by trying to describe what it meant to write in the face of death. Indeed, she had only a few more months to live. In January 1943 she and her two children were deported to Treblinka.

"We have nooses fastened around our necks," Jarecka recorded. "When the pressure abates for a moment we utter a cry. Its importance should not be underestimated. Many a time in history did such cries resound; for a long time they resounded in vain, and only much later did they produce an echo. Documents and a cry of pain, objectivity and passion do not fit together," Jarecka admitted. And the written word itself evoked mixed feelings:

> The desire to write is as strong as the repugnance of words. We hate words because they too often have served as a cover for emptiness or meanness. We despise them for they pale in comparison with the emotion tormenting us. And yet in the past the word meant human dignity and was man's best possession—an instrument of communication between people.

Perhaps the written word would also help bring the killers to justice:

> These documents and notes are a remnant resembling a clue in a detective story. I remember from childhood such a novel by Conan Doyle in which the dying victim writes with a faint hand one word on the wall containing the proof of the criminal's guilt. That word, scrawled by the dying man, influenced my imagination in the past. . . . We are noting the evidence of the crime.

Jarecka admitted that "this will not help us." But nevertheless she found a small shred of solace as she wrote. Future generations might read her essay; historians might learn lessons:

The record must be hurled like a stone under history's wheel in order to stop it. . . . One can lose all hopes except the one—that the suffering and destruction of this war will make sense when they are looked at from a distant, historical perspective. From sufferings, unparalleled in history, from bloody tears and bloody sweat, a chronicle of days of hell is being composed which will help explain the historical reasons for why people came to think as they did and why regimes arose that [caused such suffering].[18]

Jarecka, therefore, had many important reasons to write. Through the written word one could confront the terrible present with dignity of the past and recapture the themes and symbols of prewar culture. In the face of horror, language could simultaneously frustrate and console. To write was to assert precious individuality even on the brink of death. To write was to resist, if only to bring the killers to justice. To write was to complete the defeat of the killers by ensuring that future historians would use the victims' cries to change the world.

During the Holocaust hundreds of individuals wrote. They wrote diaries, laments for murdered children, essays, poetry, and fiction. In a death cell in a Krakow prison, Gusta Davidson Draenger wrote a diary on toilet paper.[19] In Krematorium III in Auschwitz, Zalman Gradowski, a member of the Sonderkommando, wrote about his conversations with victims in the anteroom of the gas chamber and buried his notes in a glass bottle.[20] In Estonia, just a few hours before his execution in the Klooga concentration camp in September 1944, Herman Kruk wrote the last entries in his diary and buried them on the spot.[21]

Some individuals decided to write entirely on their own. Others wrote because they were encouraged to do so—by a political party, a youth movement, or an underground ghetto archive. There were underground archives in several ghettos, but by far the largest was the Oyneg Shabes, organized by Emanuel Ringelblum in the Warsaw Ghetto. More than anyone else it was Emanuel Ringelblum who encouraged individuals to write, who organized and conceptualized the archive, and who transformed it into a powerful center of civil resistance.[22]

Ringelblum was a historian who, to borrow Jarecka's metaphor, tried to cast a stone under the wheel of history. He was the product of a left-wing secular culture that embraced the study of Jewish history and Yiddish literature as the building blocks of a new Jewish identity that affirmed national pride even as it reached out to the wider world. Ringelblum was absolutely convinced that the story of Jewish suffering, no matter how terrible, was a universal story and not just a Jewish one. And evil, no matter how great, could not be placed outside history.[23] The archive not only recorded crimes; it was also part of the struggle for a better future.

Shortly after the searchers unearthed the first part of the Oyneg Shabes Archive, the Polish-Jewish historian Nachman Blumenthal—one of the first to study the materials—stressed what he believed to be Ringelblum's extraordinary ability to rise above political passions and preserve his objectivity.[24] Blumenthal also praised the fact that Ringelblum—unlike others caught in the Nazi hell—had resisted the temptation to engage in meta-historical speculation or to embrace mystical, religious, or political sentiments. Ringelblum just wanted the facts. He was, Blumenthal wrote, an exemplar of historical objectivity: "He stepped out of his own persona [er tut zikh oys aleyn fun zikh]" in order to serve pure truth.

Blumenthal, however, is only partly right. Much as Ringelblum cared about facts and "objectivity," he could not entirely step out of who he was and forget the politics and ideology that shaped him. To the very end Ringelblum remained a dedicated member of the LPZ. One could see the impact of that political legacy in his Yiddishism, in his love of the Jewish masses, in his reading of modern Polish history, and in his complex attitude toward the Soviet Union. His political legacy made it very difficult for him to evaluate fairly figures like Adam Czerniakow, the head of the Warsaw Judenrat. And one does not have to look hard to notice Ringelblum's less than positive attitude toward the Bund.[25] No, Ringelblum did not entirely abandon his political beliefs.

Just as religious Jews believed in the coming of the Messiah, Ringelblum hoped that after the war a better social order would arise on the rubble of European capitalism. But it would not happen automatically. Historical knowledge and awareness would arm the struggle for a better world. And therefore one finds a certain creative tension between his political beliefs and his determination that the Oyneg Shabes be objective and fair.[26]

Long before the war one could observe a similar tension between Ringelblum's commitment to objective scholarship and his conviction that Jewish historians had a national mission—a conviction that marked the work of an entire generation of young Jewish historians in Poland. For Ringelblum and his peers, their love of history did not lead to a traditional academic career; they were fortunate to find jobs as high school teachers. But as this study will show, they were convinced that the Jewish historians had to shoulder crucial national and political responsibilities. Historians would inspire Polish Jewry to fight for equal rights. They could have a major impact on Polish-Jewish relations: Poles would realize that "the Jews" were not an undifferentiated "other" but a diverse and complex national group with deep roots in Poland.

As this book will demonstrate, Ringelblum followed in the footsteps of two great historians, Simon Dubnow and Isaac Schiper.[27] Dubnow pioneered the modern study of East European Jewish history, and Schiper, along with Meyer Balaban, led the study of Jewish history in interwar Poland and both served as mentors and teachers for younger historians. Like Dubnow, Ringelblum believed that historical consciousness could provide a cultural bulwark for secular Jews who rejected both religion and assimilation. As Dubnow admitted in his autobiography, if he could not bring himself to believe in religion, then at least he could find comfort in the record of the Jewish people, how they overcame adversity and how they maintained their national identity. But in order to compile that record, Jews had to collect and protect the raw materials of Jewish history—documents and chronicles.[28]

Long before organizing the Oyneg Shabes, Ringelblum heeded Dubnow's call. Living in the Diaspora under the sovereignty of others, Ringelblum argued, the Jews would never own their past unless they claimed it and protected it themselves. In his earliest published writings, in the mid-1920s, he complained that Gentile historians had shown little interest in Jewish history, and assimilationist Jewish historians had distorted that history to make their case that Jews were a religion, not a people. Meanwhile, he emphasized, community records and documents disappeared, folklore vanished, and national cohesion atrophied. Unlike German Jewry, the hard-pressed Polish-Jewish community, he complained, had done little to set up historical societies, collect documents, or provide financial support for Jewish historians. It was time, Ringelblum pleaded, to change the Jews' attitude toward their history and to develop a rich social history comprising the material culture, economic structure, and folk customs of the Jewish masses.[29]

Ringelblum's emphasis on social history tried to redress what he believed to be a long-standing imbalance in Jewish historiography, with its focus on what rabbis wrote, on what the rich did, on apologetic briefs for why Jews deserved to be accepted by the Gentiles. To set the record straight, the historian had to organize armies of collectors (*zamlers*) to collect the raw materials.[30] He had to encourage provincial Jews to start writing local histories. Indeed, a central goal of the historical section of the Yiddish Scientific Institute, founded in 1925, was to organize the "doing of history," to encourage *zamlers* to collect material, youth to write their autobiographies, and ordinary Jews to believe that their lives were worth studying. Jewish historians not only had to be scholars, they also had to involve the wider community in a common effort.[31] Even as a young history student at Warsaw University in the 1920s, Ringelblum joined with others in gathering and assembling documents and artifacts of Jewish history in order to sharpen national consciousness and defend Jewish claims to a distinct national identity.

Together historians and amateurs would create a new canon, a new set of texts that would both legitimize the ongoing creation of a secular national identity and undermine previous, idealized notions of "one Jewish People" (*klal yisroel*) united by religion and suffering. Clear models for such a project had emerged during the First World War. Key examples were the *Vilna Zamlbikher* (almanacs) and the Vilna War Chronicle that appeared between 1915 and 1923.[32] These almanacs and chronicles—running to many hundreds of pages—documented almost every aspect of Vilna Jewish life during a period of upheaval and war. Articles and reports brought together the past and the present: studies of traditional synagogue architecture alongside reports on new schools and soup kitchens, articles on Jewish social psychology right beside compilations of jokes and folklore, studies of new secular schools next to accounts of the Jewish book trade and publishing. The chronicles also published diaries as well as copies of official announcements and proclamations during the years when Vilna was occupied by Poles, Germans, Soviets, and Lithuanians.

This collective effort brought together religious and secular Jews, Hebraists and Yiddishists, Zionists and Bundists. By documenting the creativity and resilience of Vilna Jewry in a time of crisis, these texts highlighted the emergence of a new Jewish community and new leaders who replaced older elites that had either fled Vilna or failed to meet the challenges of wartime leadership. Implicit in these texts was the conviction that Jewish national life had outgrown traditional frameworks. Jews in Eastern Europe were too diverse, energetic, and spontaneous to fit into the procrustean bed of traditional religion or the framework of narrow ideology. The key message of these texts was that the Jews were a people, not just a religious group. The first *Vilna Zamlbukh* appeared in 1916 at a time when Vilna was under German occupation and when Jews were fighting to secure recognition as a nationality. The stakes were high: recognition for Jewish schools, permission to run a separate Jewish network of relief organizations, equal treatment with the Poles. The *zamlbikher,* which at first glance seemed little more than a collection of miscellanea, in fact became a critical weapon of national self-defense.

Implicit in the *zamlbikher* was the belief that the emerging Jewish nation in Eastern Europe was a work in progress, the sum total of what the Jews, as a people, did. Perhaps one can go further and say that hundreds and thousands of documents were each small building blocks that both recorded and facilitated the construction of a new popular consciousness. Clearly what would later become known as *"alltagsgeschichte,"* the "history of everyday life," was already a major component of this process of documentation that traced the growth of an extraterritorial Jewish nation in Eastern Europe. This concern with the details of everyday life and material history would carry into the work of the Oyneg Shabes.

In his provocative study *Zakhor,* Yosef Khaim Yerushalmi stressed the tension that he believed existed between this emerging sense of history and a Jewish collective memory that used salient archetypal events to highlight covenantal time, blur the distinction between past and present, and underscore God's special relationship with the Jewish people. The modern historian was serving up something very different from this collective memory. Jewish historians worked with facts and strove for objectivity. God receded to the background, and the Jews, in the mind of the historian, became a people to be studied like any other.

> The historian does not simply come in to replenish the gaps of memory. He constantly challenges even those memories that have survived intact. Moreover, in common with historians in all fields of inquiry, he seeks ultimately to recover a total past—in this case the entire Jewish past— even if he is directly concerned with only a segment of it. No subject is potentially unworthy of his interest, no document, no artifact beneath his attention.[33]

Although Yerushalmi's thesis has had its critics, Yerushalmi's description of the historian's task—to recover a total past and to retrieve every possible document and artifact—is strikingly similar to Ringelblum's description of the Oyneg Shabes.

The Oyneg Shabes Archive includes an anonymous document by an orthodox Jew that questioned whether Ringelblum's concern with gathering material for history was worth the effort:

> History does not teach a thing. We Jews are an unhistorical people. History has seven faces. Her true face is hard to discover. Jews have no history, all of it is only myth. We are worried about gathering material for history? Forget it. Fight hunger. Only a myth will remain of the present time. Will it be the myth of Sodom or the myth of Abraham's charity?[34]

What mattered for this author, to put the question in Yerushalmi's terms, was collective, covenantal memory, not history.

But Ringelblum would not have agreed. The Jews, he believed, needed not myth but history. The Oyneg Shabes was not concerned with elegizing a dead people. During the early phase of the occupation, before anyone suspected the possibility of mass murder, Ringelblum, to borrow an oft-used phrase, sought to create a "usable past" for a living people. At first Ringelblum saw opportunities for the socially committed historian: to reverse the debilitating linguistic assimilation of the prewar years; to discredit the Jewish bourgeoisie and expose those elites who had failed to meet the test of wartime leadership; to document the resilience of the Jewish masses; to prove that in a moment of trial the Jews had once again proven their loyalty to Poland; to use history and sociology to create a meaningful base for Jewish secular culture and to continue a work in progress—a new iconography of the Jewish urban experience—that would take its place alongside the iconography of the shtetl. The Oyneg Shabes also saw itself as engaged in active resistance: it spread the truth about German atrocities.

Yet tension existed between this faith in history and the grim reality of the unfolding catastrophe. How does a historian—who sets out to document a living community—register its destruction? If it made sense to capture a "total past" while there was still hope that Polish Jewry would survive, then what was the point of the archive after the grim efficiency of the Final Solution became all too apparent? True, just as for Jarecka, the act of writing and gathering material afforded some meager consolation. Certainly the Oyneg Shabes could help damn the killers after the war, even if it could do little to save the victims. But Ringelblum continued the archive, even after all seemed lost, for yet another reason: his innate belief that nothing was "unimportant." The ultimate surrender, the ultimate act of despair, was a failure to record what one saw. As everything collapsed all around, many Jews in the ghettos held even more tightly to their prewar ideals and hopes—if nothing else, these provided an anchor and a beacon. Ringelblum the radical did not renounce his faith in a world revolution that would sweep away the capitalist system. Ringelblum the historian did not give up his hope that historians still had something to tell a postwar world, to teach lessons that would prevent another genocide.

Ringelblum was someone who turned his weaknesses into strengths. Before the war some regarded Ringelblum's historical work as overly descriptive. Compared to Isaac Schiper or Ringelblum's close friend, Rafael Mahler, Ringelblum was seen as a competent journeyman but not as a theorist or path-breaker. One person who worked with him closely before the war considered him, somewhat unfairly, more of a facilitator than an original thinker.[35] I consider these claims in more detail elsewhere in the book. But one might ask whether Ringelblum's own sense of the historian's craft, and perhaps his own realization of his strengths and weaknesses, made the archive—a collective enterprise—possible. In a very real sense, the Oyneg Shabes reflected a kind of humility on Ringelblum's part. Clearly he had his own biases and agendas, but he knew that in addition to creating a vital historical record he was "facilitating" the work of future historians. "Collect as much as possible," he told Wasser. "They can sort it out after the war."[36]

From the very beginning Ringelblum understood the need to encourage writing "from inside the event," writing that would not be skewed by the distorting lens of retrospective recollection and selective memory. To collect material, to gather impressions, and to write them down immediately—these were the watchwords of the Oyneg Shabes. Memory was tricky, Ringelblum insisted, especially in the ghetto. Under the pressure of unprecedented events, Jewish society changed at lightning speed. In wartime, months turned into days and years into months. By December 1939 the tough prewar days seemed like a picnic. A year later, after the Jews were herded into a ghetto, the preghetto period of the German occupation evoked a kind of nostalgia. After the deportations to Treblinka began in July 1942, then even the ghetto hell of 1941–42 seemed like the "good old days." Ringelblum realized, even before he was aware of the Final Solution, how quickly trauma would efface memories of all that had preceded it, how unimportant the "everyday" would seem when viewed through the prism of greater suffering. Thus it was all the more vital to capture the "everyday" of Jewish society under German occupation, to meld thousands of individual testimonies into a collective portrait.

In one of Cecylia Słapakowa's interviews with ghetto women, part of an Oyneg Shabes study project, we read that "in the tragic destructive chaos of our present-day life we can nonetheless observe flashes of creative activity, the slow development and birth of forces that are building a base for the future."[37] This was written in the spring of 1942. Had she survived, would she have written this after the war? Some of the most vivid materials of the Oyneg Shabes Archive were reportages written by Peretz Opoczynski about features of ghetto life such as the mail and compulsory disinfection baths that humiliated the ghetto population and ruined their belongings. But had Opoczynski waited until the fall of 1942 to write about these events, would they have seemed all that important? Compared to Treblinka, how could one complain about a real disinfection chamber? But it was precisely these microcosms of ghetto life—the post office, house committees, baths, street humor—that would help serious historians reconstruct and interpret the past and understand Jewish society under the Nazi occupation.

Over time Ringelblum realized more and more clearly that survivor identity would overshadow the prewar past. The "before" would be erased by the "after." As he confronted the unfolding disaster he fought all the harder to preserve the "Now" and the "Before," to keep the a posteriori label of "victim" from effacing who the Jews were before the war. In a very real sense he saw history as an antidote to a memory of catastrophe which, however well intentioned, would subsume what had been into what had been destroyed.

In a 1981 article Yehuda Bauer pointed out that research on the Jews during the Holocaust focused on the questions of collaboration and resistance while neglecting the "intermediate organizations" in the ghettos, those that occupied the space between the Jewish Councils (Judenräte) and the resistance organizations.[38] But it was precisely these intermediate organizations that had the closest daily contact with ordinary Jews in certain ghettos. The Oyneg Shabes was embedded in, and grew out of, the single most important of these "intermediate organization," the Aleynhilf (literally, "Self-Help") that Ringelblum took part in organizing in the Warsaw Ghetto (see chapter 4). Unlike the Judenräte, which were often mistrusted, or the fighting groups, which necessarily included a hand-picked elite drawn mainly from the youth movements, intermediate organizations like the Aleynhilf had a broader social base. The record of their activities offers insight into several key issues. How did various groups in the Jewish population perceive their situation at various stages of the German occupation? What was the interplay between relief and grass-roots social mobilization? How did new leaders emerge? What was the role of the prewar Jewish leadership in the ghettos? How does one define and discuss "civil resistance"? We should also remember the real differences between ghettos and concentration camps. In the former there was still a semblance of "social space" that permitted more choice. A major focus of the Oyneg Shabes was the study of these intermediate organizations.

This book sets out to examine who Emanuel Ringelblum was—as far as the sources allow—and to explain how his personality and convictions determined the development of the Oyneg Shabes. But its story is as much about Polish Jewry as it is about a single individual. Had he survived, Ringelblum would have been the first to insist that Holocaust historiography consider not only the perpetrators and the bystanders but also the silenced voices of the victims. To hear those voices requires an understanding of who they were before the war, the cultural milieu and the political battles that shaped Ringelblum and the values of the Oyneg Shabes.

Ringelblum's formative years were spent in Galicia, where a disproportionate number of Polish-Jewish historians were born. To what degree did the specific circumstances of Galician Jewry influence his development? He remained a lifelong member of the radical Marxist political party, the Left Poalei Zion. How did Ringelblum reconcile this radical Marxism with his commitment to objective historical research? He played a growing role in the social welfare activities of the Joint Distribution Committee, becoming, in the late 1930s, a full-time employee. Can one find a direct line between the grass-roots organizing Ringelblum did for the Joint and his role as a social organizer in the Warsaw Ghetto? He also became an increasingly prominent member of the Yiddish Scientific Institute. How did the institute's research methods influence the Oyneg Shabes Archive? And, finally, Ringelblum was a committed historian. How did he modify his understanding of his mission as a historian as the war progressed?

Unfortunately available sources do not permit a comprehensive personal biography of Emanuel Ringelblum. Those who knew him best are now dead. Some of his friends wrote about him, but hagiography is not biography.[39] Some elderly survivors remember Ringelblum, but they were too young at the time to have been part of his close circle. There is little material on Ringelblum's childhood. One searches in vain for more than a few sentences about his wife, Yehudis (Judyta), or his son, Uri. In his voluminous ghetto diary he clearly avoided writing about himself. Nachman Blumenthal, perhaps rightly, complained that Ringelblum went too far in his attempt to write himself out of his ghetto narratives, but this reticence sprang as much from the cultural milieu that shaped him and the values he professed as from personal modesty.

As a "public intellectual," Ringelblum is remembered today because of the Oyneg Shabes Archive. But he had also achieved a great deal before the war, even though he was hardly a first-rank figure. He worked in three major settings: the YIVO, the Joint Distribution Committee, and the Left Poalei Zion, his political party.

The 1930s were a hard time for Polish Jewry, but Ringelblum stood out for his inveterate optimism. And he believed that what he did mattered. The YIVO, he was convinced, had an important mission, and he believed that the Joint Distribution Committee might make a difference in the economic struggle being waged by Polish Jewry. Although the LPZ lost much of its mass support during the 1930s, Ringelblum retained his unwavering faith in its ideals. In 1934 Melekh Ravitch, a noted Yiddish poet and the secretary of the Yiddish Writer's and Journalists Union, was preparing to leave Poland permanently. By chance he encountered Ringelblum in the street and told him that he, too, should leave as quickly as possible. Ringelblum laughed and told Ravitch that he was staying. Polish Jewry had a future![40] This optimism may have seemed foolhardy in 1934, but in the Warsaw Ghetto it served Ringelblum well.

As the war raged on, those Ringelblum most respected or admired had either left or were killed. He understood that now there was no one else to turn to. The time had come to fulfill an enormous national and human responsibility. With the Oyneg Shabes, Ringelblum won his place in history.

From "Bichuch" to Warsaw

GALICIA

Was it just a coincidence that more Jewish historians came from Galicia, part of the Habsburg Empire, than anywhere else in Eastern Europe? Lwów produced Meyer Balaban, Philip Friedman, and Natan Gelber. Tarnów was the home of Isaac Schiper and Salo Baron. Rafael Mahler, Ringelblum's lifelong friend, and Artur Eisenbach, his future brother-in-law, grew up in the small town of Nowy Sącz. They all came from a region that differed in many important ways from Jewish Lithuania and Congress Poland, just across the Russian border. They were the products of a cultural milieu that combined excellent Polish education with strong Jewish nationalism. Habsburg rule was milder, educational opportunities greater. During Ringelblum's formative years, Galician Jewry was undergoing a fateful process of redefinition and self-examination.

Emanuel Ringelblum was born in Buczacz (Bichuch in Yiddish) in eastern Galicia on November 21, 1900. Once a part of Poland, the province passed under Habsburg rule in 1772 before it became part of the new Polish republic in 1918–19. The area of Buczacz was also known as Podolia.

The Buczacz of Ringelblum's childhood was a pretty town, surrounded by wooded hills and nestled in a bend of the river Strypa. High up overlooking the town was an old empty castle, "der puster shlos," where, according to tradition, the legendary Polish King Sobieski staged a daring ambush of Tatar invaders. On Saturday afternoons young couples would explore the countless tunnels that lay underneath the castle.[1] The great Hebrew writer Shmuel Yosef Agnon—Ringelblum's cousin—grew up in Buczacz and left a beautiful description of his birthplace in the story "B'tokh iri" (In my town).[2] Dominating Buczacz was the splendid Ratusz, or town hall, an imposing baroque landmark built by Prince Nikolai (Mikołaj) Potocki in the eighteenth century. Buczacz had long belonged to the Potockis, one of the greatest of the Polish landowning families. Like other Polish magnates the Potockis—eager to further their economic interests—went out of their way to attract Jews.[3]

From the very beginning Buczacz was a predominantly Jewish town. In 1870, 68 percent of the population had been Jewish (6,077 out of 8,959 inhabitants); in 1900, the year Ringelblum was born, there were 6,730 Jews out of a total of 11,755 inhabitants—or 57.3 percent of the population. The surrounding countryside was heavily Ukrainian.

Buczacz was a poor town, like most towns in Galicia, with little industry. Jews dominated trade, mainly in grains and other agricultural products, but the low purchasing power of the peasant population severely limited economic possibilities. In time, the growth of both Ukrainian and Polish cooperative movements would deal another heavy blow to the economic position of the Jews. Dim economic prospects served as a powerful stimulus to emigration. Many Jews, including Jacob Freud, Sigmund Freud's father, left for Vienna. Shmuel Yosef Agnon, the future Nobel Prize winner, also left the town at a young age.

Emanuel Ringelblum's father, Fayvish, a grain merchant, was respected, if not particularly prominent in the Jewish community and regarded himself as a *maskil,* a follower of the Jewish Enlightenment. Someone who met him during World War I recalled that "he looked like an ordinary Jew [*folksmensh*], a 'Jewish Jew' [yidishlekher yid]. He was dressed half-Jewish, half-European, without earlocks but with a short, red beard."[4] Ringelblum's mother Munie, née Heler, died when he was twelve years old. In later years he would use her name as a nom de plume.

Fayvish was determined that his children—two sons and two daughters—have a solid education in both Jewish and secular subjects.[5] As a child, Ringelblum studied in a modern *heder* (Jewish elementary school)—a so-called *heder metukan*[6]—and attended one year of the local Polish gymnasium before the family fled the Russian invasion in 1914. He also participated in a Zionist youth organization led by the dynamic Zvi Heller, who later emigrated to Israel. Natan Eck, who worked with Ringelblum in the Warsaw Ghetto, recalled that Ringelblum loved to tell stories of his childhood in Buczacz.[7]

Although he never returned to live in his hometown, he would often refer to his childhood there. In some ways Buczacz was like other Jewish small towns in Eastern Europe, and the young Emanuel grew up in an atmosphere rich in Jewish folk culture. But in other ways Buczacz was different. While East Galicia and Podolia were Hasidic strongholds—the native grounds, after all, of the Ba'al Shem Tov—Buczacz stood out as a bastion of the Haska-la. Hasidim were a minority,[8] and their relative weakness made it easier for strong Zionist organizations to grow in Buczacz before World War I. A third of the students in the local Polish high school were Jews, and they received a solid grounding in classics and exposure to Polish and European high culture. Many of the high school's most popular teachers were Jews.[9] The town boasted a large Baron de Hirsch primary school, set up to give Jewish students both a general and vocational education. Some of its graduates went on to the gymnasium, others entered trades. By the beginning of the century, several alumni who had remained in Buczacz had already formed a fledgling Jewish labor movement.[10]

Although young Jews received a Polish education, they did not become young Poles. The Galician Jewish intelligentsia, however acculturated, was surrounded by a strong and vibrant Yiddish-speaking folk culture nourished in many places by deep-rooted Hasidic traditions.

Buczacz Jews—like other Galician Jews—considered themselves lucky that they did not live across the border in Russia. They did not have to worry about stiff quotas barring them from high schools and universities. The Polish political elite had built up a network of Polish high schools that freely admitted Jewish students, making Polish the preferred language of educated Galician Jews. The Galician "gymnasium" instilled discipline and orderly work habits. Meanwhile, across the Russian border, thousands of desperate Jewish young people either went abroad to study or wasted countless years trying to pass university entrance exams. Many, embittered and alienated, would join the revolutionary movement. In Galicia, only finances—not legal quotas—stood between Jewish youth and the great universities of the empire. They could choose between a German education in Vienna or a Polish university in Krakow or Lemberg (Lwów). Many attended both. A university degree did not guarantee prosperity; there were too few jobs for university graduates. (Less fortunate Jews on the other side of the Russian border liked to swap barbed jokes about the ubiquitous—and often impecunious—"doctors" who inundated the tiniest Galician shtetl.) Unquestionably, however, this university-educated Galician-Jewish intelligentsia, with its overlay of European culture, imbued Galician Jewry with a special character. In the early years of the Polish Republic, many Galician Jews, including Emanuel Ringelblum, would stream to Warsaw. There, in the new capital of the new state, they used their excellent Polish and superior educational credentials to good advantage as teachers in state schools for Jewish children, Jewish secondary schools, and administrators in various Jewish institutions.

Unlike their brothers from Lithuania, Russia, and Congress Poland, Galician Jewry had also benefited from the more congenial political climate of the Habsburg Empire. By the 1860s, they had won legal emancipation. Long before the first Duma elections in Russia in 1906, Habsburg Jews were participants in the political process. When Ringelblum was growing up in Buczacz, the town had a Jewish mayor, Berish Shtern, and a Jewish police chief.[11] Jews in Galicia felt more secure than Russian Jewry, with a relatively free press and a rich organizational life, with more legal safeguards in place. Pogroms were rarer, the resonance of revolutionary politics much weaker. Indeed Ringelblum would later recall how moved he was when, as a young man in Warsaw in 1920, he first came into contact with young Jews from Congress Poland who had participated in battles against the tsar and who had a revolutionary tradition.[12] Nevertheless, Galician Jewry saw its share of political struggle and confrontation, especially during the decade preceding World War I.

Although the Jews enjoyed the political and educational benefits of Habsburg rule, clouds loomed on the horizon, and the years of Ringelblum's childhood witnessed far reaching changes that transformed Galician Jewry. The same reforms that brought emancipation to the Jews in the 1860s also placed political power in Galicia in the hands of the Polish nobility. Most middle-class Jews shifted their allegiance from German culture to Polish. Many Jewish leaders also preached assimilation: Jews should become "Poles of the Mosaic persuasion." But by the time Ringelblum was born, support for the assimilationists had largely collapsed in Galician Jewish society. Even as they spoke Polish at home and sent their children to Polish schools, many educated Galician Jews keenly resented growing Polish anti-Semitism and the refusal to repay Jewish cultural loyalty with full acceptance. According to some memoirs, by the eve of World War I the social gulf between Jews and Poles, especially in East Galicia, had grown enormously. Polish and Jewish high school students would study together but go their separate ways after school.[13]

By the turn of the century much of the non-Hasidic Galician Jewish middle class was turning to Zionism. Zionism in Galicia had less to do with immediate emigration to Palestine than with new definitions of Jewishness. Galician Zionism, which largely conducted its business in refined Polish, symbolized Jewish nationalism, a Jewish self-consciousness that could easily coexist with the adoption of non-Jewish culture. Galicia would anticipate a characteristic development of the interwar Jewish life in Poland: growing acculturation that at the same time rejected assimilation. As tensions escalated between Ukrainians and Poles, especially in Eastern Galicia, Jewish nationalism also became an expedient way of declaring neutrality and avoiding a potentially dangerous crossfire. Aware that they had no hope of attracting Jews to Ukrainian culture, Ukrainians preferred Zionism and Jewish nationalism to overt Jewish identification with Polish culture and aims. In turn, Polish nobles preferred Jewish assimilationists or pliant Hasidic rebbes who denied separate Jewish national status and obeyed the dictates of the Polish leadership. (In Buczacz, they had long enjoyed a cozy relationship with Berish Shtern, the Jewish mayor.)

In the decade before World War I, two major events sparked Jewish-Polish confrontation and encouraged an intense process of national redefinition: the new 1907 election law and the 1910 census. The 1907 law, which expanded the suffrage, changed the rules of the political game. Zionists now saw their chance to make major gains, and the Polish elite had more reason to fear losing control over a Jewish vote that often held the balance between Poles and Ukrainians. In Buczacz and elsewhere, the elections of 1907 led to bitter charges of Polish intimidation and vote tampering. The 1910 census saw heavy Polish pressure on Jews to declare Polish as their mother tongue and thus bolster Polish claims to predominance in the area; the census authorities refused to recognize Yiddish as an option. In a test case of modern Jewish politics, many Galician Jews, even those who were actually Polish-speaking, demonstratively defied the census commission and declared Yiddish as their mother tongue. In an ironic twist, certain Yiddish-speaking Hasidic rebbes, who detested modern Jewish nationalism, urged their followers to declare themselves as Polish speakers!

All over Galicia, including Buczacz, the census battle became the symbol of Jewish independence from Polish tutelage.[14] By the time Ringelblum entered the Buczacz gymnasium, relations there between Polish and Jewish students had become quite tense.[15]

One by-product of the 1910 census fight was a renewed interest in modern Yiddish culture among a small but growing minority of the Jewish intelligentsia. They could count for support on a nascent Jewish labor movement. The Jewish labor movement was not as strong in Galicia as in Russia; Galicia had barely industrialized. But echoes of the revolutionary battles across the border in Russia certainly raised the prestige of the Bund and the Poalei Tsiyon, the party founded by Ber Borochov in 1906. On the eve of World War I both these parties had well-established organizations in the region.[16]

For workers and students who wanted to combine radical Marxism, Zionism, and Yiddishism, an ideal vehicle was the emerging Poalei Tsiyon. Several students had already broken away from a larger Zionist youth organization, the Tseirei Tsiyon, and joined Borochov's party. Among the new leaders of the Galician Poalei Tsiyon were two university students who in later years would have an important influence on Ringelblum's life: Natan Buchsbaum and Isaac Schiper. When Buchsbaum joined the party, he knew no Yiddish at all. He laboriously taught himself the language and began addressing meetings of tailors and store clerks, whom the party was trying to organize. By 1914 the party was conducting its meetings in Yiddish.

Schiper became not only one of the most important Polish-Jewish historians but also a key leader of the Galician Poalei Tsiyon before World War I. Born in Tarnów in 1884, Schiper already spoke Yiddish well and had begun to take an active interest in Yiddish culture when he read Ber Borochov's seminal article, "The Tasks of Yiddish Philology," which appeared in 1913. In December of that same year, Schiper wrote an article in the Lemberg party newspaper, *Der Yidisher Arbeter,* that elaborated on and explained Borochov's arguments in favor of Yiddish.

On the eve of World War I, therefore, Galician Jewry had undergone a marked process of political self-definition. Assimilation as an ideology had collapsed; political changes in the Habsburg Empire hastened the modernization of Jewish politics. For the first time Jewish labor parties were becoming a factor in Jewish politics. A sizable Jewish intelligentsia had emerged, well educated in Polish and German but identified with Jewish nationalism. If Galician Jewry lacked the revolutionary traditions of Russian Jewry, it did possess a large reservoir of well-educated cadres who would play a major role in Jewish political and cultural activity in the interwar Polish republic. This was the milieu of Ringelblum's formative years.

SANZ

When the First World War broke out in the summer of 1914, Emanuel Ringelblum had completed one year of the Polish classical gymnasium in Buczacz. A heavy Russian offensive in September 1914 broke the Austrian lines and headed into Podolia. Horrified by stories of maltreatment of Jews by the Russians, thousands of refugees began to flee westward. The Ringelblum family joined the stream of refugees. After a brief stay in nearby Kolomeja, the Ringelblums settled in Nowy Sącz (Nay Sanz or Sanz in Yiddish), a town on the Dunajec River in Western Galicia.

Uprooted from his home at the age of fourteen, Ringelblum had to make a painful adjustment to a new life. The family faced desperate poverty. Fayvish, who had remarried, barely eked out a living in the town marketplace. The family of six crowded into a tiny house. One of Ringelblum's new friends, the then fifteen-year-old Mendl Naygroshl, visited Ringelblum many times and remembered a "poor, depressing place: a small kitchen, a small room and every bit of space taken up with beds. . . . You could feel a quiet sadness in the house, the poverty that had taken hold and the loneliness of uprooted people."[17] According to Naygroshl, Ringelblum's new stepmother seemed especially depressed, as did his older sister.[18] Despite the family's poverty, Emanuel continued his high school studies and supported himself by tutoring younger students.

Those who befriended Ringelblum in Sanz left starkly different recollections. Naygroshl remembered the young Ringelblum—his friends called him Edek or Edzia—as sad and serious, someone who rarely laughed.[19] On the other hand, the future historian Rafael Mahler, who would become Ringelblum's lifelong friend, had a more positive recollection. "Edzia," Mahler wrote, "became the darling of Jewish working-class youth and students in Sanz. The handsome, blond student in his high school cape attracted everyone's attention. His light, hearty laughter, his Jewish folk songs and socialist songs would echo in the city park where he would spend the summer evenings surrounded by young men and women."[20] Perhaps both Naygroshl and Mahler are correct. It is possible that Naygroshl was recalling Ringelblum's early adjustment to a strange town, whereas Mahler was describing him after he had become politically active and had more friends.

At first Ringelblum had difficulty adjusting to the cultural differences between Sanz and Buczacz.[21] Unlike Buczacz, Sanz was a heavily Hasidic town. Indeed, it was the center of the great Halbershtam dynasty. As in many Hasidic centers, an enormous distance separated the Jewish intelligentsia from the Jewish masses. Another problem for Ringelblum was language. Although he had been educated in Polish, Ringelblum loved Yiddish and seemed surprised by the acculturation of his new high school classmates. Naygroshl recalled that the Jewish high school students there "spoke about Zionism in Polish, they spoke about Jewish national autonomy in Polish, and they even attacked Jewish assimilation—all in Polish."[22] According to his friend, Yakov Kener, Ringelblum immediately began a campaign to try to persuade his new classmates to speak more Yiddish.

This love of Yiddish was certainly a major factor in Ringelblum's growing interest in the Poalei Tsiyon. One student who also shared this interest in Yiddish culture was Saul Amsterdam, who recruited Ringelblum to the party.[23] A few years later Ringelblum and Amsterdam would go their separate ways. Ringelblum would remain in the Poalei Tsiyon, and Amsterdam would change his name to Gustaw Henrykowski and become a prominent leader of the Polish Communist Party (KPP)—that is, until Stalin had him executed in 1938. But when Ringelblum met him in Sanz, he found a friend who combined a mastery of political literature with a great knowledge of Yiddish secular culture. Having been recruited into the Poalei Tsiyon movement himself, by Schiper, Amsterdam knew not only the Yiddish classical writers but could also converse freely about David Bergelson, a brilliant stylist who represented a new generation of Yiddish writers. He was an excellent speaker and brilliant debater. Rafael Mahler wrote that Amsterdam was the first person in Sanz to speak "literary Yiddish."

In the local Poalei Tsiyon, Ringelblum made friends who would change the course of his life. When one considers that these friends were all teenagers in an obscure Galician town, their later achievements are quite extraordinary. Mendel Naygroshl became a respected Yiddish poet and attorney in Vienna. Saul Amsterdam went on to lead the interwar KPP. Rafael Mahler, who became one of Ringelblum's closest friends, and Arthur Eisenbach made their mark as two of the leading East European Jewish historians of the century. (Eisenbach would also marry Ringelblum's younger sister, Gisa).

As the Habsburg Empire slowly collapsed under the shock of the war, Ringelblum and his friends in Sanz searched for a political roadmap that would make sense of the upheavals that were changing their world forever. Russian atrocities against the Jewish population in eastern Galicia served as a brutal reminder of Jewish vulnerability in an unstable Europe. In a time of despair and privation, East European Jewry faced an uncertain future and eagerly sought out any sign of hope. Would the end of the war bring the victory of socialism? Would the Jews gain civic equality and cultural autonomy? The first week of November 1917 brought news of two great events—the Balfour Declaration and the Bolshevik Revolution. The former held out the hope of a Jewish national home in Palestine, and the latter promised to eliminate anti-Semitism in a new, proletarian state. Both made a powerful impact on young Jews. Many streamed into he-Haluts, a Zionist youth organization, to prepare themselves for a pioneering life in Palestine. Others looked to Moscow and the new Communist party. The Poalei Tsiyon tried for a long time to combine both: loyalty to the new Soviet state with a commitment to a Jewish home in Palestine.

One year later, in November 1918, yet another upheaval transformed the world of Galician Jewry: the rebirth of a Polish state. The new Polish constitution promised the Jews basic civil rights, but given the worsening trajectory of Polish-Jewish relations, how much would these promises be worth?

In 1920, in the middle of this period of turmoil and change, Ringelblum received a rude shock. He had finished the gymnasium in Sanz and applied for admission to Warsaw University to study medicine. The young graduate quickly learned that in the new Polish state promises of legal equality and civil rights could not be taken at face value. A rejection letter from Warsaw University medical faculty informed him that because of the "numerus clausus"—a quota on Jewish enrollments—he had to look elsewhere to study.

Embittered by this blatant discrimination—which would not have happened in Habsburg days—Ringelblum contemplated going abroad.[24] In the end, however, possibly for financial reasons, he reapplied to study on the history faculty and was accepted.

WARSAW

When Ringelblum first arrived in Warsaw in 1919, Poland's new capital was a boomtown. Hopeful migrants streamed into the city from all corners of the new Republic, causing a severe housing shortage. In the interwar period Warsaw became the cultural and political center that helped unite the long-divided Polish people. For decades the Russian occupiers had ringed the city with military fortresses and blocked its physical expansion. Now the Polish city symbolized a nation reborn. Its new residential districts, government buildings, theaters, and centers of higher learning reflected the Poles' pride in their newly won independence.

Warsaw brought together not only Poles but also Jews. Jewish political parties and welfare organizations established their central headquarters in Warsaw. The city became the home of the major Yiddish and Hebrew writers' organization as well as the most important center of the Yiddish theater. Several Yiddish dailies were based in the city. In 1923 a new Polish-language Jewish daily, *Nasz Przegląd,* began to appear. As Warsaw became the political and cultural center of Polish Jewry, it brought together the different Jewish "tribes" that had been thrown together in the new state. Important cultural differences had developed over the centuries between "Litvaks," Jews from Congress Poland, and Galicians. Now, in the new Polish Republic, friction and discord were inevitable. Nevertheless a new entity—"Polish Jewry"—steadily took shape.

Ringelblum came to Warsaw with very little money and supported himself by teaching and translating. Together with party comrade Daniel Leybel, he translated Dr. Isaac Schiper's *Economic History of the Jews in Poland during the Middle Ages* from Polish into Yiddish.[25] In the early 1920s he also taught in the evening schools of the Left Poalei Zion—for a tiny wage. In 1926 he went to Vilna for one year to teach in secondary schools there. The next year he returned to Warsaw and then procured a teaching post at Yehudia, a well-known private gymnasium for Jewish girls. Although Ringelblum would continue to teach at Yehudia until the late 1930s, he earned little and constantly sought extra sources of income.

At Yehudia, Ringelblum met Abraham Lewin, a fellow teacher and historian who later became a close collaborator in the Oyneg Shabes Archive. One of his former students at the Yehudia, Mrs. Hanna Hirschaut, remembered Ringelblum as a well-liked but shy teacher. He cared about his students and encouraged them to continue their education at a time, to quote Hirschaut, "when women's lib was not even broached." His students—well-to-do teen-aged girls from relatively comfortable Jewish families—sometimes made him the butt of their practical jokes:

> Dr. Ringelblum had a habit of coming into the classroom at the last moment a little perspired, his clothes kind of rumpled. He would always pick up a pencil holder from the nearest student desk and play with it and gesture with it. One day he came in and picked up the pencil holder and found a smelly herring inside. He dropped the whole thing to the floor and ran out of the classroom. I felt sorry for him, realizing how up-set he was. He returned after a while without mentioning the incident to the principal or discussing the matter with us.[26]

Despite Mrs. Hirschaut's fond memories, one infers that Ringelblum taught at Yehudia more out of financial necessity than conviction. Compared to the poor workers who came to his evening classes exhausted but enthusiastic, his students at Yehudia were much less likely to appeal to his idealism and sense of mission. A privately published book issued by Yehudia alumnae in Israel suggests that Ringelblum did not make as much of an impression on his students as Abraham Lewin or others. Inka Szwajger, who was the daughter of the headmistress, had recollections of Ringelblum that were much less flat-tering than Hirschaut's.[27]

Shortly after he came to Warsaw, Ringelblum met his future wife, Yehu-dis (Judyta) Herman. Four years younger than Ringelblum, Yehudis Herman came from a Warsaw Hasidic family. She joined the LPZ, and it was there that she became acquainted with her future husband.[28] In the interwar pe-riod she taught in Polish government schools and in the Borochov schools, which were run by the LPZ and formed a part of the leftist Central Yiddish School Organization (CYSHO-Tsentrale Yidishe Shul Organizatsiye). Their son, Uri, was born in 1930. Ringelblum was a concerned and loving father. Hirschaut recalled that when "we wanted to distract him from an impending test, we would ask how his little Uri was doing. A smile would brighten up his face, and he would rave about how smart Uri was and how quickly he was learning."[29]

It was when classes were over at Yehudia that Ringelblum could turn to what really interested him: politics and history. In the new metropolis Ringel-blum would find his way, as a young historian and as a political activist in the Left Poalei Tsiyon.

CHAPTER 2

Borochov's Disciple

Just six weeks before he died Ringelblum wrote a coded letter to Adolf Berman. Berman, one of the last surviving leaders of the Left Poalei Zion in Poland, and his wife, Basia, had been the Ringelblums' longtime friends. That friendship, nurtured in joint party activity before the war, became a critical source of support in the Warsaw Ghetto. As will be seen, it was the Bermans who engineered Ringelblum's escape from the Trawniki labor camp in August 1943. Now, living on the Aryan side of Warsaw on false papers, the Bermans were a crucial psychological and financial lifeline to Ringelblum, his wife Yehudis, and his son Uri, who were hiding in an underground bunker.

In this letter to Berman, written on January 21, 1944, Ringelblum spoke, in guarded terms, about "Miss Partowa"—his party, the Left Poalei Zion.[1] It was in these terrible times, he wrote, that he realized again just how much the party meant to him, the movement in which he spent his entire adult life.

The party marked him in many ways. It instilled a fervent commitment to the study of Jewish history, a love of Yiddish, a devotion to the Jewish masses, and a deep sense of moral pathos that shaped Ringelblum's development as a historian and communal leader. When Ringelblum arrived in Warsaw from Sanz he was already a committed member of the Poalei Tsiyon. When the party split into a right and left wing in 1920, he took his stand with the Left. In Jewish Poland political parties and youth movements were a second family. More than just political organizations, they provided their members with a self-contained universe of cultural activities, libraries, sports, and vacation trips. Ringelblum, his younger brother, and his younger sister all met their future spouses in the Left Poalei Zion.

The Left Poalei Zion in interwar Poland gave the Zionist idea, however modified, a solid foothold on the Left. The Communists had countered Zionism with the lure of a "promised land" closer to home—the Soviet Union. The Bund constantly hammered home its message of *doikayt* ("here-ness"): commitment to the Jewish masses, to their Yiddish speech, and to their struggle for a democratic socialist society within Poland, their home. Although many disputed the LPZ's Zionist credentials, what made the party different was its determination to combine the *do* (here) and the *dortn* (there), the Diaspora and Palestine, in a complicated, mutually reinforcing relationship. Of all the Zionist parties it was the LPZ that most ardently embraced the imperative of revolutionary struggle in the Diaspora. It struggled to meld the charisma of the October Revolution with a commitment to a territorial base in Palestine. The party emphatically rejected any suggestion that the *yishuv* (Jewish Palestine) was "better" than the Diaspora or that the labor movement in Palestine had any right to dictate to the Jewish workers in Poland. It followed that the LPZ embraced and enhanced the fervent Yiddishism of Ber Borochov, the movement's founder. To bring Palestine and the Diaspora together required a commitment to the common folk language. After all, why erect a linguistic and cultural barrier between Palestine and the Jewish workers outside? Why cripple the Jewish worker by forcing him to speak Hebrew rather than his mother tongue?[2]

It is only a slight exaggeration to say that the party attracted those workers and radical intellectuals who, but for Ber Borochov and Palestine, could easily have found their way to the KPP. In its near total identification with the legacy of Borochov, the LPZ also stood apart. Of the many Jewish political parties in interwar Poland, only the Revisionists, who followed Vladimir Jabotinsky, were so totally linked to a particular mentor.

Although the entire spectrum of Jewish political activity in interwar Poland required a high degree of personal dedication and commitment, it is fair to say that the LPZ attracted an exceptionally devoted membership. Indeed, in the very last weeks of his life, writing in an underground bunker on the Aryan side of Warsaw, Ringelblum reflected on the special character of his party, which, unlike its major rivals, could rely only on itself.[3] The Bund could count on help from the Workmen's Circle in the United States, and the Right Poalei Tsiyon enjoyed the support of the Histadrut, the Jewish labor federation in Palestine. In comparison, Ringelblum noted, the LPZ was isolated and poor. The fervor of its members had to make up for its lack of resources. Making matters worse, the party steadily lost support during the interwar period. It reached its peak in the late 1920s and then, in the 1930s, declined in influence as the Bund became ever stronger.

It is quite telling, therefore, that Ringelblum remained a loyal and committed member until the very end. His loyalty becomes especially significant when placed within the context of the party's ideological and political difficulties during the interwar period. Did Ringelblum follow every twist and turn of the party line? Probably not. But one can safely say that the teachings of Ber Borochov—as interpreted by the party—exerted a critical intellectual and moral influence on Ringelblum's development as a historian and as a public figure.

The very factors that made the party's ideology a political liability—its highly complicated analysis of the "Jewish problem"—also encouraged serious study of Jewish history. In the 1950s both Jacob Lestschinsky and Jacob Shatzky would note that more younger Jewish historians in interwar Poland belonged to the LPZ than to any other party.[4] In an essay on Isaac Schiper, written in late 1943, Ringelblum pointed out the impact of the movement's ideology on Schiper's intellectual development. An ideology that explained Jewish survival in terms of the alleged "abnormality" of the Jewish economic structure in the Diaspora encouraged a serious interest in the Jewish past and especially in economic history.[5]

Years later Jacob Kener, a friend and party comrade, remembered a bitterly cold evening in Warsaw. The LPZ had called a meeting to commemorate Borochov, who had died of illness in 1917. Ringelblum arrived after the doors had closed. Instead of going home, he stood outside in the freezing cold until the meeting was over and the doors opened. When his incredulous friend asked him why he had punished himself, Ringelblum answered that he deserved no less for coming too late to honor Borochov.[6] Another friend recalled a party demonstration in the 1930s. By this time the LPZ was suffering severe persecution from the Polish police. Knowing that Ringelblum could lose his teaching post if he were arrested, the party had excused him from participating in public demonstrations—but he came anyway.[7]

What made Ber Borochov such an attractive figure to Ringelblum and his party comrades was a powerful theoretical mind that synthesized scientific Marxism, Zionism, and Yiddishism. Since Borochov saw labor Zionism as an integral part of an international revolutionary struggle, he strongly supported Yiddish as an indispensable link that would unite Jewish workers in different countries. But Borochov's devotion to Yiddish transcended political pragmatism: it was important in its own right. Especially in the later years of his life, Borochov threw himself into the study of Yiddish philology and literature. He became one of the important pioneers of the emerging Yiddishist movement.[8] However, unlike many of his later followers in the interwar LPZ, Borochov's support of Yiddish never turned into opposition to Hebrew.[9]

In a seminal essay, "The Tasks of Yiddish Philology," which appeared in 1913, Borochov called for a disciplined, collective effort to enrich the Yiddish language and make it a suitable vehicle for intellectual expression and scientific research.[10] For too long, Borochov complained, Yiddish had "wandered the streets" and "hung around small-town-fairs" (p. 70). Banished from universities and the corridors of political power, it had failed to develop a sophisticated legal and political terminology. Yiddish also suffered from the barriers that had cut off the Jews from the world of nature; hence the inadequate vocabulary for minerals, plants, and animals.

> The paramount tasks of Yiddish philology can alternatively be formulated as the nationalization and humanization of the language. Nationalizing Yiddish entails purifying the language thoroughly and enriching it extensively, to the point where it can express all aspects of Jewish creativity. Humanizing Yiddish entails turning it into a means for incorporating into the Jewish nation all the cultural values of modern human development. (p. 70)

In this essay Borochov laid out an important and ambitious agenda for the Yiddishist intelligentsia, and it would have an enormous impact on Ringelblum. The classical Yiddish writers had begun the job of modernizing Yiddish. "Mendele Moykher Sforim," Borochov wrote, "is the Columbus of the Yiddish language, and Yitzhak Leybush Peretz is its Napoleon. Mendele discovered Yiddish, and Peretz conquered European worlds on its behalf" (p. 71). What the great writers started, however, now had to be completed by collective scholarship spearheaded by philologists and folklorists. The great treasure trove of Yiddish folk culture demanded immediate scholarly study based on a team effort.

As an adolescent, Ringelblum embraced this heady combination of socialism, Zionism, and Yiddishism. He threw himself into the study of economics and sociology. Mendl Naygroshl recalled meeting Ringelblum one evening in the street in Sanz and noticed that he seemed particularly sad. When Naygroshl asked him what was wrong, Ringelblum answered that he had just been reading a book that tried to demolish the case for socialism. "'If the book is true,'" Naygroshl remembers Ringelblum saying, "and then he made a despairing gesture with his arm—'then the only way out would be to get a rope and commit suicide!'"[11]

Borochov appealingly combined Marxist theory with a masterful and original analysis of the Jewish problem. Many Jewish socialists had long been uneasy with the Left's cavalier attitude toward the "Jewish Question." Marx had given the Jews short shrift. Lenin and Stalin also saw assimilation as the ultimate answer to the Jewish Question. Hardly anyone on the Left apart from the Bund had paid any attention to Yiddish, the language of the Jewish masses.

Borochov argued that both Marx and the Bund had fundamentally misunderstood the Jewish problem. When his important work, "Our Platform," appeared in 1906, many Jewish radicals could now breathe a sigh of relief. Here was a powerful intellect, they asserted, who embraced the Marxist tradition but who would correct its failures and shortcomings.[12] He would also put the mighty Bund—the most powerful Jewish party on the Left—in its place (or so they hoped). The Bund, Borochov's supporters complained, saw the Jewish Question in political terms, as if simply by abolishing political discrimination and establishing a democratic socialist state, the Jewish problem would solve itself. But Borochov argued that the Jewish problem was not only political but also economic and existential. The Bund, they charged, rejected the notion of a worldwide Jewish people united by common economic and political concerns. For the Bund, a Jewish worker in Russia or Poland had more in common with his Gentile comrades than with Jews in Germany or the United States. For Borochov, on the other hand, Jews everywhere shared common problems, formed one nation, and were shaped by a history whose lessons had to be mastered.

The essence of the Jewish problem, according to Borochov, lay in the fateful interconnection of economic vulnerability and extraterritoriality. The position of the Jews in the economies of the Diaspora was quite fragile. The Jews, without a territory of their own, could neither control the nerve centers of production nor win a strategic position in emerging labor movements. Growing anti-Semitism, he argued, fueled by the economic transformation of the "native population," pushed Jews away from primary industries and large factories, and exiled them to the weaker, peripheral sectors. Both the Jewish bourgeoisie and the Jewish proletariat were at risk. The rising non-Jewish bourgeoisie pushed Jewish capitalists away from strategic industries and control of raw materials, and Jewish workers became tailors and shoemakers rather than steelworkers and coal miners. Unfortunately tailors and shoemakers had little political power. Railroad workers or coal miners could shut down an economy; tailors could not.

Ultimately, Borochov argued, the native population would begin to expel the Jews from their peripheral positions and impel them to emigrate. Unlike the Bund, the LPZ stressed the decisive national importance of Jewish emigration. But emigration, too, had its limits. At some point, Borochov predicted, Jews would wear out their welcome, and immigration laws would choke off Jewish emigration to the United States and other developed countries. Thus Palestine would loom ever larger as a destination.

What then? As Jonathan Frankel, Matityahu Mintz, and others have pointed out, when it came to Palestine, there were really two Borochovs: the "determinist" or "prognostic" Borochov of "Our Platform" and a "voluntarist" Borochov, who left a very different legacy. Borochov himself unexpectedly died in 1917 at the young age of thirty-five. The battle over his legacies began immediately.

If one sees a Borochov Street in practically every Israeli town today, it is because, after the Poalei Tsiyon split into Right and Left factions in 1920, David Ben Gurion and his followers in the Palestinian labor movement followed the "voluntarist" Borochov. In their reading, Borochov endorsed Zionist pioneering and the active participation of the Jewish labor movement in the construction of a Jewish society in Palestine. He stressed the importance of dedication and commitment, the *will* to end the Diaspora.

The Left Poalei Zion, the movement Ringelblum would follow throughout his life, totally ignored the "voluntarist" Borochov in favor of the "prognostic Zionism" outlined in the 1906 "Our Platform." Deeply affected by the 1905 Russian Revolution, Borochov then sought to reconcile Jewish settlement in Palestine with radical revolution in the Diaspora, Marxism with Zionism. This he did by stripping Zionism of all romantic pathos, all semblance of Jewish nationalism. (To underscore his point, Borochov used the name "Palestine" rather than the traditional "Eretz Yisroel.") Harsh economic necessity, a stark process of elimination, and not the nostalgic yearning for Zion, would drive Jews to Palestine. Other countries would shut their doors; rising anti-Semitism would force Jews out of their home countries. Jews would therefore come to Palestine because of a spontaneous [*stychic*] process of emigration. In this new territory a "healthy" economic structure would develop, free of the deformities of the Diaspora. No longer would Jews cling to the peripheral sector. Jewish workers could now confront the Jewish middle class in open class struggle. Thus Borochov and the Poalei Tsiyon would boycott the World Zionist Organization and shun active cooperation with the Jewish bourgeoisie. As class struggle in Palestine intensified, the Jewish working class would gain a "strategic base," a territorial foundation that would radicalize the world Jewish labor movement, strengthen its relative weight in the international Left, and transform Diaspora Jewish culture.[13]

But Borochov, shortly before he died, seemed to turn his back on the prognostic Zionism of "Our Platform" and endorse a much more activist Zionism. At the party's Kiev conference, which took place in September 1917, he angered and disappointed many party members by stating that much of "Our Platform" needed revision.[14] Circumstances had changed since 1906, Borochov argued. The movement had to aggressively encourage Jewish emigration to Palestine, support pioneering settlements, and actively foster the building of a Jewish national home. This "voluntarist" Zionism was certainly better suited to the real needs of labor Zionism in Palestine, based as it was more on collective agricultural settlements than on developed industry.

Many of Borochov's followers, however, buoyed by the surging tide of revolution in Russia, reacted to his volte-face with shock and hostility. To them "Our Platform" still made sense, even if Borochov himself was having second thoughts. At any rate, Borochov's untimely death made it easier to conceal what actually happened at the September 1917 conference. With the master no longer able to assert his authority, some of his disciples decided to save "Borochovism" from Borochov.[15] Jacob Zerubavel and other party leaders deliberately created a highly biased and distorted Borochov myth that ignored Borochov's later heresies. As Zerubavel explained in 1920:

> For us it is totally unimportant what Borochov said on a particular occasion or what he did at this or that time. Because we are not concerned with Borochov as an individual. We are concerned with that Borochov that became the flesh and blood of the Poalei Tsiyon movement. Holy to us is the personification of the Poalei Tsiyon idea, Borochovism, the highest expression of our party's self image.[16]

In 1920 the Poalei Tsiyon movement split into a Left and a Right wing. The overwhelming majority of the party in Poland supported the Left—the bastion of "prognostic" Zionism—and throughout the interwar period Poland would have the largest Left Poalei Zion party in the world. There were many reasons for the split. The Right wanted to rejoin the World Zionist Organization and remain in the Second International, committed to democratic socialism. The Left wanted to join the Moscow-led Comintern and continue the boycott of the Zionist Congress. (In the end, only Moscow's insistence that the Left Poalei Zion repudiate Borochovism kept it out of the Comintern.) The Right gave a cautious welcome to the Balfour Declaration, whereas the Left dismissed it as a cheap trick of the British imperialists. Only the victory of the Soviet Union, the Left argued, could guarantee the long-term interests of the Jewish workers in Palestine.[17]

The pro-Soviet "prognostic" Zionism of the LPZ dovetailed easily with radical revolutionary politics in the Diaspora. To fight revolutionary battles in Poland was just as important, if not more so, than emigration to Palestine. In any case, the labor Zionists in Palestine and the idealistic pioneering Jewish youth in Poland were deluding themselves—or so argued the interwar LPZ. The Jewish collective settlements in Palestine were houses built on sand. To exclude Arab labor and trust the promises of the British mandate betrayed pathetic self-delusion.[18] The goal of the LPZ was a bi-national Palestine that would include both Arabs and Jews; to achieve it would require the pressure of world revolution and the collapse of British imperialism. The road to a socialist Palestine went through Moscow, not London.

In interwar Poland the party became, for a time, a major force on the Jewish Left. It had begun to grow rapidly during World War I and had built up a strong network of schools and soup kitchens. In the 1920s the party had established a solid presence in the Jewish labor unions.[19] Together with the Bund, the LPZ played a major role in the Central Yiddish School Organization (CYSHO) and maintained its own Borochov schools within that system.[20] Although the party's main strength was in mid-sized provincial towns, it had a strong presence in Lodz and elected prominent city council members in Warsaw.[21] A core of able and dedicated leaders carried the party's message.

A centerpiece of party activity—its pride and joy—was its youth organization, Yugnt, and its sports network, the Stern. Emanuel Ringelblum took part in the first congress of Yugnt in the new Polish Republic, which took place in Warsaw in 1919.[22] He became a member of its Central Committee and began to write for its newspapers, the Polish *Nasze hasła* and the Yiddish *Di fraye yugnt.*

Yugnt differed greatly from such major Zionist youth movements as Hashomer Hatzair,[23] the latter stressing emigration to Palestine. It fervently believed in the revival of Hebrew as the national language, recruited heavily from what was loosely called the Jewish middle and lower middle class, and tended to use Polish rather than Yiddish in its activities. Yugnt was a working class, Yiddishist organization that focused as much on political struggle in Poland as it did on emigration to Palestine. Furthermore, a Zionist youth group like Hashomer sought independence from adult leadership. Firmly convinced that young people were the vanguard of change, the Hashomer regarded most adult Zionist leaders in Poland with bemused condescension or even contempt. After all, what kind of Zionists were they if they were unwilling to leave Poland?[24] Hashomer Hatzair was also influenced by the European scouting tradition and this contributed to its alienation from adult politics.[25]

Yugnt, on the other hand, saw itself as an integral arm of the parent party. In this regard it was far closer to Tsukunft, the Bundist youth organization, than to Zionist youth movements. Yugnt also competed with the Bund and the illegal Communist Party for the same constituency—poor Yiddish-speaking young people from the urban Jewish working class who worked for miserable wages in small shops and factories. Many lived in the worst slums of Warsaw and Lodz, on the porous boundary line between poverty and the underworld. For a young person who lived in a cellar in Lodz's impoverished Balut or Warsaw's Smocza Street, groups like the Bund and the LPZ were far more than mere political parties. They represented a road to self-respect and human dignity, a way to strive for "something better."

Even more than their elders, Jewish youth keenly felt the sense of hopelessness and desperation that engulfed wide sectors of Polish Jewry, especially after the beginning of the Great Depression. If the adult LPZ was a radical party, then Yugnt was even more so: angrier, more combative, and more pro-Soviet. Indeed one of the biggest problems Yugnt faced was defections to the Communist Party.

For Ringelblum, serving on the Central Committee of Yugnt entailed serious risks and even some physical danger. Both Yugnt and the parent party faced growing persecution from the Polish police. The Polish authorities regarded the party as little more than a Communist front. That the outlawed KPP frequently attacked LPZ meetings did little to assuage official suspicions. The constant persecution became a major problem for the party, along with ongoing arrests of party leaders and raids on the Arbeter Heym, the party's Warsaw headquarters on 23 Karmelicka Street.

The annual May Day demonstrations were an especially dangerous time. Jacob Kener, who worked closely with Ringelblum on the Yugnt Central Committee, recalled a particularly brutal attack on the party's May Day demonstration in Warsaw in 1928. The demonstration had assembled in front of the Arbeter Heym when mounted police suddenly surrounded the crowd, blocking off all means of escape:

> Two minutes later the whole street looked like a battlefield. Heaps of wounded with beaten faces . . . lay all over . . . Suddenly I found myself surrounded by a group of drunken, excited mounted police. I bent down in order to raise a bloody red flag that lay in front of me. Just at that moment a policeman bent down to beat me with his rifle butt. I grabbed his rifle and yelled at him in Polish, "What do you think you're doing!" So the drunken policeman thought I was an agent in civilian clothes [and stopped beating me].[26]

One woman, Anna Olcanetzka, who had been a member of Yungbor, the party's children's organization, recalled a march through Warsaw streets. Ringelblum along with other party members escorted the children. Suddenly a group of anti-Semitic hooligans surrounded the Yungbor procession and began to jeer at them. Ringelblum took Anna and another child by the hand, faced down the thugs, and escorted the children to safety.[27]

Ringelblum now found a mission, an outlet for his political idealism: education and culture for party youth and older workers. Since many of these young people had only rudimentary schooling, Yugnt had to focus on something that more middle-class Zionist youth organizations could afford to ignore—basic education. Ringelblum and his comrades in the Yugnt Central Committee organized an ambitious schedule of lectures, evening seminars, and cultural activities for working-class youth. He began to give regular evening courses under the aegis of the party's major cultural arm, the *Ovnt kursn far arbeter* (Evening Courses for Workers). In 1931 he outlined a "two-year plan" to fight illiteracy.[28]

Until the Polish authorities banned it in 1933, the Ovnt kursn far arbeter was one of the most important cultural organizations in Jewish Poland. It sponsored amateur theater circles, organized sports clubs and libraries, and developed an elaborate system of adult education including rudimentary evening courses and more advanced "popular universities." A cursory survey of Ovnt kursn activities in Warsaw in 1926–27 recorded fourteen tourist excursions to other cities and several visits to Warsaw museums. The Drama Circle performed works by Moshe Leyb Halperin, Sholom Aleikhem, and S. Ansky. The library collection included 535 books in Yiddish and 437 in Polish. The library lent out 2,685 books during the year—1,987 in Yiddish and 698 in Polish.[29]

In the early 1920s the Ovnt kursn had been headed by a much beloved figure, Borukh Eizenshtat. After the Polish authorities arrested Eizenshtat and deported him to the Soviet Union in 1927, Ringelblum joined a committee that took over the running of the organization. This small group of dedicated young idealists and close friends formed an intellectual elite comprised of the young historians Rafael Mahler and Bela Mandelsberg, Adolf Berman, an aspiring psychologist who would work closely with Ringelblum in the Warsaw Ghetto, and Joseph Rosen.[30]

The group developed several comprehensive and ambitious study plans for the Ovnt kursn covering the natural sciences, literature, and history. The history course for beginners, for example, projected intensive study of geography, material culture, climatic effects on human societies, the evolution of diet, the impact of housing, a clothing survey, and many other topics. The plan stipulated that Jewish and non-Jewish history be taught together rather than as separate subjects.[31]

Along with other members of the Central Committee, Ringelblum spent his evenings and weekends giving lectures and seminars. He maintained an exhausting pace and often traveled to small towns in the provinces where, with little sleep, he would lecture on a Saturday afternoon and return to the capital the same day.[32] In the Warsaw night schools, where he taught for many years for nominal wages, Ringelblum was profoundly moved by his students' dedication to their studies. After all, they were poor workers and apprentices who staggered into class dead tired after a full day of work and yet spent their last pennies on books and library fees. Ringelblum, Jacob Kener recalled, had unlimited time for his students. He would also take them on Saturday hikes and organize extra activities during whatever spare time they could find.[33]

Ringelblum used the party press to preach the need to reform "bourgeois education," to erase artificial barriers between teacher and student, and replace rigid lectures with a Socratic method that encouraged dialogue and true intellectual curiosity. In a lurid article published in *Di fraye yugnt* Ringelblum cited an incident in Vilna, where a Polish student murdered his mathematics teacher, to point out that socialism would establish a more humane educational system that did not crush students with unbearable pressure and rote learning.[34]

The press became a centerpiece of Yugnt's activities. The Yiddish-language *Di fraye yugnt* and the Polish *Nasze hasła* gave its young readers not only numerous articles about Borochov and Lenin but also basic surveys of history, literature, and natural science. A random survey of *Di fraye yugnt* for 1925 included articles on such diverse topics as polar exploration, radio, rocket flight, and the automobile industry. As a member of the editorial board, Ringelblum also lobbied hard to involve young people in the actual running of the newspaper. It was all too easy, he argued, for an editorial board to take charge and decide on the paper's content. To avoid this, it was important to send questionnaires and ask the readership what they wanted and what they needed. His hope was that more readers could be encouraged to send articles.

The study of history played a major role in Yugnt's program. Ringelblum, writing under the pen name Munie Heler, his mother's maiden name, regularly contributed articles on such historical topics as Warsaw Jewry in the sixteenth century, pogroms in early modern Poland, the Paris Commune, Jean-Jacques Rousseau, and the peasant war in sixteenth-century Germany. In all these articles—written from a clearly Marxist viewpoint—Ringelblum tried to demonstrate the contemporary relevance of these historical subjects and stressed the interconnectedness of Jewish and general history.

In an article entitled "The Jewish Working Class and the Study of History," for instance, Ringelblum told his young readers that neither a nation nor a class could afford to ignore its own history.[35] Until now the nobility and bourgeoisie had distorted history to protect their own narrow class interests. Pliant historians had avoided social history and instead served up anecdotal accounts of kings and queens. Ringelblum cited the historical treatment of the eighteenth-century Polish hero Tadeusz Kościuszko as a blatant example of how ruling elites used history for their own ends. Official commemorations totally ignored Kościuszko's support of the oppressed peasantry and instead turned him into a symbol of Polish nationalism. Little wonder that wealthy Polish landlords blithely honored his memory. Fortunately the European working class had begun to understand how important history was to its intellectual development—and a new, Marxist-oriented history was beginning to make an important contribution to proletarian culture.

When it came to their awareness of history, however, Jewish workers found themselves in an even worse position than their Gentile comrades. "Up to now" Ringelblum, complained,

> there is nowhere where the Jewish worker can learn about the importance of historical knowledge for his own struggle . . . there is no Jewish history [that is written from the materialist viewpoint] . . . almost all the Jewish history that has been written, almost all of it in foreign languages, has been a history of persecutions, evil decrees, and pogroms that Jews had to suffer in various times and in various countries. Jewish history has been presented as an indictment of surrounding peoples and nations . . . but Jewish historians also knew that the people needed words of comfort. So they gave the people histories of rabbis and important personalities. . . . As Dr. Schiper pointed out, it is thanks to the work of Graetz [Heinrich Graetz (1817–1891)], Jost [Isaac Markus Jost (1793–1860)] . . . and Dubnow [Simon Dubnow (1860–1941)] that we have a wonderful historical picture of the spiritual leaders of the Jewish people in the Diaspora. But we lack an understanding of the hundreds and thousands who lived not from their wealth and intellect but from labor and toil . . . We know the Shabes Jew [Sabbath Jew], it is time now to study the history of the ordinary Jew.[36]

One problem, Ringelblum emphasized, was that most Jewish history had been written by German Jews, specifically Graetz and Jost, who regarded Jews as a religious group and not as a nation. What these German Jews really wanted to show was that the Jews were a chosen people whose mission was to spread ethical enlightenment and monotheistic principles.[37] Little wonder, therefore, that they had scant interest in the history of the Jewish people and of its working masses. As for the work of the assimilationist Polish-Jewish historians such as Hilary Nussbaum (1820–1895) and Alexander Kraushar (1842–

1931)—the less said the better. They were pathetic apologists who used history to convince Jews that they should become "Poles of the Mosaic persuasion." Despite some promising beginnings (Ringelblum mentioned Dr. Schiper) Polish-Jewish history was still uncharted territory.

These youthful and somewhat unsophisticated articles in *Di fraye yugnt*, written in a didactic style and accessible language, certainly reflected enthusiastic support of the party line. But they also offer valuable insights into Ringelblum's intellectual development and his growing devotion to workers' education and Yiddish secular culture. Since the Jewish bourgeoisie had turned its back on the folk language, he complained, its fate rested on a coalition of progressive leftist intellectuals (like himself) and workers.[38]

In 1926, the year after the YIVO was founded as the Yiddish Scientific Institute, an enthusiastic Ringelblum hailed the new institution in two articles in *Di fraye yugnt*.[39] The YIVO, he declared, would become the first major research institution to foster engaged scholarship in Yiddish, a vital first step in the emancipation of East European Jews from their intellectual bondage to German-Jewish scholars. With palpable enthusiasm, Ringelblum outlined for his young readers the institute's far-flung research agenda in Yiddish philology, Jewish history, psychology, economics, and statistics. Quoting Borochov, he pointed out that the time had come to revise the study of Yiddish philology. "Everything written on [Yiddish philology] in the past three hundred years now has only curiosity value . . . Modern Yiddish scholars will . . . [revise everything] . . . since they approach the study of Yiddish from a totally different perspective. They see Yiddish as a living language, not as a 'jargon' or an ugly German dialect."[40]

The YIVO, Ringelblum continued would set new agendas for Jewish historians: the study of Jewish emigration, Jewish economic history, and the history of Jewish artisans and their struggle against exploitation and social discrimination. He pointed out that the Jewish working class had a vital interest in the new historical section of the YIVO. Jewish workers who studied the history of the Jewish revolutionary movement would come away with a new feeling of pride and optimism. If they read about seventeenth-century struggles of Jewish artisans against the rapacious *kehilla* elites,[41] they would realize that Jewish history belonged as much to the masses as it did to the wealthy. This kind of history would certainly facilitate the construction of a new national and class identity.

But the mission of the YIVO did not stop there, he added. The new institute was also an indispensable ally of the new Yiddish secular school system. There was a pressing need for serious research that would help develop efficient teaching techniques for the Yiddish schools. Good pedagogy required extensive investigation of the psychological profile of Jewish children and the specific ways in which their environment and culture affected their personal development.

Ringelblum called on the Jewish workers to rally to the support of the YIVO. In order to ensure that the institute served the needs of the Jewish masses, workers had to become directly involved in YIVO activities. Ringelblum stressed the importance of *zamling,* the collecting of materials for the institute.

> The working class must collect all kinds of material for the study of Jewish folklore, ethnography, history. [It should gather] all sources that could help in the study of our language and folk tradition [*folksoytser*]: various proverbs, popular sayings, jokes, styles of speech, terms used for tools, customs, and popular oaths. This should all be collected and sent to Vilna.[42]

Tensions flared almost immediately between the leftist parties and the scholars who led the institution. Leaders of both the Bund and the LPZ accused the YIVO leadership of pursuing the tired bourgeois chimera of "objective scholarship," of trying to turn the institution into an ivory tower with little interest in the pressing needs of the Jewish masses and the Jewish working class. At the same time many Jewish teachers in the CYSHO Yiddish school system complained that the YIVO paid too little attention to their needs. They needed better textbooks, Yiddish grammars, and new rules on orthography. But, some of the teachers charged, the institute remained aloof.

In turn, the YIVO leadership—Max Weinreich, Zelig Kalmanovich, Zalmen Reyzen, and Jacob Shatzky (in the U.S.)—angrily denied these charges. Political factionalism and sectarian bitterness had paralyzed Polish Jewry. Did it make sense to politicize the one institution in the world that promoted Yiddish scholarship? Furthermore, as Max Weinreich pointed out at the 1935 YIVO conference, just because the YIVO was a scholarly institution did not mean it was an ivory tower. YIVO scholarship was engaged scholarship, committed to bringing together the past and the present. If the people were to solve their problems, first they needed thorough research to help them understand what those problems were.[43]

Weinreich's defense of the YIVO failed to impress the LPZ leadership. In 1931 several articles appeared in the *Arbeter tsaytung* that attacked "Yiddish for Yiddish's sake" and "Non-party Yiddishism" (*Klal Yidishizm*). Leading the charge was one of the party's most respected leaders, Natan Buchsbaum. Six years after the institute's founding Buchsbaum concluded that enough time had elapsed to pass judgment on the YIVO, and that judgment was clear: notwithstanding the participation of a few left-wing scholars, The YIVO had become just "another ordinary bourgeois academic institution."[44] Buchsbaum then targeted one of Ringelblum's favorite projects, the "collectors groups" (*zamler krayzn*). "These circles," Buchsbaum argued, "are useless ballast for the Jewish working class . . . they cultivate a respect for the YIVO that is not in the interests of the proletariat."[45] It is a safe assumption that a major factor in the party's growing hostility to the YIVO was the impact of the Cultural Revolution that was then in full swing in the USSR. The left turn in cultural policy had included Yiddish culture. In the USSR Yiddish scholars and the Communist Yiddish press had begun to attack "fascist Yiddishism" in general and the YIVO in particular.[46]

A month later Ringelblum replied to Buchsbaum. In a long article in the *Arbeter tsaytung* Ringelblum showed an uncharacteristic readiness to take on one of the party's most illustrious leaders. The party's rhetoric on the YIVO was so radical, so hyper-left, Ringelblum observed sarcastically, that all that was missing was some jargon about "fascist Yiddishism." No, Ringelblum admitted, the YIVO was not perfect. The leadership consisted of democratic intellectuals, not committed leftists. Yes, it would be good if workers were more involved. But this took time and required years of patient propaganda. Did Buchsbaum, Ringelblum asked, really believe that the party should boycott the YIVO? Did the party really believe that it could neglect serious cultural work until after the victory of the revolution? No, cultural work was inextricably linked to the political battle.

> Should we put off our study of the heroic Jewish labor movement until after the revolution? Should we postpone the gathering of old socialist brochures and pamphlets? Isn't this activity also political? Isn't it true that accounts of the heroic battles waged by the Jewish working class inspire younger workers to continue the struggle and to follow in its footsteps?[47]

Was it not true that the YIVO's philological section was fulfilling Borochov's legacy? Didn't the workers' children in the Yiddish schools need a clear understanding of their mother tongue? Ringelblum also defended the institute's projected studies of child psychology. Was this, too, unrelated to the needs of the working class?

If the CYSHO schools were the foundation of the Yiddish cultural system in Poland, then the YIVO, Ringelblum reminded his readers, was its roof. As Buchsbaum knew all too well, the Jewish Communists were busy doing all that they could to destroy the CYSHO schools. Ringelblum called these actions "cultural gangsterism" (*metodn fun hefkeyres*). Did Buchsbaum want to do the same thing to the YIVO?[48]

As an emerging leader of the party's cultural work, Ringelblum played an active role in the two major "culture congresses" which the party organized in 1926 and 1931. The hundreds of delegates who came to these congresses were convinced they could build a new proletarian culture that would inspire the Jewish masses and prepare the way for social revolution. In their quest for new cultural paradigms they could look to the Soviet Union and to "Red Vienna" for inspiration, but these culture congresses also reflected the tension between the quest for ideological purity and cultural integrity.[49] Although the party wanted to define "proletarian education," "proletarian sport," and "proletarian theater," what did this mean in practice? Should the "ovnt kursn" ban "bourgeois writers"? Were some sports more ideologically acceptable than others? What ground rules should the party establish for amateur theaters? These issues become the major focus of debate and the subject of a special one-time publication, *Arbeter kultur,* which the party issued in 1931.

Ringelblum took an active role in the 1931 culture congress. While he saw himself as a radical leftist, he was certainly no believer in tight, top-down centralized control. He wanted the leadership of the congress to conduct a survey of the delegates, send out questionnaires, and develop a clear sense of problems and priorities. Implicit in this stance were the convictions that successful cultural activity required collaboration rather than central control and that ideas by themselves mattered little unless they rested on a solid organizational foundation. He stressed that only meticulous organization and planning would make the congress successful.[50]

In addition to his defense of the YIVO, Ringelblum wrote important articles in the party press on the role of libraries and amateur theater in proletarian culture. Here, too, he warned against "hyper-left" radicalism that could paralyze the party's cultural work. Ringelblum advised the party to be pragmatic, not doctrinaire. He strongly opposed censorship in the libraries or establishing an index of forbidden books.[51] Libraries had to expose workers to the full range of Yiddish literature. A novel did not have to be "proletarian" to have artistic and didactic value. And even though Ringelblum believed that most books had to be in Yiddish, it was still important to stock Polish books as a bridge to the surrounding culture. The party should help the Jewish workers learn Polish and link them to their Polish comrades. Conversely libraries could bring Jewish graduates of Polish state schools closer to Yiddish culture. An increasing number of young people now read Yiddish with difficulty. Polish translations of Yiddish literature could be a first step in their return to Yiddish culture.

If Ringelblum opposed rigid censorship in libraries, he took a harder line on amateur theater groups. Here he suggested that the party should carefully vet their repertory. Theater had enormous potential to affect even the most backward worker. Unfortunately it was all too tempting—even for party groups—to exploit the popularity of the theater and stage vulgar plays for the sake of quick profit. Ringelblum advocated a leftist theater that would emphasize collective performance rather than showcasing a few "stars." He called for more choral scenes and mass recitals that would involve the entire troupe. It was also important, he warned, to keep the theater troupe from becoming a closed clique.

In the mid-1930s Ringelblum also helped lead the campaign in Poland to organize a worldwide congress on Yiddish culture. In Poland this campaign brought together Communists, members of the LPZ, and democratic Yiddishists, especially from Vilna. One leader of the campaign, Nakhman Mayzel, who edited the *Literarishe bleter,* recalled how impressed he was by Ringelblum's enthusiasm and commitment to the idea of the congress.[52] Ringelblum and other supporters of the congress argued that it was time to forget party differences and develop a united front to defend Yiddish culture by drafting a detailed action plan on libraries, publishing, schools, and theater. However, the strongest Yiddishist party in Poland, the Bund, boycotted the campaign. The Bund argued, not entirely without cause, that the Communists wanted to turn the culture congress into a party-dominated front. When the culture congress did meet in Paris in September 1937, it attracted an impressive array of delegates, including leading Yiddishist intellectuals and writers like H. Leyvik, Chaim Zhitlovsky, and Joseph Opatoshu. For some reason Ringelblum, a member of the Polish delegation, was unable to travel to Paris.[53] The congress became a forum for probing discussions about the state of Yiddish culture,[54] but the Bund's boycott severely limited its impact in Poland. The culture congress episode only sharpened Ringelblum's distaste for the Bund. One could also speculate that the campaign helped to improve strained relations between the LPZ and Jewish Communists, thus laying the groundwork for the collaboration between the two groups in the Warsaw Ghetto.

Lending a sense of urgency and relevance to the party's efforts to organize the culture congress was the Borochovian principle that the Jewish people were an interconnected whole. In stark contrast to the Bund, the party press stressed how developments in one Jewish community could modernize others. Transformation of Jewish society in the Diaspora would go hand in hand with the development of a territorial center in Palestine. Only this territorial base could guarantee the effective modernization of Jewish society in the Diaspora. In an important article in the *Arbeter tsaytung* Natan Buchsbaum emphasized how the interrelated processes of emigration and the development of a new territorial center powered the development of new models of Jewish life. The great Jewish communities in the United States, the Soviet Union, and the New Yishuv, the Jewish community in Palestine, were all creating fresh cultural paradigms that would break the hold of religious tradition and shtetl culture—a product of extraterritoriality—on Poland's Jewish masses. By misconstruing the link between emigration, territorialization, and modernization, Buchsbaum argued, the Bund betrayed the inadequacy of its ideology.[55]

Drawing heavily on the writings of Ber Borochov, Rafael Mahler made a similar connection between territorialization and the future of the Yiddish language. Territorialization not only would transform the structure of Jewish society and afford the Jewish worker a strategic base; it would also galvanize and renew the Yiddish language. The Yiddish of the shtetl, Mahler asserted, was poor and underdeveloped. A locomotive driver or steelworker in Palestine or Birobidzhan would obviously speak a richer Yiddish than a small-town shoemaker.[56]

The 1930s saw a marked decline of LPZ support. The same complex ideology that attracted true believers like Ringelblum and Mahler made it difficult to recruit a mass following. As the party tried to balance Palestine, Poland, and Moscow, it lost ground to its more focused rivals. If one were pro-Soviet, why not join the Communist Party? If one were Zionist, why not join the Right Poalei Tsiyon or one of the Zionist youth movements? And if one cared about Yiddishism and the Diaspora, why not simply join the Bund?

During the 1930s, as the LPZ struggled to define itself, the Jewish political scene in Poland changed dramatically. By the middle of the decade, the Bund had become the largest Jewish party in big cities such as Warsaw and Lodz.[57] Its message was as simple as the LPZ's was complicated—fight for equal rights where you live. This simple message became even more appealing because, in its polemics with the LPZ and other Zionist parties, the Bund seemed to offer a glimmer of optimism.

In the 1930s, for example, the Bund honed its economic platform, and one of its leaders, Victor Alter, published a detailed refutation of Borochovian economics.[58] There was no such thing, Alter argued, as a separate "peripheral" Jewish economy. What was wrong or "anomalous" about being a tailor? A Jewish tailor was no worse than a Polish coal miner. To bemoan the "abnormality" of Jewish occupations, Alter asserted, was simple self-hatred. And although the Bund admitted the worsening plight of Polish Jewry in the 1930s it took sharp issue with the LPZ's diagnosis of the problem. Bundist publications held out hope for the beleaguered Polish Jews. They were waging and slowly winning a tough war of economic self-defense. They were leaving behind the exposed and vulnerable shtetl and moving into the big cities. In the large urban centers Jews were carving out new economic positions. They were also discarding traditional prejudices and moving into factories.

Bundist successes especially frustrated the LPZ because they occurred precisely when political and economic developments seemed to be confirming the Borochovian prognosis. The Great Depression, Hitler's rise to power, and the imposition of immigration restrictions had indeed transformed Palestine into the chief country of Jewish emigration by the 1930s. Jacob Zerubavel asserted that the depression had sent more emigrants to Palestine than decades of Zionist propaganda. Meanwhile, the marginalization of the Jewish labor force in Poland also seemed to bolster the party's case. The Polish government excluded Jews from the most modern sectors of the economy, and a growing proportion of Jewish workers found themselves forced to perform contract piecework in their own homes. But the party faced a tough problem. The Bund's message, as noted, was simple and easy to understand. By comparison, the *do-dortn* (here-there) contortions of the LPZ seemed convoluted and arcane.

Even as the party sought to differentiate itself from the Bund, dramatic new developments in the USSR plunged it into crisis. In 1928 the Soviet Union offered the Jews a territory: Birobidzhan. For many party members, the promise of Birobidzhan erased the last thin barrier separating the LPZ from the Communist Party. Since the party had embraced prognostic rather than voluntaristic Zionism, there seemed to be no logical reason why Palestine was preferable to the new Jewish homeland-in-the-making in the USSR. For those who looked upon romantic Zionism with contempt, one "territorial base" was as good as another.

In 1934 Jacob Zerubavel published a series of theoretical articles in the *Arbeter tsaytung* that shattered the party. The articles were a response to a broadside by Ze'ev Abramovich, one of the leaders of the Palestinian LPZ. Abramovich had sarcastically noted that the LPZ supported every cause and every battle except emigration to Palestine and the building of the Yishuv. Palestine was a kind of afterthought, a "dessert" [*lekehkl*] that had little impact on the party's daily concerns. Abramovich went on to attack the bedrock of the party's creed, the *do-dortn* synthesis. He challenged the party to say openly and clearly that the purpose of its political struggle in the Diaspora was to prepare Jewish workers for emigration to Palestine.

Zerubavel hit back with a vengeance.[59] He reaffirmed the *do-dortn* synthesis and charged that "Palestinocentrism," as he called it, betrayed the basic principles of the movement. Why succumb to national romanticism, why turn the party into an "emigration bureau"? A new arena of Jewish territorialization had opened up—Birobidzhan. The new Jewish center in the USSR proved once again what Jews could achieve in a truly socialist state. Just as one would not ask a child whether he loves his mother or father more, one should not have to choose between Palestine and the Diaspora, especially since the Soviet Union had now assumed decisive importance in the fate of the Jewish people.

Zerubavel's article cut to the bone. By dotting the i's and crossing the t's he exposed the pitfalls of the party's ideology. If the Soviet Union was so important, then what was the point of Palestine? Zerubavel did not flinch. If the territorial base could be achieved in Birobidzhan, so be it. (That didn't stop him, by the way, from leaving Poland for Palestine in 1935!)

Other party leaders now attacked Zerubavel for blurring the line that divided the LPZ from the Communists. From Palestine, Nahum Nir-Rafalkes asked how one could keep members from bolting to the Communists if Birobidzhan was now as good as Palestine.[60] Betsalel Sherman, the leader of the American branch of the LPZ, charged that Zerubavel was taking an overly rosy view of Soviet reality. Birobidzhan was a failure, Yiddish was in decline, and Soviet Jews continued to assimilate.[61]

The Polish party now faced a full-fledged crisis.[62] Given Zerubavel's rosy endorsement of Birobidzhan, many members, not surprisingly, defected to the Communist Party. This hit the youth organization, Yugnt, especially hard. In response, Yitzhak Lev, a Warsaw city councilman and one of the party's most popular figures, called on the party to reassess its position.[63] With the future of the movement at stake, Lev appealed for a strengthening of Zionism, a greater emphasis on emigration to Palestine. Zerubavel, Lev charged, had totally misread the Soviet situation. The party leadership, he complained, had become paralyzed and could not break out of its ideological straitjacket. In the face of the growing Nazi danger, Lev warned that the party should put political realism ahead of ideological purity. If the party sharpened its Zionist message, then it could begin to reach out to the Jewish lower middle classes and especially to the youth who were flocking to the pioneering youth movements.

At the end of 1934 Lev split the Polish party and began to publish his own newspaper, the *Arbeter vort.* With that, the movement went into free fall. Membership plummeted, and finances were so bad that the party's major organ, the *Arbeter tsaytung,* halted publication for much of 1936. Faced with a total collapse of the movement, the party leadership in Poland swallowed their pride and started talking to Lev. In late 1936, Lev's group rejoined the party.

Now reunited, the Left Poalei Zion did a complete reversal and turned back to the Zionist movement. Indeed, in late 1937 the global organization of the LPZ returned to the World Zionist Organization. There were many reasons for this startling volte-face. Bad news from the Soviet Union certainly played a major role: hard on the heels of the Moscow purge trials came the news that Stalin had wiped out the leadership of Birobidzhan. The Russian leader's 1938 decision to liquidate the Polish Communist Party also undermined confidence in the USSR, just as events in Palestine forced the party to take another hard look at its policy. For a short time in 1937, the Peel Commission report suddenly raised the possibility of Jewish statehood in a part of Palestine. When a delegation of the Polish LPZ arrived in Palestine in 1937, it received red carpet treatment from the leadership of the Histadrut. Even convinced leftists like Shakhne Zagan and Natan Buchsbaum returned to Poland brimming with enthusiasm for the achievements of the Yishuv. The party press, from then on, referred to "Eretz Yisroel" rather than Palestine.[64] An important psychological barrier had been breached. The White Paper of May 1939—when Great Britain basically renounced the Balfour Declaration—also helped to bring the party closer to the Zionist movement. In the face of growing adversity—and Bundist electoral victories—the LPZ grew even more forceful in its defense of the Zionist enterprise. In 1938 and 1939 the *Arbeter tsaytung* took what seemed like a perverse pride in the party's difficulties. The lot of the Poalei Tsiyon had never been easy, Zerubavel reminded his readers. In the spring of 1939 Jacob Zerubavel effectively said: "Look at us. You can't accuse our party of taking the path of least resistance. In the middle of the Arab revolt—and just when the Bund is stronger than ever—we rejoined the World Zionist Organization. But Borochov was right and eventually the Jewish worker will see the light."[65]

During this whole period of intraparty conflict and decline, Ringelblum had steadfastly supported the Zerubavel-Buchsbaum line. When Yitzhak Lev split the party in 1934, Ringelblum had refused to go along with Lev's call for a greater focus on Palestine. A former Poalei Tsiyon member who knew Ringelblum well believed that the latter had deep reservations about what Lev was doing. When the party split, Ringelblum feared that collaboration with bourgeois Zionist parties might blur the party's message and undermine its identity as a working-class Yiddishist party committed to the Diaspora.[66] Shakhne Zagan, an important party leader whom Ringelblum admired greatly, shared the same reservations.[67] But both Zagan and Ringelblum were loyal party members and went along with the party's return to the Zionist mainstream on the eve of the war.

That Ringelblum stayed with the party during the difficult years of the 1930s is an impressive commentary on his loyalty to the movement. The logic of the party's ideology dictated a pro-Soviet position, which he took on a number of occasions. But, like others in his movement, he was deeply troubled by many aspects of Soviet Jewish reality, including rampant assimilation and the decline of Yiddish culture. Ringelblum's attitude toward the Bund also reflected his political biases. He clearly resented what he saw as Bundist arrogance and its claim to be the "sole representative of the Jewish working class."[68] His refusal to join Lev in 1934 signaled a stubborn resistance to the emotional pull of romantic Jewish nationalism and the pathos of *binyan haaretz*, the pioneering redemption of Jewish Palestine. He also had deep misgivings about renewing collaboration with Zionist middle-class parties. But like the rest of his movement on the eve of the war, Ringelblum was starting to rethink this long-held stance. In the spring of 1939 he would join in massive street demonstrations against the British White Paper.[69] Just a week before the outbreak of World War II he would be in Geneva as a delegate to the Twenty-second Zionist World Congress.

Despite the prewar rapprochement with Zionism, however, neither Ringelblum nor his party was ready to abandon the *do* for the *dortn*. They would start calling Palestine Eretz Yisroel. They would finally start marching in Zionist demonstrations. But they could never turn their backs on the Diaspora, on the Jewish masses and the Yiddish culture that they so loved. It was this facet of the LPZ that left its deepest imprint on Ringelblum: commitment to the Jewish masses and to Yiddish culture.

CHAPTER 3

History for the People

By the outbreak of the Second World War, Emanuel Ringelblum had become one of the most promising of the younger generation of Jewish historians in Poland. This generation—which included Rafael Mahler, Philip Friedman, Isaiah (Shie) Trunk, Bela Mandelsberg, and others—followed in the footsteps of Meyer Balaban and Isaac Schiper, two older scholars who served as trailblazers for the study of Polish Jewish history.

But whereas Schiper and Balaban spent their formative years of scholarship in the relative peace and quiet of Habsburg Galicia, this next generation came to maturity in the more turbulent milieu of the reborn Polish state. Like other young Jewish historians, Ringelblum had little hope of pursuing a traditional academic career. Still he deeply believed that Jewish historians in interwar Poland had multiple missions: to help in the Jewish fight against anti-Semitism and for minority rights; to build a much needed bridge between Jews and Poles; and to bring together scholars and ordinary Jews in a mutual project to shape a Yiddish secular culture. Although Ringelblum had earned a respectable record of scholarship, his forte was as an organizer. Largely ignored by their Polish colleagues and hampered by serious financial constraints as well as hostility and indifference both from Poles and within the Jewish community, young Jewish historians in interwar Poland had to shape an unofficial "counter-profession." They needed journals that would publish their work and seminars where they could discuss research with colleagues, and also the satisfaction of knowing that they were having an impact on the intense but fractious cultural life of interwar Polish Jewry. The founding of the YIVO in Vilna in 1925 was a great step forward but was only a beginning. Warsaw, not Vilna, became the center of this "counter-profession" of Polish-Jewish historians, and few people contributed more to its development than Emanuel Ringelblum.

Emanuel Ringelblum decided to become a historian shortly after entering Warsaw University in 1920. For a time he was tempted by economics and sociology but finally settled on the still largely unexplored field of Polish-Jewish history, which had become topical and relevant. Now that Jews once again found themselves under Polish sovereignty, the history of Polish Jewry took on a new urgency. Supporters of the anti-Jewish National Democratic party used historical arguments to bolster their call for a political and economic campaign against a Jewish minority which they viewed as harmful alien interlopers.[1] Articles and books by Jan Ptaśnik, Zygmunt Balicki, Father Marjan Morawski, Roman Rybarski, and others painted a damning picture of Jewish economic power and political treachery. For instance, in his 1928 study on Polish trade in the sixteenth century, Professor Rybarski, a noted economic historian, stressed the harmful impact of the Jews on the development of Polish cities and the Polish economy.[2]

In turn, Jewish historians in the young Polish republic began to see themselves as front line soldiers in a battle to convince the Polish public that anti-Semitism was not only self-defeating and harmful but rested on a totally erroneous interpretation of Polish history. Historical research quickly turned into a weapon to defend Jewish honor. Certain questions now assumed special importance. How had the Jews contributed to the economic development of Poland? How had Jews participated in Poland's struggles for independence? What truth was there to the charge leveled by Polish anti-Semites that the Jews had from the beginning constituted an alien element, indifferent to Poland's national interests and siding with her oppressors?

Aside from the battle against Polish ethnic nationalists, fierce ideological conflict within the Jewish community also engaged the partisan involvement of historians. As Jewish political parties and youth groups clashed over religion vs. secularism, Yiddish vs. Hebrew, Zionism vs. the Diaspora, historians entered the fray. Were the Jewish autonomous institutions of the sixteenth and seventeenth centuries indeed bastions of national creativity and vitality or mainly agents of exploitation and injustice allowing wealthy Jews to fleece their poorer brothers? Could religion take the credit for Jewish survival over the centuries, or should one look to economic factors? Was Yiddish culture a relatively recent creature of political radicalism, or was it rooted in a centuries-old popular tradition? For Yiddishists and Diaspora nationalists, politically committed scholars were especially welcome allies who could show that the study of the popular masses mattered no less than the study of intellectual elites.

A deep interest in history marked interwar Polish-Jewish culture. Best-selling novels like Joseph Opatoshu's *In Poylishe Velder* and *A Tog in Regensberg,* Sholem Asch's *Kiddush Hashem,* and Alter Katsyzne's play *Dukus* not only reflected popular interest in the Jewish past but also elicited important reviews and discussions in the Jewish press. The two most important Jewish historians, Isaac Schiper and Meyer Balaban, published frequent popular articles on Jewish history in the most important Yiddish- and Polish-language Jewish dailies, *Haynt, Moment, Nasz przegląd,* and *Chwila.*

Ringelblum joined a younger generation of historians who continued and expanded the revolutionary transformation of the study of East European Jewry pioneered by Schiper, Balaban, and Simon Dubnow. He did so just when Warsaw was replacing St. Petersburg as the center of East European Jewish historical scholarship.

In the last decade of the nineteenth century it was Simon Dubnow who had recognized the importance of Jewish history for the cultural modernization of East European Jewry; he had both exemplified and preached the national and political responsibilities of the Jewish historian. Dubnow's path-breaking 1891 appeal to the Jewish intelligentsia to collect and preserve the source materials of Jewish history fell on fertile ground. Dubnow defined *zamling,* the gathering of these materials, as a national mission.[3] St. Petersburg, within two decades, had become the center for the study of East European Jewish history. Younger historians like Ringelblum, although they would contest many of Dubnow's assertions, still respected him as someone who had had put the history of East European Jewry at the center of his research agenda, unlike the great German-Jewish historian Heinrich Graetz. And, unlike Graetz, Dubnow had in time moved toward what he called a "sociological" conception of Jewish history, where the central factor in Jewish history was not the Jewish religion per se but the Jewish people and its instinct for national survival.[4] Disturbed by what he felt to be Graetz's bias against the Yiddish-speaking masses of Eastern Europe, Dubnow began to stress their national vitality. For example, in a counterpoint to Graetz's negative image, Dubnow, in his trailblazing studies of Hasidism, underscored the innovative creativity that marked the beginnings of the movement. As a young literary critic, he had been one of the first Russian Jewish intellectuals to recognize the national and aesthetic importance of Yiddish literature.[5] He also emphasized the importance of studying Jewish history from the inside, not as the history of legislation enforced upon Jews but as a history of cultural, social, and political changes within the Jewish community itself. One kind of history demanded mostly non-Jewish documents, especially legal records; the other required the historian to work with Jewish sources.

Dubnow also earned the respect of the young Polish-Jewish historians for his determination to defend the centrality of the Diaspora in Jewish history, as opposed to those Zionists who saw it as an interlude between the loss of ancient independence and a future Jewish state in Palestine. Instead, Dubnow conceived Jewish history as being shaped by a succession of "national centers"—in Babylonia, Spain, and Eastern Europe—where the Jewish people proved that it did not need a territory to survive. This emphasis on the development of Jewish self-government in the Diaspora struck a responsive cord in an Eastern Europe where demands for Jewish autonomy and national rights had become a cornerstone of modern Jewish politics. The first issue of the historical journal Ringelblum would found and edit, the *Yunger historiker,* would be dedicated to Dubnow—even though, as a historian, Ringelblum and his friends would move in a very different direction.

Thanks to Dubnow, the pre-World War I Russian-Jewish intelligentsia had begun to embrace Jewish history as a basic component of modern Jewish identity. In an important 1908 speech, the prominent Russian-Jewish political leader and lawyer, Maxim Vinaver, stressed the extent to which Dubnow had influenced him and his contemporaries.[6] The St. Petersburg Jewish elite, inspired by Dubnow, organized an impressive infrastructure for the study of East European Jewish history: a historical society and important journals and collections (*Evreiskaia starina, Regesty i nadpisi, Perezhitoe*), which began to appear in Russian.

By contrast, the Polish-speaking Jewish intelligentsia took longer to develop an interest in history.[7] Before World War I the only Polish-language Jewish historical journal was the Warsaw-based *Kwartalnik poświęcony badaniom przeszłości Żydów w Polsce*—and it closed after only three issues.[8] Even in Galicia, where academic conditions were much freer than in Congress Poland and where Jewish students constituted a large proportion of the student body in Krakow and Lwów universities, Jewish university students—with a few important exceptions—had shown little interest in the study of Polish-Jewish history.[9] As Professor Lucjan Dobroszycki has pointed out, only in 1899 was the first doctoral dissertation on Polish-Jewish history submitted in a Galician university.[10]

Therefore Ringelblum arrived in Warsaw at a crucial period. Serious work in Polish-Jewish history had already begun but the field was still largely uncharted territory. There were no Jewish historical journals. A historical community in Warsaw comparable to St. Petersburg's would have to be built up from scratch, in very different conditions: where Dubnow and the Russian-Jewish intelligentsia had lived in a multinational empire, postwar Polish Jewry found itself a prominent and vulnerable minority in an ethnic nation-state. Jewish historians like Ringelblum would have to toe a fine line, showing that although Jews had put down deep roots in the Polish lands, they still remained a distinct nation entitled to equal rights and respect.

The two leading older mentors—Schiper and Balaban—helped make Warsaw the new scholarly center for Jewish historians of Eastern Europe, serving as a bridge between Dubnow's legacy and a new generation that included Ringelblum, Rafael Mahler, and Philip Friedman. Both Balaban and Schiper had begun to play a leading role well before the beginning of the First World War. As a Russian-speaking Jew based in St. Petersburg, Dubnow had had only a marginal involvement with Polish and Galician Jewry. Just before the outbreak of World War I, however, he had contacted these promising Galician-Jewish historians and invited them to publish in *Evreiskaia starina*.[11] What Dubnow had done in Russia, Balaban and Schiper would do in Poland—make the Jewish intelligentsia aware of the importance of Jewish history. Schiper especially would have a major impact on Ringelblum.

Although Balaban and Schiper differed greatly in their historical approaches, they shared one common agenda that Ringelblum enthusiastically embraced. They both consciously and decisively rejected what Ringelblum, in a 1924 article, called the old assimilationist school of Polish-Jewish history. Nineteenth-century Polish-Jewish historians such as Alexander Kraushar and Hilary Nussbaum, Ringelblum complained, had concocted a fanciful and idealized version of the Jews' status in the Polish-Lithuanian Commonwealth. Using legal documents and charters, but ignoring internal Jewish sources, these historians had emphasized the legal privileges that had made Poland a land of refuge for Jews fleeing persecution. To repay the Poles for their alleged tolerance, these historians argued, the Jews should reject Jewish nationalism and separatism and regard themselves as Poles of the Mosaic persuasion.[12]

Balaban and Schiper, Ringelblum pointed out, were different. They used history to affirm, not disparage, Jewish distinctiveness.[13] Similar to much of the Galician Jewish intelligentsia at the turn of the century, they had turned their backs on political assimilationism and had joined Zionist organizations. Indeed, as we have seen, Schiper had become one of the most important leaders of the Poalei Tsiyon in prewar Galicia. (After the First World War, however, he moved to the Right and become a general Zionist.)[14]

These two historians, and especially Balaban, stressed the critical importance of studying Polish-Jewish history both as an integral part of world Jewish history and as a key component of Polish history.[15] On the one hand, Polish Jewry had become one of the most creative Jewish communities in the world, and historians had to pay special attention to how its culture and institutions were shaped by, and in turn affected, Jewish communities elsewhere. Like Dubnow, therefore, Balaban rejected Graetz's tendency to minimize the role of Polish Jewry in Jewish history. On the other hand, Balaban and Schiper, through their scholarship, stressed the deep links between Polish Jewry and Poland and the ways in which Polish political conditions had affected Jewish development. If many of the key features of Jewish self-government in the old Commonwealth had derived from Jewish models in Germany and other countries, it was nonetheless true, Balaban believed, that Jewish autonomy had reached a new level of development and creativity in early modern Poland, largely because of the specific political conditions of the Rzeczpospolita, the pre-partition Polish-Lithuanian Commonwealth.

In the last months of his life, in the underground bunker on Grójecka Street in south Warsaw, Ringelblum wrote short biographical essays on Balaban and Schiper in which he stressed their vital role in Polish-Jewish intellectual history—and in his own intellectual development. Through his comments on the two historians, Ringelblum also revealed a great deal about himself.

Ringelblum's relations with Balaban had never been close, and the wartime essay, although full of admiration for Balaban's many achievements, reflected that distance.[16] Unlike Schiper, Balaban evidently showed little inclination to serve as a mentor to Ringelblum. Moreover, Balaban had never even flirted with leftist politics and had little interest—or so Ringelblum charged—in economic history. When Ringelblum's first book appeared in 1932, Balaban published a polite but decidedly lukewarm review in the Polish-Jewish daily, *Nasz przegląd*.[17] Their contacts were limited, even in the Warsaw Ghetto. In his essay Ringelblum mentioned that he had *heard* that Balaban had been writing an autobiography. Obviously Ringelblum had little hope of getting a copy for the Oyneg Shabes Archive. But Balaban, who died in the Warsaw Ghetto in 1942, certainly commanded Ringelblum's respect. The latter considered Balaban a brilliant writer who always managed to find just the right anecdote, the vivid personal vignette that would rivet his readers' attention. His great histories of the Jews of Lwów and Krakow crafted a superb description of Jewish culture and intellectual life. Unlike the assimilationist historians, Balaban saw a Jewish nation, not just a religious community. He pioneered the use of such Jewish sources as community records and chronicles of communal organizations [*pinkesim*]. His fine studies of the internal structure of the Jewish communal organizations of the old Rzeczpospolita facilitated the research of a new generation of historians, including Ringelblum himself. Balaban demonstrated a virtuoso command of Polish archives, both central and local, and he used them to explain the workings of Jewish self-government in a way that earlier Jewish historians had been unable to do. He published on practically every aspect of Polish-Jewish history, including studies of the Frankists, descriptions of old synagogues, authoritative bibliographies, and many other important contributions.[18]

For all his respect for Balaban, Ringelblum strongly criticized what he called the great historian's indifference to economic history and his failure to analyze social conflicts in the Jewish community.[19] Balaban, Ringelblum complained, failed to see the difference between serious social conflict and the minor squabbles that were a staple of synagogue politics. Yet their methodologies overlapped, as Rafael Mahler noted many years later. Like Balaban, Ringelblum favored a monographic approach, basing historical studies and essays on clearly defined themes and a wealth of archival material.[20] Ringelblum's own studies, also similar to Balaban's, tended to be factual and descriptive rather than polemical and theoretical. As will be seen, Ringelblum had strong political views but he expressed them in book reviews, not in his own historical work, where he eschewed sweeping theories and suggestive speculation.

Ringelblum's attitude to Isaac Schiper was altogether different. Although occasional tension marred their relationship, especially in the late 1930s, Ringelblum revered Schiper as an intellectual mentor.[21] By all accounts Schiper, one of the most important public intellectuals in interwar Jewish Poland, had a charismatic personality and incredible energy. An indefatigable historian who published several important books and dozens of articles and book reviews, Schiper also found the time to write theater criticism, popular history, and political commentary for the Yiddish- and Polish-language Jewish press. Yet somehow he also had enough energy left to pursue a political career. He had served as a Zionist deputy in the Polish parliament and had played a leading role in Al Ha-mishmar, the more radical wing of the Polish-Zionist movement that was closely identified with Yitzhak Gruenbaum. Schiper took an active interest in the welfare of Warsaw's Jewish university students. In 1928 he became the director of the Jewish Academic House in Warsaw. No one ever accused Schiper of having a phlegmatic temperament: in October 1931 Schiper, who was demonstrating against Orthodox control of the Warsaw Jewish Community Council, charged into the executive meeting room of the council and ripped the table cloth off the main table, bringing inkwells, pens, books, and bottles of water crashing to the floor.[22]

Even after Schiper left the Poalei Tsiyon, Ringelblum, as we have seen, still stressed the close connection between Schiper's old allegiance to the movement and his emergence as a historian.[23] Ringelblum quoted Schiper's introduction to his "Economic History of Polish Jewry during the Middle Ages":

> We know the Sabbath Jew with his festive spirit, but it is now high time to become acquainted with the history of the workday Jew and his workday ideas and to turn the spotlight on Jewish labor. They [the early historians] gave us a splendid picture of the spiritual leaders of Diaspora Jewry. We are, however, left completely in the dark about the history of the untold hundreds of thousands whose claim to recognition rests not on the riches of the spirit but on their toil and labor.[24]

Unlike Balaban, Schiper urged his students to "think big," to formulate daring historical hypotheses that would direct and structure their research.[25] Schiper himself was not afraid to advance sweeping theories of Jewish history, most notably his assertion that most East European Jews were descended from the Khazars. He also offered a striking refutation of Werner Sombart's theories on the Jewish role in the development of capitalism. Both contemporaries and later historians would note that quite often Schiper's conceptual boldness—his theory of the Khazar origins of the Polish Jews, for example—outstripped his scholarly caution.[26]

Nevertheless Ringelblum admired Schiper's work for many reasons. First, Schiper stressed the interrelationship of Jewish and non-Jewish history. One could not study Jews in isolation; one could not understand Jewish history unless one understood the general historical context in which they lived. This principle would remain the cornerstone of Ringelblum's historical approach. Second, Schiper laid the foundation for the study of East European Jewish economic history.[27] Third, Ringelblum wholeheartedly agreed with Schiper's "demystification" of the Council of the Four Lands (Vaad Arba Aratsot) and of the local Jewish Councils (*kahals*) in early modern Poland. Schiper disputed Dubnow's positive evaluation of these bodies as stalwart defenders of national unity and national interests. In fact, Ringelblum believed, the kahal and the Vaad had served the rich and oppressed the poor; far from being symbols of Jewish vitality and cultural independence, they served as a convenient tool for the Polish authorities to collect taxes.[28] Finally, Ringelblum admired Schiper's commitment to Yiddishism, expressed through his voluminous publications on the history of the Yiddish theater and his studies of popular culture.[29]

Ringelblum got to know Schiper in the early 1920s, when Warsaw was emerging as a new center of Polish historical studies alongside the Jan Kazimierz University in Lwów and the Jagiellonian University in Krakow. An important association, the Society of Friends for the Study of History (Towarzystwo Miłośników Historii), organized public forums and debates, helped publish monographs, and continued to publish an important journal, the *Przegląd historyczny*. Access to key archives, especially in the former Russian zone, had become much easier after the end of tsarist rule.[30] As these young Jewish historians charted their course, they had before them the example of how Polish historians had helped nurture Polish national identity and had encouraged a sober and searching examination of the national past in order to solve the serious problems of the present.

At the start of the 1920s Warsaw University boasted a first-rate historical faculty that included Marceli Handelsman, Wacław Tokarz, and Jan Kochanowski. Ringelblum was particularly fortunate to work under the supervision of one of the very best Polish historians, Professor Marceli Handelsman.[31] Handelsman, who wrote on both medieval and modern history, believed that history provided important insights into contemporary political and social problems: the formation of national identity particularly interested him.[32] He also wrote on historical methodology and the philosophy of history, stressing the importance of critical analysis of primary sources.[33] Many years later Rafael Mahler noted that Handelsman had an undeniable impact on Ringelblum's development as a historian.[34]

A scholar who also became an important public intellectual, Handelsman offered a role model for younger historians. He was not only a leading historian but also a first-rate administrator who edited journals, headed historical societies, and served in key academic posts at Warsaw University. As a young man, Handelsman had been active in the Polish Socialist Party. He then came under the spell of the charismatic Józef Piłsudski but grew uneasy with his authoritarian tendencies. In the 1930s Handelsman cast his lot with the lonely and embattled democratic liberals—the Stronnictwo Demokratyczne (SD). Only the SD represented what Handelsman believed was Poland's true self—humane, tolerant, and liberal.[35] The group bravely fought growing anti-Semitism in the universities and in the country; he himself was beaten by a band of right-wing students in 1934. Handelsman, who had been born into a Jewish family but had converted to Catholicism, took a keen interest in Ringelblum's work. It was thanks to him that Ringelblum was able to publish his first book in 1932, and, in 1934, one of his most important books, *Projekty i próby przewarstwowienia Żydów w epoce Stanisławowskiej* (Attempts to reform the Jewish occupational structure in the reign of Stanislaw August).[36] Ringelblum, who normally had little use for converts, felt deeply indebted to Handelsman, and, in the last weeks of Ringelblum's life, he wrote a short tribute to him. In the end, Handelsman's conversion to Catholicism could not save him. Right-wing Poles betrayed him to the Gestapo in 1944, and he died in the Nordhausen concentration camp in 1945.[37]

In the early 1920s Warsaw University, along with other Polish universities, began to attract growing numbers of Jewish students who wanted to study history. Political motives apart, the new Ministry of Education required all teachers in secondary schools to show proof of a university diploma in the subject they taught, offering young Jews who had no hope of finding a job in the civil service or a place on the medical faculty the promise of a modest but relatively secure career as a high school teacher.[38]

At the same time Warsaw also consolidated its position as the center of Polish Jewish history. In 1928 Meyer Balaban and Moses Schorr founded the Institute of Jewish Studies (Instytut Nauk Judaistycznych), which offered systematic instruction in Jewish history.[39] In 1936 Balaban was appointed a professor of Jewish history at Warsaw University, the first and only such appointment at a Polish university before World War II.[40] By 1939 more than fifty masters and doctoral theses on Jewish history, written under Balaban's supervision, had been completed either at Warsaw University or at the Institute.[41] Finally, owing largely to Ringelblum's initiative, Warsaw would become the real center of the YIVO's historical section in Poland.

The history professors at Warsaw University, not excluding the right-wing nationalists, treated their Jewish students fairly and even encouraged them to research Polish-Jewish history. The professors' ignorance of Yiddish and Hebrew, however, limited their ability to closely supervise their students' research.[42] Fortunately, Schiper and Balaban were both available to offer help and advice. Another development that helped bring Schiper closer to Jewish university students in the early 1920s was the contentious struggle to build a Jewish Academic House in Praga (a suburb on the eastern shore of the Vistula), which was finally completed in 1926.[43] Ringelblum became a member of its board, and it was here that his long relationship with Schiper grew even closer. In 1928 Schiper became the director of the Academic House, which was home to 300 students and boasted a lecture hall with space for 360, a reading room with 80 seats, and even a dark room for would-be photographers. At the Academic House and in the university Ringelblum found something else that the older mentors could not provide—a close community of intellectual peers who shared a common interest in Jewish history.[44]

In 1923 Ringelblum, with Mahler's help, organized the Yunger Historiker Krayz (Young Historians Circle), a club of young history students interested in sharing ideas about history and who would meet to discuss one another's research.[45] The history of this unique organization provides another important example of the cultural vitality of interwar Polish Jewry. When the Yunger Historiker Krayz first met in 1923, it was the only forum in Warsaw—indeed in all of Poland—where Jewish historians could come together to discuss ongoing research. Yet even later—well after the appearance of newer institutions such as the Institute of Judaic Studies and the YIVO—the Yunger Historiker Krayz continued its monthly meetings—right up to the outbreak of World War II.[46] According to Rafael Mahler, the circle actually attained the peak of its popularity in the 1930s. In 1926 it affiliated with the newly formed YIVO (Yiddish Scientific Institute) and in time became, under Ringelblum's leadership, the backbone of the YIVO's historical section in Poland. The Krayz began to publish a journal, *Yunger historiker*, which first appeared in 1926. After two issues, in 1926 and 1929, the Yunger Historiker Krayz changed the name of its journal to *Bleter far geshikhte* in 1934. Edited by Rafael Mahler, two issues of *Bleter far geshikhte* appeared, in 1934 and 1938, packed with articles on the history of Jewish guilds, statistics, regional studies, and other relatively neglected subjects in Polish-Jewish history.

In the interwar period the Historiker Krayz became a second home to young Jewish historians anxious for intellectual fellowship and constructive criticism of their work. As Ringelblum noted in 1938, the Krayz had become the gate of entry into the informal profession of Polish Jewish history.[47] New faces continually appeared at the monthly meetings, and new names graced the pages of the *Bleter far geshikhte*. The Krayz maintained its tradition of encouraging research on topics that were "closely linked to the everyday life of Polish Jewry":

> Their research tries to provide answers to the ongoing problems of Polish Jewry. For [these young historians] history is a vital public obligation. . . . Not one of our young historians will have a chance to pursue a university career. Not one will get a position at a research institution. But we're convinced that every one of our comrades . . . will complete their ongoing research.[48]

These young historians, Ringelblum stressed, did not choose to study narrow, arcane subjects that they could quickly finish in order to complete their degrees. Instead, they sought out historical topics that would shed light on the economic and cultural problems that Polish Jewry had to face at the time.[49]

Once a month the Krayz would meet to hear a presentation and offer criticism. One former member recalled that more often than not Ringelblum would remain silent. He preferred the role of organizer and facilitator.[50]

In the very first issue of *Yunger historiker*, dedicated to Simon Dubnow, Ringelblum declared that he and his colleagues did not regard the study of history as an abstract academic exercise. The historian was a fighter in a national struggle. "We believe," he wrote, "that we are performing a task of immense social significance [*gezelshaftlekhe arbet*], a task whose goal is not just to know the Jewish past but also to lay the foundation for the struggle that the Jewish nation in Poland is waging for its national and social liberation."[51]

The Yunger Historiker Krayz offered its members not only fellowship and intellectual companionship. It was a living affirmation of a collective determination to make the study of history into an indispensable pillar of an emerging Yiddish secular culture. In Mahler's words, the group dedicated itself to the cause of "Yiddish mass culture."[52] *Yunger historiker* was one of the first history journals to appear entirely in Yiddish in order to make history more accessible to wider sections of Polish Jewry. The Jewish community in Poland, Ringelblum complained in the first issue of the journal, still did not understand that history was important. In Germany and other countries historical societies collected documents and encouraged research. Historians enjoyed communal respect and support. Not so in Poland. Thirty years after Dubnow issued his call to gather and protect valuable communal records, Polish Jewry remained indifferent. Valuable chronicles were rotting away, Ringelblum lamented, and priceless documents remained in private hands as Jewish communal organizations showed little willingness to purchase source materials and fund historical research.[53]

Many of the members of the Krayz—and certainly Ringelblum and Mahler—also hoped to stimulate research that would reflect Marxist and Borochovist perspectives. To quote Ringelblum:

> The members of the Historiker Krayz are trying to impart a new spirit to the writing of Jewish history. They want to liberate Jewish historiography from the influence of nationalist and religious attitudes. This is a pioneering circle, since almost all its members are trying to solve the problems of Jewish history from the standpoint of historical materialism.[54]

In their search for a Marxist-Borochovist voice, these young historians grappled with one of the major problems facing the Jewish Left: If it rejected religion and nationalism, then on what basis could it justify its fight against assimilation? One important answer to this dilemma was to build an attractive and intellectually challenging secular culture based on literature, history, and folklore. The historian could use the past to transform the image of Jewish society by including previously neglected groups and by fashioning thick descriptions of everyday life that would highlight the creativity and resilience of the folk.

One key question that fascinated the members of the Krayz was the problem of Jewish survival. Why, of all the ancient peoples, had the Jews survived? Dubnow had ascribed Jewish survival to the unique vitality of the Jewish people, its ability to maintain its national will to live even after it lost both political independence and a territorial base. But Ringelblum and Mahler did not find his theory convincing.

In his article, "Why Did the Jewish People Not Assimilate?" the then twenty-four-year-old Ringelblum rejected the alleged uniqueness of the Jewish religion as the key factor in Jewish survival. He also believed it was wrong to stress the role of anti-Semitism or to look for answers in alleged peculiarities of national character. Only after Jewish historians from many different countries had completed careful studies of Jewish economic history, studies that focused on the "everyday Jew" rather than on the "Sabbath Jew," only then would real answers replace hypotheses.[55]

Ringelblum argued, like his party, that the real answer to the question lay in the economic relationship between Jews and the surrounding society. Ringelblum pointed out that where the Jews had the same occupational profile as their neighbors, they eventually melted into the surrounding population. In countries where Jews filled an economic vacuum or performed unique economic roles dictated by the host societies, the possibilities of assimilation were much smaller. Poland was an ideal case study, where the Jews' economic "isolation" made assimilation difficult.[56]

Up to this point in his article Ringelblum had merely been repeating the teachings of his political movement. But now he added a warning against an overly narrow Marxist paradigm:

> We will not make the mistake made by many who oversimplify historical materialism when they totally deny the impact of the Jewish religion and indeed of any spiritual movement. It is still too early to determine the specific role played by the Jewish religion [in the preservation of the Jewish people]. However, it is clear to any observer of Jewish history that the religion has played a colossal—though not decisive—role in the preservation of the people.[57]

In 1934, in a review of an article by Mahler in the party press, Ringelblum called for a more nuanced and sophisticated analysis of Borochovist paradigms:

> Mahler develops the theory that economic factors kept the Jewish people together. This theory has not yet been sufficiently developed [by leftist historians]. The concept of "economic isolation," which has been widely advanced as a factor behind preservation of a Jewish people, must be ex-

plained more fully by our Marxist historians. "Economic isolation" is too narrow a concept. We should look for "economic factors." . . . This is a broader concept. It includes economic competition that could erupt in the form of apparent religious persecution.[58]

Another early member in the extraordinary group of young historians, one who did not stay long, was Jacob Berman, a future leader in Communist Poland. Although the group included some Bundists and members of other political groups, members of the LPZ, as noted above, played a prominent role in the Krayz. Three members—Ringelblum, Mahler, and Bela Mandelsberg—simultaneously ran Yugnt as well as the party's educational arm, the Ovntkursn far Arbeter. Mandelsberg published important studies of the history of Lublin Jewry in the early modern period.[59] The Krayz would also come to include Artur Eisenbach, Isaiah (Shie) Trunk, Joseph Kermish, all prominent postwar historians.

If Ringelblum's energy and organizational talent held the Krayz together, it was Mahler's hard-hitting and brash attacks against older historians that spearheaded the Krayz's drive to fashion new approaches to Jewish historiography. Ringelblum cheered his friend on in fulsome review articles. Indeed, although Mahler was only one year older than Ringelblum, he served not only as a friend but also as an intellectual mentor. Mahler possessed a rare combination of qualities. In his mastery of Borochovist theory he had few peers. He had also received a fine education in both Jewish and secular subjects. Born into a well-respected Sanz family, Mahler's father had provided him with a first-class tutor; he retained a lifelong fluency in traditional Jewish texts enabling him later to launch pioneering studies of the history of Polish Hasidism and of the Karaite movement. But he also received a doctorate from Vienna University for a thesis titled "The Sociological Problem of Progress." After a few years in Lodz he settled in Warsaw in 1924, one year after Ringelblum founded the Historiker Krayz.

In 1934 Ringelblum declared that Mahler's historiographical articles were "the first attempt to develop a scholarly critique of modern Jewish historiography from a Marxist viewpoint," a bit of exaggeration that nonetheless revealed just how seriously he regarded the common project of the Historiker Krayz.[60] Especially after the decline of Jewish scholarship in the Soviet Union after 1928, Ringelblum saw his friend Mahler and their colleagues in the Krayz as blazing an important intellectual trail that would have important consequences for the development of Yiddish secular culture.[61] While acknowledging the critical intellectual influences of Karl Marx as a general theorist and Simon Dubnow as the pioneer of modern East European Jewish historiography, these young historians of the Krayz now felt the call (and the intellectual excitement) to move forward and, armed with Borochov's insights, stress the differences with their predecessors.

In the very first issue of the *Yunger historiker* Mahler published two articles—"Cultural Theories of Jewish Historical Writing" and "History and the People"—that set out to make Borochov relevant for Jewish historians. Using Borochov as well as Marx, Mahler argued that there was no contradiction between the study of general history and the study of Jewish history. Indeed, one complemented the other. Even though Marxist theory clarified the nature of the powerful economic forces that would transform all human societies, individual national cultures would survive because alongside general cultural ideals, common to all nations, each people had its own specific cultural *conditions,* shaped by the particular character of its historical development. To understand this interplay of the national and the universal, of general economic forces and specific national cultures, one needed to study national history alongside general history. Only with a thorough knowledge of their own history could Jews understand the specific problems they faced and fashion solutions to them.[62]

In this spirit Mahler later attacked the German Marxist Otto Heller, who, in *Der Untergang des Judentums* (1931), argued that the Jews were a caste, not a nation, whose peculiar traits and very survival derived from the fact that from almost the very beginning of their history, their primary economic activity had been trade and commerce. With the development of modern capitalism, this caste of traders had become superfluous. Therefore, Heller argued, the eventual disappearance of the Jews through assimilation was inevitable. Two years before Hitler came to power, Heller declared that the "Jewish Question" in western and central Europe had to all intents and purposes been solved. While the Jewish problem still bedeviled Eastern Europe, the Soviet Union was demonstrating how socialism could transform the Jews into a productive people. There, too, Heller implied that the Jews would eventually assimilate.

Mahler lambasted the book.[63] He argued, using both non-Jewish and Jewish sources, that before the destruction of the Second Temple and even for centuries afterward, Jews had been mostly peasants and artisans. Trade did not play a major role in Jewish economic life until the early medieval period, when religious prejudice and legal restrictions pushed them into a few specific economic fields.

Mahler's sharp attack on Heller shed new light on one important goal of the Krayz: to force the Left to take Jews seriously. Without a thorough knowledge of Jewish history (never mind Borochovian theory), Socialists and Communists would retain their mistaken view of the Jews and repeat groundless generalizations—supported by superficial readings of Marx and Lenin—that Jews were a "caste" and not a people. (Heller was only following in the footsteps of Marx's "On the Jewish Question," Lenin and Plekhanov's polemics against the Bund, and Stalin's writings on the nationality question.) Implicit for Mahler and Ringelblum was the conviction that historians like themselves had to convince fellow Marxists that the Jews were indeed a people. They had a language, different classes and social groupings, a history of sharp social conflicts, a rich folklore, and a creative and nuanced culture.

Mahler continued to develop his views on Jewish historiography in *Yunger historiker*; its sequel, *Bleter far geshikhte*; *Yivo bleter*, the YIVO's main scholarly journal; and *Miesięcznik Żydowski*, a Polish-language Jewish monthly that consciously reached out to Jewish historians and gave them a forum.[64] He aimed his fire not only at leftist intellectuals but also at older, established Jewish scholars like Simon Dubnow, Asher Ginzberg (Ahad Ha'am), and Yehezkiel Kaufman. Mahler praised Dubnow for his many important contributions: the recognition of the importance of East European Jewry, the attempt to demystify the role of the Jewish religion in the survival of the Jewish people, and the explicit recognition of the centrality of the Diaspora to Jewish history. But in the end, Mahler argued, Dubnow remained an unreconstructed liberal who failed to recognize the insights of dialectical materialism and who crafted a historical vision to serve the nationalist sentiments of the Jewish bourgeoisie bent on pursuing a "national revival"; his was a "klal yisroel" (all Israel) approach that privileged the myth of Jewish national cohesion over the reality of a Jewish people dominated by class conflict. The venerable historian was too prone to consider Jewish history in isolation, and he neglected economic factors.

Kaufman came in for even more criticism for his emphasis on the Jewish religion as the key link that had held the Jews together. Mahler did concede that Kaufman, in *Gola v'Nekhar*, avoided the mistake made by both Dubnow and Ahad Ha'am: he did not ascribe Jewish survival to an immanent "national will to live," nor did he view Jewish history in isolation from other peoples and cultures. But Kaufman, too, failed to grasp the truths of historical materialism and their implications for Jewish self-knowledge.

Compared to Mahler, Ringelblum wrote relatively little on Jewish historiography. Instead, he produced several carefully drawn monographs and many articles based on painstaking archival documentation. Close friends marveled at his dedication to historical research: he would finish an exhausting day of teaching and then dash off for an hour's work in a Warsaw archive.[65] Often, instead of returning home, Ringelblum would head for a meeting of the YIVO or some other cultural organization. In view of these pressures Ringelblum managed to publish a great deal.

In 1932 his doctoral dissertation on the history of Warsaw Jewry until 1527 finally appeared as a monograph in a series sponsored by the Towarzystwo Miłośników Historii (Society of the Friends of History).[66] In interwar Poland even scholarly works on early modern history could ignite controversy and protest, especially if they touched on Polish-Jewish relations. Ringelblum's first book was no exception. Professor Marceli Handelsman, who saw that the book was published in a series put out by the Society, endured abuse and criticism from right-wing members for his decision.[67] At a stormy meeting of the Society some members demanded to know why the organization lent its prestige to Ringelblum's book.

As the first academic study of the history of Warsaw Jewry, Ringelblum broke much new ground. Apart from popular sketches by Ezriel Frenk and Nahum Sokolow, no Jewish authors had touched the subject; the only Polish study, by Franciszek Sobieszczański, was little more than a sketch. The theme was difficult to research; until 1527, when the study broke off, Warsaw and Mazowsze were not a part of Crown Poland, and therefore many rich archives had only limited value as they did not cover Mazowsze.[68] Archival documents and court records, Ringelblum wrote, were scarce.

Ringelblum discussed various themes: the constant shifts in relations between the Mazowian princes and the Jews; the earliest settlement of Warsaw Jewry, including a long-forgotten Jewish street and cemetery; the economic structure of Warsaw Jewry; Jewish-Christian relations as reflected in court records; and economic relations between Warsaw Jews and Jews from other towns.

In what would become a leitmotif of his historical research, Ringelblum noted that because little Jewish material survived, he was forced to rely almost entirely on Gentile sources. Nonetheless he accomplished a lot with the scraps of material he managed to find. Based on a court record of a dispute between two Jews over the contents of a home, he provided an inventory of household possessions that yielded interesting insights into the everyday life of Jews in the fifteenth century. During his research he stumbled upon a fifteenth-century document in Hebrew and Yiddish that provided valuable information about early spoken Yiddish in Poland. On the basis of a case that showed a Jew drinking wine in the home of a Pole, Ringelblum speculated that Polish Jews might not have been as uniformly religious as was commonly believed. Elsewhere he used a court record involving a Jew playing cards with a Pole to argue that there was more social interaction between Jews and Gentiles than had been commonly supposed.[69]

The main theme of the book was the complex relationship between the Jews and the Mazowian princes, the fine balance between economic expediency—which made a Jewish presence welcome—and pressure from Christian merchants and the Church to expel the Jews. The book reconstructed the legal status of the Jews in Mazowsze and described their position as *servi camerae,* directly subordinate to the Mazowian prince. Ringelblum discussed anti-Semitism and pogroms, and stressed that the latter were more the result of economic rivalry than religious hatred; religion often served as a convenient excuse. Still, Ringelblum did not entirely ignore the issue of religious hatred. He carefully described Juan de Capistrano's visit to Poland in 1454 and the anti-Jewish riot in Krakow that was inspired and incited by the visit. Stretching the meager evidence, Ringelblum argued that Capistrano also provoked a pogrom in Warsaw. (This assertion would get him into some trouble with reviewers.) One of the most compelling aspects of the book was the light it shed on early Warsaw's trade links and the place of Jews in establishing them.

Shortly after the book appeared, Isaac Schiper published a warm review in the large Warsaw Yiddish daily, *Haynt*.[70] Schiper also pointed out, however, that the Jewish community had ample cause for shame. It was only thanks to the help of Professor Marceli Handelsman and a stipend from the Warsaw City Council that the book saw the light of day. It was a scandal, Schiper declared, that the Jewish Community Council of the biggest Jewish city in Europe refused to subsidize the publication of the first serious monograph on the history of Warsaw Jewry. What did it say about the cultural state of Polish Jewry, Schiper asked, that because of financial constraints such an important study appeared in Polish first? But Schiper reminded the readers of *Haynt* that it was not too late to right the wrong done to Ringelblum. The second part of the history of Warsaw Jewry, which took the study to 1795, was ready for publication; surely the Warsaw council [*kehille*] would subsidize its publication. In the end, volume 2 never appeared in book form—although many excerpts were published as articles. The manuscript surfaced in the second part of the Oyneg Shabes Archive that was found in 1950.

Fellow Historiker Krayz members Isaiah (Shie) Trunk in the *YIVO bleter* and Eleazar Feldman in *Miesięcznik Żydowski* also praised the book, although both questioned Ringelblum's interpretation of legal documents and the exact judicial position of early Warsaw Jewry.[71] Balaban wrote a polite review in *Nasz przegląd,* where he recognized the pioneering value of Ringelblum's book but chided the young historian for certain conclusions unwarranted by thin evidence, such as the pogrom allegedly incited by Capistrano.[72]

The most scathing review of the book appeared in the prestigious Polish historical journal *Kwartalnik historyczny*. Professor Józef Siemieński, one of the greatest Polish archivists and an expert on Polish legal history, apologized to his readers for imposing on their patience. After all, such a book was beneath criticism. But Ringelblum's ludicrous, far-fetched allegations forced him to respond. Siemieński ridiculed Ringelblum's depiction of pogroms and the very notion that a scholarly book would contain references to articles published in a Yiddish daily newspaper. Like Balaban, except much less gently, he challenged Ringelblum's use of evidence and even his knowledge of Latin. It is hard to avoid inferring from Siemieński's review the anger of a Polish patriot who deeply resented a Jewish historian's story of anti-Jewish violence, princely venality, Catholic hostility, and the economic jealousy of the Warsaw burghers.[73]

Ironically both Siemieński and Ringelblum would follow similar paths before and during the war. Both would be remembered for their devotion to archives as essential building blocks of national consciousness. From 1925 until the outbreak of the war he had served as the director of AGAD (Archiwum Główne Akt Dawnych [The Main Archive of Old Documents]). During the siege of Warsaw in 1939 Siemieński heroically fought to protect the archive from the flames that engulfed the city. And Siemieński and Ringelblum shared a parallel fate. Siemieński perished in Auschwitz in 1941.[74]

The Warsaw book launched Ringelblum as a versatile and productive historian. The journal *Sotsiale meditsin* published several of his articles on the history of Jewish medicine and physicians in Poland.[75] In the general field of Polish-Jewish relations he published three important studies on the role of the Jews in the Kościuszko Uprising, the image of Jews in the eighteenth-century Polish press, and attempts to reform Polish Jewry in the eighteenth century.[76] His essays on the history of Jewish printing in eighteenth-century Poland, published in book form in 1936, were a solid contribution to an important aspect of Jewish cultural history.[77] He published many short articles on Jewish towns in Poland in the German-Jewish *Encyclopedia Judaica*, which appeared in 1930, as well as a short chapter in a general history of Polish Jewry, *Żydzi w Polsce Odrodzonej* (1932).[78] Many articles based on the never published second volume on the history of Warsaw Jewry appeared in various journals. Ringelblum published the first study of the important and controversial Shmuel Zbytkover, a wealthy contractor who played an important role in the history of eighteenth-century Polish Jewry.[79] And Ringelblum did not neglect bibliography and pedagogy. In 1930 he and Mahler issued, in Polish and Yiddish, a book of original sources for the study of East European Jewish history.[80]

In all these works, Ringelblum insisted on the relevance of history for the understanding of contemporary problems. Class oppression in the Jewish community, Jewish poverty and backwardness, the origins of the Jewish working class, the dogged loyalty of Jews to Poland, the rigidity of tradition and religious superstition—these were all issues that Ringelblum believed could be better understood by historical study. Furthermore, what better way to refute the charges of Polish anti-Semites than to turn to history?

Certain general themes emerged from Ringelblum's historical writings, for example, the interrelationship of Jews and non-Jews. In his book on the Warsaw Jews until the year 1527, Ringelblum wrote:

> Recent studies of the inner life of the Jews have been dispelling the widely held myth of a Chinese wall that separated the Jewish community from the Christian community. Research on the history of Warsaw Jews shows us that each world penetrated the other. The results of this mutual interrelationship can be seen in every sphere. From Christians, Jews borrowed fashions [stroje], clothing, family names, first names, habits, and customs. Often they adopted the language of the surrounding country (Germany, France, Spain, etc.), and elsewhere they enriched their own language with liberal borrowings from Gentile speech (Yiddish in Poland). By the same token, Jewish culture and especially popular culture developed under the strong influence of the Christian world.[81]

Certainly this keen sense of Jewish-Christian interconnectedness was a major reason for Ringelblum's interest in the history of medicine and the social and cultural role of Jewish physicians.[82] Jewish physicians, Ringelblum argued, in early modern Poland, were the ones who most clearly straddled two worlds:

> The Jewish physicians were the only representatives of secular education in the Jewish community [oyf der yidisher gas]. Young Jewish students rarely studied philosophy . . . What practical sense would that have made? . . . So the doctors were the only ones that brought light and knowledge into the Jewish world . . . That meant bitter battles with the rabbis and with the kehilla . . . The kehilla takes revenge, not only on the living but also on the dead. These battles played themselves out in a lot of ways. The Jewish doctor becomes like his Christian colleague, especially when . . . most of his clients are Christian. He shaves his beard, he wears the same clothes as the Gentiles, he writes prescriptions on the Sabbath. In short, he breaks through the wall [of tradition].[83]

When life and health were at stake, anti-Semitic prejudice easily gave way to respect for professional competence. Therefore, of all Jews, the Jewish physician was the most likely to win the confidence of Gentile elites. Typically Ringelblum approached the subject not only as a scholar but also as an organizer: in 1936 he published a detailed précis that offered guidelines for future research into the history of Jewish medicine.[84]

In his studies of Jewish printing and the Jewish book trade in Poland, based on pioneering archival research, Ringelblum also searched for the points of contact between the Jewish and the Gentile world. What interested Ringelblum was the Jewish book as a commodity, and as a source of revenue, the latter a result of competition over the right to lease the collection of import and sales taxes on Jewish books from the Polish treasury. Jews brought so many imported editions of the Talmud and other religious texts that would-be monopolists sought the right to print them domestically; after all, as the mercantilist argument went, the fewer the imports, the more currency the country would save. Behind the dry statistics from the archives, Ringelblum's pioneering research demonstrated how essential books were to eighteenth-century Polish Jewry and how widely they were read. One did not smell a profit in selling books to an illiterate or to an uncultured people. The book industry also showed how class conflict and greed, rather than national solidarity, marked Jewish life in the Rzeczpospolita. Unscrupulous Jews and Christians alike seized on the chance to force Polish Jewry to pay dearly for the chance to read and fulfill the obligation to study religious texts.[85]

As Ringelblum continued his research, the theme of Polish-Jewish relations became ever more prominent. In the very first issue of the *Yunger historiker,* Ringelblum had envisioned history as a way of bridging the gulf between the two peoples.[86] One important mission Jewish historians could perform, Ringelblum wrote in the first issue of that journal, was to reach out to Poles. Until the very end, Ringelblum believed that it was mutual ignorance and disinterest that largely accounted for Polish-Jewish tension. He emphasized that "when a Jewish historian reads an objective historical talk in front of Polish colleagues—future high school teachers—even if the talk concerns the very distant past, he is contributing to the coming together of Polish and Jewish society."

For their part, Ringelblum wrote in his book on the Kościuszko Uprising, Polish historians had tended to see Jews as an undifferentiated mass.[87] It was the job of the Jewish historian to show the variety and complexity of the community, to demystify a group that was intimately and intricately bound up with the life of the country. Jewish historians could help revise the Polish view of Jews as an undifferentiated "Other" and thus force Polish historians to recognize that, like it or not, Jews were an integral part of Polish history.

The Kościuszko Uprising provided yet another example of historical relevance. Ringelblum argued that many historians had—for political reasons—minimized Jewish participation in the uprising and even denied the existence of the celebrated Jewish fighting unit formed by Berek Joselewicz. On the other hand, it was also wrong to focus exclusively on Joselewicz and thus overlook the allegedly widespread involvement of the Jewish masses. In his study of the Jewish attitude toward the uprising, Ringelblum called the 1794 war the first real example of Polish-Jewish fraternization. Consumed by hatred of Russia and moved by Kościuszko's appeals, the Jewish masses gave the uprising major support, especially by providing such important auxiliary services as digging trenches and supplying the army with uniforms and money. Although the Jewish community was not a monolith, Jews, Ringelblum's book implied, could indeed feel a deep loyalty to Poland, especially if that loyalty was reciprocated. On the other hand, Ringelblum argued, the Jewish elites took little interest in the Kościuszko Uprising. This was because most educated Jews, and the few wealthy Jews who lived in Warsaw, were still more connected to German culture than to Polish. The cold shoulder they had gotten from the Polish Four-Year Sejm in response to their appeals for political concessions did little to change their self-perception as enlightened Europeans rather than as Poles.[88]

Not all historians agreed with Ringelblum's arguments. After the war, both Jacob Shatzky and even his friend Rafael Mahler believed that he went too far in his thesis that the uprising enjoyed wide support from the Jewish masses.[89]

One point Ringelblum tried to make in his research, a point he hoped had obvious contemporary implications, was the inherent tension between anti-Semitic intent and the practical implementation of anti-Semitic laws. After all, according to Polish law, Jews lost their right to live in Warsaw in 1527. Yet a community continued, thanks to the economic interests of the nobility and their need of services that Jews could provide. In early modern Poland or in the interwar republic, the demands of real life and the strong goad of economic necessity often counterbalanced anti-Jewish sentiment. It was one thing to pass laws to expel Jews or to drive them out of the economy; it was an entirely different matter to suspend the concrete laws of mutual interdependence and self-interest.[90]

Just as Ringelblum wanted to demystify Jews in the eyes of Poles, he also wanted Jews to rethink their relationship to the non-Jewish world. Ringelblum had little patience with the idea that anti-Semitism was inevitable and eternal. In his review of Mahler's essay on Yehezkiel Kaufman, he praised his friend for demolishing the "false idea of eternal anti-Semitism . . . Kaufman wants to prove a religious-nationalist ideology that is based on the zoological hatred between peoples."[91]

In his books and articles Ringelblum tried to explore the myriad links that bound Jews to Poland, without idealizing Jewish-Polish relations as did some assimilationist historians. Instead, Ringelblum argued the case, through many examples, that Jews and Poles, in good times and in bad, were inextricably linked. One could not separate the "Jewish problem" from the "Polish problem." If Jews were impoverished, if in desperation they turned to crime and begging, then this was a problem for Poland as well.

In several articles Ringelblum carefully analyzed the discussion of the "Jewish problem" in the eighteenth-century Polish press and in the debates of the Polish Sejm.[92] As the Polish state struggled to reform itself, both proponents and opponents of concessions to the Jews realized that growing Jewish poverty and the alarming indebtedness of Jewish communities to Polish nobles and religious institutions had created an urgent problem. As in eighteenth-century France, Austria, and Prussia, discussions of the "Jewish Question" invariably raised wider political issues about social and political reform.

It was all well and good to discuss how Jews might become "useful" and "productive," or how to compel them to settle on the land and work in factories. But in a dying Republic vulnerable to efficient, better organized neighbors, talk was a lot easier than action. Options that existed elsewhere were foreclosed by the political realities of the Commonwealth. The Jewish reforms pushed through by the Habsburg emperor Joseph II in 1781 were not feasible, since Poland was not an absolute monarchy and the *szlachta* [nobles] did not wish to compromise their power. A French solution—a sweeping away of all estate distinctions—was not possible: neither the szlachta nor surrounding powers would allow a revolutionary Poland. But Polish conditions foreclosed yet another option: a united front of wealthy Jews with the Polish middle classes. The Polish "third estate" showed a dogged hostility to Jewish aspirations. Any increase in the power of the third estate and of the towns would hurt, not help, the position of the Jews.[93]

Ringelblum's major argument in his 1934 book, *Projekty i próby przewarstwowienia Żydów w epoce Stanisławowskiej* (Attempts to reform the Jewish occupational structure in the eighteenth century) was that only far-reaching reform of the Polish state and society could have solved the growing problem of Jewish poverty and economic decline. Had such reforms taken place, Ringelblum implied, then it was entirely possible that the Jewish question in twentieth-century Poland may well have been less acute. However, the same factors that doomed attempts to improve the position of the Jews also doomed the Rzeczpospolita. As long as serfdom existed and the szlachta enjoyed a monopoly of land ownership, attempts to engage poor Jews in agriculture would fail, not because Jews feared hard work but because they had a well-grounded fear of being reduced to serfdom. Clearly Ringelblum was making not just a historical argument but also a political statement. What was true for the eighteenth century also applied to the Poland of the 1930s. Persecution of Jews weakened the nation; anti-Semitism was a symptom of serious underlying national problems.

In many respects *Projekty i próby przewarstwowienia Żydów w epoce Stanisławowskiej* was one of Ringelblum's most impressive prewar works. It contained a wealth of information about Jewish poverty in the eighteenth century and the growing problems caused by Jewish beggars, vagrants, and thieves. As he described various attempts to employ poor Jews in productive occupations, Ringelblum enriched Jewish social and economic history by describing the Jewish role in several areas of manufacture. Using little known sources, Ringelblum argued that Jewish entrepreneurship became an important factor in the development of many industrial branches much earlier than had previously been supposed. He also furnished a great deal of information about Jewish weavers, sock makers, and other craftsmen.

Ringelblum's book was more than just an academic study of the distant past. The Institute for the Study of Nationality Problems, which published the book, brought together academics and political figures who recognized the importance of finding just solutions to Poland's serious problems with her national minorities.[94] In the years before Piłsudski's death in 1935, many Jewish leaders clung to the hope that the Polish government would show more sympathy for the plight of its Jewish citizens, who suffered greatly during the Great Depression. During this time various Jewish leaders criticized the economic policies of the Polish government, arguing that they not only hampered the nation's general economic recovery but also exacerbated the desperate position of the Jewish minority. The topics Ringelblum discussed acquired a new relevance, if only in the book's demonstration that, in the waning years of the Commonwealth, leading statesman understood the interdependence between the economic well-being of the Rzeczpospolita and Jewish poverty. In the 1930s, by contrast, many Polish politicians refused to see the problem of Jewish poverty as a national issue but instead regarded the Jews as unwelcome strangers who should be forced to emigrate. The book implicitly underscored the contrast between the eighteenth century, when Polish leaders urged the employment of poor Jews, and the 1930s, when many political figures urged a boycott of Jews and when Jews found no employment in public works projects.

The book not only contained a wealth of information about Polish-Jewish economic history, but it also reflected Ringelblum's passionate interest in researching the origins of the Jewish working class and uncovering more information about the Jewish poor. Indeed, in an article about Ringelblum as a historian that appeared in 1953, the eminent Polish-Jewish historian Jacob Shatzky argued that one of his most important contributions was to "democratize" Polish-Jewish history.[95] What Shatzky meant was that Ringelblum loved to write about ordinary people, about individuals whose lives, up to that point, had escaped the attention of most Jewish historians.

Ringelblum's books and articles included a previously ignored cast of characters that would never be confused with learned rabbis and eminent businessmen: Jewish tavern keepers, pickpockets, beggars, vagabonds, wandering jesters (*badkhanim*), musicians, and thieves, and he treated them with sympathy and admiration. Before mentioning the names of some jesters who applied for a permit to work in late-eighteenth-century Warsaw Ringelblum noted:

> These jesters can be seen as the ancestors of Jewish actors, who in hard times did what they could to amuse the Jewish masses. At the same time they enriched and disseminated popular culture [*folksshafung*]. Therefore let us mention their names so that they will be remembered [*l'zikhroyn oylem*].[96]

Ringelblum lamented how few Jewish sources he had to work with and that he had to write the history of Warsaw Jewry in the eighteenth century largely on the basis of court records. His drive to spur the Jewish masses to *zaml*, collect documents, stemmed from firsthand knowledge of how vital Jewish records were for the construction of a usable past.

Nevertheless, out of the available sources, Ringelblum constructed a fascinating tableau of Polish-Jewish relations in everyday life, where familiarity and contempt went hand and hand. Many of his sources described tense, even violent relations, but Ringelblum was more than happy to report on any sources that conveyed a more positive impression such as a sermon of an eighteenth-century Catholic priest in Praga, a Warsaw suburb, who expressed admiration for the Jews' sobriety, self-sacrifice, and exemplary family life.[97]

Notwithstanding the arbitrary and insulting treatment they often received, the Jews hardly conducted themselves like "meek lambs." Ringelblum described many earthy, tough characters who gave back as good as they got. In one case a drunken peasant, Kaspar Szarek, walked into a Jewish tavern in the small village of Szczanko and wrecked the place. Even worse, he pulled the precious cholent, a traditional Sabbath-day dish, out of the oven and hurled it to the floor. The Jewish tavern keeper, quite upset, beat the peasant to death. Luckily for the Jew, his offer to make monetary restitution to the peasant's family spared him legal punishment from a Polish court. In another case, a tough Jewish woman by the name of Szlomowa, who lived in Ujazdów, a village that later became part of Warsaw, suspected that one Kasper Mazurkiewicz had stolen her black cow. She hired a gang of Jewish toughs to bring Mazurkiewicz to her house, where they tied him to a wheel, beat him, and paraded him around the village. The Polish court, Ringelblum noted, did not impose a particularly harsh punishment: Szlomowa got two weeks imprisonment.[98]

As a deeply engaged historian, who constantly emphasized the contemporary relevance of the historical record, Ringelblum fought back against the canard that Jews were economic parasites who preferred money lending and petty trading to honest physical labor. A review of Father Aleksander Wóycicki's *Dzieje robotników przemysłowych w Polsce* (History of industrial workers in Poland), titled "A New Book with Old Lies" and published in 1929, revealed Ringelblum's outrage at the author's selective use of historical evidence.[99] Father Wóycicki was not just a historian, a professor at the Stefan Batory University in Wilno, but he was also a prominent member of the Christian Democratic Party and had chaired the Sejm's committee on social legislation. What infuriated Ringelblum was Wóycicki's tendency to ignore the Jewish entrepreneurs who built up much of Polish industry and the Jewish workers who eagerly sought the most menial labor in order to support their families. Instead, the Polish priest chose to write about Jewish middlemen and their allegedly rapacious exploitation of honest Gentile labor. Countering the canard that Jews abhorred menial labor, Ringelblum angrily documented how ordinary Jews begged for jobs in the Silesian coal mines only to be thwarted by anti-Semitic prejudice. In this review, Ringelblum clearly used history as a weapon to defend Jewish honor and combat anti-Semitism.

At the same time Ringelblum resented the myth of an idyllic harmonious Jewish community in the Commonwealth. In his introduction to a short study of the lives of Jewish apprentices in seventeenth- and eighteenth-century Poland, he wrote:

> If we read books written by bourgeois historians, we get the impression
> that Jewish history was a beautiful idyll. According to these historians
> the Jewish people always lived together in peace and harmony. There
> were never any class struggles . . . rather, unity reigned in the tents of
> Israel. . . . But if we take a Marxist approach, then the Jewish past looks
> very different. Then we see that social and class conflict was just as much
> a part of Jewish history as it was among non-Jews. Often this conflict
> was quite sharp. But we know little about it because we have few sources
> about the internal life of old Polish Jewry [from the sixteenth until the
> eighteenth centuries]. The life of Jewish apprentices in that time was very

sad. Unfortunately we know very little about their lives. After all, who cared then about how poor people lived?[100]

Ringelblum—like Mahler—was particularly scathing about the policies of the Jewish communal organs:[101]

> Our historians like to portray Jewish autonomy in Old Poland as the finest jewel [in the crown] of [Polish Jewry]. In fact, however, there were many [terrible] aspects . . . of the Jewish autonomous organs. Everywhere power lay in the hands of a clique of despots [tkifim], who treated communal assets as if they were their own private property. This clique threw the entire [tax burden] . . . on the weak shoulders of the poor masses. The abuses and the robbery of kehille barons, who ruled over the Jewish masses for hundreds of years, was a sad chapter in the history of the Jewish collective.

Ringelblum lacked the elegance of a Balaban, the conceptual sweep of a Schiper, the theoretical versatility and sophistication of a Mahler. At first glance, much of his historical writing was largely descriptive, paraphrases and summaries of court records and newspaper articles. (One should remember, of course, that he worked full-time, could manage only an hour or so in the archives after work, and had published all this work by the time he was thirty-eight.) But in the process he rendered important service to future generations of historians. Since he was in a field that had been little studied, his tendency to prefer factual description over sweeping conceptualization was certainly understandable. Ringelblum's prewar historical corpus was a major contribution precisely through its mass of concrete detail and example, based on extensive research in archives that were subsequently destroyed in World War II. For postwar historians who tried to reconstruct the history of early modern Warsaw Jewry, Ringelblum's work proved an essential reference.

To what degree could Ringelblum be considered a "Marxist" historian? Shatzky argued that Ringelblum was more of a "democratic populist," in the tradition of a Pavel Marek rather than a Marxist historian, more interested in writing the story of the Jewish masses than in writing history from a Marxist standpoint.[102] In a refutation of Jacob Kener, who emphasized the impact of Marxism on Ringelblum the historian, Shatzky wrote:

> For the most part he describes more than he interprets. He narrates in great detail and the sociology is embedded in the social theme, in the context, in the material, but not in the explanation. But this is enough to recognize that it is in this rich palette of themes that are not oversimplified and that are not prettified with the mythology of Jewish unity; in his determination to pose a problem and not just to recount the past (he

seeks explanations even when he cannot always provide an answer)—in all this lies the importance of Emanuel Ringelblum as a historian.[103]

Besides, Shatzky noted, Ringelblum held some very un-Marxist views, such as his recognition of the enormous role played by the Jewish religion in the survival of the Jewish people over the centuries.

Available evidence suggests that Shatzky's view is only half right. Yes, Ringelblum, in many ways, was a "democratic populist." But Marxism was quite salient in his book reviews, if not in his scholarly historical writings. In 1934, for example, Ringelblum reviewed an issue of *Bleter far geshikhte* that contained Mahler's hard-hitting polemic against Kaufman's *Gola v'Nekhar*. In this strongly positive review, which appeared in the *Arbeter tsaytung*, Ringelblum displayed uncharacteristic ideological venom. Kaufman, Ringelblum argued, represented the views of a Jewish bourgeoisie that was turning "Fascist":

> The Jewish bourgeoisie has not escaped the process of Fascisticization that has affected the bourgeoisie of other nations. Fascism represents a break with the progressive ideals of the nineteenth century and signifies in many respects a return to the Middle Ages. The Jewish bourgeoisie is taking the same road. In the period of "Sturm und Drang," the Jewish bourgeoisie "fought" for "progressive" ideals. But current attitudes of the Jewish bourgeoisie toward religion exemplifies the . . . [turn this class is taking] . . . Mahler succeeds in demolishing Kaufman's groundless theory that religion kept the Jewish people together.

One might argue that, since this article appeared in a party organ, Ringelblum was engaging in a bit of posturing for his political comrades. It is also true that "fascism" had different connotations in 1934 than it had after World War II, and that Marxists loved to use the term at any opportunity. But one can also cite another review written by Ringelblum that appeared in the Yiddishist, non-party *Literarishe bleter*. In this review of Philip Friedman's history of Galician Jewry in the early nineteenth century, Ringelblum argued that "anti-Jewish movements [in the Middle Ages] were not a volcanic eruption of popular anger but usually a conscious action of the burghers to gain specific economic goals. In this the clergy was usually ready to help."[104] By the same token, Ringelblum asserted, it was not Enlightenment ideals that caused the decline of anti-Semitism in the nineteenth century but rather the conscious determination of the European bourgeoisie to remove barriers to capitalist expansion. Elsewhere Ringelblum stated that the reemergence of virulent anti-Semitism in the 1930s was an outgrowth of fascism, itself a last ditch attempt by a doomed capitalist system to save itself.

Where Shatzky erred was in his tendency to exaggerate the dichotomy between "democratic populism" and Marxism in Ringelblum's historical writings. No one can deny that a tension existed on the Jewish Left in Poland between *folkstimlekhkayt* and *klasnbavustzayn*, that is, between a broad-based populism and a narrower, more focused commitment to the Jewish working class—a working class of tailors and shoemakers rather than coal miners and steelworkers.

Ringelblum resembled many Jewish "progressive" intellectuals in interwar Poland who sought a synthesis of inchoate populism and a more focused Marxism. Marxism indicated the future development of the Jewish masses: modernization and urbanization. But meanwhile a large proportion of Polish Jews lived in shtetlekh and the Jewish urban population included many recent migrants from the shtetl. The Jewish radical intelligentsia had to join a broad campaign to raise the cultural level of the masses and fashion a secular Yiddish culture that would break the hold of tradition and facilitate the political education of the people. Populism better reflected Jewish reality, whereas Marxism offered the mystique of struggle, the hope for a better future and an end to Jewish isolation.

A quick look at the weakness of the one true populist political party in Jewish Poland, the Folkspartei, offers suggestive insights. In many respects this party's teachings made much more sense than those of the Bund or the LPZ. Although it also supported Yiddish culture, it stressed that Marxism was largely irrelevant to the needs of Polish Jews who were struggling shopkeepers and independent artisans. To posture about class struggle between workers and the bourgeoisie was senseless when the "bourgeoisie" was just as poor as the "workers." Except for the Vilna area, however, the Folkspartei—after a brief spurt between 1915 and 1922—was basically moribund.[105]

Unlike the Folkspartei, Marxism offered hope of a better world and promised powerful allies: the non-Jewish working class and, depending on the party, the Soviet Union. Moreover, the Bund and the LPZ had another attractive feature—the rich tradition of revolutionary struggle, the memory of self-defense against Russian pogromists, and the heroic street battles against the Cossacks.

It was precisely the need to synthesize Marxism and Jewish populism, the poetry of the future and the prose of the present that made the struggle for Yiddish secular culture so attractive. The fight for Yiddish could transcend party differences and forge a coalition committed to the modernization and democratization of Jewish life.

Ringelblum came to see the role historians could play in this process. He wanted Jewish historians to create a new praxis of history. Deprived of a welcoming university community, they could forge a new kind of community dedicated to history and determined to bring scholars and non-scholars together in a common purpose. This new community would encourage engaged tourism (*Landkentenish*) and the gathering of historical materials (*zamling*). For the modern secular Jew, the very process of gathering documents, conducting research, or discussing ongoing scholarship was both a personal and a national act of affirmation.

THE YIVO

For intellectuals like Ringelblum, who believed in secular Yiddish culture, the founding of the YIVO in 1925 was the realization of a long-held dream. For years Yiddish scholars, including Borochov, had been calling for a university or research institute that would give the language sorely needed status and encourage serious research into the past and present of East European Jewry. In 1924 the philologist Nahum Shtif wrote a memorandum arguing for the establishment of a Yiddish academic institute. Shtif's memorandum turned out to be a vital catalyst. In 1925 the Yiddish Scientific Institute was established in Vilna. The new organization included four sections: philology, statistics-economics, psychology-pedagogy, and history.[106]

The YIVO scholars, otherwise a diverse group, shared the common conviction that there was a vital link between the East European Jewish past and present, one that required serious study—in Yiddish. In the words of Dan Miron:

> They were not to study the cultural past as a finished product, a sealed off enterprise that could now be archeologically dissected, but rather as the source of an ongoing creative activity. Therefore, they must also pay close attention to the cultural present, because it offered the only perspective through which the past could be creatively examined [107]

From the very beginning YIVO scholars saw themselves in a contrapuntal relationship to the German-Jewish scholars of Wissenschaft des Judentums, who, as Ringelblum wrote in 1924, had seen the Jewish past as a closed book, suitable for scholarly study but little more. They had sharply distinguished the Jewish past from a present where emancipation would turn Jews into Germans and Frenchmen. The YIVO scholars, on the other hand, would consciously avoid their mistakes.[108]

No one did more to shape the institution in the interwar period than Max Weinreich. Unlike some other YIVO scholars who were self-taught or lacked academic degrees, Weinreich had earned a doctorate from the prestigious University of Marburg. He brought to the YIVO not only a love of Yiddish but also scholarly discipline, first-class organizational ability, and a wide-ranging set of intellectual interests that included history, literature, sociolinguistics, social psychology, and Freudian theory. During the entire period of the YIVO's development in prewar Poland, Weinreich deftly defended what he saw as the YIVO's mission and skillfully parried incessant attacks from leftists who pushed for a more "proletarian" institution.[109]

From 1925 until the outbreak of World War II, despite financial crises and political infighting, the YIVO achieved outstanding successes. One miracle was the completion of a large and comfortable building. The YIVO also developed a major library, an important theater and literary archive, and a promising graduate program. Under Weinreich's leadership the YIVO launched an ambitious project to study Jewish youth; hundreds of young people sent in autobiographies which survived the war and remain a major source for the study of interwar Polish Jewry. The YIVO reached out to its audience with questionnaires, bulletins, meetings, and contests.

Historian Lucy Dawidowicz arrived in Vilna from New York for a year of graduate study in the summer of 1938. As she recorded in *From That Time and Place,* the building that housed the YIVO on 18 Wiwulskiego Street, with its parklike grounds, well-lit reading rooms, maps with pins showing where YIVO *zamlers* lived, library, and theater archive, impressed her greatly:

> This YIVO building was utterly unlike the institutions of the Yiddish world I knew in New York, most of which were housed in cramped, dingy and dilapidated quarters. Everything about the YIVO—its location, its landscaped setting, the gleaming immaculateness of the place— delivered a message. I interpreted it to mean that the YIVO had class, was no moldering institution, but a place from which distinction and excellence would issue. Even more: The YIVO was no seedy relic of the past; it belonged to the future.[110]

The YIVO was making a statement: Yiddish deserved to travel first-class, Yiddish had arrived, and the time for inferiority complexes was over.

Just two years later Max Weinreich, now a refugee in New York, addressed the Fifteenth Annual Conference of the YIVO and the first to be held in the United States. The YIVO, Weinreich reminded his listeners in 1940, had been much more than a center of scholarly research and a place to train future scholars, however important these two roles:

> What would, however, attract me more than anything else would have been the *myth of YIVO.* Yes, the YIVO had evolved into a myth. No one

who would examine it as a mere institution at which a few dozen people did their prescribed job and were paid for it a certain (and more often, an uncertain) salary would ever understand its role. I do not mean this pejoratively, for I have nothing against institutions where people earn a decent living. But I want to convey a difference. The young man from the town of Grodno, who roamed the streets for weeks with a group of beggars, so that he could write down their sayings and stories, did not get a penny for his pains, but he earned a *mitsve,* a substantial share in the world to come . . . People of our generation experienced elevation and ecstasy in contributing to YIVO a penny or a folkloristic write-down or just in leafing through a volume of the *filologishe shriftn.* They did these rather in the way their grandfather used to read a passage in a holy book or contribute a coin to the yeshiva of Volozhin or come out, at the reading of the gemore, with friends in the evening, with his own little talmudic innovation.[111]

One of the YIVO's goals was to change the negative, defeatist way in which many Jews looked at the Jewish present and at themselves. In *Shloyme reb Khayim's,* the great writer Mendele Moykher Sforim (Sholem Abramovich) teasingly asked a fictional Simon Dubnow why it was worthwhile to study Jews:

> None of us ever did anything to set the world on fire. Dukes. Governors, generals, and soldiers we were not; we had no romantic attachments with lovely princesses; we didn't fight duels, nor did we even serve as witnesses, watching other men spill their blood; we didn't dance the quadrille at balls; we didn't hunt wild animals in the fields and forests; we didn't make voyages of discovery to the ends of the earth; we carried on with no actresses or prima donnas; we didn't celebrate in a lavish way. In short, we were completely lacking in all those colorful details that grace a story and whet the readers' appetite.[112]

By contrast, Weinreich was certain that there were plenty of "colorful details" in the everyday life of any East European Jew. In 1931, in a review of a history of Pruzhany Jews—compiled by students and teachers in the local Yiddish school—Weinreich laid out what he thought the YIVO's agenda should be: "Only on the basis of Reb Yisroel (Mr. Israel)," Weinreich wrote, "can we learn about klal Yisroel (the people of Israel)."[113] What he meant was that without studying the Jewish individual, one could not learn much about the Jewish collective. Without studying the Jewish people in microcosm, one could not gain useful insight into the nation's larger problems. The political culture of interwar Polish Jewry had been steeped in ideologies that saw the world through the needs and perspective of the collective. Here was a voice that boldly proclaimed the importance of the individual as well.

Weinreich boldly announced the task at hand: to know the present [*der-kenen dem haynt*]. Yes, the Pruzhany volume had been a marvelous achievement, but more had to be done. The YIVO had to encourage more focus on the study of "everyday life." What changes had occurred in the clothing and diet of Pruzhany Jews? How did the Jews decorate their homes? How had hygienic habits evolved in the past few decades? Did Jews bathe more often? Were there changes in courting customs and in the giving of dowries? What factors determined a family's choice of school for its children? Was the choice of a Polish or a Zionist or a Yiddishist school largely the result of social class? Or were more subtle psychological factors at work? In a word, Weinreich was pointing the institute in a direction of more research into everyday life.[114] This approach would demand the extensive use of questionnaires and individual biographies and reports. It had clear implications for Ringelblum's later historical work in the Oyneg Shabes archive. It also fit the research agendas that the YIVO historians were setting out. Years later, Weinreich would compare the YIVO to a cabalist "who succeeded in drawing the holy sparks [*nitsotsot*] out of the broken shells [*klipot*]."

For the twenty-five-year old Ringelblum, the founding of the YIVO was a godsend. He immediately dashed off letters to Max Weinreich in Vilna and Eliyahu Cherikover in Paris offering his services and telling them that the entire Historker Krayz was eager to join the YIVO's new historical section. In 1926 Ringelblum went to Vilna to teach in the Yiddish Humanistic Gymnasium. He also used the time to work at the YIVO. With Weinreich's approval, he established a Historical Commission, helped draw up guidelines for *zamlers,* and handled correspondence with young Jews from all over Eastern Europe who were beginning to gather materials to send to Vilna.[115]

His enthusiasm was palpable. He advised, cajoled, and encouraged. In a letter to Moshe Finekind in Piotrków on March 7, 1927, who had just discovered the records of a guild [*hevre*] of Jewish workers in the eighteenth century, Ringelblum suggested some hints to guide his further research. How did the *hevre* treat apprentices and younger workers? Did the *hevres* experience the generational conflicts that were so common in the Christian guilds? What about the attitude of the Community Council (*kehille*) to the *hevre*? These questions, he told his correspondent, would lead him to one of the most important problems for modern Jewish historians: finding the origins of the Jewish working class. He told Finekind that he was sending him guidelines to help him in his research.[116]

Ringelblum quickly learned that the YIVO's historical section presented both problems and opportunities. One difficulty was that the head of the historical section, Eliyahu Cherikover, was based in Berlin, not in Poland; in 1933 he would move to France. Cherikover respected Ringelblum and encouraged him.[117] The Historiker Krayz had impressed him greatly, and he valued the young man's scholarship.[118] On the other hand, Cherikover resented Ringelblum's tendency to take initiatives without consulting him, which would be a source of ongoing tension.[119] The critical organizational meetings of the YIVO's historical section took place in Berlin, not in Poland. Moreover, there were significant cultural differences between the leadership of the historical section and the Jewish historians in Warsaw. Many of the Jewish scholars in Berlin, including Dubnow and Cherikover, were autodidacts who had been molded both by their encounter with Russian culture and with the problems of the tsarist empire. The Jewish historians in Warsaw held doctorates and had been shaped by Galicia's markedly different culture.

Another problem was that although Vilna was the natural center for the YIVO, it was far from ideal for Jewish historians. Warsaw, not Vilna, was home to the top Polish historians and had the higher educational institutions that attracted scores of Jewish graduate students. Warsaw was not only becoming a center of Polish historical scholarship, but it also had scholars like Handelsman who were ready to help Jewish students. Ringelblum returned to Warsaw and the Krayz in 1927. Using the Krayz as a base, he helped organize the Warsaw Historical Commission of the YIVO which, in 1934, was renamed the Historical Commission for All of Poland.

> Although Schiper, as the senior historian, was the scholarly authority and mentor of the entire team, it was Ringelblum who was the true architect of the commission's activity. A man of extraordinary organizational skills, never-failing inventiveness and personal magnetism, Ringelblum was behind nearly every aspect of YIVO's work in the field of history.[120]

Ringelblum lobbied the YIVO and his fellow Jewish historians to develop professional links with non-Jewish historians and win the scholarly recognition that Jewish history deserved. Convinced that history could serve as a bridge to bring Jews and Poles closer, he urged that summaries of YIVO historical journals appear in Polish and that Polish "progressive" historians receive copies of YIVO publications.[121]

Determined to put Jewish history "on the map," Ringelblum pushed hard for a Jewish presence at the Seventh International Congress of the Historical Sciences that met in Warsaw in 1933. In a letter to Jacob Shatzky in New York, Ringelblum warned that if the YIVO failed to organize a delegation, it would demonstrate weakness and poverty (*oremkayt tseygenish*).[122]

It was incredible, he later wrote, that until that Congress Jewish historians had never won the right to separate representation at major professional meetings. For that he blamed Jewish "assimilationist" historians, who, until recently, had controlled the writing of Jewish history. "They were afraid," he scoffed, "that if they appeared at a conference and gave papers on Jewish themes in [separate panels], their colleagues would view them as nationalists and separatists. So they preferred to ignore the history of a people of seventeen million rather than risk the accusation of [Jewish nationalism]."[123]

The rules of the Congress did not make it easy for Ringelblum to win the right to a Jewish panel. The Congress was organized on the basis of states and did not provide for the representation of national minorities or extraterritorial peoples. Luckily two liberal Polish professors, Marceli Handelsman and Tadeusz Manteuffel, were on the organizing committee and supported Ringelblum's efforts. There would be separate panels devoted to Jewish history and a Jewish delegation. When the Congress met in Warsaw in August 1933 many distinguished Jewish historians appeared, including delegations from the YIVO and the Instytut Nauk Judaistycznych.[124]

For Ringelblum the Congress offered a welcome chance to present his research and establish new contacts. At first he was hesitant to give a paper: in a letter to Cherikover he wondered, was he not too young to appear in such an important international congress.[125] Cherikover must have assuaged Ringelblum's fears, for he presented a paper on social and economic problems of Polish Jewry in the eighteenth century. Within the ranks of the Jewish delegation, Ringelblum and Mahler stood apart. Mahler delivered a critique of Jewish historiography from a Marxist perspective and let fly his familiar critique of Dubnow and Ahad Ha'am. The paper, not surprisingly, received a lukewarm reception from the other Jewish historians. Ringelblum, however, was quick to rush to Mahler's defense and wish him success in his future research.

Ringelblum also enjoyed meeting Soviet historians, especially Anna Pankratova, who gave a paper on her research into the history of Soviet factory workers.[126] Pankratova's use of interviews and oral histories piqued Ringelblum's interest. She encouraged factory workers to take an active role in the recording of their own past. Pankratova's work dovetailed with Ringelblum's own views that history had to be a collaborative effort between historians and the people, rather "[than the accepted view] that only professional historians with diplomas can enter the temple of historical research."[127]

If the Congress raised Ringelblum's hopes of lowering the barriers between Jewish historians and their Polish colleagues, he soon learned otherwise. After the death of Józef Piłsudski in 1935, anti-Semitism increased in Poland and particularly in the universities. Right-wing students attacked Jews and demanded "ghetto benches" in the lecture halls to segregate Jewish students. Although many eminent Polish scholars protested, the situation continued to worsen. The increasing alienation was also felt within the historical profession itself. In 1937 the major Polish historical journal *Kwartalnik historyczny* published an overview of the state of Polish historical study. Jews and Jewish history received virtually no attention.[128] Furthermore the Polish historians, Ringelblum believed, were far less forthcoming about including Jewish historians in the Polish delegation to the Eighth International Congress, which was slated to meet in Geneva in 1938.[129]

While the 1933 Congress represented a moral victory in the YIVO's battle to win outside recognition for modern Jewish scholarship, no less important for Ringelblum was the battle to mobilize the support of Polish Jewry for the YIVO's goals. With little money and hardly any organized academic base, Poland's Jewish historians had to reach out to the broad masses of the Jewish population to achieve their goals and persuade Polish Jewry that history mattered.

A top priority of the Warsaw Commission was to organize a nationwide campaign to collect community chronicles (*pinkesim*). From the mid-1920s until the outbreak of the war this effort to collect and preserve priceless historic sources remained one of Ringelblum's most important objectives but also caused him no end of bitterness. In his letters and articles Ringelblum complained that the communal leadership of Polish Jewry still showed scant interest in preserving historical sources. In Lwów the Jewish community board (*kehille*) had destroyed precious documents to save storage space, and in other towns priceless chronicles often disappeared into the hands of private individuals. The YIVO's chronic financial problems were another source of frustration. Ringelblum complained that the efforts to catalogue and preserve *pinkesim* and other historic sources could not outstrip the rate at which they were being lost.[130]

Closely linked to the *pinkesim* project was an ambitious campaign to encourage interest in Jewish art and architecture. In April 1929 Ringelblum accused the kehilles of showing as little regard for the Jewish architectural heritage as they did for Jewish documents. In many towns local Jewish leaders looked on as precious architectural landmarks, synagogues, and cemeteries decayed and collapsed, as precious murals were painted over, and unique synagogues were defaced by careless "improvements." In an effort to save what was left, the Warsaw Historical Commission joined several other organizations to organize courses and lectures on Jewish architecture and historical preservation. Throughout 1929 and 1930, the Commission presented lectures on such topics as "The Architecture of Synagogues in Poland" (Sh. Zaitchik), "The History of Synagogues in Poland" (Meyer Balaban), and "Jewish Museums Abroad" (Y. M. Neuman).[131] The Commission also organized an expedition to photograph ancient synagogues and cemeteries.

The drive to foster public interest in Jewish art and architecture brought Ringelblum into the Jewish Society for Knowledge of the Land in Poland (Yidisher gezelshaft far landkentenish). Landkentenish, literally "knowing the country," was an ambitious movement to encourage "engaged tourism," to bring Polish Jews closer to nature, and to contribute to their physical and moral development. Ringelblum was the first editor of the movement's journal, *Landkentenish/Krajoznawstwo*. In the first issue he wrote that "the centuries of urban life, the remoteness from nature, life within the narrow, stifling confines of the ghetto have caused the Jew to feel distant and estranged from the beauty and glory of nature."[132] But Ringelblum worried that the movement could easily take the path of least resistance and offer carefree recreation and "tourism for tourism's sake." He wanted a "Jewish Landkentenish Society," not a "Landkentenish society for Jews."[133] To avoid the temptation of becoming just another hiking club, the Landkentenish movement had to remember its national and cultural mission. Properly organized, tourism could bring about not only individual regeneration but also a healthy national revival. Landkentenish could become a solid pillar of an emerging secular Yiddish culture and help turn the tide of assimilation.

There were good reasons, Ringelblum explained, why Jews needed their own Landkentenish society. Polish societies showed no interest in Jewish history or Jewish architectural objects. Even if the Poles were more welcoming, there would still remain a key difference between Polish and Jewish tourism. In most countries tourist excursions visited museums, cities, and architectural sites that had already been discovered, described, and investigated by professional scholars. The tourist had no obligation to discover anything himself, only to observe and learn from prepared guidebooks. Jews, however, found themselves in an entirely different position. Almost nothing was known about Jewish local history, cemeteries, old synagogues, and regional folklore. There were no guides, no points of reference. The Jewish Landkentenish movement had to join forces with the YIVO and combine recreation with serious *zamling*.[134] "Landkentenish," Ringelblum wrote, "really means not only learning [*derkenen*] a city's past, its monuments and buildings; it also means getting to know the people [*folk*] with its centuries old folklore and creative traditions."

As an example of what Landkentenish could become, Ringelblum singled out a local history of Pruzhany produced by a dedicated group of teachers and students from the town's Yiddish school.[135] It grew out of a project that had been prepared by students and teachers for a national exhibit organized by the CYSHO. The completed volume contained a wealth of information not only on the town but also on the region: its geography, economic structure, Jewish labor, local architecture, and Jewish communal and social institutions.

Just as important as the result was the process: the Pruzhany project showed that Jewish history could be researched and written by ordinary people. Not just scholars in the big cities but also ordinary students and teachers in small towns could come together and study the Jewish past. Thus new institutions like the local Yiddish school could have an effect far beyond their immediate purpose in an emerging secular culture.

What made Ringelblum especially happy was the basic approach of the Pruzhany group. From the very beginning of the project, the Pruzhany collective refused to view Jewish history as a separate and isolated discipline. They treated the Jewish presence in Pruzhany from a comparative perspective, with the Jews perceived as an integral part of the region's social and economic system. Ringelblum wrote appreciatively: "We feel that the writers see proud working Jews. They don't feel that they are guests in Pruzhany. Rather they regard themselves as long established veterans who have put down deep roots in the local area thanks to their work and toil." This kind of history, Ringelblum argued, was a welcome change from traditional Jewish local histories that concentrated on illustrious rabbis and scholars, and ignored the general economic and social context. Ringelblum also offered criticisms. Collective efforts were fine, but they required a talented organizer and coordinator to produce the best results. In the case of the Pruzhany volume, the final product could have used better organization and conceptualization. But these criticisms did not offset Ringelblum's appreciation. The Pruzhany group had demonstrated how the YIVO and the Landkentenish movement could complement each other. Indeed the project spurred inquiries from other towns eager to write their own local histories. At a meeting of the YIVO executive board on November 27, 1932, Ringelblum expressed disappointment that the YIVO was not doing more to take advantage of this interest. It was vital to reach out to Jews in the provinces and encourage their readiness to *zaml* and write their own histories.[136]

Ringelblum's embrace of the Pruzhany project reflected a growing determination by the Historical Commission to raise its profile among Polish Jewry. More work on local and regional history would not only attract new

YIVO members but would also pave the way for a badly needed general history of Polish Jewry. In early 1938 the historical section issued detailed "directives for research into the history of Jewish communities." The directives pointed out the crucial importance of local and regional history, and appealed to the Jewish intelligentsia to start studying the history of their towns. One did not have to be a trained historian to achieve results; the Pruzhany project demonstrated what could be achieved with enough "determination, love, and understanding of the problem."[137]

Ringelblum's enthusiasm for outreach did not find unanimous support within the Historical Commission for Poland. One can infer from YIVO records that Isaac Schiper believed that, with resources limited, it was more important to think about scholars and scholarship than it was to reach out to the masses. Local histories produced by history buffs, Schiper thought, were largely a waste of time. They were certainly less critical than the development of adequate bibliographies and research guides to archives. Ringelblum strongly disagreed, and the majority of the Historical Commission supported him.[138]

The YIVO historians produced an impressive record of scholarship.[139] A centerpiece of the efforts of the historical section (not to be confused with the Warsaw-based historical commission) was the *Historishe shriftn*, edited by Cherikover. Three massive volumes appeared in 1929, 1937, and 1939, and they marked the high point of Jewish historical scholarship in Yiddish. In the introduction to the first volume Cherikover stressed one of the major goals of the section:

> The first mission of our section is not to mechanically translate into
> Yiddish what had also been published [by Jewish historians] in other
> languages but to publish new research in Yiddish. . . . Just the very fact
> that the historian uses Yiddish given the role the language plays in our
> social and cultural life. . . will result in new themes, new ways of looking
> at history and the use of new sources."[140]

The YIVO established its graduate program (the *aspirantur*) in 1935; by 1939, of the sixty-eight seminar papers that had been written for the *aspirantur,* nineteen were on historical topics. A preparatory section, designed to train young people for study in the *aspirantur,* had five students in 1938–39.[141]

This YIVO scholarship developed in the face of enormous financial obstacles. As the records of the Historical Commission for All Poland make clear, at no point did the YIVO historians have even a fraction of the funds they needed. There was not enough money to publish their books, to put out their journals.[142] By 1939 the Commission had registered more than 293 invaluable chronicles (*pinkesim*) in more than 200 communities. But hardly any had been copied, again largely for lack of money. They mostly vanished during the war.

But Ringelblum, indefatigable, developed ambitious plans to establish new links between the Jewish historians and the local communities, the credit societies, the Landkentenish groups, and Jewish student organizations in various universities. He now began to encourage provincial Jews to write institutional histories of local banks, societies, and so forth. Together with Yitzhak Giterman, Menakhem Linder, and others, he worked tirelessly to develop and expand the YIVO's Warsaw branch, which, by 1939, had more than four hundred members. He also worked with the CYSHO in the preparation of textbooks and student history exhibits.

By the late 1930s it was clear that despite shared goals and a common devotion to Yiddish culture, strains were growing between Ringelblum and the YIVO's administration in Vilna. A nasty dispute arose over a questionnaire Ringelblum had helped design; Kalmanovich and Reyzen criticized the questionnaire over what they called its faulty Yiddish.[143] A furious Ringelblum threatened to resign from the YIVO after his two critics called the questionnaire "illiterate." Shatzky and Cherikover stepped in to mediate the dispute, and Reyzen and Kalmanovich apologized, but the incident caused further damage to Ringelblum's relations with the central office in Vilna.[144] Another source of strain was the YIVO's new graduate program. Ringelblum was not convinced that the history graduate students should study in Vilna rather than Warsaw. He also had doubts as to whether the scope of the program made sense, given that most of its graduates would not have jobs.[145]

Underlying this friction, however, was Ringelblum's growing sense of self-confidence. The YIVO's Warsaw branch was prospering, thanks in large part to his own efforts. He was becoming more impatient with the need to justify his decisions to Cherikover in Paris and to the central administration in Vilna. In late 1938 he even wrote a sharp letter to Cherikover, complaining that the YIVO "seemed to care more about documents than it did about living historians."[146] He also was becoming increasingly dissatisfied with the impressive but infrequent *Historishe shriftn*. The YIVO's historical section, he felt, should be doing much more. Outreach was the top priority, as well as a journal that, although smaller, would appear more frequently.

Yet despite their divergences, in the end Ringelblum and his YIVO colleagues agreed on one essential item: the need to continue working. The late 1930s were dark times for Polish Jewry, and some questioned whether, in the gathering crisis, the scholarship of the YIVO even made sense. But in 1938, as the YIVO proudly celebrated its bar mitzvah, its thirteenth year, Max Weinreich answered that question with a resounding yes. Jews, he pointed out, had to look beyond the present crisis toward a brighter future. In response to a critic who asked how one could be busy with flowers when the forest was burning, Weinreich replied that "even in a time when forests are burning, there are firemen who put out the fire, but luckier are those who can raise flowers that will later beautify the forest."[147]

Ringelblum had come a long way from the day when, as a young historian, he sent his letters of introduction to Weinreich and Cherikover. As he came to feel more like an equal, he clearly pondered the mission and responsibilities of a Jewish historian in Poland. In a review of Philip Friedman's *History of the Jews of Lodz,* which was recovered in the second part of the archive, Ringelblum revealed his acute awareness of the pressures and dilemmas he and his friends faced.[148] Barred from an academic career in the universities, called on to use their craft to defend their people, how did the Jewish historian maintain the integrity of his unofficial profession?

Furthermore, could a committed leftist be an objective scholar? Ringelblum implicitly, if surprisingly, acknowledged a certain tension between political commitment and scholarly integrity as he discussed the problems of researching the history of nineteenth-century Polish Jewry. There were many sources, he declared, perhaps even too many, but there was also a danger posed by the subject's proximity to the present day. The more recent the period, the more the historian had to deal with political pressures and passions, especially his own. In Ringelblum's words, "The historian who has not isolated himself from public life" faces these dangers more acutely: "Although history is—to quote a handy phrase—past politics and politics is current history, it is all too possible to make history into politics, and bad politics to boot."

Could a historian also defend one's people without becoming an apologist? To write Jewish history in Poland, Ringelblum noted, exposed one to the temptation of obsessively responding to anti-Semitic attacks, or to use one's scholarship to praise the "achievements of the Jews in all fields." Friedman, Ringelblum wrote, had successfully managed to navigate between the "Scylla of apologetics and the Charybdis of nationalist megalomania."

Soon Ringelblum would find himself facing an unprecedented test, but he had prepared himself well. Working outside the traditional academic world, with few funds and little encouragement, he slowly gained in self-confidence and honed his sense of the Polish Jewish historian's mission. It was one that combined scholarship with outreach and that defended the interests of the nation not through apologetics but by trying to uncover the facts. It was a serious mission that could not be accomplished alone but demanded a collective effort, the mobilization of an entire community.[149]

CHAPTER 4

Organizing the Community

SELF-HELP AND RELIEF

Had Ringelblum remained just a historian and high school teacher, it is doubtful he could have organized the Oyneg Shabes Archive. To make the archive work, Ringelblum needed a position that gave him wide contacts and good information, as well as a certain degree of power and prestige. When the war began, his high post in the Aleynhilf, Warsaw's major Jewish relief organization, is what gave him this access to people and information. The Hebrew writer Natan Eck, who worked closely with Ringelblum in the Aleynhilf, recalled that Ringelblum attached more significance to his relief work than to anything else he had done before.[1]

Early in the 1930s Ringelblum had begun a parallel career at the Joint Distribution Committee (JDC) that would turn him into a resourceful relief worker and community organizer.[2] His new job at the Joint, the leading relief agency in Jewish Poland, put him in contact with Yitzhak Giterman, a JDC director and charismatic mentor who changed the course of Ringelblum's life. Both before the war and in the Warsaw Ghetto, Giterman served as the role model who taught his younger protégé to see the difference between self-help, based on community involvement, and traditional philanthropy. The latter, he believed, demeaned those it tried to help and reinforced traditional class divisions in Jewish society; self-help, on the other hand, galvanized the community, lifted national morale, and served as a powerful weapon against anti-Semitism.

Ringelblum quickly understood how his new job at the Joint complemented his work as a YIVO historian. Both roles stressed community involvement, and both were interdependent. Grass-roots organization provided knowledge and contacts that would afford the historians indispensable sources of information, and historical scholarship would raise communal morale and self-awareness.

Ringelblum's career as a relief worker and community organizer went through three stages. From 1930 to 1938 Ringelblum served as editor of the *Folkshilf,* the journal of the CEKABE (Centrala Kas Bezprocentowych), the network of JDC-sponsored credit societies in Poland, and he also headed the landsmanshaft department,[3] which was charged with persuading emigrants abroad to help their former communities in Poland. The second stage began in October 1938, when Giterman sent Ringelblum to the border town of Zbąszyń to organize relief for the thousands of Polish Jews whom the Nazis had expelled from Germany. The Zbąszyń experience gave Ringelblum a firsthand look at Nazi barbarism, even as it demonstrated that he had the skills of a first-rate organizer and troubleshooter. Zbąszyń bolstered his standing in the Joint and served as the springboard that put him right in the center of relief activities in the Warsaw Ghetto.

The third stage began with the German invasion of Poland in September 1939, when Ringelblum stepped forward to become a major leader of the relief effort. Just a few days after the war began he made a key decision: he would stay in Warsaw, even as most of the Jewish political and cultural elite were trying to escape to the East. The difficult weeks he had spent in Zbąszyń the previous year had left their mark: he knew he was a good organizer and could make a big difference. The task at hand was to organize relief, and who would do it if everyone ran away?

Thus began Ringelblum's fateful association with one of the most important organizations in the Warsaw Ghetto: the Aleynhilf, or the Jewish Self-Help Society. Under various names, until the Great Deportation of July 1942, the Aleynhilf supervised a network of relief agencies, soup kitchens, and house committees.

Within the Aleynhilf, Ringelblum headed the so-called "Public Sector (Gezelshaftlekher Sektor) the department that oversaw the activities of the hundreds of "house committees" in the ghetto. The house committees were the vital microcosms of ghetto society, each one its own separate world. These house committees, at first a source of great hope and a symbol of the resilience of the Jewish masses, faced an increasingly uphill battle to stay afloat in the face of dwindling resources and widespread corruption that allowed unscrupulous officials and policemen free entrée to the committees' funds. Ringelblum found himself right in the middle of this struggle, and his moral outrage grew as the committees struggled to make their meager resources count in the face of Judenrat harassment and constant shakedowns by the Jewish police and other officials.

Thanks to the Aleynhilf Ringelblum had daily contact with all segments of Jewish society and could recruit the trusted collaborators who would form the Oyneg Shabes. Practically the entire staff of the Oyneg Shabes worked in the Aleynhilf, and the symbiotic relationship between the two reflected the specific ethos of a "countercommunity"—to borrow Lucy Dawidowicz's phrase—that became particularly important in the Warsaw Ghetto.[4]

The Germans set up hundreds of ghettos in occupied Eastern Europe, no two alike.[5] They ranged from the enormous Warsaw Ghetto, with close to half a million Jews, to tiny country ghettos of a few thousand. Ghettos differed in many ways: in their internal regime, their economic functions; their cultural characteristics; their relations with the occupying authorities; the quality and composition of the local Judenrat; and their social structure. Some of these differences stemmed from the regional variations that marked prewar Jewish Poland. Others were the result of divergent occupation policies or the particular inclinations of German officials on the spot.

All ghettos saw terrible suffering, but some were better off than others. Although the enormous Warsaw Ghetto suffered up to one hundred thousand deaths from starvation and disease between 1940 and 1942, many smaller ghettos at that time were relatively well supplied with food and saw little actual starvation. Some of them were even "open," that is, inhabitants could leave the ghetto during specified hours.

Few ghettos experienced more hunger, more suffering, and more disease than Warsaw. No other ghetto had to absorb more refugees. All the ghettos in occupied Poland needed effective and well-organized social relief, but none more than Warsaw. In some ghettos social welfare was controlled by the Judenrat; in others separate relief organizations worked in harmony with the Judenrat and often shared the same membership.

But in the Warsaw Ghetto matters were different. From the very beginning of the German occupation, much of the welfare effort lay in the hands of people who tried to remain outside Judenrat control. Thus, from early in the war, the Aleynhilf came to see itself as a counterpoint to the Judenrat and gamely resisted all efforts to quash its autonomy.

The Aleynhilf's fight for autonomy benefited from the fact that the head of the Warsaw Judenrat, Adam Czerniakow, had less desire—or power—to impose the kind of tight centralized control that characterized the policies of Chaim Rumkowski, the "Elder" of the Lodz Ghetto, or Jacob Gens, the commandant of the Vilna Ghetto. In Lodz, for instance, practically the entire economic life of the ghetto was controlled by Rumkowski or German-appointed rivals, and there was little room for autonomous organizations.[6]

There was another key difference between the Lodz and Warsaw Ghettos: the Lodz Ghetto was hermetically sealed and situated on territory that had been annexed to the German Reich, whereas the Warsaw Ghetto was in the Generalgouvernement (General Government)—the central portion of German-occupied Poland that did not include areas annexed to the Reich—where the German civil administration had recognized, after a fashion, the legal status of the relief organizations. The Warsaw Ghetto also had much more contact with the "Aryan side." Whatever complaints Warsaw Jews had about Polish anti-Semitism, at least they knew that on the other side of the wall were potential smuggling partners, prewar acquaintances, and a Polish society that thoroughly detested the occupiers.

Thus the Warsaw Ghetto had more space for "autonomous" political, organizational, and cultural life than many other ghettos.[7] Indeed, a startling difference between Warsaw and other ghettos is the salient role played by the hundreds of house committees that were often elected and could create a semblance of a "public space." It was this space that the Aleynhilf tried to fill.

From a postwar perspective, applying such terms as "public sector" or "space" to the Warsaw Ghetto might seem problematic and strange. As soon as the ghettos were established, their Jewish inmates had difficulty finding the right words to describe their new reality. Terms that made sense in a normal community took on an ironic connotation in this twilight world, where people tried to live the semblance of a "normal" life even as they stepped over corpses in the street.

Some Jews in the ghettos were proud at first of the Jewish policemen and Jewish mailmen that walked the streets, occupations closed to Jews before the war. Others smiled with bitter irony about their neighbors' naïveté and joked about the "sovereignty" of the Judenrat or the "planned economy" of the Lodz Ghetto as opposed to the "liberal capitalism" of the Warsaw Ghetto. Still others found some consolation, at least in the beginning, in an idealized comparison with medieval ghettos where the walls supposedly protected Jews and gave them a chance to look inward and develop their own culture. In Lodz, Rumkowski boasted that in his ghetto Yiddish would flourish as never before.

The ghettos in occupied Poland were unprecedented phenomena, neither normal communities nor concentration camps. For a time the Germans allowed just enough space for the Jews to organize what appeared to be a societal life. Although much of ghetto existence was a grotesque distortion of a "normal" society, deep traces of prewar values and culture survived. It would be an exaggeration to speak about a "civil society" in the Warsaw Ghetto, but there was intense political life and an extensive network of organizations grouped around the Aleynhilf. Despite the mass exodus in 1939, the Warsaw Ghetto still had a large critical mass of journalists, intellectuals, social welfare workers, and other leaders. The Aleynhilf included members of various political parties and even different social classes. Parties of the Left predominated, but there were also rabbis and conservative Zionists.

Ringelblum and the Aleynhilf tried to maintain a sense of communal responsibility and social solidarity in the ghetto in the face of growing obstacles. Deep social differences, many caused by sheer chance and luck, split the ghetto. Those whose prewar homes and businesses had been on the territory of the ghetto were comparatively lucky. They had an easier time keeping their possessions, which they could eventually sell for food. Less fortunate were Warsaw Jews who had to move into the ghetto. How they fared depended largely on how much they were able to take with them into the ghetto, and some Jews, former residents of wealthy central city neighborhoods, coped relatively well. Furthermore, these individuals were in a city where they had personal contacts that could help them get by. Least fortunate were the tens of thousands of refugees who arrived in the ghetto in different waves of expulsions. Many had been solid citizens before the war, but now the Germans often threw them out of their homes on fifteen minutes' notice. They arrived in a strange city without money and contacts, and often found themselves in the dreaded *punktn,* the refugee centers that had the highest death rate in the ghetto.

The Aleynhilf also defined itself by what it opposed: the Warsaw Judenrat and the Jewish police. Not all its criticisms of the Judenrat were fair, however, for the Judenrat was in a tragic situation: the German ghetto commissar Heinz Auerswald reported with great satisfaction that the ghetto complained more about the Judenrat than about the Germans![8] Ringelblum tended to minimize the difficulties the Judenrat faced and to overlook the important welfare activities that it performed in its own right. Over time the relative weight of the Judenrat in ghetto relief would steadily increase, and this further deepened Ringelblum's anger and frustration.

But the Aleynhilf's censure of the Judenrat also reflected profound differences in their values and politics. The leaders of the Aleynhilf attacked the Judenrat and its chairman, Adam Czerniakow, for a tax policy that hurt the poor and coddled the rich; for dragging the poorest Jews to labor camps while letting the well-to-do escape; for tolerating a Jewish police that grew increasingly corrupt; for favoring converts in the allocation of key ghetto posts; and for a lack of national pride. Most Judenrat officials spoke Polish; the Aleynhilf deliberately used Yiddish as an official language.

Ringelblum and the other Oyneg Shabes members saw themselves as an integral part of a coalition that served as the "conscience" of the Warsaw Ghetto. The Aleynhilf viewed itself as the catalyst that would try to remind the ghetto population that although the war hurt everyone, some were hurt more than others, and that helping the less fortunate was not only a moral duty but also a national responsibility. Ringelblum and his circle regarded the Aleynhilf as a vital weapon—however inadequate—in the ongoing struggle against demoralization and corruption. Before the war Ringelblum and his circle had believed in the "Jewish masses," in their ability to organize, endure, and find a moral compass. Would the war belie this faith? They believed that it would not. Indeed, it was this critical tension between their faith in the Jewish masses and the proliferating pathologies of ghetto life that added drama to the Oyneg Shabes Archive. Ringelblum and his colleagues saw themselves as obligated not only to document the war experience but also to defend their national honor. The record of the Aleynhilf, they hoped, would help them do so.

THE JOINT DISTRIBUTION COMMITTEE

In 1930 Ringelblum began to work as a part-time editor of the *Folkshilf,* the journal of the free loan societies. It turned out to be one of the most important JDC programs in Poland. By 1937 the network of free loan societies (*gmiles hesed kases*) included 870 towns and cities in Poland out of a total of 1,013 settlements of more than three hundred Jews.[9] These societies often were the only source of credit for impoverished Jewish artisans and petty traders.

At the *Folkshilf* Ringelblum found a new mentor, Yitzhak Giterman, a director of the JDC in Poland. It was Giterman who had invited him to the *Folkshilf* and had imbued in him a new ideal of public service. In January 1943, shortly after Giterman was murdered at the hands of the Germans, Ringelblum wrote that "a whole book will have to be written about this very important person."[10] He considered Giterman's death one of the "two greatest individual losses"[11] sustained by Warsaw Jewry (the other was Shakhne Zagan, the leader of the Poalei Tsiyon), a remark indicating the degree to which Ringelblum idolized and respected his mentors.

Giterman was a brilliant organizer who combined many interests and skills: Yiddish culture, Jewish history, social action, and economics. At a time when political infighting and ideological bickering divided Polish Jewry and prevented unified action, Giterman tried to transcend political differences and bring people together. In an essay written a few months before his death in March 1944, a shaken Ringelblum compared Giterman to a Hasidic rebbe—a religious leader who led through charisma and spiritual magnetism and who could inspire those around him.[12] Until Giterman arrived, Ringelblum recalled, most Polish Jews had a somewhat negative stereotype of JDC officials: unsentimental, imperturbable, rather distant American Jews who smoked cigars and had a keen sense of the bottom line. Giterman was different. Ringelblum accorded him one of his highest accolades: "when a 'folksmensh,' an ordinary Jew, spoke to Giterman, he felt right at home."[13]

Giterman was, in fact, a product of the Hasidic elite.[14] A scion of two great Hasidic families, the Twerskis and the Shneoursons (the Lubavich dynasty), he was born in 1889 in the Ukraine and grew up in the court of his grandfather, R. Mordecai Ber Twerski, the Harnastopolier rebbe. Giterman was raised in a religious enclave, almost entirely cut off, he later recalled, from the outside world. Every day hundreds of Hasidim would arrive to see his grandfather, seek advice, and pray, sing, and dance. On major Jewish holidays thousands of worshipers eagerly awaited the chance to touch their *tsaddik* (holy man or rebbe). They would leave their families for weeks at a time to come and seek comfort from their rebbe and comradeship from their fellow Hasidim. Even after Giterman rebelled and left home to seek a European education, he never forgot the intense spirit of that unique Hasidic universe.

Nevertheless, at a young age Giterman realized that his family's world was not for him. He was supposed to marry a young bride whom his parents had chosen and perhaps become a rebbe himself. Instead, Giterman opted for a secular education. He moved to Kiev and learned Russian. There he befriended the future Yiddish literary critic Nakhman Mayzel. Mayzel introduced him to David Bergelson and Pinchas Kaganovich (pseudonym, Der Nister [The hidden one]), two young Yiddish writers about to make their reputation as great masters of Yiddish prose. From then on Giterman became a devoted supporter of secular Yiddish culture.

During World War I Giterman helped to organize the EKOPO (Evreiskii Komitet Pomoshchi Zhertvam Voiny [Jewish Committee to Help War Victims]), which became Russian Jewry's central relief organization. The tsarist regime had expelled hundreds of thousands of Jews to the Russian interior, and the EKOPO not only helped feed and clothe them but turned the relief effort into a powerful agent of social and cultural transformation. Soup kitchens became convenient sites for schools and cultural clubs that accelerated the development of a modern Jewish educational system. Relief for the displaced Jews transformed not only the Jewish refugees but also the Jewish intellectuals and professionals who came forward to organize the massive effort.[15] These activities brought many members of the Jewish intelligentsia back to Jewish concerns and reawakened their Jewish loyalties.

A few months after the war began, the EKOPO sent Giterman on a challenging mission: to organize relief for hundreds of thousands of desperate Galician Jews overrun by the advancing Russian army. The Russian army treated the Galician Jews more brutally than the Polish and Lithuanian Jews, for after all the Galician Jews were loyal Habsburg subjects who had no reason to love their Russian conquerors.[16]

When the war ended and bloody pogroms broke out in the Ukraine, Giterman risked his life to bring aid to the terrorized victims. In 1920 he was sentenced to death by the Soviet authorities in Rovno and narrowly avoided execution. By 1921 he had settled in Warsaw. He arrived with a well-deserved reputation as someone who combined courage, organizing abilities, and deep Jewish loyalties. Above all, he came to Poland as a natural leader. In 1926 Giterman accepted the JDC's proposal to direct its operations in Poland.

A shared love of Yiddish secular culture first brought Giterman and Ringelblum together. As soon as he arrived in Poland Giterman became a leading figure in the Yiddish cultural world. In the mid-1920s he helped organize one of the most important Yiddish publishing houses, the Kultur Lige. He warmly welcomed the YIVO, headed its Warsaw branch for many years, and served as a member of the central YIVO board in Vilna. Like Ringelblum and other historians, he fought to preserve Jewish antiquities and historical sources; in 1939 he succeeded in rescuing the treasures of the Danzig Jewish museum.[17]

Meir Korzen, who worked with Ringelblum at the *Folkshilf,* painted a somewhat unflattering portrait of Ringelblum's relationship with Giterman and portrayed him as a sycophant who sought out Giterman's opinion on even the most trivial details of the *Folkshilf*—such as the color of the cover.[18] Once Giterman came to work with a limp, and soon Ringelblum also started to limp. His colleagues, Korzen recalled, joked that this was Ringelblum's way of identifying with the boss!

More important, however, was that Giterman placed growing trust in his young protégé and eventually charged him with tasks that helped transform him into a real leader. These new responsibilities would involve Ringelblum with a broad cross-section of Polish Jewry and prepare him to work with elements outside the circles of the Left Poalei Tsiyon and the YIVO. When Ringelblum joined the *Folkshilf* he was probably little more than a glorified, part-time clerk. By 1938 he had become a key member of the JDC staff.

There was certainly enough for the JDC to do. In the 1930s Polish Jewry suffered multiple blows: the world depression, a spreading boycott, and increased government anti-Semitism that further undermined the already precarious Jewish economy. In 1936 Giterman admitted that at the beginning of that decade he had thought that the situation of Polish Jewry had hit rock bottom. But he was too "optimistic in his pessimism."[19] The situation was only getting worse.

In 1936 and 1937 a wave of pogroms devastated Przytyk, Mińsk-Mazowiecki, Brest, and other towns. Although the Polish government had no direct hand in the anti-Jewish violence, the leaders who succeeded Józef Piłsudski in 1935 had fewer qualms about ratcheting up the economic pressure on Polish Jewry; after all, they feared charges from the Right that they were coddling Jews.[20] Throughout Poland pickets began to blockade Jewish shops. The prime minister of Poland and the Catholic Church condemned anti-Jewish violence but endorsed a nonviolent economic boycott by Poles of Jewish businesses.[21]

As the mood turned bleaker, Giterman radiated a stern determination to fight back. Increasingly the pages of *Folkshilf* employed military terms to describe the tasks of the kases, the free loan societies, such as "dogged defense" or "a vital weapon in the hands of the Jewish masses," and so on. No sooner had a pogrom wrecked Jewish businesses and stalls in a small town, Ringelblum recalled, than the Joint appeared to assess the damage and give Jews loans to rebuild.[22] Often Ringelblum accompanied Giterman as they toured badly hit towns. The instigators of the pogroms hoped to drive out the Jewish population. Therefore it was important, Giterman emphasized, to send them the message that the Jews are staying put!

For Giterman, Jewish despair was as dangerous as Polish anti-Semitism; the Joint had to protect not only Jewish livelihoods but also Jewish morale. If one measure wasn't working, then one had to try another—and, above all, one had to keep trying.[23] Giterman let others discuss grand political solutions. He focused on humdrum, prosaic measures, half-steps that might made a small difference: here a course on rabbit husbandry, there a loan for a small dairy or classes to help Jewish artisans pass state-mandated exams. Often the kases worked at the margins, extending tiny credits that might help an impoverished Jewish family get by for a few more months. The Lestschinsky Archives record a typical case in the small town of Węgrów:

> A woman enters (the kase) with tears in her eyes. "Jews," she says, "you
> know that my husband is a scribe and makes eight zlotys a week. Of
> course you know that I can't live on that wage. My children don't have
> any bread . . . I would like to open a soda water stand . . . some soda

water, some apples, and I'll be able to make do [*ikh vel zikh an eyste gebn*]. But a license costs twenty-eight zlotys. Please, Jews, lend me twenty-five zlotys. I'll pay back one zloty a week.[24]

Many laughed at these attempts to sweep back the sea with a few brooms; scoffers sneered at the disparity between the tiny loans that the kases could hand out and Giterman's lofty rhetoric.[25] But Ringelblum certainly did not. Like Giterman, he stressed the positive: even when the future seemed hopeless, it was important to keep fighting. Rafael Mahler recalled that Ringelblum was totally dedicated to this campaign to "productivize" Polish Jewry. "He was full of excitement," Mahler recalled, "about every beehive, every garden that was laid out [in some obscure shtetl]."[26] The *Folkshilf* even boasted of its humdrum, practical approach, a dramatic contrast to the political radicalism of Ringelblum's own party: "The kases are . . . [organizations] for ordinary Jews who do not want to fly up to the political heavens, who prefer patching and repairing the here and now to relying on salvation from political or national messiahs."[27]

The free loan societies established by the Joint brought together Jews of different backgrounds and political leanings. The Joint was adamant about this and refused to allow political parties or unions any measure of control. It also stressed that the program offered constructive help, not charity. The Joint provided the seed money, but distinguishing these kases was the requirement that the local Jews eventually replace half the Joint's investment with their own capital. This fostered self-reliance rather than resigned helplessness.

In the struggling shtetl these kases often became a major communal institution, bolstering morale and fighting a sense of isolation:[28]

> Giterman constantly emphasized that one could not measure the effectiveness of the Joint's activities by the number of Jewish families [that were helped] . . . after all, just one government decree could destroy many Jewish livelihoods. But, Giterman would argue, what really counted was the moral aspect. The Jew in the small shtetl, who was persecuted and hounded, who had to fight off pickets and pogroms, could now see that he was not alone. There was a social force [the Joint] that thought about him and that was ready to help him out in his hour of need.[29]

To that end the Joint made a major effort to enlist the American landsmanshaftn to support the kases. Of course, help from American relatives and landsmanshaftn was already an important safety net for the Polish shtetl. But much of this money had been spent in a haphazard manner. Giterman wanted to convince the landsmanshaftn to finance a coherent program to shore up the shtetl economy. He put Ringelblum in charge of this project. In 1938 Giterman entrusted him with editing an expanded edition of the *Folkshilf* aimed at the landsmanshaftn in the United States.[30]

Each issue of the *Folkshilf* contained poignant and stirring accounts of how shtetlekh all over Poland resisted economic catastrophe. These accounts were written by ordinary Jews and provided first-rate material for historians, economists, and ethnographers. Many even had literary merit. Undoubtedly they encouraged Ringelblum in his conviction that the Jewish intelligentsia had to seek out and develop "hidden talents" among ordinary people, a pursuit that paid obvious dividends in the Oyneg Shabes Archive. Like the YIVO, the *Folkshilf* provided Ringelblum with an important counterpoint to the political divisiveness and ideological infighting that were undermining the defense efforts of Polish Jewry. In these institutions people tried to forget political differences and to work together for the good of a common cause. Almost the entire political spectrum of Polish Jewry supported the CEKABE, an important lesson that Ringelblum would remember.

Ringelblum noticed a contrast between the Jews' frequent indifference to the official community boards—the kehilles—and their interest in the kases.[31] The kases were seen as truly democratic, whereas the kehilles often became the object of government interference and manipulation. In many cities—including Warsaw—the government nullified kehille elections and appointed hand-picked boards. Even before the war, therefore, Ringelblum was quite sensitive to the tension between a "real" and an "official" community.

At the end of October 1938 Giterman entrusted Ringelblum with a new challenge. On October 25–27 the Third Reich had expelled thousands of Polish Jews by literally pushing them—at the point of a bayonet—across the Polish border. A desperate situation arose, as the Polish authorities at first refused to allow most of the victims to cross the border into Poland. At Zbąszyń, one major crossing point between Germany and Poland, about six thousand hapless refugees, hungry and cold, were stranded.[32] Giterman immediately sent Ringelblum and Shlomo Ginzburg to organize a relief effort.

This was certainly the greatest challenge Ringelblum had faced up to that time—and was also his finest hour. As Yehuda Bauer pointed out, Zbąszyń registered a basic shift in the Joint's policies.[33] Until this new crisis, the Joint had contributed money and relied on local efforts to organize and distribute relief. In Zbąszyń the roles were reversed. In an incredible effort, impoverished Polish Jewry raised 3.5 million zloty (U.S. $700,000), and the Joint actually took over responsibility for organizing the relief effort, as well as contributing 20 percent of the total funds.

When Ringelblum arrived at Zbąszyń on October 30, 1938, he entered a scene of chaos and mass confusion. The number of refugees far exceeded the permanent population of Zbąszyń. The German authorities had literally dragged many of these refugees from their beds in the middle of the night. Often they were not allowed to dress or even take anything with them. Many arrived on the Polish frontier in their pajamas or nightclothes. In the cold and damp weather, they sprawled on the floor of the overcrowded railroad station or in nearby stables. Many had no money for a bath, a meal, or a train ticket. At first they did not even have spoons to eat the soup that was offered to them. Many were on the verge of psychological collapse. Only a week earlier they had had homes and jobs; now they sat penniless and in limbo.

Michał Rudawski had been working as a secretary for the Warsaw branch of the YIVO when Ringelblum asked him to travel with him to Zbąszyń to help with the relief work. Years before, Rudawski's father had left Poland for Germany; now Rudawski heard that his father was among the milling mass of refugees. Rudawski was directed to an outlying stable where he was told that his father was wandering around the camp, too depressed to even sleep. Finally, the two found each other.[34]

Outraged and fearful, Polish Jewry responded with a massive outpouring of support. Within days the entire Jewish population began to collect money. This major effort by an impoverished and beleaguered community was much more than a natural response to the tragedy of their persecuted brethren. It was a defiant challenge to anti-Semites and a proud assertion of national dignity and solidarity.

At Zbąszyń Ringelblum proved to be a brilliant organizer. Slowly but steadily he was moving out from the shadow of others and gaining confidence in his own abilities. Applying the lessons he had learned in the CEKABE, he was careful to avoid treating the refugees as abject and passive objects of charity.[35] He led a team effort that encouraged them to take over many of the duties in the camp: a postal service, a housing department, a legal bureau, a court of honor, kitchens, an employment bureau, schools for children, classes in foreign languages for adults, and so on.[36] In his final report Ringelblum proudly noted that, of the 420 staffers of the various camp departments, all but 20 were refugees.[37]

Characteristically Ringelblum also encouraged the use of Yiddish in Zbąszyń. He sensed that many of these unfortunate Jews—some of whom had spent decades in Germany—were ready to reestablish contact with the rich folk culture of East European Jewry. Ringelblum helped organize Yiddish classes and invited a Yiddish actor from Warsaw, Noah Nachbush, to come to Zbąszyń to cheer up the refugees. Nachbush later told Rafael Mahler in New York that when he came to Zbąszyń, he saw Ringelblum teaching Yiddish folk songs to some of the younger refugees. (They especially enjoyed Itzik Manger's humorous "Rabeynu Tam.")[38]

Ringelblum became especially close to some of the young members of Zionist youth groups, whom he mobilized to help organize the camp. Arnon Fishman-Tamir, a member of He-haluts who later emigrated to Palestine, recalled Ringelblum's sincere interest and willingness to help. Ringelblum invited him to his home in Warsaw, and they corresponded after Fishman-Tamir illegally emigrated to Palestine at the beginning of 1939.[39] On December 12, 1938, he wrote to Mahler: "I miss the young people of Zbąszyń a lot. They were wonderful idealists and we became friends." Perhaps this foretold the later friendship that Ringelblum developed with the leaders of the Hashomer Hatzair, a major youth group in the Warsaw Ghetto.

Predictably Ringelblum did not neglect his duties as a historian. He encouraged the refugees to write down their experiences and hoped to use the material for future research. In fact, his insistence on interviewing the refugees led to friction with his coworkers. Meir Korzen, who accompanied Ringelblum to Zbąszyń, told Ringelblum that conducting detailed interviews made little sense. The accounts were fairly similar, and the process only aggravated the refugees' tension and depression. But Ringelblum insisted and hoped that eventually he would be able to publish a detailed study of the expulsion. He understood that this was an important subject. Zbąszyń, which was quickly followed by the Kristallnacht, the massive nationwide pogrom in Germany and Austria on the night of November 9–10, 1938, was an ominous harbinger of Nazi brutality. In a letter to Mahler Ringelblum wrote that "such a barbaric and pitiless expulsion is unprecedented in Jewish history."[40]

Korzen recalled that Ringelblum worked so hard and showed so much self-control that he actually gave the impression of someone who cared more for administrative efficiency than for the plight of the refugees.[41] But in Ringelblum's letters to Mahler and Cherikover he confessed to frequent bouts of mental anguish and emotional torment. He told Mahler that he spent an entire night weeping. In a letter to Cherikover, sent in December 1938, Ringelblum wrote, "we worked 18 to 20 hours a day. I came back—mentally and physically shattered . . . I am still not myself. It will take me a long time yet before I become a normal person again."[42] But characteristically he also saw the positive side: the youth's fervor in the camp, the interest in culture, the willingness to maintain "discipline" in trying circumstances.

His work for the Joint defined Ringelblum's course of action when the war broke out. Convinced that he had accomplished something valuable in Zbąszyń, he was more determined than ever to do his duty to the new waves of refugees created by the German invasion. Thanks to his work at the *Folk-shilf*, he now believed even more in the innate resiliency and toughness of the ordinary Jewish masses. Above all, Ringelblum had thoroughly internalized Giterman's message: the moral component of relief work was as important as its actual measurable results. This belief would give him the determination to carry on.

WAR

Just before the outbreak of war, in August 1939, Ringelblum enjoyed a rare opportunity to leave Poland. The Left Poalei Tsiyon had included him in its delegation to the Twenty-first Zionist Congress that convened in Geneva, Switzerland, on August 16. This was the very first time the LPZ had partici-pated in a Zionist world congress and it came at a dramatic moment for the movement and for world Jewry. Jews in both Palestine and Poland were fac-ing unprecedented danger. In May 1939 Great Britain had effectively canceled the Balfour Declaration with a White Paper that limited Jewish immigration, banned land sales to Jews in most of Palestine, and promised Arab majority government within ten years. Meanwhile, Adolf Hitler had finally decided to smash Poland and had told his generals to prepare Case White, a lightning campaign to destroy the Polish army. In the face of looming danger, the LPZ in Poland drew closer to its old rival, the Right Poalei Tsiyon. The two par-ties participated in a joint demonstration in Warsaw against the White Paper in the spring of 1939.

Ringelblum had joined the Polish delegation at the last minute and had few responsibilities at the congress. He welcomed the trip as a relief from the growing pressure at home. During his brief visit, he traveled to the William Tell Festival in Interlaken. The response of the Swiss audience to this his-torical drama impressed him deeply; once again he saw confirmation of how historical consciousness could develop a sense of national identity.[43] He also used this opportunity to look for old books on Jewish history. War loomed, but a friend recalled how eagerly Ringelblum rummaged through old book-stores. One day he happily returned with a copy of a valuable Yiddish pam-phlet on the beginning of the Jewish labor movement in Galicia.[44]

Perhaps many of the delegates still harbored great hope that Hitler would back down and avoid war. But, on August 22, news of the Nazi-Soviet non-aggression pact shattered any remaining illusions. A photograph of the con-gress hall taken at the exact moment the news came told the story: the congress delegates sat speechless, stunned, their heads in their hands. They now knew that war was inevitable. There could be no more delay, and the executive quickly wound up the proceedings: the Twenty-first Zionist Congress would be the shortest in history. Chaim Weizmann, speaking in Yiddish, made the farewell speech: "There is darkness all around us and we cannot see through the clouds. It is with a heavy heart that I take my leave. . . . If, as I hope, we are spared in life and our work continues, who knows—perhaps a new light will shine upon us from the thick black gloom."[45]

The Polish LPZ held an emergency meeting. One delegate suggested that they stay in Switzerland until the situation became clearer. Ringelblum insisted, however, on an immediate return to Poland. Not only was his family there, but he also believed that his civic obligation dictated he go back. According to Meir Korzen, "Ringelblum was a patriot and was tied to Poland with every part of his soul."[46] In a letter to Arnon Tamir-Fishman, written in May 1939, Ringelblum expressed confidence in the fighting power of the Polish army.[47]

Before everyone set off for home, the LPZ delegates met for one final time. Comrades from Palestine, the United States, and Poland embraced one another and wondered if and when they would ever meet again. In a poignant farewell speech, Jacob Zerubavel, now living in Palestine, said good-bye to his old friends who were about to return to Poland. He hoped that someday they would return together again. Meanwhile, Zerubavel added, he had only one request: that each party member act with dignity and courage, "so that when this war is over, we will be able to meet again and look each other straight in the eye."[48]

Ringelblum discovered that it was no simple matter to get from Switzerland to Poland. The delegates had come through Germany, but there was no way they would return there. So they decided to travel a round-about route: through Italy, Yugoslavia, and Hungary. At first the Italians turned them back at the border, but the Polish consul in Switzerland intervened and obtained Italian transit visas for them to the Yugoslav border. From there they traveled through Hungary and reached Poland just in time for the general mobilization, their trip to Warsaw slowed by overcrowded troop trains and feverish preparations for war. Just when the war began, Ringelblum finally reached home.[49]

The Germans quickly shattered the Polish lines in the south and began an armored drive on Warsaw. On Wednesday, September 6, the Polish radio in Warsaw called on all able-bodied men to leave the city and head east. This was the signal for a mass flight. That night, and for the next two nights, much of Warsaw's established Jewish leadership joined the huge throngs that crossed the Vistula bridges on their way east. Warsaw had been the political and organizational center of Polish Jewry. Now Europe's largest Jewish community lost most of the Jewish Community Council, most directors of relief organizations, and many of the leading political cadres. Of the top-level leadership of the LPZ, only Shakhne Zagan decided to stay in Warsaw. He quickly co-opted Ringelblum and Adolf Berman to form a troika that would lead the party during the emergency.[50]

On Wednesday, September 6, Ringelblum's brother-in-law, Artur Eisenbach, implored Ringelblum to join the escape to the East. Eisenbach and his wife were leaving immediately.[51] Ringelblum refused. (In a diary entry, he noted "100 phone calls" from friends who asked if he was leaving). In fact, the mass exodus made him more determined than ever to step forward and help organize relief for refugees and air-raid victims, and he tried to persuade other members of the Jewish intelligentsia to stay and help with the relief effort.[52]

On September 8 the first German tanks assaulted Warsaw and were hurled back with heavy losses. Meanwhile, Warsaw's mayor, Stefan Starzyński, and the senior military commander, General Czuma, repudiated the earlier call to abandon the city. The Poles would fight to defend their capital, even though most of the government had already left. Starzyński proclaimed the formation of a civic committee. Czuma assembled retreating military units and managed to organize a strong defense line. On September 10 a sudden Polish counteroffensive on the Bzura River temporarily relieved the German military pressure and boosted the spirits of the besieged city. Buoyed by Starzyński's moving radio appeals and cheered by rumors of Polish counterstrikes, Warsaw's population rallied in a stirring show of defiance and patriotism.[53]

Unable to conquer the city through a coup de main, the Germans began intensive shelling and aerial bombardment. For a time the Polish air force fought back, but by the second week of the war Warsaw no longer had a fighter defense to counter the German air raids. Ammunition for the anti-aircraft guns soon ran out; the Germans began to bomb Warsaw with near impunity. On September 13, the first day of the Jewish New Year, the Luftwaffe staged a particularly destructive raid against the Jewish sections of the city. Food began to run low; by the third week of September the Germans had cut the water supply and the gas mains. Fires now raged unchecked, and the dead and wounded piled up in the streets.[54]

Like many other Warsaw citizens, Ringelblum took part in the civil defense organization LOPP (Liga Obrony Powietrznej i Przeciwgazowej [League for Anti-Aircraft and Anti-Gas Defense]). Once the heavy German air raids began, the members of the LOPP faced most of the dangers of frontline combat. After herding the residents of their building into air-raid shelters they had to remain on the roofs—ready to douse falling incendiary bombs. They also had to brave bombs and shellfire to carry wounded residents to hospitals, as well as messages and supplies.

Like many other Jews and Poles, Ringelblum discovered inner reserves of physical courage that had never before been tested. One witness recalled how in the midst of a heavy artillery barrage Ringelblum carried a woman about to give birth to a distant hospital.[55] He also continued his duties with the Joint and insisted on going to his post every day of the siege. After a bomb had severely damaged the Joint's main office on Jasna Street, Ringelblum reported to new quarters on Wielka, which meant a longer journey. But even on September 25, Black Monday, when the Luftwaffe pummeled the city from early morning until nightfall, Ringelblum made his way to his office.[56]

In early diary entries made during the siege, Ringelblum noted the grass-roots mobilization of Warsaw Jewry to meet the demands of the war. Throughout the city Jews organized house committees to set up soup kitchens, to shelter bombed-out tenants, and to take care of the refugees that had begun to pour into the city.[57] These committees would eventually become the bedrock of the ghetto's so-called Public Sector and a focus of Ringelblum's activities.

By September 28 the siege was over. The city lay in shambles; about one-quarter of Warsaw's buildings had been shattered by bombs. There was no running water, no electricity, and no gas. According to some estimates, about fifty thousand citizens had been killed or injured. In the short time between the surrender of the Poles and the entry of the Wehrmacht, looters rampaged through the city and pilfered warehouses and shops. Right after the German army entered the city, the new occupiers began to distribute hot soup to a starving population. When Poles pointed out Jews in the soup lines, the Germans would throw them out. Ringelblum noted that Poles who did not know a word of German soon learned how to shout "Jude."[58]

Both Jews and Poles quickly felt the terror of the German occupation. Horrified refugees brought news of Nazi atrocities in provincial towns. Within weeks the Germans began mass expulsions of both Poles and Jews from wide areas in western Poland that were annexed to the Reich. A terror campaign against the Polish intellectual elite was in full swing by the end of 1939.

Special decrees aimed at the Jews were not long in coming.[59] Jews could not keep more than two thousand zlotys in cash; the rest of their holdings had to go into blocked accounts. Jews could not use trains without a procuring a humiliating "louse" certificate attesting that they were free of vermin. Proprietors of businesses had to turn their companies over to special Aryan "trustees." Beginning in December 1939 all the Jews in the General Government were forced to wear a visible armband that marked them as Jews. Even more troubling were the endless raids on private apartments, where German soldiers and civilians had carte blanche to loot to their heart's content. And from the very start of the occupation, various German units seized Jews off the streets for forced labor. As the German demands for forced labor steadily escalated, responsibility for providing the required contingents fell on the Judenrat. The major burden—as in so much else—fell on the very poor. At the onset of the occupation poor Jews, anxious for food, even volunteered for forced labor, but word quickly spread that at many labor sites German military personnel inflicted gratuitous humiliations on their Jewish workers.

If Warsaw Jews had any ray of comfort in the early days of the German occupation, it was only that things could have been worse. Timely intervention of German military authorities prevented the establishment of a ghetto in 1939, a calamity that finally came in November 1940. And, at least for the moment, most Warsaw Jews avoided the fate of many Jews in western Poland, who suffered wholesale expulsions from their homes.

On October 12, 1940, the Jewish Day of Atonement, the Germans informed Warsaw Jewry that they had barely two weeks to move into a crowded ghetto that included some of Warsaw's poorest neighborhoods. (The Nazis eventually extended the deadline to November 15.) For weeks Jews lived in debilitating uncertainty about the boundaries of the ghetto; some Jews spent all they had on apartments in the new ghetto, only to find out that the apartment was on the wrong street. The haggling over boundaries brilliantly exemplified the German policy of "divide and rule," as Poles and Jews fought to gain as much space as possible for their own communities. The actual ghetto suffered from a population density of about 200,000 people per square mile. Thirty percent of Warsaw's inhabitants had to crowd into 2.4 percent of its space.[60] The official size of the ghetto's population fluctuated: 380,740 in January 1941; 431,874 in July 1941; about 400,000 in May 1942. Hunger and disease claimed about 100,000 people between the outbreak of the war and July 1942. Ten percent of the ghetto population—43,000 people—died in 1941 alone.[61] During the same period—November 1940 to July 1942—the Germans drove more than 150,000 refugees into the ghetto.

On the very first day that the ghetto was established, November 16, Jews received a terrible shock when they discovered that the ghetto would be "closed": free access to the Aryan side was forbidden. This immediately dealt a crippling blow to the already shaky Jewish economy: thousands of Jews still had small businesses or hidden stores of materials on the Aryan side. Others had established economic contacts with Poles. Now all were cut off.[62]

The closed ghetto greatly complicated the problem of obtaining food. The legal food ration established by the German authorities guaranteed death by starvation. The average legal calorie allotment in 1941 was 2,613 for Germans, 699 for Poles, and 184 for Jews.[63] All food shipments, like all other imports and exports to and from the ghetto, had to pass through the German-controlled Transferstelle on the corner of Stawki and Dzika streets. It quickly became apparent that if the ghetto was going to survive, the Jews would have to forget about "legality" and smuggle in as much food as they could. More than 80 percent of all food consumed in the ghetto would be smuggled in.

Thanks to massive smuggling, the ghetto managed to hold on. Smuggling involved not only food but also large amounts of raw materials for secret ghetto enterprises which exported their products to shops on the Aryan side. These exports—the secret economy—provided employment to many thousands of Jews and partially paid for the smuggled food. Like many others in the ghetto, Ringelblum was well aware that the welfare of the ghetto depended on smugglers who in normal times might have been called petty criminals. Ringelblum and the Oyneg Shabes made the documentation and study of smuggling a major priority—not only as an economic phenomenon but also as a significant example of Polish-Jewish cooperation (see chapter 6).

To ensure efficient control over the Jewish population, the German authorities had established a Judenrat in October 1939, headed by Adam Czerniakow.[64] Czerniakow would serve in this post until he committed suicide in July 1942. Although it was the Germans who named Czerniakow to head the Judenrat, he actually became the head of the Jewish community during the siege of Warsaw; Mayor Starzyński had appointed him to replace Maurycy Meisels, the chief of the Jewish community board who had fled Warsaw in the early days of the war. Starzyński's action, Czerniakow believed, gave him a certain moral legitimacy since he could claim that his authority derived from a Polish and not a German appointment.[65]

Czerniakow had been active in Jewish politics before the war. For a time he had been a supporter of Józef Piłsudski, who had seized power in 1926, and he had also aligned himself with the General Zionists. But Czerniakow really cared more about education than he did about politics and had distinguished himself for his work on behalf of vocational training for Jewish youth. Although he was Polish-speaking—like most Warsaw middle-class Jews—he was far from being an assimilationist. By his own lights he was a proud and committed Jew.[66]

He had few illusions about his future as head of the Warsaw Judenrat. From the start he suffered heartbreak and humiliation. He dealt largely with lower-ranking German officials who had no qualms about making him wait for hours to settle Judenrat business. On one occasion he was beaten, and on another he was arrested. The finances of the Judenrat were in constant crisis, and Czerniakow had to scurry about to raise money to pay for food shipments and the wages of forced laborers. Just two months into the German occupation, the Germans showed Czerniakow that, no matter what he did, many Jews would use him as a lightning rod for their own anger and frustration. In November 1939, in retaliation for the shooting of a Polish policeman by a Jewish criminal, the Germans entered the apartment building at Nalewki 9, arrested fifty-three Jewish men, and shot them all. They then demanded that the Judenrat pay a large ransom for the men's release. Not knowing that all the men were already dead, Czerniakow ran about to collect the ransom. When the loved ones of the victims finally learned of their execution, they blamed the Judenrat chairman for his alleged procrastination.[67]

Like Ringelblum, his opposite in so many ways, Czerniakow was embittered at what he called the desertion of the community by much of the prewar leadership. But he believed that he had an obligation to serve. At the same time he became convinced that hard times demanded the services of certain kinds of questionable individuals who knew how to get things done; it was not necessarily the best or the nicest people who knew how to deal with the Germans or how to manage the unruly and undisciplined Jewish masses.[68]

The Judenrat found itself compelled to take responsibility for functions that had never been handled by the prewar Jewish community council. Before the war the kehilla had funded religious institutions and rabbis, supervised the cemetery, and to a lesser degree supported Jewish education and social welfare. After the creation of the ghetto, however, the Judenrat had to deal with matters that had been within the purview of the Warsaw city government: police, sanitation, health services, and mail delivery. Of course the Judenrat lacked enough trained personnel to do an efficient job, and its employees soon found ample opportunities for personal gain.

The membership of the Warsaw Judenrat was extremely uneven and changed over time.[69] Abraham Gepner, the head of the important Supply Department (Zakład Zaopatrywania), stood out for his personal courage and honesty. Before the war he had been a prominent industrialist. But, like Czerniakow, he did not have a natural rapport with the Yiddish-speaking masses. There were other upstanding Judenrat members: Joseph Jaszunski, a former director of the ORT (The Society for the Promotion of Vocational and Agricultural Work among Jews); Israel Milejkowski, a respected physician; and Stanisław Szereszewski who had headed the TOPOROL society before the war.[70] The Judenrat also included respected religious leaders such as Rabbis Meshulam Kaminer and Zisha Frydman of the Orthodox Agudas Israel Party. But other Judenrat members did not enjoy a good reputation, and even those members who had been respected suffered from guilt by association.

Contempt for the Judenrat grew, and the leaders of the Jewish Self-Help Society, including Ringelblum, led the attack. These differences were more than just a dispute about how to deal with the wartime catastrophe. They also symbolized the impact of prewar disputes and values on the Warsaw Ghetto. People like Adam Czerniakow and Abraham Gepner did not share Ringelblum's deep admiration of "the Jewish masses."[71] When a group of German Jews arrived in the Warsaw Ghetto, Czerniakow noted with relief that, unlike the Polish Jews, here were people who worked more than they complained.[72] And Gepner especially represented an older tradition of Warsaw Jewish philanthropy that the leaders of the Aleynhilf had grown to despise long before the war began. Like the old great leaders of Warsaw Jewry, Gepner performed his communal service from a sense of "noblesse oblige": the rich should help the poor, and the poor should be grateful. When the war came Gepner gave freely from his own pocket to help abandoned children and orphans. But Ringelblum complained that his money went to help only the children in the orphanages that he chose to support.[73] Furthermore, the same Gepner who gave so much to help the poor furiously resisted any hint of a progressive tax on income or consumption to finance public welfare activities. He saw nothing wrong with taxes on ration cards, which hurt the poor much more than the rich.

There were also stark differences between the Judenrat and the Aleynhilf on the basic ground rules for ghetto administration. Most of those in the Aleynhilf believed that all ghetto institutions should regard themselves as Jewish bodies; they should demonstrate Jewish national pride and a loyalty to Jewish culture. Most Judenrat members—certainly Gepner and Czerniakow—were also proud Jews, but they accepted the basic premise that, first and foremost, the ghetto was occupied Polish territory and they had to show their loyalty to the Polish state. In practical terms, that ruled out any discrimination against the many Catholics that the Germans had forced into the ghetto because of their Jewish origin. Indeed—much to Ringelblum's utter disgust—many prominent converts received key positions in the ghetto administration. Ringelblum saw this as evidence of a Jewish inferiority complex, a failure on the part of the Judenrat to show national pride.[74]

In a sharp conversation that Ringelblum recorded in his diary, Gepner categorically rejected Ringelblum's accusations and complaints about the Judenrat's alleged lack of national pride. Gepner reminded Ringelblum that to boycott converts in the ghetto would constitute a flagrant act of disloyalty to Poland. The differences between a Gepner and a Ringelblum reflected, in part, disagreements about how to cope with a national disaster, but they also signaled cultural conflicts that had marked Polish Jewish life before the war.[75] (It did not help that Polish remained the language of Judenrat business and of the Jewish police.)

As corruption mounted in the ranks of the Jewish police and the Judenrat, public opinion in the ghetto turned against Czerniakow. Even if people believed in his personal integrity, they accused him of countenancing deep-seated corruption throughout the ghetto "government." What especially rankled was the steady decline of the Jewish police or, as it was officially called, the Jewish Order Service (Służba Porządkowa in Polish, Ordnungsdienst, in German).[76] At first the Jewish police commanded some respect. In the early days of the ghetto, even Ringelblum had a few kind words to say about the Jewish policemen.[77] Many intellectuals, especially lawyers, joined the force, which was headed by a convert, Józef Szeryński, who had also been a former major in the Polish police. But the police received no salary, and, as time went on, fewer and fewer could resist the ample opportunities to make money by abusing their authority. They hunted down Jews for labor service and took bribes to grant exemptions. They took payoffs from smugglers and from house committees eager to avoid the dreaded disinfections and quarantines (parówki). They took regular "contributions" from bakers and restaurant owners. The slogan of the Jewish police became "feed the jukebox" (szafa gra). Not all policemen were corrupt—some members of the Order Service made sincere attempts to deal with the problems[78]—but the public image of the force grew steadily worse.

Czerniakow, though a man of integrity himself, failed to rein in the Jewish Police. It was an open question, of course, whether he or the Judenrat could have done so even had they wanted to. True, Czerniakow agreed to the demands of prominent public figures for a watchdog committee to oversee the Judenrat and the police and guard against abuses. But after a short time the members of the committee resigned, frustrated by their inability to effect any change.[79]

For his part, Czerniakow treated the leadership of the Aleynhilf with suspicion. In his diary he sneered at the pretensions of many of the Aleynhilf leaders. He also scoffed at what he saw as their penchant for cheap sloganeering.[80] (And if Ringelblum's writings were any guide, the Aleynhilf leaders indeed minimized the real efforts of the Judenrat to employ writers and artists, fight disease, and improve the food supply in the ghetto.) Although he put up a stoic front, Czerniakow knew what the ghetto thought of him. But, as he confided to his diary, "he would have to carry the cross, not drag it."[81]

On the eve of World War II Polish Jewry had managed to establish an impressive network of social welfare and self-help organizations. The CEKABE, as shown above, had made important strides in organizing Jews for economic self-defense. Meanwhile, effective collaboration of Jewish physicians and communal leaders had built up the TOZ (Towarzystwo Ochrony Zdrowia Ludności Żydowskiej [Society for the Protection of Health]), which served the health needs of the Polish Jewish community. Through public lectures, clinics, and journals the TOZ stressed "social medicine": the social and cultural context of better health. Another key organization was the CENTOS (Centralne Towarzystwo Opieki Sierot [Central Organization for the Care of Orphans]), which cared for Jewish children and orphans. The ORT made a major effort to organize vocational training.[82] All these groups had received major support before the war from the JDC.

Warsaw had served as the central base of these organizations prior to the war, and an impressive community of experienced professionals had assembled in the capital. When war came much of the professional staff fled Warsaw, but a core group of seasoned workers remained to staff these vital areas of public relief and public health. When the Germans set up the Judenrat, for a time these organizations were still able to preserve much of their de facto autonomy.

In September 1939 the Polish authorities had established a Metropolitan Committee of Social Welfare (Stołeczny Komitet Samopomocy Społecznej [SKSS]) to deal with the problems of the civilian population during the war. The Jewish leaders that were left in Warsaw during the siege established a Coordinating Committee to deal with the SKSS and take care of the needs of the Jewish population. The Coordinating Committee received funds from both the SKSS and the JDC. It would become the foundation of the Aleynhilf, which would play such a leading role in the Warsaw Ghetto. The noted actor and lawyer Michał Weichert was the first chairman of the Coordinating Committee; Ringelblum became its executive secretary.[83]

When the Germans entered Warsaw the legal status of the Coordinating Committee became unclear. It was no longer a part of the SKSS; the Poles explained to Weichert that the Germans vetoed any further links between the Polish and the Jewish relief organizations. But the Coordinating Committee had one important card to play, namely, the Joint Distribution Committee, which by now provided most of its funds.[84] That the JDC was an American institution was decidedly important, for the German authorities at that time were quite sensitive to the need to assuage public opinion in the neutral countries. The Committee set up its headquarters in the library of the Tłomackie Synagogue and displayed the Joint's emblem prominently at the entrance to the building. For their part the Germans were sufficiently impressed with the JDC's privileged status to permit director Daniel Guzik a short trip to Brussels to confer with the Joint's European division.

From the very start of the war the JDC quickly emerged as the backbone of the entire relief operation. During the siege Yitzhak Giterman had fled to Vilna, where he organized a major relief effort for the many Jewish refugees who had arrived there. In his absence Daniel Guzik, the prewar finance director, took charge of JDC activities in Warsaw. Guzik, quite unhappy that Giterman had left, met with Ringelblum and Meir Korzen shortly after the Germans entered Warsaw. He waved his foreign passport and told them that he, too, could leave at any time. But none of them had a right to do so; the Joint staff had to stay at their posts.[85] Ringelblum, of course, needed little persuading. He was at Guzik's disposal. Guzik quickly emerged as a leader of the first rank; as the war went on, he and Giterman would lead the JDC in occupied Poland, and Ringelblum would come to respect him enormously.

Meir Korzen, who worked with Ringelblum at the JDC in the early days of the war, recalled his dedication to his work and his courage. One day, shortly after the Germans captured Warsaw, Korzen was working at a JDC warehouse distributing old clothing to refugees and homeless victims of the bombing. A German soldier came into the warehouse and began grabbing old sweaters. Korzen explained that the warehouse belonged to an American institution, the Joint Distribution Committee, and asked the soldier to put the sweaters back. But the soldier ignored him and began to leave. Just then Ringelblum walked in and ordered the soldier to return the sweaters or he would complain to the authorities. "I am 'the authorities,'" the soldier replied. He kept his eyes on Ringelblum and then added, ominously, that of course he would be happy to go to the authorities with him. Without hesitation, Ringelblum got up to leave with the German soldier. Korzen, immediately afraid that the soldier would shoot Ringelblum on the way, persuaded him, with the greatest of difficulty, not to go.[86]

In April 1940 Giterman returned to Warsaw, after the Germans had intercepted his Stockholm-bound ship in the Baltic Sea. After a stint in a prisoner-of-war camp, Giterman was released, along with the Bundist leader Maurycy Orzech, who had been on the same ship. Giterman and Guzik now worked together to ensure that the Joint was able to somehow cope with the wartime emergency. They decided on a daring scheme: to raise money from wealthy Warsaw Jews by telling them that, if they lent the JDC large sums of money now, the Joint in the United States would repay them when the war ended.

Many wealthy individuals saw this as a good investment. Better that they lend their money to the Joint than risk the constant danger of German raids and requisitions. The scheme, of course, was both illegal and dangerous, but the Germans, despite suspicions, never learned the details of the plan.[87] After the war survivors were indeed able to collect their money.

With the money that continued to come from the United States and the funds raised illegally in Poland, the Joint was able to undertake major relief operations in 1939 and 1940. More than 250,000 Jews in Warsaw—about half the total Jewish population—received Passover relief from the Joint in 1940. In a later essay Ringelblum commented that the Joint might have been *too generous* in the early months of the occupation. Even the loans the JDC obtained from wealthy Jews, he implied, were only a fraction of what might have been raised. From the very beginning of the war Ringelblum refused to believe that the war had rendered Warsaw Jewry entirely destitute: enough Jews remained who could have helped mount a meaningful relief effort out of their own resources. But the JDC's relief work in 1939–1940 was so extensive, Ringelblum noted, that it gave many Warsaw Jews the impression that "the rich American relative" would take care of the community's problems. "The JDC," he complained, "got the Warsaw Jews out of the habit of helping themselves." This made relief work more difficult later on, when Joint resources began to dry up and contributions from within the ghetto itself became all the more important.[88]

During all of 1940 the Joint spent a total of 14.735 million zlotys on its Polish operations; ominously this figure fell to about 8 million zlotys in 1941. After Germany declared war on the United States in December 1941, the main source of funds dried up, but Giterman and Guzik continued to play a major role in the Aleynhilf. They also became a major support of the Oyneg Shabes Archive and later of the Jewish Fighting Organization.

In January 1940 the Coordinating Committee that had been established in 1939 took a new name—the ŻSS (Żydowska Samopomoc Społeczna-Komisja Koordynacyjna [Jewish Social Self-Help, Coordinating Committee]). In October 1940 the name changed once again to the ŻTOS (Żydowskie Towarzystwo Opieki Społecznej [Jewish Society for Public Welfare]). Later the ŻTOS came under the authority of the ŻKOM (Jewish City Aid Committee), headed by a Judenrat member and formally subordinated to the central Jewish relief organization for the Generalgovernement, the Żydowska Samopomoc Społeczna (ŻSS [Jewish Communal Self-Help]) headed by Michał Weichert in Krakow.[89]

But despite the many name changes, the Self-Help Society was known in Warsaw simply as the Aleynhilf. The legal status of the Aleynhilf rested on a

German decision taken early in the war to recognize an umbrella organization that would supervise Jewish social welfare in the entire Generalgouvernement. This was part of a general plan to oversee and control relief activities. In May 1940 the occupation authorities ordered the formation of a Central Council for Social Welfare (Naczelna Rada Opiekuńcza [NRO])—with representatives of Polish, Ukrainian, and Jewish social-welfare organizations: five Poles, one Ukrainian, and one Jew.[90] Michał Weichert, who had headed the Jewish Coordinating Committee during the siege, moved to Krakow and became the Jewish representative on the NRO. After some tough negotiations, Weichert procured a promise that Jews would receive 17 percent of all relief funds disbursed by the NRO. These funds became, after the Joint, the second major source of the Aleynhilf's income.[91]

Weichert was puzzled that the Germans paid any attention at all to the issue of Jewish social welfare. How could the Germans torture Jews and then invite them to meetings to discuss welfare and self-help? As it turned out, the Germans were responding, at least in part, to American pressure. The Commission for Polish Relief and the American Red Cross had begun to send aid to Poland and wanted firsthand assurances that the aid was reaching the entire population fairly. American relief officials actually visited occupied Poland in early 1940, which gave Weichert some leverage. Unlike Czerniakow, who had reported to both the Gestapo and the civil authorities, Weichert dealt with the slightly more civilized part of the German bureaucracy that supervised social welfare matters in the General Government. At joint meetings with Polish and Ukrainian representatives, he successfully bargained for a larger Jewish share of incoming relief funds. In conferences in Krakow, Weichert could even complain—ever so politely—about German treatment of Jews.[92]

In time the Judenrat, supported by the German authorities, increased its pressure to curtail the autonomy of the Aleynhilf. Until early 1942 real authority in the Aleynhilf rested with a small group that represented the Joint, the political parties, and the prewar relief committees, although legally it was part of the ŻKOM, which in turn was subordinated to the Judenrat. In March 1942, however, the ŻKOM began to make a more concerted effort to control the Aleynhilf and organizations like CENTOS.[93] In addition to German pressure, other factors worked against Aleynhilf autonomy. JDC resources began to decline, especially after Germany declared war on the United States. German food policy was another powerful club, since the Judenrat assumed more control over the food supplies allotted to the soup kitchens. The Judenrat and the Jewish police, as will be seen, had many ways of harassing the house committees.

But in the early days of the occupation, the Aleynhilf still enjoyed a large degree of relative autonomy and quickly became a large operation employing more than three thousand workers. In addition to its various departments, it also took in under its umbrella one of the major prewar relief organizations: the CENTOS, which had cared for orphans and poor children. In the Warsaw ghetto its role would expand enormously.

The tremendous social needs of the ghetto accounted, in part, for the large size of the Aleynhilf. But another reason was a conscious decision by Giterman, Guzik, Ringelblum, and others to use the self-help society to provide employment for the Jewish intelligentsia and cultural elite.[94] Jewish schools, newspapers, and publishing houses had been closed down because of the war. As speculators and profiteers rose to the top and the Jewish masses sank into poverty, JDC leaders did whatever they could to protect the intellectual leadership of Polish Jewry, namely, teachers, writers, and scholars. (Not all received aid, of course, and many of those who were denied leveled bitter accusations of favoritism at the leadership of the Aleynhilf.)

From the very start of the war Ringelblum led this special effort to recruit and protect members of the Jewish intelligentsia. During the siege he asked the journalist Rachel Auerbach to set up a soup kitchen under the aegis of the Aleynhilf. Auerbach had been preparing to flee to her native east Galicia. She recalled that Ringelblum remarked: "Not everybody is allowed to run."[95] When the Hebrew writer Natan Eck arrived in the Warsaw Ghetto from Lodz in late 1939 there was already a huge line outside Ringelblum's office; a large crowd of refugees, many from the intelligentsia, were hoping that Ringelblum would help them get a job with the Aleynhilf. Ringelblum, Eck recalled, kept his sense of humor and did what he could to help everyone.[96]

The Aleynhilf recruited its staff from across the political and social spectrum.[97] It took over the Judaic Library next to the great Tłomackie Synagogue. (The building survived and today houses the Jewish Historical Institute in Warsaw.) Bundists and Zionists, wealthy industrialists and poor elementary schoolteachers, all worked side by side. Jonas (Yanosh) Turkow recalled that a common sense of purpose erased political differences.[98] That was not exactly true, but awareness of the common danger certainly diminished the political infighting that had marked prewar Jewish life.

Closely associated with the Aleynhilf were two cultural organizations, Tekuma to encourage Hebrew culture and the much larger IKOR, the Yiddish Cultural Organization headed by Menakhem Linder, a statistician and economist who had worked closely with Ringelblum in the prewar YIVO. Ringelblum was also one of the founders of the IKOR and played a major role in its activities. Its executive committee, besides Linder, Ringelblum, and Yitzhak

Giterman, included Shakhne Zagan, Israel Lichtenstein, Sonia Nowogrodzka of the Bund, and others.

The IKOR reflected the determination of many Aleynhilf leaders to use the organization not only to distribute relief but also to fight for Jewish national renewal. In the Vilna Ghetto an IKOR would have been quite unnecessary: only a small minority of Vilna Jewry spoke Polish, and Yiddish was the official language of all ghetto business and most cultural events. In Warsaw, on the other hand, most of the Jewish middle class spoke Polish. Long before the war began it was the Jewish Left that had carried the brunt of the struggle for Yiddish in Warsaw Jewish life. With the establishment of the ghetto and the rise of the Aleynhilf, Yiddishists like Emanuel Ringelblum and Menakhem Linder suddenly had a potent platform to further the cause of Yiddish and to establish important precedents for the postwar period.

In his memoirs of the IKOR, Hersh Wasser, a future secretary of the Oyneg Shabes Archive, recalled that a major reason for founding the IKOR had been to teach Yiddish to Aleynhilf employees who were Polish-speaking. Now that they had to deal with masses of impoverished refugees and ordinary Jews, it was important that they learn to speak to them in their own language. Wasser emphasized that these Polish-speaking employees of the Aleynhilf had the best intentions and were devoted to their work. Still, the use of Polish "symbolized . . . disdain for the common Jew and his needs. It signified a lack of understanding—in the most literal sense—of the Jewish masses. . . . There was a danger of distorting the perception of the [Aleynhilf and its affiliated institutions]."[99] Turkow recalled that Yiddish became the obligatory language of all Aleynhilf activities. After a certain probationary period, Aleynhilf personnel had to demonstrate competence in Yiddish in order to keep their posts.[100] In their dealings with the public, Aleynhilf employees had to speak Yiddish first. The IKOR also made an unsuccessful attempt to persuade Adam Czerniakow to make Yiddish the primary language of the Judenrat.[101] Despite that failure, Czerniakow nonetheless ordered that Judenrat proclamations be in Yiddish as well as Polish.

Very quickly the IKOR's role expanded from teaching languages to becoming a major cultural institution dedicated to creating a thriving and attractive cultural life. The IKOR organized dozens of public gatherings to commemorate the great Yiddish writers Mendele Moykher Sforim, Peretz, and Sholom Aleikhem. It collaborated with the house committees in the Warsaw Ghetto to organize theater performances and poetry readings. Under IKOR guidance, many house committees voted to make Yiddish the main language of committee deliberations. In a joint effort with the CENTOS, the IKOR offered Yiddish activities for ghetto children—puppet shows, skits, and morning readings devoted to Yiddish children's literature. The IKOR also organized a Yiddish people's university that featured lecturers such as Ringelblum, Isaac Schiper, and Yitzhak Giterman. It printed Yiddish textbooks for ghetto schools and encouraged ghetto institutions to feature signs proclaiming, "We Speak Yiddish."

Ringelblum was sufficiently encouraged by the IKOR's apparent successes to note in his diary entries of December 15, 17, and 20, 1940, that perhaps the ghetto was seeing the beginnings of a "back to Yiddish movement."[102] On March 23, 1941, he wrote in his diary that "the interest in Yiddish culture is growing. To an ever increasing extent Yiddish is becoming the language of the [theater performances] in the ghetto."

A little more than a year later, on April 17–18, 1942, the IKOR suffered a terrible blow. That night the Germans shot Menakhem Linder, along with fifty-one other Jews.[103] By then, Ringelblum's early hopes for a revival of Yiddish had begun to wane—along with his former optimism about the efficacy of self-help and the ability of the soup kitchens to fight the terrible hunger in the ghetto.

The soup kitchens, headed by Shie Broyde, were another key link in the network of Aleynhilf institutions. Like many other leaders of the Aleynhilf, Broyde had been a prewar friend of Ringelblum's and had been very active in Yiddishist circles. Broyde had been a gifted teacher of classics in the Vilna Yiddish schools and had translated Plato into Yiddish. During the siege of Warsaw he had worked closely with Ringelblum. Even after German shrapnel killed his wife, Broyde continued to brave the bombings and arrange food for the Jewish soup kitchens. In the Aleynhilf, he took over the job of turning teachers, writers, and journalists into managers of soup kitchens. He organized seminars on everything from nutrition to the delicate task of dealing with swarms of hungry and desperate refugees.[104]

Within a few months the Aleynhilf had helped set up dozens of soup kitchens, most of which distributed subsidized meals to refugees and the poor; others prepared better meals at cost. The soup kitchens run by the various political parties and youth movements became the center of party life and the underground press. They not only provided meals but brought members together, serving as a meeting place and distribution point for the underground press. These soup kitchens were the physical link between the Aleynhilf and the underground political movements in the ghetto.

The Left Poalei Tsiyon, for example, ran four kitchens for adults and one for children. The central party kitchen occupied the former headquarters of the Woodworkers Union on Elektoralna 14, an old party stronghold. It fed thousands of people and was also the locale for most party meetings. Its supervisor, Pola Elster, later took part in the Warsaw Ghetto Uprising and died fighting the Germans in 1944. The children's kitchen was located in the Borochov School on Nowolipki 68. Adolf Berman called it "the apple of the party's eye." Three leading party members—the teachers Feige Hertzlich, Natan Smolar, and Israel Lichtenstein—ran the school which served as the center of the party's underground press and the hiding place of the Oyneg Shabes.[105]

While Ringelblum spent most of his time on the Aleynhilf and the Oyneg Shabes, he still maintained an active role in the LPZ in the ghetto. Natan Eck recalled that, in the first months of the occupation, party comrades pressured Ringelblum to use his position in the Aleynhilf to give them key positions in the relief network so as to improve the party's visibility and postwar prospects.[106] Although there is no direct evidence that Ringelblum did this, it was certainly true that the LPZ played a major role in the leadership of the Aleynhilf. Berman headed the CENTOS, and Zagan served on the Aleynhilf's executive committee.

The boundary line between work in the Aleynhilf and underground political work was quite permeable. In fact, leaders of the major political parties sat on a committee that the Joint set up to provide oversight of relief activities and that worked closely with Giterman and Guzik.[107]

THE PUBLIC SECTOR AND THE HOUSE COMMITTEES

Within a few months after the war started Ringelblum took on a new job in the Aleynhilf which he retained until the liquidation of the ghetto in July 1942. He became the head of the Public Sector of the Aleynhilf. This made Ringelblum the major link between the Aleynhilf and the most important grass-roots social organizations in the ghetto—the house committees.

The particular nature of Warsaw residential housing, especially in the Jewish quarter, facilitated the development of these committees to a degree. The thickly populated Jewish neighborhoods of North Warsaw had developed around the *hoyf* (courtyard). Large, multistoried, rectangular buildings often contained several inner courtyards. Traffic between the outside street and the hoyf had to pass through a gate that was watched by a custodian, creating an illusion of relative security. A typical building might house as many Jews as a small shtetl. Before the war the hoyf was a microcosm of Jewish Warsaw—a sprawling jumble of small shops, tiny factories, basement warrens for the very poor, and more spacious apartments on the higher floors. When the war began the hoyf and other kinds of apartment buildings became the basic social unit of Warsaw Jewry. During World War I many Jews from smaller towns had flocked to Warsaw where they sought the safety of numbers and the sense of protection they felt in the thick walls of the urban courtyards. In the early days of World War II, even if the hoyf provided no real safety, it was the closest semblance of a community that Warsaw Jews had. The curfew also forced Jews to seek the company of their fellow tenants; although they had to be off the street, they could stay outside within the inner squares of their own hoyf. During Hanukkah, for example, hundreds of tenants would assemble in the inner squares to light the holiday candles together and sing.

During the siege, house committees all over Jewish Warsaw had started soup kitchens for refugees, arranged shelter, and collected money for poorer families.[108] Neighbors who were virtual strangers before the war turned to one another for comfort and support. Those who had lost their apartments moved in with those who still had theirs. The tenants of large apartment buildings set up communal kitchens and looked after one another's children.

Many house committees developed out of the existing anti-aircraft defense committees, and others started up spontaneously. They varied widely in character from the casual to the formal, the latter formulating by-laws and electing subcommittees to deal with food, clothing drives, child care, and so on. Peretz Opoczynski wrote a report for the Oyneg Shabes Archive on the house committee on Muranowska 6, a building inhabited by Jewish merchants and artisans where the Jewish traditions of *tsedaka* (charity) and *matan b'seser* (giving anonymously) were still alive and well. This building, Opoczynski noted, did not need formal procedures or by-laws. Even before the war neighbors had looked out for one another. Now that the war had started, Opoczynski reported, Reb Shloyme talked to Reb Avreml; they agreed that it was wrong to abandon the poor families in the building and so invited other neighbors to come around after the end of the Sabbath, and that was how the house committee on Muranowska 6 began.[109]

When the siege was over the house committees expanded. In 1940 Ringelblum and others spearheaded an effort to organize committees in buildings that did not have them. Various reports deposited in the Oyneg Shabes describe, broadly, three principal kinds of house committees: traditional, democratic, and authoritarian.[110] The first corresponded to Opoczynski's account of Muranowska 6, where religious and traditional Jews put together a committee which was an extension of the voluntary associations that had long been an integral part of Jewish life. In the second type, which seemed to be the more numerous, leaders—professionals, intellectuals, or ordinary artisans and merchants—either stepped forward on their own or responded to their neighbors' appeals to assume the chairmanship of the house committee. These leaders answered to the tenants at regular meetings. In the third type someone, usually a wealthy tenant, would simply start a committee and run it. (Of course, this general observation does not imply that every committee fit neatly into one of these categories; it was not uncommon for a "democratic" committee to become "authoritarian," or vice versa).[111]

The house committees quickly became the basis of public life in the Warsaw ghetto. In a diary entry of November 29, 1940, Chaim Kaplan noted:

> [The house committees] are a successful organizational invention [that never existed in peacetime]. At that time no public project percolated down to the masses. This time every Jewish home from great to small has been affected. At the head of the [house committees] stand men of the people who awaken the drowsy public to give. Their words, which emanate from simple hearts, penetrate into simple hearts. They find expressions their listeners can understand and so are successful. Social action is thus diffused through all levels of the broad public, and there is no boy over ten who does not have some duty in his courtyard. There is not a tenant who is not among the members of some committee or in charge of some courtyard duty.[112]

The pressures of war quickly forged unexpectedly strong bonds between tenants. Many questions had to be decided: the payment of electric and gas bills; provisions of coal; sending help to tenants packed off to labor camps; feeding and clothing impoverished families within the building. No one could ignore the brutal application of collective responsibility. If a tenant did not pay gas or electric bills, the entire house might find its supply cut off.

The house committees exerted intense social pressure on each tenant to do his share. In addition to compulsory monthly dues, the committees demanded not only frequent donations but also a major commitment to work in subcommittees. Those who failed to give enough often found themselves on a public "list of shame." An Oyneg Shabes document records a speech in which Jews were reminded that, after the war, the Jewish community would demand an accounting from each Jew. Those who had held themselves aloof during the great crisis of their people would become pariahs.[113]

The records of the house committee on Leszno 24 that were found in the Oyneg Shabes Archive showed how ordinary Jews tried to overcome extraordinary odds.[114] The house committee elected a board that met at least weekly and made decisions on a wide range of issues. At one meeting the house board assigned to each stable family poorer tenants to feed. It revived the old tradition of *esn teg* where shtetl families used to promise to feed poor yeshiva students on a particular day. On any given day a poor family in the building would receive meals from one that was better off. The board also encouraged residents to employ tailors and shoemakers who lived in the same building. The board distributed food and coal to poorer tenants, especially before Jewish holidays. It helped arrange medical care and set up a children's corner that doubled as a soup kitchen and a school. Like many other house committees, those on Leszno 24 "adopted" nearby orphanages and refugee centers and provided them with bowls of soup and clothing. It also tried to assure that poorer tenants receive a proper burial.

Leszno 24 was a lucky building, at least in the first period of the German occupation. It does not seem to have had the "wealthy" tenants that inhabited Sienna Street, but it was certainly better off than buildings on Wołyńska or Smocza, where a third of the tenants died of typhus or hunger. The terse minutes of the house committee meetings show that the residents of Leszno 24 were trying to hang on and wait for better times. Some were employed, and others probably lived by selling possessions or by dipping into savings. The minutes also show that, as time went on, they found the conditions harder and harder.

Like Leszno 24, most of the house committees set up "children's corners," rooms where children would get a hot meal and some instruction. Quite often adolescents and young people volunteered to help out and set up "youth committees" to care for the younger children.

The house committees informally mediated tenant disputes. The committees would set up courts that seem to have enjoyed the tenants' respect. On Muranowska 6 the court appears to have functioned as a traditional *beys din*, or Jewish religious court.[115]

As the war dragged on, "Women's Circles" assumed more importance within the house committees. They often set up sewing clubs that employed poorer girls and provided clothing for children and poorer families. Frequently they also established soup kitchens for the tenants of the house. Indeed, women played an ever greater role in the running of the house committees and in the entire relief effort.[116] Hitherto unknown women stepped forward to replace men who finally gave up on their thankless task. As will be seen, the Oyneg Shabes Archive would make the study of women in the ghetto a top priority.

The house committees raised their funds from direct taxation, voluntary contributions, special fund drives, gambling parties, and especially theatrical performances, which benefited from the curfew.[117] Before long, unemployed actors and singers would come to a hoyf or any apartment before the start of the curfew, give concerts or perform plays, and then stay overnight. Early on, the house committees discovered that these musical and theatrical productions were a good source of income, especially when they set up tables for card playing and gambling.

Ringelblum and other leaders of the Aleynhilf quickly noticed both the problems and the potential benefits of these courtyard theaters. There were many instances where house committees competed for an audience by bidding up the fees of well-known actors or spending lavishly on costumes and buffets. In an essay written for the Oyneg Shabes Archive, the well-known Yiddish actor Jonas (Yanosh) Turkow also noted the tendency of many committees to use Polish rather than Yiddish, and to perform vulgar skits that were a bad influence on children.[118] Ringelblum proposed that the Aleynhilf set up a Theater Commission (Imprezn Komisye) that would take matters in hand, that is, pressure the house committees to use Yiddish and to raise the cultural level of their performances. Results were mixed, but Turkow noted some progress, especially with regard to children's theater.

Ringelblum worked in the Public Sector both as a director and a historian. He understood the importance of the house committees and arranged for the Oyneg Shabes Archive to collect house committee materials and draw up guidelines for the more systematic study of the committees' activities.[119] As only very few people who had been active in the house committee movement survived the war, these Oyneg Shabes materials became even more important. Indeed, without the archive, hardly any house committee materials would have survived. The Oyneg Shabes commissioned important reportages by Peretz Opoczynski on Wołyńska 23 and Muranowska 6, on Nalewki 23 by Celina Lewin,[120] and on Gęsia 19 by S. Szereszewska.[121] The Oyneg Shabes also collected, as we have seen, the minutes of the meetings of the house committee on Leszno 24. It is more than likely that many more house committee materials were contained in undiscovered parts of the Oyneg Shabes or in documents that were destroyed through moisture and seepage.

Luckily one survivor, Michael Mazor, wrote very important memoirs of the house committees and of Ringelblum's role in their umbrella organization, the Public Sector of the Aleynhilf. Mazor, who had no political axe to grind, recalled:

> The house committees were emphatically a national institution of the ghetto, an emanation from the masses. It would be a false interpretation of the historical truth to attribute their birth to any political party or particular person. Nonetheless one must note the preponderant role of Ringelblum: having been the first to understand the importance of the house committees, he was their prime animator, outlining the forms of their organization, and attracting the initially small number of groups of social workers—the pioneers of this great popular movement.[122]

Before the establishment of the ghetto the Aleynhilf had divided Warsaw into ten districts, each under a district commission that comprised all the house committees in a particular area and that answered to Ringelblum's Public Sector. These district commissions included circles of women and teachers that tended to the particular needs of the poorer houses in the district as well as sections for children, refugees, and the collection of money.[123] In non-Jewish neighborhoods, the Jewish tenants of several buildings would come together to form one committee. The district commissions supervised 1,518 house committees in May 1940 and almost 2,000 by September 1940.[124] After the establishment of the ghetto there were six district commissions. In January 1942 there were around 1,600 house committees that employed 6,000 to 8,000 volunteers.[125]

Legally the house committees functioned under the aegis of the Aleynhilf's Public Sector, which the German authorities recognized. The house committees themselves, however, set up their own nonofficial grass-roots organization, an elected Central Commission comprised of activists and volunteers. Relations between Ringelblum and the grassroots were sometimes strained.

At first Ringelblum intended to use the Public Sector to supervise the house committees and to mobilize them for the wider activities of the Aleynhilf, most urgently by contributing sizable sums of money to the Self-Help Society. Wealthier house committees would thus help poorer ones—a form of income redistribution that would be supervised by the Aleynhilf and its leadership, the Jewish intelligentsia. More was at stake than just money. There was also the question—especially in the early days of the occupation—of using the relief effort to reinforce national consciousness and cultural activity. The experience of relief in World War I had inspired many Jewish communal figures to work toward a "modern" model of self-help that would supplant and replace traditional charitable organizations and attitudes.

Jewish tradition had long established a basic principle: "if you have to choose between helping the poor in your town and the poor in another town, help the poor in your own town first";[126] in other words, charity began at home. Thus the poor residents of one's own building had first call on available resources.

For intellectuals like Ringelblum this approach might be effective in the narrow sense, but it also meant that Jewish Warsaw would function not as a disciplined, nationally conscious community but rather as a collection of hundreds of separate microcommunities.[127] To combat this psychology Ringelblum mobilized talented writers to issue bulletins and propaganda.[128] A 1941 speech by an Aleynhilf leader—it may well have been Ringelblum himself—reminded the audience that, like it or not, the war had given all Jews a common fate and shared responsibilities. The speech praised the house committees and called them "a consolation in the darkness" ("jest szczęściem w nieszczęściu").[129]

> But each house committee has to remember that it is a member of one large family, a part of one large whole. The house committee gives direct help to the [tenants of that house]. This is important and useful work. But it becomes harmful when the house forgets about the destitution that is spreading beyond its walls and when it thinks that it has fulfilled its obligation when it has only helped its own. There are houses where practically everyone is poor. Who will help them? There are orphanages, refugee centers, soup kitchens. . . . These institutions do not have house committees. Should each poor person be forced to depend on help from a particular benefactor to whom he has to be personally grateful? Should we turn tens of thousands of poor people into beggars? There should be a central institution that collects money and distributes it. Whoever takes help from a public institution knows that he is only taking his due . . . and does not feel humiliated.[130]

Whatever Ringelblum's initial hopes of a vast project of social mobilization based on the harmonious collaboration between the Aleynhilf and the house committees, he soon had to trim his expectations. The Aleynhilf collected money from the house committees, but not as much as it wanted.[131] As resources dwindled, the committees doggedly resisted turning over scarce funds to a central body, preferring to help their immediate neighbors.

Many did not trust the Aleynhilf to be fair with their money. Chaim Kaplan, who headed his house committee, wrote in his diary that "leftists" had taken control of the relief effort.[132] Indeed, accusations of political favoritism and cronyism in the upper reaches of the Aleynhilf were rife, and they certainly complicated Ringelblum's job. Whatever resources the Aleynhilf had, they were never sufficient to meet the need. Kaplan's accusation of "leftist" control of the Aleynhilf was not an isolated case. Eck believed that the LPZ exerted strong pressure on Ringelblum to give party insiders coveted jobs.[133] Ringelblum himself admitted that contacts and personal connections certainly helped people to get aid from the Joint.[134] Auerbach recalled that the Aleynhilf had foisted on her soup kitchen an employee who engaged in some questionable dealings with suppliers. When she complained to Shie Braude, the latter chided her for being naïve. She would have to put up with the individual because the Aleynhilf wanted to help him survive and was therefore prepared to "look the other way."[135] In his diary Kaplan stated that, even if Aleynhilf officials were not exactly corrupt, they certainly had the human tendency to take care of their friends and families. At any rate, the house committees balked at becoming integral units of the Aleynhilf system.

Differing accounts of these disputes have been left by the few survivors of the house committee movement. Natan Eck believed that Ringelblum was bitterly disappointed that the house committees had turned into some sort of monster [*goylem*] that diverted needed funds from the Aleynhilf. Eck wrote that Ringelblum turned to his "historical work" only after he realized that the high hopes he had placed in the house committees would not be realized.[136]

Other sources disagree, although they admit that Ringelblum had to trim his initial expectations. According to Mazor, Ringelblum quickly understood and accepted the spontaneous character of the house committees and backed off from his attempts to direct them. Most important, he readily accepted the legitimacy of the Central Commission—elected by the house committees rather than appointed by the Aleynhilf—and worked with it. "Gradually," Mazor recalled, "the administrative apparatus took on the character of an 'executive' of the Public Sector; Ringelblum used to say that he regarded himself as 'Prime Minister' of the Public Sector, responsible to its parliament."[137] Ringelblum, Mazor recalled, did not miss a single meeting of the Central Commission and the two bodies worked well together.[138]

Whatever his initial hopes Ringelblum certainly was heartened by the many positive features of the house committee movement. Thanks to these committees hundreds of new leaders and thousands of ordinary Jews now had a chance to come forward and contribute their individual talents for the common good. On many committee boards, professionals and artisans, ordinary workers and intellectuals, all worked together in apparent harmony.

Had matters turned out differently, the house committee movement would have produced many future communal leaders. Mazor recalled that his district secretary, Czesława Rajfeld-Pechnik, would not hesitate to stroll into a crowd of lice-ridden refugees, take their children in her arms, and console them. No warnings about typhus would stop her. "In present conditions," she told Mazor, "dying from typhus transmitted by a louse is not the worst of deaths."[139] Another of Mazor's coworkers, a former Bundist named Goldheimer, insisted on going to every weekly meeting, which was fixed for Saturday around noontime. Before the war Goldheimer had made a good living. In the ghetto he quickly suffered from hunger and grew steadily thinner. Some time later Mazor discovered that his coworker was regularly passing up a weekly lunch invitation—where he could have eaten well—to attend the Saturday meetings of the district commission. Eventually Mazor was forced to change the meeting time, since Goldheimer refused to miss them. Mazor's coworkers came from all social backgrounds, all ages, and all political parties. All were volunteers. "The existence of this united and dynamic team," he recalled, "can be likened to a miracle."[140]

In a steadily deteriorating world of hunger, corruption, demoralization, and despair, the house committees gave people a chance to come together in a disciplined and purposeful effort. The very discipline and routine of the committees and the Central Commission turned into a valiant protest against the escalating chaos of ghetto life.[141] Furthermore, as Peretz Opoczynski reported for the archive, ordinary Jews construed the house committees as a symbol of political freedom, a reminder that they could still help themselves and function as a concerned community.[142]

A revealing document in the Oyneg Shabes Archive described how the Public Sector saw its role and how its relationship with the house committees functioned in practice.[143] The date was January 15, 1942, two months after the Germans had carried out a public execution of Jews for leaving the ghetto to sell articles and buy food on the Aryan side. Now three hundred more Jews were awaiting execution, and the German authorities had just offered to commute the sentence if the ghetto delivered fifteen hundred fur coats or 1.5 million zlotys. (As the Germans had recently made all Jews give up their furs, what they really wanted was money.)

Ringelblum and Giterman called a meeting of the Public Sector and the Central Commission of the house committees to discuss an emergency fund drive to help save the prisoners. The meeting took place in the large building of the Aleynhilf on Tłomackie 5. "Hundreds of people," the protocol stated, "filled the room, the corridors, and the stairwells." The agenda concerned one issue: should the house committees join the drive to collect furs for the Germans?

Ringelblum, who presided, pointed out that the Judenrat could collect this sum from wealthy Jews and did not really need the help of the house committees. But he stressed that it would be wrong not to give the "folk masses" the chance to perform the "sacred duty" of saving fellow Jews: hence the decision to call together the representatives of the house committees.[144] After Ringelblum finished speaking, two religious leaders, Rabbis Zisha Frydman and H. B. Rogazhytsky, pointed out that saving fellow Jews from death was a holy commandment. A Judenrat representative, Henryk Rozen, told the delegates that he had just visited the condemned Jews in prison and described their joy when they learned that there was some hope that their lives might be spared. Yitzhak Giterman closed the meeting with harsh words. Warsaw Jews, he said, had earned a bad reputation among Polish Jewry, for their egotism and heartlessness. Only in Warsaw could rich Jews elbow aside their dying brothers as they hurried to dine in expensive restaurants. Warsaw Jewry should not let itself be branded with "the mark of Cain."[145]

The archival document that was uncovered noted that the meeting was successful: the delegates of the house committees waited in long lines to pick up the forms they needed to take up the collection in their buildings. This document is instructive; we learn that Ringelblum and Giterman saw themselves as leaders of the "people" but also understood that their leadership role depended on persuasion, not coercion. In view of the symbolic and moral significance of the collection, both men stressed the importance of "the masses" demonstrating their solidarity with the condemned prisoners. The subtext was that the Judenrat did not enjoy the moral legitimacy granted to the Central Commission.

Ringelblum stood side by side with Orthodox rabbis: in the Aleynhilf, political and cultural differences counted for much less than they did before the war. He and Giterman clearly had no compunctions about paying ransom to the Germans to save Jewish lives. Even though they had already received the first reports of mass killings in the East, and even though they were about to learn about the Chełmno death camp, they still did not believe that the fate of Warsaw Jewry was sealed.

DOCUMENTING DEFEAT: THE CRISIS OF SELF-HELP AND THE OYNEG SHABES

The Oyneg Shabes materials and the sparse memoir literature on the house committees all mention a "heyday" and a period of decline. Sources refer to 1940 and early 1941 as the high point of the committees' activities and vitality. On March 27, 1940, Ringelblum wrote that "the Jewish masses have not given way to despair during the occupation."[146] On April 26, 1940, Ringelblum tersely noted that "house committee people have assumed leadership."[147] The Aleynhilf and the committees were full of hope, determined to help the ghetto Jews survive, morally as well as physically.

However, by the second half of 1941, Ringelblum was becoming increasingly aware that the house committees and the soup kitchens—the very foundation of the Aleynhilf—were playing a losing game. Slowly but surely, even as their leaders tired, their resources dwindled. The soup kitchens could not save many of their clients from a slow death from starvation. The entire rationale for the Aleynhilf slowly came into question. In a diary entry of early November 1941 Ringelblum noted that a house committee on Miła Street was demanding a twenty-zloty deposit from new tenants as a guarantee that the committee would not be burdened with their burial expenses.[148] This was a far cry from the hopeful days of 1940!

Ringelblum's anger and concern grew. But he was determined to document the defeats as well as the victories. The Oyneg Shabes Archive did all it could to leave a comprehensive record of the achievements—and failures—of the massive effort made in the Warsaw Ghetto to stave off hunger and despair.

THE "PARÓWKI"

A major reason for the growing pressure on the house committees was their helplessness in the face of the blatant corruption of the Jewish police and sanitation officials, particularly in connection to the dreaded parówki, or disinfections. Ostensibly instituted to stop typhus, the parówki forced all tenants to bathe in a special shower and surrender their bedding and other important household possessions for "disinfection." Typhus was indeed one of the greatest problems facing the ghetto. As Barbara Engelking pointed out, it was a danger that, in the overcrowded streets of the ghetto, affected the rich as well as the poor. The image of the ghetto as a nest of vermin and disease also became a staple of German propaganda. In 1941 a particularly repulsive poster, entitled "Jews, Lice, Typhus," which showed lice crawling up a Jew's beard, festooned the streets of the city. But as Professor Ludwik Hirszfeld wrote, in a courageous memorandum that he sent to the German health authorities in 1941, the real cause of typhus was the German policy of forcing the Jews to live in overcrowded and unhygienic conditions. As for the disinfection measures ordered by the Germans, Hirszfeld complained that, far from curbing the disease, they actually spread it. This was especially true of the disinfection procedure, the *parówki*. Hirszfeld remarked that the spray was too weak to kill lice; if any lice died, it was "from laughter."[149]

Peretz Opoczynski called the parówki "the angel of death" for the house committees."[150] The parówki caused not only terrible material damage to tenants' possessions but also extreme psychological humiliation. This was part of the plan. The Jewish police and the sanitation squads knew that a house committee would pay handsomely to avoid them.

The Oyneg Shabes contained plenty of reports on the demoralizing effects of the parówki. An ironic but hard-hitting report by Opoczynski conveyed just why the word "parówka" struck fear into the ghetto inhabitants. The house—in this case located on poverty-ridden Smocza Street—suddenly awakened to the shouts that the "disinfectors" had arrived. The parówka team consisted of Poles and Jews. When it appeared, police would man the gates to keep people from leaving or entering—unless they paid a fat bribe. Sometimes the gates would be shut for weeks at a time.

The parówka team included "sprayers," usually Poles, and doctors and other hangers on, often Jews. If a house committee did not pay the required bribe, all tenants would be lined up and sent in relays to a bath house, where they would be stripped naked and then forced to wait in three lines: first to enter the shower, then, shivering and wet, to obtain a delousing "certificate" and finally to pick up their clothes, shriveled and ruined from the "disinfection chamber."

Opoczynski called the process "refined torture."[151] The bathhouse attendant would only let in thirty people at a time, while hundreds of freezing desperate people kept pushing from the back. There was not enough room to undress, and people's clothing got all mixed up in a chaotic pile. As if the jostling and swearing were not enough, policemen with rubber truncheons fanned through the desperate crowd to keep "order." Finally, to obtain the necessary delousing certificate, a Jew had to endure a crude and painful "haircut" with electric shears. From behind a thin wall men could hear the screams of their wives and daughters whose hair was being cut off with sadistic cruelty.

The total wait usually exceeded twenty-four hours—often without food. But there was no choice, since one needed to produce a disinfection certificate in order to receive bread ration cards from the Judenrat.[152]

The worse the reputation of the parówki, the easier it was to press money out of the desperate Jews. The corruption knew no national boundaries. Jews and Poles collaborated to make as much money as they could. The parówka team would fan out through tenants' apartments. A bribe would send them away, but if a Jewish family had no money, then the "disinfectors" would calmly pack up bed sheets, pillows, shoes, and clothing and throw them outside, where their partners would arbitrarily throw some of the articles into a bonfire, and the rest on a huge heap destined for a disinfection chamber. Tenants watched helplessly as their meager possessions lay outside in the courtyard, exposed to the rain and snow. If and when these articles finally came back from the disinfection chamber—days later—most items of value would be missing, and what was left would be ruined.[153]

The parówka reminded the tenants and the house committees that they had absolutely no rights and no protection. It showed them that no matter how much they scraped and saved to help the less fortunate and meet their moral obligations, it all counted for nothing when the parówka team arrived to demand its bribe. As time went on, the sale of household possessions became ever more important as a source of money to buy food. For many families, the parówka threatened the loss of what meager hopes they had left.

On Muranowska 6, Opoczynski compared the parówka to a "money pump." The first time the gang demanded five hundred zlotys from the house committee to call off the parówka. It returned in a couple of weeks and demanded eight hundred. The third time it wanted three thousand. When the tenants saw just how vulnerable the house committee was, their morale plummeted, as did the willingness of the leaders to continue making sacrifices. What was the point when any funds would quickly go to the parówka gang?

LABOR CAMPS

Another serious blow undermined the house committees in the spring of 1941, when the Judenrat tried to make them responsible for furnishing contingents to the dreaded labor camps. These camps supplied Jewish labor to work on river regulation, the building of roads, and other projects specified by the Germans.

As noted, the Germans began dragging Jews off the streets for forced labor at the very start of the occupation. Anxious to stop the arbitrary arrests, the Judenrat negotiated with the Germans to supply a regular quota of workers for sites near Warsaw and, beginning in 1940, for labor camps in other parts of the General Government. These camps largely worked for German subcontractors.[154] There were two major waves of impressments to the camps, in 1940 and 1941. In 1940, 5,253 Warsaw Jews were sent to these camps and, in 1941, about 8,600.

At first many Jews—unemployed and hungry—volunteered to go to the camps, lured by the promises of decent food and meager pay that could be sent to their families. It quickly turned out, however, that few workers received either. The worst camps were the river camps, where Jews had to stand in freezing water up to their chests for up to twelve hours a day. No special clothing was provided, not in these camps or in the road building camps. In some camps most of the workers became so sick that they had to be sent home. Even worse was the alarming mortality rate. Just in the spring of 1941 about 250 died in the camps. Word quickly reached the ghetto that many of these camps were indeed torture centers where Jews worked long hours, received little food, and were subject to constant beatings.[155]

The German contractors complained that the Jewish labor camps did not turn a profit. The Jews who arrived from the ghetto, they pointed out, were so weak and malnourished that they could barely hold a shovel. Their productivity was so low that, unless they were fattened up before their arrival, there was no sense employing them. After some discussion the German bureaucracy decided to provide more food and health care for the inmates—at the expense of the Warsaw Judenrat and the existing food allotments for the ghetto soup kitchens. The Judenrat was also given a bigger role within the camps. It sent doctors to examine the inmates, and Judenrat members toured the camps and reported on conditions there. Adam Czerniakow was truly shocked by what he heard and made a major effort to improve conditions.[156] He was also in a terrible position. The Germans threatened to cut off food supplies to the ghetto if the Judenrat did not come up with the required quotas for the labor camps. Eventually most of the camps were disbanded by the fall of 1941. By late summer 1941, only 2,359 Warsaw Jews were in labor camps outside the ghetto, and only 600 Warsaw Jews remained in them by October.[157]

These camps were not concentration camps. Most Jews survived them and returned to the ghetto. But many came back traumatized and injured from savage beatings. The presence of so many camp victims in the ghetto gave the Oyneg Shabes a major opportunity. The first part of the Ringelblum Archive contains a wide variety of material on the labor camps, including copies of Judenrat reports, surveys of various camps, and dozens of firsthand accounts taken from returning inmates by the Oyneg Shabes staff. The Oyneg Shabes efforts to collect materials on the labor camps produced another dividend: valuable materials on Polish-Jewish relations in 1940–41.

Ringelblum singled out for special mention the labor camp memoirs of a Rabbi Chitowski, compiled for the Oyneg Shabes by Rabbi Shimon Huberband.[158] On April 18, 1941, the seventh day of Passover, Rabbi Chitowski fell victim to a police roundup for labor camp duty. The police sent him and the others to a detention center on Leszno Street. Those who could afford a fifty-zloty bribe to the Jewish police were sent home; the rest were marched at a run to the railroad station on the other side of the Vistula. Chitowski bitterly noted that most of his group consisted of the weakest elements of ghetto society: the poor, the refugees, and the sick. "The (Judenrat) . . . intentionally sent the refugees to the camp," he wrote, "in order to get rid of them and ensure that they wouldn't be a burden on the community."[159]

They were sent to the Kampinos region west of Warsaw to work on river regulation. When they arrived at their camp nothing was organized. Food rations were absolutely inadequate, there were no blankets, and the barracks were totally unheated. The Jews were victimized both by Jewish informers and cruel Polish guards. When one Jew tried to go to a nearby peasant house to buy some food,

He was met by the master, who ordered him to return to the site. As punishment for abandoning his work, the master ordered the Jew to let down his trousers and lie flat on the ground, and told the young goyim to give him twenty lashes. The goyim were glad to carry out the sentence and gave the unfortunate man twenty lashes with their rods. The poor Jew screamed, and although his voice was muffled by the ground, it reached our ears. It was like the voice of a beaten dog.[160]

During the five weeks that Chitowski was in the camp, a Judenrat commission and a German medical commission made tours of inspection. The German commission demanded better food for the workers, but, in the end, nothing changed. The Judenrat commission expressed sympathy with the inmates' plight, but whatever interventions it made were ineffectual. Just a few days after their arrival in the camp, inmates began to collapse one by one. Within five weeks they had buried fifty-three Jews in a mass grave in a hill behind the camp. Another fifty later died in Warsaw "and the rest," in Huberband's words, became "physical and emotional invalids for life."[161]

As for the actual labor, Chitowski's account confirmed other documents: it was a waste. The Polish foremen complained of the Jews' "laziness": inmates had to stand in mud and cold water all day and push heavy wheel barrows of wet soil from one place to another in order to level river banks. Few had the strength to do so. One of the few bright spots in Chitowski's five-week ordeal was the attitude of the local Polish priest, who told the peasants in his sermons to help the Jews and who gave the inmates strong moral support.

From the perspective of 1940 and 1941, before Jews had any knowledge of the Final Solution, the camps were an important litmus test of both German intentions and the good faith—and abilities—of the Warsaw Judenrat. The evidence the Oyneg Shabes was collecting as of mid-1941 was troubling and disquieting, but it gave no conclusive evidence of a basic change in German policy at the highest level. Some Germans were sadistic, whereas others recommended better treatment. There were many cases of Polish cruelty, but many Poles did what they could to help. In sum, the camps exposed a confused and wasteful labor policy, and a pattern of "spontaneous" sadism that was not universal. Indeed, a few camps treated Jews with relative decency.

Had the labor camps been concentration camps, where people disappeared and were never to be seen again, then their impact on the ghetto would have been quite different. But most inmates, albeit in ruined health, returned. The Judenrat sent doctors, inspection teams, and supplies. In the process, it incurred a heavy burden of moral responsibility, and the camps became an important bone of contention between the Judenrat and the "Aleynhilf" which, as was often the case, tended to look past the real difficulties that Czerniakow and the Judenrat faced. Ringelblum showed no sympathy for Czerniakow, who was caught between German threats and Jewish anger, and who indeed made valiant attempts to improve conditions.

The labor camps, like the parówki, drove another nail into the coffin of the house committees. According to Opoczynski, a rumor that the Judenrat had made house committee boards responsible for furnishing workers for the camps had a devastating effect on the willingness of tenants to step forward and lead their committees.[162] Opoczynski wrote that when eight young men left for labor camp service, the house committee on Muranowska 6 had provided all of them with money, food, and clothing. They all returned broken and sick. One by one they all died. Who wanted to be forced to send anyone else?[163]

The alarming news from the labor camps infuriated Ringelblum, whose already negative attitude toward the Judenrat took a sharp turn for the worse in the spring of 1941. In a diary entry of April 26, 1941, Ringelblum compared the Judenrat to the nineteenth-century Jewish community councils that hunted down poor Jewish boys for impressment into the Russian army. Then and now the poor paid a terrible price, and the rich got off. He accused the Judenrat of neglecting the families of the labor camp inmates and doing little to ensure that conditions in the camps were bearable.

In mid-April 1941, Ringelblum wrote, the festering anger of the ghetto population against the Judenrat erupted in a tumultuous meeting of the Central Commission of the House Committees and the Judenrat. When the Judenrat representatives demanded better compliance with orders to report for labor camp duty, they were rudely interrupted with angry shouts. When Henryk Rozen, who headed the labor department of the Judenrat, declared that the house committees would be responsible for delivering workers, one of the leaders of the house committees on Leszno 2 loudly compared the Jewish police to gangsters and shouted that everyone knew they were taking bribes to let people out of labor camp duty. At that point Jewish policemen seized him but had to let him go when the enraged crowd threatened a riot.

By the second half of 1941 the Judenrat was steadily increasing its pressure on the house committees to collect various taxes and ensure compliance with Judenrat regulations. A favorite tactic of the Jewish police to intimidate the house committees was to blockade the entire building until it paid up.[164]

Not surprisingly many house committee leaders stepped down from their increasingly intolerable positions. But this was not simple. Some house committees informed their leaders that they had had a moral obligation to stay at their posts and rejected their resignations. Stefania Szereszewska wrote a report on her house committee for the Oyneg Shabes in which she described what happened when the chairman declared that he had had enough. The year 1940, Szereszewska recalled, had been the "golden age" of the committee on Gęsia 19, but matters began to fall apart in the autumn of 1941. Faced with parówki and other shakedowns, Szereszewska noted, many committees—including hers—were ready to quit. When Ringelblum's Public Sector cajoled committee leaders to stay the course, many replied that "they did not know that the war would last so long."[165]

What this meant, Szereszewska explained, was that decent people often despaired when they had to look their dying neighbors in the face and tell them they no longer could help them. Mr. Wajzer, the head of the committee on Gęsia 19, could take no more. A desperate tenant had attacked him: his hands and face were covered with cuts. "I replied quietly," Szereszewska wrote, "that I accepted his resignation but that this is meaningless since you can stop being on the house committee only when the war ends or if you die." A house committee had to continue, no matter what. The conditions of the Warsaw ghetto left no choice.

If the house committees and the Aleynhilf saw their fight as a defense of the community against Judenrat corruption, Adam Czerniakow considered their recalcitrance a major abrogation of responsibility in a difficult time. In a diary entry of January 21, 1942, he noted that "the house committees, led by incompetents, have completely failed."

In the spring of 1942 the Legal Department of the Judenrat worked out a plan to put the house committees under its formal jurisdiction. This Judenrat gambit to seize control of the house committees ran into fierce opposition from Ringelblum and the Public Sector. But the Aleynhilf had fewer and fewer cards to play. The decline in Joint receipts following the U.S. entry into the war, the steadily worsening food situation, combined with the impact of a third year of occupation wore down the resources of the Aleynhilf. But the simmering conflict between the Judenrat and the Aleynhilf over the house committees continued right up until the beginning of the Great Deportation in July 1942.

Ringelblum's comments on the Judenrat became ever harsher, replacing an objective analysis of the awful dilemmas and problems Czerniakow faced with searing condemnation that saw Judenrat behavior as just another example of the callous treatment of the Jewish masses by the Jewish bourgeoisie. In January 1942 Ringelblum angrily wrote:

> Turbulent times at least have one good result. Like a strong searchlight, they expose things that have hitherto remained hidden. The beastly face of the Jewish bourgeoisie, its cannibalistic character has recently sur-

faced during these hungry times. The whole activity of the Judenrat [Ringelblum uses the word *kehille*] is one heartrending injustice against the poor. If there were a God, he would destroy this nest of wickedness, hypocrisy, and exploitation. The whole financial policy of the Judenrat is one big scandal.[166]

But this came as no surprise. All through modern Jewish history, he wrote a few months later, ordinary Jews suffered more from their better off co-religionists than they did from gentiles.[167] By the same token, he saw the Aleynhilf not just as a source of relief but as a beacon of conscience against the depredations of the Judenrat. On November 14, 1941, he wrote:

> [The Aleynhilf], which built the house committees and awakened the entire Jewish community to the responsibility of self-help, is a thorn in the eye of the Judenrat bosses, who want to strangle it. They complain that the Aleynhilf is a stronghold of opposition against the Judenrat . . . It's true that house committee meetings criticize the Judenrat but this is because of its class bias, because it throws the burdens on the poor and exempts the rich. The Aleynhilf is the only institution where free thought reigns.[168]

But even as his anger at the Judenrat grew, he began to understand more clearly that yet another pillar of the Aleynhilf was crumbling. The soup kitchens were losing their fight against hunger.

Fighting Hunger: The Story of a Soup Kitchen

Sometime in the middle of 1941 Eliyahu Gutkowski, co-secretary of the Oyneg Shabes, asked Rachel Auerbach to write for the archive. Auerbach immediately decided to write an essay about the soup kitchen she managed on Leszno 40. The soup kitchen had already become, in a small way, one of the many pillars that supported the archive. Ringelblum would send individuals to Auerbach with a password that allowed them to get soup without having to present tickets. Some were needy intellectuals that Ringelblum wanted to save, and others were writers for the archive whom he wanted to support.[169]

Once Auerbach told Gutkowski her topic, the Oyneg Shabes secretary spared no effort in encouraging Auerbach in her work. He would periodically appear with blank notebooks and writing materials. He also offered small amounts of money, down payments on the "honoraria" that the Oyneg Shabes paid its writers. Auerbach told Gutkowski, half-jokingly, that, thanks to the Oyneg Shabes, she could again feel that she was an author who had a purpose and an audience. Although the Great Deportation kept Auerbach from completing her essay, her interim survey impressed Ringelblum greatly. He talked about it and showed it to friends.[170]

The story Auerbach told provided a gripping, behind-the-scenes look at the ghetto's desperate battle against hunger.[171] The stark statistics and official reports that existed could only register the number of deaths, the corpses piling up in the streets and in the mass graves of the Jewish cemetery. But Auerbach, like other members of the Oyneg Shabes Archive, did all she could to ensure that the victims would be remembered for who they were, not just how they died.

Auerbach managed to record the voices of the victims, both as individuals and as members of a community. She investigated the "social history" of hunger by presenting the soup kitchen as a microcosm of human relationships and human choices, so that the archive's eventual audience would understand that the Jews who came to the soup kitchen, ate there, and slowly died off were not an undifferentiated mass. Each of the daily two thousand or so "customers" and each family had its own idiosyncrasies, its own history, and its own identity. Auerbach deftly caught the phrases or the habits that made them memorable.

Auerbach also stressed that death by hunger in the Warsaw Ghetto was only the culmination of a long, slow road where the enormous national tragedy was refracted through the routine markers, the "small change" of everyday routine in the ghetto: obtaining a certificate from the house committee; taking the certificate to the Aleynhilf for a voucher; taking the voucher to register at the soup kitchen; getting a ticket that entitled one to free soup. Each stage raised hopes—but only temporarily.

The drama played itself out on many different levels. Each day Auerbach would join other soup kitchen directors at the headquarters of the Aleynhilf to compare notes, get news, and learn about nutrition. The directors attended Aleynhilf "seminars," where trained nutritionists gave upbeat lectures on how to eke out the last calorie from the marginal ingredients that the Germans left for the soup kitchens. The seminars also handed down tips on ways to make the daily soup tastier and more appealing. The implicit assumption was that somehow, with enough effort, the soup kitchens just might make a difference. But more and more directors, including Auerbach, harbored growing doubts.

Just as Auerbach tried to rescue her "customers" from total oblivion, she also attempted to ensure that in some way her staff would also be remembered: ordinary, unexceptional people who joked, quarreled, and came together to run a major operation. Auerbach remembered her bookkeeper, Halina Gelblum, as a modest and efficient woman who soothed strained nerves and gave Auerbach and the rest of the staff the strength to endure what they had to see every day. Sixteen-year-old Henie, a sprightly teenager, always had a smile and flirted with the adolescent boys who worked in the kitchen. Long after the war, Auerbach wrote, "I miss her. It was she I thought about when I wrote on the Aryan side about the Jewish girls who were like rye bread and like shirts of rough canvas (*leyvnt*) on the body of the Jewish people; they were like the happy laughter of the waving rows of grain that we Jews would walk through when we lived on the Slavic earth."[172]

Gutchke the cook often infuriated the fastidious Auerbach with her casual approach to hygiene, but she somehow made the soups taste halfway decent. In the kitchen on Leszno 40 she would sing a Yiddish ballad, bustle around, talk to the pots (she gave each a nickname: "Maciusz" was her favorite) and sample soup (with her fingers). Before the war she had run her own restaurant in Praga. Childless, she had recently married an elderly widower and scholar. Gutchke, barely literate herself, was devoted to her learned husband, for how could such a common woman have married a scholar in ordinary times? She did her best to keep him alive. Auerbach once caught her taking a tiny bit of food from the kitchen to make a meal at home. As Auerbach guiltily reported after the war, she scolded the crestfallen woman and warned her never to do that again. At the time it had seemed her duty.

> Why did I shame her and depress her? Why didn't I understand that
> through this little transgression she wanted to gladden and strengthen
> her elderly helpless husband who had become like a child? How blind,
> how stupid we were then—on the brink of extermination.[173]

However skillful the cook, there was simply too stark a disparity between the food the kitchen could provide and the food the "customers" needed to stay alive. This disparity confronted Auerbach, as the director, with serious psychological pressures and moral challenges. Like other figures in the Aleynhilf, she had seen herself as an honest public servant imbued with the moral code of the progressive Jewish intelligentsia. Very quickly, however, she discovered that for the masses of starving, desperate people who came to the kitchen each day, she, like other Aleynhilf figures, represented authority and power. In their eyes she had become an arbiter of life and death.[174] Like Ringelblum, she had come from a milieu that was imbued with love for the "Jewish masses." Now these masses, these ordinary Jews, stormed her office, blocked her in the corridors, and begged for extra soup tickets. They saw Auerbach as someone who could save them. Some confronted her in silent supplication, but others yelled and loudly reminded her of their former status. Then there were the children. Auerbach described a pack of four young orphans who would cajole her in Yiddish-accented Polish (*plosze pani* [*sic*]—please ma'am) for some extra food. The best she could do for them was to get them admitted to a children's reception center, which they promptly fled.

Increasingly frustrated, Auerbach singled out a German-speaking refugee from the Sudetenland for special attention and care. A survivor of Dachau and a former athlete, Abraham Brocksmeier won Auerbach over with his impeccable manners, good nature and spry sense of humor. For Auerbach, Brocksmeier became a test and a challenge. She bent her rules and gave him extra food. When he became apathetic, a common sign of starvation, she yelled at him that she could feed him but that he had to summon up the will to live. It was important, Auerbach felt, to win at least one victory. Ringelblum, who wanted Brocksmeier's testimony, encouraged Auerbach to try to save him.

But soon Brocksmeier developed the telltale swelling that signaled impending death by hunger. He joked and called his swollen hands *pätchenhändchen* (patty-cake hands). Auerbach tried even harder. In her diary entry of August 4, 1941, she wrote:

> Brocksmeier did not come to the kitchen today . . . the swelling has progressed so far that he can't get up. Those "patty-cake hands" and legs like logs. I have decided to do everything possible to rescue this man. I would regard it as the greatest defeat for our kitchen if we can't keep a person like this alive. What is the use of all our work if we can't save even one person from death by hunger?[175]

Six weeks later Auerbach noted his death and her own sense of frustration and defeat. She also received a rare reproof from Ringelblum, who had wanted Brocksmeier to write on Dachau for the Oyneg Shabes. "You failed to save the German" ("Ir hot farfusht dem daytch"), he told her.

She had failed to save him but she could at least give Brocksmeier one of the dearest gifts in the Warsaw Ghetto: a decent burial. Ringelblum gave her money to arrange it. She told her janitor, Pinie, to hurry to the cemetery and arrange to take custody of Brocksmeier's body before it wound up in one of the daily mass graves. But Pinie had long resented Auerbach and her favoritism. He lied to her that he had taken care of the arrangements at the cemetery. When Auerbach found out the truth, she rushed to the "shop," the place in the cemetery where all the naked corpses waited for mass burial. She held her nose and searched for Brocksmeier's body. But just as she had lost the battle to keep him alive, now she proved unable to get him a separate grave.

While Auerbach gave the Oyneg Shabes a picture of a soup kitchen seen from the eyes of a director, Leyb Goldin left the archive an extraordinary account of how a soup kitchen looked from the other side, through the eyes of a "customer." Before the war Goldin had been a journalist and a translator of world literature into Yiddish. He served time in Polish jails for communist activity, left the party, and joined the Bund in 1936. Written in October 1941, Goldin's masterful literary monologue raised many questions, including the ultimate purpose of the mutual aid.

In his "Chronicle of a Single Day," written in October 1941, a fictionalized "Arke" (a left-wing intellectual like Goldin himself) has reached the point where he has nothing left to sell and no resources to live on except his daily ticket at the soup kitchen.[176] His life and his sense of time have constricted to where nothing matters except the daily meal at 1:00 PM. At one time he had been an intellectual who had deeply appreciated modern Jewish and European literature: Peretz, Mann, and Goethe. In the good old days he could think of time as a literary trope, just as Thomas Mann had done in *Magic Mountain,* where Hans Castorp went to the mountain to pay a short visit and stayed for seven years. But now he is in the ghetto; it is 5:00 AM and time has assumed a totally different meaning. His mind can only focus on the eight hours that separate him from his daily bowl of soup at the public kitchen.

> How much longer to go? Eight hours, though you can't count the last hour from noon on. By then you're already in the kitchen, surrounded by the smell of food; you're already prepared. You already *see* the soup. So there are really only seven hours to go.

Once he could theorize about human nature. He remembered phrases from his days in the party: "the century of the masses," "the individual is nothing." But the old slogans mean little;[177] now his stomach is doing all the thinking.

> It doesn't think. It yells, it's enough to kill you! It demands, it provokes me. . . .
> Why are you yelling like that? "Because I want to. Because I, your stomach, am hungry. Do you realize that by now?"
> Who is talking to you in this way? You are two people. Arke. It's a lie. A pose. Don't be conceited. That kind of split was all right at one time when one was full. *Then* one could say, "Two people are battling within me," and one could make a dramatic martyred face.
> Yes this kind of thing can be found quite often in literature. But today? Don't talk nonsense—it's you and your stomach. It's your stomach and you. It's 90 percent your stomach and a little bit you. A small remnant, an insignificant remnant of the Arke who once was.

He finally gets up and walks—past corpses and beggars—to the soup kitchen. He understands that he is moving closer and closer to death each day. And if he dies, who will remember him? The waitresses in the soup kitchen?

> If statistics are made of the diners who died, I'll be there too and maybe one of the waitresses will say to another: "D'ya know who else died, Zoshe? That redhead who insisted on speaking Yiddish and whom I teased for an hour and, just to fix him good, didn't give him his soup. He's been put in the box too, I bet.

Finally inside the kitchen, he sits down and waits for the waitress. She gives him his bowl of soup—but forgets to take his ticket. Should he be honest and turn it in? He keeps it and gets a second bowl of soup.

> In the street the smell of fresh corpses envelops you. Like an airplane propeller just after it's been started up, which spins and spins, and yet stays in one place—that's what your feet are like. They seem to you to be moving backwards. Pieces of wood.
>
> They were looking, weren't they? Involuntarily you cover your face with your arm. And what if they find out? They can, as punishment, take away your soups. Sometimes it seems to you that they already know. That man who's walking past looks so insolently into your eyes. He knows. He laughs, and so does that man, and another and another. Hee, hee— they choke back their laughter, and somehow you become so small, so cramped up. That's how you get caught, you fool. A thief? . . .
>
> You feel that today you have fallen a step lower. Oh yes, that's how it had to begin. All those people around you apparently began like that. You're on your way. . . . The second soup—what will it be tomorrow?

As he trudges home, aware that he is sinking, he looks into a window facing the street. It is a hospital, and surgeons are operating to save a child's life. "But why, why? Why save? Why, to whom, to what is the child being brought back?" Because there is a mother, waiting and hoping to see her child again. And the corpses lying in the street, they, too, had mothers who once thought that they were the center of their world.

And suddenly Arke starts to walk faster; he starts to understand that no matter what happened to him today, the Jews in the ghetto are still human.

> Each day the profiles of our children, of our wives, acquire the mourning look of foxes, dingoes, kangaroos. Our howls are like the cry of jackals . . . But we are not animals. We operate on our infants. It may be pointless or even criminal. But animals do not operate on their young!

But whatever comfort Arke takes from this, it will not save him.

"The world's turning upside down. A planet melts in tears. And I—I am hungry, hungry. I am hungry."

Despite their different perspectives, Auerbach and Goldin underscored the tension between the Aleynhilf ethos of communal responsibility and the sheer stark reality of mass starvation, which the kitchen could postpone but not prevent. As prewar leftists and secularists, both Goldin and Auerbach had believed that one did not need traditional religion to adhere to a basic ethical code. The entire Aleynhilf was imbued with a sense of moral superiority to the Judenrat. But faced with mass starvation, what rules were left? Arke took his second bowl of soup, whatever the pangs of conscience. He had fallen a step lower not only because he had betrayed his ethical code but because his act betrayed his growing desperation and loss of control. Teetering between hope and despair, he could still take some slim comfort from the operation he witnessed. But what about the next day? And the day after that? With his mind and body now conflated into a total obsession with food, Arke was fighting his battle completely alone. There are no friends and no comrades. The rules and norms of the past still exist, but hunger is forcing him to abandon them. Yet just as the operation served as a reminder that the ghetto Jews had not yet been overwhelmed, so, too, did Arke's ability to narrate his thoughts, to provide a link—however tenuous—to prewar beliefs and standards.[178] Arke, through his words and memories, still preserved a fragile sense of self—but for how long?

As for Auerbach, she began to question the role she was called on to play. She had reprimanded her subordinates, had demanded discipline and accountability. But she, too, had her favorites, as her janitor bitterly noted. Could the Aleynhilf really meet the standards of its moral pretensions? With so much at stake, could its staff avoid the taint of corruption?

Auerbach's depression deepened:

I have been slowly coming to the conclusion that the whole balance of this self-help activity is simply that people die more slowly [śmierć na raty]. We must finally admit to ourselves that we can save nobody from death; we don't have the means to. We can only put it off, regulate it but we can't prevent it. In all my experience in the soup kitchen, I have not been able to rescue anybody, nobody! And nobody could accuse me of caring less than the directors of other soup kitchens. (February 2, 1942)[179]

A few months later Ringelblum echoed Auerbach's conclusions:

The [Aleynhilf] . . . does not solve the problem [of hunger], it only saves people for a short time, and then they will die anyway. The [soup kitchens] prolong the suffering but cannot bring salvation [because there is not enough money]. It is an absolute fact that the clients of the soup kitchens will all die if all they have to eat is the soup they get there and the bread they get on their ration cards. (May 26, 1942)[180]

So what should the Aleynhilf do? Perhaps, Ringelblum asked, the Aleynhilf had to make a hard decision and concentrate on saving the intellectual elite. But what made them more deserving than artisans and workers? What about the Jews from provincial cities who had been self-sufficient and productive and who, through no fault of their own, had been sent to the Warsaw Ghetto where they became "human scrap, debris, and candidates for the mass graves? So we are left with a tragic dilemma. What should we do? Should we try to feed everyone with teaspoons, and save nobody, or should we try to save a few?"

By now, just a couple of months before the mass extermination of the Warsaw Ghetto, Ringelblum had come to understand that his long dedication to relief and self-help counted for less and less. The lofty hopes of the house committees and of the soup kitchens gave way to the growing realization that even the Aleynhilf, for all its claims to communal leadership, also was forced to confront difficult moral dilemmas. The Jews were running out of time.

But one consolation remained: the Oyneg Shabes Archive. Without the archive almost everything might have vanished without a trace: Opoczynski's account of the parówka, Huberband's report on Kampinos, Auerbach's diary, Goldin's "Chronicle of a Single Day." When Ringelblum began the archive he was sure that Polish Jewry would survive. Now, even if it did not, the world would at least learn of its vitality, resilience, and last-ditch struggle to stay alive. It would also learn of the difficult struggle to hold onto some morality, some humanity, in the middle of hell.

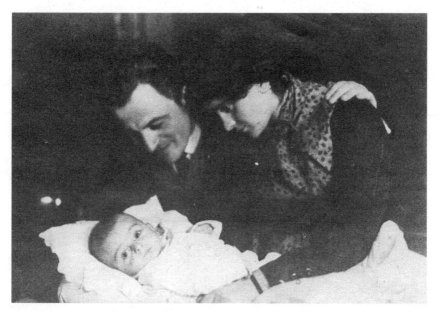

Ringelblum and wife looking at baby Uri. *Photograph courtesy Yad Vashem.*

Young Ringelblum.
Photograph courtesy Yad Vashem.

Milkcans and tin boxes. *Photograph courtesy Yad Vashem.*

Wasser and Auerbach
with a tin box.
Photograph courtesy Yad Vashem.

Workers at ZIH around a table examining part 2 of the excavated archive.
Photograph courtesy Yad Vashem.

Abraham Lewin.
*Photograph courtesy
Yad Vashem.*

Ringelblum posing with Uri. *Photograph courtesy Yad Vashem.*

Unearthing the archive, 1946. *Photograph courtesy Yad Vashem.*

Czerniakow, Winter, and released prisoners. *Ringelblum Archive, courtesy Jewish Historical Institute in Warsaw.*

Street scene in Warsaw Ghetto. *Ringelblum Archive, courtesy Jewish Historical Institute in Warsaw.*

Jewish police, Czerniakow, street children. *Ringelblum Archive, courtesy Jewish Historical Institute in Warsaw.*

Smuggling food at the wall.
Ringelblum Archive, courtesy Jewish Historical Institute in Warsaw.

In a ghetto school. *Ringelblum Archive, courtesy Jewish Historical Institute in Warsaw.*

Passover Matzo for sale. *Ringelblum Archive, courtesy Jewish Historical Institute in Warsaw.*

Collecting for the winter help. *Ringelblum Archive, courtesy Jewish Historical Institute in Warsaw.*

Selling vegetables on Miła. *Ringelblum Archive, courtesy Jewish Historical Institute in Warsaw.*

Gathering cabbages. *Ringelblum Archive, courtesy Jewish Historical Institute in Warsaw.*

Group picture of Jewish police. *Ringelblum Archive, courtesy Jewish Historical Institute in Warsaw.*

Menakhem Linder.
*Courtesy Jewish
Historical Institute
in Warsaw.*

CHAPTER 5

A Band of Comrades

The Oyneg Shabes was not just a clandestine archive; it was also a tightly knit collective, a secret but vital component of the larger alternate community that had developed out of the house committees and the Aleynhilf. Using the Aleynhilf as a base, Ringelblum slowly and methodically assembled a group of collaborators that ranged from the most prominent leaders of prewar Polish Jewry to impoverished refugees. Of all the Jewish historians in prewar Poland, it was Ringelblum who most regarded history as a collective enterprise. Now, in the middle of a national disaster, it was this collective effort that shaped the archive and imbued it with a sense of purpose. As Ringelblum wrote, probably in late 1942:

> The members of the Oyneg Shabes constituted, and continue to consti-
> tute, a united body, imbued with a common spirit. The Oyneg Shabes
> is not a group of researchers who compete with one another but a unit-
> ed group, a brotherhood where all help one another . . . Each member
> of the Oyneg Shabes knew that his effort and pain, his hard work and
> toil, his taking constant risks with the dangerous work of moving mate-
> rial from one place to another—that this was done in the name of a high
> ideal. . . . The Oyneg Shabes was a brotherhood, an order of brothers
> who wrote on their flag: readiness to sacrifice, mutual loyalty, and service
> to [Jewish society].[1]

Over time, the Oyneg Shabes brought together men and women from a wide spectrum of prewar Polish Jewry: wealthy businessmen and poor artisans, rabbis and Communists, Yiddishists and Polish-speaking intellectuals, teachers and journalists, economists and leaders of youth groups. Some were part of a small executive committee, an inner circle that raised money, made policy, and decided what to study and what to collect. A larger group contributed essays and reports commissioned by the archive. This group ranged from frequent contributors to those who only submitted one or two essays or testimonies. Some members only copied, typing or writing out duplicate and triplicate copies of incoming material; isolated from everyone else except Ringelblum and his closest secretaries, were Israel Lichtenstein and his two teen-aged helpers, David Graber and Nahum Grzywacz. They concealed the documents in the Borochov School on Nowolipki 68 and waited for the order to bury them under the school basement. Although exact numbers are difficult to establish, approximately fifty to sixty people (including copiers and transcribers) were involved in some way with the archive, from its beginning in 1940 until the ghetto uprising in 1943.

The Oyneg Shabes had more luck in saving documents than in saving people. Although thousands of pages survived in the tin boxes and in the milk cans (a significant part of the archive was most certainly lost), little more than random traces remain of the men and women who wrote the documents, gathered them, copied them, and hid them. As most of the Oyneg Shabes collaborators died with their entire families, few survivors could provide more than the barest biographical details of those who perished. The fate of the Oyneg Shabes collective reflected the fate of interwar Polish Jewry: the destruction was so complete and so calamitous that all too often only disconnected scraps of information remained. The few biographies of those who contributed to the archive, published largely in Yiddish books and journals, are short and sketchy, some little more than a paragraph, and often they are little more than hagiographies.

Some members of the Oyneg Shabes did not even have the luck to find some small memorial in an article or biographical dictionary. Those who wrote in Polish fell between the cracks: they did not merit entries in the standard Yiddish literary lexicons, nor were they famous enough for inclusion in the biographical dictionaries of Polish literature. There are scant details on the young student Salomea Ostrowska, a productive worker in the archive. Stanisław Różycki, an important essayist has left no traces beyond his penetrating essays on the ghetto streets and on his experiences in Soviet-occupied Lwów. Many members of the archive left little more than a name. Hardly any had a grave. Only three survived: Hersh Wasser, his wife Bluma, and Rachel Auerbach.

Only a small inner circle—the so-called executive committee—knew the entire scope of the archive's agendas and membership. Most Oyneg Shabes work proceeded on a need-to-know basis. Once contributors received an assignment, they were not supposed to discuss it with anyone, even if they suspected that their interlocutor was also working for the archive. They did know, however, that a secret organization with a national mission had asked them for help.

The Oyneg Shabes, although a diverse group, had particular characteristics. Although several contributors, such as Daniel Fligelman, were totally unknown figures before the war and were "discovered" by the Oyneg Shabes through the Aleynhilf or the refugee committees in the Warsaw Ghetto, Ringelblum had managed to assemble an executive committee of stature and achievement. It included prominent prewar communal leaders and well-to-do businessmen. Virtually all members of the executive committee of the Oyneg Shabes had been active in prewar Jewish cultural life. In the ghetto, the entire executive committee also served in the leadership of the Aleynhilf. Apart from the executive committee, most Oyneg Shabes collaborators were teachers, economists, and journalists, all recruited from the Jewish intelligentsia.

If any one prewar institution shaped the ethos of the Oyneg Shabes it was clearly the YIVO Institute, for prior to the war several members had worked in some way for the YIVO, in its Warsaw branch, in Lodz, or in Vilna. These included Ringelblum, Hersh Wasser, Eliyahu Gutkowski, Yitzhak Giterman, Abraham Lewin, Shie Rabinowitz, Shmuel Winter, Aaron Koninski, Shimon Huberband, Menakhem Linder, Rachel Auerbach, Cecylia Słapakowa, Jerzy Winkler, Yitzhak Bernstein, Yehezkiel Wilczynski, and others. Many were scholars in their own right who had already published work on history, literature, folklore, or economics. In the YIVO they had by now seen that political differences need not preclude collaboration to advance Yiddish culture. The Oyneg Shabes merely extended a path that they had already chosen.

But Ringelblum understood that the archive could work only by reaching out and recruiting new members. Hersh Wasser, one of the two secretaries of the Oyneg Shabes, recalled that Ringelblum had told him that the archive had to become "the property of the entire Jewish people [der kinyn fun gantsn yidishn folk]." There could be no room for ideological and political quarrels. Anyone whom the staff considered a valuable worker and able to keep secrets was eligible for membership. According to Wasser, Ringelblum never wanted the archive to be known as a Left Poalei Tsiyon archive, or even an archive with any ideological slant or bias.[2] If YIVO activists were overrepresented in the leadership of the Oyneg Shabes, they still made room for fervent champions of Hebrew (Eliezer Lipe Bloch) and for Jewish poets and writers who wrote in Polish (Henryka Lazowert, Gustawa Jarecka).

Wasser recalled that the executive committee, as part of this effort to make the Oyneg Shabes as inclusive as possible, reached out to the strongest and best-organized political party in the ghetto—the Bund. The Bund refused the Oyneg Shabes request to work together and set up its own archive.[3] As usual the Bund preferred to work alone, especially when the potential partners were Zionists or, worse, members of the LPZ, with whom the Bund had long had chilly relations.[4] But even though the Bund as a party decided to go its own way, several Bundists worked in the Oyneg Shabes Archive on their own, such as Shie Rabinowitz, who was on the executive committee; David Cholodenko, who was a judge in literary contests; Leyb Goldin, who contributed a valuable fictionalized essay on hunger; and Yehezkiel Wilczynski, who conducted interviews, transcribed documents, and left many of his own studies on the history of Polish Jewry. Furthermore, it is entirely probable—as is discussed in the next chapter—that, when news first reached the ghetto of the Nazis' extermination program, the Bund and the Oyneg Shabes worked together to inform Jews abroad and the Polish Government-in-Exile in London.[5]

Communists also joined the Oyneg Shabes. One of the most important editors of the underground Communist press in the ghetto, Yehuda Feld (whose real name was Yehuda Feldworm) played a significant role in the archive. Feld worked in the CENTOS, had extensive contact with children and refugees, and filed important and informative reports on them for the Oyneg Shabes. He also compiled a collection of short stories of ghetto life, *In di tsaytn fun Homen dem tsveytn* (In the days of Haman the Second).[6]

Ringelblum had been preparing for the archive as soon as the war began. Shortly before the Germans invaded Poland, he began a diary. This diary revealed very little about his personal emotions and practically nothing about his family. Especially in the first year of the war, it resembled the random notes and jottings of a historian who was planning a major book after the war. By day Ringelblum heard countless stories from the hundreds of people who passed through the offices of the Aleynhilf; at night he recorded them in his diary.[7]

German soldiers, in the year prior to the ghetto's establishment, frequently raided Jewish apartments to requisition them or in search of valuables. In those circumstances, Ringelblum believed, most Jews were too scared to write. Instead of keeping diaries and journals, prominent journalists and writers burned incriminating papers and books.[8] Therefore Ringelblum began keeping records in his diary fully aware that he bore a special responsibility to document events that would otherwise be forgotten.

He quickly realized, however, that these fears were exaggerated. Although the Germans did all they could in the first months of the occupation to destroy the Polish political underground, they cared little about what the Jews wrote or said. When they raided Jewish homes, they were interested in valuables, not manuscripts.[9]

That being the case, Ringelblum believed that it was feasible to organize an underground archive to study Jewish life under the Nazi occupation and to collect documentation. He knew from the beginning that it had to be a collective enterprise. No one individual could even begin to think about interviewing sources, gathering documents, and ensuring that the material would remain hidden and secure. On November 22, 1940, he convened a meeting that formally organized the archive.[10]

Over time Ringelblum and his associates built this "band of comrades" by a process of trial and error. Several people disappointed him and were quietly dropped. Others, totally unknown before the war, became indispensable. Today it is clear that the Oyneg Shabes succeeded in part because alongside an executive committee that provided direction and focus, many of the members of the archive wrote on topics they chose themselves. This interplay of central direction, focused research, and individual initiative produced an enormous variety of material. Thanks to the Oyneg Shabes, a large number of very different people, with diverse points of view and interests, ensured breadth of coverage and a variety of opinions and approaches. In the middle of a war, Ringelblum believed, it was best to cast as wide a net as possible. How could one know, after all, what information future historians would find "important"? In the archive Ringelblum came closest to realizing his prewar dream of a history "of the people and by the people."

THE SECRETARIES

The two most important members of the Oyneg Shabes, apart from Ringelblum, were both refugees from Lodz: Eliyahu Gutkowski and Hersh Wasser. Gutkowski and Wasser were the co-secretaries who ran the daily affairs of the Oyneg Shabes.[11] Once the executive committee decided to send someone on an interview, or to solicit a particular essay, usually Wasser or Gutkowski followed through, routinely working with Ringelblum to draw up the research agendas and questionnaires that became so important when the archive decided to complement *zamling* with focused studies of Jewish life under the Nazi occupation. Evidence suggests that it was Wasser who took the actual archival materials to Israel Lichtenstein at the Borochov school on Nowolipki

68.[12] Wasser's wife, Bluma, not only interviewed but also joined a pool of typists who made duplicate and triplicate copies of the testimonies and accounts streaming into the archive. When the staff at the Jewish Historical Institute in Warsaw opened the first tin boxes of documents in September 1946, Rachel Auerbach recognized the telltale notebooks that Gutkowski would distribute to writers who received assignments from the Oyneg Shabes. Gutkowski, she recalled, would also come around to prod writers to stay on task and meet their deadlines.

Wasser had been a member of Ringelblum's party, the LPZ, and an important leader of its Lodz organization. An economist by training, he had also directed the party's Borochov library in Lodz. In December 1939 he and his wife decided to flee Lodz for Warsaw. After a harrowing train ride, where German soldiers beat and robbed passengers, the Wassers arrived in Warsaw. Hersh Wasser went immediately to Ringelblum, who recruited him for the Aleynhilf.[13] Wasser ran the landsmanshaft department, which directed the refugee organizations based on town of origin. This very important job gave him valuable contacts with the hordes of refugees pouring into Warsaw. Thanks to Wasser the Oyneg Shabes could now collect a wealth of data about what had been happening to Jews in the provinces.

Wasser kept lists of Oyneg Shabes collaborators and distributed small stipends to them.[14] He also maintained a running inventory of material flowing into the archive.[15] Later on, after news arrived of the "Final Solution," Wasser, along with Ringelblum and Gutkowski, compiled Oyneg Shabes bulletins on the mass murders and put together reports to be sent abroad.

Alongside his work in the Oyneg Shabes, Wasser remained active in the LPZ. According to his daughter, Leah, he was passionately devoted to his movement—before, during, and even after the war.[16] He helped edit its underground press and sat on its Central Committee. In the second half of 1942, as a representative of the LPZ, he attended key meetings that concerned the ŻOB, the Jewish Fighting Organization.[17] Thus Wasser constituted one of several links that would develop between the Jewish resistance movement and the Oyneg Shabes.

During the ghetto uprising, Wasser fell into the hands of the Germans who put him on a train to Treblinka. He jumped from the train and made his way back to Warsaw.[18] He and his wife eventually found a hideout in the northern part of Warsaw. They shared it with Hersh Berlinski, the former commander of the LPZ fighting groups in the ghetto uprising; Pola Elster, a charismatic party leader who had escaped from the Poniatowa labor camp in 1943; and Eliyahu Erlich, a party member. On September 1944 the Germans discovered their hideout. In the shootout that followed, Berlinski, Elster, and

Erlich were killed, but Wasser and his wife survived.[19] It was thanks to Wasser, who owed his life to a series of miracles, that the Oyneg Shabes Archive was eventually discovered.

The other secretary of the archive, Eliyahu Gutkowski, had been a leading member of the Right Poalei Tsiyon.[20] Gutkowski's prominence in the Oyneg Shabes reflected Ringelblum's determination to put aside political differences for a common cause. Like Wasser, Gutkowski had lived in Lodz, where he acquired a solid reputation as a teacher and as an expert in Hebrew culture. He received much of his Hebrew erudition from his father, Rabbi Jacob Gutkowski, and had lived in Palestine for many years.

Gutkowski was a gifted writer who had worked in his party's press. It was probably thanks to Gutkowski that the Oyneg Shabes managed to recruit one of its best writers, Peretz Opoczynski, who had worked alongside Gutkowski in the Right Poalei Tsiyon's major newspaper, *Dos vort.*

Like Wasser, Gutkowski did not let his ties to the Oyneg Shabes interfere with his political activities. In the ghetto he helped edit the major underground newspaper of the Right Poalei Tsiyon. He also drew closer to one of the most important youth organizations in the ghetto, Dror-Frayhayt.[21] While political and perhaps personal considerations prevented some of Dror's leaders from entirely trusting Ringelblum, they did feel quite close to Gutkowski.[22] In time, as the idea of resistance crystallized, these connections to the youth movements would become very important to the Oyneg Shabes.

Especially warm relations developed between Gutkowski and Dror's Yitzhak Zuckerman, who would later serve as deputy commander of the ŻOB.[23] Zuckerman recruited Gutkowski to help teach seminars that Dror organized in the ghetto. Together they compiled an anthology of Jewish history and martyrdom, *Payn un gvure* (Pain and heroism), that was avidly studied in Dror's seminars.[24]

The ninety-eight-page anthology was a rich collection of historical and literary writings on the Crusades, the expulsion from Spain, the Khmelnitsky massacres, the pogroms of 1903–21, World War I, and Jewish fighters in mandatory Palestine. It certainly attested to Gutkowski's deep knowledge of Jewish literature and history—and perhaps underscored why he would see the Oyneg Shabes as a national mission of critical importance. Precisely at the time the Germans were trying to crush the spirit of the Jews, the study of Jewish history could remind them that the Jews belonged to a great nation. Issued in the summer of 1940, just following the fall of France, *Payn un gvure* admitted that there seemed to be little hope for the Jewish People in this most difficult period of their history. The Nazis seemed to be winning everywhere. However,

we Jews, an ancient nation rich in culture, with a great spiritual tradition from which we draw enormous strength—we Jews cannot and do
not want to perish. During our three-thousand-year history we have gone
through many difficult times—sometimes even harder than now. But
we have survived, much to the dismay and outrage of our oppressors.
The history of our nation shows that we are a great people. . . . One can
oppress such a people only for a short time, but it is impossible to wipe
it off the face of the earth. . . . This [collection] will instill in us a will to
live and a determination to hang on in this difficult time. Our forefathers
died as martyrs and withstood terrible tortures because they believed in
a higher idea. With all our successes and failures, we are like the mythic
phoenix that rises again from the dust.[25]

After the war Zuckerman recalled that the anthology made an enormous impact on the members of the youth movements. But, as time went on, it was
also a reminder that what they were experiencing was entirely unprecedented.
Whatever the lessons were of Jewish history and literature, Zuckerman believed that they were of limited value in the Warsaw Ghetto, with one exception: the lesson that Jews had to fight for their honor.[26]

Gutkowski constantly pumped Zuckerman for material for the Oyneg
Shabes, and after the war Zuckerman found many of his seminar notes in
the archive.[27] Thanks to Gutkowski, the Oyneg Shabes was probably able to
procure several important ghetto writings of the Hebrew-Yiddish poet Yitzhak Katzenelson. In the Warsaw Ghetto, Katzenelson was like a member of
the Dror family.[28] Gutkowski's links to this dynamic youth movement would
complement Ringelblum's growing ties to Dror's main rival, the radical-left
Hashomer Hatzair.

Gutkowski himself wrote extensively for the archive. He composed a long
memoir of Lodz Jewry during the early days of the German occupation, and
in 1941 and 1942 he compiled important essays on economic trends in the
ghetto and on currency trading. When the Oyneg Shabes began its systematic study of Jewish life under the occupation ("Two and a Half Years"), Gutkowski wrote many of the detailed questionnaires that guided interviewers.
In the spring of 1942 he wrote reports that summarized the development of
the German extermination program.

During the Great Deportation, Gutkowski, like many other members of
the Oyneg Shabes, found temporary shelter in the woodworking shop run
by Alexander Landau on Gęsia 30. Deeply concerned about his own survival and about hiding his only son, Gutkowski still continued to work for
the Oyneg Shabes. In early September the Germans sent him to the Umschlagplatz. On the train to Treblinka, he found himself in the same boxcar

as Michael Mazor, who had worked with Ringelblum in the house committees, and Nathan Asz, a functionary in the Aleynhilf.[29] They noticed that
the barbed wire that sealed the opening of the boxcar was loose and jumped
from the train. Gutkowski made his way back to Warsaw and rejoined the archive. He was probably killed in the ghetto uprising in April 1943 at the age
of thirty-nine, together with his wife, Luba, and their four-year-old son, Gabriel-Ze'ev. According to Zuckerman, they died trying to escape the burning
ghetto through the sewers.

THE PROTECTORS

The Oyneg Shabes executive committee charted policy and raised money.
The membership of this committee shifted over time, but it included Ringelblum, Wasser, Gutkowski, Yitzhak Giterman, Menakhem Mendel Kon, Shie
Rabinowitz, Shmuel Winter, Alexander Landau, Lipe Bloch, Daniel Guzik,
Abraham Lewin, and others. The Oyneg Shabes badly needed people who
were well connected, relatively wealthy, and powerful enough to protect it
from outside interference. All the members of the executive committee were
in a position to provide this help, and they were all committed to Ringelblum's project. The account book of the Oyneg Shabes showed that, in particular, Landau, Winter, and Rabinowitz contributed sizable amounts regularly to the archive's treasury (more on this in the next chapter).

Menakhem Mendel Kon

Ringelblum and Wasser agreed that when it came to keeping the Oyneg
Shabes in business, few people were more important than Menakhem Mendel Kon (1881–1943). The archive's treasurer and one of its chief fund-raisers,
Kon also had to keep key members of the Oyneg Shabes alive. When Peretz
Opoczynski and Rabbi Shimon Huberband contracted typhus in the course
of their work, Kon procured expensive medicines and arranged for extra food
rations to enable them to recover.

In a diary entry of May 27, 1942, Hersh Wasser wrote:

> I am very upset that our dear Menakhem Kon is still here in the rot-
> ten ghetto. He needs, according to his doctor's advice, a sanatorium and
> fresh air. I'm going mad looking for a way to get him to Otwock. All his
> reservations, all prompted by legitimate worries about his obligations and
> responsibilities, must be waived because his health is the guarantee of
> Oyneg Shabes work. Without him it vanishes like a soap bubble. A per-
> son of such heart and character as Kon must be guarded like a precious

gem. Together with me, Rabbi Huberband is also looking for a solution. I hope we will persuade him in the end.[30]

Kon, like many others, emerged from obscurity to leadership in the ghetto. A native of Ostrołęka, he had been a wealthy merchant who arrived in Warsaw as a refugee. Ringelblum got to know him in the Aleynhilf, where he acted as a gadfly who called on his colleagues to spend less time on meetings and more on actually helping the poor.[31] Kon seems to have had good contacts with religious circles in the ghetto.[32] Rabbi Huberband, he wrote in his diary, was "his best friend."[33]

Kon saw the Oyneg Shabes as a vital national mission:

> I consider it a sacred duty for everyone, whether proficient or not, to write down everything he has seen or heard from others about what the Germans have done. . . . It must all be recorded without a single fact left out. And when the time comes—as it surely will—let the world read and know what the murderers have done. When the mourners write about this time, this will be their most important material. When those who will avenge us will come to settle accounts, they will be able to rely on [our writings].[34]

Among the many documents that Kon deposited with the Oyneg Shabes was a fragmentary diary that he kept of his experiences during the Great Deportation. This diary contained some negative, even damning judgments about Jewish behavior, but a basic rule of the archive was to record everything— good and bad. In the middle of panic and despair, fighting to stay alive and avoid German manhunts, Kon wrote down what he saw and felt—constant fear and often bitter disappointment in his fellow Jews.

The roundups and blockades produced such panic that even Kon, a respected and well-known figure in the ghetto, was refused help by close friends. On August 6, 1942, he found himself in the middle of a German roundup. Desperately seeking a hiding place, he found a cellar but decided to leave it to make room for children. ("The children should be saved before anyone else.") He then ran to the carpentry shop of Alexander Landau on Gęsia 30, where he had many friends and which would soon shelter the remnants of the Oyneg Shabes and the leaders of key Zionist youth movements. But on that day friendship counted for less than terror. (This may have been just after the German raid on the shop described by Natan Eck; see below.) In an unemotional tone Kon recounted how his friends turned him away, probably afraid that hiding an elderly man without documents might compromise their own illusory security in the shop. ("I see that there is no place for me;

my friends of yesterday are casting such eyes on me, strange, unrecognizing pricking looks . . . as if I had intruded by force into their territory where they have the exclusive right to be. One has to run somewhere else.")[35] Back on the street, Kon soon encountered Ringelblum and Lipe Bloch, both distraught and afraid that their families had been captured. Finally, Kon found a hiding place: at Nowolipki 68, the "safe house" of the Oyneg Shabes, where Israel Lichtenstein, David Graber, and Nahum Grzywacz took him in and gladly gave him food and shelter. Just a couple of days before, Lichtenstein and the two boys had buried the first cache of the Oyneg Shabes Archive.

Kon found a job in Emil Weitz's brush factory, where he worked alongside Rabbi Huberband. But illusions of safety quickly vanished. Kon witnessed the SS select Huberband for death, and on September 7 he fell into the German net. Driven under a hail of blows to the Umschlagplatz, Kon told the people around him to escape. ("We should rather be killed on the spot than go to the death camp.") Kon dropped his bags, dashed off, dodged German bullets, and returned to the brush factory, hoping to hide there. In his last diary entry, on October 1, 1942, Kon wrote that the remnants of Polish Jewry were going to their deaths with one hope—that after the war the Jewish people would exact retribution and justice. That, he wrote, was the main reason why Jews had to keep writing down what they were seeing. Kon continued to work for the archive until his death in April 1943.

Shmuel Winter

Like Kon, Shmuel Winter (1891–1943), another important member of the executive committee, arrived in the Warsaw Ghetto from the provinces early in the war. Born in Włocławek in 1891, Winter grew up in a rabbinic family and received a traditional religious education before he left for Frankfurt to study commerce. Winter made his fortune exporting grain and seeds, and headed one of Poland's largest import-export firms, Nasiona. He occupied major positions in both Polish and Jewish business organizations and served as one of the leaders of the Jewish Merchants Union (Yidisher Soykhrim Fareyn).

Shmuel Winter defied established stereotypes.[36] He was a wealthy businessman who contributed to the socialist Bund. According to Rachel Auerbach, Winter helped the Bund because of its stance on Yiddish culture rather than its politics.

> Winter probably had his political sympathies . . . but just like a faithful husband is [true to only one woman], Winter devoted his entire passion and his heart to one idea—secular Jewish culture. He carried on his

shoulders the burden of responsibility for its very existence, for its every need. And because he left no heirs, no political party to bask in his achievements and in his memory, his name has been forgotten.[37]

The Jewish business elite of central Poland was largely Polish-speaking, but Winter's stubborn insistence on using Yiddish in his business dealings and on his letter heads earned him the sobriquet "Don Quixote." Winter was one of the founders of the YIVO and served on its executive board. It was the YIVO that brought Winter, Giterman, and Ringelblum together long before the war began. Even as his business prospered, Winter found the time to *zaml* for the YIVO and to publish many articles in the *YIVO bleter* and the Yiddish press on Jewish folklore and Yiddish literature. Max Weinreich recalled that he had a particular interest in Yiddish dialects, especially his own Kujawy patois. Winter became a regular contributor to the *Vilner tog,* a newspaper known for its high standards and interest in Yiddish culture.[38] He also amassed an enormous private library of thousands of volumes. In addition to folklore, he loved Jewish history. When the war began, he had still not completed a project he had been working on for many years—a history of the Jews of the Kujawy region.

Winter arrived in the Warsaw Ghetto with his wife and three children early in the war and became part of the Oyneg Shabes inner circle as well as a mainstay of the IKOR, the Yiddish cultural organization. With Winter, the Oyneg Shabes made a glaring exception to its ironclad rule barring collaboration with people who had ties to the Judenrat. The Judenrat, probably impressed with his prewar standing in the business community, recruited him to a key post in the semi-autonomous and critical Department of Provisioning and Supply (Zakład Zaopatrywania [ZZ]), which became an independent agency in September 1941.[39] There he worked closely with the respected Abraham Gepner, who headed the ZZ and was also one of the most important Judenrat members. Winter thus served as an indispensable unofficial link between the "official community" and the Aleynhilf, since he was able to help procure food allotments for the soup kitchens—and, one can assume, to funnel information to Ringelblum about Judenrat intentions.[40]

The Israeli historian Israel Gutman, whom Winter helped in the ghetto after he lost his family, recalled that,

> [Winter] was a special kind of character in the Ghetto, even in his external appearance. He was very tall, with a wide back that was curved like a round bow. He was always looking toward the ground. A huge nose jutted out of his yellowish face and perched on it were a pair of spectacles.[41]

Two of Winter's sons were in the Hashomer Hatzair, despite their father's op-position to Zionism.[42] In time this would create an important personal link between Winter and the resistance movement.

Available evidence suggests that Winter's role in the Oyneg Shabes be-came especially vital after the Great Deportation of 1942. In the shrunken and devastated ghetto, Winter continued to work for the ZZ. After September 1942 normal movement in the ghetto was no longer possible. The ghetto had been split up into isolated blocks of "shops"; one needed special passes to go from one to the other. Right after the Great Deportation Ringelblum and Lichtenstein were in Bernhard Hallman's carpentry shop on Nowolipki 59, close to the site where Lichtenstein had buried the first part of the archive. Wasser and Gutkowski were at Alexander Landau's shop, the OBW (Ost-deutsche Bautischlerei-Werkstätte), on Gęsia 30. On the pretext of arranging supply matters for their shop kitchens, the leaders of the Oyneg Shabes could come to Winter's Office on Franciszkańska 30, where they could also discuss and exchange archival material. Winter provided money and food for Ringel-blum and his staff—and a priceless telephone to communicate with the Ary-an side.[43] He could also procure jobs for people whom the Oyneg Shabes wanted to save—such as Rachel Auerbach and Shie Perle. It was through Winter's telephone, with its link to Adolf Berman (who had left for the other side in September) that Ringelblum, Auerbach, and others were able to pre-pare their eventual escape from the ghetto.

In the fall of 1942 Winter arranged a job for Auerbach to provide cover for her new Oyneg Shabes assignment—to collect and write down the stories of various Jews who had escaped from Treblinka. Now Auerbach saw him more often. He was now living in a small apartment with his surviving son Julek, his daughter Marysia and her beau.

The charred, fragmentary pages of Winter's diary reveal the terrible pain of his last months. During the Great Deportation the Germans had sent his wife, Tobke, and his youngest son, Heniek, to Treblinka, and he felt guilty that he had failed to save them.[44] He wrote that he could not sleep and was in such great emotional pain that he was ready for the end. But then he revealed: "I don't want to leave the world when we can see from afar . . . a possibility to live to see . . . revenge against the killers." According to Ber Mark, Winter expressed a deep faith in the Soviet Union and was angry at the Western al-lies for allegedly dragging their feet in fighting the Germans.[45]

When the first armed resistance electrified the ghetto on January 18, 1943, Winter was still unsure whether it was more important to fight or to preserve the Oyneg Shabes—which an all-out battle might endanger.[46] But within a couple of days he expressed full support for the young fighters. He only regretted that, during the Great Deportation, hundreds of thousands of Warsaw Jews had let themselves be taken like sheep to the slaughter and had failed to put up any resistance. But now, in January, the young fighters were helping to save Jews. Thanks to them, the Germans were afraid to go into the cellars and hideouts to look for hidden victims. Firmly committed to resistance, Winter joined a committee that included Ringelblum and that collected money to buy weapons for the Jewish Fighting Organization. He handled large sums, and even complained in his diary that he was not used to taking and handing over so much money without a paper record.[47] He also sent consignments of bread to the ŻOB.

Although other Jewish leaders were now beginning to look for hideouts on the Aryan side, Winter adamantly refused to leave the doomed ghetto. Auerbach urged him to try to get out:

> "What do you mean leave? Not everyone has the right to just pick up and go. What will happen to those who have no way of getting out?"
>
> "But isn't there some fund to help people get out?"
>
> When I mentioned this fund, which was supposedly set up to help the intellectual and political elite to escape, Winter became even angrier and his face grew red.
>
> "Who should take it upon themselves the right to decide who goes and who stays?"[48]

Unquestionably tension was developing in those final weeks between Winter, who was ready to die in the ghetto, and Ringelblum, who was torn between his desire to save his wife and child and his sense of duty. Ringelblum wanted to collect money to save "the intellectual and political elite." Winter preferred to collect money for arms.[49] And in another fragment of his diary, Winter complained that, in the general rush to leave the ghetto, some leaders of the Oyneg Shabes were forgetting their higher responsibilities to the archive.[50] Ringelblum had already sent his wife and son out of the ghetto. He joined them in a hideout on the Aryan side sometime in February 1943, but he made frequent forays back into the ghetto and was trapped there when the uprising began on April 19, 1943.

When the uprising broke out on April 19 Winter joined his surviving children in a well-equipped bunker under Franciszkańska 30. After some persuasion, a proud Abraham Gepner also joined them. Israel Gutman recalled that, in the first few days of the battle of the ghetto, as the buildings aboveground went up in smoke and the air inside the bunker turned acrid and it was difficult to breathe, Winter sat in a corner and wrote in his diary. After Gutman was wounded in the eye, Winter came to visit him, and it would be their last meeting. For the first time Winter spoke to the young Gutman as an equal. His life was finished, the older man told him, and besides, after the loss of his wife and son, he was a broken man. But one question bothered him and gave him no rest: Where was the outside world as the Jews went to their deaths?

> They, the Jews abroad and the world in general know what [is happening here]. We hear the radio station Świt boast about the uprising in the Warsaw Ghetto. So if they know, what are they doing, how are they reacting? Do they just get out of bed, read the newspapers, drink their morning coffee, and complain about the bad weather? Does nothing bother them? Does not one bit of our pain reach them? . . . [Winter] wanted to ask Jews after the war, what did they do?[51]

After the war Rachel Auerbach heard from the Bundist fighter Marek Edelman how Winter had died. On May 3, 1943, Edelman and his fighters saw from their perch on Franciszkańska 30 how the Germans discovered the bunker where Winter, Gepner, and other Jews were hiding. They threw tear gas into the opening, and the Jews began to crawl out. Edelman saw Winter and Gepner marched away, along with the others.[52]

Alexander Landau

Another major protector of the Oyneg Shabes, also a member of its executive committee, was Alexander Landau. An engineer by training, Landau had established a successful lumber factory before the war. In his youth he had been a member of the Poalei Tsiyon, and in the years before the war he had drawn closer to the pioneer youth organization He-haluts.[53] Landau became an important member of the Aleynhilf in the ghetto and also continued to run his woodworking establishment. According to Natan Eck, since the factory was formally owned by a brother who lived in the United States, the Germans did not confiscate it until the U.S. entered the war. After December 1941, although it now assumed a new German name, Ostdeutsche Bautischlerei Werkstätte, the Landau brothers continued to run it.[54]

Unlike many Jewish entrepreneurs in the ghetto, Landau used his energy, money, and contacts to encourage civic and later armed resistance. After the beginning of the Great Deportation, many activists of the Oyneg Shabes and the youth movements found a refuge in Landau's shop on 30 Gęsia Street. Landau gave them papers that offered at least temporary exemption from deportation. Although he could have earned enormous sums of money by selling these precious places in his shop, he apparently helped activists without taking any compensation. Natan Eck arrived at Landau's shop in early August with his wife and child. He begged Landau to let him in. The shop was crammed with people. Landau reproached him for not coming earlier, when it might have been easier to find him a place. Nevertheless, he agreed to take him in.

Many of Landau's "real" workers—carpenters and woodworkers—deeply resented what their boss was doing. They believed that he was endangering their lives to save intellectuals and activists. In early August 1942 Germans and Ukrainians entered the shop and seized a large number of men, women, and children who had found refuge in an inner courtyard and thought they were safe. After they left, the Jewish craftsmen blamed Landau for the tragedy and started a riot. Unless Landau convinced the Germans to release their wives and children, the workers threatened, they would tell the SS that he was using the shop to shelter outsiders. Landau tried to use his contacts with the Germans, but it was too late to save the women and children. In the end the workers did not carry out their threat.[55]

In fact, any safety Landau could provide was only temporary. When SS barged into shops and snatched Jews for deportation, they rarely bothered with such details as actual work skills or documents. On January 18, 1943, during the so-called Second Action, when the Germans met with armed resistance, Landau himself was hustled off to the Umschlagplatz. He was released a short time later.

Landau's own daughter, Margalit (Emilka), was a member of the Hashomer Hatzair, and her father spared no effort to help the youth movements and, later on, the ŻOB. On January 18 Margalit joined Mordecai Anielewicz and other Jewish fighters who were marching in a column to the Umschlagplatz. When Anielewicz gave the signal Margalit threw a grenade, and the fighters attacked the Germans. Margalit died on the spot. After her death Landau, his wife, and surviving son went over to the Aryan Side. Along with other Jews who had procured foreign passports, including the well-known poet Yitzhak Katzenelson, the Landaus were sent to the internment camp of Vittel, in France. In April 1944 the Nazis shipped them to Drancy and from there to Auschwitz, where they were gassed.[56] People who remembered him from Vittel recalled that he constantly spoke of his daughter.[57]

Shie Rabinowitz (1888–1943)

Like many other members of the Oyneg Shabes executive committee, Shie Rabinowitz had been active in the prewar YIVO. Like Yitzhak Giterman, Rabinowitz was also a scion of the leading Hasidic families of Eastern Europe.[58] To the utter horror of his family, Rabinowitz refused to become a Hasidic rebbe. Instead, he joined the Bund! Arrested during the Revolution of 1905, he was released only thanks to a hefty bribe paid to the Russian police by the Bialer Hasidim.[59]

Although Rabinowitz remained a lifelong Bundist, his real interest was Yiddish culture. Like Winter, Rabinowitz used his successful business—in this case roofing tiles—to finance his support of the YIVO. It was in the Warsaw branch of the YIVO that he likely came to know Ringelblum. One can assume that he was able to keep some of his money in the ghetto, and he gave generously to the Oyneg Shabes.

In the ghetto Rabinowitz also joined the Aleynhilf and IKOR.[60] According to Michael Mazor, Rabinowitz worked closely with him in the Central Commission of House Committees.[61] Just as Winter served as a de facto link between the Judenrat and the Aleynhilf, Rabinowitz possibly played a similar role between the Oyneg Shabes and the Bund.

In January 1943 Rabinowitz and his family tried to hide on the Aryan side. Disaster soon overtook them. The Gestapo caught his wife and younger daughter and shot them. Rabinowitz returned to the ghetto with his son-in-law and tried to save himself by buying a false South American passport. In 1943 the Germans sent him, along with a group of other Jews who had foreign passports, to Bergen Belsen. Survivors recalled that in the camp Rabinowitz gave lectures on Yiddish culture and Jewish history. On October 11, 1943, the Germans deported him and his son-in-law to Auschwitz—probably in the same transport that included the Yiddish writer Shie Perle and the leader of the LPZ Natan Buchsbaum. The entire transport was gassed.

Lipe Bloch

Ringelblum scored a major coup when he recruited Eliezer Lipe Bloch to serve on the executive committee of the Oyneg Shabes. Bloch had long been a major figure in his own right, an important leader of the General Zionist Party in Poland and the director of its major fund-raising arm, the Keren Kayemet (the Jewish National Fund). Unlike the Yiddishist Ringelblum, Bloch had long been a fervent supporter of Hebrew. Before the war he had helped run the Tarbut, the highly regarded network of Zionist schools in Hebrew.

After the war started he and Ringelbum worked closely in the Aleynhilf, where they shared a common interest in the house committees. They became close friends.[62] Bloch was an excellent speaker, a respected leader, and an amateur scholar who had a deep interest in Jewish history and who appreciated the importance of clandestine documentation. When the Oyneg Shabes planned its major study project, "Two and a Half Years," Bloch was slated to be its coeditor along with Ringelblum (more on this in the next chapter). Needless to say, as the former director of the Keren Kayemet, he was also an experienced fund-raiser. Like many others in the Oyneg Shabes, he enjoyed close relations with a Zionist youth movement—in this case, Dror.[63]

In the weeks before the outbreak of the ghetto uprising Bloch worked on a committee to raise money for the ŻOB. The Germans caught him during the uprising and sent him, along with eight hundred other Jews to the Budzyn labor camp near Lublin, where the German firm Heinkel had an airplane factory.[64] Besides Bloch, this group also included Kolonymous Shapiro, "the Piaseczno rebbe," who was well known for his writings and talks during the war. Adolf Berman tried to rescue Bloch the same way that he had rescued Ringelblum from the Trawniki labor camp—by sending the Polish railway worker Tadeusz Pajewski and his Jewish friend, Emilka Kossower, to smuggle him out. But Bloch and fifteen other Jews—including Rabbi Shapiro—had taken a solemn vow that they would all stay together, come what may. Pajewski could take out no more than two Jews, and certainly not fifteen. In August 1944 the Germans sent Bloch to the feared Mauthausen camp in Austria. He died sometime before the end of the war.

The Young Activists: Joseph Kaplan and Shmuel Breslav

In 1942 the Oyneg Shabes added Joseph Kaplan and Shmuel Breslav, two leaders of the leftist Zionist youth group Hashomer Hatzair, to its executive committee. At first glance this decision is hard to explain. Unlike Bloch or Winter, they were not established businessmen or well-known prewar leaders. But the inclusion of Kaplan and Breslav on the Oyneg Shabes reflected the growing importance of the youth movements in the ghetto. Moreover, by that time Ringelblum had become personally close to the leaders of Hashomer.

Before the war adult leaders and the youth movements usually had little to do with each other. By 1942 the distance had lessened considerably.[65] The youth movements and their couriers became critical sources of information for the Oyneg Shabes after the first reports arrived of German massacres in the eastern territories in the fall of 1941. In time, these youth movements would provide an all-important link between the Oyneg Shabes and the ŻOB.

As Israel Gutman and others have pointed out, the youth movements stood out for their inner cohesion and their ability to maintain intellectual and moral standards in the chaotic and demoralizing conditions of the ghetto. The members, having known one another long before the war began, trusted and relied on one another. They established closely knit communes and for a time even wangled German permission to live and work together on farms outside the ghetto. Until the spring of 1942 the youth groups focused their energies on their clandestine press, underground seminars, and classes.[66] They did not challenge the hegemony of the political parties and showed little interest in competing with them for political leadership. But when news of the mass murders began to penetrate the Warsaw Ghetto, things began to change. The leadership of Dror and Hashomer Hatzair turned away from cultural work and began to prepare for armed resistance. In the process the youth movements acted with growing independence and self-confidence.

In the Warsaw Ghetto the LPZ and Hashomer Hatzair drew closer together, but before the war serious differences had divided these movements. The Hashomer disdained Yiddish, emphasized Hebrew, and infused its young members with a determination to immigrate to Palestine at the earliest possible opportunity. Unlike the LPZ, which reached out to Yiddish-speaking youth from poor families, the Hashomer Hatzair attracted Polish-speaking Jewish youth, many from middle-class backgrounds. It was an elitist movement that had little interest in the *do* (here), the daily life, and the concerns of Polish Jewry. Ringelblum, like many of his party comrades, had believed that the prewar Hashomer prepared *tlushim* (uprooted misfits).[67] Hashomer, its critics in the LPZ charged, imbued its young members with enthusiasm and giddy self-confidence—and then left them uprooted and disappointed. One could not stay young forever, and one could not wait indefinitely for the chance to go to Palestine. Eventually all too many *shomrim* (members of Hashomer) found themselves psychologically unprepared for the hard life of a Jewish young adult in Poland. Once they left the intense experiences of the *ken* (the local Shomer organization) they had nothing to fall back on.

Hashomer and the LPZ started to bury the hatchet with the coming of the war in 1939. Both groups realized that, apart from the Communists, they were the most pro-Soviet organizations in the ghetto. Neither group idealized the Soviet Union, but when the war began both agreed that, whatever its faults, the Soviet Union was the Jews' best hope. True, Britain was fighting Hitler but that did not make London an ally of the Jews. After all, in 1939 Britain had betrayed Zionism with the White Paper. Zionism's best chance depended on the collapse of British rule in the Middle East; only world revolution and the Soviet Union could make that happen.[68]

So while Dror and the Bund supported Britain as she fought alone against Hitler, the LPZ and Hashomer wrote in their underground press about an "imperialist war" between Germany and Britain. Difficult as it may be to believe that these Jews in the Warsaw Ghetto saw no difference between Hitler and Churchill, the fact remains that under the conditions they faced they desperately needed ideological certainties and dogmas that afforded hope and a shred of optimism. Ringelblum did not discuss these views much in his diary, but his party preached these notions in its underground press, which was co-edited by Hersh Wasser.

Once Hitler attacked the Soviet Union in 1941, all Jews naturally hoped for a Red Army victory. Hashomer and the LPZ could now dispense with the unnatural cant about the imperialist war and cheer on a USSR that was allied with Britain and the United States. In March 1942 the LPZ, Hashomer, Dror, and the Right Poalei Tsiyon joined the Communists in the formation of an "Anti-Fascist Bloc." As Raya Cohen has pointed out, the new situation forced Hashomer to become less focused on Palestine and more concerned with the "here": the ghetto, the war, and the situation in Europe.[69] Although the movement's hostility to Yiddish never disappeared, it began to issue a Yiddish publication (*Oyfbroyz*), a sign that for all its elitism and isolation it was at last reaching out to those outside its narrow circle. Thus the ideological gap between Hashomer and the LPZ continued to narrow.

As Ringelblum became personally close to some of the key leaders of Hashomer in the Warsaw Ghetto, they began to invite him to their meetings. In his diary he recorded his growing admiration for the movement's spirit and idealism.[70] Despite the risks, he allowed the Hashomer to use the second floor of the Aleynhilf headquarters on Tłomackie 5 for its meetings, which attracted more than five hundred members. In a diary entry of November 23, 1941, Ringelblum noted "the incredible courage of the members of Hashomer. They are organizing conferences . . . are carrying out a wonderful educational program, and are publishing a journal that is on a very high level."[71]

Ringelblum became especially close to Mordecai Anielewicz and, one can assume, to Breslav and Kaplan as well. In his memoirs Adolf Berman recalls the personal bonds that developed between him and Ringelblum and these young leaders of Hashomer. All three—Anielewicz, Breslav, and Kaplan—would become major proponents of armed resistance, and Anielewicz would lead the Jewish Fighting Organization, the ŻOB. Ringelblum recalled that one time Kaplan and Anielewicz asked him to come to Hashomer's headquarters on Nalewki 23. There they showed him two revolvers which they were using to train young people in the use of weapons.[72]

The impulsive and romantic Breslav, the main editor of Hashomer's clandestine press, was a gifted writer and a born journalist.[73] Zuckerman recalled that he acted "like a young Pole." When the war began, Breslav took the Hashomer flag with him when he fled Warsaw and carried it three hundred miles to Vilna! (The flag eventually made it to Palestine.) On orders from the movement Breslav returned to Warsaw and became one of the most fervent advocates of armed resistance. When the Great Deportation began, he wanted Jews to resist with every means at their disposal, including their bare hands. According to Zuckerman, when the Jewish Fighting Organization was founded six days later, on July 28, 1942, its command staff consisted of himself, Zivia Lubetkin, Breslav, and Joseph Kaplan.[74]

Joseph Kaplan, born in 1913, was older than Anielewicz and Breslav and was one of the most beloved and respected leaders of the Hashomer. Unlike most of his comrades, Kaplan actually liked Yiddish culture and seemed closer to the ordinary Jewish masses.[75] Despite his markedly Jewish appearance, Kaplan fearlessly traveled through occupied Poland, where he visited various branches of Hashomer and relayed information.

The known contributions of these two activists to the archive include an important interview conducted by Breslav of a Polish woman regarding Polish-Jewish relations; a study by Breslav of a young Jewish woman active in the house committees; a large amount of Hashomer Hatzair correspondence and materials; and the bulk of the Hashomer Hatzair illegal press in the ghetto.

The Germans killed Breslav and Joseph Kaplan on the same day, September 3, 1942. According to Zuckerman, a Jewish informer had revealed Kaplan's whereabouts. After the Germans took Kaplan away in a car, Yitzhak Zuckerman rushed to inform Giterman, hoping that Giterman might be able to raise ransom money. That same day Breslav was walking along Gęsia Street with a switchblade in his pocket and spotted a car full of Germans. He and his companion ran, but the Germans caught him. Breslav attacked them with his knife. They beat him to death on the street.

Ten days earlier, in his diary entry of August 24, 1942, Abraham Lewin wrote:

> A meeting of the Oyneg Shabes at the Hashomer Hatzair with the participation of R-m, G-n, G-k, B-ch, L-n, G-ski, W-r, Josef, B-au. Rabbi H. was missing; he had been seized at the broom factory. The place, the time, and the appearance of the participants underline the special tragedy of the meeting.[76] [Josef was Kaplan, B-au was Breslau.]

The Rabbi: Shimon Huberband

In his essay on the Oyneg Shabes Ringelblum recalled that when he first organized the archive, finding good collaborators had been a process of trial and error. Therefore the arrival of Rabbi Shimon Huberband (1909–1942) was especially welcome. Before the war the rabbi had lived in Piotrków but had come to know Ringelblum at the Warsaw branch of the YIVO.[77] Just a few days after the war began German bombs killed Rabbi Huberband's wife and children near Piotrków, but his deep religious faith helped him to bear his loss. In 1940 he moved to Warsaw. Ringelblum found Huberband a job in the Aleynhilf, where the rabbi headed the Department of Religious Affairs. He also remarried.

In the Aleynhilf, more than any other ghetto institution, Orthodox and non-Orthodox Jews worked closely and effectively. Certainly Huberband deserves some of the credit for this. In a moving eulogy for Huberband, delivered shortly after his deportation to Treblinka in August 1942, Menakhem Mendel Kon said:

> Considering his devout piety one could only marvel at his tolerance of [atheists and leftists]. He always looked at the whole man, this is what determined his attitude. He respected his opponent if the latter was sincere in his beliefs. He despised falsehood. A great scholar, highly erudite in the Torah, Mishna, and Talmud, a man of noble virtue, a fervent Hassid with a flaming heart, he nevertheless always tried to use common sense. . . . Every day I would spend a few hours with him on Oyneg Shabes matters—and I can say that Rabbi Huberband was one of the finest personalities of our times. Committed heart and soul to the archive, nothing was too difficult for him. . . . It was Dr. Ringelblum who influenced and guided him in his writing. Woe to you, teacher and master![78]

Before the war many Orthodox journalists and rabbis in prewar Poland had already begun to take their first, halting steps toward modern literature and even secular culture.[79] Without in any way compromising their devotion to the Torah, they began to express an interest in secular Yiddish writing, world literature, and the YIVO.

The YIVO and a shared dedication to the history of Polish Jewry had brought Ringelblum and Huberband together before the war. Both Ringelblum and Isaac Schiper were convinced that the young rabbi had the makings of a superb historian. They were especially excited by Huberband's mastery of rabbinic "Responsa Literature,"[80] which contained a treasure trove of material on the social history of Polish Jewry and had been under-utilized by historians with little yeshiva training. In 1939 Rabbi Huberband published an important study in *Sotsiale meditsin*, titled "Jewish Physicians in Piotrkow from the Seventeenth Century to the Present," where he used both Jewish and non-Jewish sources. But the young rabbi's interests were not confined to history. He showed a deep interest in the problems of reconciling traditional Judaism with modern science and had published an article on the subject. He had also written stories, in Hebrew, about Hasidic life and Talmudic luminaries.[81]

A serious historian who understood the importance of the archive, Huberband was a methodical collaborator and interviewer who carefully adhered to the guidelines worked out by the Oyneg Shabes staff. Discreet and careful, he was afraid at first to write in notebooks; he would scribble his essays in the margins of holy books in case the Germans made a search. (Gradually Ringelblum convinced him that there was little risk.) No one in the Oyneg Shabes worked on as wide a range of topics as Huberband: religious life, labor camps, ghetto folklore, Jewish women, and Jewish life under the Soviet occupation.

Huberband shared with Ringelblum the conviction that the Oyneg Shabes bore a special responsibility to record the German destruction of Jewish synagogues, cemeteries, artwork, and markers of material culture. In a diary entry of February 27–28, 1941, Ringelblum remarked that when the Germans forced Jews to destroy a historical Torah ark in the synagogue in Plonsk, they were also trying to erase the physical evidence of the centuries of Jewish life in Eastern Europe, "in order to show that the Jews were an alien element that had no claims [to live in Poland]".[82] For his part Huberband wrote a special report for the Oyneg Shabes listing what had been destroyed up to then and the steps Jews might take to hide valuable books, documents, and artifacts.[83]

Huberband was most indispensable to the Oyneg Shabes as a conduit to the religious community. He conveyed material on many aspects of religious life under the Nazis. He was especially close to one of the most important religious thinkers in the Warsaw ghetto, Rabbi Kalonymous Shapiro, the Piaseczner Rebbe. It was possibly because of Huberband that the archive procured many of Shapiro's wartime sermons and writings.[84]

Although Ringelblum and Kon remembered Huberband as a self-effacing rabbi and scholar, his writings were often hard-hitting and controversial. Like Ringelblum, Huberband saw himself as a historian, not as a hagiographer, and he pulled no punches. He could describe young Gerer Hasidim as self-centered drunks, and atheistic Bundists as courageous martyrs. Like many other writers in the Oyneg Shabes, Huberband did not believe that German persecution excused Jewish corruption. Some titles of his essays speak for themselves: "Moral Lapses of Jewish Women during the War" and "The Extortion of Money from Jews by Jews." In the latter, Huberband wrote:

The Talmud permits the killing of informers, and that is also the opinion of the Shulkhan Arukh. In the Responsa of Reb Asher b. Jehiel, it is mentioned that Reb Asher ordered an informer's tongue cut off to prevent him from continuing his murderous activity. In the response of Reb

Meir of Lublin the fact is noted that, in the days of R. Shachna of Lublin, Jewish informers were drowned in the *mikveh* [ritual bath]. But today there aren't enough *mikvehs* to suffice for all the Jewish informers.[85]

Huberband's work in the Oyneg Shabes became even more important in light of the widespread agreement among many observers that the war had seen a major decline in religious observance. In a survey of Jewish intellectuals and cultural leaders, discussed further in the next chapter, Hillel Tseitlin had dwelt on the failures of Orthodox Jews. Ringelblum repeatedly noted that during this war, compared to past trials, Orthodox Jews showed much less willingness to become martyrs, that is, to die for Kiddush Hashem, sanctification of the holy name. Huberband did not explicitly defend religious Jewry against these charges. Indeed, he added his own accusations—as seen by his indictment of the young Gerer Hasidim. His work rested on the conviction that ultimately the facts would make a more lasting impression than hagiography or apologetics.

Alongside accounts of corruption and moral decline, Huberband compiled stories of Kiddush Hashem, which, he explained, could be performed in three ways:

> A. a Jew sacrifices his life when others attempt to make him abandon the Jewish faith. B. a Jew gives his life to save a fellow Jew, and even more so—to save a group of Jews. C. a Jew dies while fighting to defend other Jews. Maimonides rules that if a Jew is killed, even without any overt attempt to make him abandon the Jewish faith, but because he is a Jew, he is considered a martyr.[86]

Huberband described the rabbi of Włodawa, Reb Avrom Mordkhe Maroco.

> On the second day of September 1940 a group of officers entered the rabbi's home and carried out a search. During the search they found a Torah scroll. They ordered the rabbi to tear apart the scroll, or else they would burn him alive. The rabbi refused. They poured gasoline on his body and set fire to him alive. When the rabbi was transformed into a blazing torch, they threw the Torah scroll on top of him. The rabbi and the Torah were burned together.[87]

In his essay *Kiddush Hashem* Huberband included secular Jews such as Dr. Josef Parnas, the chairman of the Lwów Judenrat, who refused a Gestapo demand for a list of Jewish professionals and intellectuals. He was hanged. Huberband also mentioned the Bundist leader in Piotrków, Avrom Vayskof, who risked his life to save Torah scrolls.

Thanks to his many contacts in the ghetto, especially in the religious community, Huberband gathered testimonies and accounts that humanized and individualized the tale of collective suffering. In the process he also uncovered important examples of how ordinary Jews faced death with dignity and quiet courage. One such person was Yosef Peykus, who had a wife and a small child and who had borrowed 180 zlotys to sneak out to the Aryan side to buy food for his family. Peykus was caught and was among the first group of Jews sentenced to death by the Germans in November 1941 for leaving the ghetto illegally. From his death cell he wrote a final letter to his wife, which he gave to a rabbi who visited him. The rabbi passed the letter on to Huberband.

Peykus told his wife where he had hidden their nest egg—a sack of jewelry—and reminded her that she had to repay the 180 zlotys that he had borrowed.

> We must pray to God that our son will grow up to be a mensch and that he will know the prayers. . . . If I am shot, may my father arrange a burial plot for me. A separate grave with new shrouds, everything as it should be. Things haven't worked out well; for young blood to go to earth so early. I could still have lived a bit, and instead to be buried in the ground. To be a young widow so early, with a sweet son whose father lies in the ground. . . . This letter is made of blood, not words. If I have done any wrong to my parents, may they forgive me. May Khayele and her daughter forgive me. Shloyme, take care of my wife. Dovid Volfshtayg, I thank you very much for your kind heart, and the deeds you have done for me.[88]

The Oyneg Shabes spared no effort to keep Huberband safe. When the Great Deportation began, the rabbi procured a job in Emil Weitz's brush makers shop. But the SS raided the shop in August 1942, carried out a selection, and sent Huberband directly to the death trains at the Umschlagplatz. There was no time to send someone to try to bribe guards and get him released.[89]

THE TEACHERS

It was only natural that Ringelblum would recruit many teachers to work in the archive: Bernard Kampelmacher, Israel Lichtenstein, Aaron Koninski, and Abraham Lewin. For many years this had been his own milieu; he knew these people and could trust them. Israel Lichtenstein—as the physical guardian of the archives—had perhaps the most sensitive job in the entire Oyneg Shabes; Koninski provided the archive with some of its most valuable material on Jewish children in the ghetto; Lewin served not just as a contributor but as a trusted member of Ringelblum's inner circle; and Kampelmacher had been a respected school principal in Grodzisk before the war, and became an indefatigable collaborator of the Oyneg Shabes after his arrival in the Warsaw Ghetto.

Abraham Lewin

Lewin and Ringelblum were old friends. Both had been teachers at the Yehudiah high school for girls in Warsaw; the students deeply respected Lewin, a master teacher who was able to establish a unique rapport with his pupils.[90] Lewin headed the youth division of the Aleynhilf in the ghetto and was one of the archive's most important members. Not only did he do a great deal of interviewing but he also kept a diary that Ringelblum considered one of the most important holdings of the Oyneg Shabes.[91]

Lewin was a firm believer in the importance of cultural resistance, and knew Jewish history and Hebrew well.[92] Both he and his wife, Luba, were children of the Polish Orthodox Jewish elite who had found their way to Zionism and to modern secular culture. Luba, the daughter of a famous rabbi, even went to Palestine to settle on a kibbutz, but poor health forced her to return. The couple had one daughter, Ora, who would later join Hashomer Hatzair. All three would perish.

Lewin and Ringelblum differed politically—Lewin was a General Zionist, a party detested by the Left Poalei Tsiyon—but both men shared a passion for Jewish history and they had worked together in the Warsaw branch of the YIVO. Like Ringelblum, Lewin "lived" Jewish history. He was especially moved by its pathos and by the suffering of the "forgotten Jews," the Jewish poor.

In 1934 he published *Kantonistn,* which he called a history book "of the folk for the folk."[93] This was a survey of the dreaded *rekrutchina,* the impressment of Jewish boys into the Russian army during the reign of Nicholas I (1825–1855). What had prompted Lewin to write the book was a passage in the memoirs of the famous Russian revolutionary Alexander Herzen. Herzen had described a convoy of young Jewish boys, who would probably never see their homes again, and the image of those children gave Lewin no rest.[94]

Kantonistn, less a historical monograph than a large anthology of contemporary memoirs and folk songs, documented the trauma suffered by the poorest sectors of the Jewish population. Like much of Ringelblum's own work, Lewin's *Kantonistn* had a marked populist tilt, with the Jewish masses cast as heroes and the Jewish elite as villains. Rich Jews, Lewin charged, protected their own children at the expense of the poor. They hired kidnappers (*khapers* in Yiddish) to track down their prey and wrest them from the arms of their desperate and helpless parents. For Lewin, the *rekrutchina* represented one of the greatest national calamities in modern Jewish history precisely because of the breakdown of national solidarity and the moral failure of the Jewish elite. Indeed, Lewin wondered why Jewish historians had not written more about this disaster, which he compared to the expulsion from Spain in 1492 and the Khmelnitsky massacres of the seventeenth century.

> We should gather all the tears of the Jewish children of that time in one
> cup and put it alongside all the other cups overflowing with our blood
> and tears from previous persecutions. Our people should never forget its
> young martyrs.[95]

In the ghetto both Ringelblum and Lewin would draw parallels between the *khapers* and the behavior of the Judenrat and the Jewish police.[96] If Lewin could be moved so deeply by a nineteenth-century Russian's depiction of Jewish suffering, then one can well imagine how he reacted to the Warsaw Ghetto—and later to the deportation of his beloved wife in the summer of 1942. His moral sensitivity and willingness to commit his innermost feelings to paper made him an especially valuable member of the Oyneg Shabes and lent his Warsaw Ghetto diary extraordinary power.

Lewin recorded honestly a subject that surfaced only rarely in the ghetto diaries: his own personal fear.[97] As the German vise tightened, his terror grew. On May 16, 1942, with reports flooding into the Oyneg Shabes about German massacres in the provinces, Lewin wrote:

> An unremitting insecurity, a never-ending fear, is the most terrible aspect
> of all our tragic and bitter experiences. If we ever live to see the end of
> this cruel war and are able as free people and citizens to look back on the
> war years that we have lived through, then we will surely conclude that
> the most terrible and unholy, the most destructive aspect for our nervous
> system and our health was to live night and day in an atmosphere of un-
> ending fear and terror for our physical survival, in a continual wavering
> between life and death—a state where every passing minute brought with
> it the danger that our hearts would literally burst with fear and dread.
> (p. 73)

Whereas Ringelblum rarely abandoned the tone and voice of the objective historian, Lewin gave the Oyneg Shabes a diary that recorded what it felt like to see Jews dragged off to the cattle cars, to lose one's own family, and to face the prospect of a terrible death. On August 12 Lewin returned to find that a German blockade of Landau's shop had swept up his wife:

Eclipse of the sun, universal blackness. My Luba was taken away during a blockade on 30 Gęsia Street. There is still a glimmer of hope in front of me. Perhaps she will be saved. And, if God forbid she is not? My journey to the Umschlagplatz—the appearance of the streets—fills me with dread. To my anguish there was no prospect of rescuing her. It looks like she was taken directly to the train . . . I have no words to describe my desolation. I ought to go after her, to die. But I have no strength to take such a step. Ora—her calamity. A child who was so tied to her mother, and how she loved her. (pp. 153–154)

Lewin struggled to find the right words, the right tone, to convey the double blow of a national catastrophe and personal disaster. With the Great Deportation, Lewin switched from Yiddish to Hebrew, the language of the *pinkesim,* the traditional chronicles of Jewish suffering and woe.[98] On November 11, 1942, he railed yet again against his probable fate: to be remembered as a "martyr."

How terrible it is that a whole generation—millions of Jews—has suddenly become a community of "martyrs," who have had to die in such a cruel, degrading and painful manner and go through the torments of hell before going to the gallows. Earth, earth do not cover our blood and do not keep silent, so that our blood will cry out until the ends of time and demand revenge for this crime that has no parallel in our history and in the whole of human history. (pp. 206–207)

Lewin held on. He still had his daughter. But he was acutely aware that his own milieu, that of the Warsaw Jewish intelligentsia, was already largely gone. And he realized with growing dread that the catastrophe might have irrevocable consequences for the nation. If Polish Jewry went under, what would happen to the Jewish people? What would be left? Dread of approaching death mingled with despair about the destruction of his entire people. On December 29, 1942, Lewin wrote:

Warsaw was in fact the backbone of Polish Jewry, its heart, one could say. The destruction of Warsaw would have meant the destruction of the whole of Polish Jewry, even if the provinces had been spared this evil. Now that the enemy's sword of destruction has run amok through the small towns and villages and is cutting them down with murderous blows—with the death agony of the metropolis, the entire body is dying and plunging into hell. One can say that with the setting of the sun of Polish Jewry the splendor and the glory of world Jewry has vanished. We, the Polish Jews, were after all the most vibrant nerve of our people. (p. 232)

As Lewin continued to work for the Oyneg Shabes, interviewing escapees from Treblinka, he struggled to cope with his fear. On January 9, 1943, he wrote:

> When I hear these accounts of Treblinka, something begins to twist and turn in my heart. The fear of "that" which must come is, perhaps, stronger than the torment a person feels when he gives up his soul. Will these terrible agonies of the spirit call up a literary response? Will there emerge a new Bialik able to write a new Book of Lamentations, a new "In the Town of Slaughter?" (p. 237)

His final diary entry is dated January 16, 1943. He probably died in Treblinka later that same week. His daughter, Ora, also perished.

Aaron Koninski

Another teacher who made an important contribution to the archive was Ringelblum's brother-in-law Aaron Koninski.[99] Koninski had gained a reputation before the war as a fine teacher who took a lively interest in the problems of Jewish education. A member of the Right Poalei Tsiyon and an active member of its school movement, the Shul Kult, Koninski showed a flair for social service and administration. He took over the running of the deficit-plagued Jewish Emigration Society (JEAS) on Mylna 18 and turned its finances around. In 1939 Koninski opened up Mylna 18 to many of the refugees from Zbąszyń and gave them help and support. Many of these refugees died from a direct hit on the building during the siege of Warsaw in 1939.

When the war began the Aleynhilf turned Mylna 18 into a children's center under Koninski's supervision. He developed a good rapport with the children and with the teachers. Often the Aleynhilf and the CENTOS could not provide all the children's institutions with enough food, but Koninski always found some way to keep the children from going hungry.

Koninski wrote a major essay on the Jewish child in the Warsaw Ghetto for the Oyneg Shabes.[100] Based on comprehensive research, this essay analyzed the situation of Jewish children in the ghetto and concluded that "of the hundred thousand children in the ghetto, 80 percent require help" (more on this in chapter 6). But only half the needy Jewish children were receiving any kind of assistance. Koninski concluded with a sudden shift from objective, dispassionate analysis to moral pleading: unless the Jewish community acted fast, Koninski warned, the children of the ghetto would become physical, mental, and moral cripples. Jewish society was responsible for its children. Would history record that Warsaw Jewry failed to do all it could?

As a member of the Oyneg Shabes and as Ringelblum's brother-in-law, Koninski had an inside account of the massacres that had started in 1941. He certainly would have known the real meaning of the words "deportation to the East." Nevertheless, when the Germans collected his "children" for deportation, Koninski decided to accompany them on their final journey. Together with his wife, the teachers, and the rest of the staff, Koninski marched with the children to the Umschlagplatz. He was forty years old.

Bernard Kampelmacher

Before the war Kampelmacher had been a respected school principal in Grodzisk. After he arrived in the ghetto as a refugee, the archive gave him his bearings and a sense of purpose.[101] His many contributions to the archive— an essay on education in the ghetto, interviews with refugees, a detailed study of his hometown in the early days of the war—show a careful, methodical, and thorough man. Thrown into the chaos of the Warsaw Ghetto, Kampelmacher coped by developing an orderly routine. He helped run the association of Grodzisk refugees in the ghetto. He worked hard on a detailed plan to improve schooling for ghetto children. Unlike some other members of the Oyneg Shabes, he stuck closely to the guidelines and questionnaires prepared by the Oyneg Shabes when he interviewed refugees about their hometowns. The raging typhus epidemic made this dangerous work. In early 1942 Kampelmacher came down with the disease and died.

THE ECONOMISTS: MENAKHEM LINDER (1911–1942) AND JERZY WINKLER (D. 1942)

When he wrote Menakhem Linder's obituary, Max Weinreich, the director of the YIVO, stressed that "we loved Linder in a special way because Linder was one of us."[102] One of the first products of the YIVO graduate program in Vilna, Linder quickly became the institution's rising young star. With his gift for languages and his law degree from Lwów University, Weinreich noted, Linder might have become a successful lawyer. But he came to the YIVO not because he had no other options but because he wanted to serve his own people. Like Ringelblum and Rachel Auerbach, Linder was a native of Galicia who defied the prejudices of Polish-speaking Jewish intelligentsia and embraced modern Yiddish culture.[103] (Linder's turn to Yiddish was all the more startling because earlier he had been a member of the Hashomer Hatzair.) In the new YIVO graduate program, Linder won an award for his study of the economics and social profile of his native town, Śniatyń. He fell in love with Vilna, found a wife there, and even began to speak Yiddish with a Vilna accent. His deep interest in the economic problems of Polish Jewry led him to take a position with the CEKABE in Warsaw, where he worked under Giterman's supervision and came into close contact with Ringelblum. Linder soon became the editor of the YIVO's major economic journal (*Yidishe ekonomik*), and published several important studies on the economic problems of Polish Jewry in the late 1930s. He also became secretary of the Warsaw branch of the YIVO.

After the start of the war Linder headed the Aleynhilf's statistical section. In the Oyneg Shabes he chiefly coordinated and organized the gathering of economic materials. In early 1942 Ringelblum gave him a key assignment—to write the economic section of "Two and Half Years," the large-scale study of Jewish society in wartime which the Oyneg Shabes planned but never completed.

Linder's first love in the Warsaw Ghetto was the Yiddish cultural organization, the IKOR; he found encouragement in the new interest in Yiddish culture that he had observed in the Warsaw Ghetto.

> He had the vision of Jewish cultural autonomy in the lands of the Diaspora. He believed that out of the curse of the ghetto would come a blessing in the form of a general shift of the Jewish intelligentsia to the living language of the masses . . . that a new energy would invigorate a Jewish creative spirit forged and tempered by the ordeals [of the war].[104]

In the large hall of the Aleynhilf building on Tłomackie 5 (now the site of Warsaw's Jewish Historical Institute), large crowds came to hear Yiddish lectures organized by the IKOR. The indefatigable Linder was fascinated by how Yiddish responded to the new wartime conditions. He even coined new words to describe unfortunate ghetto realities.[105] Along with Ringelblum, Linder worked tirelessly to ensure that Yiddish became the standard language of the house committees, and he also found time to lecture for the underground seminars of the youth movements. Zuckerman recalled that Linder was one of the most popular lecturers.[106]

On the night of April 17, 1942, Gestapo agents knocked on Linder's door and politely asked him to come with them, reminding him to take a toothbrush and a change of clothing. He entered their car and, when they arrived at the building of the former Evangelical hospital, the agents told Linder to get out. There they shot him. He did not die quickly. Witnesses reported that he struggled for a long time. But it was after curfew, and no one dared go out to help him. They could only watch helplessly from the windows as he struggled and suffered. His terrified widow burned his diary before Ringelblum could acquire it for the archive.[107]

With Linder gone, the economist Jerzy Winkler assumed major responsibility for the economic research of the Oyneg Shabes.[108] Before the war Winkler had studied economics at Vienna University and had also been active in the YIVO's economics section. Thanks to his YIVO ties, he got to know Joseph Jaszunski, who became a member of the Warsaw Judenrat and who procured a job for Winkler in the Judenrat's statistical bureau. This post gave Winkler access to many Judenrat documents as well as to Judenrat correspondence with the German authorities. The first part of the Oyneg Shabes Archive contains several such documents and letters that Winkler copied by hand.

Winkler's most important contribution to the Oyneg Shabes was his splendid essay, in Polish, on the ghetto economy, "The Ghetto Struggles against Economic Enslavement."[109] Here Winkler painstakingly documented how Jews doggedly worked to acquire raw materials, set up workshops, and export goods to the Aryan side. The money earned from these exports, based on a myriad of business relationships with Poles and Germans, helped keep tens of thousands of Jews alive.

Winkler also completed valuable statistical studies for the archive. In 1941 he wrote a study in Yiddish on the health of the ghetto population and on the reasons for declining physical resistance to epidemics.[110] That same year he compiled a statistical survey of those who were sent off to the labor camps.[111]

Obviously impressed, Ringelblum (and probably Linder) asked Winkler to coauthor the economic section of "Two and a Half Years."[112] After Linder's murder, Winkler took over the project, but when the Great Deportation began in July he had an emotional breakdown. Disabled with a crippled arm, he knew that he had little chance of surviving a "selection." At the very beginning of the Great Deportation he was sent to the Umschlagplatz but his coworkers in the Judenrat were able to obtain his release. His reprieve was short-lived, however. He and his wife perished a short time later.[113] Winkler was in his mid-thirties.

THE REFUGEE: DANIEL FLIGELMAN

In 1941 the Oyneg Shabes recruited a young refugee, Daniel Fligelman, who became one of the archive's most productive contributors. His many essays and reports in the first part of the archive suggest an interesting and erudite man in his twenties who knew foreign languages, read widely, and had a mordant sense of humor. His essays, written in Polish, were sprinkled with Latin phrases.[114] He had strong opinions and did not hide them; for example, on the cover sheet of an interview he had conducted with a refugee in the Warsaw Ghetto who had been the chief of the Jewish police in his hometown, Fligelman wrote that the interview had been a waste of time, as the man was probably a liar. Usually Fligelman used the code name Fligar, but his style was unmistakable. In a report on the small town of Nieszawa, in western Poland, Fligelman described the public flogging of several Jews:

> After they whipped him the Jew Jagoda asked the officer a question straight out of Tolstoy: "Why?" Instead of an answer Jagoda got a blow in the face from a baton. . . . The officer then ordered another 60 lashes for Jagoda, whipped another Jew, and then beat Jagoda again. When it all ended, all the Jews were allowed to go home except Jagoda, who was taken to jail. A few days later, despite repeated efforts by the local Jews, he was shot along with two Polish thieves. So Jagoda died the death of Christ.[115]

As Ruta Sakowska speculates, Hersh Wasser probably noticed Fligelman in the course of his work with the refugees and recruited him for the Oyneg Shabes.[116] For all his intellectual acuity, Fligelman impressed Ringelblum as someone who was quite helpless in everyday life: "The quiet dove Daniel Fligelman would have perished [long before he did] had it not been for the constant help and concern he received from our dear comrade Menakhem [Kon]."[117] Kon's account book recorded many disbursements that helped keep Fligelman alive: 90 zlotys on November 20, 1941; 150 zlotys in January 1942; and 140 zlotys . . . on February 25, 1942.[118] Kon also procured medicine to treat Fligelman when he became infected with typhus, probably as a result of his extensive interviewing in the refugee centers.

Although Fligelman only arrived in Warsaw around the middle of 1941, he quickly became one of the archive's most important workers. Ringelblum called Fligelman's essay on Jewish prisoners of war from the September 1939 campaign the best study of the subject in the archive.[119] Fligelman's contribution to the archive was immense when it came to interviewing refugees and producing accounts of events in the provincial towns, He conducted two crucial interviews that provided the archive with its first detailed accounts of German massacres in the East. One interview, with Hashomer member Aryeh Vilner, contained ominous news of the mass killings in Vilna. Another interview described the massacre of the Jews in Slonim. Both accounts found their way into the material that the Oyneg Shabes sent abroad in early 1942. Fligelman died in Treblinka in the summer of 1942.

THE TRANSLATOR: CECYLIA SŁAPAKOWA

To write a study of Jewish women in the ghetto, the archive approached Cecylia Słapak.[120] Married to a successful engineer, Cecylia Słapakowa was someone who easily crossed many of the cultural boundaries that marked prewar Jewish Warsaw. A native of the Vilna region, she was part of the old Russian-speaking Jewish intelligentsia that had been dispersed by the 1917 Russian Revolution. She was also involved with the Yiddish literary elite. According to Auerbach, she maintained close ties with the prominent Yiddish critic Shmuel Niger and his brother, Daniel Charny, as well as with Marc and Bella Chagall. Usually "Litvaks" like these had little involvement with Polish culture. But Słapakowa was different. She attracted attention with her translation into Polish of Simon Dubnow's monumental *World History of the Jewish People.* She was also a frequent contributor to the Polish-language Jewish daily *Nasz przegląd.* Like many other members of the Oyneg Shabes, she was linked to the Warsaw branch of the YIVO and publicized its activities for the Polish-speaking circles of Warsaw Jewry.

Rachel Auerbach remembered how, in the first winter of the German occupation, Słapakowa decided to arrange Sunday afternoon "coffee hours" that brought together Jewish intellectuals, actors, and writers, a decidedly dangerous activity when German patrols were routinely barging into private apartments in their search for valuables and forced laborers. But Słapakowa was determined to fight the prevailing mood of fear and depression. Her "five o-clocks" resembled a prewar salon where good conversation and modest food enabled the fifteen or so guests to forget the war for a few hours. Sometimes guests performed chamber music.[121]

After the Germans forced the Słapaks to move from their spacious apartment on Elektoralna 1 in the spring of 1940, the salon ended. Auerbach often met Słapakowa in the Aleynhilf offices on Tłomackie 5, and during one visit to her apartment, Słapakowa asked Auerbach about her work in the soup kitchen. The tone of the questions led Auerbach to guess, correctly, that Słapakowa was researching an assignment for the Oyneg Shabes. After the war, in the tin boxes that housed the part 1 of the archive, Auerbach and others found the records of the interviews that Słapakowa was conducting for her unfinished study of Jewish women during the war.

The Słapaks had one young child of school age, a daughter who resembled her mother. Both perished in Treblinka during the Great Deportation of 1942. According to Auerbach, her husband survived.

Several members of the Oyneg Shabes had known Ringelblum and Wasser from the Left Poalei Tsiyon. In addition to the teachers Israel Lichtenstein and Natan Smolar, this group of LPZ members included Nehemia Tytelman, Mordecai Schwartzbard, and Yekhiel Gorny.

Before the war Tytelman had been one of the leaders of the Warsaw Shtern, the sports organization of the LPZ. Although he suffered a breakdown at the onset of the war, he recovered and remained an active member of the underground party in the Warsaw Ghetto.[122] He was also courageous. Angered by the abuses in the labor camps and by Judenrat venality, he sent an open letter to the head of the Judenrat's labor department in which he demanded fairer treatment of the poor.[123]

Tytelman made many important contributions to the archive, including essays on smuggling, interviews with refugees, and street sketches. His specialty, however, was ghetto folklore: courtyard songs, jokes, and the milieu of the all-important smugglers. Tytelman wandered the ghetto with pen and paper, always ready to write down the songs of a child singer or of a wandering "comedian," along with vivid descriptions of the singers themselves.

In a typical reportage, Tytelman described an encounter with an eighteen-year-old street singer, Shayne Eisenberg. In Rypin, her father had been a tanner and the family had enough to live on. But as soon as the Germans took the town, they arrested her mother and the family never saw her again. The family finally arrived in Warsaw, at the notorious refugee center on Stawki 9. Shayne's father soon died of starvation and her brother wandered off. Now she had only her ten-year-old sister left, whom she supported by street singing.

> When Shayne mentions her mother she breaks out in prolonged crying. "If they had not dragged mother away things would not be so bad." She is awfully lean, looks like a corpse, is already dulled, does not . . . understand what people say to her. . . . The shoes, obviously her father's, are thrice her size. . . . All the time, whether singing or talking, she keeps begging [for food]—one notes that her song is garbled, she does not know all of it.
>
> To the tune of "Mame libe, mame getraye," she sings:
>
> Oh oh oh oh / oh oh oh dear father
> Why, why, why must we Jews so suffer
> Suffer so much suffering, suffer, suffer
> Why, you promised us, long ago didn't you
> To elect us for your beloved nation.[124]

Tytelman, who also used the pseudonym NR (Natan Rocheles, Natan the son of Rachel) was killed sometime in 1943.

Little is known of Yekhiel Gorny except that he was a member of the archive who could be trusted to carry out many different assignments: interviews, short reports, and copying. He kept a diary that he continued even during the chaotic and terrible days of the Great Deportation. He also wrote one of the first descriptions of the January 1943 action. It was thanks to Oyneg Shabes members like Gorny that historians have a day-by-day account of what happened in the Warsaw Ghetto after July 1942, at a time when fear and terror paralyzed many surviving writers and chroniclers. Gorny continued to write even after the Germans took away his wife and child on August 7, 1942.

Gorny tersely recorded the things he witnessed. On November 25, 1942, eight Jews were shot. On November 26 a German gendarme warned Jews to avoid the next street: "Don't go, there's an SS man over there and he'll shoot you." Later that same day Gorny noted that thirty people had been shot the day before and that "at 5:00 PM a Jew was shot near Miła 55."[125] On November 29 Gorny noted that "an unknown hand" had killed Israel Furst, a notorious Jewish collaborator for the Gestapo.[126] In these last weeks of his life Gorny described, day by day, how the remaining Warsaw Jews wavered between hope and despair. When news came of the Allied landings in North Africa, Gorny wrote that "the mood of the Jews is getting happier, that hope is rising that the handful of survivors . . . might see Hitler's downfall." But two days later the mood was "very depressed."

Gorny expressed hardly any emotion, except when he wrote about the Jewish police. "Their conduct," he wrote in October 1942, "can be answered by one word only, 'J'accuse.'" How should the Jews punish them after the war? This would be a problem, because Gorny believed that Jews "were not capable of taking revenge through murder, burning, or extermination . . . not even against our mortal enemies, the Germans. We would not be able to do it." No, after the war "the Jews of Warsaw" should lead the surviving Jewish police to Treblinka and make them stand there—on the site of the gas chambers—with a placard attesting their complicity in the "greatest disgrace of the twentieth century."

During the ghetto uprising, Gorny fought in the combat group of the LPZ commanded by Hersh Berlinski. He was killed on May 10, 1943, with a group of fighters who were trying to leave the burning ghetto through the sewers.

In memoirs published after the war one LPZ veteran called Mordecai Schwartzbard "one of the most intelligent leaders of the Jewish labor movement in Poland."[127] Before 1939 Schwartzbard served on the central committee of the Lodz Poalei Tsiyon, a party stronghold. Arrested several times by the Polish authorities, Schwartzbard gained a reputation as an excellent speaker and a tough fighter.[128] In November 1939 Schwartzbard left Lodz for Warsaw. He continued to work for the party and directed a soup kitchen for Lodz refugees.

In the Oyneg Shabes Schwartzbard conducted interviews with refugees; wrote many reports, especially on conditions in various labor camps in 1940 and 1941; recopied Ringelblum's diaries and notes; and made copies of many other documents. His most important contribution to the archive, however, was his own diaries and chronicles. Schwartzbard wrote a detailed chronicle of the early days of the German occupation in Lodz, where the Germans seized him twenty-two times for forced labor. His chronicles continued after he arrived in Warsaw and then stopped in 1942.

Schwartzbard probably died in Treblinka in 1942, along with his wife, Miriam, and his son, Daniel. All his writings were contained in part 1 of the archive, which stopped in August 1942.

THE POLISH LANGUAGE WRITERS:
HENRYKA LAZOWERT AND GUSTAWA JARECKA

Although Ringelblum as a fervent Yiddishist frequently criticized the growing use of Polish among Jews, he nonetheless readily recruited trusted members of the Polish-speaking Jewish intelligentsia to work in the archive. Two important collaborators were the young poet Henryka Lazowert and the leftist writer Gustawa Jarecka. The Oyneg Shabes also collected many of the writings of the most popular Polish-language poet in the ghetto, Władysław Szlengel. But although Ringelblum thought Szlengel important enough to write a short essay about him (more on this in chapter 8), Szlengel did not appear to be an actual collaborator of the Oyneg Shabes, probably because of his membership in the Jewish police which he quit at the beginning of the Great Deportation.

Henryka Lazowert (Łazowertówna)

Before the war Henryka Lazowert had been a promising young poet who had won an academic fellowship to study in Italy. When the war started Ringelblum brought her into the Aleynhilf, where she wrote "propaganda": leaflets, appeals, and so on. He then recruited her for the Oyneg Shabes. At a time of so much suffering in the refugee centers, when tens of thousands of families were slowly starving to death in shocking conditions, Ringelblum praised Lazowert for her ability to bring to life the individual family tragedies that lurked behind the dry statistics of mass suffering contained in the Aleynhilf reports. Ringelblum singled out Lazowert's essay on a single Jewish family's struggle for survival in the ghetto. This essay won a first prize in a secret contest sponsored by the archive.[129]

Lazowert continued to write poetry in the ghetto. Her most popular poem was "To the Child Smuggler," which was translated into Yiddish and sung by the well-known performer Diana Blumenfeld.

> Through walls, through holes, over ruins, through barbed wire I'll still find a way. Hungry, thirsty and barefoot I slither through like a snake: by day, at night, at dawn. No matter how hot. No matter how much rain. You can begrudge me my profit. I am risking my little neck.[130]

During the Great Deportation Ringelbum wrote that Lazowert voluntarily went with her mother to the Umschlagplatz. The Aleynhilf tried to rescue her, but when she discovered that she would have to leave her mother, she chose to accompany her to "the East."[131]

Gustawa Jarecka

It is not clear how well Ringelblum knew Gustawa Jarecka (1908–1943) before the war. She had not taken part in any Jewish cultural activities; her reputation rested on leftist novels about working-class life and political struggle. Forced into the ghetto with her two children, she found a position as a typist with the Judenrat. There she worked closely with Marcel Reich-Ranicki, who after the war became a popular television personality and literary critic in Germany. Ringelblum asked both of them to furnish copies of Judenrat documents for the Oyneg Shabes.[132]

As they worked together in the Judenrat offices Reich-Ranicki and Jarecka developed a deep friendship. They loved to talk about French and Russian literature. Reich-Ranicki admired the older woman's poise and self-possession, and began to develop strong feelings for her.

> Did I love her, this Polish writer Gustawa Jarecka? Yes, but this was an entirely different relationship from the one I had with Tosia. I knew very little about Gustawa's past. Before the war, little tied her to the Jewish world. She was one of those Polish Jews, for whom religious matters were totally foreign. She arrived in the ghetto with her two children: an eleven or twelve year old from a short-lived marriage and a two year old about

whom she never told the father. Czerniakow (and we have to credit him for this) selflessly supported many intellectuals who were in the ghetto without work and found them employment in many offices of the Judenrat. Since Gustawa knew German and knew how to type, she wound up in my office. I can still see her before me: a chestnut haired, blue-eyed woman, a bit over thirty, composed and quiet.[133]

On July 22 Reich-Ranicki and Jarecka were both at work in the Judenrat offices when SS officer Hermann Höffle barged into Adam Czerniakow's office with an order to begin the deportation of Warsaw Jewry. Reich-Ranicki and Jarecka were ordered to type transcripts of the meeting—and of the fateful deportation order—in German and in Polish. Höffle told Czerniakow that if the Judenrat did not carry out the order, he would hang all its members: "right there," he said, pointing out the window at a recently opened children's playground.[134]

Thanks to her job in the Judenrat, Jarecka managed to avoid the first wave of selections in the summer of 1942. Ringelblum then asked her to write about what she had seen. She entitled this essay, "The Last Stage of Deportation Is Death." Living through the hellish fear of the daily blockades, Jarecka recalled at the start of her essay, was easier than writing about what happened. Then the senses were numbed. Now she could look back on the horror and know that even as she sat and wrote her reprieve was only temporary. Writing just brought back memories:

> memories of mothers crazed with pain over losing their children; the memory of the cries of little children carried away without overcoats, in summer clothes and barefooted, going on the road to death and crying with innocent tears, not grasping the horror of what was happening to them, the memory of the despair of old fathers and mothers, abandoned to their fate by their adult children, and the memory of that stony silence hanging over the dead city after the sentence, passed upon 300,000 persons, had been carried out.[135]

But Jarecka believed that the written word was a link to a "before" and an "after." After the war the details of mass murder might shock the world and keep such a crime from recurring. What had happened to the Jews, she implied, could well happen to others. In order to grab the attention of future readers whom she knew she would never see, Jarecka did her best to tell the truth and conceal nothing, even if it caused her pain.

Why, she asked, did the Jewish masses not resist? She admitted that the Germans found it easy to fool the Jews and that Jewish solidarity quickly collapsed as individuals looked for ways to save themselves through "exemptions." But she implied that no one could afford to ignore another factor, and that was the Jews' misplaced optimism in mankind. They simply refused to believe that mass extermination was possible. They continued to accept the assumption that "organized communities had a right to life. . . . Wearily and slowly most of us, who had been brought up on illusions, learned to consider facts from the viewpoint of subordinating justice to politics. Too long we had believed in the importance of life."

Jarecka's essay remained half-finished. Either she ran out of time or found the effort unbearable. According to Hillel Seidman, who writes that he talked to her in December 1942, Jarecka expressed regret that she did not know Yiddish or Hebrew. She told Seidman that if she survived the war, she would learn these languages and write in them.[136]

Reich-Ranicki clearly remembered the last time he saw Jarecka. It was on January 18, 1943, the first day of the January action, when the Germans first encountered armed resistance in the ghetto. Jarecka, her two children, and Reich-Ranicki and his new wife were all in a crowd that was marching to the death trains. Reich-Ranicki and his wife decided to run. He told Jarecka to run with them, and she said that she and her children were ready. But when Reich-Ranicki and his wife made their mad dash, Jarecka remained in the column. Perhaps her youngest child, then a boy of four, was unable to run.[137]

THE YIDDISH WRITERS AND JOURNALISTS

In his essay on the Oyneg Shabes Ringelblum declared that he preferred amateur writers to professional journalists:

> The majority of our permanent collaborators, which totaled a few dozen [etlekhe tsendlik] were mostly recruited from the folk intelligentsia [folksintelligentn], mainly from the proletarian parties. We purposely avoided inviting professional journalists because we didn't want our work to become cheapened and distorted. We wanted the simplest most unadorned account possible of what happened in each shtetl and what happened to each Jew (and in this war, each Jew is like a world in itself). Any superfluous word, any literary exaggeration grated and repelled. Jewish life during the war is so packed with events that it is unnecessary to add an extra sentence. And then again, there was the problem of secrecy. As is well known, journalists have a hard time with that.[138]

In fact, however, Ringelblum did involve several Yiddish writers and journalists in the archive, both as interviewers and authors, including Peretz Opoczynski, Shie Perle, Rachel Auerbach, Leyb Goldin, Yehuda Feld, and Moshe Skalov. Generally all were leftists or at least shared a populist identification with "the Jewish masses." Except for Perle, none had belonged to the literary elite before the war. Many other Yiddish and Hebrew writers did not work for the archive, but their works were preserved by the Oyneg Shabes: Yitzhak Katzenelson, Joseph Kirman, Kalman Lis, Shlomo Gilbert, and others.

While testimonies and eyewitness accounts remained the foundation of the archive, Ringelblum and his associates understood the importance of other genres: reportage, poetry, essays, and synoptic stories. The Oyneg Shabes encouraged literary life in the ghetto by sponsoring competitions and awarding prizes.

Although the reality of the war exceeded the worst of horror fiction, writers in the ghettos understood that the catastrophe had not made fiction and poetry superfluous. Well-crafted language and synoptic stories could bring out the truth in new and compelling ways. And though factual testimonies constituted the bedrock of the archive, reportages also proved effective in conveying information, making a point, and gripping the conscience of a hypothetical reader. In the entire Oyneg Shabes there was little question that the master of ghetto reportage was Peretz Opoczynski.

Peretz Opoczynski: The Ghetto Mailman

In Peretz Opoczynski the Oyneg Shabes found a brilliant reporter and one of its best writers. Opoczynski was born near Lodz in 1892. His father died when Opoczynski was only five, and he grew up in terrible poverty. He spent his youth in various yeshivas, sleeping on benches in synagogues, and living on meager meals in strangers' homes. Drafted into the Russian army during World War I, Opoczynski spent most of the war years as a POW in Hungary.

His mother had hoped that he would be a rabbi, but Opoczynski decided to become a writer. After the war he supported himself as a shoemaker and, on the side, began to write short stories, poems, and reportage. These attracted some notice, and Opoczynski became part of the Lodz literary scene.

Just when it seemed that he had a secure career as a journalist, Opoczynski lost his two children to polio and suffered serious bouts of depression. In 1935, citing an old Jewish saying that a change of place means a change of luck, he left his comfortable apartment in Lodz and moved, with his wife, Miriam, to Warsaw where he took a job with *Dos vort*, the newspaper of the Right Poalei Tsiyon. In 1938 his sister came to visit him from the United States. She recalled that he lived in an attic apartment on Wołyńska 21 in shocking poverty. The walls were covered with mold and damp. His stubborn pride caused him to refuse any financial help from his sister. But Opoczynski and his wife had one consolation: they had a new son, Daniel, who was intelligent and healthy. Opoczynski's sister recounted that "Danchik," born in 1935, was an adorable child who filled both parents' lives.[139]

The war deprived Opoczynski of his meager livelihood as a journalist. Natan Eck and Hersh Wasser both remembered Opoczynski in the ghetto as very poor and frail. He could not earn enough from his job as a ghetto mailman to feed his family. His feet were swollen from hunger. Still, he found the strength to play an active role in his party, the Right Poalei Tsiyon, and to write, in both Hebrew and Yiddish, for the Oyneg Shabes.[140] Opoczynski also was active in his house committee on Wołyńska 21.

Long before the war Opoczynski had tended to see writing as a mission and a calling rather than as a career. Although he had been widely published, he apparently did not frequent writers' circles such as Tłomackie 13. Conveying the impression of being an ordinary artisan rather than the gifted journalist that he was, Opoczynski was exactly the kind of writer that the archive could use.

Hersh Wasser recalled that, in the Warsaw Ghetto, the Oyneg Shabes helped Opoczynski survive with small stipends. When he contracted typhus, Menakhem Kon provided medicine. (In appreciation, Opoczynski dedicated a Hebrew story to Kon.) Perhaps it was the Oyneg Shabes that helped Opoczynski aquire his job as a mailman.[141] In any case, the "investment" was well placed, as Opoczynski helped the archive in several important ways.

Once the extermination process began in the provinces, Opoczynski may have been one of those who gave the archive a priceless source of documentation: final postcards and letters that Jews awaiting "resettlement" sent to loved ones in Warsaw.[142] He also wrote important reports on the ghetto post office and kept a diary that covered the period from May 1942 to January 1943.

Opoczynski's greatest contribution to the archive, however, was his skill with reportage.[143] As he walked the streets and knocked on people's doors to deliver mail, he encountered, and later described, the ghetto's concerns and tensions, the array of characters and social types that had made Jewish Warsaw so diverse: Hasidim, Polish-speaking doctors, Jewish workers, smugglers, housewives, neighbors, and friends. Underpaid and starving, Opoczynski crafted a masterpiece, "The Ghetto Mailman," written in October 1941. Here he skillfully dissected the deeper social and cultural ramifications of a seemingly straightforward relationship between a mailman and the people on his route.[144] He was the object of envy and jealousy at first. Before the war there had been no Jewish mailmen or Jewish police; now the ghetto had both—surely a sign of Jewish autonomy! And what a job! Of course the uniform might have been better. A sword would have looked nice, but a mailman's cap would do. This was a good job, people thought enviously, secure, with plenty of opportunities for bribes.

The truth, Opoczynski bitterly remarked, was quite the opposite. In the post office, as in so much else in the ghetto, corruption reigned. A small clique of Polish-speaking Jews ran the post office and grabbed all the lucrative jobs for themselves. A martinet who was in charge took care of his friends and terrorized his underlings. As for Opoczynski, on a good day he might deliver as many as 100 to 150 letters but earn only 6 to 9 zlotys, little more than the price of a loaf of bread.

Many desperate Jews regarded this simple mailman as a messenger of hope, a direct link to better places, better times. Opoczynski reported how the letters and packages he delivered created both a physical and emotional lifeline between starving Jews in the ghetto and children or husbands who had fled to the Soviet zone or who had emigrated. How Jews dealt with their mailman exposed the wide cultural and social gaps that marked the ghetto. Polish-speaking Jewish professionals treated him with condescension and arrogance, which, he commented acerbically, only reflected their own pathetic inferiority complexes. As undelivered mail piled up in the central ghetto post office, these acculturated Jews made cutting remarks about Jewish incompetence. For different reasons, Opoczynski had equally few good words to say about the Hasidim. They were hypocrites and skinflints who refused him the tips he needed to get by. He empathized with the *amcho*—ordinary Jews like himself who spoke Yiddish, who did not put on airs, who understood how hard it was to live, and who gave him decent tips—at least in the beginning.

Like his other reports on the house committees, children, and the parówki, his story of the ghetto postal service described a tough struggle for survival that the Jews were slowly losing. Inexorably and ominously, conditions worsened. Hitler's invasion of the Soviet Union and Pearl Harbor put an end to the vital food packages from the Soviet zone and remittances from the U.S.[145] As the mail service deteriorated and the Judenrat raised its fees for each letter and package, many people blamed Opoczynski and began to treat him with hatred and contempt.

Because he was not part of the privileged inner circle, Opoczynski's route included some of the poorest streets of the ghetto as well as the refugee centers where hundreds of people lived in a few large rooms; the sick often lay all day in their excrement. Locating a person in these conditions was far from easy. Hallways were dark, stairs were polluted with filth, and often there was no list of tenants' names. All too often Opoczynski would bring a precious letter only to learn that the person lacked the thirty groszy to pay the delivery fee. They would ask him to lend them the money, which he could not afford to do. In these circumstances the mailman might have to spend precious time going to neighbors for small contributions to "redeem" the letter.

These reports were unlike anything Opoczynski had written before the war. Then he knew who his audience was and when they would read his piece. Now there was no newspaper, no guaranteed audience, and no certainty of personal survival. Yiddish, the very language that had bound writer and reader in a circle of mutual understanding, was itself being destroyed. But Opoczynski wrote as if there would be a tomorrow, as if he and his readers would meet again in the morning newspaper. He presented the ghetto experience by dividing it into understandable, discrete themes and incidents to be shared with trusted readers who in turn recognized the reporter's authority. In the midst of a collective and an individual disaster, Opoczynski confronted rupture by seeking continuities with the known past: language, shared experiences, social spaces, and social conventions.

Without glorifying the ghetto inhabitants, Opoczynski described their rough humor and grim struggle to survive—and to maintain some modicum of social solidarity. Along with his keen powers of observation, he had a wonderful sense of language. He remembered and recorded conversations between Jewish mothers and their children; the slang of the Jewish smugglers; the pleas of young beggars on the street; housewives' petty quarrels; grim humor in a long line waiting to enter the parówka. Without in any way disguising their foibles or embellishing their virtues, Opoczynski made it clear that these were the people he was comfortable with: *folksmenshn,* ordinary Jews. He understood the importance of the social microcosms of the ghetto: the courtyards, the house committees that had become the arena of a desperate struggle that Jews were fighting not only for physical survival but also for dignity and to gain a foothold in conditions of growing chaos. Writing with no firm knowledge of a final outcome, Opoczynski conveyed how Jews saw and reacted to events as they unfolded. Quiet and unthreatening, he could win people's trust without monopolizing their attention; so they let him observe their lives and report what they did to survive in the ghetto.

Overall, his reportage reveals an inexorable deterioration of ghetto life, a grim realization that day by day, the battle to survive was becoming harder and harder. A new note crept into his writings. In most of his reporting Opoczynski had maintained the voice of a detached observer. When he wrote about particular individuals—ordinary people he knew—he could describe them with admiration and sympathy. But when he wrote about Warsaw Jewry as a collective, he became increasingly angry, and in "Children on the Pavement," written in November 1941, he became an accuser. Since Opoczynski had lost two of his own children, he was especially sensitive to this subject. In normal circumstances, he wrote, people approached children with an instinctive love and protectiveness. For any normal community, preserving children ranked as the most important priority. Now, in the Warsaw Ghetto, it was the Jewish child that was bearing the brunt of the suffering. Future generations, he implied, would not only blame the Germans. They would also blame the Jews.

In "Children on the Pavement" Opoczynski poured out his outrage at his fellow Jews for allowing Jewish children to sleep in the streets, starve to death, and degenerate into wizened and decrepit beggars. Like Ringelblum, he was especially bitter at the Judenrat and the Jewish police for sending only poor Jews to labor camps, a policy that exposed the children of the poor to particular hardship. But not just the Judenrat and the Jewish police were to blame. The plight of the Jewish child exposed the moral bankruptcy of much of Jewish society. Yes, the Germans bore ultimate responsibility. But that did not excuse Jews who had lost their sense of community and their feelings of mutual responsibility. The war had made Warsaw Jews—selfish to begin with—even more egotistical and self-absorbed.

> All sense of community began and ended with the four walls of one's
> own apartment. It is the tragedy of the Polish Jews that the war found
> them so unprepared, so unorganized, so unable to rise to the needs of the
> times. Polish Jewry—divided into thousands of separate tribes [eydes]—
> and each person a tribe unto himself.[146]

Had Polish Jewry been better organized, Opoczynski wrote, it could have accomplished so much in the early months of the war. Jewish possessions and wealth could have been used to stockpile large reserves of food and clothing to help the poor and to protect Jewish children. Polish Jews should have learned from the experiences of their brethren in Germany and Czechoslovakia that there was no point in hanging onto one's wealth. Sooner or later—"guided by gentile or Jewish informers"[147]—the Nazis would find it anyway. Jews were supposed to be a people with intelligence and common sense. What happened? And now, why weren't Jews doing more to help the children? There were still plenty of people in the ghetto who could do something: the smugglers, the bakers who were earning so much.

His reportage included both dry statistics and heartrending incidents that he witnessed or heard about. One such incident concerned a child whose accent marked him as a refugee from the provinces. An older woman noticed that he was wearing a decent coat. Taking advantage of the child, she told him that she could find him a place in a children's shelter—and she would also get him a bicycle. But it was raining, and she needed to cover the bicycle with something. If the child would only lend her his coat, she would come right back. The child never saw his coat again.

> [The suffering of the Jewish child] should have shaken us to our core, yanked us out of our passive paralysis and blindness and moved us all to protect our children. But so far that has not happened. As I write these lines [November 1941] we are going through the most critical time of the ghetto: new expulsions, more streets being taken away, less room, a tighter noose around our necks, walls, new walls. There is no room to move. Winter, damp, cold, poverty and death-will we be able to save the Jewish child?[148]

Opoczynski discussed Poles and Germans as well as Jews, conveying his belief that no one people had a monopoly on righteousness, just as no one people had a monopoly on evil. In his description of the parówki, Opoczynski wrote that the Nazis accused the Jews of spreading typhus in order to isolate them from Poles and Germans. The Nazis were afraid to let German soldiers wander through the ghetto. Opoczynski knew that many came to steal and rob, but he also knew there were exceptions:

> Many German soldiers came to visit the ghetto because they were decent ordinary folk [*erlekhe folks menshn*], workers and peasants, who had no interest in Hitler's ideology. . . . [T]hey would come to the Jewish street markets and talk to the Jewish traders in Yiddish-German. Like common people everywhere they [found a common language], began to feel comfortable with one another and even began to say what they thought of Hitler and his gang.[149]

In the same reportage, corrupt Jews eagerly joined Germans and Poles in extorting money from their unfortunate brothers.

In "Smuggling in the Warsaw Ghetto" and "Gentiles in the Ghetto," Opoczynski described how smuggling and illegal trade drew Poles and Jews together. Of course, smugglers and traders were not saints. The Poles who entered the ghetto knew the Jews were hungry, and they used their buying power to get the best deal they could. They wanted to make a profit. No matter. Not only did they foil the German plans to isolate the Jews behind ghetto walls and separate the two peoples, they actually kept the ghetto alive.

> The bridge that linked Jew and gentile was made of bad material—speculation—but it served a good purpose—to save many Jews from starva-

tion . . . these Polish smugglers [worried about their own pockets] but still played a national role . . . by maintaining the ties between loyal citizens of Poland and by stretching out a brotherly hand to the persecuted. Thereby they sow the seeds of morality in a time of major moral degeneration.[150]

Their actions, Opoczynski believed, also served as an implicit repudiation of the widespread economic boycott that had figured so prominently in prewar Poland. The war proved once again that the two peoples needed each other ("The Poles cannot live without the ghetto"). Painful as it was for Jewish women to part with wedding dresses, candlesticks, and family heirlooms, they had already lost their homes; now they had to keep their families alive. Smuggling and trading created personal bonds, a form of community that somehow gave the Jews in the ghetto a sense of comfort, a reminder that they were not completely alone. After all, the Poles themselves took risks to enter the ghetto. Often, after the Polish peasant women made a deal for merchandise they wanted, to ward off bad luck they tried to do a good deed such as giving bread to starving Jewish children.

> The "kind lady" would reach into her bosom, take out her purse and would give the poor Jewish child a zloty or even two zlotys or even some bread. At the same time she would whisper in his ear and ask him to say a prayer to the "Jewish God" to help her get back on the Aryan side.[151]

After the Great Deportation, Opoczynski continued to keep his diary and traced the destruction of Warsaw Jewry in short, laconic comments. On September 3 he recorded the death of Shmuel Breslav: "Shmueli, a leader of the Hashomer Ha-tzair, a talented fellow, a great idealist and a man of action was shot in the street yesterday." The next day he noted the rumors that the Germans intended to wipe out all the Jews of Europe: "Our end had come. This is the thought that is on everyone's mind. We're facing annihilation and no one has the courage to lead a resistance, so that we would at least die with honor."[152]

On September 8 he described the bedlam of the "cauldron," where all the remaining Jews of the ghetto had to wait in a small area for a final registration and selection:

> The impression left by this registration was terrible and was symbolized by one- and two-year-old children sitting on a sofa in the middle of the road and crying "mama" while Jews, their hearts bleeding, were passing by, watching the horrible scene and crying. The Germans had probably done it deliberately. They could have taken the children away, but they did not. On the contrary—they let the Jews see and grieve.

And on September 30:

> We are now seeing beautiful days. The sunshine is unusual for September. The heart is full of feelings. Scenes and memories of the past fill up the soul on this eve of Hoshana Raba [the seventh day of the fall Sukkot festival]. This gold in the sky, the colors, the beauty of the sunset—the heart is so strong—will we live to see redemption?

On October 9 Opoczynski reported rumors of a "giant electric chair" in Treblinka, designed to kill ten thousand Jews and Poles a day. "The Germans like to brag about their industrial prowess, and so they also want to run their killing industry with American efficiency."

In the last months of his life, Opoczynski continually returned to the theme of resistance. Apparently unaware of the ŻOB and its preparations for armed resistance, he gave vent to his anger in his diary. On December 4, 1942, he discounted a rumor sweeping the ghetto about Jewish workers in a labor camp near Lublin who had supposedly killed their German guards; 180 Jews were said to have escaped.

> We are more than certain that this rumor is not true. It had been produced by our deep sense of shame that in Warsaw, this mother city of Israel, in this city with its great masses of tough working Jews, and its traditions of political struggle—the Jews should have let themselves be led like sheep to the slaughter.

Even as Opoczynski wrote of his growing despair, he retained his faith in the basic decency of ordinary Germans. For him, faith in "the German masses" represented a last shred of hope and a lingering trace of prewar humanism that assuaged the growing sense of terror and isolation. On December 22, 1942, he reported widespread rumors that fifty thousand Warsaw Jews had turned up as workers in Bobruisk in White Russia, a sign that Jews still wanted to believe that the Germans really were deporting Jews to "the East" and not to Treblinka. The Gestapo spread these rumors, Opoczynski believed, not to comfort the Jews but to deceive ordinary German soldiers.

> [The Gestapo is afraid] . . . that ordinary German soldiers, who are finding out the truth about the "resettlements" from their conversations with Jews, might revolt. . . . The German soldier really did believe the SS when it said that Jews were being sent to the East [to work]. But when he hears [from us] about the death factory at Treblinka, he starts to tremble and denies it all. But now that the British and the American radio is broadcasting the news, the SS has to work harder to cover up the terrible truth.

His last diary entry is dated on January 5, 1943. He was probably seized during the roundups in mid-January. Nothing is known about the fate of his wife, Miriam, and of his son, Danchik. Much of his prewar literary archive was found in the second part of the Oyneg Shabes.

Shie (Yehoshua) Perle: The Accuser

Before the war Shie (Yehoshua) Perle had been one of the most talented writers in Yiddish literature. Overcoming the personal tragedy of his wife's suicide in 1926, he went on to write *Yidn fun a gants yor,* a superb novel of Jewish life in a provincial city seen through the eyes of an adolescent boy.[153] The novel won the Bund's top literary prize in 1937 as well as the first prize of the Yiddish Pen Club. (Critics like Dan Miron and David Roskies have compared it to Henry Roth's *Call It Sleep.*) While many Yiddish novels had a historical or a political focus, Perle's narrative examined interpersonal relationships, family dynamics, and psychological tensions. Instead of national pathos the novel described the everyday, with its problems and small victories. If there was any implicit political message in this autobiographical novel, it was subtly embedded in Perle's depiction of Polish Jews as being totally at home in their surroundings. The characters in the novel, struggling to make ends meet, do not see themselves as a people in exile. Poland is their home, its streets, villages, and landscapes are their own. They differ from their Polish neighbors, but they are neighbors all the same. Perhaps this sense of *doikayt* ["hereness"] explained Perle's growing closeness to the Bund, which he formally joined just before the war.[154]

But as one of his close friends noted, Perle paid little attention to politics. His constant flirtations with the Left never overshadowed his deep interest in Jewish tradition and his respect for religion. When Dovid Nomberg, a prominent Yiddish writer, died in Warsaw, many leftist writers attended his funeral bareheaded. Perle wore a skullcap. (This is the way we Jews honor the dead, he said.) While vacationing in a Polish resort in August 1939, he would go to hear the sermons of nearby Hasidic rebbes.[155]

Perle was as controversial as he was talented. Long before the publication of *Yidn fun a gants yor,* Perle had gained a certain notoriety for his serialized stories in the Yiddish press, which contained sexual motifs that shocked straight-laced critics and self-appointed guardians of the moral purity of Yiddish literature. (Some of the most memorable passages of *Yidn fun a gants yor* involved adolescent sexual awakening and fantasies.) In 1935, when Perle appeared to speak at the Second International Conference of the YIVO in Vilna, he was booed off the stage. Writers of *shund* [trash], the crowd yelled, were not welcome at the YIVO.[156]

When the war began Perle fled to Soviet-occupied Lwów. The Soviets treated him well, and, according to Melekh Ravitch, Perle became the chairman of the Yiddish section of the writers' union.[157] But he also realized that Soviet Jews had little interest in Yiddish culture, and their future as a distinct nationality seemed bleak. After the Germans invaded the Soviet Union, he returned to Warsaw in late 1941 and shared his impressions and concerns with Ringelblum.[158] In the ghetto Perle lived next door to Shakhne Zagan, the leader of the LPZ. Perhaps this also brought him into closer contact with Ringelblum. Ringelblum mentioned that Perle wrote a long report on Soviet-occupied Lwów for the Oyneg Shabes.[159]

The war changed Perle. In the spring of 1942 the Oyneg Shabes asked Perle to participate in a survey of Jewish intellectuals and writers about the future of Polish Jewry after the war. Of all the participants, Perle was among the most pessimistic—and angry. Perle, deeply committed to Polish Jewry, to its folk culture and its language, understood that the war was irreparably destroying it all. He greatly resented the "Jewish bourgeoisie" and its lack of self-respect and sense of national honor. The ghetto experience, as shown by the plague of informants and deep demoralization, mercilessly exposed the rot that had infected large sections of Polish Jewry long before the outbreak of the war.

> Among Poles you certainly would not see the pestilence of informers that we have in the ghetto. I find it hard to believe that any nation endowed with national pride would sink to such shameful depths. . . . . [The Germans] shut the Jews up in the ghetto with the hope that they would kill one another. And they have been proven right; we bury each other alive.[160]

This abject lack of national honor extended to their own language, which Jews "hated," even in the Soviet Union, where Yiddish received state support. Only the Jewish working class, Perle believed, the "only group which was not rotten," offered a ray of hope. As for the postwar world, he believed in some kind of Jewish state, "but a Communist one." "Only the Soviet Union," he stressed, "could give the Jews a country."

In early August 1942 the Germans entered Perle's courtyard and shouted for everyone in the building to come down. Trusting in their documents, Shakhne Zagan and his family obeyed the command, only to find themselves hauled directly to a Treblinka-bound train. Perle ignored the order and stayed put in his room; he evaded that particular roundup.[161]

In August 1942 the Oyneg Shabes asked Perle to write about the Great

Deportation. He started writing on August 31 and completed it on October 2. The essay, "Khurbm Varshe" (The Destruction of Warsaw) hurled bitter accusations at the Judenrat, the Jewish police—and all of Warsaw Jewry itself.[162]

> We must ask: my God, who raised these [policemen], how can the sons of Jewish fathers turn into such killers? Which Jewish mothers nursed them? The only answer is that the fathers were murderers and the mothers were whores.

Perle cited the case of a Jewish policeman who had already caught four Jews. One short of his quota, he spied a small child whimpering in an abandoned apartment. He raced to hand the child over to the SS—and to take his well-deserved rest for the day. But the SS man looked at the child with disgust and then quickly shot him with his revolver.

> No, the German executioner said. This "head" does not count. I shot the little dog. Anyone I shoot does not count as a "head." So you owe me one "head." Go catch someone or you'll pay.
> The Jewish bastard left without a word and brought in a fifth "head."

Why had there been no leadership? Why hadn't the people fought back? Czerniakow's suicide had been an act of cowardice. Why had he not issued a public call for resistance before he decided to kill himself? The Judenrat had played such a shameful role that its members, Perle believed, deserved to be hanged from lamp posts.

> We could have defended ourselves, not let ourselves get slaughtered like stupid oxen. Had all Jews just run into the streets, had we all just climbed over the ghetto walls, had we all flooded the Warsaw streets carrying knives, axes, even stones—then maybe they would have killed 10,000, 20,000, but they would never have killed 300,000! We would have died with honor.

His conclusion was bleak:

> If a community of 300,000 Jews did not try to resist, if it exposed its own throat to the slaughterer's knife, if it did not kill one German or one Jewish collaborator—then maybe this was a generation that deserved its bitter fate!

In September 1942, as Perle was writing "Khurbm Varshe," Shmuel Winter secured him a job in the artificial honey factory on Franciszkańska 30—the same factory that would also employ Rachel Auerbach.[163] Now only Jews with numbers—hung abound their necks like dog tags—had a right to live, working up to fourteen hours a day for meager rations. The Germans handed out

30,000 numbers in all, and Perle wrote another essay about his new name, "4580." The Bible had admonished Jews to blot out the name of Amalek, the treacherous tribe that had attacked the Israelites in the desert. Now the Germans, with the consent and connivance of the Judenrat, were turning the tables on the Jews.[164] They had already killed 300,000. And now they were blotting out the names of the few they allowed to linger on in the ghetto shops.

Once his name, Perle wrote, had served as his conscience and his moral guide. Before the war his name had provoked anger and derision—and then honor and recognition. In the worst moments of his life—following the death of his young wife—it was fear of bringing dishonor on his name that had prevented him from committing suicide.[165] A name meant autonomy, it symbolized a small measure of dignity, and it linked its bearer with past and future generations. One could mourn a name; could one mourn a number?

In this essay, written in a tone of ironic self-mockery mixed with self-deprecating humor, Perle discussed the new status that gave him a temporary right to life—the tin tag that hung around his neck with the number 4580.[166]

> And just as Sholom Aleikhem's Motl, the son of Peyse the Cantor, runs
> around barefoot and happily proclaims, "I'm alright, I'm an orphan,"
> so I walk around in the tenement courtyard on Franciszkanska Street,
> which had become the great wide world, and proclaim: "I'm alright, I'm
> a number."

In "Khurbm Varshe," Perle had bitterly noted that it was the worst who had gone into the shops and survived—the hustlers and *makhers* who paid big money for their dog tags and preferred self-preservation to resistance. But in the end, Perle implicitly admitted, he himself had acted no differently. He, too, had survived thanks to pull. Instead of rushing into the streets and attacking a German, as he urged in "Khurbm Varshe," he had became one of the "lucky ones." And what now? For the few weeks of extra life, one paid a heavy price in guilt. His neighbor ("as clever, as learned, as polite as I—maybe even more polite") did not get a number. He kept his name: "but a beautiful human name has the same value today as a beautiful human heart or a beautiful human virtue."

> In order to become a number, my fifty-three years had to be jabbed at
> until they bled. Jabbed at, mocked, raped. In order for me to become
> a number, they had to destroy my house first. Destroy it, tear it up by
> the roots. Under my number lies three times a hundred thousand Jewish martyrs. Three times a hundred thousand Jewish lives that Amalek
> slaughtered with the consent of the head of the kehilla and his servants.

From under my unfortunate number leaps out the cry of tens of thousands of poisoned, strangled Jewish children.

Traditional Jewish texts of lamentations and mourning could not describe what was happening now.

> In the dark nights I hear the great weeping of the mother of all our mothers, our Mother Rachel. She walks across the desolate fields and wraps her children in burial sheets. With her beautiful delicate hands she washes the blood off her sons and daughters. But can she wrap ALL of them in burial sheets. Can she wash them ALL? Blood cries out; and the earth, in all its length and breadth, is dissolved in lamentation.
>
> They lay, the slaughtered creatures, naked and shamed, scattered and spread, impurified for burial, without a kaddish, without a gravestone, violated by the murderous hands of Amalek, with the consent of the holy congregation of Warsaw. I'm alright. I'm a number.

In 1943 Perle and his son, Lolek, a member of the Polish Communist Party and an engineer by training, left the ghetto to hide on Aryan papers provided by a friend of Lolek's.[167] Like many other Jews in their position, Perle and his son clutched at a chance to buy Latin and Central American passports and thus possibly save their lives. Those who bought the passports assembled in Warsaw's Hotel Polski, from where the Germans sent many to camps in Germany and France while deciding whether these newly minted "Latin Americans" could be of value, either for exchanges or money.[168]

The Germans first sent Perle and his son to Bergen-Belsen.[169] There months passed as Perle nursed the hope that the Germans would let him leave Europe. A fellow inmate recalled that Perle loved to attend lectures on the Bible and other Jewish texts given by an Orthodox Jew. After one lecture Perle loudly complimented the Jew on his insights and on his excellent Yiddish. Another religious Jew mordantly repeated the well-known saying: "God, the Torah, and the Jewish People are one" (Kudsha borukh hu, araysa v'yisroel khad hu). Perle immediately understood the meaning and began to cry.[170] If the Jewish people were being destroyed, the Jew seemed to be saying, then what was the point of the Torah? And if a religious Jew could make such a statement, then who was left to show moral steadfastness? Perle despaired. Caught between his nostalgia for Jewish tradition and his vague left-wing sympathies, what he most believed in were the Jewish masses of Poland. And whatever happened to him, they, he knew, were gone forever. His essays had been filled with allusions to the Bible and the Prophets, to Sholom Aleikhem and to Peretz. His Polish Jews would have understood them. Would anyone else?

In October 1943 the Germans told Perle, his son, and a group of other Jews to pack their bags. They were being transferred to a transit camp and then to freedom in Switzerland. Perle seemed hopeful and promised those left behind that he would do all he could to publicize the German crimes. The train actually took the group to Auschwitz, where Perle and his son were gassed.[171]

After the war, when the Warsaw Jewish Historical Institute published "Khurbm Varshe" in its journal without naming the author, the Yiddish literary critic H. Leyvik questioned its authenticity and charged that Ber Mark, the director of the Institute, had falsified the document. Why did the "anonymous author" reserve his bitterness and anger at his fellow Jews and hardly mention the Germans? And despite all his calls for resistance, where was the evidence that he himself had done any fighting? Surely, Leyvik argued, this was an example of scurrilous Communist subversion of the truth.[172]

Indeed, Ber Mark was not averse to tampering with and censoring published documents. But, on this occasion, Mark easily rebutted Leyvik's accusations. For Leyvik, still reeling at the destruction of East European Jewry, the murdered Jews were *kedoyshim*, martyrs. He had trouble grasping the anger and bitterness that engulfed Warsaw Jewry as it surged to its death. But the Oyneg Shabes preferred a record that told the entire truth—thus ensuring that the Jews would be remembered as they were and not as elegists preferred to see them.

Rachel Auerbach: The Survivor

As one of only three survivors of the Oyneg Shabes Archive, Rachel Auerbach had the rare opportunity not only to retrieve her wartime reportage but to rewrite and publish her reports in such books as *B'hutsot varshe, Varshever tsvoes*, and *Baym letstn veg*. The differences, some subtle, some great, between her wartime writings and their postwar versions reflected a personal journey of survival and an evolving search for the meaning of Holocaust memory. As she handed over her first cache of writings to the Oyneg Shabes on July 26, 1942, in the chaos of the deportation to Treblinka, she attached a note that exposed her feelings: raw fear, violent anger, despair. "I am handing over this unfinished essay to the archive. The fifth day of the 'Aktion'. Perhaps such horrors have already occurred before in Jewish history. But such shame, never. Jews as tools [of the killers]. I want to stay alive. I am ready to kiss the boots of the worst scoundrel [*dem gemaynstn kham*] just to be able to see the moment of revenge. REVENGE REVENGE remember."[173]

In that same note she also wondered whether her writings would share the same fate as the scribblings of a coal miner trapped in an accident with no survivors, whose body would never be found. Would anyone read them, would anyone care? And besides, she complained, she had lost her ability to write coherently. Her style, she felt, was confused, disjointed. Had it not been for Ringelblum, she would have written nothing. And yet, maybe it was best if she died. As a survivor, what good would she be to anybody?

By early 1944, living under false papers on the Aryan side, she was writing her memories of the Warsaw Ghetto at the request of the Jewish National Committee. This time there were no questions, no doubts about why she was writing. She owed it to the dead to tell what had happened. But her writing had to be exact:

> The mass murder, the murder of millions of Jews by the Germans, is a
> fact that speaks for itself. It is very dangerous to add to this subject inter-
> pretations or analyses. Anything that is said can quickly turn into hope-
> less hysteria or endless sobs. So one must approach this subject with the
> greatest caution, in a restrained and factual manner . . . this had been
> my intention: not to express but to transmit, to note only facts but not to
> interpret.[174]

She quickly added that she realized immediately than this mandate was impossible—even for her.

After the war, in Poland and in Israel, after she had recovered her wartime manuscripts, her writing would take on yet another purpose: to ensure that the Jewish people remembered not only to keep faith with the dead but to use the lessons of the Holocaust to strengthen the nation and tighten the bonds between Israel and the Diaspora.

For Auerbach, memory and mourning demanded a painful return to the intense, vibrant world of prewar Warsaw Jewry which one of her mentors, the Yiddish poet Melekh Ravitch, had called a sprawling mosaic of different Jewish tribes and subcultures.[175] Auerbach took its shattered bits and shards and reconstructed a mosaic of memory based on a poignant evocation of dozens of individual vignettes. And thus she spoke for those who had no one to remember them: the ordinary Jews she came to know in the ghetto as she ran the soup kitchen on Leszno 40 and the Jewish writers, artists, and actors whose milieu she shared in the 1930s and in the ghetto. The more one knew about what and whom the Germans had murdered, the more one could grasp the enormity of the national *khurbm* [holocaust].

Before the war she had been active in Warsaw Yiddishist circles and had written articles on literary criticism and psychology for the Yiddish- and the Polish-language Jewish press. Like Ringelblum, she was a native of Galicia.

Before moving with her family to Lwów, she had spent her childhood in a remote shtetl in Podolia, Lanowitz, where she acquired a love of Jewish folklore and the Yiddish language. The great Jewish folklorist and ethnographer, Shmuel Lehman, had interviewed her many times about the folksongs and customs of the rural Jews of Podolia.[176] Auerbach, like Opoczynski, was a superb observer of the Jewish everyday. She had a fine sense of the nuances of the behavior and speech of the diverse panorama of Polish Jewry. Auerbach conveyed what she saw and observed in evocative, powerful language that made her writings an indispensable source for any cultural or social history of the Warsaw Ghetto.

Like many other Galician Jews, Auerbach combined a deep Jewish identity with a first-class Polish education and cultural sensibility. At Lwów University in the early 1920s she studied psychology and befriended the young poetess Dvora Fogel and her friend, Bruno Schulz. Indeed, it was Auerbach who was instrumental in launching Schulz's literary career as one of the most promising writers of the Polish avant-garde.[177] In Lwów in the 1920s she served on the editorial board of *Tsushtayer,* a literary journal that tried to encourage Yiddish culture in a region where most of the Jewish intelligentsia spoke Polish.

Auerbach moved to Warsaw in 1933. She began to publish literary and theater criticism in the Polish-language Jewish daily *Nasz przegląd* as well as in Yiddish journals such as *Literarishe bleter.* She also published articles on psychology and supported herself with part time copy editing. In Warsaw Auerbach became the companion of the brilliant and tempestuous Yiddish poet Itzik Manger. After Manger was forced to leave Poland in 1938, Auerbach preserved many of his manuscripts and hid them in the Ringelblum Archive.

Thus much of the power of Auerbach's reportage stemmed from her ability to navigate cultural boundaries, derived from a life that straddled different worlds: village, shtetl, and city; Yiddish and Polish; Poles and Jews; Galicia and Warsaw; the milieu of the Jewish literary elite and the world of the Jewish masses; religious and secular; diaspora nationalists and Zionists. (This negotiation and mediation would continue after the war, as Auerbach began speaking up for the murdered victims in her controversies and arguments with Ben Zion Dinur about the agendas of Yad Vashem and Jacques Steiner over his book *Treblinka*.)

Auerbach and Ringelblum had known each other before the war but had not been especially close. Therefore Auerbach was quite surprised when Ringelblum mobilized her for the Aleynhilf and then for the Oyneg Shabes. In addition to her essay on the soup kitchen Auerbach kept a diary of her life in the ghetto and, at Ringelblum's request, began to write a report of the literary life of the ghetto.[178]

In her diary Auerbach gave free rein to her growing fear of death, as reports of mass executions in the provinces streamed into the Oyneg Shabes. In the past, she wrote on March 6, 1942, Jews had gone to their deaths knowing that they could have saved themselves had they only chosen to renounce their faith. Now Polish Jewry did not have the comfort of Kiddush Hashem, of dying to sanctify God's name. Like a convict on an American death row, they were waiting for their date with the executioner. In her diary Auerbach betrayed her uncertainty and her dread as her thoughts flitted back and forth between despair and hope.

> How will our ordinary Jew get the strength to meet such a death, what will hold up his spirit as he waits week after week for his execution? . . .
> I am sure that our age-old spiritual capital, this golden pillar of our community, has not been totally shattered[179]

During the summer of 1942 Auerbach had several close calls but managed to survive.[180] In the fall of 1942, during the lull in the killing, Shmuel Winter summoned Auerbach to his office on Franciszkańska 30. Winter told Auerbach that he had found a new job for her in an artificial honey factory in the same building. What he really wanted her to do, however, was to fulfill a new assignment for the Oyneg Shabes—to interview and write down accounts of escapees from Treblinka for the archive. Several of them had already made their way back into the ghetto. Using her job as cover, Auerbach began to interview one of these escapees, Abraham Krzepicki. When Krzepicki's detailed account surfaced in the second part of the Ringelblum archive, it came to almost one hundred typed pages. Winter and Ringelblum closely followed Auerbach's work. The Oyneg Shabes had hoped to issue it as an underground publication (more on this in chapter 8).

In February 1943 Auerbach escaped to the Aryan side. Helped by Polish friends, she procured Aryan documents and became a courier for the Jewish underground. Carrying a basket with hidden money and manuscripts, covered by vegetables, Auerbach crisscrossed the city on various missions.[181]

After the ghetto uprising, Auerbach continued the legacy of the Oyneg Shabes.[182] She not only wrote a constant stream of essays but also became part of an underground Jewish archive on the Aryan side. At the request of the Jewish National Committee she wrote essays on the Great Deportation and on the murdered Jewish intelligentsia. With the help of Polish friends, Auerbach buried her writings in two different locations in Warsaw, on the grounds of the Zoo and in a field in the southern district of Mokotow. Both caches survived the war.[183]

Auerbach had been close to the circles of the prewar YIVO, and her wartime writings stressed the close links of the Jewish intelligentsia and the masses. The first title of her essays on the murdered writers, musicians, and artists was "Tsuzamen mitn folk" (Together with the people). Her work followed in the footsteps not only of Emanuel Ringelblum but also of YIVO director Max Weinreich who made special efforts to incorporate the insights of Sigmund Freud and social psychology into the study of Polish Jewry. In a world hitherto dominated by traditions and ideologies that stressed the primacy of the collective over the individual, Auerbach, like Weinreich, believed that one could not understand *klal yisroel* (the collective) without grasping the needs of *reb yisroel* (the individual): the aspirations, drives, obsessions, and hopes of the many individuals who made up the Jewish masses in Poland. (In her masterly 1935 review of Shie Perle's wonderful novel of adolescent awakening—*Yidn fun a gants yor*—she lambasted a prudish Bundist critic who panned the book because it suggested that adolescent boys thought about sex.)[184]

And so, too, in her Holocaust writings she highlighted the complex interplay of psychological factors in individuals, families, and entire social groups. She told a complicated story: resilience, vitality, and self-sacrifice on the one hand, and corruption and moral collapse on the other.

Auerbach stressed the Germans' brilliant use of psychological factors to effect the destruction of Warsaw Jewry and to use the Jews' strengths against them. The Germans played with the Jews and with their natural human instincts of self-preservation and hope. In her cogent observations of the mass hysteria that gripped the Warsaw Ghetto in the summer of 1942, she described how the very qualities that had served Jews so well in the past—practicality, pragmatism, hard-headedness, "seykhel," and natural optimism— now accelerated their journey into the abyss.

> And still other Jews. Broad-shouldered, deep-voiced, with powerful hands and hearts. Artisans, workers, wagon drivers, porters, Jews who, with a blow of their fists, could floor any hooligan who dared enter their neighborhoods.
>
> Where were you when your wives and children, your old fathers and mothers, were taken away? What happened to make you run off like cattle stampeded by fire? Was there no one to give you some purpose in the confusion? You were swept away by the flood, together with those who were weak.
>
> And you sly cunning merchants, philanthropists in your short fur

coats and caps. How was it that you didn't catch on to the murderous swindle?[185]

Would other peoples, confronted with a similar massive assault, have acted better? She did not think so. Did Warsaw Jewry eventually recover from the shock and fight back? Yes. Should one blame the Jewish masses for not having fought back earlier? Only those who had not been there, Auerbach implied, would do so. Was armed resistance the only way the Jews stood up to the Germans? Absolutely not.

In November 1943 Auerbach was sitting in a Warsaw trolley car and saw a woman, her head thrown back, talking to herself. Like the biblical Hannah in her silent prayer, she at first conveyed the impression of being drunk. It turned out that she had just learned that the Germans had shot her son.

> "My child," she stammered, paying no attention to the other people in the streetcar, "my son. My beautiful beloved son."
> I too would like to talk to myself like someone mad or drunk, the way that woman did in the Book of Judges [sic] who poured out her heart unto the Lord and whom Eli drove from the Temple.
> I may neither groan nor weep. I may not draw attention to myself in the street. And I need to groan; I need to weep. Not four times a year. I feel the need to say Yizkor four times a day.[186]

Unlike the Polish woman, she could only mourn in secret. She returned to her room, locked the door, and began to write "Yizkor" (Remember).[187] Most of the time Auerbach wrote in Polish; this she wrote in Yiddish.

She poured out her soul as she tried to describe the murder of Warsaw Jewry: the toddlers, the children whom she remembered from the ghetto schools, the tough Jewish workers, the hardened women shopkeepers, young scouts, courting couples, intellectuals, all gone, gone. Even if a few individuals survived, the vibrant, raucous, and diverse mosaic of Warsaw Jewry had been destroyed. "Yizkor" humanized the victims by recalling not only their individuality but also their city, the specific urban milieu that had shaped them and that had made them "Varshever."

As she groped for images in "Yizkor" to explain the sheer magnitude of the catastrophe, she used the example of a flood and evoked the oath "If I forget thee, O Jerusalem" of Psalm 137:

> I saw a flood once in the mountains. Wooden huts, torn from their foundations were carried above the raging waters. One could see lighted lamps in them, men, women, and children in cradles tied to ceiling beams. Other huts were empty inside but one could see a tangle of arms

waving from the roof, like branches blowing in the wind waving desperately toward heaven, toward the riverbanks for help. At a distance one could see mouths gaping, but one could not hear the cries because the roar of the waters drowned out everything.

And that's how the Jewish masses flowed to their destruction at the time of the deportations. Sinking as helplessly into the deluge of destruction.

And if for even one of the days of my life I should forget how I saw you then, my people, desperate and confused, delivered over to extinction, may all knowledge of me be forgotten and my name be cursed like that of those traitors who are unworthy to share your pain.[188]

Auerbach offered no explanations for the catastrophe. This secular writer could only end her essay by repeating the Hebrew words of the traditional Jewish prayer for the dead. As David Roskies has pointed out:

Only someone who was flesh of the people's flesh yet thoroughly trained in analytic observation could have produced—fourteen months after the events described—a chronicle of destruction that combined reportage and liturgy, the documentary sweep of Lamentations and the individual pathos of Psalms. Only someone standing on the other side of the ghetto wall could possess such total recall.[189]

In other essays written in 1943–44, Auerbach regretted the lack of resistance. But "Yizkor" was different. Unlike the works of some other writers of the Oyneg Shabes, such as Perle, Lichtenstein, or Opoczynski—Auerbach's "Yizkor" was suffused with empathy and stunned bewilderment rather than anger. By using the imagery of a flood, a natural disaster, she anticipated future questions that those who were not there would pose.

No, the mass murder was not a metahistorical event. But its enormity was too horrible and too unprecedented to allow for glib theories and facile questions that might compromise the memory of the Jewish masses that she cherished so deeply. How does one resist a flood or an earthquake? What befell the Jewish masses was so unthinkable and so calamitous that they were psychologically unprepared. Implicitly Auerbach was anticipating the invidious distinctions that many would make after the war between the few who fought back with weapons and the masses that had allegedly died without a fight. It was the people she wrote about in "Yizkor," not the fighters who had risen up just months before.

Now all she could do was defend their memory and take her place, once more, among those who could no longer speak for themselves. As a child in the synagogue her grandfather had built in Lanovitz, she recalled how on major holidays the Torah reader, Meyer Itsik, would loudly bang the podium and cry out "We recite yizkor." And then even the less devout would return to pray. For Auerbach, "Yizkor" was a return not to religion but to the place of her birth, to a world that did not have to invent new words to describe pain and loss. They were already there, in the prayers.

After the war Auerbach desperately told everyone she could about the archive hidden under the ruins. Well aware that she, Wasser, and his wife were the only survivors, she implored people to start the search. At first people did not take her seriously. There was so little money, the dimensions of the disaster were just beginning to sink in, and traumatized survivors had other priorities.

In April 1946 Auerbach spoke at a meeting in Warsaw to commemorate the third anniversary of the ghetto uprising. The Yiddish writer Mendel Mann recalled a tiresome and disappointing evening, full of phrase mongering and political sloganeering. Then Auerbach, the only woman on the rostrum, got up to speak:

> She did not make any speeches, she did not "explain the meaning" of the uprising. She implored! With a stubbornness that deeply affected me, she demanded, she called: Remember, she cried out, there is a national treasure under the ruins. The Ringelblum Archive is there. We cannot rest until we dig up the archive. . . . Even if there are five stories of ruins, we have to find the archive. I'm not making this up. I know what I'm talking about! This isn't just talk! This is coming from my heart. I will not rest, and I will not let you rest. We must rescue the Ringelblum Archive![190]

Mann remembered that Auerbach met with a cool reception. People had their own troubles, and many did not understand why the archive was so important. Everybody knew what happened, and survivors reckoned that they did not need any historians to tell them about the disaster.

But Auerbach disagreed. Now more than ever, survivors had to organize a systematic and collective effort to record the past and continue the work of the Oyneg Shabes. The traditions of the Ringelblum Archive could counteract disturbing trends she had already noticed in early postwar memoirs. The memoirs of the eminent biologist Ludwik Hirszfeld, a convert to Catholicism, or the pianist Władysław Szpilman, she felt, presented a skewed and distorted picture of the ghetto.[191] But what could one expect, she asked, from individuals who had been so distant from Jewish society before the war? On the other hand, Auerbach also attacked the memoirs and writings of many nationally conscious survivors for their tendency to settle political scores and nurture ideological jealousies. Auerbach held up the model of the Oyneg Shabes, where, she felt, a shared sense of national mission trumped narrow agendas. In the aftermath of the catastrophe, a wounded nation had to look at its record, the good as well as the bad. To tell the whole truth, to add and subtract nothing, was a debt owed not just to the victims who had died but to the nation that had to recover and rebuild.

Auerbach and Wasser persisted, and with money from the Jewish Labor Committee in New York the search finally began in earnest in the summer of 1946.

For the rest of her life Auerbach guarded Ringelblum's legacy. Immediately after the war she threw herself into the work of the Historical Commission of the Central Committee of Polish Jews, which later became the Jewish Historical Institute (ŻIH). Even before the war ended, the Commission, which besides Auerbach included such scholars as Philip Friedman, Joseph Kermish, and Nachman Blumenthal, collected survivor diaries, memoirs, and testimonies. It published several important books of documents and testimonies. Auerbach helped publish Leon Wieliczker's memoirs of the Janowska concentration camp near Lwów and a book on Treblinka, based on survivor testimony.[192]

After her immigration to Israel in 1950, she helped organize the collection of survivor testimony and support for Yad Vashem, the Israeli Holocaust Archive and Museum. There, too, people remembered her as a tough, uncompromising, and single-minded woman who was determined to protect the memory of the victims—and Ringelblum's legacy.[193] She was convinced that the study of the Holocaust should not be limited to professional scholars. Researchers had to reach out to survivors, mobilize them, and harness their need to recount what they saw. Unlike some scholars who regarded survivor testimony with suspicion, Auerbach believed that for many aspects of the Holocaust their testimony was a critical resource. Ringelblum had shown the way, she argued, with his call for history to be a collective and popular enterprise, and Philip Friedman had continued this approach after the end of the war. Furthermore, Ringelblum had reminded the Jewish people that the writing of their history should not depend on gentile documents and hostile sources. After the war this charge had become even more important. Auerbach was not only worried about Holocaust denial, although that too concerned her greatly. She fretted that Jews, Israelis in particular, were forgetting just how powerful a force Holocaust awareness could become in strengthening national identity and cohesion.[194] The Six Day War was just one example. Because of the Holocaust, the Jewish soldier knew that he had no choice but to win.

In 1958 Auerbach became involved in a nasty, public battle with the dean of Israeli historians, Ben Tziyon Dinur, who also served as the director of Yad Vashem. Dinur had attacked Auerbach for her allegedly poor performance in her job and fired her. Auerbach hit back with a public rebuttal that questioned Dinur's priorities and the entire direction of Yad Vashem. Instead of focusing on research and study of the Holocaust, she charged, Yad Vashem was neglecting its basic mandate in favor of projects that had little to do directly with the Holocaust.[195] The very fact that it allocated far more money to German-language rather than Yiddish-language testimony, Auerbach pointed out, spoke for itself.[196] Research on the internal life of the ghettos, on social conflicts within Jewish society, whether or not Jews outside Europe had done all they could to rescue their brethren—all these vital questions were not getting the attention they deserved. Indeed, in a draft of a memorial article for Philip Friedman, she wrote that right after the war she and her comrades who were working in the postwar Historical Commission in Warsaw had regretted that they had been able to publish only a fraction of what they should have. But however inadequate, she now realized that, in retrospect, their efforts in postwar Poland constituted a "golden age" of Holocaust research.[197]

Auerbach also condemned what she feared was premature normalization of German-Jewish relations and refused to allow her biography to appear in the *Leksikon fun der nayer Yidisher literatur* because the project was partly financed with German reparations money.[198] In 1966 she became involved in a bitter dispute with Jean Steiner about his fictionalized account of Treblinka. Steiner, she charged, had distorted the truth and had defamed the memory of the victims and the honor of the camp survivors.[199]

Before she died in 1976, Auerbach published three books of memoirs on the Warsaw Ghetto. In the tension between her wartime writings and postwar emendations, one can discern a marked shift not in subject matter but in emphasis and attitude.

In her wartime writings and reportage for the archive, Auerbach judged herself harshly. The soup kitchen had been a failure, the Aleynhilf largely an exercise in futility.

After the war, when she retrieved these wartime writings, she took a more positive view of what she had done. She admitted that no one who depended *only* on the soup kitchen could have survived. But the kitchens had provided a critical margin for those who had some other source of food and had helped many people to survive; the Aleynhilf had done yeoman work in keeping up the struggle for human dignity.

By the same token she changed her views on the state of Polish Jewry and its cultural future. In the 1930s she shared the doubts of many of her friends about the future of Yiddish culture in Poland. But as she redacted her wartime writings, she realized that here, too, she had been overly pessimistic. During the war she had written about the last days of such Yiddish cultural figures as the librarian Lev Shor, the poets Hershele, Kalman Lis, and Joseph Kirman, the actors Miriam Orleska, singers like Marysia Eizenshtat, composers like Yankel Glatshteyn. After the war, as she reread her essays on the Warsaw Jewish cultural elite, she asserted that this new generation of writers, poets, artists, and singers would have taken the place of those who had gone before—if only the Germans had not killed them all. Furthermore, she wrote, her work in the Aleynhilf was an epiphany. The Jewish masses had more strength than she had believed, and they would have provided a deep reserve of people and spirit to counteract assimilation and cultural decay.

This was her way of keeping faith with a band of comrades who had almost all perished.

Between the outbreak of the war and the summer of 1942 Ringelblum had managed to assemble a group of teachers, rabbis, scholars, writers, businessmen, and idealistic young people. This group, for all its differences, represented the finest traditions of Polish Jewry. It reflected the extraordinary cultural ferment that had transformed so much of East European Jewry in the first decades of the twentieth century.

One of the strengths of the Oyneg Shabes derived from its collective character. Ringelblum conceived the archive, probably wrote most of the questionnaires, and his views certainly carried great weight. But a sense of shared purpose clearly animated the Oyneg Shabes. This was not a group of disciples but, as Ringelblum himself wrote, a collective imbued with a common ideal. Over time as the archive evolved it was able to capitalize not only on its ability to organize and define topics but also on its success in drawing on the diverse talents of its members and in encouraging their individual creativity.

Based in the Aleynhilf, the archive had conduits to all sectors of the Jewish community and sources that brought in information from all over occupied Poland. The members of the Oyneg Shabes, whatever their political differences, worked under the most difficult circumstances to leave a record for future generations. True to the legacy of Peretz, Dubnow, and Ansky, these *zamlers* worked to the very end to ensure that future generations would view Polish Jewry through the prism of history rather than hagiography and elegy. In good times and bad, Polish Jewry spoke in many different voices; the men and women of the Oyneg Shabes did all they could to record those voices and ensure their survival until someday someone would listen.

CHAPTER 6

The Different Voices of Polish Jewry

In a diary entry of May 1942 Rachel Auerbach reported that German film crews were busy in the ghetto. This time they forced young girls and elderly men to undress together in a Jewish ritual bath. Just a few weeks before, the German movie makers had lined Jews up before a table loaded with food and ordered them to eat—but not before they stepped over hungry children who were begging at the door.[1] Meanwhile, all over occupied Europe, the German propaganda ministry was showing "The Eternal Jew," a film that compared Jews to rats and that showed them living in filth. The Nazis wanted to inscribe for future generations the image of Jews as a depraved and unscrupulous race of subhumans.

The German film crews arrived in the Warsaw Ghetto just in time. Within a few months the Great Deportation began. The Jews were unable to resist the murder machine, but they did foil the Nazi plan to destroy their traces and blot out their memory.

A generation earlier, in the middle of the First World War, the Yiddish writer Y. L. Peretz had urged his fellow Jews to document their wartime experiences. A nation that had pride and self-respect did not leave the writing of its history to enemies. Jews, Peretz warned, had to ensure that future historians would work with Jewish sources and not depend on hostile documents and testimony.[2] Until early 1942 the Oyneg Shabes, like Peretz in the First World War, had believed that the end of the war would see a revitalized Jewish community in Poland with the archive a buttress to national self-awareness and a means to create a "usable past" for the future. But by the spring of 1942 the workers of the Oyneg Shabes began to realize that, instead, they might be writing the last chapter of the eight-hundred-year history of Polish Jewry. Nonetheless their work had a purpose. Even if they did not survive, they could still determine what that last chapter would say and who would write it. Their work and sacrifice would create a record that would bring the killers to justice. They might still leave a legacy for future generations.

In the summer of 1943, in the Majdanek concentration camp, Isaac Schiper told a fellow inmate that,

> Everything depends on who transmits our testament to future generations, on who writes the history of this period. History is usually written by the victor. What we know about murdered peoples is only what their murderers vaingloriously cared to say about them. Should our murderers be victorious, should they write the history of this war, our destruction will be presented as one of the most beautiful pages of world history, and future generations will pay tribute to them as dauntless crusaders. Their every word will be taken as gospel. Or they may wipe out our memory altogether, as if we had never existed, as if there had never been a Polish Jewry, a ghetto in Warsaw, a Maidanek. Not even a dog will howl for us.
>
> But if we write the history of this period of blood and tears—and I firmly believe we will—who will believe us? Nobody will want to believe us, because our disaster is the disaster of the entire civilized world. . . . We'll have the thankless job of proving to a reluctant world that we are Abel, the murdered brother[3]

Ringelblum, more optimistic than Schiper, had no doubt that the world would believe what had happened—if confronted with the proper evidence. He intended to amass a record whose thoroughness, objectivity, and sheer scope would force "future generations" to look the truth in the face.

THE UNIQUENESS OF THE OYNEG SHABES

The Oyneg Shabes Archive was the largest secret archive in Nazi-occupied Poland, but it was not the only one. In the Vilna Ghetto, Jewish librarians and writers—for example, Herman Kruk, Avrom Sutzkever, and Shmerke Kaczerginski—gathered and buried books and documents.[4] In the Białystok Ghetto, a young resistance leader, Mordecai Tenenbaum, who had almost certainly learned about the Oyneg Shabes during his brief stay in the Warsaw Ghetto, set up a ghetto archive and incorporated it into the Jewish underground organization.[5] In the Lodz Ghetto, Ghetto Elder Chaim Rumkowski established an archive as a separate department of the ghetto administration—and seemed to turn a blind eye as it became a major center of testimony and documentation.[6] There was also a secret archive in the Kovno Ghetto, working closely with the Judenrat.

After the war much of the material gathered by these archives survived. Most of the Lodz Ghetto Archive was unearthed from a dry well and from a secret burial place under the former ghetto fire department. (The Germans discovered a third cache and destroyed it.) In 1944 Avrom Sutzkever and Shmerke Kaczerginski returned to Vilna and dug up many of the documents they had buried—as well as Kruk's important diary. In Białystok Mordecai Tenenbaum had entrusted the archive to a sympathetic Pole. The Pole disappeared but, miraculously, many of the archive's documents surfaced after the war.

Countless individuals worked on their own to record what they saw. In hundreds of ghettos, hiding places, jails, and death camps, lonely and terrified Jews left diaries, letters, and testimony of what they endured. For every scrap of documentation that surfaced after the war, probably many more manuscripts vanished forever.

But the secret archives could accomplish much more than solitary individuals. They drew their strength from the collective energy of dedicated workers who could pool their talents and establish a hierarchy of priorities and objectives. The more diverse the archival staff and the greater the range of their prewar political and cultural backgrounds, the more likely it was that the archive would develop fruitful contacts and sources of information. Archives, although not entirely free of politics, generated a sense of common purpose that helped allay political rivalry. A collective could mobilize financial resources and gain the protection of important people in the Jewish Councils or social welfare organizations more easily than individuals. In some ghettos the official Jewish leadership and the archival staffs came together in a complex relationship fraught with mutual suspicion and mutual need. Ghetto leaders might feed the archive important documents—even as they concealed others.

In some important respects the Oyneg Shabes Archive resembled the archives in other ghettos. All collected documentation and testimony, and all worked in varying degrees of secrecy. Many leaders had earned respect before the war and claimed some authority in the ghetto community. In Lodz, for instance, Henryk Neftalin had been a prominent and esteemed attorney. Herman Kruk had headed one of the largest Yiddish libraries in Poland, the Bund's Grosser Library in Warsaw; in the Vilna Ghetto he not only organized the library but turned it into a major institution of the ghetto's cultural life and used it as the base for his documentation project.[7] Avrom Sutzkever and Shmerke Kaczerginski had already made their mark in prewar Vilna as promising young poets in the literary group Yung Vilne, and if few people outside his youth movement, Dror, had heard of Mordecai Tenenbaum before the war, in the Białystok Ghetto he headed the Jewish resistance, acquiring authority and status that gave the archive legitimacy.[8]

But there were also important differences between these other archives and the Oyneg Shabes. In Lodz, Vilna, and Białystok the archives enjoyed varying degrees of official "cover" and encouragement, and received financial help—some more than others—from the official ghetto leaders, who in turn used the archives to convey information and tell their side of the story. The Oyneg Shabes, on the other hand, had only minimal contacts with the Judenrat. Indeed, it saw itself as an integral part of the ghetto's alternative community.

In the Lodz Ghetto the archive functioned simultaneously as an official department and as a semi-clandestine organization. But it was obvious that the archive staff did not feel free to criticize Rumkowski or gather any material it wished.[9] In the Vilna and the Białystok ghettos, the archives were not under Judenrat control. However, both Jacob Gens, the commandant of the Vilna Ghetto, and Ephraim Barash, the head of the Białystok Judenrat, maintained contact with the archives. Barash gave Mordecai Tenenbaum financial help and a place to work and handed over valuable Judenrat records even as he withheld other particularly sensitive documents.[10] In Vilna relations between ghetto commandant Jacob Gens and Herman Kruk were quite cool. But Gens knew about Kruk's diary and archive, and he occasionally sought him out in order to tell his side of the story.[11]

The Oyneg Shabes, on the other hand, gave the Judenrat a wide berth. (Shmuel Winter was an "exception that proved the rule.") Ringelblum noted that more than once the Oyneg Shabes had passed over potential recruits just because they had connections to the Judenrat. Ringelblum and Judenrat president Adam Czerniakow had little in common. Ringelblum knew that Czerniakow was keeping a diary, and Ringelblum's name was in Czerniakow's address book, but there is no evidence that they shared any confidences or that Czerniakow called Ringelblum in for the kind of secret meetings that took place in Vilna or Białystok with Gens and Barash. The Oyneg Shabes did interview the Judenrat officials Israel Milejkowski and Henryk Rozen as part of its survey of Jewish leaders and intellectuals (see below), but here, too, no evidence suggests that either Milejkowski or Rozen knew that this was an Oyneg Shabes project.

CHANGING PRIORITIES:
THE EVOLUTION OF THE OYNEG SHABES

Ringelblum's sweeping and ambitious agenda for the Oyneg Shabes outstripped in scope and ambition those of other archives. Over time this agenda came to embrace the collection of artifacts and documents, the study of Jewish society, the gathering of individual testimony, the documentation of German crimes, and the alerting of the outside world to the German mass murder. These goals often overlapped and were pursued simultaneously by the archive.

The Oyneg Shabes Archive collected both texts and artifacts: the underground press, documents, drawings, candy wrappers, tram tickets, ration cards, theater posters, invitations to concerts and lectures. It took copies of the convoluted doorbell codes for apartments housing dozens of tenants. There were restaurant menus advertising roast goose and fine wines, and a terse account of a starving mother who had eaten her dead child. Carefully filed away were hundreds of postcards from Jews in the provinces about to be deported to an "unknown destination." The Oyneg Shabes preserved the poetry of Władysław Szlengel, Yitzhak Katzenelson, Kalman Lis, and Joseph Kirman. It preserved the entire script of a popular ghetto comedy, "Love Looks for an Apartment," and long essays on the ghetto theaters and cafes. The first cache of the archive also contained many photographs, some seventy-six of which survived.[12]

The Oyneg Shabes retained hectographed readers used in the ghetto schools and reports that nurses wrote in the ghetto orphanages. After July 22, 1942, the archive collected the German posters announcing the Great Deportation, among them one promising that anyone who voluntarily reports for deportation will be given three kilograms of bread and a kilogram of marmalade. Crammed into the milk cans of the second cache were penciled notes whose shaky handwriting betrayed the desperation of their authors. These scraps of paper—smuggled out of the Umschlagplatz—were frantic appeals for a last-minute rescue. Among the last documents buried in the second cache were posters calling for armed resistance.

The Oyneg Shabes commitment to comprehensive documentation went hand in hand with another important commitment, namely, postwar justice. Its model in this regard was Eliyahu Cherikover, who had established the remarkable archive that documented the Ukrainian pogroms of 1919–1921. The evidence amassed by Cherikover had helped acquit Shalom Schwarzbard, who in 1926 had assassinated Ukrainian leader Semyon Petlura and was subsequently tried for murder in a French court. This quest to gather evidence explained why the archive collected enormous amounts of material from as many localities as possible. At first glance much of this material was repetitious. But it did confirm, town by town and village by village, exactly what the Germans did, when they did it, who gave the orders, and who helped them do it. If the Oyneg Shabes did not keep these testaments, then who would?

In time the Oyneg Shabes, unlike most of the other archives, also acquired a new role as a center of "civil resistance."[13] Eventually the Oyneg Shabes turned into an information center of the Jewish underground, disseminating news about the extermination of Polish Jewry via the Polish underground abroad, issuing bulletins, and warning surviving Jews to drop their illusions about German intentions.

Priorities of the Oyneg Shabes constantly shifted to reflect changing circumstances. Broadly speaking, the Oyneg Shabes went through different periods. From the outbreak of the war until the establishment of the ghetto, Ringelblum kept his notes, gathered information, and scouted out potential collaborators.

When the ghetto was established in the fall of 1940 the work of the archive, paradoxically, became easier. Fear of German searches lessened; the Nazis, intensely following the activities of the Polish underground, seemed to have little interest in what Jews said or wrote. Thus, in addition to the "social space" created by the house committees and the Aleynhilf, a new kind of "cultural space" emerged in the ghetto that made it easier for Ringelblum to develop the archive.

One manifestation of this "cultural space" was the expansion of a large and varied underground press published by the political parties and youth groups.[14] The archive made the collection of these newspapers a major priority; indeed, without the Oyneg Shabes, very few newspapers and pamphlets would have survived. Like the archive, they provide priceless information about life in the ghetto, political debates, Polish-Jewish relations, and how Jews followed the military situation.

The underground press and the archive covered many of the same themes: daily life in the ghetto, complaints about Judenrat and police corruption, escalating mortality from hunger and disease, problems in the labor camps, events in the provinces, the plight of children and refugees, street humor, and ghetto folklore. Ultimately a complementary relationship developed between this underground press and the Oyneg Shabes. The press put out edited versions of reports for the archive. Several members of the executive committee of the Oyneg Shabes—including Hersh Wasser, Eliyahu Gutkowski, and Shmuel Breslav—also edited underground newspapers. In October 1941 it was the underground press that began to publish the first accounts of mass executions. By the spring of 1942 the Oyneg Shabes would publish an underground bulletin of its own, full of information about the oncoming "Final Solution."

While the archive itself had to remain secret, it indirectly benefited from the ability of the underground press to disseminate information, remind readers of prewar values and moral codes, and foster a community. The flow of information disseminated by the underground newspapers helped create an awareness of the need to record what was happening, and their moral and political exhortations bolstered a determination to use this testimony to bring to justice not only Nazi perpetrators but also Jews who had failed the moral tests of national solidarity and honesty. The underground press, through its articles on the military situation, became the major source of information in the ghetto about the war. Even when things looked bleakest, such as after the fall of France in June 1940, the underground press furnished commentaries that kept hope alive.

By the fall of 1941 a new period began when the Oyneg Shabes decided to institute a major study of Jewish life under the Nazi occupation—the "Two and a Half Years" project, as noted earlier. No sooner had the Oyneg Shabes begun this project than news began to arrive about Nazi massacres, first in the eastern territories, then in Chełmno, and then in the provinces surrounding Warsaw. Racing against time to complete the "Two and a Half Years" project, Ringelblum and the staff now faced a new challenge—to gather and disseminate information about the Nazi killings.

As we have seen, the Oyneg Shabes Archive was uncovered in two separate caches: the first in September 1946 and the second in December 1950. The first cache covered the period from the beginning of the war until August 3, 1942, the day Lichtenstein Grzywacz and Graber buried the documents.[15] A third cache, never found, was buried under Świętojerska 34 and would have documented the critical months of March and early April 1943, when the ghetto was preparing for armed resistance. Despite dogged searches, it was never found.[16]

Unfortunately the physical condition of the first and second parts of the archive differed considerably. The first part had been packed into boxes of tin or sheet zinc. Lichtenstein did not have the time to weld them shut, and water seeped into all the boxes.[17] Many documents that had been written in ink were illegible, and many photographs were destroyed. Paper clips corroded, further damaging the materials. Much of the first part of the archive was covered with a thin fungus. The whole collection required years of painstaking restoration work, which remains incomplete. Indeed, only in the late 1980s, thanks to a grant from the United States Memorial Holocaust Museum, were major resources available for physical restoration.[18]

The second part of the archive, discovered in December 1950, had been packed in aluminum milk cans which protected the contents from water seepage. Therefore the condition of these documents was much better. The materials of the second cache reflected the vastly different conditions that the Oyneg Shabes faced after the onset of the Great Deportation. The archive was no longer in a position to conduct the careful studies of ghetto life begun in 1941. The children were gone, along with the schools, orphanages, and house committees. On the other hand, compared to the first cache, the second contained a much higher proportion of official records: Judenrat documents, German correspondence and orders, and records of the Aleynhilf. Before the onset of the Final Solution, Ringelblum did not assign priority to the collection of German documents or even Judenrat materials. The Germans, he figured, would preserve these records in their own files. But after the Great Deportation began the Oyneg Shabes tried to collect as many official records and Judenrat materials as possible. Ringelblum also asked Yitzhak Zuckerman to procure archival materials from Michał Weichert's Jewish Self-Help Society, whose central offices were in Krakow.[19] The second cache contained as much material as the archive was able to gather about Treblinka, the Great Deportation itself, and the reactions of the surviving Jews. It documented psychological transformations that marked the ghetto inhabitants after the conclusion of the first stage of the extermination process in September 1942: anger at the Jewish police and the Judenrat, shame at the lack of resistance, determination that "the next time" the Jews would fight back. The Oyneg Shabes painstakingly documented the world of the "shops" that had replaced the ghetto after the Great Deportation. The second cache also contained important materials about the first armed confrontation between the ŻOB and the Germans in January 1943. And as the last members of the Oyneg Shabes faced death, they put their own personal documents in the second cache: university diplomas, personal writings, and so on. Ringelblum left the entire manuscript of his unpublished "History of Warsaw Jewry," and Opoczynski left many of his prewar writings.

Neither Wasser nor Auerbach believed that the ten boxes of the first cache contained all the material that the Oyneg Shabes had collected by August 1942. Even taking into account documents that had been damaged by water, they still believed that Lichtenstein and his young helpers must have buried other boxes.[20] Indeed, certain essays that Ringelblum cited in his essay on the

Oyneg Shabes did not turn up.[21] In his letter to the YIVO written on March 1, 1944, Ringelblum mentioned "more than twenty [*tsvey tsendlik*]" boxes.

We will probably never know the answer.

WORKING IN SECRET

The Oyneg Shabes staff was small enough to ensure efficiency and secrecy but large enough to fan out all over the ghetto in search of material. Ghetto teachers brought in children's essays in neat copybooks, and postal workers submitted the last postcards sent by provincial relatives before their deportation to an "unknown destination." In the pestilential refugee centers Oyneg Shabes interviewers risked their health to collect firsthand accounts of brutal expulsions and of the desperate efforts to hang on to life in overcrowded former synagogues and schools that often housed hundreds of starving people. The staff of the Oyneg Shabes interviewed Jewish intellectuals about the future of the Jewish people, and children about their dreams for "after the war." When refugees arrived in the Warsaw Ghetto from the Soviet-occupied zone, the Oyneg Shabes spared no effort to obtain their testimony.

The Oyneg Shabes quickly established a distinct organizational framework. The executive committee supervised the everyday work of the archive. Grouped around the executive committee were a few dozen writers and copiers. One list of Oyneg Shabes workers in Hersh Wasser's handwriting includes thirty-seven names and addresses.[22] Many of those listed had no recorded writings in the archive and were probably copiers. The list was far from complete; missing were such names as Kon, Winter, Giterman, Landau, Auerbach, and Słapakowa. Judging by who was included and who was absent, a plausible assumption might be that those on the list were receiving regular payments from Wasser but not those with sufficient means or stable employment.

Ringelblum and the executive committee, at their customary Saturday meetings to discuss the activities and plans of the archive, formulated questionnaires that were used to guide the "Two and a Half Years" project, and presumably they discussed the recruitment of new members. The committee probably reviewed the inventories of archival materials that were compiled by Hersh Wasser and Menakhem Kon's account book of income and expenditures.[23] By 1942 the executive committee as a whole, rather than individual Oyneg Shabes members, often met with refugees and survivors, and heard firsthand accounts of the escalating mass murder.[24] The executive committee must have approved the decision to issue an Oyneg Shabes underground publication in the spring of 1942 that publicized the German killings. At the height of the Great Deportation in August 1942 the executive committee met to decide the eventual destination of the archive, the YIVO in New York City.[25]

Secrecy was paramount. The staff constantly worried that the slightest mistake, the smallest misjudgment could destroy the entire project. Prospective recruits were carefully scrutinized.[26] The archive rejected some potentially valuable contributors because of their links to the Judenrat, to the Jewish police, or to the "Thirteen."[27] Perhaps this explains the absence of the great historian Isaac Schiper as a member or contributor to the archive: Ringelblum noted with some consternation in his diary that Schiper had accepted invitations for dinner with Abraham Gancwajch, the leader of the "Thirteen."

The few diaries left by members of the Oyneg Shabes clearly revealed the importance of secrecy. In the hundreds of pages of the Ringelblum diaries, the Oyneg Shabes is barely mentioned—and then only in the most roundabout way. In the diary Hersh Wasser kept in the Warsaw Ghetto, he refers to "interesting OS meetings" and nothing more. Abraham Lewin in his diary also avoided any discussion of the inner workings of the archive. Rachel Auerbach had known the writer Peretz Opoczynski before the war and would see him from time to time in the Warsaw Ghetto. She learned only after the war that Opoczynski was, like herself, one of the major contributors to the Oyneg Shabes.

After the onset of mass extermination, when personal survival appeared more doubtful than ever, Ringelblum decided to write about the archive in an essay contained in the cache of documents discovered in 1950. That essay, along with terse memoirs by Hersh Wasser and postwar essays by Rachel Auerbach, constitute the only sources on the archive written by insiders. Considering that only three members survived the war, such a paucity of sources is not surprising.

Underpinning the activities of the Oyneg Shabes was a group of copiers and transcribers.[28] Sometimes authors would hand over compositions to the Oyneg Shabes, which would then be copied. Another category of materials consisted of interviews that were conducted by an Oyneg Shabes member. Depending on the interviewer and the circumstances, these ranged from almost verbatim transcripts to loose paraphrasing.[29] The archive tried to make multiple copies of each document to safeguard the information, whether the document was an original composition or the transcript of an interview. Copies were sometimes typed and sometimes handwritten. Of course photographs, posters, or original artifacts could not be copied. Coded letters in various alphabets or symbols appear on the front of documents, as well as abbreviations that refer to various members of the Oyneg Shabes. Certain symbols, for instance, designate "transports" of documents that Hersh Wasser classified, organized, and transferred to a hiding place.[30]

After the war, when the archive was unearthed, it became very difficult to distinguish between originals and copies. In the first cache many copies survived but the originals did not. Documents often had names or initials, but in many cases it was impossible to know whether these names referred to the original author or to the name of the person who made the copy or who transcribed the interview. Thus, after the war, certain essays thought to have been written by Rabbi Huberband were actually his transcriptions of what he heard from a second party. After the war Hersh Wasser identified authorship of certain documents, but these notations were not always correct.[31]

To ensure secrecy, Ringelblum and the staff decided to build a "firewall" between the inner circle of the Oyneg Shabes and Lichtenstein's group, the three men who would receive physical custody of the materials, and, at a signal, bury them. As the materials from Wasser slowly piled up in the hideout in the school, Lichtenstein and his teenaged helpers would read the documents and discuss what they meant. Just before he helped bury the first cache on August 2–3, 1942, David Graber, nineteen years old at the time, recalled,

> My own work was rudimentary—I would pack and hide the material.
> But nevertheless it was so interesting. There was so much variety, so
> much that one could learn. Until late into the night we would sit with
> Comrade Lichtenstein, look through the documents and talk. . . . First
> were the photographs of Jews being beaten . . . there were many photo-
> graphs. Then came the reports of the lives of Jews in the provinces, in
> Lodz. This was hard to read. . . . How horrible was the report about the
> gassings in Chełmno, told by Grojanowski. We were so shaken . . . that
> we could not work the whole next day.[32]

It is now clear that when they buried the first cache of the archive on the night of August 2–3, 1942, they worked in great haste. Staring death in the face, they had no time to classify the materials or to sort out copies from originals, which should have gone in different boxes to increase the chances of survival. In fact, when the boxes were opened, many documents were jumbled together, copies along with originals.[33]

From the very beginnings of the archive, the entire staff of the Oyneg Shabes knew they had to risk their lives to collect information. As noted earlier, it was especially perilous to go into the disease-ridden, squalid, and overcrowded refugee centers, and many members of the Oyneg Shabes indeed came down with typhus. Some such as Rabbi Huberband and Peretz Opoczynski recovered, but others, like Bernard Kampelmacher, died. Still, despite the dangers, the Oyneg Shabes was a godsend for many of Ringelblum's recruits. It provided a moral lifeline, an occupation, and a reason to go on living. Members felt needed and part of a community.

The staff of the Oyneg Shabes had to find a way to gather material without compromising security. The far-flung activities of the Aleynhilf provided excellent cover, since practically the entire Oyneg Shabes—and especially the inner circle—worked in this organization. The Aleynhilf's activities allowed members to gather descriptions of practically every forced labor camp in the General Government and helped to camouflage one of the archive's most important projects, the collection of information on events in cities and towns outside Warsaw and in the Soviet-occupied zone. Under the guise of ascertaining the needs of the refugee population, Hersh Wasser and others arranged hundreds of interviews, investigating each interviewee's background and, Ringelblum noted, often waiting until the interview ended to make notes.[34]

The soup kitchens were another major resource from which the Oyneg Shabes gathered material. Rachel Auerbach would identify "clients" who could provide important information, and Ringelblum would send useful individuals to the kitchens for extra food.

Public writing contests proved another excellent source of material and provided a welcome degree of subterfuge. In January 1942 the "Jury and Executive" of a writing contest (which actually consisted of key members of the Oyneg Shabes staff) announced a public competition on a number of themes: a monograph on Jewish life in a city; Polish-Jewish relations; Jewish converts to Catholicism in the ghetto; schools; children; bribery and corruption; smuggling; any particular aspect of the ghetto economy; house committees; entertainment and dissolute behavior in the ghetto; the refugee shelters; the September 1939 campaign; and the Jewish police. There were other themes as well, but much of the document is illegible. The "jury" also announced that it would consider themes that were not on the list.[35]

The prizes, ranging from one thousand zlotys for first place to one hundred for sixth place were a significant incentive at a time when a common wage was four to six zlotys a day. The jury reserved the right to divide prizes. Still another competition invited young people to write about their life in the ghetto: essays, diaries, edited correspondence, or even fiction from working youth, middle-class youth, members of the intelligentsia, and students.[36]

The executive committee, and especially Menakhem Kon, collected the money that the Oyneg Shabes needed to function. Expenses included paper and supplies, honoraria for essays, and money to buy food and medicine for key members of the project. There were also many extraordinary expenses that could not be anticipated. For example, when "Szlamek" escaped from the death camp in Chełmno in January 1942, it was Hersh Wasser who took him in hand, found him a place to stay in the Warsaw Ghetto, and then sent him to the provinces. Kon recorded that the Oyneg Shabes gave Szlamek payments totaling about one thousand zlotys in February and March 1942. Further, in 1942 and 1943 the Oyneg Shabes published information bulletins in Yiddish and in Polish—presumably at its own expense.

One account ledger for the Oyneg Shabes, in Menakhem Kon's handwriting, lists disbursements of at least 55,298 zlotys between November 1940 and July 1942.[37] Other account books probably existed, as the archive continued to work after July 1942. This one extant account book establishes that the archive was spending at least 2,500 zlotys a month and probably much more. Most of the disbursements seem to have been small regular payments to the members of the archive plus periodic purchases of paper and ink and other incidentals. On August 28, 1941, the book recorded an outlay of 390 zlotys to procure tin boxes—no doubt for storing the documents.

There is no question that many—perhaps most—of the archive's expenses were also tucked into the much larger budget of the Aleynhilf, as most of the Oyneg Shabes worked there. Although their salaries were meager, these were monies the archive did not have to account for. The same held true of food. As we have already seen, Ringelblum, Gutkowski, or Wasser would send up to sixty people a day to Rachel Auerbach's soup kitchen. It is likely that the kitchen on Leszno 40 was not the only one the Oyneg Shabes used.

Where did the Oyneg Shabes get its funds? Although Yitzhak Giterman was on the executive board, Hersh Wasser insisted in his postwar account that the Oyneg Shabes received no direct help from the Joint Distribution Committee. Wasser's memory must have failed him, since Kon's account ledger shows several payments of 750 zlotys from the Joint as well as regular income from the "SPS" (perhaps the Aleynhilf?). Kon's ledger also showed regular and sizable donations from three individuals in particular: Shmuel Winter, Shie Rabinowitz, and Alexander Landau.

Ringelblum kept reminding the men and women of the Oyneg Shabes that they "had to work badly." In other words, the collaborators had to remember that "the best was the enemy of the good." Given the conditions in the ghetto, it was pointless to pretend that writing, research, and interviews could meet the prewar standards of a university or a scholarly journal. And security came first. If getting a particular piece of information proved too risky, then it was better to forgo the opportunity.

As time went on Ringelblum worried that too many Jews were becoming complacent about alleged German lack of interest in their political activities and in the underground press. Ringelblum was present at a noisy meeting of the Hashomer Hatzair held a short distance from German gendarmes. The cheers and singing could easily be heard outside the building, and the whole scene reminded Ringelblum of a raucous prewar rally. He began to fear that the Germans might indeed care about this clandestine activity, especially if they suspected a possible connection between the Jewish and the Polish secret press.[38] At any rate, the Germans shattered the widespread sense of false security on the night of April 17–18, 1942, when they suddenly descended on the ghetto in the late hours of a Friday evening with lists of names. The lists seemed random, although later many Jews believed that many of the victims had been connected in some way to the underground press. Small groups of Gestapo agents knocked on apartment doors, politely asked certain individuals to come with them, and then shot them in the street. The bodies were left lying in pools of blood. One of the most prominent victims, as we have seen, was Ringelblum's longtime comrade from the YIVO and the IKOR, the Oyneg Shabes activist Menakhem Linder. Yitzhak Zuckerman, a future leader of the Jewish Fighting Organization, narrowly escaped the same fate. That evening Ringelblum had been planning a lecture in Rachel Auerbach's soup kitchen on the subject of martyrdom (Kiddush Hashem) in Jewish history. Forewarned that something was afoot, he abruptly cancelled the lecture.[39]

What would the Germans do next? If they were onto the underground press, surely they would be doubly anxious to track down the secret archive. At least one member of the Oyneg Shabes executive committee, Menakhem Kon, urged Ringelblum to leave the Warsaw Ghetto as soon as possible.[40] Ringelblum ignored these pleas, but the archive decided to lay a false trail to deceive the Germans. Shortly after the April massacre, the Oyneg Shabes put out the word that it had stopped its activities. Then, in absolute secrecy, Ringelblum and the executive committee invited a much smaller cadre to continue working.

The onset of the Great Deportation in July 1942 threw the Oyneg Shabes into temporary disarray, but Ringelblum and his staff soon regained their bearings. Although the Germans deported many important members, much of the core group survived the first phase of the deportation, which halted on September 12, 1942. Even during that terrible summer the Oyneg Shabes held meetings and charted its future course of action. It now began to pay special attention to documenting the deportation process. When the first escapees from Treblinka appeared in the Warsaw Ghetto, the Oyneg Shabes sat them down to give detailed accounts. When the temporary lull began in September 1942 the Oyneg Shabes resumed its work, composing more questionnaires and learning as much as possible about the state of mind of the remaining Jews. The archive paid special attention to the "shops." It also began to issue an informational bulletin in Polish, *Wiadomości*. Sometime in February 1943 Ringelblum ordered the burial of a second cache—the milk cans that were found in 1950.[41]

The archive had failures as well as successes. The great musicologist Menakhem Kipnis had amassed a large archive of Jewish folk songs and cantorial compositions, but the Oyneg Shabes could not persuade him to part with it; it disappeared when he boarded the boxcars for Treblinka.[42] Menakhem Linder had kept a valuable diary. Ringelblum tried to get it after his murder, but his widow had already burned it.[43] Joseph Kaplan also kept a diary, but for a long time he hesitated to let the archive copy it because of confidential material on Hashomer Hatzair. Finally, he agreed to let the archive copy excerpts. Before this could be done, however, the Germans murdered him, and all trace of the diary was lost.[44] And there were other gaps. Jonas (Yanosh) Turkow wrote an essay for the archive on theater in the Warsaw Ghetto, but he did not give the archive all the material he had gathered. Ringelblum had heard that the great historian Meyer Balaban was writing an autobiography, but somehow no one on the Oyneg Shabes was close enough to Balaban to ask for a copy. Ringelblum noted that Isaac Schiper was working on various historical studies, but, as far as we know, the archive never tried to procure any copies. Shmuel Winter kept a diary that he did not give to the Oyneg Shabes. Burned fragments surfaced in the assumed hiding place of the missing third cache after the war. There were other puzzles that will probably never be explained.

One of the greatest setbacks for the Oyneg Shabes was Ringelblum's failure to secure the collections and archives of the folklorist Shmuel Lehman. Lehman was one of the pioneer Jewish folklorists in Poland and had traveled to the farthest corners of Eastern Europe in search of material.[45] He was something of an eccentric and favored bizarre headgear. In the slums of Jewish Warsaw, where he would pay pickpockets, pimps, and a wide assortment of street characters to sing him their songs, the tough characters on Stawki Street liked to call him "Der yold in der kapelyush" (The weirdo with the hat) In 1923 Lehman published a classic collection of songs of the Jewish underworld. He generally collected more than he published. After the start of the war in 1939 Lehman began to supplement his already large file on Polish-Jewish relations with new material on how the war had affected mutual perceptions of these two peoples.

Ringelblum, Isaac Schiper, the poet Itzik Manger, and other Jewish intellectuals deeply appreciated Lehman's talents. According to Wasser, Lehman was present at the meeting on November 22, 1940, in Ringelblum's apartment that formally created the Oyneg Shabes Archive. Obviously Ringelblum nurtured hopes that Lehman would play a prominent role in the archive, but he soon became sick. Both Ringelbum and Giterman helped support him in the ghetto, and Rachel Auerbach, who had been one of his best informants on Jewish rural folk culture, would visit him regularly.

When Lehman died Ringelblum organized a dignified funeral. He bitterly remarked in his diary that, Czerniakow, when told of Lehman's death, did not even know who he was.

Shortly after Lehman's death Ringelblum went to his apartment and asked his widow for Lehman's folklore archives. Unwilling to share the secret of the Oyneg Shabes, Ringelblum could only say that he would protect the materials but could give no details. Lehman's widow refused to entrust the collection to Ringelblum. Thus none of Lehman's writings showed up in the Oyneg Shabes Archive. It was all lost.[46]

The archive suffered other defeats. Once the mass deportation to Treblinka began Ringelblum would rush members of the Oyneg Shabes to the empty and looted apartments of writers and artists, hoping to find papers and manuscripts. More often than not, these efforts proved fruitless. Yet despite such setbacks, and spurred on by Ringelblum, the Oyneg Shabes prepared for even greater tasks: the study of the ghetto and the chronicle of catastrophe.

CHAPTER 7

Traces of Life and Death

TEXTS FROM THE ARCHIVE

Determined to document the Jewish experience in the war, the Oyneg Shabes collected artifacts, texts, and testimonies that reflect an ongoing tension between prewar ideals and escalating chaos; between a yearning for collective solidarity and rampant social fragmentation; between idealism and debasement; between continuity and rupture—material as disparate and varied as the experiences of the Jews who gathered and wrote them. There were outlines of studies that were never completed, sketches of projects cut short by the Great Deportation; fragments and pieces remain the only traces of individuals who vanished forever. Taken together, these materials tell a collective story of steady decline and unending humiliation, interspersed with many stories of quiet heroism and self-sacrifice. The postwar reader sees Polish Jewry disappearing in an ordeal where the todays were worse than the yesterdays but still better than the tomorrows: from the siege of Warsaw to the early days of the occupation; from the imposition of the ghetto to the Great Deportation; from the Great Deportation to the final months of the ghetto. It is a collective story composed of hundreds of smaller narratives, accounts of everyday horrors from different individual perspectives, yet illuminated by moments of reprieve, of dignity and courage.

As the situation became increasingly desperate many individuals broke, collapsing into depression, anger, rage, shame, and fear. The members of the archive were not immune. Yet somehow, no matter how bad things became, the collective enterprise of the Oyneg Shabes went on, flexible, inventive, and determined to make sure that nothing escaped its attention.

STUDYING THE GHETTO:
"THE TWO AND A HALF YEARS" PROJECT

During the first year of its activities, as the archive collected material, the Oyneg Shabes debated priorities and guidelines. Ringelblum at first wanted the Oyneg Shabes to amass as much as possible without reference to particular agendas or preconceived hypotheses. The war was changing Jewish society so fast and events were so unpredictable, Ringelblum believed, that it would be foolish to try to skew the collection of material to fit one's own view of what was important or to try to anticipate what would be pertinent. He also felt that to write monographs or conduct studies would waste time and leave little of lasting value; such work would become quickly outdated when the war was over. More important was for the archive to create a resource and database for future historians.[1]

By mid-1941, however, so much material had flowed into the archive that the Oyneg Shabes staff began to rethink this reluctance to study and prioritize. The executive committee decided to begin a new project—a massive study of the wartime experience. They borrowed YIVO methodology, with the limits imposed by the need for secrecy: comprehensive questionnaires, interviews, and essay contests. Ringelblum called the project "Two and a Half Years":

> The Project was divided into three [*sic*] parts: a general section, an economic section, a cultural-scientific-literary-artistic section, and a section devoted to mutual aid. This project, which was started at the beginning of 1942, was directed by me, Menakhem Linder, and Lipe Bloch. I directed the first and the third sections, Linder the economics section and Bloch the section on mutual aid. [We involved new people . . .] The project was slated for over 1,600 printed pages, and it would have been one of the most important documents of the war. At meetings of the Oyneg Shabes staff, which would last for many hours, we worked out [theses and guidelines] to direct [the study of the topics].[2]

In late 1942 or 1943 Ringelblum wrote a brief note that was included in the second part of the archive: "Two and a Half Years . . . which goals? [*velkhe tsvekn*] A photograph of life. Not literature but science [*visnshaft*]."[3]

The scope of "Two and a Half Years" was enormous. A partial outline in Eliyahu Gutkowski's handwriting, concerned mainly with the Warsaw Ghetto itself, contained eighty-one separate subheadings dealing with the Warsaw Ghetto alone (see appendix B). A partial list of the theses and guidelines worked out by the Oyneg Shabes staff included studies of women, youth, children, corruption, Jews in the Soviet-occupied zone, religious life, the life of writers and intellectuals, Polish-Jewish relations, German-Jewish relations, economic life, the social history of the ghetto, the ghetto street, opinions about the future of the Jewish people, house committees, soup kitchens, wages, prices, the Jewish police, and so on.[4]

The questionnaires underscored the archive's determination to set high standards for objectivity and comprehensiveness. For example, one of the two different sets of guidelines to frame the study of German-Jewish relations began: "the belief that all Germans are bad-false."[5] Rather than lump all Germans together into one undifferentiated mass, the guidelines stressed the need to collect information on possible differences in behavior between various groups: Austrians, Volksdeutsche, and Reichsdeutsche; party members; "radicals" and "non-radicals." Did Germans who treated Jews with conspicuous hostility change their tone when their countrymen left the room? How did Germans see the problems of the ghetto? What did individual Germans know about Jews before the war? Did they believe the news about expulsions and massacres, or did they dismiss it as "Jewish atrocity propaganda"? Were there "righteous gentiles [hasidei umoys ha'oylem]" among the Germans? Did the encounters that Germans had with Jewish workers change their attitudes toward Jews? Someone scrawled "Facts!" in the margin of the guidelines and questions. A second set of guidelines for the study of German-Jewish relations contained twenty-eight topics arranged in chronological order.[6]

Another controversial subject was the topic of rampant corruption in the ghetto: bribe taking, informers, widespread theft from the refugee centers, the looting of food packages in the post office, the abuses of the parówki. The Oyneg Shabes planned to investigate not only the Judenrat and the Jewish police but wide sectors of ghetto society: doctors, janitors, porters, the ghetto post office.[7] And despite the special ties that linked the Oyneg Shabes to the house committees and the Aleynhilf, the guidelines did not exempt these bodies as targets of investigation. The archive told its informants to gain the trust of various hustlers and agents (makhers), to conduct extensive interviews, and to write individual profiles that highlighted how the system of bribes worked. Had bribery become standardized, with set prices for specific services? What about the causes of corruption, such as low pay and fierce competition for posts? In any given institution, was the corruption systemic or was it confined to relatively few individuals?

High on the agenda of the "Two and Half Years" project was the sensitive issue of Jews in the Soviet-occupied territories and Jewish attitudes toward the Soviet system, an issue that figured prominently in Polish-Jewish relations, especially in view of widespread Polish allegations of massive Jewish collaboration with the Soviet occupiers, which is examined in chapter 9. The topic also had important ramifications for internal Jewish politics. In many towns in eastern Poland, previously ardent members of Zionist youth groups quickly deserted their former comrades and joined the Komsomol, the Communist youth organization. In Vilna, Zelig Kalmanovich, one of the leaders of the YIVO, bitterly noted the alacrity with which many secular Yiddishists rushed to embrace the Soviets.[8]

The Soviet occupation brought both benefits and calamities to Jews. Jews saw the Soviets as a welcome alternative to Nazi occupation. Jewish youth, especially from the poorer strata, embraced new opportunities for education and employment largely denied them in prewar Poland. Jewish artisans and craftsmen, especially in the economically backward shtetlekh of eastern Poland, discovered, in many cases, that the Soviet system gave them better economic opportunities and improved social status. On the other hand, the Soviet system destroyed most of the foundations of religious life and Hebrew Zionist culture, and subjected Yiddish culture to rigid ideological supervision. It destroyed Polish Jewry's rich network of associational and political life and ruined well-to-do merchants. The Soviets deported many Jewish political leaders as well as members of the middle classes and professional elites. As one Zionist leader remarked, the choice between the Nazis and the Soviets resembled a choice "between a death sentence and life imprisonment."[9]

Although both Ringelblum and Wasser belonged to a pro-Soviet party, they knew all too well the stories of repression, rampant assimilation, and the parlous state of Yiddish mass culture in the Soviet Union. Consistent with its approach to other difficulties, the Oyneg Shabes aimed for a fair and objective appraisal of all facets of the problem.[10] How did the Jews adapt to the Soviet occupation? How did they cope economically? What were their attitudes toward communism? How did the Soviet occupation affect Yiddish culture and schooling? What impact did the occupation have on relations with non-Jews? In addition, Abraham Lewin compiled a memorandum summarizing the legal status and problems of Jews who had fled from western and central Poland into the Soviet-occupied zone between 1939 and 1941.[11] Looking back, Ringelblum believed that the Oyneg Shabes had achieved a fair balance: "We have enthusiastic accounts written by supporters of the new [Soviet] system, but also writings of those who thoroughly detested [the Soviet regime]. These writings will help future historians ascertain the attitudes of various social groupings during the war."[12]

The archive tried to procure information representing various social backgrounds, political affiliations, and ages, and, to that end, mobilized many of its best interviewers, including Rabbi Shimon Huberband, Abraham Lewin,

Yekhil Gorny, and Daniel Fligelman. Testimonies and memoirs ran the gamut from sincere praise of the educational opportunities under Soviet rule to bitter criticism of persecution and wretched living standards. For dedicated Yiddishists like Ringelblum, the interviews confirmed what he already knew: that the Soviet system offered little future for Yiddish culture. Many accounts stressed that Jews themselves demanded Russian schools for their children and tried to assimilate as fast as they could. A former Bundist who settled in Vitebsk before returning to the Warsaw Ghetto described the dismal wages and working conditions, the lack of freedom and the general demoralization that he encountered among Soviet workers. Within a few months this Bundist began to dream of returning home, to the German zone.[13] On the other hand, a young middle-class Jew from Warsaw wrote a thoughtful account of the idealism and dedication that he found in the Soviet school system.[14] Before the war in Poland, he had felt like a pariah with no hope and no future. The Soviet system treated him as an equal, offering prospects for a profession and a productive life. He told the Oyneg Shabes interviewer that he evaluated the Soviet system with "open eyes" and had no illusions about its shortcomings: the suspicion and regimentation, the tyranny of petty bureaucrats, the low level of culture displayed by Soviet youth. But his general impression was positive. What Soviet youth lacked in knowledge and culture, they made up for in idealism, patriotism, and lack of petit-bourgeois cynicism.

Some of the most important and informative contributions on this topic were the essays of Stanisław Różycki, who fled to Lwów in 1939 before returning to the Warsaw Ghetto in the fall of 1941. In a study of the Soviet educational system in Lwów between 1939 and 1941, for instance, he pointed out both positive and negative aspects but stressed that, as a whole, Jewish youth welcomed the newly available educational opportunities.[15] He also outlined the dilemmas faced by Jews who had to decide whether to accept Soviet citizenship or try to rejoin their families under German occupation.[16] Różycki also provided a great deal of information on a topic that had not been well covered by the Oyneg Shabes: Ukrainian-Jewish relations.

Unfortunately the beginnings of "Two and a Half Years" coincided with the escalating and alarming reports streaming into the archive about German mass murder in the provinces. What had started as a well-planned, well-structured study of Jewish life had turned into a race against time, a race shadowed by death. Still the work moved forward, spurred by Ringelblum, Gutkowski, and Wasser. By the late spring of 1942, the situation had become so dangerous that the Oyneg Shabes decided to call in all the materials, finished or not. For that reason most of the "Two and a Half Years" project remained in the form of raw data and unfinished essays. Still it forms one of the most important parts of the Oyneg Shabes.

The following examples of this ambitious project highlights what the Oyneg Shabes tried to accomplish—and how quickly it found itself rushing to stay ahead of events.

THE FUTURE OF THE JEWS: A SURVEY

When the Oyneg Shabes began the "Two and a Half Years" project, Ringelblum and his associates were still convinced that Polish Jewry would survive the war—exhausted, battered, but alive. Just as the prewar YIVO had used scholarship to help a living people, the Oyneg Shabes hoped that its efforts might help change postwar Jewish society. Therefore one of the first goals of the project was to record Jews' thoughts about the postwar future. Most Jews in the ghetto were too preoccupied with simple survival to think about their national future, but the Oyneg Shabes felt that a survey of interim opinions about the state of Polish Jewry and its postwar prospects would constitute an important historical document and be a marker for a nation taking stock of events when the war ended.

Most members of the Oyneg Shabes had been shaped by the Jewish secularism which had envisaged a new Jew who did not need religion to feel ethnic pride and to act morally. Bundists and Zionists alike had embraced European humanism while rejecting assimilation. Some of the most creative energies of interwar Polish Jewry—in the youth movements, the trade unions, the schools, the YIVO—had been dedicated to this cultural and psychological transformation.

But in the late 1930s, as fascism swept large parts of Europe and as anti-Semitism intensified, some Jewish intellectuals had begun to question this Jewish secular revolution along with its faith in the European Enlightenment. In 1939 Eliyahu Cherikover edited a collection of essays titled *Oyfn sheydveg* (At the crossroads). This collection included many contributors who were well known to Ringelblum such as Simon Dubnow and Zelig Kalmanovich of the YIVO. Cherikover and others expressed their deep fears for the future of European Jewry and called for the Jewish intelligentsia to deepen their understanding of Jewish values and traditions. In the past Jews had faced persecution firmly anchored in their own identity and culture. Modern Jews, on the other hand, were stranded between two shores, alienated from their own traditional culture and rejected by a Europe whose character they had tragically misread.[17] The Enlightenment, Kalmanovich argued, might have offered great opportunities to the Jews as individuals but it certainly weakened the solidarity of the Jewish people. Fractured and confused, the Jews were hard-pressed to meet the blows they were suffering everywhere.

Simon Dubnow dissented, reaffirming his faith in the future of rationalism and Enlightenment. However bleak the present, he believed that to return to the ghetto was a counsel of despair.

> In our epoch of counter-emancipation we dare not pose the ironic question: "Well, what has emancipation brought us?" True it brought assimilation, but also freedom and human dignity. It revived the free person in the Jew. . . . Two years from now we will commemorate our first emancipation [1791] and we will remind the world that during the most recent period we added to this elementary civic emancipation national or auto-emancipation. We stand or fall with the progress or regress of mankind as a whole, and not with a few of its degenerate parts.[18]

The concerns that worried the intellectuals who contributed to *Oyfn sheydveg* surfaced in the Warsaw Ghetto. The trauma of the war became a test, not only of the moral level and social cohesion of Polish Jewry but also of the very viability of the attempt to provide a new basis for Jewish identity. For some individuals, including Ringelblum, the war confirmed and strengthened the political faith forged in the prewar period. But the war forced others to revise their convictions. In the Vilna Ghetto Zelig Kalmanovich expanded on the ideas he had laid out in *Oyfn sheydveg* just three years before, confiding in his wartime diary that the Yiddish secular revolution had been a mistake and that only religion and Zionism could save the Jewish people.

In the Warsaw Ghetto the pathologies of the ghetto—the Jewish police, the informers, the indifference to starving beggars and children—partly explain this soul-searching. After decades of effort to build a new Jewish culture in Yiddish and Hebrew, how did one explain that more and more Polish was being spoken in the ghetto streets? Were the pathologies of the ghetto an inevitable result of wartime conditions? Or did they signal, as some intellectuals believed, an ominous disintegration of a Jewish society that had been in crisis long before the war?

Even before the Oyneg Shabes organized "Two and a Half Years," intellectuals and political leaders had been holding informal conversations about these problems. One such individual, Aaron Einhorn, a former editor of the Yiddish daily *Haynt*, asserted that not all the alarming horrors of the ghetto could be blamed on the Germans. The Jews also bore much of the blame. Previous generations of Jews had acted with more dignity and self-respect; the medieval ghettos, with all their problems, had been centers of national creativity and examples of self-sacrifice and heroism that sustained the nation for centuries. By contrast, the Warsaw Ghetto had exposed a long-festering rot.[19] Others disagreed. Shakhne Zagan, the leader of the Poalei Tsiyon, was more optimistic. The Jews would hold out, he believed, survive the war, and realize that they had passed an important test.

For the Oyneg Shabes, these questions assumed added urgency because of the important differences between the Polish Jews and other occupied peoples such as the Poles, French, or Norwegians. All occupied nations experienced soul searching and the need to take stock, exacerbated by the often vague boundaries between accommodation, adaptation, and collaboration. Corruption, too, was universal; in order to survive one often had to break the law, steal or trade on the black market. But other occupied peoples could feel part of a common community of moral and national obligation. They could look forward to ultimate liberation, when the nation would settle accounts with collaborators, rethink the mistakes of the past, and construct a better society. In the underground press, convenient narratives of the occupation were already emerging. Corruption and collaboration would be ascribed to deviant individuals or classes; resistance and heroism would redound to the credit of the entire nation. No one questioned the existence of the people, its links to the land, its very future.

This was not so with the Polish Jews who had neither a secure homeland nor even a basic consensus about their identity and national destiny. Most Poles before the war had regarded them as strangers and had wanted them to emigrate. The war found Polish Jewry deeply divided linguistically, culturally, and politically, all its major ideologies facing serious challenges. The British White Paper seemed like a death sentence for political Zionism, and the Bund's call for a Jewish future in a democratic, socialist Poland was based more on hope than on concrete evidence. Even Orthodox Jews were in crisis. Their leaders had long asserted that if Jews simply accommodated themselves to the Polish government and rejected Bundist and Zionist demands for national autonomy, then the Poles would leave them in relative peace. But the 1936 legislation to limit Jewish ritual slaughter exposed the hollowness of this strategy as well. Everywhere the Jews turned, they seemed trapped.

But although social distance between Poles and Jews widened in the interwar period, Jewish acculturation grew and with it knowledge of a Polish culture and literature that prized honor, romantic nationalism—and resistance. For some middle-class, Polish-speaking Jews, this exposure to a culture that rejected them produced an inferiority complex that made the privations of the war even more difficult to bear.[20] Many Oyneg Shabes documents refer to the corrosive effects of this sense of inferiority and repeatedly noted the alleged overrepresentation of such individuals in the Jewish police and various ghetto institutions. Consumed with self-hatred and contempt for the Jewish masses, these Jews—many of whom had been former attorneys—consciously or subconsciously internalized the disdainful attitude of the Poles, who accused the Jews of a lack of pride and unwillingness to fight back.

Just over the wall, Polish society was responding to occupation by retreating into time-tested national myths that had helped to preserve the nation during the long period of foreign subjugation. Whatever the personal behavior of individual Poles, the collective myth served to create the impression of a people proudly united to protect their national honor and to fight the occupier. There was an underground state and a code of behavior that bound the nation in a common cause. But Jews were excluded from this "moral community."

Thus the Oyneg Shabes began its survey of Jewish intellectuals amid serious concerns. What national narrative would the wartime experience create? What comfort would they be able to find? Had Jewish society met the moral challenge? What place would they find in a postwar Poland? How would their neighbors see them?

The archive wanted a record of how Jewish society in the Warsaw Ghetto saw these issues. Implicit in the project was the assertion that the Jews were still a vital people, not a passive collection of helpless victims who were too numbed to look the truth in the face and think about their present and their future.

The fragmentary outline of this part of the "Two and a Half years" project proposed interviews with fifty Jews—writers, artists, intellectuals, and also "ordinary Jews [*Yidn fun a gants yor*]." The interviewer would ask the subjects to "unburden their souls [*opredn zikh fun harts*]." This project

> will not only allow people to unburden themselves but it will also have major historical significance . . . a first-class document will emerge that will describe the inner life of Jewish society in the Warsaw Ghetto. . . . Two and a half years of war have produced as many changes for European Jewry as previous generations might have experienced in decades. Many new truths have emerged for us, some of them quite painful. We have experienced many bitter disappointments and deep shocks that have undermined our faith in humanity and our belief in truths which had been the credo of entire generations.[21]

The Oyneg Shabes asked the interviewees to comment on negative and positive developments they had noticed in Jewish society during the war. What would the future of the Jewish people be like after the war? Should the Jews look to a state in Palestine, or should they pin their hopes on the Diaspora?

Did the interviewees think that after the war anti-Semitism would strengthen or decline? Another question indirectly probed the effects of modernization and urbanization on Jewish society. Had Warsaw Jews acted worse than others, the questionnaire asked; had they been less willing to help the poor than had Jews in the provinces who were closer to Jewish tradition and religion?

> What kind of social order will reign after the war and what lessons can our two-and-a-half-year experience teach us to prepare for the [postwar] era. How should we educate our youth in [this regard]. These are the questions that torture Jews during the long sleepless nights of 1941–42.[22]

From the half-destroyed document one can make out the names of thirty-one people whom the archive planned to interview as well as the names of the Oyneg Shabes members who would talk to them. The list included people from the entire cultural spectrum, including rabbis, Bundists, leaders of Zionist youth movements, and journalists. Ringelblum himself had undertaken to interview three people: Maurycy Orzech and Sonia Nowogrodzka, who were Bundist leaders in the Warsaw Ghetto, and Rabbi J. L. Orlean, who before the war had led the Beis Yankev schools for Orthodox girls.

Only nine responses survived in the first cache of the archive. They came from a cross-section of the Warsaw Jewish intelligentsia: two anonymous religious Jews; Hillel Tseitlin, a well known religious thinker and journalist; Shie Perle, the Yiddish writer; Henryk Rozen, the head of the Judenrat's labor division; Edmund Stein, a well-known Hebrew scholar; Shaul Stupnitzki, a prominent journalist; Aaron Einhorn, a former editor of *Haynt;* and Israel Milejkowski, the head of the Judenrat's health department. In normal times a sample of nine people in a population of 440,000 would hardly constitute a meaningful research document. In the conditions of the ghetto the Oyneg Shabes did the best it could and elicited information that would otherwise have been entirely lost.[23]

Not surprisingly opinions differed about the behavior of Polish Jewry and its postwar prospects. Most of the respondents were quite pessimistic about the postwar era. The Poles, they believed, would not welcome the Jews back, would not return their businesses and shops to them, and would pressure them to emigrate.[24] No matter who shaped the postwar era, most respondents felt, the Jews would lose. If the Communists won, Dr. Milejkowski warned, they would destroy what was left of Jewish culture. But the triumph of liberal democracy would offer small comfort, since Hitler's anti-Semitism "was so enticing that the nations liberated from Hitler's regime will not deny themselves the chance to imitate Hitler's policies toward the Jews." Some respondents, such as Henryk Rozen, predicted a wave of conversions: Jewish youth already demoralized by life in the ghetto, and corrupted by smuggling and hustling, would try to seek an easy way out. Optimism was in short supply. Would the Jews secure Palestine after the war? Most respondents were doubtful.

The little hope that remained came from two entirely different directions. Shie Perle pinned his faith in the victory on the Soviet Union, even as he recognized that this would not halt the rampant process of Jewish assimilation. At the opposite end of the spectrum, several interviewees hoped that the Jews would respond to the war by returning to their religious tradition, the source of their national strength and the foundation of their identity. Tseitlin believed that "without a religious awakening, without a messianic idea, there will be no help for the Jews."

Henryk Rozen hoped that young Jews would regain their sense of national honor:

> We must awaken in our young people a sense of Jewish national pride, offer them an ideal for which it would be worthwhile to suffer, show them that we took a major part in the worldwide fight against Hitler. They should see that Hitler had good reasons to hate the Jewish spirit . . . and that our dead were not passive victims whose sacrifices were pointless. The mere fact that we do not die as quickly as the German would like is a form of resistance. . . . We should use the period of the ghetto to uproot the particular Jewish faults that spark [anti-Semitism] . . . such as the pursuit of pleasure and the easy life.

On the question of Jewish behavior in the war, a division emerged between "accusers" and "defenders." An anonymous religious respondent, one of the "accusers," hurled a question back at the interviewers: What does it mean to be Jewish in these circumstances? "In the past [these words meant] living righteously, drawing inspiration from a spiritual approach to life . . . just as heaven commands." But what now? Where was the public conscience that was "supposed to keep us from becoming a Sodom and Gomorrah?" Secular Jews had revolted against religion and had promised a higher morality and a renewed Jewish nation. What had they really achieved? Secular Jews had looked to new sources of cultural authority such as the great Yiddish writers Mendele Moykher Sforim and Y. L. Peretz. If these writers were alive today, what would they say about Jewish behavior in the Warsaw Ghetto?

> And where are all the proud nationalist Jews, how do they allow such a large part of our nation to die? Where are all those whose closets are bursting full of clothes [that could be sold for food]? They just watch as

others freeze to death, naked. I looked at the world through the eyes of Jews who freeze in the streets from hunger and cold. I suffered with Jewish women who keep restlessly running trying to save their children, like lionesses after their cubs. Anyone who listens to the wail of the tens of thousands, who hears the cries of pain and [knows the] fear of the suffering, must conclude that *no one may speak of Jews, of being Jewish, of Jewish culture in our present society.*

Whoever this respondent was, the transcript of his answer showed that he was on good terms with important secular Jewish leaders like Yitzhak Giterman, Shakhne Zagan, and presumably Ringelblum himself. Nonetheless he issued a direct challenge to Ringelblum and all those who tried to make history into the foundation of a new, secular Jewish identity. What was the point of history? Why gather materials for a secret archive? History has taught nothing and, in fact, Jews were "an ahistorical people"; they only had myth based on their covenantal memory. And now only one task, one priority, remained: to fight hunger: "All those who are great and small in deeds, fight hunger. In Yiddish, Polish, and Hebrew, fight hunger! This is our culture, this is being Jewish. There is no other culture now, but to help those who fall down in the streets and who die at home from hunger."

In the survey religion did not fare much better than secularism. Hillel Tseitlin, deeply pessimistic about Polish Jewry and its prospects, reported a steep decline in religious observance in the ghetto. Of the 220 families in his building, maybe 2 or 3 observed the Sabbath. Perhaps if the Germans forbade religious observance, Jews would try harder to keep the laws. But since the Germans did not care, neither did the Jews. In fact, Tseitlin noted, many religious Jews were rebelling against God, perhaps a consequence of the prewar religious leadership who had always harped on the need to keep Jewish law but did little to imbue the masses with a true understanding of the Jewish faith. In the ghetto, he complained, religious Jews had shown little spiritual nobility. All they cared about was getting some more money from the Aleynhilf. The best that could be said was that Jews from the provinces—more anchored in Jewish folk tradition—far surpassed Warsaw Jews in their compassion and their basic moral instincts.

Had he seen any positive moments in the ghetto? No, Tseitlin answered. He agreed with most of the other respondents that the ghetto had exposed rampant acculturation. Jews loved to speak Polish, perhaps to spite those who had crammed them into a ghetto in order to isolate them from the wider world. On the whole, Tseitlin confessed, "the Jews have shown themselves to be far weaker, far less capable of resistance, than was thought. The Jews have shown themselves incapable of withstanding the slightest trial."

And the postwar period, he believed, looked grim. The Poles would not tolerate a return to the prewar days, and Britain would certainly betray the Zionist movement. Jews needed a territory, and they needed to teach their young people productive vocations. But the only real hope, Tseitlin believed, had to come from within, from a return to the spiritual traditions of the Jewish people.

Even the "defenders" expressed little real optimism, but they did try to put the tragedies of the ghetto streets in a different perspective. The well-known journalist Shaul Stupnicki refused to condemn Jews who walked past beggars and corpses. What choice did they have? They were not callous; they were just fighting for their own lives:

> What about the indifference with which people pass the dead on the streets? Maybe what I say will sound strange but I see it as a positive phenomenon. It's a miracle that people do not become depressed and break down at these macabre scenes in the streets. . . . Were it not for that cruel cold-bloodedness, scenes like these could paralyze [us] . . . and drive people into hopeless depression. So I see it as a positive [sign] that people in the ghetto have become so toughened, so hard-hearted that they pass by the dead and keep fighting for life.

Henryk Rozen also found glimmers of reassurance. The Jews in the ghetto had shown admirable discipline. There had been few robberies or murders. Given the miserable German food allocations, it was a miracle that even more Jews did not die. Yes, there were serious moral lapses. The rich were not paying enough to help the poor, the Judenrat tax policy was indeed unfair, and the Aleynhilf was not up to the job. But even if all these institutions worked perfectly, Rozen asked, would they be able to solve the most pressing problem, that of hunger? To feed the ghetto adequately required 180 million zlotys a month, and, even if such sums were available, the Germans would never have agreed to allocate the food. Thus the contention that Jews could combat famine on their own, which Ringelblum and others held, was a pipe dream, But one should not hurry to blame the victim. Ghetto conditions created want and encouraged lawlessness, but surely any other people, in the same conditions, would have acted the same.

An anonymous religious respondent was also reluctant to condemn his fellow Jews. The truly religious trusted in God even more than before. The only ones to rebel were those who observed the commandments out of habit rather than conviction. God was testing the Jewish people: "A nation of prophets, a people who produced Moses, created the Scriptures, may be faced with tougher demands than other nations, and therefore we are being punished more severely than others." As to the future, this devout Jew was hopeful:

> We are passing through the period of the birth pangs of the Messiah. Who knows how long this will last? Will these trials end for the Jews when the war is over? There is no clear answer. But in the end the Jews will pass this fiery test cleansed and purified, and they will once again become a spiritual people.

Dr. Israel Milejkowski, the head of the Judenrat's health department, insisted that, in judging any aspect of Jewish behavior in the ghetto, one had to consider two levels of ghetto reality: first, the visible phenomena that casual observers would readily notice; and, second, the deeper, less apparent processes that more realistically depicted the true character of the Jewish masses. An outside observer, Milejkowski conceded, would indeed come away with a devastating impression. But the ghetto was like a boiling cauldron: "the upper layer seethes and sizzles and bubbles all over its surface. The bottom layer also seethes but more quietly, with less fuss." This "bottom layer" included the ongoing work of the house committees, "where the true Jewish qualities of mercy and compassion are realized." Deep below the surface other important work was going on such as running soup kitchens and providing schooling. Milejkowski also singled out an area he was deeply involved in: extensive medical research into the effects of hunger that various physicians were conducting in the ghetto.[25] Indeed, he pointed out that even as he was writing his response a medical conference was taking place where researchers were presenting scientific papers.

Milejkowski had no illusions about the ghetto. It was a curse, where Jews had to become hustlers and manipulators in order to survive. Milejkowski had a modest goal: "to show the world, after the war, that these terrible ordeals did not break us." When the Germans put him in a line for the death train on January 18, 1943, Milejkowski shouted, "Murderers! Our blood will fall on your heads!"[26] According to another account, after this fiery speech Dr. Milejkowski and other Jewish doctors gave themselves lethal injections of morphine rather than enter the wagon.[27]

Although he had no way of knowing it, Milejkowski's shrewd observation that much of the important and positive communal activity in the ghetto remained hidden from view coincided with Ringelblum's own convictions. In his diary Ringelblum addressed some of the issues raised by the survey.

I believe that the assertion that we are more demoralized than other peoples is exaggerated, especially if we remember the particularly difficult situation [that the Jews find themselves in] where so many face the choice between hustling [*geyn oyf krume vegn*] or dying of hunger. So let's [not] draw the picture darker than it really is. It's dark enough anyway. (May 18, 1942)[28]

Indirectly the pessimism uncovered by the survey reinforced two perceptions. First, in a situation where Jews could not find ready solace, as did the Poles, in a myth of national solidarity or in hopes for postwar regeneration, the political parties and especially the youth movements stood out all the more for their ability to imbue their followers with belief in a better future. Second, the survey reinforced the perception that the real ray of light in the ghetto hell was the ongoing record of the self-help society and the constant but unheralded efforts of ordinary Jews to endure and help one another. After the war Natan Eck commented in reference to this Oyneg Shabes survey that people like Ringelblum and Milejkowski, who were active in the Mutual Aid Society or in the fight against epidemics, had a more nuanced—and less pessimistic—understanding of Jewish society than those who were less active, like Einhorn, Tseitlin, or Perle.[29]

To study these "deeper layers" of ghetto society became an ever more important priority of the Oyneg Shabes, as this dimension could reveal the true character of Jewish society in wartime, its capacity to resist and endure. Yes, the archive would not flinch from evidence of widespread corruption and demoralization. But it would also document the dogged determination of ordinary Jews to survive, to endure, and to maintain their basic dignity in terrible conditions. And in this quiet, hidden struggle, the Jewish woman played a significant role.

THE JEWISH WOMAN

To study and describe the role of Jewish women in wartime became a major priority of the "Two and a Half Years" project.

The future historian will have to devote [much attention] . . . to the role of the Jewish woman in the war. She will receive an honored place in Jewish history because of her courage and powers of endurance which enable thousands of families to survive this bitter time. Lately we have seen an interesting phenomenon. In many house committees women are replacing men who are leaving because they are burned out and tired. There are now house committees where women comprise the entire leadership. This reservoir [of fresh cadres] is very important for the [Aleyn-hilf]. (June 10, 1942)[30]

One should not read Ringelblum's notation through a modern feminist lens. If gender is, in Joan Scott's words, "a constitutive element of social relationships based on perceived differences between the sexes,"[31] then discussion of gender issues in prewar Jewish public discourse in Poland was relatively rare and took a back seat to other problems such as ideology, economics, culture, and mutual help. Religious and mainstream Zionist parties had shown little interest in rethinking traditional gender roles.[32] The Bund, the strongest Jewish party in Warsaw by the mid-1930s, did issue special electoral appeals to women but its leaders took little note of the pleas of their women's organization (Yidishe Arbeter Froy [YAF]) to respond to their special needs. When the Bund did discuss women's issues, it was usually in the context of other concerns such as assimilation: what to do, for instance, about Jewish women who brought Polish language and culture into the home. In the words of Daniel Blatman, "many political groups retained their traditional assumptions about Jewish society and women's place in it. The processes of change were only beginning in interwar Poland, and the change in ideology did not have enough time to produce far-reaching effects regarding the role of women in Jewish society or in Jewish political settings."[33]

The Oyneg Shabes was predominantly male, and some of its members, when they referred to women, still adhered to traditional stereotypes, both negative and positive. Shimon Huberband (see below) expected Jewish women to be paragons of Jewish morality and was disappointed when they failed these expectations. In his diary entry of May 21, 1942, Abraham Lewin criticized Jewish women and girls ("few in number, it must be said") who dressed ostentatiously and behaved immodestly.[34] Another Oyneg Shabes member, Yehuda Feld, singled out the role of women "semi-professionals"—nurses and teachers—in helping to care for starving and often brutalized ghetto children.

Ringelblum's call for research into the role of Jewish women derived in part from the YIVO. In the 1930s the YIVO promoted an ambitious agenda of research into the problems of Jewish youth, which included a well-known autobiography contest that gave many Jewish girls a chance to write about their lives.[35] Although the YIVO did not stress gender categories or modes of analysis based on gender differences, its research agendas did reflect a growing sense that unprecedented changes, requiring serious study, were taking place in Polish-Jewish society. Young people were marrying much later, a development that facilitated the growth of a distinct youth culture and youth movements. Pauperization and the economic crisis were taking a toll on the stability of Jewish family life. At the same time new educational currents beckoned Jewish youth, as did Jewish and non-Jewish literatures that undermined many traditional values.

From the very first day of the war Jewish women began to assume unprecedented responsibilities. Politics—the domain of men—quickly took a back seat to the challenges of the everyday: finding food and maintaining moral and psychological equilibrium in conditions of rupture. The war had also produced a marked decline in the proportion of able-bodied men in the overall Jewish population, and with it a basic change in the relative importance of women in bearing the burden of ensuring family survival.[36] At the end of October 1939 the Jewish population of Warsaw numbered 164,307 men (46 percent) and 195,520 women (54 percent). If one only counted those between the ages of sixteen and fifty-nine, then the disparity expanded to 44–56 percent in favor of women. On January 31, 1942, out of a total Jewish population of 368,902, there were 157,410 males and 211,492 females. But among the twenty to twenty-nine year olds, women constituted 65 percent! Several factors caused this demographic imbalance. On the eve of the war many men had been drafted into the Polish army; a large percentage were either killed or did not return from German POW camps. On September 6, 1939, after the Polish government called on all able-bodied men in Warsaw to cross the Vistula and head east, many left their families and did not return. Even after the start of the German occupation many men continued to go east, believing they were more vulnerable to German arrest than their families. In 1940 and 1941 constant manhunts to fill the forced labor camps took many men and left others afraid to be seen on the street. Therefore it was their wives and daughters who had to earn money. Ringelblum observed:

> the toughness of women. The chief earners. The men don't go out. When they [catch a man for labor], the wife is not afraid. She runs along, yells, screams. She's not afraid of the soldiers. She stands in long lines [for food]. (early January 1940)[37]

As several scholars have pointed out, war and its massive assault on Jewish society led to a reversal of gender roles and a new emphasis on values that had traditionally been the purview of women. The Germans had rendered men powerless, unable to protect their families. They had become "women," and the women had to become "men."[38]

The Oyneg Shabes study plan on Jewish women recognized that the war had had a major impact on traditional gender roles, even as it carefully avoided gross generalizations. Gender counted for the Oyneg Shabes, but so did social class. The study plan analyzed women as breadwinners and as the catalysts of grass-roots social activity, even as it gave short shrift to psychological and perceptual differences based on gender. The plan stressed the importance of studying women from different social backgrounds as they reacted to various stages of the Jewish war experience.[39] Had the Oyneg Shabes been able to complete what it started, and had Polish Jewry survived the war, this study of Jewish women might well have become a landmark project.

On this subject the Oyneg Shabes wanted to elicit as broad a range of opinions and observations as possible. Some judgments were harsh, such as Rabbi Shimon Huberband's "The Moral Decline of the Jewish Woman during the War." Huberband lambasted the moral failings of Jewish society in the war and singled out Jewish women who gave themselves to German and Soviet soldiers or who seemed indifferent to starving children in the ghetto.

> In addition—and this is not, God forbid, a smear campaign of horrors against all Jewish women—I saw the following with my own eyes. Near a display window of a large concern of various pastries, wines, liquors, grapes, and other delicacies, there lay the dead body of a Jew, some thirty years old. The dead body was totally naked. It was a truly ironic scene. . . . Nonetheless this did not prevent the dressed-up ladies from walking across the dead body to enter the store and then leave it with packages of goodies, which, if only a fraction of the contents of those packages had been given to the hungry, this Jew would not have died of starvation.[40]

Polish anti-Semites, Huberband remarked, did not fail to notice the enormous social gaps in the ghetto and the callousness of the Jews: "Yes, the illusions of 'Jewish unity' and 'Jewish compassion' have been broken. One must only add [. . .] it is painful and a disgrace; I am ashamed [. . .] of the decline of the Jewish woman."[41] Huberband's anger stemmed partly from disappointment: in a time of social and moral crisis, he expected Jewish woman to be exemplars, to outshine men and display what he saw as their traditional qualities of charity and empathy. Yet other observers, including Ringelblum himself, stressed women's resourcefulness and courage, as they filled roles formerly assigned to men. As noted, they became the breadwinners and increasingly the leaders of grass-roots mutual help.

A basic theme of the archive's accounts of the 1939 siege was, in fact, the bravery, courage, and staying power of women. While some men cowered in shelters in the middle of a bombardment, women ventured out to find food.[42] Several accounts of women's activities during the siege were contained in the archive. They were air-raid wardens and firefighters, and did not run away even in the worst air raids. Women also organized the first house committees, set up kitchens for refugees and for people who had lost their homes, and staffed the refugee centers, day care centers, and orphanages.

Cecilia Słapakowa, a principal contributor to the project, saw her study as a contribution to what she hoped would be a necessary and healthy reawakening of Jewish society after the war.[43] "In the tragic destructive whirlwind of our present situation we can still discern signs of creative energy: the slow development and consolidation of forces that are building the foundations of the future. Women are playing an important role in the positive trends of our life [sic]."[44] Słapakowa considered women a buttress against the escalating pressures of moral collapse: they were helping to preserve a modicum of basic communal values. And far from interpreting the war-induced inversion of gender roles as a "measure of atrocity," as Sara Horowitz does, Słapakowa saw it as a good sign for the future. After all, why shouldn't women be more independent, especially if their energy and drive were combined with superior intuition and adaptability? Any final judgment on the role of Jewish women in the war, Słapakowa believed, would have to await the more balanced evaluation of future historians but certain tentative conclusions stood out. She believed that women were showing an amazing capacity to adjust to changing circumstances:

> Women's individuality, so long hemmed in by ethical-cultural norms, has now become [a source of dynamic strength]. The particular circumstances of our socioeconomic life have impelled the Jewish woman to positions in the fight for life that are far more prominent than those occupied by women of other nationalities. The Jewish woman has penetrated into almost every aspect of life. In many areas she has acquired a dominant position [*osiągnęła dziś hegemonię nad mężczyzną*] and has become the positive factor in the formation of our new economic and moral reality. In her individual and communal activity she brings forward many models of behavior from the past; however, with a subtle and amazing sense of intuition she adapts this experience to new conditions, thus achieving very positive results. It is important to remember that the Jewish woman wants more than to simply "endure" [*przetrwać*]. She also wants to   construct the foundations for the future socioeconomic rebirth [of our people]. Therefore we see the drive to acquire skills and professions. . . . But the influence of the Jewish woman is also strong in the moral sphere. She is imparting a ray of hope and courage into our dull and dark life, a touch of humanity and . . . even of heroism.[45]

Motivated by a strong sense of obligation toward their families and toward their own sense of self, women learned to do many things at once: care for their children, learn new skills, and risk leaving the ghetto to engage in smuggling.

Following the Oyneg Shabes guidelines mentioned above, Słapakowa carefully questioned these women about every stage of their experience: their prewar life, the outbreak of the war, the siege, whether their husbands had fled or stayed, how they coped with the beginning of the occupation, and how the establishment of the ghetto affected their lives. She was conducting interviews as late as May 1942 and possibly later. Słapakowa probably handed the notebooks to Gutkowski or Wasser just after the beginning of the Great Deportation on July 22, 1942, and before August 2–3, 1942, when Lichtenstein buried the first cache. Słapakowa and her children died in Treblinka in the summer of 1942.

Słapakowa's surviving notebooks included interviews with seventeen women, referred to only by their initials. They were a highly diverse group. Some had had a higher education and spoke several languages; others had stayed at home or had helped their husbands in their business. They ran the gamut from Basia Temkin Berman, a librarian and an important figure in the Jewish underground, to Ms. P, who survived by becoming a high-class prostitute in a ghetto nightclub.

Słapakowa began her survey with a vivid description of a random moment in the ghetto streets:

> It's ten o'clock . . . a hot sunny day. The Jewish street pulsates with
> the intense rhythms of its anemic life. People push, hurry, shove, [and]
> stand close against the wall. A mix of faces, voices, smiles—"Rolls,
> fresh, tasty, white, [and] cheap!" "Morena, your eyes glowed like two
> stars!" "Warschauer Zeitung, Reich." "Cheap cigarettes!" . . . "Dear good
> people, have mercy on a mother of three orphans!" "O my God, catch the
> thief!" "I have a hairdresser's appointment." "Thank God, I earned some
> money this week." "They're behind on paying wages in the office, how
> will I support my family?" . . . "It's such a beautiful spring. You so much
> want to live. We have to survive." It's ten o'clock, and the Jewish street is
> full of voices of need and of hope.

It was on those streets that many of Słapakowa's subjects waged their battle to survive, with varying degrees of luck. Ms. C and Ms. F, Słapakowa's first two subjects, both came from lower-middle-class backgrounds: Ms. C. had made corsets, and Ms. F had sold shoes. Since the beginning of the war neither woman's husband could provide much economic help. Mr. C cowered in the house, constantly sick and afraid to go outside, and Mr. F had been beaten so badly during a stint of forced labor that he was unable to work for a long time. Both women relied on their prewar contacts with friendly Poles in order to trade and support the family. After the ghetto was established, both would slip out to the Aryan side to smuggle. In November 1941 the Germans announced the death penalty for Jews caught outside the ghetto. Ms. C had a number of close calls. After being caught by a police agent who freed her in exchange for a bribe of fifteen hundred zlotys, she finally decided to give up smuggling, even though she had been earning her up to seven thousand zlotys a month. She told Słapakowa that she was now surviving by petty trade and by selling personal effects. But the risk of getting shot was not worth it. "Because," Ms. C declared, "the most important thing is life. Before, I took risks in order to live. But what's the sense of taking risks in order to die?"

Her associate, Ms. F, was not so lucky. She had three children to support, and the oldest was thirteen. In 1941 she had another child—and redoubled her frantic journeys that took her under the ghetto walls to the Aryan side. ("She was haunted by the fact that now she had to feed one more soul. She tried to store reserve supplies of food.") Making matters worse, her husband came down with typhus in September 1941. Ms. F took enormous risks to crawl out of the ghetto, through holes and cracks she found in the ghetto walls. Even the announcement of the death penalty did not deter her. Caught in November, Ms. F did not have the money to pay the high bribe that the agent demanded. She was among the first group of Jews executed in November 1941 for exiting the ghetto illegally.

Słapakowa did not shrink from presenting strategies for survival that violated established prewar conventions. One interviewee, Ms. C, had grown up in a home marred by alcoholism and "sexual brutality." She married a dental technician shortly before the outbreak of the war. She found herself alone when her husband fled to the East on September 6, 1939. Since her parents owned a restaurant, they did not suffer from food shortages during the siege of Warsaw. After the Germans entered Warsaw, her husband sent word from Vilna, where he had found refuge, instructing her to meet a certain guide who would take her over the German-Soviet demarcation line. But her attempt to cross the border illegally nearly ended in disaster, as rifle fire from Soviet border guards pushed her back to the German side. When she finally returned to Warsaw she discovered that her parents' restaurant had collapsed; the Germans had requisitioned all the food supplies that the family had hidden. Unfazed by this new disaster. Ms. C. seized on a new opportunity. Her parents had rented out a room in their apartment to a Volksdeutsche, a Polish citizen of German origin. Ms. C. became his lover. Her paramour, able to freely travel in occupied Poland and in the Reich, would return with goods that Ms. C could sell for a handsome profit. The establishment of the ghetto ended this cozy arrangement, but Ms. C once again landed on her feet—this time as a waitress in a restaurant which she started with the food supplies smuggled in by her Aryan lover until his ardor cooled and the restaurant collapsed. Once again she picked herself up and began to smuggle on the Aryan side. Like many of the Jewish women in Słapakowa's study, Ms. C relied on the collaboration and help of Polish acquaintances. A house that bordered the Aryan side provided a convenient passage out of the ghetto. Once, when a German gendarme caught her, she broke away and ran; a bullet missed her by inches.

When the Germans changed the borders of the ghetto in October 1941, Ms. C could no longer use the house that gave her access to the other side. She found herself a new job, as a waitress in a ghetto restaurant. This time she combined her knack for petty trade with a new skill: conducting erotic conversations with customers over copious amounts of vodka. When Słapakowa met her, she had already worked herself up from a lowly waitress in the establishment to the "top girl," who survived through a profitable combination of trade and sex. "For the price of having to sell herself . . . she can ensure her own and her family's economic survival."

The story of Ms. G. was similar in some ways.[46] Ms. G, too, acquired Aryan lovers who helped her to live. Her father condemned her affairs, but her mother believed they were necessary for the family's survival and even helped entertain Ms. G's Aryan lover, Mr. J, who also boarded with the family. Mr. J and Ms. G remained close for a long time, even though, as a Volksdeutsche, Mr. J was taking a great risk by being involved with a Jewish woman. During a search of the apartment, the Gestapo caught Mr. J, tortured him, and then released him. Yet, for a time after his release, he continued to see Ms. G. When the relationship ended, the family restaurant collapsed and Ms. G found a new lover, a Polish tailor who also helped her smuggle goods. After she found a job as a bar girl in a restaurant of dubious reputation she took up with another Pole, a police inspector named Bolek. Pretty soon Ms. G and Bolek were conducting an ostentatious ménage. They ran up enormous bills in the most expensive ghetto cafes. Thanks to this relationship, Ms. G was able to earn money on the side by trading on Bolek's ability to free Jewish prisoners. Bolek was also able to free Ms. G's brother the first time that he was sent to a labor camp in April 1942. The second time, in May 1942, she was not so lucky, and Bolek's interventions failed to keep her brother from being sent off in an "unknown direction."

This relationship bothered even the normally unflappable Słapakowa. The open pleasure Ms. G took in Bolek, the expensive wines they consumed together, and the fact that Ms. G felt no embarrassment in front of her friends all puzzled Słapakowa. She wondered whether Ms. G's behavior might be explained by a tendency she noticed on the part of many Jewish women to "eat, drink, and be merry." Perhaps she thought her brazen behavior would reassure Bolek and tie him more closely to her. Słapakowa admitted that there was something "repellant" in what her subject was doing. But she also quoted Ms. G's mother: "If it hadn't been for Guta," she said "our whole family would have been in the Gęsia cemetery long ago."

Some of Słapakowa's most effective interviews were with women who came from her own social class. One such case was Ms. F, a refugee from Lodz who had a doctorate in philology, was fluent in four languages, and had had a comfortable position as an executive secretary in an artificial silk factory.[47] Ms. F, a woman who valued her autonomy, left her job when the factory changed hands and she lost many of her former responsibilities. She then took a new job where she was able to use her fluent French. Like other women interviewed by Słapakowa, Ms. F got help from prewar Polish acquaintances. After the Germans occupied Lodz and imposed restrictions on Jews, including curtailed shopping hours and access, Ms. F's Polish friends brought her food and necessities. Nevertheless, she decided to flee Lodz for Warsaw after the Germans announced their plans for a ghetto in April 1940. Together with her sister, Ms. F risked a harrowing and horrible journey across the border that separated the Reich and the General Government. The border guards forced her to strip naked and then beat her. Thrown off the bus and forbidden to cross the border because she was a Jew, she ignored the danger and crossed on foot, even though she was grazed by a border guard's bullet. After some adventures she finally arrived in Warsaw. Unsuccessful as a street trader, she decided to learn how to give manicures and pedicures.

By 1942 Ms. F had tried many different ways to survive. She had worked in a box factory and an ink factory, earning about six zlotys a day and a bowl of soup. She refused a better job because she did not want to help the German war effort. Working in a factory that employed both Polish and Jewish workers, she suffered from petty anti-Semitism. When she tried to earn extra money by giving manicures and even reading fortune cards, Poles denounced her and made her stop.

As Słapakowa concluded her interviews with Ms. F, the former elegant business secretary was now selling candies on the street. As she explained to Słapakowa, women from the intelligentsia had to start thinking about what they would do when the war was over. She could not count on regaining her former social position. Therefore it was all the more important to have something to fall back on. Ms. F was afraid that women in her position might become "spiritual cripples." She would probably emigrate, and so a marketable skill made sense. "The woman of tomorrow," Ms. F declared, "will be a skilled craftswoman" ("Rzemieślniczka, to zdaniem moim, wogóle kobieta jutra"). In the meantime, Słapakowa noted, Ms. F evinced a "biological drive to survive" while preserving her own moral standards and individual dignity. She was not ashamed to take on any job or do anything at all, as long as it did not compromise her integrity.[48] That meant that she firmly refused to ask for help from the Aleynhilf. She would support herself, no matter what.

Some women derived energy from a sense of being useful to others. Ms. B, forty-eight years old when the war started, performed heroic service during the siege of Warsaw as an anti-aircraft warden.[49] She helped put out fires, took care of refugees, and nursed the wounded. During the terrible air raids of September 26 and 27, 1939, she stayed at her post: even when she knew her own house was being bombed, she refused to try to save her possessions. After the start of the occupation, Ms. B worked in an orphanage of the CENTOS, and then in the ghetto as a hygienist in a refugee shelter. The death of her husband in November 1941 did not break her. Her evenings were devoted to working in the house committee; during the typhus epidemic she risked her life to help the sick. Słapakowa saw Ms. B as the kind of woman who needed her volunteer activities in order to keep fighting for her own survival.

Basia Temkin Berman, the only woman in the study known to have survived, and hence her real name may be used, also threw herself into the service of others.[50] In the ghetto she overcame innumerable obstacles to set up a children's library. Before the war she had been one of the few Jewish employees in the Warsaw public library. She had many fine Polish colleagues (who would help her during the war) and excellent working conditions. But she told Słapakowa that her work in the ghetto gave her much more satisfaction both because of its immediate achievements and because she was helping Jewish children prepare for the postwar world. Berman saw the job of a librarian as being a friend, a teacher, and a trusted intellectual guide. By preparing attractive exhibits and posters, and by organizing readings and discussions, she would awaken children's interest in books. She particularly tried to attract ghetto children to Yiddish books. As she told Słapakowa, enjoying their own literature and reconnecting with their language would make them happier and better-adjusted human beings.

For some educated women the war actually presented new opportunities that were not available in peacetime. Before the war Ms. R, thirty-seven years old and married, had been a trained agronomist and had worked for the CEKABE in its agricultural department. But the work bored her; she wanted something more challenging and more exciting. She recalled that a female colleague of hers, equally restless, had even blurted out that she wished for the dreaded war to break out so that women like themselves would be challenged, would take on important tasks like organizing soup kitchens and war relief. ("We'll do things. We'll live!") Indeed, when the war began, Ms. R sprang into action. Even though she was pregnant, she ignored the incessant bombardments and threw herself into organizing relief for refugees. On September 15 an air raid destroyed her building. She continued to work. After the birth of her child, she successfully juggled, according to Słapakowa, the difficult roles of relief worker, wife, and mother. Forced into the Warsaw Ghetto, Ms. R decided to do something that would make a difference for the postwar era. She returned to her prewar specialty and began to teach agronomy to young Jews in the ghetto.

All the women Słapakowa interviewed had fought to hang on with varying success. While Ms. D cleaned houses and did laundry, she carefully rummaged through garbage for scraps of food to eat. Before the war she and her husband had led a modest lower-middle-class lifestyle. At the very beginning of the war they lost their home and found themselves in the one of the dreaded *punktn* (centers for refugees). Ms. D did all she could to maintain a sense of dignity and autonomy. She hung a blanket around their space in the refugee center to preserve the illusion of privacy. She dreamed of leaving the center and becoming a maid where she could at least live "in a real room." When her husband came down with blood poisoning after engaging in forced labor for the Germans, she donated blood to help save him but he died anyway. As Ms. D searched through the garbage she told Słapakowa, "You know, I so much want to survive!"

The story of Ms. K shows the fragility of the ghetto's "economic security."[51] Ms. K was a deeply religious woman. Before the war her husband ran a successful shop that sold ladies' coats, while she cared for their ten-year-old daughter and seven-year-old son. During the siege of Warsaw a German bomb destroyed their house and all their possessions. With her husband afraid to leave the house, Ms. K joined forces with her two sisters and opened a vegetables and fish stand. The work exhausted her, but she was happy she could feed her two children. Although her marriage collapsed, her strong family ties enabled her to weather new economic shocks, such as the establishment of the ghetto. The move into the ghetto forced her to leave her old stand, but she and her sisters went into business again, this time selling bread. The three sisters would take loans each morning, buy their stock of bread, and clear about twenty-five zlotys a day. That barely sufficed to feed three families, but they survived. Life was bearable—until August 1941.

Then her life began to fall apart. No matter how well one coped or managed, one could not avoid the crowded streets and jostling people; typhus remained a constant threat, and Ms. K fell ill in August 1941. No sooner had she recovered than her two sisters both became ill and died. Now forced to support her sister's four children in addition to her own son and daughter, Ms. K sank deeper and deeper into poverty. She sold all her possessions. In the winter of 1941–42 she had no money even to light the stove; the children spent all their time lying in bed in their layers of clothing. Ms. K and her children were quickly sinking to the bottom. On days she worked, she earned five zlotys; a loaf of bread cost twelve. In a desperate gamble, she began to sell all the families' ration cards for bread, sugar, and soap. She then used the money to buy porridge, supplemented by potato peels donated by neighbors. On days she did not work, they ate nothing.

Ms. K knew that her appearance had deteriorated. She told Słapakowa that not long ago she had wanted to buy candy for her children. The stall keeper took her for a beggar and chased her away. Ms. K, who had been scrupulous about Jewish dietary laws, now ate what she could get.

> But the war has not distorted her soul or spoiled her sense of right and wrong, her ideas of honor and morality. Even in the worst times, even when she faced the death of her loved ones, she never went into the street to beg or to steal. She never sent her children out to beg. (A neighbor has confirmed this.)

Słapakowa's account breaks off with the story of Mrs. K. Did the Oyneg Shabes receive all her notebooks before she perished? It is impossible to say. Clearly Słapakowa did not have time to conclude her study. What did survive, however, demonstrates that Słapakowa was taking dead aim at what she considered to be the social and cultural pressures in Jewish society that had limited women's aspirations and ambitions. Following the traditions of the YIVO, Słapakowa's interviews strove to "study the present" in order to change the future. Before the war Jewish women had had a hard time getting political and communal leaders to take them seriously. Perhaps Słapakowa believed that studies like hers would encourage a new willingness to rethink social attitudes in the postwar era.

One cryptic comment hastily written by Ringelblum sometime in late 1942 or early 1943 suggests that he realized that Słapakowa's study remained incomplete and that he would have liked to have collected even more materials on Jewish women in the war. In the notes in the second section of the archive is the following inscription: "Women, not enough [*mangl*], ZTOS [Aleynhilf?], Slapak."[52]

A few months before his capture by the Gestapo, when he was writing in his underground bunker, Ringelblum made one more comment about Jewish women in the war, this time in connection with the bravery of the young girls, members of the Zionist combat groups, that he had personally witnessed during the battle of the Warsaw Ghetto. "Their courage, ingenuity, and combat skills left the men far behind."[53]

THE FACE OF THE GHETTO

Although the Oyneg Shabes focused on people, ideas, and organizations, it also understood the physical environment of the ghetto as a critical part of any social history of the occupation and developed an ambitious plan to describe the sights, sounds, and atmosphere of the public spaces of the ghetto. The teeming, overcrowded streets with their jarring contrasts, cacophony of sounds, and ever-present macabre scenes of public death and filth epitomized the visible face of the ghetto. As soon as one entered the street, the armbands that everyone wore delivered a stark reminder that, at least in the eyes of the Germans, all the inhabitants of the ghetto belonged to one people. Initially some Jews in the ghetto were relieved to find themselves in an all-Jewish environment. Some Orthodox Jews, at first anyway, regarded the ghetto as affording a measure of protection and security.[54] Nonetheless, the streets also provided constant reminders of national abasement and humiliation. The very layout of the streets sowed disorientation and confusion. Streets led nowhere, suddenly cut off by arbitrary walls and gates that blocked access to parks and trees. To walk in the streets posed unending moral challenges—tiny children begging for food, a dead body covered with a newspaper—and physical danger: exposure to crowds, contact with hordes of unwashed, lice-infested strangers, and typhus. Some streets were relatively quiet, others quite dangerous, but there was no such thing as a safe street, and no one, rich or poor, could avoid the misery of the ghetto. The choke points—narrow passages people had to traverse to get from one part of the ghetto to another—exposed them to deadly encounters with German police who might beat them, force them to do calisthenics, even shoot them. Karmelicka, which the Jews nicknamed "the Dardanelles," was especially risky.

No longer a prewar city, not quite a concentration camp, the ghetto represented a phenomenon that the Oyneg Shabes wanted to study from as many different angles as possible. Ringelblum especially wanted to record and collect impressionistic details of sights, sounds, and clothing. Characteristically, in late 1942, he wrote a short essay titled "Boots" as an example of how fashion reflected social changes and moral values. Many Jews liked to wear boots, he noticed, because they conveyed a message of authority and power. They flaunted the wearer's self-confidence, implying that he or she had connections and money. Members of the Jewish police, barred from carrying weapons, wore their boots as a symbolic compensation for guns. Boots—and the habit of shouting and barking orders and commands—were examples of how Nazi values had infiltrated and influenced a certain category of Jewish society.[55]

Ringelblum's concern with external details dictated the scope of a major study of the Oyneg Shabes, titled "The Street," which examined both its material and social history:

1. The external appearance. First impressions. A comparison with the prewar Jewish street. Exoticism and Europeanism 2. Buildings (as seen from the street). Gates. Windows. Shops. Displays 3. The walls. Outlets. Gates and passages. Little bridges, breaches, smuggling 4. Street traffic. Pedestrians. Difficulties of moving on foot and in conveyances (walls, bridges, blocked streets). Vehicle traffic (autos, trams, horse-drawn trams [*konhellerki*], hearses, ambulances . . . rickshaws. People blocking the street) 5. People in the streets. White-collar workers, peddlers, unemployed, beggars, functionaries, women, children, Aryans 6. Street trade. Stores, cafes, restaurants, gardens, bazaars, stalls, shelves, trade in old clothes, food, bread, cigarettes, candies, books. Middlemen. The oriental character of street trade. 7. The aesthetic aspect of the street. Sights and sounds. Cries of beggars and peddlers. Music, street songs and monologues. Noise of conversations and arguments—of sellers and buyers. Colors: bright colors, variety of clothes. Armbands, hats, uniforms. Advertisements and placards. The stench. External contrasts of rich and poor. Theaters, cabarets, open-air cafes. Exoticism. 8. Public life on the street "Aristocratic streets" and their "splendid isolation" [English in original] Churches and clubs of converts. The lords and the beggars. Rulers and prisoners. The useful worker and the superfluous others. Proletarian and semi-proletarian streets. "All Equal [*ale glajch*]" Equality on the bottom. Social differences marked by clothes, religion, language, . . . and a less gaunt appearance. The hunt for protection and work. Street diversions. The performances of the beggars, a walk and relaxation . . . loudspeakers, rumors, cafes 9. the morality of the street. Thefts and swindles. Healthy and pathological impulses. Vigilante justice. Indifference and empathy. Alms, Punishments. Ordinary lack of shame. Urinating and defecating in public. Spendthrifts, alcoholism, prostitution, corruption, contrasts in way of life. 10. The emotions of the street. Optimism and pessimism. Joy and sadness. Hope and despair. Fear and terror: beatings, jail, manhunts for forced labor and camps. Panic and rumors.[56] Sympathy and empathy. Vengefulness and hatred. Cowardice and courage. The most exalted and the lowest feelings: humanitarianism, dedication, martyrdom, heroism, religiosity, rationalism, Jewish anti-Semitism, egotism, bestiality. General deaden-

ing of feelings. 11. External poverty . . . lack of air and plants, lice, dirt, illness and death on the streets. 12. Different streets. The large and the small ghetto. Different sections. Central and peripheral streets. Main arteries. Lively and dead streets. Streets cut off, divided, cut off. The street as a jail.[57]

Within the framework of this ambitious project the archive adopted a variety of approaches including impressionistic surveys, transcriptions of street songs, essays dealing with the ghetto streets, and even a study of the ghetto's cafes.

Stanisław Różycki made a particularly important contribution to "The Street" study project with four essays: "The Street," "This Is the Ghetto," "Street Scenes," and "Cafes."[58] "This Is the Ghetto" was written in December 1941 and survived in relatively good condition; many pages of "The Street," written in July 1942, were illegible. All these essays, however, were clearly written to accord with the guidelines of the Oyneg Shabes.

Różycki, probably a high school teacher, had fled from Warsaw for Soviet-occupied Lwów in 1939 and returned to Warsaw in October 1941. He quickly went to work for the archive. In addition to essays about the streets, Różycki would also write important studies on Jewish life under the Soviet occupation.

Różycki's first impressions of the ghetto were a terrible shock. During his long months of exile in Lwów, he had heard rumors and stories about the ghetto but still longed to return to his home. Exile from his family, from his apartment and friends, had convinced Różycki that even a ghetto was preferable to a rootless life in a strange city. As he made his way through the Aryan streets of Warsaw, Różycki breathed a sigh of relief. Life went on, and the city and its inhabitants seemed in better condition than he had feared. Then he entered the ghetto. A Jewish policeman immediately pounced and demanded a bribe to release him.

> I entered. I crossed the boundary not just of a residential quarter but of a zone of reality, because what I saw and experienced cannot be understood by our reason, thoughts, or imagination. . . . The very act of crossing reminded me of some rite of passage, a ceremonial initiation, a crossing into the realm of Hades. ("This Is the Ghetto," AR I, no. 428)

Różycki, a Warsaw native who knew every nook and cranny of the city, was lost. The walls, the barriers separating streets or running through the middle of streets, forced enormous detours to travel tiny distances and created crowded choke points and culs-de-sac. He became disoriented and depressed.

By the time he made his way to his old apartment and saw his wife for the first time in two years, he felt deep despair.

As a newcomer, who had not yet become crushed and hardened by ghetto reality, Różycki noticed that even the shortest walk in the ghetto streets became an ordeal of dehumanization, humiliation, and macabre dissonance, a horrifying blend of the worst of two eras: the middle ages and the twentieth century. In the ghetto, Różycki pointed out, one could not avoid the ordeal of the streets. Hardly anyone had telephones, and the smallest errand now took hours. People no longer had the time or the space to receive guests in their crowded "homes" unless they lived in the same building and did not have to worry about the curfew. It was in the streets that one met friends, heard rumors, received vital information about which streets might be removed from the ghetto, when new roundups for the labor camps might begin. Inside the ghetto apartment buildings, the house committees offered a small measure of solidarity and decency. In the streets, however, Różycki saw nothing but filth, demoralization, petty theft, and social disintegration: passersby gaunt and filthy, beggars everywhere, yet the shops bulged with food. But when one entered a store, one plunged into a chaos of jostling, shouting, and arguments between harried sellers and hungry customers. Różycki observed the ghetto police, ironic symbols of the "autonomy" that the Germans had bestowed on the Jews. Before the war hardly any Jews had been mailmen, municipal workers, or policemen. Now they were everywhere, their pathetic attempts to wield power a hideous and absurd counterpoint to the reality of Jewish impotence. Civility and any sense of public decorum had completely disappeared.

Revolting scenes occurred at every step:

> Brazen public manners: Beggars and other poor people relieve themselves on the street: if not on Leszno, then on Orla; if not on Karmelicka, then on the side streets. One can frequently see a young woman, young or old, who would spread her legs, raise her petticoat and relieve herself in public view, without being ashamed to look straight in the eyes of embarrassed passersby. The children do the same . . . The beggars often expose their private parts. They do this on purpose, because they want to show off all the parts of their bodies that are infected, injured or swollen. ("The Street," AR I, no. 154)

Most vestiges of social solidarity, Różycki believed, had broken down. The Jewish population had splintered into "castes." One cared only about one's own caste: prewar friends, members of one's own party or profession. Beggars, outcasts, shunned and ostracized by everyone else, "cease to be human":

They lose all feelings except for the animal urge to eat. They place themselves beyond good and evil, and they become "color blind" with regard to morals, emotions, culture, and social obligations. An average beggar won't even respond with a glimpse of gratitude toward the donor, won't look at him, won't say thank you. ("The Street," AR I, no. 154)

Like many other members of the Warsaw Jewish intelligentsia, Różycki, sickened by the rampant corruption and demoralization he encountered as he tried to settle himself in the ghetto, had scathing words to say about his fellow Jews. No sooner had he returned to Warsaw than a plague of informers and blackmailers accosted him and demanded hefty bribes—or else they would inform the authorities that he had arrived from the Soviet zone without permission. One had to admire, Różycki wrote, the Jews' resourcefulness, vitality, and sheer determination to survive. But the terrible suffering of the average ghetto inhabitant, Różycki believed, was made even more painful by the realization that much of his agony was being caused by other Jews: "What we suffer from [the Germans] . . . well, that's that [*dopust Boży*], there is not much we can do about that. But to suffer at the hands of our own people, that hurts, that causes people to throw up their hands, to turn away from everybody" ("This Is the Ghetto," AR I, no. 428).

There are no "ideal communities," Różycki wrote, and wartime brings out the bestial instincts latent in all societies: "And yet . . . in vain does one seek to justify, to excuse, to look for mitigating circumstances. No, the Jews have failed the test of political maturity, organizational competence, public courtesy and ethics. This is a fact that no one will be able to refute, and no one will be able to change" ("This Is the Ghetto," AR I, no. 428).

His polished and well-written essays, in an excellent Polish, reveal a highly educated observer with a refined sensibility. He expected certain minimum standards of behavior and decorum, even in the terrible conditions of the ghetto. Różycki gave the impression of standing apart from the ghetto's political and communal life. In the world of Polish Jewry, he seemed like an outsider, a cultivated European liberal who was skeptical about ideologies, who had a highly developed sense of morality and civic conduct, and who had no illusions about the future. For Różycki, the war was an especially bitter blow not only because it devastated him personally but because it demonstrated that the values of the Enlightenment had never been deeply rooted in European society. The "law of the jungle" reigned everywhere, whether one happened to be in Nazi-occupied Poland or in the supposedly humane Soviet Union, where venality, corruption, and fear were rampant.

Had Różycki been a member of a left-wing party or a religious Jew or a member of a Zionist youth group, he might have been able to cling to some source of hope for the future: the revolution, God, or a Jewish state. For a humane liberal and an outsider, the ghetto and the war were—simply put—unmitigated disasters.

The Oyneg Shabes also collected other accounts of the streets that to some degree counterbalanced Różycki' s negative and depressing appraisal. Where Różycki saw social disintegration, other observers of the streets ferreted out evidence of Jewish grit and solidarity. What in normal times might seem an insignificant detail, such as how peddlers hawked their wares, now assumed new significance. Sh. Shaynkinder's "In the Streets" described the inventiveness of the street peddlers. In the cries and routines of the various peddlers, and in the way the crowd reacted to them, Shaynkinder discerned the resilience of ordinary ghetto Jews. (He was, however, describing the early days of the ghetto.) A common language and a shared ability to decode the puns and double entendres of Warsaw Yiddish patois created moments of shared community and humor. Here a seller of armbands hawks his wares to an appreciative crowd:

> "Fresh armbands, Jews get 'em right away—they'll make a fine souvenir!" And while the people gathered around smile, the young man shouts with more vigor: "My armbands are white and clean, no one's gone with them into the Judenrat or into a labor camp. My armbands have never been worn by Aleynhilf big shots."

On another street Shaynkinder came across a candle seller (in Warsaw Yiddish dialect, the word for candles (*lakht*) was pronounced the same way as the imperative "to laugh"):

> "Candles [laugh], Jews, candles [laugh] for 20 groshen.
> They burn day and night without mercy. Candles [laugh], Jews, candles (laugh) . . ." While a smiling crowd gathers in the narrow lane, the peddler shouts louder: "Buy, Jews, and may they burn on memorial days, and during festive occasions, on days commemorating the dead, and God be willing, on days to commemorate the scoundrels! Candles [laugh], Jews, candles [laugh] for 20 groshen and may the Jews at long last be able to celebrate! Jews are eager to buy candles like these."[59]

Even starving children, Shaynkinder reported, composed clever rhymes to win the crowd's sympathy:

> Mir hobn nisht oyf keyn zapasn
> Mir voynen in a keler a nasn
> Mir darfn nisht keyn tsuker, keyn shmaltz
> Git unz a shtikl trunkn broyt un zaltz.[60]

[We have nothing saved,
We live in a damp cellar,
We're not asking for sugar or fat,
Just a piece of dry bread and salt.]

Nehemia Tytelman, the archive's major collector of street songs and beggars' chants, reported that the two most popular songs in the ghetto were "Di Bone" (The ration card) and "Moes" (Money), with endless variations on the lyrics and different ways to dance to the beat.[61] A song like "Moes," sung to a snappy American jazz tune, provided an opportunity for strangers to come together and listen to biting satire directed against the Judenrat, the Jewish police, and all those who were better off than they: bakers, Pinkert the funeral czar, the people on the house committees, and all the "Jewish manufacturers" who were supposedly making a fortune from the war. The song reminded the street crowds that, in the ghetto, money determined who lived and who died:

Mues, mues mues iz di beste zakh!
Hostu nisht keyn mues,
Hob ikh far dir a plan
Shik nokh Pinkert's kestl un rik zikh dortn aran.[62]

[Money, money, money is it!
If you don't have money,
You might as well just kiss it all good-bye.]

While money determined the fate of the individual, the smugglers' success or failure decided the collective fate of the ghetto. One verse of "Moes" wished "the best of luck to our smugglers, may the only German they see be blind."

While Moes expressed the rampant cynicism about the division of the ghetto population into "haves" and "have nots," "Di Bone" (The ration card) was a poignant plea for life. Sung in a mixture of Yiddish and Polish, the message was simple and direct:

I don't want to give up my ration card,
I'm still young.
I want to see something good in life,
I want to survive the war,
Please give me something![63]

Just one month before the start of the Great Deportation, Tytelman collected anecdotes illustrating the volatility of popular moods that could switch instantaneously from dark pessimism to hope for victory and revenge. In one story, which referred to German advances in North Africa, one Jew asked another if he had registered with the Judenrat for permission to go to Palestine. No, replied the second, by the time the Judenrat completed the registration, there would be enough time for the Germans to send the Jews of Palestine to the Warsaw Ghetto. In the second story three Jews mused on the pleasures and amusements they would seek after the war. One would eat his fill; a second would happily visit all German military cemeteries. A third said that he would buy a bicycle and travel all over Germany. "Why?" his friends asked? "For a trip of a couple of hours?"[64] But Jewish optimism itself could become the butt of jokes. As two Jews were walking to the gallows, one remarked that if the Germans had no bullets to shoot them, then they really must be in a bad way.

In its efforts to document street life, the Oyneg Shabes consciously cast as wide a net as possible—from random impressions and short sketches to more comprehensive essays. One report, titled "Sketches from the Ghetto," contained the impressions of an anonymous contributor during a random walk in the ghetto:

> 1. A very thin boy walks along Grzybowska Street. He walks bent down, scours the mud with his hand, and puts stuff in his mouth. In the mud were some kernels of ersatz coffee made out of wheat. Then he walks some more and puts something else into his mouth. The boy does not yell, he does not beg, he just walks on, looking down, searching for what he might find.
>
> 2. On Karmelicka Street a baby about a year and a half old sits on a pillow. It sits quietly. A short distance away a girl is standing, watching the baby. Men and women go by, no one pays attention; no one takes any interest in the ghetto's youngest beggar. A small beggar girl goes by with a piece of dried fish in her hand . . . she breaks off a piece and stuffs it into the baby's mouth. The baby eats it greedily.
>
> 3. On my way from Orla along Zamenhofa, I passed two corpses covered with paper, one on Orla, the other on Karmelicka.
>
> 4. On Sienna 38 the notice of a youth circle is posted in the gateway. It is written in Polish. "The management of the youth circle calls on all members to cooperate closely in the anti-beggar campaign. Any member, on meeting a beggar in the gateway or on the stairs, is asked to inform him or her that alms are given only on Friday and that going through the whole house is not necessary.[65]

Oyneg Shabes member Yehuda Feld titled his sketches "Scream, Jews, Scream: Scenes from the Street." Although he did not indicate whether the sketches were fiction or eyewitness accounts, his descriptions differed little from what many others saw in their daily walks through the ghetto streets. One such sketch juxtaposed the tension between the persistence of basic social norms and their total collapse. Feld described how a child beggar quickly snatched a piece of bread from a passerby. Totally indifferent to the blows that rained down on his head, he crouched into a fetal position and devoured the bread. Suddenly a mother who was watching the scene began to savagely beat and curse her own child. The onlookers protested and tried to stop her. One stranger warned the mother that unless she stopped beating her child, he would hit her. Only then did the mother stop and turn around. She fixed the man with a glare, glanced at the small thief who had stolen the bread, and then started hitting her own child again:

> "That's how you should steal bread and stuff your face with other people's food! I don't have anything for you! I can give you only my troubles and heartbreak. She gave him a shove. Hey, eat my skin, chew it up! There's no flesh left on me to eat! So learn to do what he did, learn to steal food and feed your face [*fresn*]! I'll teach you." And the blows resumed. The passersby fled with fear in their eyes.[66]

Yet not far from this scene were posh cafes and restaurants, described for the Oyneg Shabes by Różycki. If one had the money, one could walk past the corpses on the streets and enter an oasis of peace and quiet. In these cafes one could order a mocha, as good as in the prewar days, listen to live music and cabarets, and feast on the finest foods. But sooner or later one had to return to the street—and see the children.

THE CHILDREN

It was the plight of the children that brought out the best and the worst of ghetto society. True to its mission, the Oyneg Shabes committed itself to document one of the most painful aspects of ghetto life—the agony of the Jewish child and the stark moral challenge that agony presented to ghetto society. One could force oneself to ignore dying adults, but not a begging child. In August 1941 Ringelblum wrote about young beggars who disregarded the curfew and yelled from the courtyards for people to throw down a piece of bread:

> In the silence the screams of a hungry beggar child produce a shattering effect, and no matter how callous you have become, in the end you will throw down a piece of bread. If you don't you won't be able to sit quietly.

. . . It often happens that begging children die at night on the sidewalk. I just heard about a terrible scene on Muranow 24, where a six-year-old beggar lay dying all night, unable even to crawl to eat a piece of bread that someone had thrown to him from the balcony.[67]

The numbers of children were staggering. Of the ghetto's one hundred thousand children under the age of fourteen, as many as 80 percent needed help. Many children were orphans, as their parents had died of hunger. Children who lived in the dangerous typhus-ridden refugee centers had to be taken out of that environment and given clean clothing and food. As the streets filled with dying children, many turned to petty thievery. Parents, unable to feed their children, became increasingly desperate and ultimately left them at the door of an orphanage or children's center.

The plight of the children moved all the Jewish institutions to respond. The Judenrat, the Aleynhilf, and even the Jewish police joined forces to help. The house committees set up many day care centers and gave meals to the children of their buildings. The CENTOS, the main children's relief agency, poured resources into the desperate battle to save Jewish children, setting up orphanages, a network of soup kitchens, and day care centers where children could spend a certain number of hours a day. It also sponsored major fundraising campaigns, called "Month of the Child." Adolf Berman recalled that the first "Month of the Child," in the fall of 1941, was a great success. Not only did it raise a million zlotys but it turned into an important demonstration of communal solidarity. Top artists made attractive posters. The campaign included several presentations and recitals by children from various institutions.[68]

In a rare example of collaboration between the Aleynhilf community and the Jewish police, policemen collected street children and packed them off to special homes, where they were washed, fed, and cared for. Various political groups established a school network that not only taught children but also fed them. Both the schools and the CENTOS sponsored theater and puppet shows, drama groups and choirs, special Hanukkah parties and Passover Seders. In conjunction with the Judenrat and Toporol, an agricultural society, CENTOS found places in the fetid ghetto to plant flowers and where children could get some fresh air.

But the heroic efforts made by the CENTOS and other groups in the ghetto could not save all the children, especially given the growing disparity between available resources and the needs of the children. There were not enough kitchens and not enough food. In winter, children often could not get to their designated soup kitchens because they had no shoes or warm clothing. A cursory survey of imperfect statistics for October 1941 shows that little more than half the needy children in the ghetto were receiving some kind of help.[69]

While Berman, in his memoirs, preferred to focus on the heroic struggle to keep Jewish children alive, others blamed the CENTOS, the Judenrat, and the house committees for not doing enough. Opoczynski's "Children on the Pavement" turned into a savage indictment of Warsaw Jewry for its alleged indifference. Even Ringelblum pointedly criticized the CENTOS, an institution directed by one of his closest friends and colleagues. When the "Month of the Child" campaign was in full swing, in November 1941, Ringelblum wrote:

> The most terrible thing is to look at the freezing children, children with bare feet, bare knees, and tattered clothes, who stand mutely in the streets and cry. Today in the evening I heard the wailing of a little tot of three or four years. Probably tomorrow morning they will find his little corpse. [Even in October] they found the bodies of seventeen children in the stairwells of destroyed buildings. Frozen children are a common occurrence. The police are supposed to open a special place on Nowolipie 20 where street children will be collected, but in the meantime children's corpses and children's crying are the constant backdrop of the ghetto. The public covers the children's corpses with beautiful posters made for the "Month of the Child" campaign, posters that bear the slogan, "Our Children Must Live: The Child is our Holiest Resource!" In this manner the public wants to protest the fact that the CENTOS does nothing to gather up these children and save them from death, especially when it has become known that the CENTOS has collected close to one million zlotys.[70]

In order to tell the story of the Jewish child in the Warsaw Ghetto, the archive made extensive use of its many ties to the CENTOS and the schools: Berman; Ringelblum's wife Yehudis, who directed the provisioning department of the CENTOS; and Ringelblum's brother-in-law, Aaron Koninski, who ran one of the most important children's institutions in the ghetto, on Mylna 18. Several other members of the Oyneg Shabes worked directly with children. The communist writer Yehuda Feld worked in the CENTOS, and Israel Lichtenstein and Natan Smolar taught in the ghetto schools and compiled textbooks. Basia Berman ran the most important children's library in the ghetto. Gele Sekstein, who helped organize children's theater performances, was Israel Lichtenstein's wife.

The first part of the archive contained guidelines for the study of the problem of "street children": interviews with members of the CENTOS, the Jewish police, directors of orphanages and children's institutions. There were questions for the children themselves. Where had they lived before the war, and what had their parents done? Did their parents encourage them to go out and beg, or did they try to stop them? Why did many children seem to prefer living in the streets to a relatively secure life in an institution?[71]

Supplementing these guidelines, Ringelblum's brother-in-law, Aaron Koninski, wrote a comprehensive essay on the problem of children in the Warsaw Ghetto, titled "The Face of the Jewish Child" (November 1941). The report summarized and mostly praised all the efforts of the house committees, the CENTOS, and the Judenrat. The children's homes and orphanages run by the CENTOS were superb institutions where the children had full-time care, teachers, a nourishing diet, and clean rooms. But the fourteen homes only had room for two thousand children, and the centers for street children, equally well run, could only accommodate eight hundred children out of the two thousand who lived in the streets. The CENTOS had set up 30 "children's corners" in the refugee centers, where more than three thousand children received extra meals and the supervision of care givers, usually young women, who taught them drawing, read aloud to them, and supervised games and dancing. But these children's corners could take in only a fraction of the needy refugee children. The house committees set up an additional 164 children's corners for forty-five hundred children and engaged better-off tenants to give four thousand children a daily meal. A network of playgrounds gave six thousand children daily supervised activities.

Nonetheless, Koninski warned, Warsaw Jewry was losing the battle to save the children from disease, hunger, and psychological degeneration. The closing of the schools at the start of the war had been a disaster, and efforts to start clandestine schools were largely ineffectual. Parents, worried and harried, failed to give their children attention and care. Children in turn began to steal, swear, or simply give up, spending whole days in bed, staring at the walls and doing nothing. Children who were Warsaw natives were relatively lucky, but even they were showing the effects of the war. Koninski observed a game they played called "German and Jew," where the "German" kicked and cursed the Jew. As for the refugee children, whose parents had lost everything, Koninski cited one case of a mother and child he knew who had been expelled from Kalisz. Before the war they had been of the middle class. In the ghetto the child had become completely obsessed with food. He greedily stalked his mother, ever fearful that she might keep some of his meager bread ration for herself. Many other refugee children took to the streets, especially after their parents died from hunger or typhus.

Like Opoczynski's "Children on the Pavement," Koninski's essay ended with a fervent plea to save the children, the future of the nation. Could War-saw Jewry look on with a "clear conscience" as the next generation turned into physical cripples and petty criminals?

> After all, the child is the holy of holies of any community; it is its fu-ture, its vitality and its mainstay. The Jewish community must bear re-sponsibility for the state of the younger generation; it should consider no burden too great; it should accept every challenge and effort to save the Jewish child from destruction. The concern for the state of the younger generation is the historic obligation of Jewish society. It is also our most pressing concern today. Each lost day hastens the specter of catastrophe; help must come quickly and effectively. Jewish society has the responsi-bility to feed the hungry child, clothe the naked, care for the abandoned and provide shelter for the orphans and the homeless children. [Only if this happens] will Warsaw Jewry be able to stand before the tribunal of history with a clear conscience, knowing that it had done all it could and did not allow the destruction of the younger generation to take place.[72]

The Oyneg Shabes tried to give these children a chance to speak for them-selves, gathering the essays and writings of younger and older children under the guise of a school exercise. The archive asked the children to write about their wartime experiences, about the saddest and the happiest moments of their lives, about what they hoped to do after the war. They were also asked: "What does war mean"? Some responses were written down by teachers, based on interviews with the children, and others the children wrote themselves.

In September 1941 the archive collected thirty-four essays from the chil-dren in the day care center on Nowolipki 25.[73] The director of the center, Genia Silkes, had been a teacher in the Borochov school on Nowolipki 68; she was a member of the LPZ and a friend of Ringelblum's. The essays, which ap-pear to have been written by ten and twelve year olds, all bore the title "How the War Changed Our Lives." The children described how they remembered their prewar lives and what their families had experienced since the begin-ning of the war.[74]

In April 1942 the archive collected a number of accounts of older chil-dren who were living in the refugee centers. Fourteen-year-old Chil Brajt-man, from Maciejowice, wrote that his family was deported to Warsaw in November 1940. They lived in a refugee center, where the windows were bro-ken and where it was so cold that the soup froze. His father died of starvation in March 1941, and his mother starved to death in June.

> During the course of the day I would not eat until two in the afternoon, at the CENTOS. Hunger tortured me, I knew that I would die of hun-

ger, I did not want to beg so I started to smuggle. That was a tough way to earn one's bread. Once a Polish policeman beat me [very badly] . . . but better a beating than death. Often gendarmes would put the barrel of a pistol to my skull. . . . Then I would return hungry and tired, unable to eat.

I have saved myself so far, my 17-year-old brother died in February 1941, my sister died in March 1942 of dysentery. My oldest sister is still in the refugee center, where she is starving. I am sorry that here in this children's home, my smuggling skills have gotten rusty, because I would like to be able to help my sister.

My worst memories? I'll remember the refugee center my whole life . . .

Best memories? The Jewish holidays at home, long walks in the fields in the summer.

What does war mean? No work, that's war. Just hunger.

Plans after the war? None. I think that as long as I live, nothing will change.

Fourteen-year-old Israel Lederman had come from a religious family. Both his parents had died. He did not mind the children's center but would have liked a more religious atmosphere. His happiest memories before the war were heder [a Jewish religious school] and visits with his father to see the Gerer Rebbe, an important Hasidic leader.

What does war mean? Well, there are two kinds of war, the war against hunger and the war with bullets. The hunger war is worse because then everybody suffers, a bullet will kill you quickly.

Plans for the future? I'll become a watchmaker, an easy job.

For fifteen-year-old Sara Sborow, her worst wartime experience was "the night mommy died. I slept beside her in the same bed. During the night I felt that my mother was cold and stiff, but what could I do, I lay close to her until morning and then a neighbor helped me carry her out of bed and lay her on the floor." Sara wrote how she tried to keep her sister alive by giving her raw cabbage. But her sister swelled up from hunger and died. Sara wrote that she would rather die than beg. She had seen many bad people during the war, and in the ghetto she was robbed of everything. When asked to describe what war meant to her, she replied, "I know it all, but I cannot put it into words."

The archive supplemented Koninski's report with firsthand accounts from caregivers, nurses, and teachers who were in the front lines in the battle to save Jewish children. One of the key institutions that fought for the lives of the children was the Berson and Bauman Hospital for Jewish Children, which had been opened in 1878. For many years, one of the chief doctors of the hospital was the legendary Anna Braude-Heller, who stayed at her post until she was killed in 1943. Among the other doctors who worked in the children's hospital was Adina (Inka) Szwajger, who later became an underground courier and survived the war. (Coincidentally Szwajger's mother had been the principal of the Yehudiah gymnasium, where Ringelblum had taught before the war.) When the Germans ordered the final liquidation of the children's hospital on September 12, 1942, Dr. Szwajger decided to poison all the children and thus spare them the horrors of Treblinka.[75]

Nurse Dora Wajnerman gave the Oyneg Shabes a revealing document, "Scenes from the Children's Hospital" (between March and May 1941). On the night of March 3, 1941, Wajnerman and her assistant were deluged with work. They had to wash, feed, and give injections to fifty children. Suddenly the telephone rang: ten new children had arrived. But there were no beds, blankets, or clothing. The hospital had no heat. Each bed already contained two children. Wajnerman was told to add a third child to each bed.

The ten children had just arrived from a small town, their families having been dumped in the ghetto. They all had the measles. After checking them in, she inspected all the beds. In one bed three small children lay in a pile of feces. All three were crying.

> A swollen five year old is lying in the corridor. He is dying of hunger. He came to the hospital yesterday. Two swollen eyes, hands and feet like little pumpkins. We did all the tests. Kidneys? Heart trouble? But it's neither. The child barely moves his lips and asks for a piece of bread. I give him something to eat. Maybe he'll swallow? But no, his throat is swollen, nothing goes down, it is too late. The doctor asks, "Have you eaten something at home?" No. Do you want to eat now? Yes. After a few minutes, for the last time, he says "a piece of bread," and with these words he dies.

Not everyone on the staff could cope with the pressure and daily heartbreak. Nurse Wajnerman reported how a desperate mother appeared at the hospital with a dying child. The attending physician explained to her that the hospital could not admit her child unless the mother left a fifteen zloty deposit for funeral costs. The hospital simply had no money to bury children. But the mother was a refugee, lived in one of the shelters, and did not have a penny.

> The weeping mother suddenly lets loose a torrent of anger. All her misery and pain that had been building up since the beginning of the war is unleashed at the doctor.
> "You are not a doctor, you are a murderer, you want to kill my child,

you have no heart, human feelings, for fifteen zlotys you want to sentence my child to die. They have expelled me four times already. Where am I going to find money?' She clasps her heart and sobs. The child is lying on the table, its face already blue, gasping and choking for its last breath. The doctor can no longer endure this scene and runs out of the room. The mother is left alone with the dying child, she screams until the guard comes and asks her to leave. She takes the child and curses: "This is supposed to be a hospital? Let it burn! Doctors without hearts, killers, bandits!"

Such scenes occur very often.[76]

Some caregivers cracked under the pressure. Others redoubled their determination to help the children. Many children had been so traumatized that it took extraordinary patience and skill to reach them and win their trust. Many of the teachers and nurses had hungry children of their own at home, and it was difficult for them to forget their personal worries and devote themselves to the children in their care, especially because their own salaries were so low. Oyneg Shabes member Yehuda Feld gave the archive a short story, probably based on a true incident, of a harried caregiver who refused to give up on a street child who spoke to no one at the center and stole anything in sight. The supervisor of the institution wanted to expel the child, but the caregiver would not agree. Even after the boy stole some food that she had bought to feed her own children, she still continued her efforts to gain the child's trust, and finally she succeeded.[77]

In 1941 the archive collected several reports from the directors of the child care centers established by the CENTOS to work with the refugee children.[78] These caregivers faced one of the most difficult jobs in the CENTOS network. These children did not have even the semblance of a home and lived in some of the worst conditions of the ghetto. Their refugee parents were more likely than native Warsaw Jews to suffer from apathy and depression. Caregivers quickly realized that many hungry parents were forcing their children to hide some of the food they received in order to bring it home. The staff quickly learned to supervise all the meals and make the children eat their entire serving. They also warned the parents not to hang around the day care center in the hope that their children might give them some food. G. Kon and Sima Rydyger, who worked at the center at Stawki 9, wrote that some children hoped that their remaining parent would soon die so they might get an extra ration as an orphan.[79]

To help the children required not just money and food but also an investment of time and commitment. Yet conditions made it extraordinarily difficult to focus on a particular child and forge a psychological bond. Many of the children had lost their childhood and were contemptuous of playing and games and the skits the caregivers tried to organize. Yet, as one caregiver stressed, that was precisely what had to be done: to break down their defenses and get them to play and laugh once again. Cecylia Apel, a CENTOS worker who visited children in their "homes," recalled one eleven year old who had lost both parents, had become apathetic and listless, and spent entire days in bed. Apel did not give up on the child, roused him from his lethargy, and reported that she managed to send him to a day care center where his emotional state improved and where he participated in activities.[80]

Many caregivers took pains to turn filthy, neglected rooms in refugee centers and overcrowded buildings into bright, welcoming locales for the children. They struggled to find small ovens, coal, tables, and chairs. Once they acquired these essentials, they then bombarded the CENTOS with requests for chalk, paper, and books.

A major part of the struggle for the Jewish child was to maintain morale. Many children had even forgotten what rivers, hills, forests, and parks looked like. The ghetto poet Władysław Szlengel, in his poem "A Talk with a Child," asked:

But how to explain it to a child,
what does it mean the word: afar
while he does not know what is a mountain,
and he does not know what we call a river . . .
and he has not like mother . . . and has not like me
the images under the eyelids,
then how to explain it to a child,
what does it mean the word: afar.[81]

The teachers and caregivers tried. In a report of December 17, 1941, Esther Karasiówna explained her work with refugee children in the shelter at Śliska 28. For a project entitled "Children of the World," they heard stories and learned songs from China, Africa, and other places. She also taught them songs about winter animals such as squirrels. Of her eighty-six children, all but fifteen had lost either one or both parents.[82] Initially traumatized by their losses, they were improving: they were now playing and singing, and the older ones wanted to study. Karasiówna, like other caregivers, asked the CENTOS for chalk, books, and paper. But serious problems remained. Fifteen children were sick and could not come to the shelter; sixteen simply had no clothing at all. Four children had taken to begging in the streets. She was trying her best, but there were limits to what she could do. The ghetto's institutions, she wrote, had to step in and provide more support.

The caregivers tried to remind the children that even though they had lost their homes and even their parents, the world had not yet dissolved into total chaos. Rules, routine, and decorum signified that they were still part of a community: not everything had collapsed. Karasiówna made the children observe certain basic rules of politeness and etiquette. Before the children sat down to eat, they had to wash and stand quietly by their tables, wish one another "Bon appetit" (*smacznego*) before they ate, and say thank you when they were done. Children took turns cleaning up.

Filed in the first part of the archive was the invitation to the last children's performance in the ghetto, in the orphanage directed by Janusz Korczak. The performance took place on July 18, 1942, and it featured the children's presentation of Rabindranath Tagore's "The Postman." Szlengel helped write the invitation:

> It transcends the test—being a mirror of the soul
> It transcends emotion—being an experience
> It transcends mere acting—being the work of children.

The main character of "The Postman" is Amal, a very sick orphan whom the doctor forbade to leave the house of his adoptive parents. Amal has a dream that the king's doctor comes to see him and that the King himself will come pay a visit. Happily anticipating the prospect of rescue and new life, Amal dies. Betty Lifton speculates that Korczak was trying to teach the children to overcome their fear of death.[83]

As we know, Korczak and his colleague, Stefania Wilczyńska, accompanied their charges to Treblinka. So did Aaron Koninski, who ran the children's home on Mylna and who stayed with the children on their final journey. And so did Esther Berenhholtz.

The second part of the Oyneg Shabes Archive contains very little material on children. As one of the archive's statistical reports noted, of the children who had been living in the ghetto just before the Great Deportation, 99 percent were gone.

THE SHTETL

A major priority of the "Two and a Half Years" project was to collect as many essays and reports as possible on the experience of various small towns (*shtetlekh*) and provincial cities during the war in order to make the archive a record of Polish Jewry and not just of Warsaw. Spurring them on was the knowledge that, as the Germans expelled Jews to larger ghettos, shtetl after shtetl became Judenrein: who knew if and when they would return?

Ringelblum realized that these shtetlekh, with their centuries-old history of Jewish life, had been important bastions of Jewish folk culture, small close-knit communities that had nurtured a sense of Jewish peoplehood in Eastern Europe. He had grown up in Buczacz and Sanz, and his work on the Folkshlif in the 1930s had given him a deeper appreciation of the rich folk culture of the shtetl.

In early 1943 Ringelblum called the studies of the small towns "the most important treasure [of the Oyneg Shabes]." He stressed that the staff had worked out careful and detailed theses to guide the essays (see appendix C), which would examine "all aspects of [the shtetl's collective experience]," for example:

> economic life, how Germans and Poles related to the Jews, the Jewish councils, mutual aid, the most important events in the history of the town such as the arrival of the Germans, pogroms, expulsions, atrocities during Jewish holidays, religious life, forced labor and labor camps, the labor departments of the Judenrat, how Germans treated Jews doing forced labor, etc.[84]

In the first part of the archive alone, the Oyneg Shabes filed away close to four hundred essays, reports, and brief testimonies from shtetlekh and provincial cities. Given the conditions under which the archive worked, the number of writings collected fell somewhat short of Ringelblum's high hopes for a geographically comprehensive record. The bulk of the essays were from Congress Poland and the Warthegau, indicating that most of the respondents were refugees from these areas. There was much less material on Galicia and eastern Poland.

Ringelblum wanted these studies of the shtetl to reflect the diversity and cultural ferment that characterized Polish Jewry:

> Aside from adults, young people and, in exceptional cases, even children worked with the Oyneg Shabes. The Oyneg Shabes tried to give a comprehensive [alzaytig] picture of Jewish life during the time of the war. What we cared about was to be able to convey a photographic picture of what the Jewish folk masses lived through, thought, and suffered. So in describing, for example, the experiences of a shtetl, we tried to have the narrative of an adult and of a young person, of a religious Jew, who cares about the rabbi, the synagogue, the cemetery . . . and of a secular Jew, who chooses to emphasize other themes that are no less important.[85]

In fact, as Ringelblum admitted, relatively few of these essays strictly adhered to the Oyneg Shabes guidelines. Many were individual testimonies all the more powerful and convincing for their unstudied quality: the authors were obviously ordinary provincial Jews unaccustomed to composing an essay or a narrative. Quite a few came from adolescents who were fifteen years old and even younger.

Nevertheless Ringelblum believed that the essays, some concise and spare, others lengthy, successfully conveyed what Polish Jewry was going through.

> The essays are written with feeling [*zaynen geshribn mit a varem harts*]. Often one wonders how the writers can relate with such epic calm the most tragic events that occurred in the shtetl. But the calm is the calm of a cemetery, a calm that is the result of the feeling of resignation caused by terrible suffering. The only people who can write that way are those who know that you can expect anything from the Germans.

For many of these Jews, the chance to write down their experiences or recount them to an Oyneg Shabes member afforded a welcome opportunity to feel useful and to remember that, despite their refugee status, impoverishment, and degraded living conditions, someone believed that what they had to say was important. It was a chance to reaffirm their former identity as valued members of a community and to remind the relatively fortunate Warsaw Jews that they had not shown the goodness and charity expected of fellow Jews. Meir Medzinski, a folk poet and refugee from Sieradz, told Oyneg Shabes worker Zalmen Skalov:

> Yes, now about the expulsion from Sieradz. I would like to leave a document after I'm gone. Let someone think about what we have gone through. A document for the future, let a future generation think about our sufferings. May our own wealthy brothers here in Warsaw understand the sparks that sparkled in the hearts of the "beggars" [*shnorrer*] who have ended their lives as lepers on the bare boards of the lice-infected refugee centers.[86]

What they had seen and lived through, the refugee informants were told, was significant, not only for Jewish history but also to ensure that justice would be done after the war, when the world would be whole again.

Unlike the postwar *yizker bikher,* memorial books compiled by Holocaust survivors on their destroyed towns, these essays were written during the war itself, at a time when most Jews still had no knowledge of the Germans' intention to destroy European Jewry. Although the writers were uprooted refugees, they were still a part of a living community. Polish Jewry had not yet been destroyed. They were not yet writing as "Holocaust survivors," and their perspective was shaped less by the need to memorialize and eulogize an entire civilization than it was to testify and record specific incidents and events, and, in the process, defend what was left of their own individuality and dignity.

Many of these accounts described the very first months of the war and the first experiences with the German occupation, and they convey the shock and trauma of events that were dwarfed by subsequent horrors. The writers of these accounts, ordinary, provincial Jews, tried to tell what they saw: the killing of a neighbor; the beating of a boy; the sadistic torture of several dozen Jews by a group of German soldiers; the burning of a synagogue, often with Jews herded inside. There were accounts of Jews being forced to spit on Torah scrolls and to dance on them, and descriptions of how Jews were buried alive or hanged. Oyneg Shabes worker Leyb Skalov recorded two cases where German soldiers forced Jews to strip and simulate sexual acts.

The hundreds of shtetl essays told a story of wanton and gratuitous face-to-face brutality that began with the entry of German troops. The beatings and the sadism preceded the Final Solution. They underscored the extent to which many German soldiers, gendarmes, and police took pleasure in spontaneously assaulting and even killing Jews. Only very few accounts mentioned how Germans expressed shame at what their countrymen were doing and even helped Jews.

The shtetl project elicited contributions from traditional Orthodox Jews. An essay on the shtetl Skempa depicted it as a *kehilla kedosha* (holy community), religious Jews led by a saintly rabbi, Joseph Gelernter, who protected his flock, shared their sufferings, and accompanied them into exile.[87] The Oyneg Shabes essay recorded the rabbi's sermons, as he explained to his fellow Jews that their ordeal had nothing to do with their sins or their faults. Their generation was fated to suffer as Jews had not suffered before. The age of liberalism and enlightenment was about to give way to a darker time. But this was God's test. And hadn't the saintly Rabbi Akiba, the martyr of the second century, reminded Jews that "there is a time when tortures are welcome. Do you know, my dear friends, when? When the ordeals are not experienced just by individuals, because of particular sins or crimes, but when they happen to us because we belong to a people that is trying to bring the light of the Torah to a dark world." This essay, like many others in the collection, expressed the poignant grief of refugees who wanted to remind their unknown readers— and perhaps themselves—that, until recently, they had homes, a stable community, responsibilities, a station in life. As the Skempa Jews prepared to leave their town for the unknown, just after receiving the German expulsion order, they asked their rabbi to give them personal letters attesting to their past status in order to remind strangers that they, too, were once respected householders, not beggars.

Often the refugees lovingly describe the history and the past glories of these towns. A writer from Kutno, Josef Piotrkowski, carefully enumerated not only the great rabbis who had lived there but also Yiddish writers like Sholem Asch and Y. Y. Trunk.[88] An essayist from Kozienice recounted the pride that all the town's Jews supposedly felt in the heritage of the great "Kozhenitser Magid," an important early-nineteenth-century Hasidic leader.[89] A Jew from Nowy Dwor reminded his readers that his was an ancient town, and that Napoleon had once stayed there.[90] This was not just nostalgic pride. In a time of displacement and catastrophe, it recalled the deep ties that had linked the Jewish individual to the community and, through it, to the glorious past of Polish Jewry.

Other essays depict social tensions that were often missing in elegiac postwar memorial books, just as these contemporaneous essays much more readily describe and condemn the behavior of fellow Jews than the memorial books.

One Jew from Głowno, refracted the war through a mass of ordinary, seemingly petty details that traced his struggle to hold on to his prewar routine. The war began on a Friday morning, and his first worry was how to celebrate the Sabbath. He reported in great detail how he managed to find a duck for that first Sabbath and, with fighting raging all around, how he had gone to look for a ritual slaughterer. He recalled his efforts, in the first months of the German occupation, to visit the synagogue, to continue communal prayers, and to keep his business going. For him, as for probably many others, the war could only be faced one day at a time.[91]

Many accounts repeated the familiar Golgotha of the refugees: the summary expulsion order, with little or no time to pack possessions; the trek in columns watched by guards who beat and shot at them at whim; trips in unheated railroad cars; and the final arrival at a filthy refugee center in the Warsaw Ghetto. A report from Tłuszcz described the expulsion and the march:

> The rabbi was led out to the market, told to remove his shoes and dance barefoot on one foot around the market. When he did so, they flogged him mercilessly. When he fell to the ground, wounded and pouring blood, they shot a bullet at his foot, beat him again and then shot him in the hand, then in the buttocks, and finally in the head.[92]

At first women and children were told to get into carts, and the men had to run.

> Among the women was twenty-year-old Miss Lustig, renowned for her beauty not only in Tłuszcz but in the entire region. When she tried to get into one of the carts, the Wachmeister approached her and called

out: "Jews should not have such beauties." He pulled her off the wagon and shot her then and there. Then they called over the chairman of the Judenrat, Meir Traub, and shot him, too.

The men waited an hour, and then had to run after the wagons. All laggards were shot. Jews who paused to help a father or a child were killed immediately by the gendarmes mounted on horses or bicycles.

> Ten kilometers after Tłuszcz we saw two gendarmes standing in a field with machine guns in their hands. Their horses stood nearby. When we arrived at the site, we heard them shout: "This is how Jews walk! Run! Run!" We started to run with all our might. At that moment there was a heavy barrage of machine-gun fire . . . the terrible cry of "Shma Yisroel" [Hear O Israel, the Lord is our God, the Lord is one] rose up as people fell on top of one another. . . . Not of our own strength but out of fear of such a terrible death we continued to run until we caught up with the vehicles just outside Radzymiń. . . . I thought, only yesterday you were rich, you had husbands, your children had fathers; now you are widows, orphans, and impoverished.[93]

Many of these provincial Jews had been confident that, thanks to their resourcefulness and strong family ties, they would survive, just as Jews had somehow managed to survive past wars. The Oyneg Shabes interviews captured the trauma, the sense of disbelief, the sudden panic that resulted from losing not only close loved ones but also the community that had been a source of identity and strength.

A Jewish couple (Simon and Sara Powsinoga) from Okuniew, not far from Warsaw, described how, for the first two years of the war, the four hundred Jews of their little town had been lucky. The Germans did not establish a ghetto in their town, they could move around, and best of all there were many opportunities to work—Simon was a shoemaker—and to trade with the peasants. Finding food was also not a problem. On March 26, 1942, their luck ran out. After weeks of rumors about an imminent expulsion of the Jews, German gendarmes suddenly appeared and ordered all the Jews to gather in the town square. The gendarmes, aided by local Poles, helped themselves to the Jews' possessions. Then the Jews were driven out of town, the women and children in carts, the men on foot. The Jewish men had put on many layers of clothing and were all loaded down with heavy packages, hoping to have something to sell in the future in exchange for food. But the mounted gendarmes began to beat the column of men with whips and forced them to run. Sweating and out of breath, the Jews dropped their packs and struggled to keep the pace. The gendarmes shot anyone who dropped behind.

The Powsinogas carefully named all the Jewish victims they could remember, including their only son, seventeen-year-old Mates-Borukh. (They also had a fifteen-year-old daughter.) Mates, like the other men, was wearing many shirts and was also dressed in a heavy winter coat. He had just returned from a labor camp and was sick and very weak. A gendarme beat him on the head with a whip and then shot him in the head.

At this point the Oyneg Shabes interviewer asked Simon Powsinoga if he thought that the Germans had made a special effort to target young people.

> I don't know, I simply don't know what's happening with me. I still can't believe that I no longer have my boy, my beloved Mates. My only son and helper. Two days ago I was still a human being [*mensh*]. I was the head of a family and a household [*balebos*]. Because of my hard work I had laid away supplies not only for Passover but also for the whole summer. I could support my own family and even help others. Now look at how I look. [He shows the interviewer swollen legs with bloody and painful wounds.] When I came here my boots were full of blood. [How will I work? For now we're staying with relatives.] How long will I be able to hold out? Maybe my son is better off than we are? [The Oyneg Shabes interviewer notes that at this point his wife begins to sob.] You know, I just don't care now. I don't have Mates, what's the point of living?[94]

Because the German expulsions had ended the Jewish presence in many small towns, Ringelblum thought it was important to collect as many eyewitness accounts as possible. He especially valued the collection of shtetl monographs for its information on Polish-Jewish relations:

> There is a widespread opinion [among Jews] that anti-Semitism has increased sharply during the time of the war and that most Poles are happy about the misfortunes that have beset the Jews in the cities and small towns of Poland. But the attentive reader of our materials will find hundreds of documents that show the opposite. In more than one report from a shtetl he will read about how warmly the Polish population treated Jewish refugees. You will find hundreds of examples of peasants hiding and feeding Jewish refugees from nearby shtetlekh.[95]

When he began the shtetl project, Ringelblum had understood that there was a different texture to Polish Jewish contact in small towns than in big cities, where familiarity tempered distance and where Polish and Jewish families had often lived side by side for generations. As Eva Hoffman has observed:

Morally and spiritually, the two societies remained resolutely separate, by choice on both sides. Yet they lived in close physical proximity, and, willy nilly, familiarity. In the shtetl pluralism was experienced not as an ideology but as ordinary life. Jews trading horses in a small market town, speaking in haphazard Polish—that was the shtetl. Poles gradually picking up a few words of Yiddish and bits of Jewish lore—that was also the shtetl. Jewish bands playing at Polish weddings and local aristocrats getting financial advice and loans from their Jewish stewards—all that went into the making of the distinctive, mulchy mix that was shtetl culture. This was where prejudices and bonds were most palpably reenacted— where a Polish peasant might develop a genuine affection for his Jewish neighbor despite negative stereotypes, and, conversely, where an act of unfairness or betrayal could be most wounding because it came from a familiar [face].[96]

In an anonymous Oyneg Shabes shtetl essay on Tarczyn, a small town south of Warsaw, the author described how peasants and Jews would buy from each other. They would look over each other's wares, chew straw, take their time, bargain and draw matters out.

Even though the peasants are sure that the Jews would love to cheat them, still they are in no hurry to end the bargaining. They also would not think of buying from a non-Jew, because that's the way things have been for generations. Even the [prewar] pickets did not deter them from trading with the Jews whom, half-jestingly, half-seriously, they would call swindlers.[97]

These shtetl monographs, which mostly deal with the 1939–41 period, reflect the complexity of Polish-Jewish relations before the great break of 1942, that is, before the onset of mass annihilation. Several accounts describe rabid Polish anti-Semitism, but many essays also recorded Polish sympathy and kindness. In Chełm, when the Germans imposed a heavy levy on the Jewish community in late 1939, the local Polish intelligentsia contributed food and money to the Jews.[98]

An informant from Sochaczew noted that before the war anti-Semitism was strong in the area, and right-wing agitators pressed for an economic boycott of the Jews. Nevertheless, even if peasants said harsh things about "the Jews," they all had their particular Jewish friends and business partners. Despite the boycott, they would trade with Jews when no one was looking.

Lately, after the expulsion of the Jews from many areas, the attitude of the peasant of Mazowsze and Kujawy has become much friendlier toward the Jews. Because of common sufferings . . . his soul has been changed. He is more understanding of Jewish sufferings, he wonders how he would feel if the Germans expelled him from his home . . . all he has to do is to see a suffering Jew and he will invite him into his hut, even though he doesn't know him and is seeing him for the first time. There have been cases where former Endeks [National Democrats, an anti-Semitic party] become quite merciful, seeing a poor Jewish wanderer, and more than one Volksdeutch has also given help.[99]

Other shtetl monographs also noted that in their towns Poles ignored the pre-war boycott and continued to trade with their Jewish neighbors. One writer from Turobin maintained that the local Poles detested the boycott, which was organized and carried out by "outside Poles," especially newcomers from the Poznan region.[100] Several of these monographs recorded, for example, good relations between the Polish army and local Jews both before and during the September campaign.[101] One informant from Kalisz reported that on the eve of the war the Polish attitude toward Jews had changed for the better.[102] Daniel Fligelman from Aleksandrów spoke of the friendly attitude of the Polish Army toward the Jews, better, he added, "than might have been expected."[103] The peasants, on the other hand, were less friendly to hungry refugees, but they were just as callous to Poles.

One frequent theme in the monographs concerned the aid that Jews received from peasants. When a young Jewish adolescent from Serock was marched off with a column of Jews in the fall of 1939, he was unable to keep up the pace. A German soldier shot him by the side of the road and left him for dead. After crawling to a nearby village, he was nursed back to health by a kindly peasant.[104]

A barber from Wiskitki who had been deported with his family to the Warsaw Ghetto, described how beginning in the spring of 1941 he would illegally leave the Warsaw Ghetto and return to his native region to try to earn money to feed his family.[105] He would wander from peasant village to peasant village, approach families he knew, and cut their hair, for which they would give him money and food to take back into the ghetto. He began to leave the ghetto regularly and live among the peasants, whose attitude to him was "extraordinarily good." In his account for the archive, he mentioned all the different families who took him in. Sometimes peasants would ask him whether Jews would help and feed Poles if their situations were reversed. In November 1941, when the Germans began to mete out the death penalty for Jews caught on the Aryan side, the barber stopped his illicit journeys. He did observe that although the peasants were happy to feed him and take him in for a short time, there was no question that they would not be willing to hide him for a longer period.

The shtetl monographs, of course, produced much contrary evidence as well. The following accounts were derived mainly from the outbreak of the war until the end of 1939. In Kozienice a group of hungry, barefoot Polish POWs received permission from the Germans to take footwear from nearby Jews.[106] The anonymous Jewish chronicler had noted that, only a few minutes before, the bedraggled Poles and the terrorized Jews had looked at each other with mutual sympathy, as "brothers in sorrow." But the illusion quickly shattered as soon as the Germans gave the Poles permission to rob the Jews of their shoes. One Jewish account from Radomsk described how Poles happily watched Germans humiliate Jews in the public square.[107] The anonymous writer of this report repeated the biblical phrase, "Let my soul die with the Philistines." Poland was such a wicked country, he wrote, that he was happy to see it burn, even if Jewish property also went up in smoke.[108]

Almost all the shtetl monographs were buried in the first part of the archive, and there is relatively little shtetl material in the second part—from the period that marked the height of the extermination process—that described Polish-Jewish relations. But there is no question that Polish-Jewish relations worsened. The Polish writer Zofia Kossak-Szczucka, who despite her past anti-Semitic views would call on her fellow Poles to help save Jews during the war, wrote a revealing report about her travels through the Polish countryside in the fall of 1942.

> At first the behavior of the peasantry in the face of German atrocities against the Jews was humane, logical, and reasonable. It was expressed in a Christian readiness to help hungry Jews who were leaving the ghettos. That was still in 1941 . . . However, in the second half of 1942 (that is, at the time that the Hitlerites proceeded to mass murder) these attitudes have changed radically. Today German bestiality has dulled the moral sensibilities of the country, has undermined moral instincts of judgment. Thunder does not strike from the sky to slay the killers of children, blood does not cry for vengeance. Perhaps [the peasants think] it is true that the Jew is damned, someone one can kill without fear of punishment. Therefore there are more and more cases of active collaboration [among the peasants] in the German murder of the Jews. This is a very dangerous precedent.[109]

One document from the second part of the archive describes the deportation from Łuków on November 8, 1942.[110] Once the mass murder started, there were Poles who preyed on desperate Jews—with little apparent resistance from their own community. The informant from Łuków, Finkelstein, recounted how he jumped from a train that was taking him to Treblinka. The Jews broke the door and began to jump. Many received terrible injuries as they hit the ground. For those who survived the jump, however, their ordeal was just beginning.

> Finkelstein jumped from the train—near the village of Krinka. For a short time he lost consciousness and, when he regained it, with the desperation of a chained animal he began to run along the tracks. He ran into a gang of local peasants, aged 20 to 40, armed with sticks and iron rods, who were catching the Jews who had escaped and were beating them to death, after which they robbed the body of everything, including clothes. Still some 250 beaten and injured Jews survived and milled about. [Finkelstein] lost his boots and jacket.[111]

No sooner had the peasants finished beating and robbing the Jews than they called the railway police in Łuków to tell them that many Jewish escapees were huddling in a nearby wood. The police came immediately, searched the wood, and shot them. Another group, including Finkelstein, was led to the Jewish cemetery, made to lie down, and then shot.

> Our informant, being in the second group, undressed, lay down, and waited for his death. Apathetic and indifferent to it all, he only wished for it to end as fast as possible. He had no idea why, but the shot only covered his head with soot. He remained on the ground. Eight groups followed him. After the execution the Schupo [German police] checked to see that all were dead. They shot him again in the shoulder and throat. As soon as the executioners went off, a crowd of Poles ran over to rob the clothing and shoes. Finkelstein got up, put on somebody's pants and shoes, and dragged himself to a Christian acquaintance. Two weeks later [he arrived in the Warsaw Ghetto].

In short, had the war ended in mid-1941 or even in early 1942 the picture of Polish-Jewish relations conveyed by the Oyneg Shabes Archive, and especially the shtetl monographs, would have been of complex ambiguity but certainly not of unbridgeable national hatred or bitter resentment.[112] From the second half of 1942, however, the archive registered a definite deterioration in how Jews perceived their Polish neighbors. The December 23–31, 1942, edition of the Oyneg Shabes bulletin *Wiadomości* reported that the local peasant population was systematically robbing and attacking escapees from Treblinka—a marked contrast from the positive tone of many earlier reports.[113]

THE STRUGGLE TO SURVIVE:
THE ECONOMICS OF THE GHETTO

All Jews knew that in order to survive they had to defy German laws and edicts. The official rations could not sustain life. Jewish businesses were requisitioned, and Jews could only keep two thousand zlotys in cash. Their bank accounts were frozen. The ghetto not only cut them off from their Polish customers and suppliers, but it also established a formidable customs barrier that turned the ghetto into the equivalent of a foreign country in the middle of Warsaw. All "imports" and "exports" had to go through a German agency called the Transferstelle. This included food, heating materials, and raw materials for production. The Transferstelle set prices and levied hefty taxes for its "services." Just as each Jewish family had to find the financial resources to pay for basic food supplies, so, too, did the ghetto economy as a whole have to cover its massive "imports" of food with "exports" of various goods—or cash payments. Yet the rates set by the Transferstelle made it practically impossible for the ghetto to cover its expenses through "legal" means.

Obviously the ghetto quickly developed a massive underground economy. The illegal trade with the Aryan side dwarfed the legal trade that was coming through the Transferstelle. In his diary entry for December 6, 1941, Czerniakow told a German official,

> We received legally 1.8 million zlotys worth of food monthly and illegally 70 to 80 million zlotys worth. The first figure refers to the provisions through the Transferstelle and some Aryan suppliers, who make up only a small fraction of the imports. In the ghetto, one might reckon, there are 10,000 capitalists, plus or minus 250,000 who earn their living by work, and 150,000 who have to rely on public assistance.[114]

Clearly if the ghetto was importing 70 to 80 million zlotys a month worth of food, it had to find some means to pay for it.

In his diary entry of August 1941 Ringelblum raised pointed questions about the Jews' ability to survive economically. Why, he asked, in the face of such massive mortality from hunger and disease, did so few Jews attack food stores and steal? Jews died quietly. What explained this passivity? One answer, he believed, was that many of those dying were refugees from the provinces, without resources or contacts. Death from hunger was so slow and so insidious that its victims lost their energy and initiative long before they died. However, Ringelblum pointed out, there was another side to the story. A large percentage of the poor Jews in the ghetto, especially the natives of Warsaw, had somehow found a way to survive by exploiting new economic opportunities: smuggling, working in German shops, or working in the underground economy.

In its ambitious plans to study the economic position of Polish Jewry in wartime, the Oyneg Shabes paid special attention to the underground economy. In the guidelines for the "Two and a Half Years" project, the archive had stated:

> At a time when the [German] economic policy aims to [isolate the Jews], Jewish determination not only protects previous economic positions but also creates new employment opportunities. While the Germans want to immure the Jews behind the ghetto walls, the drive to survive impels Jews . . . to reach out across to the Aryan side and to develop entirely new economic branches aimed at the Polish consumer.
>
> Despite terrible difficulties and obstacles Jewish stubbornness and ingenuity are able to find raw materials or to come up with necessary substitutes.[115]

Ringelblum regretted that the archive only partially succeeded in studying the economics in the ghetto. To do this sprawling subject justice, researchers had to have resources and the scholarly detachment that did not mesh easily with hectic wartime conditions. The murder of Menakhem Linder, to whom Ringelblum had entrusted the economic section of the "Two and a Half Years" project, was an especially serious blow.[116] Nevertheless the Oyneg Shabes commissioned several studies of the "ghetto economy," including essays on trade in various items, specialties such as brushmaking, carpentry, upholstering and clothing manufacture, the rise and fall of prices for foodstuffs, the black market trade in foreign currency, and various aspects of the lifeblood of the ghetto: smuggling.[117]

Jerzy Winkler's "The Ghetto Fights Back against Economic Enslavement" stands out for its careful attention to detail and to the vagaries of German attitudes and policies toward exploiting Jewish economic potential.[118] When the Germans arrived in Poland they immediately banned Jewish participation in the textile trade and restricted Jews to collecting scrap, junk, and old materials. But the German authorities in the General Gouvernement quickly discovered that the Polish Jews, far from being unproductive parasites and hucksters, contained a high proportion of artisans and skilled workers. If they wanted to derive maximum benefit from the Polish economy, they would not only have to use Jewish labor but also, indirectly, to recognize that, despite the wartime restrictions, Jewish entrepreneurial skill and ingenuity mattered. Winkler showed how in various fields of production—textiles, brushmaking, carpentry, shoemaking—German and Polish contractors found themselves dealing with Jewish middlemen, who in turn linked them to the Jewish workers they needed. Jewish craftsmen and artisans in the ghetto worked for miserable wages. On the other hand, economic necessity and the self-interest of the Germans brought these Jewish workers back into the wider economy. The salient role of Jewish entrepreneurship and craftsmanship became especially important in the first half of 1941, when the German army placed enormous orders for basic field furniture, brushes, mirrors, and so on. Networks of Polish businessmen and Jewish middlemen sent raw materials into the ghetto and received back finished goods in a web of transactions that usually bypassed the legal framework of the Transferstelle. Willy-nilly, a "gray economy" emerged in the ghetto that allowed thousands of Jews to feed themselves and their families. After the German army invaded the Soviet Union in June 1941 and most German troops left Polish territory, the important military market contracted. But it was replaced, Winkler pointed out, by a growing market of Polish consumers who bought various goods made in the ghetto.

Winkler stressed that the economic relationships between Jews and Poles were unequal, and that Jews were the exploited party. Nevertheless, under the circumstances, it was a relationship that ultimately benefited both sides: "The Jews' ingenuity overcame obstacles and walls. The Jew worked at a loss, but he managed to hang on to life. The mere fact of his existence proved that the Jewish role in the . . . economy of partitioned Poland has not been completely eliminated."

The archive not only sought to record the economic struggle waged by the Jews but also to describe its socio-cultural context. In the conditions of high risk and high reward that prevailed in the ghetto, key occupations fell into the hands of closed guilds marked by a distrust of outsiders and a determination to guard their hard-won profits. Tytelman's description of the brush makers, Gutkowski's essay on the currency speculators, and Peretz Opoczynski's reportage of smuggling provided rich and detailed descriptions of sub-communities with their own slang, customs, and ethos. The smugglers aroused emotions that ranged from admiration to disgust. Various observers condemned the lavish lifestyle of the smugglers and noted the high proportion of former underworld characters that controlled this dangerous but highly lucrative occupation. Others, including Ringelblum, felt that, despite everything, the ghetto owed the smugglers a deep debt of gratitude. Were it not for them, the ghetto would starve.

The archive also studied the German shops. The establishment of these shops reflected a slowly dawning realization on the part of the German authorities that they could benefit from Jewish labor. In its turn the Judenrat set up a Production Division to stimulate economic activity and to attract German employers. By the eve of the Great Deportation, four thousand Jews were employed in these shops. However, wages were too low to support a family. Thus, before July 1942, the shops were not attractive options.[119]

The Oyneg Shabes, anxious to document the "everyday" of the Warsaw ghetto, gathered information on wages, family budgets, and prices. In describing how "ordinary" families coped, the Oyneg Shabes showed how precarious their position really was. In his important essay, "This Is the Ghetto," written in December 1941, Oyneg Shabes member Stanisław Różycki illustrated the budget of a typical family fighting to stay afloat. In this hypothetical family of four, the father, an employee of the Judenrat, earned 235 zlotys a month and another 245 zlotys through various extra jobs. His son, an office assistant, earned 120 zlotys, thus bringing the family income to 600 zlotys—quite good for the ghetto. The mother stayed at home and cared for a ten-year-old daughter who had a "ravenous appetite." Of this 600-zloty monthly income, half went to buy a daily portion of one and a half kilos of the cheapest black bread. Another 105 zlotys went to buy a daily kilo of potatoes. Thus, even allowing for four cheap meals at the soup kitchen every day, the family was spending two-thirds of its budget just on bread and potatoes. Forty-five zlotys a month went for saccharine and ersatz coffee, 70 zlotys for rent, 54 zlotys for a kilo of lard once a month, and 20–30 zlotys for electricity and gas. Thus a bare bones budget, without any provision for heating, laundry, soap, medical care, or cigarettes, would come to 600 zlotys. More fortunate than most, this was a family that did not starve. But any unforeseen expenses would force the family to sell furniture—its only reserves.

> Next month there won't be any furniture left. But this is a normal budget of a fortunate, middle-class citizen of the ghetto. There is some income, it is steady, and that in itself arouses the envy of many ghetto inhabitants. Yet the diet is skimpy, based mainly on bread and potatoes, and soon there will not be the money to pay the rent. And when sickness comes, which is inevitable in the conditions of the ghetto, even this budget will collapse.
>
> I have no idea how people live who do not have steady incomes. I think they don't really have a budget. They sell something, buy bread and potatoes, pay rent. When the money runs out, they sell more of their possessions. When there is nothing left to sell, that's the end. And that fate awaits most of us, because all savings will run out sooner or later. It is only a question of time and frugality. But the end is the same, and when it comes is simply a question of who will die sooner and who later . . . Each of us is waiting in the queue.[120]

Yet, ironically, in the months before the Great Deportation, there were signs that the ghetto economy had stabilized and that the Jews' dogged battle to stay alive was finally beginning to show some results. The monthly death toll had begun to drop, and slowly new sources of employment were opening up. From the beginning of the war until July 1942 close to one hundred thousand Jews had died of starvation and disease. But about 70 percent of the original ghetto population was still alive. As Israel Gutman points out [on the eve of the Great Deportation]:

> The population of the ghetto had actually managed to overcome the worst. The incidence of fatal disease began to decrease; the weaker elements of the population had already succumbed to death; more sources of employment and subsistence had been created; and the expectation grew that, in spite of everything, the majority would succeed in surviving the war.[121]

Unfortunately the Germans now had other plans for Warsaw Jewry.

Picture of resistance leaflet. *Ringelblum Archive, courtesy Jewish Historical Institute in Warsaw.*

Rachel Auerbach.
*Photograph courtesy
Jewish Historical
Institute in Warsaw.*

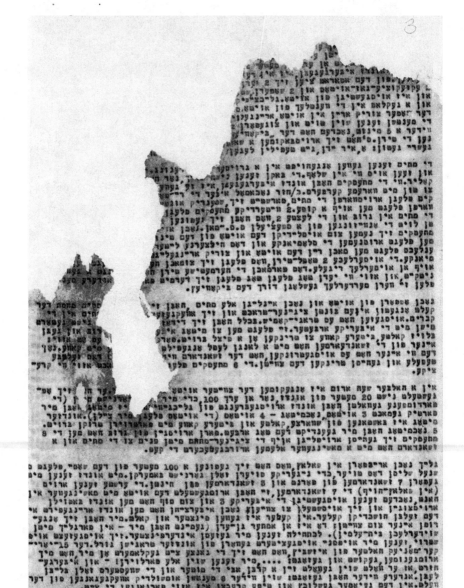

Manuscript of Szlamek's testimony about Chełmno. *Ringelblum Archive, courtesy Jewish Historical Institute in Warsaw.*

פון רעליגיעזן לעבן

1. ‏ ‏דאַוונען – שולן, חדר־מדרשים, סטיבלעך, בית־מדרות, באנו צו דער ארבעט פון די מגילים, נדרים.

2. בית־הוורה – צרייסענע און געשענדעטע.

3. רבים – קראַנען חדירות, ביטן, עמיסלען, שלו מעוורות, סלוח־סלבחה.

4. רבנים – רין־תורות, חשמות, גטין, שמרדכירות (שמא), חברי־ שלירות (חמץ), מאלוה.

5. ‏ ‏געשלט. לאַנג פון ראַביינדם: חהוזה־א־סן, מעברן־קעי, אירנעל דונגען.

6. גערר – געשוירן, וואָנגערגעזוננדענע, מבוען פאר בערד.

7. תלמושה – דאָס אויברבשן, די ברודעריאצעעעלע לאנגע סלבושים און ירושת דרך־עלעך א דין־מראשעיס־קלירונג, ז־דעע וועס־יעס, חגר־ל און ארויין־שמרלעך.

8. יומה – וו־ שוו ן זואנ אגעל געמערן חהוונות, בריחן, בו־בצחנות.

9. הרום – חבית שי, קליים־סזעגן.

10. מקוואות – בקרות מה מ־פאות, מערן א־ן געענבע הבשחה, רי מקואות.

11. שמיבה – מהם סה מ־ן, א־ן קמובן, בו־רעמען קעלעא.

12. תהרנגים – א־ן יצר ח.

13. מצות – א־ן י־ן.

14. יה־חתים בהרם־ ־ים, קבורה א־ן שמח און א־ן ־ן און ברי־ין צוזאמען, לען.

15. ימים־סוב־ם־ דוכות, חנוקה, פורים שמ, מון די י־ון ח־ים־א און א חס־א.

16. ש־ל מעזן חדרים, וואָס לערנען א־ן סמיבלעך, ־ן סגג.

17. שמירה־שבת חלול־שבת רעלי־שבל יעס ארן, ־רי־ ־יבה, סעגטלעקער חלול שבת־ ־ול לעי־ע־ו אן ־י־ווע־ אויר קארוזר־קלעבונג.

18. דאָס לעבן פון די ־קראַ־ער ־ים אין מאַרשע ־י געשטע־נ־בי־ע ־ור ר עפרה תרגנ־ם.

19. רי־סוזלעען מ־לעער י־כן.

20. רעלי־זע פעסטערן גר־ ־ו־א, קהלא, לענער ב, ־ צעגם־ס. קירוח־חשם.

Guidelines for study of Jewish woman. *Ringelblum Archive, courtesy Jewish Historical Institute in Warsaw.*

RE UDZIELICIELA CI... Kl, Warsza...
Wydział Opieki nad Dzieckiem
...
...ałna 92
...ba 9

Warszawa, dnia 15 lipca 1942 r.

Nie jesteśmy skłonni obiecywać, nie mając pewności.

Pewni jesteśmy, że godzina pięknej bajki myśliciela i poe-
ty da wzruszenie - "najwyższego szczebla" drabiny uczuć.

Przeto prosimy na sobotę dn. 18 lipca 1942 r. godz. 4,30 pp.

Dyrektor Domu Sierot

/ Z nienapisanej recenzji "Żywego Dziennika"/

.... Pierwszy prawdziwie artystyczny spektakl od 1939r.

Coś więcej niż tekst   - bo nastrój;
Coś więcej niż emocja - bo przeżycie;
Coś więcej niż aktorzy - bo dzieci;

/ - / Władysław Szlengel

Wejście bezpłatne.

Invitation to children's play at the Korczak orphanage, July 15, 1942. *Ringelblum Archive, courtesy Jewish Historical Institute in Warsaw.*

Sketches of street scenes by Rozenfeld. *Ringelblum Archive, courtesy Jewish Historical Institute in Warsaw.*

David Graber's last testament. *Ringelblum Archive, courtesy Jewish Historical Institute in Warsaw.*

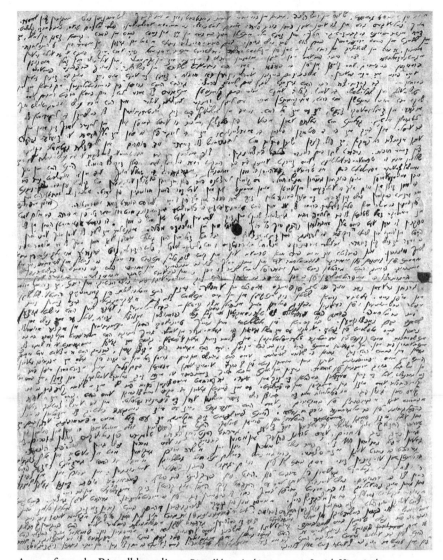

A page from the Ringelblum diary. *Ringelblum Archive, courtesy Jewish Historical Institute in Warsaw.*

Letter from Szlamek to Hersh Wasser. *Ringelblum Archive, courtesy Jewish Historical Institute in Warsaw.*

Instructions for cooking frozen potatoes. *Ringelblum Archive, courtesy Jewish Historical Institute in Warsaw.*

Candy wrappers. *Ringelblum Archive, courtesy Jewish Historical Institute in Warsaw.*

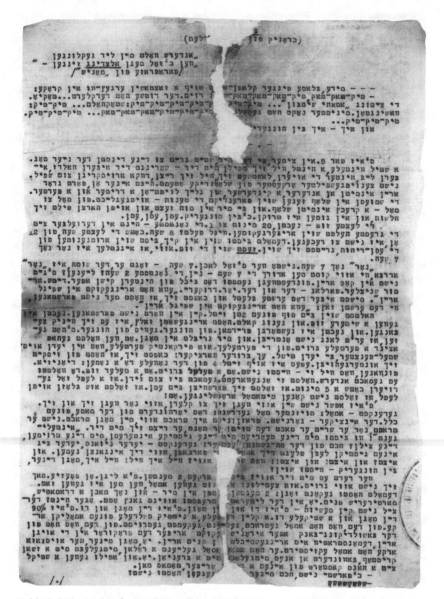

Goldin's "Chronicle of a Single Day." *Ringelblum Archive, courtesy Jewish Historical Institute in Warsaw.*

Gela Sekstein's testament. *Ringelblum Archive, courtesy Jewish Historical Institute in Warsaw.*

Front and back of postcard
thrown out of boxcar by
deportee from Plonsk.
*Courtesy Jewish Historical
Institute in Warsaw.*

Photo of Gela Sekstein.
*Ringelblum Archive, courtesy
Jewish Historical Institute in
Warsaw.*

Gela Sekstein's
drawing of a young girl.
*Ringelblum Archive, courtesy Jewish
Historical Institute in Warsaw.*

Photo of Shmuel Winter.
Courtesy Jewish Historical
Institute in Warsaw.

The Tidings of Job

The "Two and a Half Years" project was just getting into high gear when disquieting news arrived in the Warsaw Ghetto about German massacres in the Soviet-occupied eastern territories. As early as the summer of 1941 the underground press in the ghetto began to report eyewitness accounts of shootings in Slonim and the burning of a synagogue, crammed full of Jews, in Białystok. But the clandestine newspapers categorized these killings as "pogroms," the latest in a long chain of anti-Jewish violence in Eastern Europe. Some of these articles even questioned whether it was the Germans or local anti-Semites that bore major responsibility for the violence.[1]

More ominous reports soon arrived from Vilna of mass shootings in Ponar, a small wooded area near the city. Shortly after the German invasion of the Soviet Union, both Dror and Hashomer Hatzair had been able to establish contact with Vilna, thanks to trusted couriers from the Polish scout movement.[2] In October Aryeh Wilner, a member of Hashomer, arrived in the Warsaw Ghetto from Vilna and corroborated the Poles' grim reports. Within a short time, other envoys from the Vilna youth groups also arrived in Warsaw.

In October 1941 *Neged Hazerem,* the underground newspaper of the Hashomer Hatzair, carried Grabowski's account of the mass killings in Vilna:

> In the last three months the Jewish population of Vilna has dropped
> from seventy thoussnd—the number during the Soviet occupation—to
> thirty-five thousand. Only a few Jews succeed in escaping from the city.
> The small ghetto has been almost completely destroyed by mass killing.

The Jewish population is terrified and depressed. All are convinced that death is near, and all they can do is wait for their turn.[3]

Shmuel Breslav, the editor of the paper, did not seem entirely sure what to make of the news. In a rare departure from his common practice, he prefaced the article with a brief note explaining that a comrade had arrived from Vilna on October 16 and that *Neged Hazerem* was relaying his account of what had happened. Clearly Breslav was still not ready to believe what he was hearing.

Shortly after Aryeh Wilner returned to Warsaw, the Oyneg Shabes assigned Daniel Fligelman to debrief him and record his detailed testimony for the archive. Wilner, a trusted member of the inner circle of Hashomer Hatzair, described how the Germans seized thousands of Jews on the streets and in their homes and transported them to an unknown destination. At the beginning of September a Jewish woman, who had escaped from the killing grounds of Ponar, gave the ghetto its first eyewitness account: in large pits that the Soviets had dug to store oil, the Germans and Lithuanians were shooting thousands of Jews every day. It was this witness who convinced Vilna Jewry that something terrible was happening.[4] The Jewish population of Vilna, Wilner told Fligelman, had already dropped from seventy thousand to twenty-five thousand: "The tidings of Job are coming from provincial Lithuania. In town after town—Landwarów, Troki, Święciany, Niemenczyn, Nowo-Wilejka, Ejszyszki—the entire Jewish population has been wiped out. Even infants have been killed."[5]

As other refugees from Vilna arrived in Warsaw, they, too, were interviewed by the Oyneg Shabes staff—Huberband, Gutkowski, Fligelman, Salomea Ostrowska, and others. Rabbi Huberband, who took down a young woman's reports of shootings in Ponar, prefaced his transcript with a brief statement: "It was not regrettably an empty dream nor a mad fantasy or an evil tale but naked bitter reality."[6]

Horrible as these testimonies were, what did they actually mean? Was this a sign that the Germans had decided to wipe out all European Jewry? The first Jews who indeed grasped that they were seeing the beginning of the Final Solution were the leaders of the youth movement in the Vilna Ghetto, including the Hashomer leader Abba Kovner. On January 1, 1942, they issued an appeal to the Jews to resist. The Germans, they warned, were going to kill all the Jews of Europe.[7] But even in the Vilna Ghetto, and even in Kovner's own youth movement, not everyone was ready to believe that the Germans planned total genocide. Perhaps, some argued, the massacres in Lithuania were a local phenomenon, caused by Lithuanian anger at Jews for their alleged cooperation with the Soviets. Even Kovner himself found it hard to explain why the Germans were killing Jews in Vilna and leaving them alone in Białystok and other cities.[8] And even if the killings were a prelude to a wider operation, did they forecast the elimination of European Jewry or only of "unproductive elements"? Adding to the confusion, many of the reports stressed the ferocity of the Lithuanians or Poles rather than the Germans.

In Warsaw political leaders, activists in the youth movements, and the leaders of the Oyneg Shabes were slow to comprehend the portent of the massacres in the East. One exception, Yitzhak Zuckerman, a native of Vilna, understood immediately and almost suffered a psychological breakdown; his own family, who had remained in Vilna, was in mortal danger.[9] But Zuckerman was an exception. Many leaders in the Warsaw Ghetto still could not believe that the Nazis were planning total extermination.

On November 17, 1941, a month after the Oyneg Shabes heard the first news from Vilna, the Germans executed eight Warsaw Jews who had been caught buying food on the Aryan side. In his diary a shaken Ringelblum noted that this execution was worse than the shootings in Vilna and Slonim. "We have gone through quite a lot," he wrote, "in Warsaw and especially in Lithuania, where mass executions are taking place. But this pales before the fact that [the Germans] killed eight people only because they left the ghetto."[10] Why would Ringelblum regard the shooting of eight Jews as being worse than the mass executions in Lithuania? Probably because he, like many others, tried to delude himself into thinking that the massacres in Lithuania were a feature of the "wild East" and the violent atmosphere of the Soviet-German war. Ringelblum still did not think that the massacres were part of a cold-blooded plan. The killing of eight Jews in Warsaw, however, took place in a "judicial framework."

When a group that represented different Vilna youth movements arrived in Warsaw in December 1941, "not a single person believed their stories about the outright extermination of Jews, and no one wants a war or a revolt against the Germans."[11]

It was the arrival of "Szlamek," a religious Jew from Izbica, in late January 1942 that finally dispelled whatever doubts the Oyneg Shabes or Ringelblum might have had about German plans.[12] Szlamek was an escapee from Chełmno, the killing installation in the Warthegau that had begun murdering Jews in gas vans in December 1941. Szlamek had worked in the Chełmno Sonderkommando and gave the Oyneg Shabes the first eyewitness testimony from a German death camp.[13] No one could explain this away as the work of a roving execution squad or a localized pogrom. Szlamek told Hersh and Bluma Wasser that high-ranking SS officers observed the killings and congratulated the German staff on their work.[14] Chełmno seemed well organized and terrifyingly permanent.

Szlamek told Wasser that on January 7, 1942, he received a summons from the Judenrat to report for forced labor the next day. On January 8 German gendarmes loaded a group of about twenty Jews from the town into a truck and took them to an old castle in nearby Chełmno, where they were locked in a dark cellar with other prisoners. The next day, heavily guarded (about thirty guards watched twenty-nine prisoners), they were taken to a forest clearing. To make escape difficult the prisoners had to remove most of their outer clothing, despite the cold. The prisoners were issued pickaxes and shovels and told to dig large pits. Then a large van pulled up near the pit. This was one of two gas vans at Chełmno. When the vans approached the forest clearing where the prisoners were digging, the drivers stopped their vehicles and released the exhaust gas into the rear cargo compartment of the van. Szlamek heard terrible screams, as the people inside the van began pounding the walls. After a few minutes, when the victims had suffocated, the Germans opened the doors of the van. A coarse SS man snarled, "Jews, put on your phylacteries [Ihr Juden, geht tfilln legen-*sic*]" and ordered them to unload the dead, excrement-covered bodies. The prisoners had to clean the filthy gas vans with their own clothes. The Germans carefully inspected the body orifices of the corpses for hidden valuables.

The first few days, Szlamek remembered, the victims were gypsies; then transports of Jews began arriving from nearby towns and from the Lodz Ghetto. In a procedure that would be repeated every day that Szlamek was in Chełmno, each morning the Germans would select eight Jews for "bottom work." Those selected would have to jump into the pit and arrange the corpses that the others threw down from the top. The bodies of little children were crammed into empty spaces in the rows of corpses. Each evening, the Germans would shoot the eight Jews who had been selected for the "bottom work." One day, for a few minutes, Szlamek managed to snatch a conversation with the "bottom Jews" (*hamisamkim,* in Yiddish).

> Among them was Abram Zielinski from Izbica, thirty-two years old; Bravman from Izbica, aged seventeen, Zalman Jakubowski from Izbica, aged fifty-five, Gerszon Prashker from Izbica. About three o'clock, when there was a lull . . . Prashker pulled out a prayer book, covered his head with his hand . . . they called to us: we are about to die a terrible death, let this be a redeeming sacrifice for our loved ones and for the whole Jewish people.

Szlamek gave a detailed account of how Chełmno operated, and how the Germans fooled the victims until the very last moment. The victims would be taken from the train station or by truck to the old castle. There an older SS man smilingly helped women get off the trucks and even carried their little children. He told them that they would have to undergo disinfection prior to "resettlement" and should therefore undress down to their underwear. Inside the castle genial smiles suddenly gave way to kicks and blows as the Germans herded them down a corridor and into a waiting van.[15] The van drove to a nearby forest where it stopped. The drivers then pulled a lever that directed the gas fumes into the back compartment and killed all the victims. In the time that Szlamek was in Chełmno the pace of the killing quickly increased. Soon they were unloading up to nine vans a day. At first the Germans had jammed sixty people into each van, and then more than ninety. After dark, the Germans would set up lights and the "work" continued without letup.

The Wassers were skillful interviewers. They let Szlamek speak in his own voice, the voice of a highly intelligent, thoughtful young Orthodox Jew suddenly confronted with something inconceivable. His Yiddish was that of a religious Jew from a small town, with many Hebrew expressions, but he also spoke Polish confidently. After his escape from Chełmno he told the first peasant he met that he was a Pole and even used traditional peasant greetings. During his time in the camp, he appeared to have been a natural leader whom other prisoners respected. Judging from the many spelling mistakes that Szlamek made in written Polish (in a later postcard to Wasser), it was also clear that he had received little if any formal secular education.

Szlamek's account gained credibility through its wealth of personal detail. For protection from the freezing cold, the doomed "bottom Jews" wrapped themselves in bits and pieces of the gypsies' colorful clothing as they arranged their bodies into neat rows: Szlamek called the effect "tragicomic." The first night in the cold cellar, the German guard suddenly ordered the prisoners to sing. Szlamek told all the prisoners to cover their heads, and then he led them in the "Shma Yisroel." Not satisfied with just one "song," the German ordered them to sing again. Szlamek led the prisoners in the singing of "Hatikva," a song that became the national anthem of the state of Israel.

The first Sunday, the Germans unexpectedly announced a day off.

> After the morning prayers and *kaddish,* the prayer for the dead, we were left pretty much to ourselves in our underground paradise. Once again we began to talk about politics, God, and our own situation. Everyone wanted to survive to see the liberation but, more than that, our greatest desire was for the survival of the Jewish people [*klal Yisroel*]. Each one of

us would have given up his life with the greatest of pleasure if only that would guarantee the future of our people.

Szlamek told Wasser that the prisoners sometimes argued about the existence of God. One day two prisoners angrily asked how God could stand by and allow these horrors to take place. Szlamek responded that it was not their place to question the ways of God. Perhaps the horrors they witnessed portended the coming of the Messiah. While some angrily denied their religion, Szlamek and many of the other prisoners doggedly came together to say the confessional prayer each morning before their daily ordeal—and the evening prayers after their return. In keeping with Jewish law, before they began their prayers they would cover the open slop bucket with a shirt.

The worst moments came when the prisoners recognized their own loved ones among the corpses. Szlamek saw the bodies of his parents. Mechl Podchlebnik, who also escaped, recognized his wife and two children; he describes the experience in Claude Lanzmann's film *Shoah*. Aizensztab from Kłodawa buried his wife and his fifteen-year-old daughter, his only child.

> Aizensztab silently sobbed . . . he said that he now had nothing to live for. He was going to ask the Germans to shoot him so he could rest with his loved ones. But we talked him out of it, saying that there was no reason to hurry and that, anyway, he might escape and get a chance to take revenge.

Some Jews committed suicide. One evening one of the prisoners, Krzewacki, made a noose out of some rope, put it around his neck, fastened the rope to the ceiling, climbed up on a bundle, and then kicked it away. The other prisoners noticed that he died quickly. Another Jew, Shwetoplawski, immediately decided to hang himself as well. Just as he began to dangle, a German guard came close by, and a young boy, Moniek Halter, quickly cut Shwetoplawski's rope. Shwetoplawski fell and writhed on the floor in great agony.

> On the one hand we did not want to rescue him (What was the point?). On the other hand we couldn't bear to watch him suffer. So we asked Brzonstawski to end his suffering. Brzonstawski put a rope around Shwetoplawski's neck and pulled with all his might.

The prisoners asked themselves why they didn't resist. Shouldn't they simply attack the Germans and at least meet a quick death? Were they indeed cowards? But others responded that what was important was that at least someone escape and survive, in order to "save the Jewish people." They were convinced that if news of Chełmno got out, Jews elsewhere would do something to foil the extermination. Meanwhile, the Germans brought in new groups of prisoners to replace the ones they shot each day.

One day one of the prisoners, Abram Roy, escaped through a cellar window. In reprisal the Germans shot sixteen prisoners. Nevertheless Szlamek was determined to escape, sure that his fellow prisoners would support him and help him—even at the risk that the Germans would probably kill them in retaliation. When he found out that one prisoner had money, he asked him to give him his money to help his escape. The prisoner willingly agreed. On January 19 Szlamek finally saw his chance. That day no car followed the vehicle that was taking the prisoners to the killing ground. Szlamek opened the car window and quickly climbed out. The other prisoners covered for him. They were probably all shot that same day.

Szlamek knocked on the door of a Polish peasant hut and received food and directions to the nearest settlement, Grabów. In Grabów Szlamek immediately asked to see the rabbi, Jacob Sylman. Dirty and unkempt, he knew the Grabów Jews thought him deranged. He told the stunned rabbi that he was a Jew from "the other world." As the rabbi and other Jews listened, he recounted all that he had seen in Chełmno. The rabbi then proclaimed a day of fasting and prayer. He also advised Szlamek to make his way to Warsaw, where contacts eventually put him in touch with Hersh Wasser and the Oyneg Shabes. On his way to Warsaw in late January 1942, Szlamek, using the name Jacob Grojanowski, spread the news in the various ghettos that he passed through.[16]

Rabbi Sylman dispatched letters of warning to other towns, including Warsaw and Lodz. In his letter to relatives in Warsaw (probably taken into the ghetto by Szlamek himself) Rabbi Sylman stressed that there was not a minute to lose. Warsaw Jewry, he reminded his relatives, was still a force to be reckoned with, the largest Jewish community in Europe. The Jews now had to "alarm the world and devise methods and stratagems to save those threatened by the terrible decree." Clearly, the rabbi believed, this news was so terrible that as soon as the world heard of it, it would force the Germans to stop.[17]

Szlamek probably arrived in Warsaw at the very end of January or the beginning of February 1942, after a trip that led him through Piotrków and other cities. Wasser and the Oyneg Shabes took him in hand and gave him shelter and money. Although no documents describe how Szlamek met Wasser, the latter, as director of the Aleynhilf's landsmanshaft department, would undoubtedly have been well known to Jews in the ghetto who hailed from Szlamek's hometown. Szlamek developed a great liking for Wasser as well as for Menachem Kon, the treasurer of the Oyneg Shabes. Kon recorded several disbursements to Szlamek (under the name Jacob Grojanowski). Preserved in the archive is a signed photograph of Szlamek, dated March 8, 1942, inscribed to Hersh Wasser and his wife.[18]

The Oyneg Shabes relayed Szlamek's account of Chełmno to other leaders in the ghetto. Gutkowski gave Zuckerman a detailed summary.[19] Given that the Oyneg Shabes executive committee was directly linked to the Bund, the Zionists, the Joint, and the youth movements, Szlamek's story soon became common knowledge among the political and cultural leadership of the ghetto.

The leaders of the Oyneg Shabes knew that the Germans would spare no effort to track down Szlamek as well as two other escapees from Chełmno and decided to send him out of the Warsaw Ghetto to Zamość, where he had a sister-in-law. He was to write to the Oyneg Shabes using the name and address of one of Ringelblum's former students in the Yehudiah gymnasium, Dvora Shtatman.[20] The Oyneg Shabes arranged for a certain individual in Zamość to help Szlamek financially in exchange for Oyneg Shabes disbursements to that person's relatives in the Warsaw Ghetto.

No sooner did Szlamek arrive in Zamość in 1942 than he sent a letter imploring Wasser to get him back to Warsaw. His putative helper did not keep his word. Unwilling to break the strict Passover dietary laws and unable to afford the proper food, Szlamek told Wasser that he had not eaten for the first two days of the holiday. In that same letter, written between April 5 and 12, Szlamek added chilling news. The Germans, he wrote, had built another death camp very close to Zamość, near the town of Bełżec. Using Hebrew-Yiddish words to try to fool the censors, Szlamek wrote Wasser that "the cemetery is in Bełżec, it's the same death as Chełmno [das Beys olem ist in Belzyc to jest same mise co w Helmnie]."[21] Unless Wasser helped him quickly, Szlamek implored, he would soon be meeting Chaim Rywen Izbicki. (Izbicki had been a member of the Chełmno Sonderkommando that Szlamek had mentioned in his account and he was now dead.) Szlamek casually added the names of three towns—Lublin, Rawa Ruska, and Biłgoraj. In the closing sentence, in a mixture of Polish and Yiddish (in Latin characters), Szlamek warned Wasser that the Jews in each town mentioned in the letter were put to death (in Bełżec) in the same way as the victims of Chełmno.[22]

Wasser wrote back, but it was too late: Szlamek was gassed in Bełżec along with the other Jews of Zamość. On April 24 Wasser received a postcard from Szlamek's fourteen-year-old nephew, Abram Beiler (Bajler?). Abram told Wasser that all the Jews had been sent away. He and his younger brother had remained because they were working. "Imagine," Abram told Wasser, "how hard it is for me, a fourteen-year-old boy to be left alone without any parents and to be forced to care for a younger brother. But we'll cope. It's difficult, we must accept our fate."[23]

In those early months of 1942 the Oyneg Shabes was filing an ever growing number of postcards and letters to Jews in the Warsaw Ghetto from Jews in the provinces who were about to be deported. Some of the writers guessed their fate and wrote to take leave of their relatives and to warn them of impending extermination. The stories of the three escapees from Chełmno obviously spread quickly, since several postcards and letters came from Jews in the Warthegau, who guessed the worst. The German postal rules forbade any letters or postcards in Hebrew characters, so many of the postcards were in mangled Polish or in a Germanized Yiddish. The writers often used a clumsy code to implore their relatives in the Warsaw Ghetto to do something. Through the landsmanshaftn, these letters found their way to the archive.

The Oyneg Shabes also received news of new German death camps in Sobibór and in Treblinka. One letter from Włodawa, written in Yiddish, was smuggled into the Warsaw Ghetto sometime in June 1942. It reported the gassing of the Jews of Włodawa in Sobibór in May 1942 and mentioned one particular victim, the famed Radzyner Rebbe, Shlomo Velvel Lajner. (As will be seen below, legends quickly began to circulate in the Warsaw Ghetto about the rebbe's heroism.) The letter warned that the "uncle" (the Nazis) was preparing "the same kind of wedding for the children that we had here." He was building a new house "very near to you" (Treblinka), and it was very much like the house that was close to Włodawa (Sobibór). The writer stressed that the "best remedy for this illness is *yoshev beseiser* [Hebrew for going into hiding]."[24] Shortly thereafter Eliyahu Gutkowski debriefed two women couriers (Frumka Plotnicka and Chava Folman) who corroborated the accounts of Sobibór.[25]

For the political parties and the youth movements in the ghetto, the news from Vilna, from Chełmno, from Lublin, and from other towns began a period of painful stocktaking. Disbelief and skepticism slowly yielded to the realization that Warsaw's turn would come. Until now the youth movements had focused their activities on culture, education, and self-help. But the news from the provinces convinced the leaders of Dror and Hashomer that seminars and classes now made little sense.[26] Major youth movements now began to reach out to the wider ghetto population, circulating publications that reported the mass killings. Dror, for example, started to publish a new underground newspaper, *Yedies* (The news), based on information provided by Gutkowski and the Oyneg Shabes.[27] In a hard-hitting June 1942 article, *Yedies* criticized the Jews of the Warsaw Ghetto for their determination to shrug off bad news and try to live a normal life, and chided communal and political leaders for continuing to worry about schools and soup kitchens. All that mattered now, the article warned, was to accept the truth and prepare for resistance. (The entire arsenal of the Dror and Hashomer combined consisted of a few pistols at that time.)

The growing realization that the Germans had changed their plans for the Jews injected a new sense of urgency into attempts to unite the political parties and the youth movements in order to prepare for resistance. The Zionist youth movements took the lead by inviting representatives of major political parties and youth groups to a joint meeting in March 1942. The meeting included representatives from Dror, Hashomer Hatzair, the Right and Left Poalei Tsiyon, and the Bund. According to Zuckerman, the agenda included the establishment of a Jewish fighting organization, the formation of a Jewish body that could negotiate with the Polish underground, and the preparation of a unit on the Aryan side that would procure and manufacture arms. Immediately after the meeting, Zuckerman gave Gutkowski a report on what had taken place, which Gutkowski deposited in the Oyneg Shabes.[28]

Since the Bund was the best-organized political party and had the best contacts with the Polish underground, its cooperation was essential to the establishment of any viable Jewish fighting organization and to any supply of arms. At the March meeting, however, citing its traditional doctrinal unwillingness to collaborate with other Jewish parties, the Bund refused to be part of a joint organization.

Although the Bund's attitude was a bitter disappointment, high hopes came from another direction—the Communists and their newly organized Polish Workers Party (PPR). For the leaders of both the Right and Left Poalei Tsiyon and of the youth movements, the Communists represented a vital bridge to the Soviet Union and its Red Army, a guarantee that the Jews in the ghetto were not alone. The charismatic PPR leader Andrzej Schmidt, who had fought in the Spanish Civil War, added to the mystique; in turn, it was mainly in the Warsaw Ghetto that the PPR, organized in January 1942, could find even a modicum of support. The leaders of the PPR opened talks with the LPZ and the two groups in turn made overtures to the Hashomer, Dror, and the Right Poalei Tsiyon. Together these organizations set up an Anti-Fascist Bloc.[29] The non-Communists at this time had an exaggerated idea of the actual strength of the PPR and its access to weapons and Soviet support. The Bloc began to issue a Yiddish newspaper, *Der Ruf,* and organized groups of "fives" for military training. Whereas the youth movements wanted to prepare for a battle in the ghetto, the Communists wanted to train for partisan war in the forests. Militarily the Anti-Fascist Bloc accomplished nothing. Its pro-Soviet orientation and the Bund boycott precluded any hope of support from the Polish underground—which, in any case, had little interest in Jewish fighters. The PPR had virtually no weapons and no support among the Polish population. Making matters worse, the Germans penetrated the PPR and arrested Andrzej Schmidt in May. This crippled the Bloc's ability to recruit and train fighters. Contrary to communist postwar propaganda, therefore, the Bloc was not the organizational precursor to the Jewish Fighting Organization that was founded by the Zionist youth groups in August 1942. On the other hand, Ringelblum considered the Bloc to have been a direct catalyst for the Jewish Fighting Organization. Just one week before he died, he reiterated the importance of gathering information about the role the LPZ had played in the organization of the Bloc.[30] This claim enabled his own party and its beloved leader, Shakhne Zagan, to garner some credit for the turn to armed resistance.

For the Oyneg Shabes, the founding of the Bloc cemented and strengthened the ties between the major Zionist youth movements and both branches of the Poalei Tsiyon, and thus imbued the organizational core of the archive with a new sense of solidarity and purpose. Of course, long-standing rivalries did not disappear overnight, but they paled in the face of the common danger. Over time the Oyneg Shabes began to see itself as the documentary arm of a wider Jewish resistance movement.[31]

The Oyneg Shabes now adopted new priorities and responsibilities: to document the extermination program, to provide material for the Jewish and Polish underground press, and to get that information out of Poland.[32] The careful studies of "Two and a Half Years" now became less urgent than the need to document mass murder.[33] The Oyneg Shabes began to issue a new Yiddish-language bulletin, *Miteylungen,* that reported the news of the killings. Its first issue appeared in April 1942 with the headline: "The Jewish Population in the Face of Physical Extermination, a report from Lublin, where thousands of Jews had been deported to an unknown destination."[34] There were rumors, the article added, that the Germans were sending the Lublin Jews to Bełżec to be gassed. *Miteylungen* also described deportations from Izbica, Lwów, Okuniew, Wawer, Wawolnica, and Mielec. The tone of *Mitteylungen* was spare and factual, without superfluous commentaries.

As Hersh Wasser noted after the war, the Oyneg Shabes at this time also set up a press bureau to feed material to both the Jewish and Polish underground press.[35] The first section of the archive contained several weekly bulletins as well as a longer report by Gutkowski that summed up what was known about the German extermination program.[36] Right after Wasser's interview with Szlamek, Wasser, Ringelblum, and Gutkowski began to prepare digests of materials to be sent abroad, to the Polish Government-in-Exile in

As Ruta Sakowska has argued, the Oyneg Shabes had two potential chan-
nels for getting this information out of Poland. Both ran through the Polish
underground. One channel involved Aleksander Kamiński, who headed the
Bureau of Information and Propaganda of the Polish Home Army (Armia
Krajowa [AK]), and was also the editor of the AK's major underground newspaper, the *Biuletyn Informacyjny*. As we have seen, Kamiński was a friend of
Irena Adamowicz, who had close ties to Hashomer and to Dror. The Oyneg
Shabes provided much of the material that the Bureau of Information and
Propaganda was publishing about the killing of the Jews.[40] The internal in-
formation bulletins issued by the AK often spelled the names of localities as
they were written in Oyneg Shabes reports. In several cases the Polish reports
were almost a verbatim copy of the Oyneg Shabes bulletins.[41]

A second channel involved the Bund. Ringelblum certainly viewed the
Bund with suspicion and disappointment, but political rivalries paled beside the obvious need to alert the outside world.[42] Many personal ties linked
the Oyneg Shabes and the Bund. Thanks to its long-standing relationship
with the Polish Socialist Party, the Bund was the only Jewish organization
in the Warsaw Ghetto with good links to the higher levels of the Polish underground. The Polish underground, in turn, was using sympathetic Swedish
businessmen living in Warsaw to get reports out of Poland in late 1941 and
early 1942.[43] These businessmen—Carl Wilhelm Herslow, Sven Normann,
and Carl Gustafsson—had lived in Warsaw for many years. Trusted by the
Polish underground, they traveled regularly between Sweden and Poland,
conveying information on rolls of 35-mm film. According to Laqueur, this is
how the Chełmno report and the Bund letter on German atrocities reached
London. Normann's last visit to Poland took place in May 1942. The Gestapo
arrested the two other Swedes in July, just as the Great Deportation was beginning.

By late May 1942, therefore, the first two Oyneg Shabes reports had arrived in Britain, as had a detailed report compiled by the Bund. On June 2,
1942, the BBC broadcast the news that the Germans had murdered seven
hundred thousand Polish Jews (by that time the actual figure was much higher). Other broadcasts followed, to Ringelblum's satisfaction: In his diary entry of June 26, 1942, he wrote:

> Friday 26 June was a great day for the Oyneg Shabes. Today at dawn we
> heard a British radio broadcast about the Polish Jews. It mentioned ev-
> erything that we know so much about: Slonim and Vilna, Lemberg and
> Chełmno. For months we have been suffering because we thought that

the world was indifferent to our tragedy, which is unprecedented in human history. We were angry at the Polish community [*efentlekhkayt*] and at those in contact with the Polish government because there were no transmissions about the murders of the Polish Jews, and the world remained in ignorance of what was happening. We blamed the Polish leaders for deliberately suppressing the news of our tragedy because we suspected that they did not want that news to overshadow what was happening to them. But now it is clear that all these efforts have achieved something. [In June there have been several broadcasts about Belzec, Chełmno, Vilna, etc.] The BBC mentioned the figure of seven hundred thousand murdered Jews. It also warned that these crimes would exact revenge and justice.[44]

Ringelblum allowed himself some optimism that the BBC broadcast had vindicated the work of the Oyneg Shabes and might even have saved the remnants of Polish Jewry:

The Oyneg Shabes has [through sending this information] performed a great historical mission. It has alerted the world to our fate and perhaps rescued hundreds of thousands of Polish Jews from extermination. The near future will show whether these hopes [of rescue] will come true.

I don't know who from our group will remain alive—who will be fated to live to work on the gathered materials. But one thing is clear to all of us; our effort and our toil and our dedication have not been in vain. We have dealt a blow to the enemy. Even if [the news has no effect] we know one thing: we have done our duty. We overcame all the obstacles and barriers and achieved what we set out to do. Even our death won't be as meaningless as the deaths of tens of thousands of other Jews; at least [we will die] knowing that we hurt the enemy. We have unmasked his devilish plan to destroy Polish Jewry, something he wanted to do in secret. We have upset his plans and have revealed his cards. And if England keeps its word and goes through with its threats . . . then maybe we'll be saved after all.

IN THE FACE OF DEATH

As Ringelblum was writing these words, the ghetto was experiencing escalating German terror and mounting fears of an imminent deportation. Almost every night Gestapo agents would enter the ghetto and murder victims either at random or from a prepared list. "The forty days of the ghetto," referring to the Franz Werfel novel about the Turkish genocide of Armenians, became a common topic of conversation both in the ghetto and on the Aryan side.[45]

At the weekly Saturday meetings of the archive, each member told of the interviews he had conducted that week, with their tidings of new massacres and death camps. In his diary entry of June 6, Abraham Lewin summarized that afternoon's meeting. There was news from different provincial towns, none of it good. Dr. Aharon Soloveitchik, a well-known Warsaw physician who had just returned from Lida, told the group that the Germans had shot a young girl and her entire family because the girl had lost her armband. In Pabianice, before the Germans shot all people aged sixty and over, a German officer taught the elderly Jews to sing a German-Jewish song, "Moses." Only after they learned it to his satisfaction did he shoot them. In Zduńska Wola, just before the festival of Shavuot, the Germans hanged ten Jews, among them the rabbi of the town. The rabbi asked the doomed Jews to rejoice, since they had the privilege of dying for Kiddush Hashem, a death of martyrdom. A report from Krakow stated that most of the Jews had already been liquidated. The number of letters and telegrams coming into the Warsaw Ghetto from desperate relatives in the provinces who were begging Warsaw Jews to save them kept growing. But, Lewin asked, what could the Jews of Warsaw do when their own lives were hanging in the balance?

> We gather every Sabbath, a group of activists in the Jewish community, to discuss our diaries and writings. We want our sufferings, these "birth pangs of the Messiah," to be impressed on the memories of future generations and on the memory of the whole world. . . . These stories always fill me with deep gloom and my head begins to ache, as if a heavy lead weight was pressing down on me. This is how it was today, too. They talked and talked and I felt a chillness and despondency.[46]

Later that month Ringelblum described the fear and apprehension that gripped the ghetto, despite German assurances to Czerniakow that the ghetto was safe. Ringelblum himself had no faith in these German promises. But he clung to the belief that the ghetto—or at least a large part of its population—might win some reprieve by working for the German war economy. Although the Oyneg Shabes report sent to London had expressly stated that the Germans killed Jews even when it contradicted their economic self-interest, Ringelblum was not ready to renounce all hope.[47]

Meanwhile life in the ghetto somehow continued. Even as the members of the Oyneg Shabes were learning of Sobibór, of Bełżec and Treblinka, the archive still chronicled life as well as death: how Jews in the ghetto went on with their lives, worked in their house committees, and did their best to care for helpless children. As winter gave way to spring and summer, teachers and caregivers tried to forget the news and ubiquitous rumors by continuing to put on children's plays and recitals. Filed away in the first part of the archive was an invitation to a children's program at the Femina Theater on May 5, 1942. The pupils of the school on Nowolipki 22 recited a Hebrew poem, "Spring Has Come." The school on Gęsia 9 recited a Polish fable, "The Orphan's Ball." The school on Nowolipki 68, run by the LPZ, presented "The Seasons of the Year" in Yiddish.[48] On May 30 the day care centers that cared for the poorest children put on a major children's evening at the Femina. Children from a variety of centers, orphanages, and shelters sang, recited poems, and acted.[49] On July 14 an invitation went out for the grand opening of a Hebrew-language preschool on Leszno 11. The children of the school, named after the Hebrew poet Chaim Nachman Bialik, performed an all-Hebrew program of songs and poems. On July 18, just four days before the beginning of the Great Deportation, the children of Janusz Korczak's orphanage staged a special artistic evening.

During much of July Czerniakow had gone to one German office after another, trying to verify the rumors of deportation. Various German officials assured him that the Warsaw Ghetto was safe from deportation. On Wednesday morning, July 22, the squad of SS officers led by Hermann Höffle burst into his office and announced that the "Resettlement" of Warsaw Jewry had begun. The Germans had deceived Czerniakow until the very last moment. On July 23 Czerniakow killed himself.[50]

The Germans cunningly announced that a number of categories would be exempt from deportation: employees of the Judenrat and the Aleynhilf, those with work in German enterprises, and others who were gainfully employed. Those deported, the Germans stressed, would work in the East. The Resettlement Squad, faced with the mammoth task of deporting hundreds of thousands of people, set Jew against Jew and fooled the Jews into believing that a document or a job would actually save them.

Later, a close friend of Ringelblum's, Natan Smolar, would write for the archive that even though Warsaw Jewry knew quite well that the Germans were wiping out the provincial Jews, they could not believe that the Germans would dare to destroy the Jews of Warsaw. The homeless, the beggars, perhaps . . . but Warsaw, "the mother of generations of Jews"?

> But then it began. The placards appeared: "All Warsaw Jews . . . with the exception . . ." "The exception" was the main thing. . . . Had Jews not read that part, perhaps there would not have been as many victims. Perhaps the Jews would have defended themselves, perhaps we could have avoided the disaster, where three hundred thousand Jews, including tens of thousands of young and healthy people, let themselves be driven to the slaughter.[51]

Gestapo agents also spread rumors that the deportation would end in one week, then two. The roundups, agents whispered, would end when the SS caught seventy thousand Jews, then one hundred thousand. Throughout the deportation, rumors, illusions, and fear divided and paralyzed Warsaw Jewry.

Many, probably the majority, could not believe that the Germans would actually exterminate the enormous Warsaw Ghetto. Even after the news of Chełmno and Vilna, few could grasp the notion of genocide. As Gustawa Jarecka points out in her essay on the Great Deportation (more on this in the final chapter), believing the worst was difficult for those raised to believe that God looked after the world or that decency and humanity ultimately triumphed in human affairs.

During the first phase of the deportation, few Germans actually participated in the roundups. The Jewish police did the job for them; each had a fixed quota of "heads" to deliver. Since nonfulfillment of the quota threatened the policeman and his family with deportation, Jewish policemen, many of them university-educated professionals, turned into cruel bloodhounds. Desperate to meet their quota, policemen wielding axes and sticks ran through the ghetto buildings smashing doors and cutting locks. Often they would tear up a Jew's work papers and ship him off to the Umschlagplatz.[52] Most pocketed fat bribes during the course of their work.

The Germans tricked the Jews into a diabolical race to procure the "right" papers, to find a place in the "right" German shop. People relinquished all their savings for a place in a shop or a precious work document which usually became useless within a couple of weeks. When the Germans needed to fill empty boxcars, even the "best" papers in the "best" shops proved worthless. Meanwhile the shops became a gold mine for their German owners and for the Jewish foremen and hustlers who sold openings. The influx of newcomers without proper job skills enraged the Jewish craftsmen who were already employed and who feared that the Germans would close down their shops and deport them all. Ugly scenes were common. The crowded shops quickly turned into death traps when the SS barged in, ignoring documents and work qualifications, and carried out brutal selections for the Umschlagplatz. Nevertheless, despite these dangers, the shops represented a last slim hope for many Jews, better than hiding, better than death.

With or without papers, sheer survival now became exceptionally difficult. The smuggling of food into the ghetto practically ceased, and food prices soared. In April a kilo of black bread had cost about seven zlotys, potatoes between three and four. On July 26 Abraham Lewin recorded that a kilo of bread cost fifty zlotys and a kilo of potatoes cost twenty. By the next day the price of bread had already increased to sixty zlotys a kilo—ten times the average daily wage in the ghetto just before the deportation began. As the Germans removed block after city block from the ghetto boundaries, thousands of Jews lost their apartments, their possessions, and the hiding places they had so carefully built. Eluding the manhunts became even more difficult when one was hungry and dispossessed. And on top of it all the Germans curtailed postal service into and out of the ghetto at the beginning of the Great Deportation. Although the delivery of incoming mail was later resumed, the ban on outgoing mail remained in place.

The nightmare culminated on September 6, the first day of the "cauldron."[53] Early that day all Jews who remained in the ghetto were ordered to assemble in a small area of streets adjoining the Umschlagplatz. For three days a massive selection took place, as employees of each shop and workplace had to march past SS officers who would decide who would die and who would receive a precious "work number." The Germans planned to issue only thirty-five thousand numbers. The SS separated children from parents and wives from husbands. Some Jews, given "numbers" that would save them but not their wives or children, turned their backs on their loved ones and abandoned them. Others voluntarily joined the crowds selected for death. In many cases parents tried to save their babies by drugging them and carrying them in backpacks until the SS began to probe the packs with bayonets. In six days the SS sent about fifty thousand Jews to Treblinka. Then, except for a one-day roundup on September 21, the manhunts temporarily ceased. But daily shootings and the reign of terror went on, day after day.

The beginning of the Great Deportation confronted the Oyneg Shabes with the dilemma of its own future. On July 25, at a "tragic meeting," to use Lewin's words, the executive committee decided that after the war the archive would go to the YIVO in the United States.[54] Almost certainly at the same meeting the committee also decided to bury the collections as soon as possible.

The members of the Oyneg Shabes, like all the other Jews of Warsaw, were now in imminent physical danger. Although the Germans had promised that Aleynhilf workers would not be touched—and during the first week of the Great Deportation Ringelblum and others gave out hundreds of Aleynhilf work certificates—within a week the Germans stopped recognizing these documents.

The members of the archive were not immune from the panic and fear that gripped everyone. When the Aleynhilf papers failed to protect all but a few senior employees, most Oyneg Shabes members had to save themselves by finding a place in a shop. The archive tried to save its people; for example, Ringelblum found Rabbi Huberband a place in the brush makers' shop. But ultimately little could be done. This seeming refuge, like so many of the shops, quickly turned into a trap. The Germans took away many members of the Oyneg Shabes. On August 8, 1942, a dragnet sent Bluma Wasser to the Umschlagplatz, but she managed to escape. Many others, who found temporary refuge in Landau's shop on 30 Gęsia Street or in Bernhard Hallman's woodworking shop on Nowolipki 59, still lost their loved ones as the Germans descended on the shops and hauled off the women and children.

Desperation spawned anger and mutual recriminations. Menakhem Kon railed in his diary at his friends who did not want him to hide in Landau's shop. Ringelblum understandably did what he could to save his wife, Yehudis, and his son, Uri, provoking a bitter reproach from Israel Lichtenstein, who hid in Nowolipki 68 with Nahum Grzywacz and David Graber as he waited for the order to bury the archive:

> Today [July 31, 1942] I saw Dr. Ringelblum sitting in the carpentry shop on Nowolipki 59 [the shop of Bernhard Hallman]. He's hiding with his family. Is this the plan? Should we have allowed ourselves to reach the point where the leaders [eskonim] worry only for their private lives and leave everything else to fall apart [hefker]?[55]

Lichtenstein may not have been entirely fair, but his outburst reveals the atmosphere in which the Oyneg Shabes had to function once the Great Deportation began. Strained friendships and mutual suspicions might well have ended the work of the archive, especially after Lichtenstein buried the collections in early August.

Instead, the "band of comrades" continued its mission. Given the danger, the persistence of the Oyneg Shabes required incredible presence of mind. Of course, the terror left its mark. Ringelblum himself stopped making his usual journal entries in July and August. He later noted that for a few months the archive all but halted its activities. In late July even as Gutkowski tracked down outstanding assignments from Oyneg Shabes workers, he was also trying to find a hiding place for his four-year-old son and his wife. Incredibly several Oyneg Shabes members—Abraham Lewin, Yekhil Gorny, and Peretz Opoczynski—kept up their diaries, even as they lost their loved ones or were running for their lives. It was these members of the Oyneg Shabes who, just when writing became especially difficult, left a day-by-day account of the ghetto in July and August, and continued the most important work of the archive during the Great Deportation.

By August the ghetto broke up into disconnected enclaves. Forced to hide or find a place in a shop, the members of the archive maintained contact only with great difficulty. During the daylight hours, when the blockades took place, the streets were downright dangerous. Soon free movement within the ghetto became practically impossible, as Jews were forced into noncontiguous mini-camps. Shop workers were confined to their workplaces and adjoining apartment blocs. Whole stretches of the ghetto became a kind of no-man's-land, where any Jew could be shot on sight.

Ringelblum seems to have enjoyed relative freedom of movement. His prominence and senior position in the Aleynhilf apparently afforded him some protection. Able to move among the different shops that housed members of the Oyneg Shabes, Ringelblum was a key link that kept the archive going.

During this period Shmuel Winter's role in the archive became especially critical. His high post in the Provisioning Agency gave him relative immunity from deportation. By sending people to different parts of the ghetto on agency business, Winter was able to provide Oyneg Shabes workers the cover they needed to move through the ghetto. As we have seen, he also had access to one of the few telephones left in the ghetto. When the archive needed to protect someone who was performing a particularly important job, it was Winter who made the arrangements.

But the Oyneg Shabes certainly had to change its methods and its mission. Until July 1942 the archive, with its many links to the Aleynhilf, had depended on the "social space" of the Warsaw Ghetto, which, for all its miseries, was far from being a concentration camp. The house committees, political parties, underground press, Aleynhilf, landsmanshaftn, schools, and orphanages all enabled the survival of organizational networks that preserved prewar values and moral codes, and maintained a measure of cohesion and solidarity during a time of rupture. These networks not only created a reservoir of workers for the archive but imbued it with a sense of purpose and even framed its agendas, for example, documenting the lives of the children, the work of the Aleynhilf, and the struggles of the house committees. Countless documents conveyed hundreds of individual stories, *petits-recits* of struggles against the odds and hopes for a better future. The crowning measure of this hope for the future was the "Two and a Half Years" project.

But almost everything changed on July 22.

The "social space" of the ghetto shriveled. Since the beginning of the war Jews had been herded into ever narrower confines. First they were forced into overcrowded ghettos that offered little privacy. Then the ghettos themselves shrank. Finally, after July 22, the ghetto gave way to shops and attached housing blocs, which destroyed the tiny modicum of privacy that had existed before. By mid-September the surviving Jews in the ghetto were atomized and terrorized. Most had lost their loved ones. Herded into barracks and working up to sixteen hours a day for no wages, they felt humiliated and angry with little to anticipate except probable deportation. In comparison, life in the pre-deportation ghetto was a relative paradise.

For the Oyneg Shabes, such projects as "Two and a Half Years" were now tragically beside the point. The house committees and schools, the Aleyn-hilf and landsmanshaftn, were all gone. Few children remained. It looked increasingly unlikely that Polish Jewry would survive. After the war what would be left? Within a few short weeks, Abraham Lewin lost his wife, most of his friends, most of his community, the Warsaw Jewish intelligentsia. In his entry of December 29, 1942, Lewin wrote:

> In general one sees rough faces and vulgar types from the common folk. Members of the middle class, the intelligentsia, and the more educated elements are not to be seen. Very few have survived from bourgeois and cultivated Jewish Warsaw. Teachers, for example, have been almost completely wiped out. I am the only survivor from my school. Out of all the female teachers, the directress, and the male teachers who were working in the classroom until recently, none survive.[56]

Yet the archive regrouped, with new agendas and new priorities. Shortly after the beginning of the Great Deportation, the Oyneg Shabes decided to collect as much Judenrat and German correspondence and proclamations as possible in order to document the step-by-step process of bureaucratized mass murder. Now every scrap of paper became important, and Gustawa Jarecka and Reich-Ranicki provided Ringelblum with as many copies of Judenrat documents as they could. The second part of the archive contained their transcript of the July 22 meeting where Höffle dictated German orders to the Judenrat concerning the deportation.[57] A copy of the proclamation informing the population of the deportation was also in that part of the archive. On July 24 another Judenrat proclamation "reassured" the Jews of Warsaw that,

> In view of unfounded rumors about the resettlement that are spreading through the Jewish Quarter, the Jewish Council in Warsaw has been authorized by the authorities to announce that the nonproductive elements of the population are indeed going to the eastern territories for resettlement.[58]

Jews were urged not to hide but to report voluntarily for deportation. On July 29 a proclamation announced that anyone voluntarily reporting to the

Umschlagplatz would receive three kilograms of bread and a kilogram of marmalade.[59]

The Judenrat report of its activities for the period from July 22 to October 27, 1942, also went into the archive.[60] Similar in style and tone to a quarterly corporate report, complete with organizational charts and tables, the report dryly summarized the various stages of the resettlement action and outlined its own cooperation, including its cooperation in its own demise: as the number of Jews in the ghetto decreased, the Germans ordered a major reduction of Judenrat employees: "among the most important tasks faced by the Jewish Council in connection with the resettlement order was the task of furnishing seven thousand people, Judenrat employees and their families [for deportation]." Each department head had to prepare lists of employees who would remain. All the others, according to the report, were "obligated, together with their families, to present themselves at noon, August 10, at the Umschlagplatz in order to be deported." A helpful table demonstrated that between July 10 and August 27 the total number of Judenrat employees declined from 9,030 to 2,527.

The archive saved the scraps of paper that desperate people at the Umschlagplatz wrote to friends, begging for a last-minute rescue. On one such scrap, in a hasty scrawl, the Yiddish poet Joseph Kirman implored Yitzhak Giterman to save him.

> Dear, dear Giterman, I beg you to save me. There is still time. They grabbed me on the street and took me to the Umschlagplatz. I want to be able to someday see my wife and two children again. Save me. Fast!

When a Jewish policeman seized Kirman on the street he resisted ferociously but was overpowered.[61] On that day at least, the note helped. Giterman intervened and managed to extricate Kirman from the Umschlagplatz.

The postcards collected from Treblinka were altogether different. In order to fool the ghetto residents, the Germans forced many deportees to write to relatives that they had arrived safely at Treblinka and were gainfully employed. On October 5, 1942, for instance, Hersch Lepak wrote to his wife in the Warsaw Ghetto that he had been in Treblinka since August 31, was healthy, and had found gainful employment as a carpenter.[62]

The archive managed to procure a German tabulation of the daily deportations: 6,250 on July 22; 7,300 on July 23; 7,400 on July 24; and so on.[63] Except for one hiatus, from August 28 to September 2, the deportations continued every single day until September 12. The data also included the number of Jews who were shot in the streets or in the Umschlagplatz, perhaps indicating instances of individual resistance to deportation or attempts to escape.[64]

The total German tabulation came to 255,936 "resettled" and another 11,780 sent to transit camps (Dulags).[65] The Oyneg Shabes believed that the actual number was much higher.[66]

Even in documenting the destruction of the ghetto, Ringelblum and the Oyneg Shabes tried to maintain a systematic methodology that would not only bear witness to the disaster but would also help future historians. During the temporary respite that began in September, the archive prepared an outline for a study of the Great Deportation, specifying nineteen different topics for description and study. How exactly did the Jewish police and the Germans carry out their daily blockades of the apartment buildings? What role did the Ukrainians and Jewish Gestapo agents play? How did the Jewish masses assess the rumors that swept through the ghetto before July 22? The archive wanted research on the frantic effort to secure places in "shops," examples of resistance, detailed descriptions of the Umschlagplatz and what went on there. The Oyneg Shabes also wanted to examine the failure of the Judenrat to lift a finger to save the Jewish intelligentsia as well as the role of the Jewish police. Finally, the archive called for a statistical reckoning of the destruction. How many Jews were shot every day in the streets, in their homes, at the Umschlagplatz?[67]

Statistics, carefully collected by the Oyneg Shabes, now spoke volumes about the scope of the horror. As noted by Gustawa Jarecka, who probably supplied these statistics to the Oyneg Shabes: "Statistics and official proclamations are the fundamental documents of the [Great Deportation]. Written accounts can only provide some additional details about events and specific incidents. But basically nothing is more expressive than statistics!"[68] Wasser recalled that, even now, Ringelblum insisted that the archive tabulate the statistics for reports that would avoid pathos and excess emotion. The numbers would speak for themselves.[69]

In November 1942 the Oyneg Shabes published a breakdown by sex and age of the ghetto's population. At that time only 1.3 percent of males and 1.6 percent of females in the ghetto were between the ages of one and nine. Only 12.1 percent of males and 7.1 percent of females were over the age of fifty. Before the deportation females outnumbered males in the ghetto, but after September 1942 the opposite was true. With regard to age, 99.1 percent of children from newborns to the age of nine had been deported. Before the deportation there had been 51,458 children; in November 1942 there were 498—93.8 percent of males and 98.3 percent of females between the ages of ten and nineteen had been deported. For those between twenty and twenty-nine years of age, corresponding figures were 89.5 and 87.3 percent; for those between thirty and thirty-nine, 76.9 and 88.3 percent; and for those between forty and forty-nine, 79.6 and 91.6 percent. These figures reflected the greater difficulty that women faced in getting places in shops, as well as the effects of the German raids on the shops that took away women and children.[70]

The archive staff prepared the groundwork for thorough studies of the shops, with particular attention to the mostly Jewish shop police, the hated Werkschutz, who hunted down hidden Jews and enforced German rules.[71] Remarkable, too, was that given the desperate conditions the archive procured several journals and diaries that described the horrors of the September selection, the "cauldron."[72]

The Oyneg Shabes managed to interview several escapees from Treblinka, including David Nowodworski, a leader of Hashomer, and Jacob Rabinowitz, a cousin of Shie Rabinowitz.[73] By far the most comprehensive testimony about Treblinka came from Abraham Jacob Krzepicki, who had been deported on August 25 and who spent more than two weeks in the camp before he escaped and returned to Warsaw. Ringelblum and Winter assigned Rachel Auerbach to interview Krzepicki and record his testimony. They provided her with paper and carbide lamps for light. Winter was able to grant Auerbach an indefinite "sick leave" from her nominal job so that she could finish the project as quickly a possible. They hoped to publish it as a clandestine book that would convince Jews to resist the Nazis in any way they could.[74]

Abraham Krzepicki, originally from Danzig, was about twenty-five years old and a member of the Zionist youth group Ha-Hoar Ha-Tsiyoni. Krzepicki's account, which ran to more than ninety typed pages, recounted his entire ordeal, from the moment he and his group of shop workers were seized on the street to his escape from Treblinka. Like many others, Krzepicki had been sure that his work papers would protect him. But as he and his fellow workers were marching from their factory, the Germans surrounded them and loaded them into the trains. He and many other Jews in the boxcar refused to believe the worst, even on August 25, five weeks after the start of the Great Deportation.[75] Throughout the harrowing journey, and even when they arrived in Treblinka, many continued to hope that they would be sent to work. Krzepicki described the arrival, the beatings, the herding of victims into the gas chambers. Just when he was about to get in line for the gas chambers, the Germans selected him to join a work detail. He sorted clothes, moved corpses, and helped to meet the new transports of Jews and collect their shoes. During his two-week stay in Treblinka, he memorized the layout of the camp.

Krzepicki wrote out a detailed plan of Treblinka and even described the inside of the gas chambers. His story of terror and brutality dwarfed anything the ghetto inhabitants had seen or heard from the survivors of the labor camps. As he described how the women and children were forced to undress at breakneck speed under a hail of blows and screams, Krzepicki told Auerbach that perhaps the victims were lucky it all happened so fast—had they had time to think about what was going to happen to them, they would have suffered even more.

> As I stood behind the open door and watched the wild scene before me, a blond girl pretty as a blossom came running over to me and asked in great haste, "Yehudi [Mr. Jew] what are they going to do with us?" It was hard for me to tell her the truth. I gave a little shrug and tried to answer her with a look, to calm her fears. But my bearing filled the girl with even more terror and she cried out: "So tell me right now, what are they going to do with us? Maybe I can still get out of here!" I had no choice but to say something, and so I answered her with one brief word. "Scrap!" The girl left me and started running all over the barracks like a mouse caught in a trap. She was looking for loose boards, doors and windows. Back and forth she ran, until her turn came to hand in her clothes and an SS man began to hit her with his whip so she should strip naked.[76]

An older woman stood in the undressing barracks and led others in a prayer. After she uttered the Shma Yisroel (Hear O Israel) she raised her hands to the heavens and intoned: "God, You One and Only God, take revenge on our enemies for their crimes! We are going to die to sanctify Your name. Let our sacrifice not be in vain!"

A little boy yelled out that he wanted to "say good-bye to daddy." A Ukrainian guard picked the boy up and took him to a separate line of men who were waiting to be gassed. The father embraced the boy and kissed him. The boy returned quietly to the undressing barracks.

Like Szlamek in Chełmno, Krzepicki related how his fellow prisoners discussed the lack of resistance. One reason, Krzepicki believed, was that the German terror proved so overwhelming that the Jews feared the Germans more than death itself.[77] But Krzepicki also saw what happened when Meir Berliner, an Argentinean citizen who had been stranded in Poland at the beginning of the war, stabbed an SS man, Bielas: the Germans and Ukrainians hacked Berliner to death with shovels.

On September 13 Krzepicki managed to escape from Treblinka by hiding in a boxcar full of clothes that left the camp. Some kindly Poles helped him to return to the Warsaw Ghetto. Krzepicki later joined ŻOB, the Jewish Fighting Organization, and died during the ghetto uprising in April 1943. He was wounded in the leg and unable to move, so his fellow fighters had to leave him in a basement. He told Auerbach that, "in the event of my death, please inform others what happened to me."

In the fall of 1942 the surviving political leadership in the ghetto, organized as the Jewish National Committee (ŻKN), the political counterpart of the ŻOB, asked the Oyneg Shabes to prepare a comprehensive report on the Great Deportation to send abroad.[78] Wasser recalled that the Jewish leaders had been frustrated by the response elicited by the previous Oyneg Shabes reports; perhaps this one, full of new details on the extermination process, might galvanize the Allies and world Jewry into action. In late October 1942 Ringelblum went to the OBW shop where Wasser and Gutkowski worked and told them to prepare the report which consisted of two major sections: the Great Deportation, prepared by Wasser, and the eyewitness accounts from Treblinka, prepared by Gutkowski. Ringelblum would appear three times a week to look over and edit the draft. He improved the Polish style and made the tone of the report more matter-of-fact and less emotional.[79] The report also contained a precise account of the Great Deportation and detailed statistics on the numbers of Jews who were deported or shot by Germans in the streets. It also included the sketches of the death camp that the escapees had furnished to the archive. The report implored the outside world to intervene. In particular, the Oyneg Shabes asked that the Allies threaten retaliation against Germans living abroad.[80]

In late 1942 the Oyneg Shabes began to publish a Polish-language bulletin, *Wiadomości*.[81] Like *Miteylungen,* issued the previous spring, the six issues of *Wiadomości* that appeared between mid-November 1942 and mid-January 1943 were blunt: Treblinka was still working at full capacity; Jews should not believe rumors about a suspension of the extermination program. According to Rachel Auerbach, these bulletins had one basic purpose—to rouse the Jews to resist and support the Jewish Fighting Organization.

The Oyneg Shabes also hoped that the journal might reach a Polish readership, and it warned the Poles that the Germans planned the same fate for them as for the Jews:

> We stand at the brink of the abyss. We see no help from anyone or anywhere. But we want to emphasize, even at this moment, how closely interwoven are the fates of the Jews and of the Poles. . . . The continuation of German rule will mean not just the destruction of the remaining Polish Jews but also the physical liquidation of the Polish nation.[82]

INDIVIDUALIZING DISASTER

Perhaps the hardest part of the Oyneg Shabes mission was to ask individuals to describe the indescribable: what they felt as they lost their loved ones, witnessed the destruction of their community, and awaited the probability of a painful death. The archive collected testimony from as wide a range as possible. The material is hard reading. Many religious Jews had dealt with the German persecutions by putting them in historical context as a repetition of earlier disasters that had befallen the Jewish people. In his weekly sermons on the Torah portion of the week, the Piaseczno rebbe, Kalonymous Shapiro, had taken this tack.[83] Once the Great Deportation began, however, he, too, had to admit that he was witnessing a catastrophe without precedent in Jewish history.[84]

The poet Yitzhak Katzenelson wrote a poem, "Vey dir" (Woe to you), cursing the German people, pronouncing that they would be haunted forever by the murder of the Jews. Murdered Jewish children would not simply disappear and crimes would not be unavenged; the dead victims would return and devour the lives and souls of the German nation:

> We will stand on all the roads.
> Quiet. quiet like the grass.
> Quietly stand and quietly ask,
> Why did you kill us, why?
>
> Bloody and filthy you will scurry
> Engulfed in wild terror;
> But we the dead will block all your roads
> Wherever you run, you will see us.
>
> We the murdered will look at you silently
> In our agony we will mutely stare;
> And looking at you we will silently devour you
> And gnaw at your bones.[85]

Another Yiddish poem pulled out of the milk cans of the second part of the archive, written by an unknown author, was titled, simply, "Where Is God?" The spelling mistakes in the poem and the Polish-Yiddish dialect indicated that the writer was a simple, religious Jew:

> Angels and spirits
> Smash the commandments
> Darkness all around
> Is God anywhere?
> In chaos and confusion
> A people goes under.
> They destroy the highest commandment
> And where is God?[86]

Many Jews chose to express not only hatred of the Germans but also anger at their fellow Jews and deep shame. Shie Perle's outburst cited earlier was far from an isolated case. Peretz Opoczynski and Yekhiel Gorny expressed outrage at the lack of resistance. On the fifth day of the Great Deportation, Rachel Auerbach lashed out at the shameful complicity of the Jewish police. Israel Lichtenstein wrote that the Jews had been betrayed by their leaders.[87] The Jews, Lichtenstein wrote, should have followed the example of the ancient Germanic warriors, who preferred to set their homes on fire and die in the blaze rather than to surrender to an enemy.[88] Shmuel Winter wrote in his diary that when the Great Deportation broke out, the Jews should have burned the ghetto and stormed the walls.[89]

The loss of loved ones made anger and shame even more difficult to bear. Some tried to assuage their grief by memorializing their loved ones in the essays they wrote for the archive. The teacher Natan Smolar, Ringelblum's close friend and longtime pillar of the LPZ Borochov school, wrote in December of his torment during the Great Deportation: he began by eulogizing his three-year-old daughter whom the Germans had taken away in August:

> Dedicated to the bright memory of my only, beloved daughter Ninkele.
> It wasn't so long ago, on July 11, 1942, that we all celebrated your third birthday. Dear friends came. . . . There were so many toys, so much noise and play, so much happiness and children's shouting. And as we drank a cup of tea, we all wished you, from the bottom of our hearts, that you celebrate your fourth birthday in freedom. And today there is no more Ninkele, her mother is gone, along with my sister Etl. They would, with so much admiration, get her to say phrases and show her intelligence, they loved her ingenuity when she played. And to think that that three year old already knew what a blockade meant, and what a Jewish policeman, a snatcher of old people and children, was. She knew that you had to hate them.[90]

Smolar wrote that if he did not survive, then perhaps his sister who lived on 1468 Leyland Avenue in the Bronx might someday read this message. Smolar did not survive. The last time Ringelblum saw him was Sunday, April 18, the night before the beginning of the ghetto uprising, as the teacher joined Israel Lichtenstein in a walk back to Nowolipki 68. Smolar probably died together with Lichtenstein and his family during the uprising.

THE POETS OF A DYING GHETTO: YITZHAK KATZENELSON AND WŁADYSŁAW SZLENGEL

Among the most revealing documents of the ghetto's final months are several poems of Władysław Szlengel and Yitzhak Katzenelson who read their poems to their fellow Jews in the shop barracks and in makeshift apartments. The consciousness of a shared tragedy and a shared fate linked writer and listener. They did not write their poems for literary journals or critics. They wrote as they watched the Jews marching to the Umschlagplatz, as they sat in dark hideouts with the SS just a few yards away—and, in Katzenelson's case, as he struggled to stay sane after having lost his beloved wife, Chana, and two of his three sons. They hid their poems for posterity.

In the last months of the ghetto, words could only go so far; but they were welcome nonetheless.[91] At a time when the Germans had shattered the frail bonds that had held Jews together—family, circles of friends, even the comfort of a crowded but familiar apartment—poetry helped forge, however fleetingly, moments of shared values in a ravaged community. As the shrinking social space of the ghetto eroded the distinction between the individual and the collective, the poets of the dying ghetto showed that the written word—unadorned, spare, matter-of-fact—could help Jews mark their sense of loss and anguish. A common fate bound these poets to their audience and endowed their poetry with a legitimacy and authority that no degree of artistic virtuosity or aesthetic creativity could have equaled. "Art"—the subtle interplay of rhythm, verbal imagination, and poetic structure—now belonged to another time, another place. In a world of humiliation, destruction, and death, even the fertile imagination of an Edgar Allen Poe could not convey a fraction of the horror that everyone had witnessed, the sense of loss and rupture that the remaining Jews—temporarily reprieved—felt to their very core.

Thus Szlengel's "Pomnik" (The monument), a memorial for an ordinary Jewish woman, a mother and a wife, deported to Treblinka, leaving behind a husband and a son who were working in a German shop:

> For heroes—poems and rhapsodies!!!
> For heroes—the homage of posterity,
> Their names etched in the plinths,
> for them a monument of marble.
> But who will tell you, the people of the future,
> Not about bronze or mythic tales
> But that they took her—killed her,
> That she is no more.

This woman had lived a plain, undistinguished life. In the great scheme of things she did not stand out.

> Was she good?
> Not really.
> She often quarreled,
> She would slam the door,
> She would scold,
> But . . . she was.

This unremarkable woman gave her husband and son a home. In the ghetto they would return to her, to "warm soup, or a white towel."

> And they took her,
> She left just as she was,
> Standing near the kitchen stove;
> She did not finish the soup.
> They took her, she went,
> She is no more, they have killed her.[92]

Now the husband and son return to an empty room, to unmade beds, to their loved one's only monument—a cold pot on the stove.

The Jews, left in the ghetto, including Abraham Lewin or Yitzhak Katzenelson, had no graves to visit, and few had had a chance to say good-bye. They simply returned one day to find their wives gone, their children gone. How their loved ones suffered in their final hours, they now knew far too well: the hell in the boxcar, the ramp at Treblinka, the stampede to the gas chambers. As Szlengel wrote in "It Is Time":

> And when the killers will have pushed you and forced you
> And dragged, stuffed you into the steam chamber
> And sealed the hatch behind you,
> The hot steam will begin to suffocate you, to suffocate you,
> And you will scream, you will try to run—
> And after the torture of dying will have stopped,
> Then they will drag you out and throw you in a horrible pit;
> They will put your stars out—the gold teeth in your jaw—
> And you will turn into ashes.[93]

This was a kind of poetry with few metaphors, no catharsis, and certainly no illusions. Brutally honest, it offered only one small solace: that by bringing together poet and listener, the written word reaffirmed their common humanity—even in the face of death. Just as Leyb Goldin, in "The Chronicle of a Single Day," pointed out that animals did not operate on their young—and thus the Germans had not yet turned the Jews into animals—so, too, could the Jews in the dying ghetto believe that people who needed poetry, even this poetry, hadn't lost everything yet.

The two poets of the dying ghetto, Szlengel and Yitzhak Katzenelson, were each quite different. Szlengel wrote in Polish, Katzenelson in Hebrew and Yiddish. The former had just begun his career before the war, whereas Katzenelson had already gained fame as an important Hebrew poet. Katzenelson's poetry was shaped by a profound consciousness of Jewish traditional literature and history, whereas Szlengel reflected the sensibilities of the acculturated but unassimilated Polish-Jewish intelligentsia, caught between genuine Jewish pride and love of a Poland that would never extend true acceptance. Together they left a searing epitaph for Warsaw Jewry.

"What I Read to the Dead": The "Document-Poems" of Władysław Szlengel

In the final months of Ringelblum's life, as he wrote his essays on the major figures of the Jewish intelligentsia of Warsaw, he composed a detailed and admiring portrait of Władysław Szlengel, whom he called "the poet of the ghetto."[94] It may seem surprising at first that Szlengel, who wrote in Polish rather than Yiddish, sparked Ringelblum's interest. He believed that Szlengel's poetry was more important as testimony than as art.[95] Unlike many of the other subjects of Ringelblum's final essays, Szlengel had not played a major role in prewar Jewish life, although his published poetry, often filled with foreboding about the future of Polish Jewry, attracted growing interest.[96] In the pre-deportation ghetto he read his satires and ditties in the Café Sztuka on Leszno, which also featured the pianist Władysław Szpilman, the protagonist of Roman Polanski's 2003 film, *The Pianist*. Szlengel's "Living Newspaper" was especially popular, a funny commentary on current events. He satirized many of the bigwigs in the ghetto, who often came to the café to enjoy the young poet's cheeky lampoons.

Szlengel had also been a member of the hated Jewish police. But when the Great Deportation began he quit the force, recognizing that there were moral lines he would not cross.[97] Szlengel freely admitted that he was no hero and that, without the seeming protection of his "policeman's hat," he was frightened. But as the ghetto dissolved, Szlengel overcame his fear to write poems that reached out to the dwindling remnant of Warsaw Jewry.

In "What I Read to the Dead," written shortly after the first armed confrontation with the Germans in January 1943, Szlengel described his determination to be a voice for the dead and the dying. He recalled a prewar Soviet film about trapped sailors on a sunken submarine. The last survivor, about to suffocate, scrawls a final message affirming his faith that he is dying for a higher cause. But the Warsaw Jews, Szlengel wrote, could take no such comfort in their deaths.

> With all my being I feel that I am suffocating as the air in my sunken boat slowly gives out. [Unlike the Soviet sailor] the reasons I am in this boat have nothing to do with heroism. I am here against my will, and without any reason or guilt.
>
> But here I am, in the boat. And although I am no captain, I still think that I should at least write the chronicle of those who have sunk to the bottom. I don't want to leave behind only statistics. Through my poems, sketches, and writings I want to enrich (a bad word, I know) the historical record that will be written in the future.
>
> On the wall of my submarine I scrawl my poem-documents. To my companions, I, a poet of AD 1943, am reading my scribblings.[98]

One by one, Szlengel wrote, his companions, the ones who listened to his poetry, were taken away. Just a few hours after he recited poems to a group of friends, most of them became victims of an SS dragnet. "It is high time," he remarked, "that I sort my papers."

After the Great Deportation, Szlengel's poem-documents became a running chronicle of the moods, hopes, and fears of those left in the ghetto. As the Polish literary critic Irena Maciejewska noted, before the deportation Szlengel's poetry had entertained and diverted. After July 1942 his poetry became a beacon of protest and resistance.[99] The different versions of his poetry multiplied, as did the number of copies, a tribute to their importance at this time. Grammatical and spelling mistakes were indications that many Jews who wrote down his poems were not native Polish speakers.[100]

In "Things," a poem that reads like a bill of lading, Szlengel traces the descent of middle-class Warsaw Jews by listing the possessions they take with them as they leave one home after another.[101] The inventory grows smaller and smaller, along with the ghetto itself. The journey begins with a nice apartment on Marszałkowska or Hoża or Wspólna, three of Warsaw's best streets. When they leave for the ghetto, they manage to take along many of their things in carts as they move into a smaller but relatively comfortable apartment on Sienna Street:

> From Hoża and Wspólna and Marszałkowska Streets cartloads . . .
> Jewish cartloads on the move . . . furniture and tables and stools, small valises and featherbeds, suits, portraits, bedding, pots, rugs and draperies. Cherry wine, big jars, little jars, glasses, silverware, teapots, books,

toys, knickknacks, moved from Hoża Street to Street Śliska. In the pocket a bottle of vodka and a chunk of sausage. In carts, rickshaws and wagons the motley mob rides.[102]

Then the Germans exclude Sienna Street from the ghetto, and they move again into the central ghetto, now with fewer things:

Furniture, tables, and stools,
Small valises and bundles,
Bedding pots—yessiree!
But already without rugs,
No sign of silverware,
No more cherry wine,
No suits, no featherbeds,
No little jars, no portraits,
All these trifles left on Śliska.

From there they squeeze into a grim shop block:

No more furniture, no stools,
No pots, no bundles.
Lost are the teapots,
Books, featherbeds, little jars.
To the devil went
The suits and knick;
Dumped together in a rickshaw
A valise and a coat,
A bottle of tea,
A bite of caramel;
On foot without wagons
The gloomy mob rides.

The circle grows smaller and smaller, and finally they find themselves on "the Jewish road" (i.e., the road to Treblinka)—with nothing but some water and a capsule of poison. But the "things" remain. Slowly normalcy returns, the "things" find a home with their new, non-Jewish owners.

But one day, when everything seems to have been forgotten, Szlengel has a surrealist vision: all the former Jewish possessions, the things, the tables and chairs, trucks and bundles, the suits and kettles, everything will jump out of the windows and march down the street and gather on the highways, along with the black railway tracks and will disappear, and no one will know what it all means—only the little poison pill will bear evidence.[103]

An interesting sidebar to this poem is that one of the "things" in the poem—a discarded table—contained many of Szlengel's poems; in the 1960s a Pole in a small town near Warsaw, Ryszard Baranowski, was chopping up the table for firewood when he discovered packets of manuscripts in the double table-top whose contents included Szlengel's poems.[104]

In his essay on Szlengel, Ringelblum recalled a poem titled "Four Sons," which the last remaining Jews in the ghetto sang to the tune of the popular Yiddish folk song "Oyfn Pripetchik." The poem suggests the enormous scope of their national tragedy—including what they saw as the indifference of their brothers and sisters who lived in safety abroad. One son fought in the Red Army; a second hid on the Aryan side of Warsaw, but Polish blackmailers had turned his life into a living hell; a third son was in a German concentration camp, and the fourth son lived in New York.

> [The fourth son] is sitting by a Hanukkah menorah. The radio is broadcasting a memorial meeting for the murdered Jews of Europe. The son lights the candle and turns on the radio. . . . During the broadcast an advertisement reminds listeners that when they need candles to mourn . . . that they should remember to use only the candles of Firm X. And thus the materialistic American Jews exploit the tragedy of the Jews in Europe.[105]

Ringelblum considered Szlengel's poem "Reckoning with God" an accurate description of the erosion of religious faith in the ghetto. In the poem Szlengel and God meet around a table. The poet opens a big ledger, and God pulls out his Waterman pen. A "gray elderly gentleman, with a look full of kindness," God's clothes are unremarkable, except that he does not wear a Jewish armband. Happily, instead of the coveted German Aryan ID card, the Kennkarte, God is the proud bearer of something even better—a Uruguayan passport. As God listens, the poet reminds him that he has kept the Jewish commandments and has observed the major holidays, has fasted and donned his phylacteries. But in the ledger, the balance is all one-sided. The page that lists God's favors is blank.

> What did you give me today for all my deeds?
> This barrack, this tin number, the Umschlagplatz,
> The coupons or Treblinka?
>
> Do you still expect that I,
> The day after tomorrow, like in the Bible,
> When I go under the Prussian gas
> Shall I say Amen to you?[106]

Like many Jews in the Warsaw ghetto, Szlengel tried to retain faith in a common humanity that included even Germans. In "Two Men in the Snow," a Jewish worker and a German guard stand outside on a snowy day. The snow and the cold affect both. At the moment neither has a home.

> Because of you I can't move a step
> But neither can you
> Who is holding whom?
> Perhaps a third party holds us both.[107]

Szlengel, again like many Warsaw Jews, felt a deep tie to Polish culture and cared deeply for the opinions of the Poles: the sting of perceived abandonment and betrayal exacerbated his loneliness and dread. In two of his poems, "The Telephone" and "The Window Facing the Other Side," Szlengel expressed his feelings of longing for the Polish side of the wall. Once he had Polish friends. Now, sitting by a telephone in a ghetto office, wanting to pick up the receiver and speak to a Polish friend—there is no one to call. He and his Polish friends had all gone their separate ways in 1939. And now, as Szlengel looks at the phone, the only number he can dial is . . . the automatic time signal.

> How great it is to talk to you
> No quarrels, no words
> You are nicer, my little time clock,
> Then all my former friends.[108]

Many Jews in the ghetto felt deeply hurt by Polish accusations of cowardice that only deepened the trauma of mass annihilation. In "Two Deaths," Szlengel contrasted the common perceptions of Polish death and Jewish death during the war: Poles died with courage, in battle, for a cause and a future, unlike the death of the Jews:

> Your death is a death by bullets
> For something . . . for a country;
> Our death is a stupid death
> In a garret or a basement.
> Our death is like a dog's
> In a corner of a street.
> Your death comes with decorations
> And communiqués;
> Our death is wholesale death.
> They bury you—and good-bye.
> Your death—face to face

You meet in the open;
Our death is a hidden death
Buried in a mask of fear;
Your death is an ordinary death
Human and easy;
Our death is a garbage death
Jewish and—vile.[109]

Szlengel eagerly sought and welcomed any act that contradicted that bleak image, any sign of dignity and resistance such as Janusz Korczak's last march with the children of his orphanage. In a poem composed on August 10, 1942, "Kartka z dziennika akcji" (An entry in a deportation journal), Szlengel wrote:

On this battlefield where death does not sanctify,
In this nightmare dance in the night,
There was one proud soldier,
Janusz Korczak, the guardian of the Orphans.

Do you hear, you neighbors beyond the wall,
Who watch us die through the bars of our cage?
Janusz Korczak died
So that we, too, could have our honor.[110]

Szlengel's greatest hope was that someday, after the war, Poles as well as Jews would read his poems. He included among his buried papers a short note, "To the Polish Reader," as he was sure that some of his poems would be offensive to Polish readers.[111] But if one day Poles did read his last poems, they should remember that he had loved Warsaw and Poland as much as they.

It is important to [remember] the entire one-sidedness and hopelessness of this love [for Poland] in order for the Polish reader to understand and forgive the hurtful tone of such poems as "Things" [and] "The Window Facing the Other Side" or the accusations in "The Janitor Has the Key."[112]

Desperate to salvage Jewish honor, and eager to see the Jews fight back, Szlengel was galvanized by news of the armed resistance on January 18, 1943. He quickly wrote his best-known poem, "Counterattack." The poem passed from hand to hand in the ghetto, and survivors knew it by heart.[113] The poem begins with a description of the deportations which, by then, had become, for the Germans, a tedious routine: the Jews, passive as cattle, would move dumbly to the cattle cars, where an SS officer, just to relieve the boredom, might shoot one of them and throw his own empty cigarette pack on the corpse. Thus an advertisement for a popular German cigarette pronounced. "Why Junos are Round."

> They plodded calmly to the cars,
> As though disgusted with it all,
> Gazed like dogs at the guards' eyes,
> Cattle!
> Dapper officers smirked to see
> That nothing got under their skin.
> That hordes moved with torpid step
> . . . and only for sport
> lashed their snouts with whips
> . . .
>
> And the gentlemen on the corpses let fall in a casual way
> Cigarette boxes that said
> "Why Junos are round."[114]

Suddenly, gunshots! The Jews—the cattle—were fighting back!

> On twisting stairs where a mother
> Was dragged down by the hair
> Lies SS man Hantke
> Strangely tensed, as though
> He found death indigestible.
> This revolt like a bone in his throat—
> Choked in bloody drool—
> And a box: Junos are round
> Round, round.

The "cattle," the "meat," had revolted.

> REVOLT OF THE MEAT!!! SONG OF THE MEAT!!!
> . . . .
> We ask of you God a bloody battle,
> We implore you, a violent death—
> May our eyes before they flicker
> Not see our tracks stretch out
> But give our palms true aim, Lord,
> To bloody the coats of blue.
> Allow us to see before
> Dumb groaning chokes our throats.
> In those haughty hands—in those paws with whips
> Our everyday human FEAR!

Whereas earlier Szlengel had glorified Janusz Korczak, whose quiet dignity and courage in the face of death had given Jews their own Westerplatte, now he took as his hero the Jewish fighter, who could make the Germans taste fear and who could exact revenge.

The Jews could now die like Poles—honorably, in war:

> Block-numbers flutter on breasts,
> Our medals in the Jewish War,
> The shriek of six letters flashes with red,
> Like a battering-ram it beats REVOLT!
> And on the street a package
> Crushed and sticky with blood!
> JUNOS ARE ROUND

Galvanized by the January fighting, Szlengel began to see his poems as a new weapon to encourage resistance.[115] For the vast majority who could not join the ŻOB, this new will to live and to resist meant building a bunker. In his "What I Read to the Dead," Szlengel described the aftermath of the January fighting:

> Cement and bricks are being brought, the nights resound with the pounding of hammers and pickaxes. Water is pumped, wells are dug in basements. The shelters. A mania, a rush, a cardiac neurosis of the Warsaw Ghetto. Lighting, underground cables, drilling the passages, bricks again, ropes, sand . . . lots of sand. Sand. Bunks, cots. Supplies sufficient for months. Electricity, waterworks . . . Twenty centuries are written off by the SS man's whip. The cave epoch returns, oil lamps, village type wells. The long night has begun. People are going back under the ground. To escape from animals.[116]

The bunkers now became redoubts, symbols of Jewish determination. In his final poems between January and April 1943 Szlengel brought together the themes of Jewish and Polish resistance. As Rut Shenfeld points out, Szlengel, in his poem "Five Minutes to Twelve," paraphrased "Reduta Ordona," Adam Mickiewicz's paean to the last stand of a group of Polish rebels in the Polish Uprising of 1830–31.[117]

Szlengel died during the ghetto uprising in April 1943. He had taken refuge in the bunker of the well-known underworld figure Szymon Katz on Świętojerska 36. According to one eyewitness, Leon Naiberg, as the heavy fighting raged all around him, Szlengel spent his last days in Katz's bunker writing poems to encourage the Jews to fight back. In his diary entry of May 8, 1943, Naiberg wrote: "Yesterday evening the poet was still writing his poems, in which he praised the heroism of the fighters and mourned the fate of the Jews. But this was the last time [I saw him] because the bunker was captured."[118]

A Yearning for Heroism:
Yitzhak Katzenelson's "The Song of the Radzyner"

Yitzhak Katzenelson and Władysław Szlengel, as noted above, came from different worlds. Whereas Szlengel had absorbed the values of Polish culture and admired Poles for their sense of pride and honor, Katzenelson's moral compass was tuned inward, to Jewish culture and Jewish values. His belief in the nobility of Jewish culture carried much authority, given his knowledge of and regard for European literature. And as his audience—especially the leaders of the youth movements—prepared to fight, Katzenelson reminded them that before they fought to defend Jewish honor, they first had to remember what made their nation different.

Katzenelson, who had fled Lodz for Warsaw in November 1939, went through a profound transformation in the Warsaw Ghetto. Before the war this committed Zionist poet had written mostly in Hebrew; he had been called the "golden boy" of Hebrew letters.[119] He ran an important Hebrew school in Lodz and always identified himself as a teacher as well as a poet.[120] In the Warsaw ghetto, however, he switched to Yiddish, the language of the Jewish masses. He directed a theatrical studio and threw himself into cultural work with children. Katzenelson could and did bridge the "language gap"; he cooperated with both the Yiddishist IKOR and the Hebraist Tekuma.

In the ghetto Katzenelson became a mentor and intellectual guide to the Dror youth movement. He lectured at their seminars and spent much of his time at the Dror commune on Dzielna 34. Survivors of the ghetto remembered his spellbinding lectures on Hebrew literature and the Bible, especially on the Prophets. He and his students developed close ties of friendship and mutual respect.[121] Katzenelson depicted the horrors of the ghetto in several important poems that were passed hand to hand.[122] In a wartime memoir, Mordecai Tenenbaum-Tamaroff, who later died commanding the Jewish Uprising in the Białystok ghetto, wrote that he had had little interest in Katzenelson before the war, but in the Warsaw Ghetto the poet became "like our brother," someone who surpassed the great Hebrew poet Bialik. "A new Katzenelson, a 'Yiddish' Katzenelson, was born to us in the ghetto":

> He cursed better than [Bialik], his prophecies were more far-reaching,
> and his hatred inspired us more. We would give him a bit of the despera-

tion we were feeling and he would turn that into something that reached the skies and [through poetry] made it eternal. We created as a team. We took joy in each of his rhymes—we saw it as a collective achievement.[123]

Through Eliyahu Gutkowski, the Oyneg Shabes received some of Katzenelson's most important poems. Many other poems were buried in the Dror's archive and were retrieved only after the war.[124] (Ringelblum himself may have had a tense relationship with Katzenelson.)[125]

Like Abraham Lewin, Katzenelson suffered the shock of returning home one day in August 1942 to find that the Jewish police had taken his wife, Hannah, and two of his three sons, fourteen-year-old Bentzion and eleven-year-old Benjamin, to the Umschlagplatz. The loss shattered Katzenelson and threatened his sanity. He could not keep his thoughts from dwelling on their final agonies as they entered the gas chambers. Had the Germans killed the children separately from the adults, perhaps the gullibility and trusting optimism of childhood might have spared them the final moments of terror. But he knew that the Germans killed the children along with the adults, and so they knew full well that they would die with their parents.[126]

He found some comfort in his oldest son, Tzvi, and in the young people of Dror. But for all their talk of resistance, the youth movements, including Dror, were stunned by the Great Deportation. Throughout August and September each day seemed to bring greater humiliations and defeats. On September 3 the Germans not only killed Joseph Kaplan and Shmuel Breslav of Hashomer but seized the paltry cache of arms that the new Jewish Fighting Organization had managed to collect. This blow brought the Zionist youth movements to the brink of total despair. Many of the young Zionists now wanted to launch a suicidal attack on the Germans with nothing but their bare fists and knives. Finally, Yitzhak Zuckerman prevailed on his comrades to stand strong and rebuild the fighting organization.[127]

At least the young people plotted resistance. Older leaders, on the other hand, simply felt helpless, humiliated. On September 4, 1942, as the Germans ordered all the Jews remaining in the ghetto to gather in the "cauldron," Katzenelson was in a hideout with the two leaders of the Joint, Daniel Guzik and Yitzhak Giterman. With their access to relief funds, Guzik and Giterman had long been among the most respected, and powerful, in the ghetto. Long lines of people would wait patiently every day to see them. Now they, too, were helpless, cowering in the dark. Every now and then, when Katzenelson lit a match, the two men would glance at him—and quickly look away.[128] Only a few yards away the Germans were destroying the remnants of Warsaw Jewry—and they could do nothing but hide.

Dror "adopted" Katzenelson and Tzvi, arranging hideouts and protecting them. Katzenelson was with the Dror and Gordonia fighters on Zamenhof 58 when the Germans suddenly entered the ghetto on January 18, 1943. As they heard German jackboots climbing the stairs to their apartment and all seemed lost, Katzenelson told the young people that he was happy to die in the ranks of the fighting Zionist youth and that he believed in the eternal survival of the Jewish people. A moment later the door burst open, and a group of armed Germans entered. Zecharia Artstein and Hanoch Gutman calmly sat in a chair, Artstein seemingly absorbed in a book of Sholom Aleikhem stories. The Germans glanced at them and quickly entered the next room. Artstein pulled out a revolver, opened fire, and killed one of the intruders. As the startled Germans ran from the room, the young fighters killed a second German, whose body tumbled down the stairs.[129]

Soon after this incident Katzenelson and his son escaped to the Aryan side. For a short time they hid in the underground bunker that would later shelter Ringelblum and his family. In May 1943, having procured Honduran passports for himself and Tzvi, he joined the transport of "Latin American Jews" whom the Germans sent to the internment camp in Vitel, France. In April 1944 the Germans, informed that the original issuers of these passports did not recognize their validity, sent the "Latin Americans" first to Drancy and then to Auschwitz. Katzenelson and his son were gassed on May 3, 1944.[130]

From August 1942 right up to his own death, Katzenelson constantly wrote about his murdered loved ones, about his grief, about his hatred of the Germans, and about his love of the Jewish people. Today Katzenelson is remembered mainly for the important works he wrote in Vitel, France: the *Vitel Diary* and his masterpiece, "The Song of the Murdered Jewish People," which a friend, Miriam Novich, buried under a tree and retrieved after the war. What he wrote in the Warsaw Ghetto—including the important poetry buried in the second part of the Oyneg Shabes Archive—has received much less attention.[131] Yet in a time of unprecedented humiliation, when the very future of the Jewish people was at stake, Katzenelson told the condemned Jews to remember that they belonged to a great people, a nation that had given the world the legacy of the Bible. The Germans, not the Jews, should feel ashamed, because they had committed a crime that would forever sully mankind. Indeed, in April 1944, when the Jews in Vitel learned that they were going to Drancy, some committed suicide. Katzenelson would not. He told Nathan Eck that he wanted the burden of his death to be on the Germans, and he refused to absolve them of even a small measure of guilt ("Zoln zey zayn mer shuldig!" [Let them be more guilty!])[132]

Whereas many Jews in the ghetto compared the alleged spiritual superiority of previous generations to the demoralization of their own, Katzenelson rejected this simplistic assertion of national decline. Of course, his scorn and anger found many targets: certainly the Germans but also the Jewish police, the anti-Zionists and Bundists, and the acculturated Polish-speaking Jews. But for Katzenelson the Jewish nation itself had not lost its capacity for moral regeneration. Jews carried a spark that endured over time. And Katzenelson implored future generations to remember that the Jews of the Holocaust were as good as the best of the prophets and the greatest heroes of the Bible. In his "Song of the Murdered Jewish People," written in 1943–44, he described one of the many children he worked with in the Warsaw Ghetto: "He spoke a mix of Yiddish and holy tongue. No it was all the holy tongue. Listen! Listen! See his Jewish eyes, his forehead, how he raises his head . . . Isaiah! You were not as small, not as great, not as good, not as true, not as faithful as he."[133]

Two important poems on Jewish heroism and spiritual resistance, "The Song of Shlomo Zhelichowski" and "The Song of the Radzyner," found their way to the second part of the Oyneg Shabes Archive. Both poems were based on true stories and reflected Katzenelson's belief in the vitality of the nation, even in the face of death.

In May 1942, on the eve of the Jewish festival of Shavuot, the Germans hanged ten Jews in the market square in Zduńska Wola, including the pious Gerer Hasid Shlomo Zhelichowski. According to eyewitness accounts, Zhelichowski told his fellow Jews that they should be happy to have the chance to die for the sanctification of the name. On their last night he led them in the Yom Kippur prayers and suggested that they say the concluding service, Neilah, just before the Germans led them to the gallows. As the Jewish population of the town stood and watched, Zhelichowski went to his death singing his prayers.[134]

> Let us sing, Jews! To die like a Jew, such an honor / We are blessed. We die for our people, for the sanctification of the name / it is our great merit to hang on the gallows / let us sing Jews / let's sing a tune!

"The Song of the Radzyner," written between early July 1942 and January 1943 and read aloud by the poet to the members of Dror as they prepared for the armed uprising—was a clarion call for leadership to restore national pride and honor. Katzenelson told his friends in Dror that the spark of heroism was in each and every one of them and that their people had unique values and a distinct definition of heroism:

I will sing you a song of a hero / No, don't laugh, brothers / how does
a Jew come to sing songs of heroes?

Songs of heroes . . . sure! / why are you afraid? / such songs are for a
gentile / they belong to him.

Gentiles . . . to them belongs victory / only they have heroes / they
kill in war / and destroy entire worlds.

So it will be hard for me / There is a Jew, with no weapons and no
spurs / he does not shoot / His hands are pure, his heart is pure / and
pure, pure is his conscience.

And if this Jew spills any blood / it is only his own / so I am singing
you a song of a hero / but one in a very different tune.[135]

The subject of the poem was Shmuel Shlomo Leiner, the rebbe of Radzyn
and the scion of an illustrious Hasidic dynasty.[136] Early in the war Leiner fled
Radzyn for the town of Włodawa. Leiner's exemplary behavior during the
occupation became well known: Ringelblum mentions in his diary entry of
May 8, 1942, that Leiner had urged his fellow Hasidim to sell their personal possessions and give the proceeds to charity.[137] The Hasidim did not heed
his advice, and the Germans eventually confiscated the wealth that might
have helped the poor. Word also reached the ghetto that Leiner had told his
followers to flee to the forests and resist the Germans.[138] In June 1942 the
Dror bulletin *Yedies* reported that the Germans had arrested the Rebbe in the
Włodawa Ghetto. In an act of self-sacrifice, the bulletin reported, a young
man tried to save the rebbe by telling the Germans that he was Leiner. The
Nazis shot them both.[139] According to the Włodawa Memorial Book, German security Chief Nietschke arrested Leiner, released him in return for a
hefty ransom paid by the local Jews, and shortly thereafter shot him in the
Jewish cemetery. Soon other stories about how he died began to circulate. As
he faced execution, he was said to have spit in the faces of the Germans.[140]

Katzenelson's poem depicted sublime courage and self-sacrifice just a few
kilometers from the death camp Sobibór. The poet described how the rebbe spurned an opportunity from his followers to flee Włodawa for Warsaw,
where his disciples thought he would be safer.[141] Instead, he told his wealthy
followers from Warsaw to give him a large sack of money. The rebbe then dis-
guised himself as a simple peasant and trudged to the railroad line hauling
the sack. When he came upon a trainload of Jews on their way to the death
camp, most of them already dead, he offered the local peasants money to help
him carry the dead Jews for a Jewish burial, and even more money if they
found a Jew who was still alive.[142]

In the poem's lyrical descriptions of Lublin, Warsaw, and the Jewish shtetl,
Katzenelson evoked all the past glories of Polish Jewish history to especially

emphasize the massive scale of the disaster. Now more than ever a Jew had to remain a Jew and remember that he had work to do. One could mourn, one could cry, but one could not succumb to passivity and helplessness. To give the dead a proper burial was one of the most important commandments and one of the greatest acts of kindness, a "hesed shel emet."[143] When one did right by the dead, one acted entirely without selfish consideration.

In the boxcar full of Jewish bodies, the rebbe heard God crying in a corner. It had come to this: a murdered people and the rebbe and God all alone in a dark car filled with corpses. But the Radzyner was too busy to comfort God, who had to watch the murder of his people.

> Who is crying there? Who? And he entered the freight car,
> Sat in a dark corner, in silent pain, and he listened to God's sobs.
> The rebbe stayed in the corner a long time,
> In the empty, dark cavern of the wagon.
> He did not move, listened bravely to God's crying,
> Stayed still, and did not utter a word of comfort.[144]

God looked on in grief while the rebbe proved, to the very last, his love of the Jewish people. Could the very idea of God survive without Jews? Did transcendence come from God—or from each individual Jew? For Katzenelson, there could only be one answer. Without Jews, who would be left to comfort God?

The rebbe returned to the ghetto and proclaimed a fast. The Germans summoned him. His wife begged him to flee, but he willingly went to his death.

> If I could die like Rabbi Akiba
> They flay me with an iron comb
> My wife do not sin . . . like Rabbi Akiba, for God's name
> Don't cry . . . if I could have the honor
> For my Jews, for God . . . what joy
> And he left and did not return.[145]

Katzenelson, through the story of a Hasidic rebbe, at once confronted the disaster of his people and affirmed Polish Jewry and its national pride, based on an age-old fusion of religious and ethnic identity. Katzenelson was a passionate Zionist, whereas most Hasidic rebbes had fiercely fought the movement. But, by 1942, Hasidism had become for Katzenelson an important symbol of the spiritual vigor of East European Jewry, and a reminder of past Jewish resilience and vitality. In a time of religious and social crisis, in the eighteenth century, Hasidism had offered a new kind of religious experience and

section of "Song of the Murdered Jewish People," titled "To the Heavens," asks:

> Have we changed so much that you don't recognize us as of old?
> But why, we are the same—the same Jews that we were, not different,
> Not I . . . Not I will to the prophets be compared, lo and behold!
> But they, the millions of my murdered ones, those murdered out of hand . . .
>
> It's they . . . they suffered more and greater pains each one.
> The little, simple ordinary Jew from Poland of today . . .
> Compared to him, what are the great men of a bygone past?
> A wailing Jeremiah, Job afflicted, Kings despairing, all in one—it's they!
> . . . .
> You have no God in you! Open the doors, you heavens, open wide,
> And let the children of my murdered people enter in a stream.
> Open the doors for the great procession of the crucified,
> The children of my people, all of them, each of them a God—make room![150]

Katzenelson desperately hoped that these writings would survive. He elicited a promise from Natan Eck that, if Eck survived, he would do everything to find them and publish them. The Jews of the world had done so little to help their doomed brothers during the war: at least let them read their writings later. Or so Katzenelson hoped.

At about the same time that Eck made his vow to Katzenelson, Emanuel Ringelblum was busily writing essays and letters in his underground bunker in Aryan Warsaw. Both men, the fiery poet and the dedicated historian, spent their last weeks composing a final testament. For Katzenelson, it was "The Song of the Murdered Jewish People"; for Ringelblum, it would be his important historical work "Polish-Jewish Relations during the Second World War" and his equally significant work on the Jewish intelligentsia. Ringelblum and Katzenelson, who differed in so many important ways, now struggled to complete a final task that was strikingly similar: to leave a final testament that would defend the memory and honor of a murdered nation.

CHAPTER 9

A Historian's Final Mission

By late 1942 Ringelblum's worst fears were coming true. As he watched the destruction all around him, he probably realized that his chances of saving the archive, small as they were, were still better than the odds of saving Polish Jewry. Jewish survivors, especially returnees from the Soviet Union, might rebuild a postwar community but the rich, vibrant Polish Jewry of prewar days was gone forever. After the war there would be no more Historiker Krayz seminars in Warsaw, no more graduate students in the Vilna YIVO to discuss and study the treasures of the Oyneg Shabes.

The tense and depressing meeting of the executive committee on July 26, 1942, when it was resolved to send the archive to the YIVO in New York after the war—marked a stark contradiction to earlier hopes that the archive would be a vital resource for postwar Polish Jewry. When the committee authorized Lichtenstein to bury the archive right after that July meeting, it signaled its doubts about the community's survival.

Facing constant danger, shaken by the murder of his closest friends, torn between his work in the archive and his obligations to his family, Ringelblum summoned up great reserves of inner strength to continue his work. He did so because he knew that even if Polish Jewry did not survive the archive was still necessary. Without it, posterity would read the records of the killers but forget the voices of the victims. But what had been possible in the predeportation ghetto was now infinitely harder. Ringelblum worked under growing pressure and tension, his anguish manifest in the writings he left behind after the end of the Great Deportation.

After the deportations ceased for a time in September 1942 Ringelblum found a new focus. Instead of daily, weekly, and monthly notations that had recorded impressions and events, Ringelblum tried to analyze Jewish behavior in extremis, especially the reasons for the shift from stunned terror during the summer months to a grim determination to resist. The fighting organizations prepared for battle, and the remaining Jews built bunkers and hideouts. By 1943 few Jews were prepared to listen to German promises.

In his last months, from his return from the Trawniki camp in August 1943 until his death in March 1944, Ringelblum began his final mission as a historian. The ghetto lay in rubble, and his closest friends and mentors were either dead or out of reach. The old Oyneg Shabes no longer functioned—although it had a reincarnation of sorts in the archive of the Jewish National Committee that Hersh Wasser, Adolf Berman, and others continued on the Aryan side.[1] Ringelblum, a consistent proponent of history as a collective enterprise, now became a lonely chronicler. He sat in a corner of a crowded underground bunker and wrote nonstop. It was under these agonizing conditions that Ringelblum the historian wrote one of his best works, *Polish-Jewish Relations during the Second World War*. Ringelblum, the passionate Yiddishist, wrote this in Polish, perhaps subconsciously reaching out to a Polish readership, the same readership that had ignored him and his fellow Jewish historians before the war. Whatever happened to him personally, he hoped that postwar Poland would be a different country. And, besides, after the war, how many people would be left to read Yiddish?

IN EXTREMIS

During the summer of 1942 Ringelblum had neither the time nor the heart to make his regular journal entries. Instead, he scribbled cryptic phrases, random notes, whose very lack of coherence paralleled the fragmentation and destruction of the world around him.

> One goes before 5 o'clock, before the sentries. In order to be shot. The reason for Czerniakow's death . . . Hostages. 10,000 a day. The story about orphanages for 10,000 children. The behavior of the police. Threw the sick on the carts. People report [for deportation] because of hunger . . . 70 zl [zlotys] for bread. Judenrat employees as voluntary kidnappers. July 26 120 shot at the Umschlagplatz—sick and weak. Terrible conditions there.[2]

Disjointed notes such as these betrayed Ringelblum's own anxiety and confusion as his world disintegrated, and as his comrades and friends disappeared, one by one, into the boxcars.

The notes were also a reminder that he was human: in that terrible time he could be inconsistent in his judgments and unfair. For example, in one of these terse notes, perhaps written after the end of the first phase of the Great Deportation in September 1942, Ringelblum jotted down: "The suicide of Czerniakow. Too late—a sign of weakness."[3] Like several other leaders of left-wing parties and youth groups, Ringelblum clearly believed that Czerniakow, before his suicide, should have issued a public appeal to the Jewish population to resist the deportation.[4] Ringelblum, from the very start of the war, had been critical of Czerniakow. Although some of his attacks were justified, others revealed more about his own biases than about his objective judgment.[5]

If Czerniakow failed to call for mass defiance in July, neither did Ringelblum's own party or, for that matter, the leadership of the Aleynhilf. Moreover, at that point, since there were no arms in the ghetto, what did resistance actually mean? Did it mean a mass escape into Aryan Warsaw, incineration of the ghetto, or maybe individual attacks on Germans with knives or boiling water?

For at least six months the inner circle of the Oyneg Shabes had been compiling reports on the Final Solution, and Ringelblum knew in May and June that Warsaw would not avoid the fate of Lublin and other cities. Still, the Nazi assault of Warsaw Jewry caught Ringelblum off-guard, and for a few days he clung to illusions that he must have known were false. Michael Mazor recalled that when the Great Deportation began he told Ringelblum and Shakhne Zagan that the ghetto Jews should storm the walls and scatter through the city. But Ringelblum (along with Zagan) still hoped that the SS was planning only a partial deportation.

> My interlocutors [Zagan and Ringelblum] replied that there was hope
> of saving a part of the population, that it had not been proven that the
> Germans intended to carry out a total extermination, that they took into
> consideration certain exemption papers. As an example they cited the city
> of Rovno, where some twenty thousand Jews were brutally massacred,
> yet where six to seven thousand artisans together with their families lived
> and worked in tranquility, etc.[6]

Some indirect evidence supports Mazor's account. Both Ringelblum and Zagan attended a July 23 meeting of Jewish leaders to discuss how to react to the deportation order. Rabbi Zisha Frydman, who represented the Orthodox Agudas Yisroel, and Isaac Schiper strongly counseled against resistance. Rabbi Frydman proclaimed: "I believe in God and in miracles. God will not let his people, Israel, be destroyed. We must wait and a miracle will happen." Schiper also warned that resistance would cause the total liquidation of the

Warsaw Ghetto. Schiper's response at the meeting was recorded in the memoirs of Hersh Berlinski, the leader of the LPZ fighting group in the ŻOB, who was probably briefed on the meeting by Zagan or Ringelblum:

> I believe that we will be able to preserve the essence of the ghetto in Warsaw. We are in the midst of a war. Every nation sacrifices victims; we, too, are paying the price in order to salvage the core of the people. Were I not convinced that we can succeed in saving that core, I, too, would come to a different conclusion.[7]

In his own recollections of the meeting Ringelblum stressed the difficult responsibility that a call for resistance would have entailed; he did not mention whether he or Zagan supported such a course. Memories differ: Yitzhak Zuckerman wrote that the left Zionist parties supported the call for armed resistance, whereas Bundists Marek Edelman and Bernard Goldstein claimed that only Hashomer and Dror favored this course.[8] In any case, the July meeting broke up without having reached a decision. The participants intended to meet again, but the terror and chaos of the Great Deportation prevented them from doing so.

All available evidence suggests that Ringelblum basically agreed with Schiper. If one could not save the masses, then one should at least try to save a "core"—the intellectual and creative elite. Ringelblum strongly supported the controversial plan to use money from the Joint and other organizations to create a reserve fund to save the intelligentsia.[9] Also telling was Ringelblum's reaction to the death of Shmuel Breslav on September 3, 1942, which revealed that Ringelblum, at that time, saw resistance as a romantic pipedream: "The role of youth—the only ones who remained on the field of battle, *romantics, dreamers*—Shmuel, he couldn't take the tragedy of the ghetto."[10]

From the very first day of the Great Deportation, Ringelblum was being pulled in many different directions. He had to protect his wife and son but also had to worry about his own safety. He sought protection in his papers from the Aleynhilf, as well as in a work certificate from Bernhard Hallman's shop, an enterprise that did carpentry work for the German army. (The shop, notably, stood on a critical site: right beside the former Borochov school where Lichtenstein had buried the first part of the archive.)

Any illusions Ringelblum may have had that his high position in the Aleynhilf or his shop documents would guarantee his safety ended when the Germans hauled off Shakhne Zagan and his family on August 5, 1942. Zagan, the leader of the Left Poalei Tsiyon, had been one of the most prominent figures in the ghetto; even the Jewish police and notorious Gestapo agents like Yossele Kapote treated him with respect. But when the Germans, and not the Jewish police, were conducting manhunts, no one was safe. Zagan might have saved himself had he been willing to abandon his family. But, instead, he accompanied them to the Umschlagplatz.[11] Zagan was such an essential figure that, for a time, many Jews refused to believe he was dead; rumors floated that he had been sighted on the Aryan side. Only when Zagan failed to surface, Ringelblum recalled, did the realization sink in, even among skeptics, that deportation meant death.[12]

Zagan's deportation stunned Ringelblum. Yet another of his mentors, the leader of his party, was gone. Ringelblum idolized Zagan, and, except for Giterman, there was no one he relied on more for inspiration and advice. In September he lost two more of his closest friends, when Adolf and Basia Berman left the ghetto for the Aryan side.

The Bermans quickly became indispensable leaders of the Jewish underground in Aryan Warsaw, and provided the critical contacts and logistical support that enabled Ringelblum's family, Rachel Auerbach, and others to leave the ghetto. But, in the short run, their departure, coming so soon after the deaths of Zagan and Shimon Huberband, surely increased Ringelblum's already heavy psychological burden and sense of isolation.

Zagan's death also caused tensions within the party. The Bermans, in leaving the ghetto, had defied the wishes of the party organization.[13] Hersh Berlinski, one of the figures who now stepped forward to lead the party, was idealistic and brave, but survivors described him as "tough" and "hard"— significant sobriquets in a party that had never been distinguished by mild-mannered liberalism.[14] The abrasive Berlinski made high demands of himself and of others.[15] Although Ringelblum respected Berlinski, there was none of the closeness that had characterized his relations with Zagan or the Bermans.[16] During the ghetto uprising Berlinski would command the combat group of the LPZ.[17]

The evidence shows that, although Lichtenstein blamed Ringelblum for a failure to lead, during the Great Deportation Ringelblum often endangered himself trying to save as many people as he could. In the early days of the "Action," when the Germans promised exemption to employees of the Aleynhilf, he tirelessly produced and distributed Aleynhilf work certificates.[18] Once again, he worked under inhuman pressure. On July 23 Natan Eck witnessed an argument that took place in the Aleynhilf headquarters between Ringelblum and Menakhem Kirshenbaum, a leader of the General Zionists, over who had the authority to distribute the Aleynhilf certificates. As tempers flared, Kirshenbaum insulted Ringelblum by reminding him that he, Kirshenbaum, had been an established leader before the war, unlike "certain parvenus" who had come from nowhere. In a rare outburst of anger Ringelblum retorted that after the war people would be free to judge which of them had done more in the ghetto.[19] But in an instant the two men calmed down, both realizing the foolishness in arguing about status and honor when the Germans were wiping out the ghetto. As long as Ringelblum believed that Aleynhilf workers could evade the deportations, he did all he could to save them. Mazor recalled that Ringelblum fought hard to include in the exempted category not only full-time salaried workers but also Aleynhilf volunteers.[20]

Within a week, however, Ringelblum and everyone else in the Aleynhilf understood that none of this mattered: except for a few top leaders, who remained exempt from deportation for now, the Aleynhilf was doomed. Within a few weeks the Judenrat reduced the Aleynhilf exemption quota from three thousand to seventy-five.[21]

Ignoring the risks, Ringelblum was constantly at the Umschlagplatz, where his status as a top Aleynhilf leader—one of the lucky seventy-five—permitted him to distribute supplies to the trapped Jews. He did his best to rescue whoever he could. It was a grim ordeal, trying to save a chosen few—intellectuals, writers, teachers, and artists—from among the masses waiting their turn to enter the death trains.

One day, at the Umschlagplatz, Ringelblum noticed Leyb Shur, a renowned book collector, publisher, and librarian. Shur had devoted his whole life to Yiddish literature and to Yiddish books. In the Warsaw Ghetto he collected discarded books, rescued private libraries, and began a lending library in his apartment. He was especially helpful to Basia Berman when she needed Yiddish books to start a children's library in the ghetto.[22] When Ringelblum saw Shur, he asked a Jewish police officer, whom he knew well, to free him. He was successful with Shur, but at the very same time he failed to secure the release of two women teachers who had taught in the CYSHO schools.[23] Their screams and cries haunted him. As for Shur, his reprieve was short-lived. Unable to endure the constant manhunts and unable to afford bread which now cost one hundred zlotys a loaf, Shur soon hanged himself inside his beloved library, surrounded by all his books.

Ringelblum's vigils at the Umschlagplatz exposed him to insults, even violence, at the hands of Jewish collaborators. On one occasion he unsuccessfully tried to persuade Mieczysław Szmerling, the degenerate Jewish police commander of the Umschlagplatz, to release Dr. Yitzhak Lipowski, an economist who had worked with Ringelblum in the Joint before the war. Szmerling threatened Ringelblum and refused to let Lipowski go. A few days later Szmerling beat Ringelblum with his truncheon when the latter tried to secure the release of the pianist Halina Dickstein and the painter Regina Mundlak.[24] Ringelblum also mentioned that he received a beating at the hands of

Israel First, head of the economics section of the Judenrat and a notorious Gestapo agent.[25] (The ŻOB executed First on November 29, 1942.)

Genia Silkes, a party comrade, recalled how Ringelblum rescued her during the terrible selection at the "cauldron" in September 1942. She and her family found themselves trapped in an enormous courtyard near the headquarters of the Jewish police. Just when they were about to give up, they saw Ringelblum.

> He saw us, went up to us, and warned us to get out of that courtyard, since the first victims would be deported from there. We should try to get to the neighboring courtyard of the Judenrat on Zamenhof 19. Once there, he said, "we'll see." We were in a bad state. Being with Emanuel gave us strength. His presence eased our fear. Ringelblum goes forward and tells us to walk behind him. As we leave the courtyard we are stopped. Ringelblum tells the guards that we are his sister and brother-in-law. We find ourselves in the courtyard of the Judenrat. Ringelblum is worried; he does not rest. He tells me that it is dangerous to be here as well. We have to get out of here. He gives us an address, Mila 64, which contains the living quarters for the workers in Alexander Landau's shop. He tells us that when we get there to use his name and implores us to build a good hiding place. Emanuel helps us find an exit from the courtyard.[26]

With the temporary halt in the Great Deportation after September 12, Ringelblum resumed both his writing and his public activities. The Aleynhilf had disappeared during the Great Deportation; now he tried to revive a mutual aid organization among the Jews who were left in the ghetto.

At first glance Ringelblum's determination seemed quixotic. There were no more house committees, and hardly any children or old people. The sixty thousand remaining Jews were divided into two categories: "legal," those employed in shops or in other German enterprises both within and outside the ghetto; and "wild," those without the work numbers conferring legal status. Compared to the new situation in the ghetto, the pre-deportation days now seemed downright idyllic. How would a mutual aid organization function? What would be the point?

Yet Ringelblum also understood, precisely now, the absolute need for some kind of social organization that could maintain a minimal level of morale and cohesion. Practically everyone had lost a wife, parent, or child. Those few with close family members had to hide them in the shops and hope that the Germans or the *werkschutz*—the police force that guarded the shops—did not find them during their frequent searches. Many of the survivors were wracked with guilt for remaining alive after their loved ones had been taken away. They were also filled with anger at the Jewish police and shame that they themselves had offered no resistance to the deportations.

Adding to their humiliation, they now lived and worked in conditions that were worse than ever. By now everyone had heard of Treblinka, and few had any illusions about their ultimate fate. Just a few weeks earlier, hundreds and thousands of Jews had lived in the ghetto. Now they were gone. Discarded bedding and pillows, old clothing, broken furniture littered the courtyards. The Germans established a new enterprise, the Werterfassung, charged with looting anything of value. A new word entered the Jewish vocabulary, *shabreven* (to look for abandoned property).[27] Many Poles now came into the ghetto to buy up the possessions of the murdered Jews. The Poles drove hard bargains, reminding the Jews that soon they would be "turned into soap." Why, then, they asked the Jews, not just grab the few zlotys they offered for a jacket or a dress and at least have a good feed?

The Jews knew they were living on borrowed time. Life in the shops was filled with constant terror as the Germans kept returning to take more victims. In the course of a single day, the workers' moods oscillated between hope and resigned despair.[28] Most shops had orders and stocks of raw materials that guaranteed work for only a couple of months. The SS was constantly shutting down individual shops and deporting the Jewish workers. Nothing mattered now, many Jews thought, except to eat, drink, and be merry, and so they engaged in alcoholic debauches or in sexual promiscuity.[29] When Jews had lived in family units, Ringelblum noted, at least women tried to maintain minimal standards of cleanliness, but now, in the new apartment blocks allocated to each shop, they lived in squalor and despair. Earlier standards had broken down.[30] An anonymous author, in a memoir about the shops written for the Oyneg Shabes, stressed that the Germans had destroyed one of the most important pillars of moral support and cohesion: the family.[31]

The actual conditions in the shops and in other German workplaces threatened to destroy what slim shreds of dignity and self-respect remained. The Jews were totally at the mercy of the German shop owners and the Jewish foremen, and they knew it. Most shops paid no wages and did not even provide a minimal level of nutrition. Indeed, harried Jews paid out their last pennies to get a coveted "number." Ringelblum himself composed a short essay describing the extent to which the shops had degraded their workers.[32] No matter what happened to the surviving Jews, he wanted posterity to understand the exact conditions under which they had lived.

As for the "wild" Jews, they could be shot at any time. The slightest movement around the ghetto had become extremely dangerous. Jews could only remain in their shops or proceed under escort to their German workplaces.

No one else was allowed in the ghetto streets, which were now carved into noncontiguous sections.

Mutual aid, in Ringelblum's thinking, could help reestablish a modicum of decency and responsibility. Together with Yitzhak Giterman, as well as Abram Gepner and Gustaw Wielikowski from the Judenrat, he founded the Central Committee to Support Work in the Shops (CKPPwS). Its purpose— as stated in an official memorandum to the Germans—was to increase the productivity of the Jewish population by establishing new employment opportunities for those still unemployed, especially wives of shop workers and children over the age of ten.[33] The committee would also try to improve sanitary conditions in the housing blocks, help the sick, arrange medical care, provide clothing, find extra rations for those engaged in heavy labor, and arrange loans. The committee stressed that only a ghetto-wide organization that united all the shops could cope with the challenges of increasing productivity in the ghetto. Therefore the project proposed a central board, composed of delegates from all the shops as well as from the Judenrat that would meet regularly and allocate resources. The project also outlined a grandiose table of organization that encompassed shop committees and regional committees.

Since the German authorities would read Ringelblum's draft proposal, he had to pretend that he was suggesting ways to solve the routine concerns of a normal urban community and not the extraordinary problems of a ghetto that in only six weeks had lost 80 percent of its population. Indeed, the German officials responsible for the ghetto—Karl Georg Brandt and Gerhardt Mende of the local Gestapo—insisted on what they knew full well was a pretense of normalcy and missed few opportunities to engage in cynical humor. In the fall of 1942 Brandt had urged the Jews to reopen coffee houses and places of entertainment. He also reminded them to open schools for children, since "children are the future of the nation."[34] Although Oyneg Shabes statistics showed that 99 percent of the ghetto's children had been deported, the CKPPwS project nonetheless stressed that one of the committee's major goals had to be the provision of day care for children so that their parents could work more productively.

Ringelblum had few illusions about German plans for the remaining Jews. Nonetheless he and Lipe Bloch built up the self-help organization in Bernhard Hallman's shop. They interviewed destitute Jews and then allocated money, food, and clothing, distributing more than fifty thousand zlotys.[35] This project also gave Ringelblum the chance to work closely with Yitzhak Giterman. Now that Zagan was gone, Giterman's friendship and support were more important than ever.

Ringelblum knew that less than 1 percent of the sixty thousand Jews left in the ghetto could join the ranks of the active fighters in the ŻOB or in the Revisionist ŻZW. For the others, left outside the fighting organizations, the youth movements and the political parties, as well as the mutual aid committee, might give them a sense that they still constituted a community.

> The shops that had more "takers" than "givers" were supposed to get help from the shops that were better off. The meetings of the representatives of the mutual aid committees of the various shops constituted a new attempt to organize the communal energies of what was left of Warsaw Jewry. Mutual aid would provide a cover to discuss the basic questions facing the Jewish community. The shop committees began to organize communal drives; for example, a collection of clothing for Jews that were returning from the labor camps had excellent results. Other projects were planned, including collections of money . . . but this all came to an end after the January 1943 action, which also took the life of Dr. Giterman.[36]

The CKPPwS enabled Ringelblum to move from shop to shop, meet the various self-help committees, and enjoy free access to everyone, including Wielikowski on the Judenrat, Abraham Gepner and Shmul Winter in the provisions department, and the leaders of the ŻOB combat units that were hurriedly being formed. Thus he became an eyewitness to the preparations for armed resistance.

"WHY DIDN'T THEY RESIST?"

A cornerstone of Ringelblum's prewar historical credo had been his admiration for the Jewish masses and his determination to use history to record their resilience and creativity and to rescue forgotten Jews from oblivion. In his essay on Schiper written in the last months of his life, he repeated what had so impressed him in the 1920s: Schiper's call to remember not only the "Sabbath Jews" but also the ordinary weekday Jews, those who not only prayed and studied but also slaved to earn their daily bread.[37] Before the war Ringelblum had worked hard to preserve the memory of these Jews; as a young volunteer in the YIVO, he had opened the envelopes in which young Jews in remote shtetlekh sent their documents and local histories. As editor of the *Folkshilf* he had printed the letters and reports sent by shopkeepers and shoemakers. As soon as he arrived in Warsaw as a poor twenty-year-old student, he had taught tired young workers in the slums about history and Yiddish culture. Now, in 1942, he stood at the Umschlagplatz and watched the Jewish masses go to their deaths. If he had felt a moral obligation before the war to protect the memory of seventeenth-century Jewish apprentices and eighteenth-century wandering beggars, then how could he feel as he watched the destruction of Polish Jewry?

The temporary lull gave Ringelblum a chance to gather his thoughts and think more deeply about Jewish responses to German persecution and mass murder. From the very beginning of the war, he had heard serious charges leveled against Polish Jewry: moral weakness, corruption, callousness, lack of national pride. Now a new accusation had joined the litany: that the Polish Jews had let themselves be destroyed like "sheep to the slaughter."

Ringelblum understood the bitter anger of many of his friends and associates at Jewish "passivity." He had certainly read what Perle had written in "Khurbm Varshe." At about the same time another essay, written for the Oyneg Shabes by a Jew who was working in Brauer's shop, emphasized the enduring shame of the Jewish police:

> [These were] the offspring of a people that called itself the "merciful
> and the children of the merciful." In the provinces the Jewish police
> also [helped the killers]. Could such a thing have occurred with another
> people? I cannot imagine that something similar could have happened
> with Englishmen or Americans. Perhaps such a people is not worthy of
> a better fate. Warsaw Jewry had cared little for the plight of the refugees
> from the provinces. Now it has perished together with them.[38]

The author of this essay, composed in elegant Yiddish, was well versed in both European and Jewish culture, and quoted copiously from the Hebrew Bible; he cited both Rousseau and Tolstoy as he questioned whether "progress," technology, and science had any impact on human morality. Until the very last moment, the writer had not believed that war would break out or that such mass murder could happen 150 years after the French Revolution.

If this author, who experienced the horror himself, could echo Shie Perle and question—however rhetorically—whether the Jews deserved their fate, then what would future historians say? And what judgments would they render? As the anger and self-reproach increased among the survivors, Ringelblum felt a growing responsibility to leave a sober, balanced historical record.

But the task grew ever more difficult. Ringelblum himself struggled to explain the collaboration of the Jewish police:

> People here keep trying to figure out [*men brekht zikh itzt dem kop iber
> der retenish*] how Jews, who were mostly educated people, former law-
> yers . . . could murder their own brothers. How could it happen that
> Jews could load women and children, the sick and the old, onto the
> trains, knowing as they did that all were going to their deaths. There

are those who believe that each people gets the police they deserve, and that the malignancy—helping the occupier kill three hundred thousand Jews—has affected the whole society and not just the police, which is after all just one part of that society.[39]

No matter how sordid the record of the Polish police, at least they did not hunt down their brothers. The Jewish policemen did their dirty work and gave no sign that they felt any guilt or regret. Day by day they caught more Jews than their daily quota, in order to build up a reserve credit for the next day. And Ringelblum noted that they looked happy, smug, overjoyed at the loot they would share with the Ukrainians.

The horror of what he had seen and suffered at the Umschlagplatz was taking its toll. Those around him were full of rage and anger. Could Ringelblum, who was seeing the murder of his people, still rise above his emotions and continue to record the facts? As a Marxist, he had rejected the notion that entire peoples could hate or that eternal and implacable anti-Semitism would always govern relations between Jews and non-Jews. The archive's treatment of German-Jewish relations had been the preeminent example of Ringelblum's determination not to let the war erode prewar values. The guidelines that the Oyneg Shabes prepared for the "Two and a Half Years" project on German-Jewish relations had explicitly ruled out any blanket condemnations of the German people. Several testimonies in the archive described Germans who had helped Jews and were revolted by Nazi behavior. The Oyneg Shabes guidelines stressed the need to see the Germans not as an undifferentiated mass but to take into account social and regional differences and to develop a nuanced approach to understanding the reactions of various Germans to Jewish suffering. This approach also fit the Marxist and humanist predilections of people like Ringelblum, Wasser, and Gutkowski.

Ringelblum could not forget that millions of Germans had, in the past, voted for the SPD and the Communists.[40] In 1940 he still believed that even the many Germans who hated Jews did so out of ignorance. More than once he cited a story, which he had probably heard from Yitzhak Giterman, about Jewish POWs who had been sent to work on German farms in 1939–40 and had impressed the German peasants with their industriousness. One German farmer was supposed to have told a Jewish POW that "you came to us as 'dirty Jews' but you are leaving as honored children of Israel."[41] In a diary entry of March 28, 1940, Ringelblum noted that, although German civilians and soldiers began to treat Jewish POWs with respect and even warmth, relations between Jewish and Polish POWs were much less cordial.[42]

In May 1942 he mentioned accounts of growing unrest in Germany, of pamphlets calling on the "soldiers, workers, intelligentsia and the popular masses to revolt against the regime."[43] His explanation of Nazi anti-Semitism was quite close to what later scholars would call the concept of generic fascism—that Jew hatred and extermination were the desperate tools of an ideology fighting to protect a dying capitalist system, and certainly did not express the views of the German masses.

On June 30, 1942, shortly after hearing, on a BBC broadcast, that the Nazis had already murdered seven hundred thousand Polish Jews, Ringelblum wrote the following in his diary:

> All those who have a chance to meet Germans know quite well that they do not know about the murders and slaughters that are being carried out outside the cities or in murder factories like Belzec. The Occupier is afraid that the German population, even the German soldiers, might learn of the murder of the Jews. Therefore he is trying to kill the Jews in secret. . . . If the foreign countries only react [to the news of mass murder] with speeches and threats, then what might really save us is the [Nazi] fear of German public opinion.[44]

He recalled that when certain Germans heard the news of Chełmno they openly worried about what would happen to their wives and children when the world learned of these atrocities.

Although he had always tried to maintain a historian's objectivity, even when assessing German behavior, by September 1942 Ringelblum had seen too much and a new tone crept into his comments regarding the German people. He no longer believed, as he had in June, that the Nazi regime was trying to hide the news of the Final Solution from the German people. The first issue of the new Polish-language Oyneg Shabes bulletin, *Wiadomości,* dated November 14–21, 1942, stated that "the Germans are no longer concealing their criminal plans concerning the Jews. On November 10, 1942, the *Deutsche Allgemeine Zeitung* . . . wrote that 'the answer to the Jewish bid for world domination has been a necessary struggle to exterminate European Jewry, a process that is already quite advanced.'"[45]

On December 22, 1942, *Wiadomości,* referred to the "brutalization [*zezwierzęcenia*]" of the Germans. It printed accounts of German sadism perpetrated not by the SS but by ordinary German civilians and soldiers. In Modlin, thirty-two Jews were clubbed to death for arriving five minutes late to work. The German killers "were German soldiers, not SS men!" The bodies of the victims were horribly disfigured: brains oozed out of shattered skulls, and faces and limbs were smashed beyond recognition—and all this the soldiers did in full view of the other Jewish workers. In Siedlce, *Wiadomości* reported, an incident occurred that "only those who knew the 'Herrenvolk' firsthand would believe." In the course of its normal operations the German construction firm, Rechmann, would murder Jewish workers who were too weak to continue working. But recently,

> [The firm] allowed itself the following novelty: three Jewish workers were immured alive in the concrete of a building under construction. The screams of the suffocating victims sent the perpetrators into paroxysms of joy. We emphasize that these acts were committed by German civilians [that is, neither the SS nor the Wehrmacht].[46]

In its issue of January 1–8, 1943, *Wiadomości* reported that the murder of the Jews, which the Oyneg Shabes saw as a prelude to the forthcoming German murder of the Poles, forced "hard conclusions" about the Germans (*groźnych dla Niemców wniosków*):

> We would to leave this issue to experts—political leaders, educators, psychologists. But we want to stress that in the whole course of human history, from the Stone Age until the present day, on every continent and in every culture, it is impossible to find even the slightest precedent [for this genocide]. What made this possible was the tragic combination of particular factors: the psychological collapse following the [defeat of 1918], the breakdown of moral and ethical norms, nationalist megalomania strangely combined with an inferiority complex, [and] the effects of modern technology.[47]

And in the underground hideout, sometime in late 1943 or early 1944, Ringelblum wrote to Berman:

> No other people has produced as many sadists, perverts, and butchers . . . as the German people. We will not take up the question of punishing the SS, SD, Volksdeutsche, civil servants, and, in general, all Germans directly responsible for the murder of Jews and Poles. The greatest punishment would not compensate for what happened to Polish Jewry.[48]

After the war, Ringelblum added, Germans who had stood by and done nothing should be forced to wear a red mark, the mark of Cain, on their foreheads.[49]

But this outburst of anger and rage did not necessarily mean that Ringelblum had renounced his Marxism or even that he now believed in essentialist readings of national character. After all, in his essay on Yitzhak Giterman, written about the same time as his letter to Berman, Ringelblum recalled what Giterman had said just after the latter's return from German internment in 1940. The two had met for a Passover Seder at the apartment of Shakhne

Zagan, and the conversation around the table turned to the question of taking revenge on the Germans after the war. As Ringelblum recounted:

> Even leftist Jews said that the Germans, for the most part, were a people of murderous instincts who had to be eliminated from Europe. Giterman opposed the idea of collective revenge. . . . He met a lot of humane Germans in the camp. . . . There will be no end to the mutual cycle of killing . . . if we try to take revenge. The Germans will then try to take revenge [and the vicious circle will continue]. Others who sat around the Seder table said that the new social order [that will follow the war] will take revenge on the classes that are guilty for Hitlerite Imperialism and for the murders of Jews, Russians, and other peoples.[50]

This private letter to his friend Berman indeed revealed Ringelblum's inner turmoil and grief, but ultimately he rose above his feelings and continued to fulfill his mission. He had set himself a task, one that could be accomplished only if he remained true to the scholarly principles he had learned from Handelsman, Schiper, and others. Friends like Perle were composing bitter threnodies for the archive. He understood, and perhaps even sympathized and certainly believed, that they should form an essential part of the historical record. But in the shrinking Warsaw Ghetto, he would remain what he had always been—a historian. From the very beginning of his career as a historian, Ringelblum had seen no contradiction between his obligations as a scholar and his duties to his people. Objective scholarship that avoided apologetics, bitter accusations, and blatant emotion was the best way to serve the nation.

Ringelblum's writings at this time showed a particular concern with three issues: the moral level of Jewish society, the problem of Jewish resistance, and Polish-Jewish relations. In the early years of the war Ringelblum expressed a basic optimism about the moral level and psychological resilience of Polish Jewry—even as he recorded a disturbing pattern of corruption and informing, especially among certain groups such as doctors, porters, and the Jewish police. He saw this resilience evinced in several ways: in the house committees and the self-help organization; in the appearance of new, hitherto unknown leaders; in smuggling; in the low suicide rate; in Jewish evasion of German legal decrees; and in what he saw as the growing ability of a large section of Warsaw Jewry to find economic niches that would enable them to survive.

On March 27, 1940, he noted that "the Jewish masses have not fallen apart [*hobn zikh nisht ayngebrokhn*]."[51] In May 1940 he wrote, "It would be bad indeed if the war lasted as long as the Jews can hold out, because the Jews will be able to hold out longer than the war will last."[52]

This belief in the resourcefulness of the Jewish masses accompanied a reluctance to join those who interpreted the corruption and callousness in the ghetto as symptoms of a deeper crisis of Jewish society as a whole. Ringelblum consistently warned against overstating the moral failings of the Jewish masses. Matters were bad enough, he wrote, without making them seem even worse. On the other hand, as the crises of the Aleynhilf and house committees deepened, he expressed a growing anger at both the Judenrat and the Jewish bourgeoisie for failing the basic test of morality and decency.

By 1941 and 1942 Ringelblum had lost the cautious optimism of the first year of the war. The onset of mass murder coincided with his realization that the Aleynhilf was failing to save the poor, and that the best he could hope for was to save a chosen elite. His diary entries in the spring of 1942 sound a new note of urgency, even desperation. One reason for his momentary elation at the BBC broadcast of the news of German mass murder was his belief that the Jews were reaching the end of their tether. On May 8, 1942, he asked, "When will the war end? The Jews cannot hold out much longer."[53]

As he mulled the ongoing extermination of Polish Jewry, he noted that desperate Jews were turning for comfort to the study of history. Historical novels like Tolstoy's *War and Peace* had become very popular in the ghetto, as were stories of previous Jewish martyrdom. Jews loved to think, he wrote, that Hitler would meet the same fate as Napoleon.[54] But in the weeks that preceded the Great Deportation Ringelbum himself realized that what the Germans were doing to the Jewish people was so unprecedented that history could offer few easy lessons and very small comfort. In June 1942 he wrote that fascism, the last great spasm of a dying capitalist system, had staked its final card on radical anti-Semitism and genocide.[55] He was certain that Hitler would lose the war, but, as he implied in June 1942, he may well win his war against the Jews.

The paradigm of Fascism helped Ringelblum explain Nazi persecution, but it hardly explained Jewish responses to it. Could Jewish history offer any helpful perspectives? As he searched for precedents he focused his attention first on "Kiddush Hashem," the sanctification of God's name. In the past Kiddush Hashem had been an important model for Jews facing persecution. Rather than betray their faith, Jews chose death.[56] Such martyrdom in the past had asserted Jewish acceptance of death as proof of ultimate devotion to God (*yesurim shel ahava*).[57] Kiddush Hashem, not armed resistance, had become the valorized Jewish response to attempts to make Jews renounce their faith.[58] The rabbis remembered Rabbi Akiva for his willingness to die for the glory of God, not for his support of the Bar Kokhba revolt. By the early twentieth century, however, the concept of Kiddush Hashem had become more problematic. In his important poem, "City of Slaughter," H. N. Bialik savagely parodied the passive behavior of Jewish men in the Kishinev pogrom and inspired a new determination to resist anti-Semitic assaults.[59]

Ringelblum's diary referred to discussions on the subject among the ghetto intelligentsia. Indeed, Rachel Auerbach noted that on the night of April 17, 1942, just before the Germans murdered Menakhem Linder and fifty-two others, Ringelblum had been scheduled to give a lecture in the soup kitchen on Kiddush Hashem in Jewish history.[60]

Ringelblum's ongoing interest in the problem of Kiddush Hashem cannot be explained by a sudden fascination with the fine points of Jewish religious law. Nor was his primary aim to disparage religious Jews or make invidious comparisons with the behavior of their ancestors. Rather, the problem of Kiddush Hashem exemplified Ringelblum's growing awareness that the suffering of Polish Jewry had no precedents in Jewish history. In previous generations Jews could die for Kiddush Hashem precisely because their killers gave them a choice. If they renounced their faith, they could save themselves. The Nazis, on the other hand, did not care whether Jews observed their religion or converted. In those circumstances, what did this traditional form of spiritual resistance mean? If Kiddush Hashem was irrelevant, then how should Jews respond?

A diary entry of March 23, 1941, introduced an intriguing new slant on this subject. "Today," he wrote, "Kiddush Hashem is being sublimated into a determination to keep the Jews alive [vyfisuhuln di yidishe bafelkerung]."[61] Ringelblum was referring to what others called "Kiddush Hahayim," the sanctification of life. In the past when the enemy wanted to convert Jews, resistance meant to refuse apostasy, even at the cost of one's life. In this war, when the Nazis wanted to kill the Jews, resistance meant doing what one could to stay alive and to keep other Jews alive.[62]

In December 1942, after he had witnessed the destruction of most of Warsaw Jewry, Ringelblum posited a historical alternative to Kiddush Hashem: the subterfuge of the Marrano. In early modern Spain, Jews had pretended to convert to Catholicism in order to save their lives.

> If we study our history carefully, we will see that Kiddush Hashem is not the norm. Just the opposite. Marranodom, pretending to be a Christian [was quite common]. Jews always adapted to difficult circumstances, always knew how to survive the most difficult times.[63]

The Marrano, who lacked the sublime heroism of the Jew who died for Kiddush Hashem, survived to build Jewish communities elsewhere. Reading carefully, it was clear that Ringelblum preferred survival to martyrdom.

By the spring of 1942 irrefutable evidence of mass murder impelled Ringelblum to confront another option: active resistance. Why, he asked, were Polish Jews not fighting back against their killers? He had heard reports that strong, healthy Jewish POWs had let themselves be murdered without raising a hand. Dror couriers Frumka Plotnicka and Chava Folman had told the Oyneg Shabes that in Hrubieszów they had seen young Zionist pioneers marched to their doom guarded by a handful of men.[64] The Zionist youth had made no effort to escape.

In June 1942, when he knew that the liquidation of the Warsaw Ghetto might start at any time, Ringelblum wrestled to understand this apparent Jewish passivity. An acquaintance from Biała Podlaska who had witnessed the deportation of the local Jews to the Sobibór death camp, had asked Ringelblum:

> How long? How long will we go like sheep to the slaughter? Why are we quiet? Why doesn't anybody launch the call to go into the forests, to fight back?[65]

In his struggle to answer these questions, Ringelblum betrayed his own uncertainty. He noted that when the Germans liquidated a ghetto they usually took the old, the sick, and the children first. Those best able to resist were lulled into thinking they might survive. But he also admitted that three years of brutal occupation had produced terrible psychological scars, including "spiritual collapse." Ringelblum reluctantly admitted that the stories and rumors about Jewish resistance were probably false: young Jews were going to their deaths without a fight.[66]

In the end, Ringelblum found an explanation that redounded to the credit of the Jewish masses:

> Jews did not resist anywhere, they passively went to their deaths and they did so in order to let the other Jews remain alive. Because each Jew knew that to raise a hand against the Germans meant that he was endangering fellow Jews in another city and perhaps even in another country. For this reason three hundred POWs let themselves be shot on the road from Lublin to Biala, even though these were soldiers who had fought bravely for Poland's freedom. To be passive, not to lift up a hand against the Germans, this has become the quiet, passive heroism of the ordinary Jew [iz gevorn dos shtile passive heldentum fun dem yidishn masnmensh]. This, it seems, had been the quiet vital instinct of the masses, which tells everyone that they should act in this way and in no other. And I think that no agitation or propaganda can help here. It is impossible to fight a mass instinct, one can only submit to it.[67]

Thus, in the same entry in his diary, Ringelblum offered two contradictory explanations of the Jewish refusal to fight back, one attributable to the cost of years of horrors, the other a morally grounded active choice of the Jewish masses who, in order to protect their fellow Jews from German reprisals, renounced the urge to resist. This contradiction reflected Ringelblum's own confusion and the difficulty he faced when trying, in June 1942, to describe and understand a crime whose enormity and novelty had taken him—and his fellow Jews—completely by surprise. Like writers in other ghettos, Ringelblum was struggling to find the right words—and the right thoughts—to grasp what was happening.

After the end of the first phase of the Great Deportation in the fall of 1942, Ringelblum returned to his analysis of Jewish responses to Nazi genocide. A short note entitled "WHY?" written on October 15, 1942, reveals pain and puzzlement:

> Why was there no resistance when they [Germans] deported three hundred thousand Jews from Warsaw? Why did the Jews let themselves be taken like sheep to the slaughter? Why did the enemy have such an easy and smooth task? Why did the executioners not suffer even a single death? Why could fifty SS men (some say even fewer), with the help of a detachment of two hundred Ukrainians and Latvians, carry this out without difficulties?[68]

Yet within a couple of months, just as he had done in the "Two and a Half Years" project, Ringelblum once again weighed the evidence and tried to rebut some of the more extreme condemnations of Jewish behavior. In contrast to his essays of June and October, or to his hurried notes of the summer, Ringelblum now had the time and relative perspective to analyze the absence of resistance. By way of answering his own series of questions, Ringelblum did not exculpate the Jews, but he did try to put their passive behavior into an understandable context. First, Ringelblum wrote, the Jews faced a cunning and ruthless enemy who used a lethal combination of guile and overwhelming force. He compared the German extermination program to a well-planned and well-executed military campaign based on surprise, deception, overwhelming power, and speed. Second, the Germans also exploited internal divisions within Jewish society and made expert use of a fifth column—the Jewish police and an army of informers. Third, the Germans also exploited the admirable wish to protect the weak and vulnerable, so that people accompanied children and parents to their deaths, even at the cost of their own lives.

Implicitly Ringelblum defended Polish Jewry against the accusations hurled by Perle and others that the Jews were a pariah people that had lost its dignity and self-respect. Rather, he argued, the speed and brutality of the German campaign had caught the Jews off-guard. Was it so surprising, Ringelblum implied, that a military machine that had smashed entire armies in weeks could also crush the Jews, at least for a time?[69]

Conversely Ringelblum reiterated his belief that Jews had resisted as best they could, by trying to stay alive, for few committed suicide, and by trying to avoid psychological collapse.

> The people . . . and the great majority of the intelligentsia did not allow itself to collapse psychologically and fought a passive battle for as long as possible. The answer to the question of why Jews did not defend themselves should be this: the Jews waged a strong, successful [*gelungenem*] resistance on the psychological front. No other people on earth would have been able to show the psychological staying power of the Jews.[70]

The Jews who were left in Warsaw after the Great Deportation were quickly regaining resourcefulness and determination, spurred in part by the shame they felt—heightened by Polish taunts—for not having resisted those who killed their loved ones, and also by a total mistrust in German promises and assurances.

> We are seeing the corroboration of the well-known psychological law that slaves who are totally beaten down cannot revolt. Now it seems that the Jews are recovering a bit from the heavy blows; they have sobered up as a result of their sufferings and have concluded that [passively] going to the slaughter did not make the number of victims smaller but, on the contrary, it made the number larger. No matter whom you talk to now, you hear the same thing: we should not have allowed the Great Deportation to have taken place. We should have gone into the streets, we should have burned down everything, blasted the walls and run to the other side. The Germans would have taken their revenge. It would have cost tens of thousands of casualties, but not three hundred thousand. Now we are covered in shame and ignominy, both in our own eyes and in the eyes of the entire world, since our passivity gave us nothing. This should not happen again. Now we must resist. Children and adults must defend themselves against the enemy.[71]

In late 1942 Ringelblum wrote a short essay, "Will We Stay?" which showed just how much he had changed since July, when he still believed that the Germans might spare a small core of productive Jews. Now he had no illusions.[72] The Nazis planned to kill all the Jews regardless of economic considerations. Why, then, did the Nazis leave tens of thousands of Jews in the Warsaw

Ghetto? It was to preserve an "alibi," a scapegoat to blame for whatever went wrong. But if the Nazis faced final defeat, one of their last acts would be to kill the remaining Jews.

As Ringelblum noted in his essay "Hideouts," once the Warsaw Jews lost their illusions and their faith in German promises, they expressed their determination to resist by building hideouts. These hideouts became ever more elaborate. Resourceful Jewish engineers connected many of them to the city water supply and even to the city electricity and gas supply. Many were cooperative ventures, where people pooled their resources to build comfortable bunkers with adequate ventilation systems and enough food supplies to last for months. For many Jews, the hideouts no longer were intended just to help them survive the next German "action." With the war news lifting their hopes—Allied victories in Stalingrad and North Africa—many even let themselves think that a good hideout might allow them to live to see the final German collapse.[73]

ARMED RESISTANCE

As feverish efforts to procure weapons and organize Jewish fighting groups continued, Ringelblum stepped forward to raise money for the fighters and to document and explain why the surviving Jews swung their support to the fighters. The Germans interrupted Ringelblum's work on a history of the Jewish resistance in Warsaw with his arrest on March 7, 1944.[74]

In the fall of 1942 most of those who comprised the executive committee of the Oyneg Shabes—Ringelblum, Giterman, Menakhem Kon, Lipe Bloch, Winter, and Landau—joined a new finance committee of the ŻOB, formed to raise money for weapons.[75] It is hard to say how much money the group raised, but it was probably far less than what the fighting organization raised at gunpoint from shakedowns of wealthy Jews ("exes"), an activity for which people like Ringelblum were temperamentally unsuited. Ringelblum acknowledged that, because his committee collected money by voluntary donations, it raised relatively little cash. Still, Shmuel Winter's diary records the disbursement of sizable funds to the ŻOB and of Ringelblum's role in it.[76]

Two separate Jewish fighting organizations arose in the ghetto, the ŻOB and the Revisionist ŻZW (Żydowski Związek Wojskowy [Jewish Military Union]).[77] The ŻOB, with a wider political base, was organized around combat units based on political parties and youth groups. Aligned with the ŻOB were two other organizations, the Jewish National Committee (ŻKN) and the Jewish Coordinating Committee. (ŻKK). The ŻKN arose because the

Polish underground government stipulated that it would enter negotiations only with an authoritative body that represented the major Jewish political parties. It did not want to talk to youth organizations. The Bund, for ideological reasons, would not join the ŻKN but agreed to sit on a special "coordinating committee," thus declaring that its cooperation with Zionists was a tactical move and not a betrayal of principle. Long and complicated negotiations to include the Revisionists in the ŻOB failed. As a result, they set up their separate fighting organization, the ŻZW (Jewish Military Union).[78]

Ringelblum, determined to chronicle the entire story of Jewish resistance, tried to establish closer ties with both the ŻOB and the ŻZW. Surprisingly the ŻZW was quite forthcoming. The Left Poalei Tsiyon, like the other parties and youth groups in the ŻOB, despised the Revisionists and often referred to them as Jewish fascists. But somehow the ŻZW leaders overlooked their political differences with Ringelblum, perhaps regarding him as a respected and trusted communal leader who was not blinded by political animosities. At any rate, they invited him to their headquarters and showed him their arsenal. He was quite impressed:

> . . . I saw the ŻZW weapons cache. It was located in an uninhabited
> house on Muranowska 7 in a six-room apartment on the first floor.
> A first-rate radio was installed in the headquarters. There was also a type-
> writer. For several hours I spoke with the military leadership, who were
> armed with revolvers shoved into their belts. Weapons of all kinds hung
> on hooks along the walls: light machine guns, rifles, various kinds of re-
> volvers, hand grenades, ammunition belts, pouches with bullets, German
> uniforms . . . the room buzzed with activity and resembled a military
> headquarters. They received reports of expropriations which the different
> groups carried out to make rich Jews pay for weapons. I witnessed a deal
> with a former officer of the Polish army where the ŻZW paid 250,000
> [zlotys] for weapons with 50,000 as a down payment.[79]

In the very last months of his life, Ringelblum redeemed the trust that the Revisionists had shown in him. In a letter written to Adolf Berman on December 28, 1943, he insisted that any future history of the ghetto uprising include the role played by the ŻZW.[80]

Ringelblum also described his visit to the fighting group of the Left Poalei Tsiyon, affiliated with the ŻOB. Not everyone in the ŻOB was willing to welcome him and share secrets. Yitzhak Zuckerman, the deputy commander of the ŻOB, kept him at arm's length.[81] We can only speculate on the reasons for this reserve, if Zuckerman's account is indeed accurate. Relations between Ringelblum and Dror had never been close and, as we have seen, it was Gutkowski who had served as the main contact between Dror and the

Oyneg Shabes. The LPZ also bickered with Zuckerman and Anielewicz over the allocation of weapons and the proper relationship between the political parties and the youth groups in the ŻOB .[82] And while Ringelblum and Mordecai Anielewicz, the ŻOB commander, had become friends during the war, it was during this time that Anielewicz and Ringelblum apparently disagreed on financial priorities. Ringelblum believed that it was important to establish a fund to finance the rescue of the remaining "elite": writers, scholars, and political leaders. Anielewicz (and also Shmuel Winter) opposed Ringelblum's plan, believing instead that every available zloty had to go to buy arms.

Still, although there may have been some tension between Ringelblum and the ŻOB, it would be an exaggeration to speak of a serious estrangement. By the end of 1942 the Oyneg Shabes had become a constituent part of the Jewish National Committee, the political arm of the Jewish underground. It was Ringelblum, Wasser, and Gutkowski that continued to prepare reports on the Final Solution for transmission abroad, including the comprehensive document that was sent in November 1942. *Wiadomości,* the new bulletin put out by the Oyneg Shabes, rallied support for armed resistance through its blunt and unadorned presentation of the German extermination program. Through Wasser and Gutkowski, the Oyneg Shabes still enjoyed important sources of information about ŻOB activities.

The differences between Anielewicz and Ringelblum should also not be overstated. The ŻOB commander still confided in his older friend. Shortly before the ghetto uprising, Anielewicz told Ringelblum that he understood that no one from the ŻOB would survive the coming battle: the ŻOB fighters, he said, would "die like abandoned dogs, and no one would ever know their burial place."[83] Anielewicz also trusted Ringelblum enough to involve him in at least one important operation to punish a Jewish collaborator. In January 1943 the ŻOB poured acid on a former Jewish policeman who was working in the Bernhard Hallman shop on Nowolipki. The shop police detained one of the men who carried out the attack, Avraham Zandman. Anielewicz approached Ringelblum, who was also living in the shop, and told him of a plan to free the detained fighter. Five members of the ŻOB overpowered the shop police and freed Zandman.[84]

On January 18, 1943, the uneasy lull that had begun in mid-September ended as SS officers, aided by Ukrainian and Latvian auxiliaries, stormed into the ghetto. Himmler had visited Warsaw a week earlier and had ordered the deportation of eight thousand Jews. By this time, unwilling to believe German promises that they were being sent to labor camps, most Jews went into hiding.

For the first time in the history of the Warsaw Ghetto, the Germans encountered armed resistance. The ŻOB still had few weapons, and the German assault on the ghetto startled the fighting groups. Nevertheless individual fighting groups hit back, greatly surprising the Germans. One group of Hashomer fighters, commanded by Anielewicz, attached itself to a group of Jews being led to the Umschlagplatz and then attacked their guards. Another battle took place on Zamenhofa 58, where Dror and Gordonia fighters, commanded by Yitzhak Zuckerman, awaited the Nazis with an arsenal of four revolvers, four grenades, clubs, steel pipes, and sulfuric acid. The groups managed to kill two Germans before the remaining Nazis fled.[85] Yekhiel Gorny's account of these dramatic events of January 1943, titled "Action Number Two," was one of the last documents to be deposited in the second cache of the archive.[86]

The Jewish resistance astounded the Germans, who suddenly lost their enthusiasm for entering the maze of hideouts to roust out concealed Jews. Although the Aktion lasted four days, the number of victims fell well short of Himmler's goal: sixty-five hundred out of a planned catch of eight thousand, the vast majority nabbed on Monday, January 18, before the Jews could recover from their surprise.[87]

The resistance galvanized the fighters and the civilian population. The Germans had suffered casualties and had retreated. The ghetto Jews, who had been blaming themselves for their lack of resistance, became more determined than ever to build hideouts and do whatever it took to avoid future German roundups.

Even Jews skeptical about surviving the war, valued the fighting in that it restored a bit of pride and self-respect. Until now, the Germans had treated the Jews like cattle destined for the slaughter house. Now they had to be careful. The impact of the January fighting helped ensure that, when the final showdown came in April, the ghetto uprising would have wide support from the surviving Jews. In this respect, Warsaw was very different from Vilna and Białystok, where, in July and August 1943, the ghetto Jews refused to support armed resistance.[88] One of Ringelblum's more important contributions as a historian would be to describe how this process occurred.

But, for Ringelblum personally, the January action was also a terrible shock. On that first day, January 18, the Germans shot Yitzhak Giterman, who was running to warn his neighbors on Miła 69 that the SS had entered the ghetto. Within a few months Ringelblum had lost two revered friends and mentors, Zagan and Giterman. He felt Giterman's murder so deeply that he allowed himself to show a very rare outburst of personal emotion. Not long before Giterman's death, the two men had read through and edited lists of murdered Jewish leaders and intellectuals:

Now to this list, which includes entries in his handwriting, I have to add the name of Yitzhak Giterman. My hand shakes as I write these words; who knows if a future historian, reviewing this list, will not add my name, Emanuel Ringelblum? But so what, we have become so used to death that it can no longer scare us. If we somehow survive the war, we'll wander around the world like people from another planet, as if we stayed alive through a miracle or through a mistake.[89]

Giterman's murder ended a long period of hesitation for Ringelblum. Giterman himself had been thinking about crossing over to the Aryan side. The Bermans had been pressuring Ringelblum to leave the ghetto and help them with their underground work on the Aryan side. Ringelblum had already begun to leave the ghetto regularly, joining groups of Jewish workers who were going to their workplaces on the Aryan side. Using the phone in Winter's office, he would arrange a rendezvous with the Bermans. He would then return to the ghetto with the workers. Sometimes, Hersh Berlinski, the commander of the LPZ fighting groups in the ŻOB, would accompany Ringelblum on these excursions out of the ghetto.[90]

Apart from the possibility of working in the underground, Ringelblum also understood more clearly than ever that he could save Yehudis and Uri only if he found them a hideout outside the ghetto. The Bermans were ready to help. But what would happen to the archive? And if he saved himself and his family, what about those left behind?

In late January and early February Ringelblum prepared to leave. Through the Bermans he found a religious Polish Catholic family who agreed to shelter Uri. His son did not want to leave his parents and agreed go only when Ringelblum explained to him that Jewish children had an obligation to stay alive and to ensure a future for the Jewish people.[91] Ringelblum put Uri into a sack and gave him to Paweł Hormuszko, a Polish peasant from Grodno. Hormuszko took Uri to a hiding place in Praga.[92] The Bermans then found a hiding place in Izabelin, a suburb of Warsaw, for Ringelblum and Yehudis and Uri, but Yehudis preferred to accept an invitation to hide in a large bunker that had been built at Grójecka 81 (more on this below) The bunker contained more than thirty people, and Berman had grave misgivings about its long-term safety. But Yehudis was determined to stay there and Ringelblum decided to join her. (Ironically the Jews who took the Izabelin hideout that Yehudis rejected survived the war.)[93]

Sometime in early February Ringelblum gave orders to bury the second part of the archive beneath the basement of the Borochov school on Nowolipki 68. Did he do so himself? Did Lichtenstein help? The sources are silent. What is clear, however, is that the very last materials in the second part of the archive, buried in two aluminum milk cans, date from late January and early February 1943. Among these last materials were a few pamphlets from the ŻOB and the ŻZW, and Ringelblum's essay on the Oyneg Shabes Archive itself.

Ringelblum knew that his decision to leave the ghetto would cause some bitterness. At about the same time Hersh and Bluma Wasser also left for the Aryan side.[94] In a diary entry probably made sometime in February 1943 Shmuel Winter complained that the work of the Oyneg Shabes had practically stopped, because too many of its leaders were thinking more about saving their own lives than about continuing the archive.[95] The archive still continued to document the Jewish resistance, but Ringelblum's and Wasser's departure certainly hurt its work.

Even after he left for the Aryan side, Ringelblum would frequently return to the ghetto, despite Yehudis's deep fears for his safety. Two major projects preoccupied him. First, he was trying to rescue as many Jewish children as possible, and, to that end, he helped organize meetings to discuss an offer from Catholic clergy to hide Jewish children in monasteries. According to Jonas (Yanosh) Turkow, the well-known Jewish actor, Ringelblum embraced this project as early as August, at the height of the Great Deportation, though he did not entirely trust the motives of the Church.[96] He suspected that the Church wanted to convert the children, wanted the financial compensation the Jews offered, and wanted to show world opinion that it had done something to help Jews during the war.

The church's offer, Ringelblum himself noted, provoked heated discussions among surviving Jewish leaders. Some were adamant that the Jewish leadership should not cooperate with any action that risked the conversion of Jewish children.[97] Citing previous eras in Jewish history, they stressed that, as a community, Jews should embrace the precedent of Kiddush Hashem. Let individuals make their own decision about their children but on no account should Jews as a collective body accept the Church's offer.

An anonymous memorandum written in Hebrew in December 1942 reminded the group that,

> Our people fought for many generations, from the time of the Maccabees, through the Middle Ages up to the present against the invasion of alien cultures. We defended our identity whenever we were threatened [with assimilation]. Are we now going to give this up, renounce our heritage? I am sure that if we could ask our people, the unanimous answer would be not to make our children pass through the heathen fire.[98]

But Ringelblum also reported the opposing viewpoint, which, in all likelihood, he shared: Marranodom was not surrender. With most of Polish Jewry destroyed, how could Jews pass up a chance to save the lives of Jewish children? Besides, the postwar era would see a marked decline in the influence of the Church. Even if the children converted, the conversions would not last.[99]

Besides the children, Ringelblum determined to rescue the members of the Jewish cultural and intellectual elite. This triage also ran into bitter opposition, on both moral and practical grounds. As we have seen, Shmuel Winter did not believe that one should decide who was worthy of life and who wasn't; Mordecai Anielewicz absolutely opposed any diversion of funds from the purchase of weapons. But Ringelblum resolved to save a core group. The tide of war had turned, the Germans were about to surrender at Stalingrad. Even if Polish Jewry perished, perhaps there was a chance to rescue its distinguished actors, scholars, and writers. Jonas (Yanosh) Turkow recalled that in March 1943 Ringelblum slipped into the ghetto to give him one thousand zlotys that the ŻKN had set aside to rescue the intellectual elite. Ringelblum also confided to Turkow plans to build a gigantic underground bunker on the Aryan side to hide the political and cultural leadership. Turkow replied that his wife, Diana Blumenfeld, was in emotional turmoil, convinced that the final destruction of the ghetto might start at any time. Ringelblum then told him that he would help them leave the ghetto immediately and gave them the telephone number of Adolf Berman.[100]

Ringelblum kept making these dangerous visits to the ghetto partly to try to save his close party comrades—including Natan Smolar and, in all probability, Israel Lichtenstein, his wife Gele Sekstein, and their daughter Margalit.[101] A few days before the uprising began on April 19 Ringelblum was back in the ghetto; he attended a conference of the LPZ on Saturday, April 17.[102] He met with the fighting group of the LPZ and conferred with Smolar, Lichtenstein, Genia Silkes, and Fela Herzlich-Blit. Ringelblum's major concern at this point was rescue. Just before the fighting started, Smolar and Lichtenstein tried to get back to their hideout on Nowolipki 68. Ringelblum never saw them again.

The first day of the uprising, April 19, Ringelblum was in Brauer's shop on Nalewki 32, perhaps to confer with Menakhem Mendel Kon, who was working in that shop.[103] Ringelblum was trapped in the flaming ghetto, unable to get back to Yehudis and Uri. From the fourth floor of Brauer's shop he saw some of the fighting firsthand, especially on the first day of the uprising.[104] A short time after the beginning of the battle he was caught and sent to the

Trawniki labor camp near Lublin. Available sources do not detail how he was captured and when he was sent to Trawniki. In all likelihood, the Germans sent him there directly from the Warsaw Ghetto in late April.

After repeated efforts, the Bermans finally learned where Ringelblum was and managed to contact him. Luckily they knew two intrepid couriers, Teodor Pajewski, a Pole, and Emilka Kossower, a Jewess, who were willing to smuggle prisoners out of Trawniki.[105] The pair had successfully managed to rescue Pola Elster, a key member of the LPZ. In August 1943 they traveled to Trawniki to help Ringelblum escape.

The timing of the plan was carefully coordinated with Ringelblum. Pajewski, wearing a railway man's uniform, and Kossower went to a bakery just outside the camp.[106] They bribed one of the Ukrainian guards to look the other way as Ringelblum managed to slip away from his work detail and quickly enter the bakery. There he put on an extra railway worker's uniform that Kossower had brought for him. The three then started to walk to the train station. On the way they encountered SS men, who flirted with Kossower and asked her why she was wasting her time with two older men. Kossower playfully blew them a kiss and kept on going. (Ringelblum gripped Kossower's arm so tightly that it left a slight bruise!)[107] The threesome then caught a train to Warsaw, where Kossower and Pajewski handed Ringelblum over to Adolf Berman.

The three months in Trawniki had left their mark. The day he arrived in Warsaw he met Rachel Auerbach. Mussolini had just been arrested, the Allies had nearly completed their conquest of Sicily, and Auerbach cheerfully told Ringelblum that the end of the war might be in sight. Ringelblum was somber. Only with Liberation, he replied, would they really begin to realize what they had endured, and then their real pain would begin.[108]

The Bermans gave Ringelblum a new Polish name, Pan Rydzewski: he could easily pass for a Pole, and they wanted Ringelblum to work on the Aryan side for the Jewish National Committee. But Yehudis, who had been frantic with worry after Ringelblum failed to return from the ghetto in April, would not hear of it. She wanted her husband back with Uri and her—in the bunker on Grójecka 81. She wrote to the Bermans that if they insisted, then she would agree to her husband's leaving the bunker. But in her state of mind, she would find that almost unbearable.[109] Ringelblum gave in to his wife's entreaties and stayed. Besides, the Bermans believed, what he really wanted to do was to write history and not go to meetings and run a conspiracy.[110]

Even after Ringelblum descended into the bunker, the Bermans, who maintained regular contact with him, kept pressuring him to change his mind. After dark, they would meet him in the yard of Grójecka 81. Ringelblum would hand over his writings and in turn receive letters and copies of the underground press. They informed Ringelblum that the Polish underground might be able to smuggle him across the Hungarian border. But Ringelblum refused the offer.[111]

On January 4, 1944, three Gestapo agents accosted Berman on Marszałkowska Street as he was hurrying to a meeting. He had to pay an enormous bribe for his freedom, and the Bermans immediately fled their apartment.[112] Forced to lie low in a new hideout, the Bermans now found it harder to carry on their underground activities. At the same time the Gestapo was hunting Yitzhak Zuckerman and Daniel Guzik, who also had to go into hiding for a while. Faced with a real crisis in Jewish underground work, Berman increased his pressure on Ringelblum to come to the surface. Ringelblum promised to leave the hideout and take a more active role, but he kept on postponing his move.[113] In the meantime he wrote feverishly and copiously.

He had confided to the Bermans that one of his first projects was to write a detailed study of the Trawniki camp, which would have been one of the first serious academic surveys of a Nazi concentration camp. He and the Bermans maintained regular contact with a core resistance group in Trawniki. They were able to send and receive letters that were smuggled in loaves of bread. On the basis of these letters Ringelblum carefully gathered information about the resistance movement in the camp, folklore, jokes, and even such intimate details of prisoner life as sexual practices, accumulating more than two hundred pages. Whatever description Ringelblum gave of his own personal experiences disappeared with the manuscript.[114] Scattered references in letters he wrote to Berman from his hiding place indicate that he was deeply shaken by what he had seen in Trawniki, even though he mentioned that Trawniki was the "Jerusalem" of the labor camps, where conditions were better than elsewhere.[115]

Through Berman, Ringelblum kept urging the resistance group at Trawniki to escape as quickly as possible. But they kept delaying their planned escape. Then, on November 3, the Germans suddenly surrounded the labor camps in Poniatowa and Trawniki and murdered all forty-two thousand Jews there in a killing spree they dubbed "Erntefest" (Operation Harvest Festival).[116] Ringelbum, who had formed deep friendships there, learned that none of the inmates survived.

The terrible news from Trawniki spurred him on to finish his other historical projects, including a major study of Polish-Jewish relations during World War II. For him these projects now assumed the urgency of a moral obligation.

The hideout that became Ringelblum's final refuge, from August 1943 until his death in March 1944, nicknamed Krysia, was an underground bunker that concealed up to forty Jews.[117] It was built under a long rectangular greenhouse behind Grójecka 81, the residence of the Wolski family that housed the family matriarch Małgorzata and one of their sons, Mieczysław Wolski.[118] The family had delivered vegetables to the ghetto and had established contacts with certain members of the Aleynhilf, including David Klein. Jewish leaders trusted the family who had hidden, without compensation, a poor Jewish seamstress.[119] Wolski had been active in the Polish Socialist Party (PPS).[120] During the Great Deportation they proposed that the family build a large hideout under the greenhouse on their property. For a handsome sum of money Wolski agreed to do so.[121] In order to explain the large food purchases that he would have to make, he had a relative open a grocery store in his house. Although the arrangement enriched Wolski, Jacob Celemenski, a Bundist activist, emphasized that he was honest and kept all the promises he made. Ringelblum, who understood the enormous risks that Wolski ran, did not mention the issue of money when he wrote about him in *Polish-Jewish Relations during the Second World War*.

Each Jew who entered the hideout had to agree to pay 10,000 zlotys up front, in addition to regular charges for food and other expenses. Most of the Jews in the bunker were fairly well off, but the group included some members of the intelligentsia, including Itke Lazar-Melman, who had been a teacher in the CYSHO schools in Lodz, and Marek Passenstein, an economist who had worked with Yehudis in the CENTOS in the ghetto.[122] The Ringelblums had heard about the bunker from Guzik and Lazar-Melman. In February 1943 Yehudis eagerly accepted their invitation to hide there.[123] They joined the group sometime in February 1943.

The Krysia, seven meters long and five meters wide, contained two rows of double bunk beds along the sides and a long table down the middle.[124] Ventilation was barely adequate and the air reeked. The Jews cooked at night and vented the smoke through a chimney concealed in a thick stand of shrubbery. During the day people lay in their bunks or sat at the long table. At night one person at a time could climb the stairs to breathe some fresh air. Bedbugs were a constant problem, and every so often all the "inmates" had to hold a flame to the bunk planks in order to kill the vermin.

Wolski's sisters and mother, as well as his seventeen-year-old nephew, Janusz Wysocki, assisted in the maintenance of the Krysia. Janusz would bring the food and carry out the chamber pots and garbage. During the daytime hours, Janusz would always hover near the hidden entrance to the Krysia and warn of possible danger. When German soldiers were in the vicinity Janusz would whistle the opening bars to "Besame, Besame Mucho," a popular song at the time. When the danger passed, Janusz would whistle the first lines of another hit song.[125]

In time a deep friendship developed between Janusz and one of the Jewish boys who was hiding, Szymek. The two boys would spend hours together, talking and playing chess. Szymek planned to go to Palestine after the war, and Janusz wanted to visit him there.[126] Janusz, a gardener, was captivated by Szymek's stories of the kibbutzim and of Jewish agricultural achievements in Palestine.

Wolski frequently visited the hideout at night and reassured the hidden Jews about their prospects of surviving the war. The hideout, he believed, was foolproof.

> Sometimes he stayed until late into the night and, together with the people in the Krysia, used to spin out fantasies for the future—when the war ends and Nazi Germany is defeated; how everyone will leave the Krysia and go up to greet the daylight and the sunshine and start a new life as a free man; how he himself will become famous for having dared to oppose the Nazis and save the lives of forty people. The bunker will be preserved as a relic of the past and a warning for the future. Not only Jews and Poles will come to see it but also tourists from all over the world. "If any of you invite me to Palestine, I will come to see your country, the holy places, the kibbutzim," mused Mieczysław.[127]

But there were also some close calls. Once a Gestapo agent visited Wolski and asked him if he was hiding Jews. Luckily Wolski cleverly tricked him. Another time an inmate carelessly left an opening uncovered in the hothouse. One of the women workers was chasing a hen, stumbled upon the opening, and heard voices. Frightened, she told the other workers that the hothouse was infested with ghosts. Usually Wolski allowed no one to enter the hothouse during the day. This time he resorted to a desperate stratagem. To counter the rumors flying among his Polish workers, he decided to invite a Polish policeman into the hothouse to sample mushrooms. He warned the Jews that during the visit they had to remain absolutely quiet. Each child was assigned an adult who was responsible for ensuring total silence. Wolski's stratagem was successful and the rumors abated—for the moment.[128]

With thirty-eight people jammed into such a tiny space, conflicts were inevitable. During the daylight hours, Wolski demanded special vigilance, and no cooking or loud talking was allowed. Most people simply lay on their bunks, with the only light coming from two carbide lamps. When nightfall came, Janusz or Mieczysław would appear, open the flap that allowed the inmates to breathe some fresh air, and deliver food. There were unending petty quarrels, constant battles over food and space. Lording it over the inhabitants of the Krysia was "Borowski," who collected money for food and enforced the communal rules.[129] The Jagurs, who left the Krysia shortly before the Gestapo uncovered it, remembered him as an insufferable bully.

"Borowski" was responsible for an incident that deeply affected all the Jews hiding in the Krysia. One of the inmates was Basia, a thirteen-year-old girl. Her mother had been killed in Treblinka and her father had left her in the Krysia in the care of M., a woman to whom she was very attached. The father vanished and was probably killed by the Germans. One day "Borowski" called a group of people together and informed them that the money left by the girl's father had run out; he suggested that the other Jews cover her and M.'s expenses. He let slip that M. had been Basia's father's long-time lover. The girl overheard this, became profoundly depressed, and refused to eat. She simply lay on her bunk and stared at the wall. She threatened that if the residents tried to force her to eat, she would scream and give the hideout away. No cajoling helped, and after an agonizing three weeks she died. That night, Wolski and his nephew Janusz buried her under a tree in the garden.[130] Ringelblum and his wife were deeply affected by the incident, which also almost led to the discovery of the Krysia when a stranger, digging for clay, came close to discovering Basia's grave.[131]

There were occasional breaks in the gloom and depression. On Christmas eve, 1943, Wolski and Wysocki appeared with a Christmas tree, wine and cakes. "The bunker," Orna Jagur recalled," was suddenly full of light, warmth, and coziness."[132] On the first anniversary of the Krysia, all the Jews enjoyed a festive meal.

Day after day, Ringelblum sat at one corner of the long table, surrounded by documents and papers, tried to shut out what was happening around him, and wrote.

> Dr. Ringelblum was only physically present in Krysia. His thoughts were far away from there. He did not take part in the everyday life of the bunker. He showed no excitement or involvement in moments of danger or relief. He did not take part in discussions or quarrels. His intensive work and the presence of his family were, evidently, his escape from the gray monotony of the passive existence in the bunker, which was to become the last stage of his life.[133]

In fact, he was far from detached. On the contrary, he was very conscious of the tensions and quarrels that often poisoned the atmosphere, and he asked Berman to try to procure money for residents whose funds were running out.

In the early days of his hiding, Ringelblum would emerge at night to meet one of the Bermans or Guzik. Later his main contact became Wanda Elster, Pola's sister.[134] His night visitor would bring money and documents, and leave with letters and Ringelblum's completed essays. Ringelblum was anxious for Berman to read the essays and make comments and suggestions, which he would then incorporate in a second draft.[135]

Ringelblum appreciated the risks that his Polish protectors, the Wolskis, were running, and wrote about them with warmth and gratitude in "Polish-Jewish Relations during the Second World War": "Mr. Wladyslaw is a fellow of excellent fancy, with a liking for liquor and brawling. He has something of the Mazowian in him, is bold and courageous, and enjoys taking risks for their own sake."[136] He was especially grateful to Małgorzata, Wolski's mother, for the emotional support she gave to Yehudis after he left the Krysia on the eve of the Ghetto Uprising and was deported to Trawniki.[137] On the other hand, the constant danger created inevitable tension with Wolski, which Ringelblum alluded to in his letters to Berman but not in his study of Polish-Jewish relations.

On November 25 Yehudis wrote to the Bermans: "We are engulfed by terrible depression, by the feeling that we are in a jail with an indefinite sentence." Yehudis, who suffered from major health problems, also wrote to Berman that Trawniki had taken a great toll on her husband. There were constant worries: about money, about Uri, about retaining sanity in the conditions of the Krysia. Both Yehudis and Ringelblum suffered from bouts of despair. Nevertheless he again refused an offer to be smuggled out of Poland and was determined to stay and finish his mission.[138]

APOLOGIA PRO VITA SUA:
A HISTORIAN TAKES STOCK

Ringelblum wrote four major studies in the Krysia: on the Jews in Trawniki, on Polish-Jewish relations during World War II, on the Jewish intelligentsia, and on the Jewish armed resistance in Warsaw. The Trawniki study was lost, the essay on the resistance was probably left uncompleted, but the other two projects survived. This corpus not only comprised Ringelblum's conclusions about the history of Polish Jewry in World War II but also served as a final way to take stock. Ringelblum had never written about himself, and he did not start now, but his choice of subjects constituted an intrinsic substitute for an autobiography. His essays on the intelligentsia included sketches of Isaac Schiper and Marceli Handelsman,[139] the historians who had molded his intellectual development; Meyer Balaban,[140] whom he deeply admired despite political differences; Shakhne Zagan, the leader of his party; and Yitzhak Giterman, his mentor and protector.[141]

He also wrote about leaders of Yiddish culture in Poland: the economist Menakhem Linder, the folklorist Shmuel Lehman, the teacher and translator Shimon Lubelski, and the Yiddish scholar and translator Shie Broyde.[142] He devoted a particularly significant essay to Mordecai Anielewicz, the commander of the ŻOB. History, politics, and mutual aid had been the major themes of his life. All three had been inextricably linked to Jewish resistance and, as such, formed the leitmotif of his final writings.

In addition to the longer essays mentioned above, Ringelblum wrote several shorter essays and sketches of the Polish-Jewish intelligentsia—teachers, folklorists, writers, poets, and journalists. Less than forty years separated Sholom Aleichem's first Yiddish literary journal in 1888, the *Yidishe Folksbibliotek,* from the founding of the YIVO in 1925; fifteen years later the Germans began the destruction of East European Jewry. Only twenty-five years separated the birth of modern secular school systems in Hebrew and Yiddish from the Nazi onslaught. Yet this short period had produced a new intelligentsia of East European Jewish writers, teachers, economists, and journalists—an intelligentsia cut down so quickly, exterminated so totally, that Ringelblum feared that it would be totally forgotten. Years later, long after the war, the Israeli poet Nathan Alterman would underscore the magnitude of the loss in a poem that featured the beloved characters of Sholom Aleikhem's stories, now murdered along with their readers: "My Sheineh Sheindel, white snow is falling. There is no one. Everyone is gone. Understand. Tevye is dead. And dead is Mottel the Cantor's son. Dead is dear Uncle Pinye."[143]

In a letter to Berman on November 25, 1943, Ringelblum wrote, "I think that it is our most sacred duty that something remains [to remember them]."[144] Ringelblum worried that the Germans had destroyed not only the writers and teachers but also the physical traces of the Jewish presence in Poland. In a report to Berman, probably written in September or October 1943, Ringelblum noted the German determination to wipe out old synagogues, cemeteries, and libraries.

> History knows of no other example where the enemy has been so determined to wipe out every trace of the vanquished. After the Romans destroyed Jerusalem, they left the "Wailing Wall." After the barbarians

invaded Rome, they left everywhere the [material traces] of Roman culture. The Moslem invaders, after they captured Christian Spain, turned churches into mosques. But what the Germans have done to Jewish cultural [antiquities] has no precedent in history.[145]

Was it this fear that the Germans were destroying the last traces of an entire culture as well as a people that lay behind Ringelblum's determination to save what could be saved of the cultural elite, perhaps in the slim hope that they might help renew a shattered nation after the war? He had, as we have seen, used the Aleynhilf to give jobs to writers, teachers, and artists. In one of his rare attacks on the Joint, he had criticized that body for not doing enough to save the intelligentsia during the Great Deportation.[146] Perhaps a special fund to distribute bribes at the Umschlagplatz, he wrote, might have rescued a few more people. He also attacked the Judenrat for its indifference to the Jewish intelligentsia.[147]

In his essay "How the Jewish Intelligentsia of Warsaw Went to Its Death," written in December 1942, Ringelblum paid tribute to the renowned children's writer and pedagogue Janusz Korczak, who accompanied the children of his orphanage to the Umschlagplatz, even though he could have saved himself. Other teachers and directors of children's institutions—including Ringelblum's brother-in-law Aaron Koninski—followed Korczak's example. This led, Ringelblum commented, to a martyrdom that was "futile and perhaps unnecessary."[148] Martyrdom interested him less than the possibility of saving a few remnants of a world whose murder he was forced to witness.

SHAKHNE ZAGAN: A FINAL POLITICAL TESTAMENT

If his essays on the Jewish intelligentsia tried to memorialize a murdered culture, his essay on Shakhne Zagan underscored the political commitment and idealism that Ringelblum believed had enabled that culture to endure in the face of terrible obstacles. The essay on Zagan, a key leader of the Left Poalei Tsiyon, not only praised a man whom Ringelblum deeply admired. It also constituted a manifesto reaffirming Ringelblum's lifelong loyalty to his party.

For Ringelblum, the war transformed Zagan from a political figure into the "recognized leader" of the Warsaw Jewish community.[149] Thanks to Zagan's moral authority and courage, basic norms did not completely collapse and ordinary Jews could find some ally against the corruption of the Judenrat and the Jewish police.

In writing about Zagan, Ringelblum underscored the critical role in the ghetto of the political Left in general and his party in particular:

During the war the Party became a major force [*groyse zakh*]. Before the war countless threads—unions, public organizations—linked the conscious elements of the community. Now [with the outbreak of the war], only the Party remained. It gave a refuge to Warsaw Jews and Jews from the provinces, active and passive members, young and old. The Party—decimated by the occupier, terrorized by traitors, emptied of its . . . [leading cadres] who fled to the Soviet Union—remained the sole important factor on the Jewish street [*iz geblibn der eyntsiger virkndiger koyekh oyf der yiddisher gas*]. Forced to hide in private apartments, in soup kitchens and elsewhere, the Party acquired a magical force. It became the only organization that frightened the Jewish Gestapo agents. They bothered and harassed the rich, but they dared not lay their dirty hands on the Party. . . . The Party was the word that the Jewish masses uttered with the greatest respect. They saw in it the epitome of all that was the most beautiful, an oasis of justice in the surrounding sea of wickedness. The Party was the force that did not allow surrounding Jewish life to turn into Sodom. . . . It did not allow the Jewish Gestapo agents to take control of Jewish life.[150]

Whereas most of the leaders had fled, Zagan stayed and quickly convinced his party to adapt to the new circumstances. The Jewish Left had been suspicious of "charity" before the war. Now Zagan understood that the network of mutual aid—especially soup kitchens—would have to take the place of the prewar trade unions as the backbone and foundation of a political community.[151] Ringelblum credited Zagan's leadership with ensuring that the wealthy merchants and industrialists did not seize control of the mutual aid organization and turn it into a copy of the hated prewar philanthropic organizations.

In his essay on Zagan, Ringelblum recalled the party's "Last Supper," the last time that his beloved comrades all came together in the Warsaw Ghetto. On a Saturday in March 1942, the LPZ had gathered together to mark the opening of the party's new soup kitchen:

We all ate our midday meal seated at nicely set tables. Comrade Zagan presided. Just to be safe, there were no speeches. But it was enough for all the comrades to come together to feel all the words that did not have to be said. It was like the scene in the New Testament, "Where two gather, I am with them." Zagan's tall, broad-shouldered figure towered over the large room. His hearty laughter made everybody happy. For a few hours we forgot about the Germans, we even forgot about the ghetto walls, which, in fact, bordered the building where we sat. Only a few shots from police patrols at smugglers reminded us that we were in occupied territory. This was the last ray of sun before the sun set. The last meeting of the Poalei Tsiyon in Warsaw.[152]

In a telling passage Ringelblum stressed that Zagan, "along with the entire Poalei Tsiyon movement," believed that the present war would end with the collapse of the capitalist system and with the victory of the Red Army. Zagan was "also certain that the working class in so-called democratic countries would not repeat the mistakes of 1918 and not let the fruits of victory slip away."[153] There is little doubt that Ringelblum considered "mistakes of 1918" to be the decision of the German Social Democratic Party to set up the Weimar Republic instead of a Soviet state and the failure of workers in other countries to help the Bolsheviks. Convinced that dying capitalism had spawned Nazism and, with it, the murder of European Jewry, this belief in world revolution gave Ringelblum a rare glimmer of hope.

The LPZ had long found itself in the rather difficult position of supporting a country—the USSR—whose mistakes and shortcomings it knew all too well. Ringelblum also had few illusions about the future of Soviet Jewry, and he reiterated his conviction that only the solution advocated by the LPZ—a territorial base in Palestine—could preserve the Jewish people.[154] Still, Ringelblum, along with his party, clung to the hope that the road to Jerusalem led through Moscow. Only a world revolution, directed by the Soviet Union, could procure a socialist, Jewish Palestine.

Perhaps some of the intensity with which Ringelblum pursued his final mission as a historian derived from the tension between his faith in the Soviet Union and his deep loyalty to the Jewish people. The revolution might create favorable conditions for a socialist Palestine, but neither the Soviets nor the Polish Communists gave any indication that they regarded Yiddish culture or the future of the Jewish people as a major priority. Indeed, in a letter to Adolf Berman on December 28, 1943, Ringelblum expressed his disappointment that the underground press of the PPR was devoting little attention to the Jewish tragedy.[155] Perhaps, he guessed, its leaders did not want Poles to think that Jews dominated the party. And without one of their most important communities, the Yiddish-speaking Jews of Eastern Europe, Jews would enter the postwar era not only physically decimated but culturally eviscerated.[156]

To save what could be saved, and to reconstitute a basis for a Jewish secular culture after the war, a strong historical consciousness, buttressed by a gripping chronicle of national suffering and resilience, would be essential. And Ringelblum badly wanted that record to include the Left Poalei Tsiyon, whose achievements, he feared, might be forgotten after the war or minimized by political rivals. So in the last week of his life, Ringelblum wrote Berman about how much the party had meant to him and how important it was that future historians remember what the LPZ had done in the ghetto and in the armed uprising.

It is important to emphasize the role and position of Mister Stolarski. There is no doubt that Mr. Chal. played the leading role in all this, but as long as Mister Stolarski does not bring up his own role in all this, the record will be distorted. I ask you to get Jelenski to recount from memory the exact details of the conference of Saganski with Paprocki . . . as well as all attempts . . . and [our role] in the ob.[157]

A PAEAN TO A FIGHTER: MORDECAI ANIELEWICZ

Ringelblum first got to know Anielewicz in the early days of the war. A leader of Hashomer Hatzair and only twenty years old, Anielewicz visited the older historian to borrow a book. That meeting led to many discussions about history and economics. As we have seen, Ringelblum and his party drew steadily closer to the young leaders of Hashomer, especially as both groups shared a pro-Soviet orientation. Ringelblum stressed, however, that this faith in the Soviet Union "did not in the least lessen their positive attitude to the land of Israel [Eretz Yisroel] and to the idea of Palestinism as the solution of the Jewish question."[158]

In addition to this shared political orientation, Ringelblum admired Hashomer because many of its members turned their backs on their comfortable middle-class homes and chose a life of self-sacrifice. Too many young people, Ringelblum believed, had decided to live for the moment and had lost themselves in cards, alcohol, and lascivious behavior.[159] Even young people who worked in the Aleynhilf, he believed, often did so with ulterior motives. But Hashomer was different. Even though he had opposed the movement before the war, he now saw it as a valued elite that could serve as a model for others.

While Anielewicz and Ringelblum developed a growing political affinity, they also had their differences. And once Anielewicz learned of the mass extermination, Ringelblum wrote, he had only one focus: armed resistance. He immediately lost interest in cultural work: seminars, literary and historical discussions, and so on. He now regretted the time that he could have spent learning how to use weapons. At the time, the leaders of other youth movements agreed with him.[160]

In writing about Anielewicz Ringelblum expressed both pride and remorse: pride in the friendship and respect that bound him to these young people in the ghetto and remorse that it was they, and not his own generation, that led the preparations for armed resistance. An unmistakable note of self-reproach and regret surfaced as Ringelblum wrote about Anielewicz's fierce determination to organize an armed uprising:

Our comrade Mordecai made a second mistake that took its bitter revenge on the history of the Warsaw Jews and the Polish Jews. [The youth] . . . paid too much attention to the opinions of the adult generation—the experienced ones, the wise ones, those who weighed and considered and had at hand a thousand well-reasoned arguments against fighting the occupier. A paradoxical situation arose. The adult generation, which had already lived half its life, spoke, thought, worried about surviving the war. The adults dreamed about life. The youth—the best, the most beautiful, the noblest element that the Jewish people possessed—spoke and thought only about an honorable death. They did not think about surviving the war, they did not arrange "Aryan" Papers, they did not get apartments on the other side. Their only worry was about the most honorable death, the kind of death that a two-thousand-year-old people deserves.[161]

Was Ringelblum thinking of himself here? Or thinking of Zagan? Was he recalling the July 1942 meeting that postponed a decision on armed resistance? Who, after all, were the adult leaders whom Anielewicz and his friends, disciplined as they were, had mistakenly obeyed? Whether or not Ringelblum was too hard on himself, his writing revealed a certain degree of guilt, perhaps unjustified but nonetheless real. Later Ringelblum, discussing the lack of resistance in July and August 1942, wrote:

We are not trying here to excuse the socially and politically active members of Warsaw Jewry for not coming up to the mark, for letting themselves be terrorized by the SS, and for allowing the mass murder of Warsaw Jewry to happen without shedding a drop of blood of the Germans and Ukrainians.[162]

Unfortunately, Ringelblum noted, the youth movements had been "too disciplined." What he meant was that for too long they had deferred to the adult leadership. Therefore the Germans were able "to kill three hundred thousand Jews at no cost to themselves." These young people in the ghetto, Ringelblum noted with regret, should have studied the history of liberation movements in more detail. Throughout history, he noted, it was the young who led revolts, not those who had to worry about their family responsibilities. Ringelblum, who praised the young people who did not get Aryan papers or apartments on the other side, while he himself was trying to save his family and his own life by doing exactly that, fully understood what it meant to live in what Lawrence Langer calls a world of "choiceless choices."[163]

After describing how Anielewicz met his death in the command bunker on Miła 18 on May 1943, Ringelblum concluded with words that once again underscored just how intently Ringelblum looked for revolution to provide some partial redemption for catastrophe:

> And so died one of the best, one of the noblest, who had from the beginning of his life dedicated himself to the service of the Jewish people, to protect its honor and dignity. The working class will remember that he was one of the few who had, right from the first moment, tried to serve the world revolution and the first proletarian state in the world.[164]

COMING FULL CIRCLE: POLISH-JEWISH RELATIONS

At the very end of his life, Ringelblum the historian returned to what had been one of the major themes of his scholarship: Polish-Jewish relations. His first book had described how Warsaw Jewry began, and now he would be among the first to record how Polish Jewry perished.

Ringelblum knew that this study, "Polish-Jewish Relations during the Second World War," was hardly a conventional scholarly work. Even though Adolf Berman regularly sent him material, including the underground press, Ringelblum obviously had no access to research libraries or archives, including relevant Polish documents. On the other hand, he had been closely involved with the Oyneg Shabes project on Polish-Jewish relations and probably remembered many of the important essays and sources collected by the archive, especially regarding economic cooperation and smuggling. He was also in regular contact with two of the most important leaders of the underground Jewish National Committee, Daniel Guzik and Berman. At once informants and friends, they most likely provided Ringelblum with valuable up-to-date information on their own negotiations with the Polish Home Army and the Delegate's Office. Berman, also a treasurer of the joint Polish-Jewish Committee to Help Jews, Żegota, had good information both about the Żegota's successes and its many setbacks.

Still, Ringelblum realized that the book would have serious limitations; as his preface states: "The material on which this work is based is still too fresh, too unripe to permit objective judgment by a historian. Much official information, press material and the like, which will be needed to supplement this work after the war—all this is still lacking."[165] Further, he feared that his incarceration in Trawniki had affected his memory; he asked Berman for help in checking sources.[166] He also feared that he might not survive and that the book represented an awesome and pressing responsibility, for was there another Jewish historian who had seen what he had seen? Balaban, he knew, was dead; Schiper had perished in Majdanek; Philip Friedman was in hiding in Galicia; and, of course, Ringelblum had no way of knowing that he would survive the war.

Ringelblum knew that an eight-hundred-year era of Polish-Jewish history was nearing its end in a surge of horror intensified by the bitterness of perceived betrayal and the pain of mutual estrangement. He had always hoped that history would act as a bridge to bring the two peoples closer together. The least he could do at this time was to perform a historian's final mission: leave a study that would force future generations to confront the past honestly and openly. He also hoped that his book might serve as a resource for future historians, who would undertake their own research in vastly different circumstances.

The essay "Polish-Jewish Relations during the Second World War" was the culmination not only of the intensive work on the subject carried out by the Oyneg Shabes in the Warsaw Ghetto but also represented, in many ways, a final synthesis and reappraisal of Ringelblum's prewar scholarship. As we have seen, Ringelblum, in those earlier endeavors, had tried to counter two starkly different perceptions of Polish-Jewish relations. The first was the myth of Poland as a land of asylum and refuge, distinguished by age-old traditions of liberalism and tolerance. The second was the contrary myth of eternal anti-Semitism, the notion that Polish-Jewish relations were rooted in unbridgeable antagonism and mutual alienation. In truth, Polish-Jewish relations reflected a constant interplay of rivalry and cooperation, religious alienation and close personal ties, economic tension and mutual collaboration. It was the historian's role to explain this story, to undercut long-held prejudices and thereby build mutual understanding between Jews and Poles.

This remained Ringelblum's view throughout the first part of the war, at least until the beginning of the genocide. From the time the war began, and certainly until the onset of the destruction in 1941–42, Ringelblum's work on Polish-Jewish relations looked to the future, to a time when the historical record might assuage shared misunderstandings. Both before the war and beyond, Ringelblum sincerely believed that one reason for Polish-Jewish tension was a lack of mutual knowledge. He was an optimist, convinced that Poles and Jews could overcome their differences and that historians could help bring them closer together.[167]

Ringelblum's prewar writings on Polish-Jewish history had also sought the true story of Polish-Jewish relations that lay hidden beneath the visible evidence of legal decrees and political intent. Theory and practice were often quite different. Building on the economic research of the Oyneg Shabes, Ringelblum saw Polish-Jewish relations between 1939 and 1941 as a continuation of this enduring conflict between, in his words, "gray theory" and the "tree of life [*ets khayim*]."[168] For generations, both personal ties and economic interests had linked Poles and Jews. For Ringelblum, neither the boycott campaign of the 1930s nor the German decrees of 1939 or 1940 could easily destroy the enormous interlocking web of economic relations built up over centuries. There may not have been much love between Poles and Jews but they did need each other.

For Ringelblum, until the onset of mass extermination, the combination of economic self-interest and Jewish resilience sabotaged the Nazi determination to strangle Polish Jewry through ghettos, starvation rations, and punitive economic decrees. The ghetto developed important "export markets" with the Aryan side, and Polish-Jewish economic ties flourished.[169] Little wonder, therefore, that Ringelblum regarded the massive smuggling that helped sustain the Warsaw Ghetto as a major milestone in Polish-Jewish cooperation.[170] He admitted, however, in a May 1942 diary entry, that it did attract characters of the "lowest type."[171] Nonetheless he endorsed the proposal by the noted attorney Leon Berenson for a postwar monument to the "unknown smuggler." Many documents of the Oyneg Shabes Archive described how the establishment of ghettos helped isolate Jews from Poles and tore asunder the web of daily contact.

But the archive also offered ample testimony that when it came to trade even ghetto walls failed to break Polish-Jewish relations. An Oyneg Shabes report on conditions in the ghetto's Gęsia Street jail, which contained many Jews caught for smuggling and buying food outside the ghetto, described prisoners' reactions when asked about the Poles:

> Asked about the attitude of Poles, they utter spontaneous exclamations of gratitude and friendliness. This—from everyone in the crowd, such as, "They gave me to eat!"—"I could even spend a night!"—"Yes, the Poles are a kind people"—etc. One feels that the Jewish proletariat will not soon forget kindness encountered.[172]

Ringelblum intended that the Oyneg Shabes Archive give top priority to the study of Polish-Jewish relations. As part of the "Two and a Half Years" project, he wrote extensive and detailed guidelines to ensure comprehensive coverage taking in the period from the beginning of the war until early 1942.[173] The guidelines, quite detailed even by the exacting standards of the Oyneg Shabes, reflected Ringelblum's obsession with laying out a painstaking, objective, and scholarly approach to the complexity of problems that comprised Polish-Jewish relations. Since one of the major initial goals of the archive was to improve these relations in the future, the collection of documentation on the September 1939 Polish-German war figured prominently in Ringelblum's guidelines. The battles of September 1939, he wrote, reminded him of the insurrection of 1863, a high point in Polish-Jewish rapprochement, when young Jews, along with their fellow countrymen, rushed to fight for Polish independence.[174] In that spirit, Ringelblum and the Oyneg Shabes doggedly collected every possible scrap of information about Jewish heroism on the battlefield, and about Jewish civilians who fought fires and tended the wounded during the siege of Warsaw.[175]

No clear consensus emerged. A cursory glance at what members of the archive were writing about the Poles on the eve of the Great Deportation shows a wide difference of opinion. On June 7, 1942, Abraham Lewin wrote in his diary that the war had favorably influenced Polish-Jewish relations:

> The majority of Poles have been gripped by philo-Semitic feelings. . . .
> I see Polish-Jewish relations in a bright light. I think that this war will
> wash this earth of ours clean of much filth and savagery. . . . There
> will be no refuge here for anti-Semitism, at least not for public aggressive anti-Semitism. They will be ashamed to deal in it. I believe that
> the Polish people, too, have been purified by the terrible fire that has
> swept the face of the earth. Let us not forget: the Poles are in second
> place in the table of tragic losses among the nations, just behind the
> Jews.[176]

But two weeks later *Yediot,* the Dror newspaper, declared:

> A certain stratum—and to tell the truth a very thin one—of the Polish public displays sympathy with the tormented Jews of Poland and
> even extends them active assistance. But the masses, the Polish "street"
> is well pleased with all the new repressions. "At least that's one good
> thing Hitler is doing for us—getting rid of the Jews." Talk like this is
> heard in the trains and in the market, in the trams and on the streets.
> Eyewitnesses tell harrowing stories of how the Poles behaved during the
> deportations and the slaughter [in the ghetto]. The noble actions of the
> Poles who have not lost elementary feelings of humanity stand out all
> the more against this dark background.[177]

As for Ringelblum, a diary entry he made in that same month, June 1942, placed him somewhere between Lewin's optimism and the Dror's pessimism. He noted that the Germans were indeed doing all they could to drive a wedge between the two peoples, that German anti-Semitic propaganda was intensifying, and that leaving the ghetto was becoming increasingly difficult. Nevertheless, every Sunday afternoon a Jewish symphony orchestra would play on the border of the ghetto. Crowds of Poles would come to listen and collect money for the Jewish musicians. Every half-hour Poles would leave and allow other listeners to take their place. The crowds would remain right up to curfew.

> The same thing happens elsewhere, wherever there is the slightest possibility of contact between Jews and Christians. For example, each evening a group of musicians plays in front of the Hospital of St. Sophia, entertaining the sick prisoners. Music knows no boundaries of race and religion. It brings together the two peoples who have been separated by force. It is a symbol of the unbreakable commonality of the Polish-Jewish fate.[178]

The Oyneg Shabes principle of contemporaneous study and testimony was rarely more consequential than in the study of Polish-Jewish relations. Events occurred so rapidly that if one did not record something today, it would be overshadowed, even rendered irrelevant, by the horrors of tomorrow. Once the mass murder began, and with it growing Jewish bitterness at alleged Polish indifference, then it became all the more difficult to recall that between 1939 and 1942 there had been many positive as well as negative moments in the relations between the two peoples.

Before the mass murder began, Ringelblum approached the problem of Polish-Jewish relations from much the same perspective that had informed his prewar scholarship. The Jews had a future in Poland, he believed, and historians could help bridge differences between the two peoples. In this spirit, as soon as the war began, he had to absorb and understand a vast amount of often contradictory material. On the one hand, there was a great deal that was positive: the marked decline of anti-Semitism in the summer of 1939; the correct and loyal attitude of most Polish military units and relief agencies in 1939; and dozens of accounts by Jewish refugees of help received from Polish soldiers and civilians. Ringelblum was also impressed by examples of rabid anti-Semites who called a truce in their Jew baiting in order to keep their distance from the common enemy. On the other hand, he was also aware of much that was less favorable: an upsurge in anti-Semitism as Warsaw capitulated; strained relations between Jewish and Polish soldiers in German POW camps; the indifference of Polish bystanders to the Easter 1940 pogrom in Warsaw; a growing tendency of Poles to take advantage of Jewish friends who had entrusted them with property; and the realization that, after the war, Poles who had inherited Jewish shops and businesses would be in no hurry to return them.

Amid this welter of conflicting observations, one particularly disturbing pattern stood out from the very onset of the German occupation: the disparity between the "personal" and the "civic" behavior of the Polish population.

On the one side, many Poles showed great kindness to individual Jews and to starving Jewish children; on the other, even shared suffering at the hands of the common enemy did not soften their tendency to regard "Jews" in the abstract as an alien, even hostile body, quite outside the sphere of Polish moral responsibility. In other words, Polish kindness to Jews all too often rested on individual rather than "civic" or "political" considerations, notwithstanding the Jewish record in September 1939. An early example was the notorious March 1940 pogrom in Warsaw.[179] While most Poles had nothing to do with the anti-Jewish violence, Ringelblum was bothered by the passivity and indifference of Polish onlookers.[180] Few seemed to care that such anti-Jewish violence played into German hands and enabled the Germans to score important propaganda points at the Jews' expense. On November 15, 1940, with the creation of the Warsaw Ghetto, he wrote that "a small part [of the Poles] feel sympathy, the majority [are] passive. Others are happy and believe that this will force the Poles to learn commerce."[181]

Other essayists working for the Oyneg Shabes echoed Ringelblum's concerns. Stanisław Różycki's essay "Polish-Jewish Relations," probably written for the archive in early 1942, stressed that "some Poles" helped Jews and that Jews "do not want to remember the meanness, the insults, and the humiliations. They trust the Polish people." But Różycki did not paint a pretty picture. Certain groups of Poles whose work took them into the ghetto regularly—employees of the gas and electricity works, tax collectors, and Polish policemen—shamelessly and ruthlessly squeezed money out of helpless Jews and humiliated them with slaps and blows. Many Poles whom Jews entrusted with their possessions refused to return them. Jews knew that if a Pole cheated them in any way, they had no recourse. But, for Różycki, the worst blow was the realization that the Polish masses remained deeply anti-Semitic.

> It suffices to look at the faces of the youngsters, rascals, peasant women, and artisans who cross the Jewish quarter by tram: they are happily amused, they cheerfully crack shameless and crude jokes, betraying full satisfaction and malicious joy at the fact that the Jews "got what they deserved" and what everybody wished them.[182]

An interview conducted for the archive by Shmuel Breslav provided some insight into Polish-Jewish relations from the viewpoint of "an intelligent, well-educated woman" who was a religious Catholic and traveled in liberal, democratic circles in Polish society.[183] The interview probably took place in May or June 1942, since the woman mentioned news of the killings in Vilna and the mass deportation from Lublin. Breslav's interlocutor stressed that much of the Polish elite, even those who rejected the programmatic anti-Semitism of right-wing circles, believed, as they had before the war, that the Jews had no future in Poland and should emigrate. If Jews stayed after the war, they should enjoy equal rights but on no account should they regain the property they had lost: without question, the Jews could not resume their prewar economic status. Poles knew that they had profited from the expulsion of Jews into ghettos; indeed, the material benefits had been considerable. The sudden disappearance of competitors and the easy acquisition of Jewish property were tangible benefits of German anti-Semitism.

According to Breslav's informant, many ordinary Poles were afraid that if the ghetto walls disappeared they would suddenly have to give up what they had gained. Thus they welcomed the news that Jews were being deported, even though by this time they had surely guessed that the Jews were going to their deaths. Their feelings of relief were undeniably tinged with guilt, but as they pondered what was happening to the Jews, the Poles embraced a convenient alibi to justify their indifference—the stories of alleged Jewish collaboration with the Soviets between 1939 and 1941.

Ringelblum understood, from the very onset of war, that these ugly accusations of Jewish collaboration with the Soviets had provided many Poles with a ready-made excuse to see the Jews as a disloyal, alien element.[184] For a time Ringelblum tended to approach this explosive issue carefully; his writings reflected the intellectual caution of a historian who understood the extent to which this question would weigh on future relations between the two peoples, as well as his hope that the September campaign had ushered in a new chapter in those relations. But, until the beginning of the mass murder, Ringelblum approached this problem as an issue deserving of serious analysis and study. The war would end, charges and countercharges would fill the air, and historians could help provide perspective on this and other sensitive issues. After all, similar controversies had raged about Jewish-Polish relations after the Lwów pogrom in 1918 and the Vilna pogrom in 1919.

In this spirit of trying to gather as much material as possible for future historians, Ringelblum readily recorded Polish complaints that Jews had acted disloyally to Poland. He doubtless had also read several Jewish accounts given to the Oyneg Shabes Archive that seemed to corroborate some of these Polish claims.[185] In April 1940 Ringelblum cited Jewish testimonies from Białystok and Zamość that described how Jews had jeered at Polish officers and former civil servants. He also described a conversation he had had with a Polish writer who had been friendly to Jews. The writer had returned from Soviet-occupied Poland and had seen how a Russian soldier and a newly minted Jewish commissar had searched the suitcases of two Polish students. Suddenly the Jew spied a crucifix in the suitcase; it had been given to the student by his mother. The Jewish commissar threw it away, but the soldier retrieved it and gave it back to the student. "You see," the writer told Ringelblum, "I can understand something like this, but is it a great surprise if an uneducated seventeen-year-old becomes an anti-Semite? Why must the Jews be more Catholic than the pope?" Ringelblum noted this without comment or protest, except to add that many Jews were also coming back with similar stories.[186]

When the mass extermination of the Jewish population began, however, Ringelblum's handling of the problem changed markedly. No longer was this a quarrel that could be understood by reasoned and patient analysis. This was no longer 1940, when mass expulsions of Poles from the Warthegau and brutal German-Soviet repression of the Polish intelligentsia gave many Poles ample reason to think that their fate was as bad as the Jews'. Instead, an enraged Ringelblum saw the canard of the "Żydokummuna" (the Jewish-Communist cabal), as a convenient alibi that Poles used to rationalize and excuse their indifference to the mass murder of their Jewish neighbors. He now dismissed the Polish complaints of Jewish collaboration with the Soviets as exaggerations, "groundless nonsense."[187] The Żydokummuna had become one of the most reliable staples of German propaganda, and most Poles had fallen for the bait. Confronted with the hatred and contempt of the Polish population, the Germans nonetheless had managed to find one sure link to the Polish "street"—anti-Semitism. After the German discovery of the grisly mass murder of Polish officers by the Soviets in Katyn in April 1943, German anti-Semitic propaganda became even more effective.[188] The Katyn revelations coincided with the ghetto uprising and with a mass flight from the ghetto to the Aryan side. Just when Jews needed Polish support more than ever, hostilities hardened.

After the mass murder began, Ringelblum's determination to remain an objective historian vied with his grief at the annihilation of his people. In his introduction to "Polish-Jewish Relations during the Second World War," he revealed his emotional turmoil and deep sense of responsibility toward future generations. This left-wing, Marxist historian thus began his essay by comparing himself to a Torah scribe:

> When a Jewish sofer [scribe] sets out to copy the Torah, he must, according to religious law, take a ritual bath in order to purify himself of all uncleanliness and impurity. This scribe takes up his pen with a trembling heart, because the smallest mistake in transcription means the destruction of the whole work. It is with this feeling of fearfulness that I have begun this work with the above title. I am writing it in a hideout on the Aryan side. I am indebted to the Poles for having saved my life twice during this war: once in the winter of 1940 when the blessed arm of the Pol-

ish underground saved me from certain death, and the second time when it got me out of an SS labor camp, where I would have met my death either in an epidemic or from a Ukrainian or SS bullet. . . . I, in my own person, am concrete evidence of the lack of truth in the assertion made by some Jewish circles that the entire Polish population rejoiced over the destruction of Polish Jewry and that there are no people on the Aryan side with hearts that bleed and suffer over the tragic fate of the Jewish people of Poland. On the other hand, Polish circles may be hurt when I say that Poland did not reach the same level as Western Europe in saving Jews. I am a historian. Before the war I published several works on the history of the Jews of Poland. It is my wish to write objectively, *sine ira et studio,* on the problem of Polish-Jewish relations during the present war. In times so tragic for my people, however, it is no easy task to rise above passion and maintain cool objectivity.[189]

Ringelblum's essay was a unique synthesis of the immediacy of contemporaneous testimony with the analytic dispassion of retrospective historical analysis. The essay reflected the tension between the imperative of historical objectivity and shock at the enormity of the crimes he had witnessed not as a bystander but as a direct victim. Detached historians could make necessary distinctions between perpetrators and bystanders, between Polish and German anti-Semitism, between active complicity and indifference. But for a member of a victimized people to do so required a major effort of intellectual discipline. Ringelblum, writing both as a historian and a witness, wrote an essay that decades later retained its scholarly relevance.

Ringelblum, acutely aware of his lack of access to sources, understood the limitations of his study. Some of his more problematic assertions and conclusions reflected his political views. For example, he tended to rely too much on the paradigm of generic fascism to explain the intensifying anti-Semitism in Poland in the 1930s. The government, he believed, afraid to undertake real agrarian reform and change the dysfunctional capitalist system, turned to anti-Semitism as a way to garner support. To be sure, Piłsudski's successors, afraid of being outflanked for support from the Right, did implement anti-Jewish policies.[190] But Ringelblum tended to downplay the idea that, far from being a tool used by a frightened or cynical government, anti-Semitism reflected the feelings of large sectors of Polish society that needed no outside agitators to teach them to be suspicious of Jews. Nor did Ringelblum appreciate the fact that agrarian reform would probably have done little to solve Poland's structural economic problems. Another area where political considerations skewed Ringelblum's conclusions was his assertion that workers and the intelligentsia played an outsized role in saving Jews. This is not borne out by more recent research, which has found that no particular class or social group stood out in this regard.[191]

One scholar, Gunnar S. Paulsson, has also argued against Ringelblum's assertion that Jews hiding in the Netherlands and in other Western European countries could count on a proportionally far greater number of non-Jews willing to hide them and help them.[192] It was certainly true that in comparing Dutch Nazis with Polish members of the extreme right-wing Polish nationalist political party, the ONR (National Radical Camp), Ringelblum treated the former much too charitably. But the fact remains that over 10 percent of Dutch Jewry survived the war in hiding. The comparative figure for Warsaw Jewry, even accepting Paulsson's figures, is certainly no more than 3 percent of the prewar population and even lower for Polish Jewry as a whole. (This does not include Jews who survived the war in the USSR.) Paulsson also believed that the prospects for survival of Jews hiding in Warsaw in 1943 and 1944 were not quite as hopeless as Ringelblum made them appear. Here Paulsson's arguments are more cogent, but the discrepancies are not major.

Generally most, though not all, of Ringelblum's major assertions and arguments stood the test of time remarkably well. Given the limitations he faced as he wrote the book on Jewish-Polish relations, his estimates of the numbers of Jews in hiding in Warsaw in late 1943, and the number of Polish helpers, were somewhat understated but not by a large margin:

> It is hard to estimate the number of Jews hiding in the country In Warsaw they speak of 10,000–15,000 hidden Jews; some people estimate 25,000–30,000 which, in my opinion, is considerably exaggerated. Supposing that 15,000 Jews are hiding in the capital . . . at least 10,000–15,000 Polish families in Warsaw are helping Jews hide, which comes out to 40,000–60,000 people, counting four people to a family. . . . In all of Poland, including Warsaw, there are probably no more than 30,000 [Jews in hiding].[193]

One of Ringelblum's most important achievements was to use his credibility and moral authority both as a scholar and an eyewitness to remind posterity that Polish society was not a monolith, that the Poles were not Nazis, and that the Germans, not the Poles, started and executed the mass murder. Ringelblum recognized that the Polish people could neither have averted the Holocaust nor saved most of their Jewish neighbors. He paid tribute to their national pride and their highly developed sense of national honor.

He also took great care to note the terrible risks involved for Poles who hid Jews:

The life of a Pole hiding Jews is not an easy one. Appalling terror reigns in the country, second only to Yugoslavia. . . . Arrests and roundups at every step and constant searches for arms and smuggled goods in the trains are common in city streets. Every day the press, radio, etc., infect the masses of the population with the venom of anti-Semitism. In this atmosphere of trouble and terror, passivity and indifference, it is very difficult to keep Jews in one's home. A Jew living in the flat of an intellectual or a worker or in the hut of a peasant is dynamite liable to explode at any moment and blow the whole place up. Money undoubtedly plays an important role in the hiding of Jews. There are poor families who base their subsistence on the funds paid daily by the Jews to their Aryan landlords. But is there enough money in the world to make up for the constant fear of exposure, fear of the neighbors, the porter, and the manager of the block of flats, etc. Idealists exist who devote their whole lives to their Jewish friends who cause them a great deal of trouble! A Jew is a little child, incapable of taking a single step by itself![194]

A salient risk included being denounced by one's own countrymen. Ringelblum mentioned that, more than once, Germans chasing a fleeing member of the Polish underground caught their suspect by yelling in the street: "Catch the Jew!"[195]

Given his recognition of Polish courage, all the more telling are his accusations of indifference and moral abandonment by the Polish underground, the Home Army, and the majority of the Polish population. The Polish-Jewish solidarity of the 1939 war, which had so reminded Ringelblum of 1863, quickly faded. Ringelblum discerned during the war what many postwar scholars have later described as the Polish failure to include Jews in their sphere of moral responsibility.[196] In standing up to the Germans, the Poles showed great courage. Confronted with the mass murder of their fellow citizens, however, they turned away.

Even in the relatively straightforward matter of suppressing the blackmailers and informants who plagued Jews on the Aryan side, the Polish underground did much less than it could have. In theory Jews, as citizens of the Polish Republic, should have enjoyed the protection and concern of the Polish underground. Although this would not have changed their ultimate fate, at least it would have assured them that they were not alone.

The Polish people and the government of the Republic of Poland were incapable of deflecting the Nazi steamroller from its anti-Jewish course. But the question is permissible whether the attitude of the Polish people befitted the enormity of the calamities that befell the country's Jewish citizens. Was it inevitable that the Jews, looking their last on this world as they rode in the death trains speeding from different parts of the country to Treblinka or other places of slaughter, should have to see indifference or even gladness on the faces of their neighbors?[197]

Isolated and beleaguered, the Jews could not resist without the backing and support of the Polish Home Army. But the AK refused to provide any meaningful support, at least until after January 1943, and even then weapons deliveries were sparse and grudging. But, perversely, the Poles accused the Jews of passively going to their deaths and taunted them for their alleged lack of pride and honor. The pattern of condemning Jews for not fighting and then denying them weapons continued well after the end of the ghetto uprising. Adolf Berman and Yitzhak Zuckerman sent a bitter letter to the command of the Polish Home Army in late 1943 complaining of an AK edict that banned the use of relief money from abroad to buy weapons for Jews. Given Ringelblum's ties to Berman, he certainly knew about this as he was writing his book. He was also probably well informed about the many complaints made by both the Żegota and the Jewish National Committee concerning the unwillingness of the Polish underground to take harsher measures against blackmailers and informers.[198]

With one important exception—Żegota, the Council to Aid Jews—Polish help to Jews was largely a private matter, conducted by heroic individuals acting on their own initiative. Ringelblum admired Żegota as a noble enterprise but considered its activities too little and too late.[199] Żegota, Ringelblum noted bitterly, did not even have the funds to save Isaac Schiper.

In Ringelblum's judgment, the record of Polish behavior on the civic level, expressed in the actions of the Polish underground, failed the important tests of solidarity and basic human decency. His final verdict was harsh: "Polish fascism and its ally, anti-Semitism, have conquered the majority of the Polish people. It is they whom we blame for the fact that Poland has not taken an equal place alongside the Western European countries in rescuing Jews."[200]

Nevertheless Ringelblum remembered that, as a historian, he bore important responsibilities to future generations. That he wrote in Polish, hoping for Polish readers as well as the handful of Jewish survivors who would emerge after the war, represented the last action Ringelblum could undertake in the fight for a better Poland.

BETRAYAL

In early March 1944 the Krysia's luck ran out. According to three different sources, Wolski was betrayed by his girlfriend after a falling out.[201] The Jagurs stated that the Krysia was betrayed by an eighteen year old named Jan Łakiński, who was subsequently executed by the Polish underground.[202] On March 7 Germans and Polish police appeared at the Wolski house. They knew exactly where to look. While one group burst into the house, another ran toward the garden and into the hothouse. Some of the Germans threw themselves on Mieczysław and yelled, "You damned Jewish stooge, you wanted to hide Jews, you will pay for it, you fool!" Wolski implored the Germans not to touch his mother or his sisters. It had been his idea, he said, and he alone was responsible. The Nazis beat Wolski, dragged him to the entrance of the hothouse, then repeatedly smashed his head against the door and yelled for the Jews to come out. For a moment nothing happened. The Germans then fired into the air and yelled that they would poison them all like rats unless they came out.

> Finally, the flap concealing the entrance to the bunker was raised from the inside, and, in the opening, the victims started to appear one by one. First, the mothers came out with their children. The poor kids blinked, dazzled by the daylight and the glare of the sun, which they had not see for such a long time. Some of them were crying; their mothers hugged them helplessly and desperately. They were followed by the adults, who came up in deadly silence, interrupted now and then by a woman's sob, drowned by the screams of the Gestapo men. At the end the two boys, my grandson Janusz and Shimon, came to the surface."[203]

The Gestapo men loaded all the Jews into trucks and drove away. Meanwhile, one of the Jews, Orna Jagur's father, had managed to swallow a cyanide capsule. They loaded his body onto the truck as well. That afternoon Wolski's sister caught a final glimpse of her brother Mieczysław. For some reason the Germans took him back to the site. He was dressed only in a long shirt and had been badly beaten. For a brief moment he cast a long glance at the window of the house. That was the last time she saw him.

Mieczysław Wolski and his nephew, Janusz Wysocki, were soon shot. Many years later Wolski's sister recalled that their friends shunned them, and they were made to feel as if they had committed some crime. "Until this very day [1988] we never speak with anyone about the Krysia. But, after all, it wasn't a crime to try to save human lives, was it?"[204]

The truck took all the captured Jews, including Ringelblum, Yehudis, and Uri to the Pawiak Prison, in the area of the now destroyed ghetto. Men and women sat in separate cells. News quickly spread among the inmates of the Pawiak that Ringelblum had been captured. Some of the Jewish inmates tried to make a last ditch effort to save him. Perhaps, they believed, it might be possible to smuggle Ringelblum out of his cell and into a regular prison work detail.

One of these prisoners was the Yiddish writer Yekhiel Hirschaut. He went into Ringelblum's cell. Ringelblum's son, Uri, was sitting on his lap. Ringelblum looked as if he had been badly beaten; he told Hirschaut that the Gestapo had tortured him to find out about his contacts in the Jewish underground. Quickly Hirschaut told Ringelblum that the Jewish prisoners wanted to try to save him. Ringelblum glanced quickly at Uri and gave Hirschaut a questioning look. What about his son and his wife, he asked Hirschaut? No, Hirschaut said, it would not be possible to save them. He knew immediately that Ringelblum would not accept his proposition.[205]

Hirschaut remembered Ringelblum's words as he looked at his son: "The little one, why is he guilty? My heart breaks because of him [Vos iz er shuldik, der kleyner? Tsulib em veytigt mir shtark dos harts]."[206] And Ringelblum asked Hirschaut a final question: "Is death difficult?"

Within a couple of days, somewhere in the ruins of the Warsaw Ghetto, the Germans shot all the prisoners of the Krysia, Ringelblum, Yehudis and Uri among them.

A FINAL MESSAGE

About ten days earlier, on March 1, 1944, Ringelblum and Berman finally completed a project that Ringelblum deemed vital, a letter to London describing Jewish cultural activities during the war and listing the murdered writers, teachers, actors, rabbis, and scholars who had formed the cultural elite of Polish Jewry.[207] The letter was addressed to the YIVO in New York as well as to the Yiddish PEN Club, to the writers Sholem Asch, H. Leyvik, Joseph Opatoshu, and their own friend Rafael Mahler. The letter opened with the stark declaration that 95 percent of Polish Jewry had already been murdered and that the few who were still alive had little chance of surviving the war.

In the letter Ringelblum and Berman proudly described the far-flung mutual aid activities conducted by the Aleynhilf and other organizations that had recruited devoted helpers from across the political spectrum. The principle of mutual help had inspired Jews even in German concentration camps like Trawniki and Poniatowa. Only with the onset of mass murder did Jews change their focus from mutual aid to armed resistance. Mindful that the Bund was already claiming much of the credit for the uprising, Berman and Ringelblum reminded their readers that Zionist youth had taken the lead in the fighting. In the battles of the Warsaw Ghetto, in Białystok, in the uprisings in Sobibór and Treblinka, "Jews showed the world that they could fight with weapons and that they knew how to die with honor in the battle against the arch-enemy of the Jewish people and humanity."

The watchword of the Jewish public leadership, Ringelblum and Berman stressed, had been "'to live with honor and die with honor.' . . . A sign of this was the wide-ranging cultural activity that developed despite terror and hunger, and that grew . . . along with the martyrdom of Polish Jewry." Even in the concentration camps, "the outpouring of cultural and social activity continued as long as the Jewish collective remained alive. Please remember that the last surviving cultural leaders remained faithful to the ideals of your culture—until the very end. The banner of culture as a weapon in the battle against barbarism remained in their hands until they died."

The letter also described the "twenty or so" boxes of "documents, diaries, memoirs, reportage, and photographs" that were in the Oyneg Shabes Archive. "Most of the material that was sent abroad originated from the archive," they wrote. "We alarmed the world with detailed information about the greatest crime in history, and we are continuing our archival activity." In concluding the letter, Ringelblum and Berman expressed their doubt that they would survive the war and see their friends in New York.

Only fifty years separated the beginning from the end. In 1891 the Jewish historian Simon Dubnow issued his famous appeal to East European Jews to collect documents and study their history. In 1940 Ringelblum organized the Oyneg Shabes Archive to document the ordeal of Polish Jewry under the Nazi occupation. During the half-century that separated the Dubnow appeal from the Oyneg Shabes, East European Jewish historians—with no support from governments, state archives, or universities—turned the collection of sources and documents [zamling] into a mass movement and the writing of history into a national mission for the Jewish people of Eastern Europe. If there was any tension between this view of history as objective scholarship and history as nation building, these Jewish historians did not let it interfere with their task.

Ringelblum followed in the footsteps of Dubnow, although in tragically different circumstances. By recording the most painful chapter of Polish Jewish history in all its detail and variety, a task carried on not by one historian but by a dedicated collective, the archive reminded posterity that in death, as in life, East European Jewry was a people, not a religious group or a community of martyrs. As a people it had its heroes and villains, its share of failures and successes.

Right after the end of the Holocaust, Mark Dvorzhetsky, who had survived the Vilna Ghetto and a number of German concentration camps, published an article titled "Should We Hide the Truth?" Should survivors, Dvorzhetsky asked, tell the world about the Jewish police, about the Kapos, about ugly behavior in the ghettos?[208] Indeed, this fierce anger against other Jews was expressed far more frequently during the war than after. Ringelblum's answer, through the Oyneg Shabes, would have been a simple yes, for by telling the entire truth, as far as that was possible, the Oyneg Shabes underscored the quiet heroism of the thousands of ordinary Jews who helped their neighbors and struggled to hang onto their personal and national dignity. The Warsaw Ghetto produced the Jewish police, but it also created the house committees. Some Jews betrayed their own people; others fought heroically to help dying children.

Ringelblum also believed that the archive, by historicizing and individualizing disaster, would make future generations remember that genocide can truly be grasped only by understanding and remembering what and who was destroyed. As he told Hersh Wasser:

> I do not see our work as a separate project, as something that includes only Jews, that is only about Jews, and that will interest only Jews. My whole being rebels against that. I cannot agree with such an approach, as a Jew, as a socialist, or as a historian. Given the daunting complexity of social processes, where everything is interdependent, it would make no sense to see ourselves in isolation [kon nisht zayn keyn reyd vegn opshlisn zikh in unzere daled omes]. Jewish suffering and Jewish liberation and redemption are part and parcel of the general calamity [umglik] and the universal drive to throw off the hated [Nazi] yoke. We have to regard ourselves as participants in a universal [almenshlekher] attempt to construct a solid structure of objective documentation that will work for the good of mankind. Let us hope that the bricks and cement of our experience and our understanding will be able to provide a foundation.[209]

Ringelblum was not trying to "universalize" the Holocaust by blurring the differences between the mass murder of the Jews and the sufferings of others. Indeed, a great part of his life had been spent fighting "Red assimilation," the refusal of much of the Left to respect Jewish claims to a separate national identity. But neither would he abandon the ideals and beliefs that had shaped him before the war and that provided an anchor of hope and stability as his world collapsed around him. He shared his party's conviction that a revolution would cleanse the world of evil, and that in the new socialist era there would be a place for the Jewish people, especially if historians gave them a record that would help them know who they were and what they had done.

As Israel Lichtenstein buried the first cache of the archive in 1942, he concluded his testament with the following words: "We are the redeeming sacrifice for the Jewish People. I believe that the nation will survive. We the Jews of Eastern Europe are the redeemers of the People of Israel."[210] At the very end of his life Lichtenstein reaffirmed his belief in the future of the Jewish people. And he reminded posterity that Jews were not just victims: they were people and part of a living and resilient nation. So Ringelblum also believed, and so his legacy—the legacy of the Oyneg Shabes Archive—reminds us today.

Guidelines for a Study of Polish-Jewish Relations (AR I, no. 492)

THE POLISH-GERMAN WAR

The Period Preceding the Siege of Warsaw

- The difference in how the authorities, especially the military authorities, regarded Jews before the war and [after the war began]
- How different political parties regarded and spoke about Jews after the outbreak of the war
- How the "man on the street" related to Jews
- The impact and reaction to Jewish participation in the fighting
- The participation of Jews in organizations of public welfare and civil defense
- Scenes of Polish-Jewish friendship on city streets
- The attitude of the Polish population, especially peasants, to Jewish refugees fleeing from areas threatened by the Germans

DURING THE SIEGE OF WARSAW

- Attitudes toward Jews of various classes of the Polish population— workers, the lower middle class, intelligentsia—during the siege
- The portrayal of Jewish participation in the defense of Warsaw by the military, the press, radio, and various social classes
- The aid organized by the Jews—without regard to nationality—to soldiers, the wounded, those whose homes had burned, and refugees (the different forms of aid, concrete examples)
- Rumors and slanders about Jews during the time of the siege— especially accusations of profiteering. Blaming the Jews for the fall of

Warsaw, especially by right-wing elements. Anti-Semitic undertones in Starzyński's speech
- The Polish radio about the Jews
- The city government about the Jews
- The looting of Jewish stores in the final stages of the siege
- The marked rise in anti-Semitic attitudes in the period just after the capitulation and before the Germans entered the city

CREATION OF THE GHETTO

- German policies aimed at worsening relations between Poles and Jews. Can one say that the Germans attempted to use anti-Semitic propaganda to build a bridge between themselves and the Polish population? The forms and results of German anti-Semitic propaganda. Polish-German cooperation in anti-Jewish outbreaks
- Can one speak of a change in attitude toward the Jews on the part of Polish reactionary political parties? The reasons for and examples of this change in official statements (for example, in the matter of introducing an "Aryan Paragraph" in the Bar)
- The Warsaw city government and the Jews
- Polish youth and the Jews. Students in the schools, lower middle class youth, working class youth. The Polish hooligans
- The January pogrom: its course, evil manifestations (*zło*), street scenes, the attitude of the Polish community and particular political parties
- Polish-Jewish economic cooperation. Polish representatives and partners in Jewish firms. Trade between Poles and Jews
- The distressing story of Polish doctors and health authorities' attitude to the Jews
- The problem of converts as seen by Poles and Jews
- Clerical protection of converts
- What is said about Jews: in school, the Church, satire (cabarets), in illegal organizations, on the radio, in the daily press, in Polish-language publications, in non-published [illegal] Polish literature
- The attitude of Polish official bodies toward the problem of the ghetto. The fight for territory. The exchange of flats and exploitation by Christian tenants
- The role of reactionary Polish economic unions during the creation of the ghetto (the role of the Union of Merchants, the memoranda of Polish artisans)
- Which Polish groups profited from the establishment of the ghetto?

- The safeguarding of Jewish property by Polish friends
- The attitude of Polish lawyers toward their Jewish clients and colleagues
- How did Polish society react to the formation of the ghetto: what was said while waiting in line, the attitude of workers, artisans, merchants, the professional intelligentsia
- The issue of the converts. Family tragedies connected with the establishment of the ghetto

AFTER THE ESTABLISHMENT OF THE GHETTO UNTIL THE GERMAN-SOVIET WAR

- [The attitude of] Polish official circles and political parties toward the situation of the Jews in the ghetto
- [The attitude] of Polish society toward the situation in the ghetto: workers, artisans, merchants, professional intelligentsia. What kind of gossip is exchanged while waiting in line: stories about the riches of the ghetto, about the power of the Judenrat, etc. The Polish police in the ghetto. Altered spheres of competence
- The theft of Jewish property, blackmail, corruption, the collaboration of the criminal police with the Gestapo. The Police and the Jewish Order Service. The attitude and behavior of the Polish police toward Jews caught outside the ghetto. Polish hooligans around the ghetto walls
- Polish officials (tax officials, municipal workers, etc.) in the ghetto
- [Polish officials'] attitude toward Jews. Blackmail, corruption
- Evidence of sympathy and friendship toward Jews outside the ghetto
- The attitude toward Jewish beggars outside the ghetto
- Polish-Jewish collaboration in smuggling
- Polish-Jewish economic cooperation. Trade ties, the form, character, which period

FROM THE OUTBREAK OF THE SOVIET WAR UNTIL THE PRESENT MOMENT

- How did the outbreak of the German-Soviet war change Polish-Jewish relations? Heightened anti-Semitic propaganda on the part of the Germans, its form and character. How beneficial was it to the Germans?
- The reception on the Polish street of the news of the physical liquidation of the Jews. How well is Polish society informed about events like Wilno, Chełmno, Lublin, etc.

- How are Poles reacting? Polish official circles about the future of Polish-Jewish relations. What do different political parties say about this? How does the Polish "man on the street" see the future of Polish-Jewish relations?
- The attitude of workers, artisans, merchants, smugglers, traders, the professional intelligentsia
- Polish-Jewish relations in the provinces: the rural population employs Jewish workers, youth, even children. Landowners' attitude toward *halutzim*.* The attitude of the rural population toward Jewish refugees
- What do Poles think about how Germans treat the Jews? What do they say about the attitude of Jews toward the Poles in Białystok during the Soviet occupation?

*Members of Zionist youth movements; they sought agricultural work to prepare themselves for a life in Palestine.

Guidelines for a Study of the Warsaw Ghetto (AR I, no. 98)

HISTORICAL OVERVIEW

Demographics: Apartments, Living Conditions

Economics
- Workers
- Handicraft and small industry: guilds (*tsekhn*)
- Trade and industry under Aryan trustees
- Free professions: doctors, lawyers, teachers, engineers
- Trade
- Smuggling
- Owning and managing apartments
- Shops
- Employees in ghetto institutions
- Wages and salaries
- Finances and currency exchange
- The ghetto as an economic phenomenon
- From what do Jews live (questionnaire: legal and illegal [occupations])
- Labor unions and the cooperatives

SOCIAL HELP

- General overview
- The organizations: ŻTOS, CENTOS, TOZ, Aleynhilf
- House committees
- Feeding
  Soup kitchens (Leszno 40, Nalewki 23, Twarda 15, Leszno 29, Zamenhofa 15, Nalewki 22, Nowolipki 68, Karmelicka 29)

- Expellees (*goylim*) and refugees
- Refugee centers (*punktn*)
- Help for children
- Epidemics
- Sanitary services
- Provision of clothing
- TOPOROL*
- Help for relatives (*kroyvim hilf*)
- The Judenrat and class tension
- Constructive help: free loan *kases* [credit societies]
- Hospitals
- Religious department

SOCIAL AND CULTURAL LIFE

- General overview
- Social life (*gezelshaftlekh lebn*)
- Literature
- Scholarship and science (*visnshaft*)
- Folklore: sayings, jokes, letters
- Music choirs
- Schools: private schooling (*kompletn*)
- handicraft training
- Students and classes
- Religious life
- "Them" [the Germans]—attitude to Jews
- Converts
- Converts in the Judenrat
- Converts in artistic life
- Youth
- Libraries
- Women
- Demoralization and corruption
- Housing department
- Inspiring (*derheybene*) moments of Jewish life

*Before the war the TOPOROL was an organization that fostered agricultural education among Jews. In the Warsaw Ghetto it organized the planting of vegetable gardens in vacant lots.

POLISH-JEWISH RELATIONS

THE JUDENRAT (KEHILE)

- Organization of the Ghetto (Jewish residential quarter)
- Legal position of the Judenrat
- Development of the Judenrat
- Territorial changes in the boundaries of the Jewish Quarter: topography, geography, names
- Food supply
- Coal Supply Commission
- Post Office
- Jewish police (converts in the police)
- Insurance
- Banks
- Pharmacies
- Health department
- Labor Department
- Cemetery
- Trash and waste removal
- "Protected buildings"
- Industry and trade
- Finance department
- Social aid
- Statistical department
- Housing department

EXPELLEES AND REFUGEES (the sociological problems stemming from being uprooted from one's home)

ARTISTS (ARTISTN)

PAINTERS

MUSICIANS

DAILY LIFE OF WORKERS, ARTISANS, SMUGGLERS

THE JEWISH CHILD

SHOPS

Guidelines for a Study of the Jewish Shtetl (AR I, no. 155)

THE LIFE AND APPEARANCE OF THE SHTETL JUST BEFORE THE OUTBREAK OF THE WAR

- Polish-Jewish relations
- Polish-German relations
- Reporting in the local press

THE BEGINNING OF THE WAR AND THE SITUATION IN THE SHTETL BEFORE "THEY" ARRIVE

- Events in the first days after the outbreak of the war
- Facts and descriptions of special interest
- Bombardments, fires
- Casualties of military action
- Communal life
- Attitudes of Poles toward Jews
- Fleeing. (*Dos loyfn*). Who gave the signal? Who ran? The attitude of the peasants toward those who fled
- How many returned?
- How many remained in the shtetl, and why?
- Which classes and age groups fled?
- List of victims (*kedoyshim*) of the military operations
- Battles around and within the shtetl

THE ARRIVAL OF "THEM" [THE GERMANS]

- The first days after their arrival
- Their attitude toward Poles and Jews

- Jewish loss of legal rights
- Arson, attacks on Jews
- The attitude of the Polish population
- What happened with the main synagogue, prayer houses, societies (*hevres*), the cemetery, chronicles (*pinkesim*), religious objects (tora scrolls, religious books), the rabbi
- Jewish markings [armbands or star]: shape, inscriptions, when introduced?
- Beards, Jewish traditional dress
- Tribute (*kontributsie*): how did it happen?
- Synagogues and prayer houses, burning synagogues (with or without Jews inside)
- Public burning of books
- Roundups for forced labor
- Deportation to concentration camps: who, how, why?
- Examples of martyrdom (Kiddush Hashem) and self-sacrifice (*mesires nefesh*)
- List of martyrs killed by "them"
- Incidents of resistance (*kegnvirkungs aktn*)

PUBLIC JEWISH LIFE UNDER "THEM" [THE GERMANS]

- Ghetto: open or closed?
- Judenrat and its makeup
- New strongmen (*tkifim*), communal leaders and their actions
- Jewish police: composition and powers. How did they wield their power?
- Legal status of the Judenrat. Documents. Daily functioning
- How did the Judenrat get its revenue? What were its expenditures?
- What did the kehille give to "them"?
- What did "they" take from the Jews?
- How did Jews try to influence "them"?
- Labor duty . . .
- Labor camps: their organization and how they took Jewish workers
- Jewish work. How did "they" related to it?
- Jewish artisans working for "them"
- Jewish women working for "them." How were they treated? Pretty women, ugly women
- Brothels for "them"
- Jewish social aid and "their" reaction to it: soup kitchens, refugees from the immediate vicinity, refugee shelters

- Aspects of help for the poor: permanent help, special drives for Passover and the holidays, help in winter, medical help, legal advice, help from abroad
- Schools, religious schools
- How "they" acted to Jews: to workers, wealthy Jews, merchants, artisans, religious figures, etc.
- Religious life: prayer quorums, prayer houses, Hasidic life, the Sabbath, the third meal of the Sabbath, Melave Malkes (ceremony of ushering out the Sabbath), . . . Sukkot, citrons, holidays
- Special days
- Informers and thugs (*voyle yungn*)
- What happened to the local shtetl intelligentsia?
- New converts and their attitude toward Jews
- The condition and the attitude of German (Jewish) refugees to the shtetl Jews

THE ECONOMIC SITUATION

- Bourgeoisie, industry, handicrafts, workers, petty trade, businesses, trade now, new forms, new materials, joint ventures with "them." Smuggling: what form did it take?
- The newly rich. How did they make their fortune? Names of the newly rich
- What happened to the prewar rich and to their fortunes?

THE EXPULSION (GIVE DATE)

- Rumors about the expulsion (planned or sudden)
- How many were expelled?
- The process of the expulsion. Where to?
- The population: the elderly, youth, children
- Kindnesses and cruelty from "them"
- The attitude of the Poles
- What happened to the insane and to the patients in the hospital?
- What was the approximate value of the lost Jewish wealth?
- Arrival in Warsaw and the reception (First aid, life in the refugee shelter, etc.)

POLITICAL, LABOR, AND OTHER ORGANIZATIONS

- How many members did the organization have before the war?
- What happened to the members at the beginning of the war: mobilized, left the shtetl, etc.

- What happened to the local party archive, flag, library, Jewish school, party seal, etc.
- Interesting episodes in the life of the organization during the (Polish-German) war and in the first days of the occupation
- How many members fled to the Soviet zone (*oyf yener zayt*) and what happened to them?
- A list—as detailed as possible—of party martyrs. Under what circumstances were they killed? Did they receive a Jewish burial?
- What happened to the youth organizations and to their property? He-halutz, hakhshara (training) bases, etc.
- What happened to other proletarian and bourgeois organizations?
- Did a discussion take place in the local organization about whether to stay or flee to the Soviet side?
- Were there any attempts to escape to Palestine?
- Contacts with other parties: Jewish, Polish
- The participation of the organization in the defense of Poland
- What kind of help did the party members get from their comrades after they arrived in Warsaw?
- After their arrival in Warsaw, did they maintain contact with their comrades back in the shtetl?

NOTES

The originals of the Ringelblum Archive are in the ZIH in Warsaw, with copies of most documents in Yad Vashem Archive in Jerusalem and the United States Holocaust Memorial Museum in Washington. Often a particular copy might be more legible in one archive than in another and in some cases, to read a particular file, one needed to consult all three archives. Therefore, all cites from the Ringelblum archive will follow the ZIH citation system, explained in note 8, page 402, even though documents actually came from all three archives.

INTRODUCTION

1. In Yiddish Oyneg Shabes (Oneg Shabbat in Hebrew) literally means the "Joy of the Sabbath." Ringelblum used this code name for the archive, because the staff usually held its meetings on Saturday afternoons.

2. See Rachel Auerbach, "Vi azoy iz oysgegrobn gevorn der Ringelblum Arkhiv," *Arbeter vort,* June 27, 1947.

3. Rachel Auerbach, *Varshever tsvoes* (Tel Aviv, 1974), p. 196. Ringelblum had told Auerbach that someone on the Aryan side had been informed about where the archive had been hidden. But sources indicate that after the war no one came forward except Wasser to locate the archive. Auerbach herself recalls that during this meeting with Ringelblum, which took place in early 1943, Ringelblum did not reveal where the archive was buried and she did not ask. "Legende" was a term historians used to indicate the description and location of a historical document. But it also meant "legend."

4. The organization was founded in 1925 in Vilna, Poland (now Vilnius, Lithuania), as the Yiddish Scientific Institute and is now the YIVO Institute for Jewish Research, headquartered in New York City since 1940.

5. Letter from Emanuel Ringelblum to Adolf Berman, March 1, 1944, Berman File, no. 358, Ghetto Fighters Museum Archive (Arkhiyon Beit Lohamei Ha-getaot); henceforth, GFMA. In this same letter Ringelblum expressed the hope that the archive would eventually be sent to the YIVO: "W razie gdyby nikt z nas nie przeżył wojny należałoby już teraz wymienić Rafała oraz ciocię IWO jako spadkobierców. Niech przynajmniej to po nas zostanie, naturalnie że włączam tu skład pod 68" [If none of us survives the war, then it would be good to appoint Rafał or Aunt YIVO as the heirs. At least let that remain after we are gone, and of course I am including the collection under 68]. The number 68 refers to where the archive is hidden, and Rafał to the Jewish historian Rafael Mahler who was then in New York. At the height of the Great Deportation from the Warsaw Ghetto, the Oyneg Shabes discussed the possibility that the archive might find its way to the YIVO after the war. See Abraham Lewin, *A Cup of Tears: A Diary of the Warsaw Ghetto* (Oxford, 1988), p. 141; diary entry of July 29, 1942.

6. Auerbach, "Vi azoy iz oysgegrobn gevorn."

7. Israel Lichtenstein, like Ringelblum, was a longtime member of the Warsaw Left Poalei Zion organization. Born in Radzyń in 1904, Lichtenstein studied in the Vilna Yiddish Teachers Seminar. After moving to Warsaw in 1932, he headed the Borochov school and contributed to several Yiddish journals including *Literarishe Bleter* and the children's magazine *Grininke Boymelekh.*

8. Ringelblum Archive, part I, no. 132. Reprinted in Joseph Kermish, ed., *To Live with Honor and Die with Honor: Selected Documents from the Warsaw Ghetto Underground Archives Oyneg Shabbath* (Jerusalem, 1986), p. 66. Loyal to his political movement until the very end, Graber asked that those who find the archive send it to a Borochov Museum in a "United Soviets of Palestine." (Hereafter, AR I refers to the first part of the Ringelblum Archive; AR II refers to the second part. The document numbers were those established by the catalogue of the Jewish Historical Institute [ZIH] in Warsaw. Although a new catalogue is being issued, with some new numeration, it has appeared too late to be used in this present work.)

9. Gele Sekstein grew up in a poor Warsaw neighborhood and was orphaned at an early age. Her artistic talents attracted the attention of her teachers at the Bund's Grosser school, where she received her primary education. The noted Yiddish writer I. J. Singer also noticed her gifts and helped her exhibit her work. Eventually she became an art teacher in the Borochov school in Warsaw. Her prewar portraits of Jewish children, many drawn in the famous Medem Sanitarium, earned her a growing reputation. As her husband emphasized, she devoted herself in the Warsaw Ghetto to helping children. Many of her portraits were hidden in the Ringelblum Archive.

Gele Sekstein also left a testament, dated August 1, 1942. When the Great Deportation started, Sekstein had been planning a large exhibit of her many portraits of Jewish children. She regretted that only a small part of her work could be hidden in the archive. She asked that after the war her portraits be exhibited in a Jewish museum that would be established to restore Jewish culture. Like her husband, she hoped that her daughter would be remembered. "Now I am at peace," she ended. "I must die, but I accomplished what I wanted to. I try to hide some trace of my work. Be well, my comrades and friends. Be well, Jewish people. Don't ever allow such a catastrophe to happen again!" See Khaim-Shloyme Kazdan, ed., *Lerer Yizkor Bukh* (New York, 1954), pp. 285–288. See also Auerbach, *Varshever tsvoes,* p. 200.

10. AR I, no. 1018.

11. AR II, no. 258. Reprinted in Ruta Sakowska, ed., *Archiwum Ringelbluma: Getto Warszawskie, lipiec 1942-styczeń 1943* (Warsaw, 1980), p. 175.

12. Auerbach, *Varshever tsvoes,* p. 201.

13. Emanuel Ringelblum, *Ksovim fun geto,* 2 vols. (Tel Aviv, 1985), 2:222–223.

14. Auerbach, *Varshever tsvoes,* p. 201. It is logical to assume, although without absolute certainty, that Auerbach was correct when she wrote that Lichtenstein was the one who buried the second part of the archive.

15. This date is given by Hersh Wasser. See his "Arkhiyon ha-geto: mifalo shel Dr. E. Ringelblum," *Yediot Beit Lohamei ha-Getaot,* nos. 9–10 (1955): 26.

16. The former Świętojerska 34 became the future site of the Chinese Embassy in Warsaw. In April 2003 searchers from Israel and Poland received permission to dig underneath the embassy and look for the archive, but they found nothing. See the *Jerusalem Post,* April 4, 2003.

17. Ringelblum, *Ksovim fun geto*, 2:186–187.

18. AR II, no. 197 ("The Last Stage of Resettlement Is Death"). Reprinted in Kermish, *To Live with Honor*, p. 704.

19. Gusta Davidson Draenger, *Justyna's Narrative* (Amherst, Mass., 1996).

20. Ber Mark, *Megiles Oyshvits* (Tel Aviv, 1977), pp. 286–351.

21. Herman Kruk, *The Last Days of the Jerusalem of Lithuania,* ed. and introduction by Benjamin Harshav, trans. Barbara Harshav, (New Haven and London, 2002).

22. Ruta Sakowska of the Jewish Historical Institute in Warsaw was the first scholar to see the Oyneg Shabes Archive as a center of civil resistance. See her "Opór cywilny getta warszawskiego," *Biuletyn Żydowskiego Instytutu Historycznego* [hereafter, *BŻIH*], nos. 86–87 (1973): 79–81.

23. On this point, see also David Roskies, *Against the Apocalypse: Responses to Catastrophe in Modern Jewish Culture* (Cambridge, Mass., 1984), p. 200.

24. Nakhman Blumenthal, "Der historiker—tsu der ferter yortsayt," *Arbeter tsaytung,* no. 3 (1948).

25. In 1953 a harsh attack on Ringelblum appeared in the Bundist journal *Unzer tsayt.* The writer, Y. Hart (Sholom Hertz), lambasted Ringelblum for being a "dictator" who abused his authority in the disbursement of relief funds and who turned the Oyneg Shabes Archive into a narrow clique of Poalei Tsiyon hacks. According to Hart, the Ringelblum diaries "are not and cannot be the chronicle of the life and death of Warsaw Jews during the Second World War. They cannot be because of their chaotic nature, because of their haphazard composition, because of their inaccuracies and in many cases because of the falsehoods that they contain. Because of what's missing and because of what the diaries contain. Ringelblum's portrayal of the Jews is distorted [*bashmirt*] and false. Many notations are included with evil intent [*mit a beyzn viln*]. The writer of these dairies, unfortunately, did not possess the sense of responsibility and the vigilance necessary to write the tragic chronicle." See Y. Hart, "Vegn Ringelblum's notisn fun Varshever geto," *Unzer tsayt,* no. 7–8 (1953); and idem, "Nisht di khronik fun di tragishe Varshever yidn," *Unzer tsayt,* no. 9 (1953). In an interview in 1999 Marek Edelman, a leader of the Bundist fighters in the Warsaw Ghetto Uprising, asserted that Ringelblum was "not a historian. He was a Communist hack in the Jewish sector. His history can only please the Communists." See "Kwestia moralności," *Midrasz,* November 1999.

26. On this point, see also Raya Cohen, "Emanuel Ringelblum: Between Historiographical Tradition and Unprecedented History," *Gal-ed,* nos. 15–16 (1997).

27. Other common versions of Schiper's first name were the Yiddish "Yitzhak" and the Polish "Ignacy."

28. S. M. Dubnow, "Ob izuchenii istorii russkikh evreev i ob uchrezhdenii istoricheskogo obshchestva," *Voskhod* (April–September 1891): 1–91; see also his autobiography, *Kniga zhizni* (Jerusalem and Moscow, 2004), pp. 168–169.

29. Emanuel Ringelblum, "Dray yor seminar," *Yunger Historiker,* no. 1 (1926); idem, "Di yidishe arbetershaft un di geshikhtsvisnshaft," *Di fraye yugnt,* no. 1 (1924).

30. A highly suggestive essay on the importance of organizing the study of local history can be found in Ringelblum's review of a local history of Pruzhany. See "Der Ershter Pruv," *Literarishe bleter,* no. 15 (1929). Ringelblum saw the study of local history as a collective effort based on groups of local volunteers. On the other hand, he emphasized that one person—a trained historian—should be responsible for advising and directing the enterprise.

31. In fact, as Jacob Shatzky has pointed out, there was always a certain tension in the interwar YIVO between the amateur ethos of collecting and the professional ethos of academic scholarship. See Shatzky, "Finf un tsvantig yor YIVO," in idem, *Shatzky bukh* (New York, 1958), p. 305. See also Cecile Kuznitz, "The Origins of Yiddish Scholarship and the YIVO Institute for Yiddish Research," Ph.D. dissertation, Stanford University, 2000.

32. See Tsemakh Shabad and Moshe Shalit, eds., *Vilner Zamlbukh*, 2 vols. (Vilna, 1916/1918); Zalmen Reyzen, ed., *Pinkes fun der Geshikhte fun Vilne in di yorn fun milkhome un okupatsiye* (Vilna, 1922).

33. Yosef Yerushalmi, *Zakhor: Jewish History and Jewish Memory* (New York, 1989), p. 94.

34. AR I, no. 88; reprinted in Kermish, *To Live with Honor*, pp. 732–733.

35. Meir Korzen, "Emanuel Ringelblum lifnei ha-milhama u'biyameha harishonim," *Yediot Yad Va-shem*, no. 21–22 (1959).

36. Hersh Wasser, "A vort vegn Ringelblum Arkhiv," unpublished manuscript, YIVO Archive (hereafter, YA), New York.

37. AR I, no. 49, notebook 1.

38. See Yehuda Bauer, "Jewish Leadership Reactions to Nazi Policies," in *The Holocaust as Historical Experience*, ed. Yehuda Bauer and Nathan Rotenstreich (New York, 1981), pp. 173–189.

39. In 1948 Yakov Kener, a close friend of Ringelblum's and a leader of the Left Poalei Zion, published a short pamphlet titled *Emanuel Ringelblum: A held in legion fun di giburei Yisroel in Geto* (Munich, 1948). Relying heavily on Kener for details of Ringelblum's early life, Jacob Shatzky wrote "Menakhem ben Fayvish Ringelblum (1900–1944)," which was the introduction to a collection of Ringelblum's writings that Shatzky edited; see Emanuel Ringelblum, *Kapitlen geshikhte fun amolikn yidishn lebn in Poyln*, ed. Jacob Shatzky (Buenos Aires, 1953). A third biographical article on Ringelblum can be found in Rafael Mahler, *Historiker un vegvayzer* (Tel Aviv, 1967), pp. 274–302. John Hersey wrote a fictionalized account of Ringelblum in his underrated novel of the Warsaw Ghetto, *The Wall*.

40. Melekh Ravitch, *Mayn Leksikon*, 3 vols. (Montreal, 1945/1947/1958), 2:85.

1   FROM "BICHUCH" TO WARSAW

1. Yehuda Mozner, "Mayne yugnt yorn in Buczacz," *Pinkas Galitsie* (Buenos Aires, 1945), p. 476.

2. Sh"Y Agnon, "B'tokh iri: perek ehad shel sipur ehad," in *Sefer Buczacz*, ed. Yisroel Cahan (Tel Aviv, 1955), pp. 9–14. On Agnon's early years in the town, see Dan Laor, *Khayei Agnon* (Tel Aviv, 1998), pp. 13–49. In a personal interview Shlomo Shweitzer, an old friend of Ringelblum's from the Left Poalei Zion, told me that Agnon, whose real name was Shmuel Yosef Czaczkes, was a cousin of Ringelblum's and had warm childhood memories of him.

3. A worthwhile article on Buczacz Jewry by the noted historian Meyer Balaban is in the Brokhaus-Efron Encyclopedia. See "Buczacz," in *Evreiskaia entsyklopediia*, ed. L. Katsnelson and Baron David Ginzburg, Vol. 5 (St. Petersburg, n.d.), p. 135.

4. Mendl Naygroshl, "Vegn E. Ringelblum's yugnt yorn," *Zhurnal tsum tsen yorikn yoyvl fun Dr. Emanuel Ringelblum Arbeter Ring Tsvayg 612* (New York, 1957), p. 33. One

might infer from the absence of any discussion of the family in the Buczacz memorial book that the Ringelblums were not among the most prominent Jewish families.

5. Kener, *Emanuel Ringelblum,* p. 8.

6. Unlike more traditional schools, this type of heder stressed the study of the Bible and Hebrew grammar. Maskilim considered it more modern and sent their children there.

7. Natan Eck, "Mit Emanuel Ringelblum in Varshever geto," *Di goldene keyt,* no. 24 (1955): 120.

8. David Pohorila, "Pirkei hayai," in Cahan, *Sefer Buczacz,* p. 194.

9. Mozner, "Mayne yugnt yorn in Buczacz," p. 476.

10. Kener, *Emanuel Ringelblum,* p. 9.

11. Mozner, "Mayne yugnt yorn in Buczacz," pp. 477–478.

12. Ringelblum, *Ksovim fun geto,* 2:217.

13. Natan Eck, "In baginen fun yorhundert," in Tsentral Farband fun Galitsianer Yidn in Argentine, *Galitsianer Yidn: Yoyvl Bukh,* ed. Nokhem Lindman and Mordecai Kaufman (Buenos Aires, 1966), p. 173.

14. Ibid., p. 144.

15. Ibid.

16. A valuable study of the Poalei Tsiyon in Habsburg Galicia is Shabtai Unger's *Poalei Tsiyon b'keisarut ha-Ostrit* (Beersheba, 2001); on Schiper in this period, see also Julien (Yehhil) Hirschaut, *In gang fun der geshikhte* (Tel Aviv, 1984), pp. 173–180.

17. Naygroshl, "Vegn E. Ringelblum's yugnt yorn," p. 33. Mendl Naygroshl (1903–1965) would leave Sanz for Vienna, where he earned his law degree and practiced law until the Anschluss of 1938. He also became a Yiddish poet and wrote on the history of Yiddish literature in Galicia. Like many of Ringelblum's close friends, he would play an active role in the YIVO.

18. In Naygroshl's words, "Ringelblum's step-mother made a sad impression. Worried, looking like a lost soul, hair always askew, she seemed like someone who had given up on everything and everybody. One never saw her go outside; it's as if she lived on some forgotten shore" (ibid., p. 33).

19. Ibid., p. 31.

20. Rafael Mahler, " Doktor Emanuel Ringelblum, historiker fun poylishe yidn un fun zeyer umkum un gvure," in *Sefer Sanz,* ed. Rafael Mahler (Tel Aviv, 1970), p. 647.

21. Kener, *Emanuel Ringelblum,* p. 9.

22. Naygroshl, "Vegn E. Ringelblum's yugnt yorn," pp. 30–31.

23. Rafael Mahler, "Shaul Amsterdam," in idem, *Sefer Sanz,* p. 584.

24. Both of these letters are contained in an unnumbered file in the archives of the Żydowski Instytut Historyczny (Jewish Historical Institute) in Warsaw.

25. According to Leybel, when Ringelblum received this assignment, shortly after arriving in Warsaw, he felt that his literary Yiddish was still too shaky to do the job alone. Therefore he asked Leybel, whom he met in the Poalei Tsiyon, to help him. Leybel remembers playing only a secondary role in the translation. Still Ringelblum insisted that he be listed as a co-translator. See Daniel Leybel, "Mit Ringelblumen," *Nayvelt,* April 1954.

26. Hanka Warhaftig Hirschaut, "Emanuel Ringelblum: Hero as Teacher," *The Forward,* January 4, 1985.

27. Anka Grupińska, *Ciągle po kole* (Warsaw, 2000), p. 204. Like Edelman, Szwajger was repelled by Ringelblum's ultra-left politics, "more communist than the communists."

She also remembered what she called his heavy-handed jokes [*końskie dowcipy*] and his sycophantic tendency to favor her because she was the director's daughter.

28. For a short biography of Yehudis Herman, see Kazdan, *Lerer Yizkor Bukh,* p. 411.

29. Hirschaut, "Emanuel Ringelblum: Hero as Teacher."

2   BOROCHOV'S DISCIPLE

1. Letter from Emanuel Ringelblum to Adolf Berman, January 24, 1944. Adolf Berman Collection, Archive of Kibbutz Lohamei Ha'Getaot, File 358.

2. This is one of the major themes of the party press. For examples of the party's Yiddishism, see Y. Zerubavel, "Poalei Tsiyonizm kontra Palestinatsentrizm," *Arbeter tsaytung,* no. 28 (1934); see also N. Buchsbaum, "Tsum YIVO Tsuzamenfor," *Arbeter tsaytung,* no. 35 (1935).

3. Ringelblum, *Ksovim fun geto,* 2:104.

4. See Jacob Lestschinsky, "Emanuel Ringelblum," *Forverts,* December 20, 1953; Jacob Shatzky, "Emanuel Ringelblum der historiker," in *Zhurnal tsum tsenyorikn yoyvl fun Dr. Emanuel Ringelblum Arbeter Ring Tsvayg 612* (New York, 1957). Lestschinsky noted that "as left-wing Zionists, it was natural that they would take an interest in Jewish economic problems (and history). For the Bund the solution to the Jewish problem was simple: bring on democracy and socialism, and, presto, all Jewish headaches will disappear! A left Zionist had to somehow find a way to combine these two clashing theories."

5. Ringelblum, *Ksovim fun geto,* 2:152. "Dr. Schiper's historical researches were closely linked to his political activity. Dr. Schiper, the leader of the Poalei Tsiyon in Galicia, which put the anomaly of the Jewish economic structure at the center of its platform, looked to the past to find the explanation for the present Jewish economic profile" (ibid.). Although many young Jewish historians indeed belonged to the LPZ, Natalia Aleksiun, who studied the backgrounds of students in Meyer Balaban's Jewish history seminar at Warsaw University in the late 1930s, has failed to find evidence that the LPZ was overrepresented in this group (personal communication with Natalia Aleksiun).

6. Jacob Kener, *Kvershnit* (New York, 1947), p. 240.

7. Khaim Brand, "Emanuel Ringelblum," in *Zhurnal tsum tsenyorikn yoyvl fun Dr. Emanuel Ringelblum Arbeter Ring Tsvayg 612,* p. 5.

8. On the tenth anniversary of Borochov's death the important Yiddish cultural journal *Literarishe bleter* marked the occasion with two articles, one by Zalman Reyzen, the editor of the Vilna *Tog,* and the other by Eliyahu Cherikover, who would head the YIVO's historical section. Neither Reyzen nor Cherikover were members of the LPZ but both emphasized Borochov's pioneering role in the study of Yiddish philology and literature. See Eliyahu Cherikover, "Ber Borochov, vi ikh ken im"; and Zalmen Reyzen, "In rekhtn oyfbli," both in *Literarishe bleter,* no. 51 (1927).

9. What Borochov objected to was not Hebrew or the Hebrew revival but what he called "militant Hebraism" marked by an aggressive negation of Yiddish. Indeed, he warned, this militant struggle against Yiddish would backfire; the Jewish masses might well reject not only the Hebrew fanatics but also the language itself. See Borochov's 1915 essay, "Hebraismus miltans," in *Class Struggle and the Jewish Nation,* ed. Mitchell Cohen (New Brunswick, N.J., 1984), pp. 143–147. For Ringelblum's own attack on Hebraismus militans, see Emanuel Ringelblum, "Yidishe Kultur Konferents," *Vilner Tog,* no. 235 (1926).

10. Ber Borochov, *Shprakh-forshung un literatur geshikhte* (Tel Aviv, 1966), pp. 53–76.

11. Naygroshl, "Vegn E. Ringelblum's yugnt yorn," p. 32.

12. Worthwhile treatments of Borochov can be found in Matityahu Mintz, *Ber Borochov: Ha-ma'agal ha-rishon* (Tel Aviv, 1978); and Jonathan Frankel, *Prophecy and Politics* (Cambridge, 1981), pp. 329–365.

13. See, for example, Frankel, *Prophecy and Politics,* pp. 344–351; see also "Our Platform," in Ber Borochov, *Nationalism and the Class Struggle: A Marxist Approach to the Jewish Problem* (Westport, Conn., 1972), pp. 183–205.

14. For an excellent discussion on this issue, see Matityahu Mintz, *Naye tsaytn, naye lider* (Tel Aviv, 1993), pp. 501–540.

15. The definitive study of the Left Poalei Zion in Poland is Bina Garncarska-Kadari, *Bihipusei derekh: Poalei Tsiyon Smol b'Polin ad milhemet ha'olam ha'shniya* (Tel Aviv, 1995).

16. Jacob Zerubavel, "Tsum dritn yortsayt," in *Unzer lebn* (Warsaw, 1920), p. 4; quoted in Matityahu Mints, *Naye tsaytn, naye lider* (Tel Aviv, 1993), p. 490.

17. Along with Garncarska-Kadari's *Bihipusei derekh*, a good summary of the split can be found in Ezra Mendelsohn, *Zionism in Poland: The Formative Years, 1915–1926* (New Haven and London, 1981), pp. 136–161.

18. "Tsum 10tn yoyvl fun Histadrut," *Arbeter Tsaytung,* no. 1 (1936).

19. Pockets of LPZ strength in the Jewish labor movement included, in Warsaw, the Woodworkers, the Chemical Workers, Store Clerks and Porters; in Lodz the LPZ either controlled or had strong positions in the Needle Workers, the Chemical Workers, and the Waiters. See Kener, *Kvershnit,* p. 157. According to Kener, the LPZ dominated the Jewish unions in such mid-sized towns as Brest Litovsk, Chełm, and Nowy Sącz (Sanz).

20. See ibid., pp. 187–193; and Garncarska-Kadari, *Bihipusei dereh,* pp. 210–226.

21. The LPZ reached its peak strength in the late 1920s. In the municipal elections of 1927 and 1928, according to Kener, the party received about 50,000 votes and elected 140 delegates to various city councils. In Brest, Chełm Bendin (Będzin), and Kalisz, the LPZ was the dominant Jewish party. The Bund, on the other hand, outpolled the LPZ in Warsaw and Lodz.

22. On the Yugnt, see Rafael Mahler, "Yugnt-tnuat ha'noar shel poalei tsiyon smol b'Polin," *Ha-tsionut,* no. 6 (1973): 247–257; Kener, *Kvershnit,* pp. 200–217; and Garncarska-Kadari, *Bihipusei dereh,* 329–337.

23. A useful introduction to the study of Jewish youth movements in interwar Poland is Moshe Kligsberg, "Di yidishe yugnt bavegung in Poyln tsvishn beyde velt milkhomes," in *Studies on Polish Jewry,* ed. Joshua A. Fishman (New York, 1974), pp. 137–229. On tensions between the LPZ and Zionist youth movements, see Israel Oppenheim, "Yahas Poalei Tsiyon Smol b'Polin l'rayon ha-halutsi u li'he-haluts: ha-reka ha'rayoni," *Gal-ed,* no. 6 (1982): 81–96.

24. See, for example, Raya Cohen, "Ha-emnam derekh ahat? Od al mikoma shel hitnagdut ha-mizuyenet b'getaot," in *Ha-shoah: historiyah vezikaron: kovetz maamarim shai le-Yisrael Gutman,* ed. Shmuel Almog et al. (Jerusalem, 2001), pp. 31–32.

25. Mendelsohn, *Zionism in Poland,* pp. 126–130.

26. Kener, *Kvershnit,* pp. 196–197.

27. Personal conversation with Anna Olcanetzka, New York, June 1999.

28. E. R. [Emanuel Ringelblum], "Tsvey-yorplan in kamf mit inalfabetizm," *Arbeter kultur* (1931).

29. "In di varshever ovntshuln," *Di fraye yugnt,* no. 9 (1926).

30. Garncarska-Kadari, *Bihipusei dereh,* pp. 298–302.

31. *Di fraye yugnt,* no. 2 (1925).

32. Mahler, "Yugnt," p. 255.

33. Kener, *Kvershnit,* pp. 238–239.

34. Emanuel Ringelblum [Munie Heler], "A blutige vorenung," *Di fraye yugnt,* no. 3 (1925).

35. Emanuel Ringelblum [Munie Heler], "Di yidishe arbetershaft un di geshikhts-visnshaft," *Di fraye yugnt,* no. 1 (1924).

36. Ibid.,

37. In fact, Ringelblum's assertion that Graetz discounted Jewish peoplehood was not quite accurate. See, for example, Shlomo Avineri, *The Making of Modern Zionism* (New York, 1981), p. 35.

38. Emanuel Ringelblum, "Der Yidisher Visnshaftlekher Institut un di arbeter yugnt," *Di fraye yugnt,* no. 7 (1926). It was telling, Ringelblum noted, that the Jewish bourgeois press had ignored the establishment of the YIVO in 1925 even as it hailed the simultaneous founding of the Hebrew University. But he saw this bourgeois interest in modern Hebrew culture as a sham, a convenient alibi to justify abandoning Yiddish in favor of Polish. Unlike the Bund, the LPZ did not boycott Hebrew per se. Children in the party's Borochov schools studied the language. But both the party and Ringelblum strongly opposed the persecution of Yiddish in Palestine and the use of Hebrew to supplant Yiddish.

39. "Der Yidisher Visnshaftlekher Institut un di arbeter yugnt," *Di fraye yugnt,* no. 7 (1926); "Der Yidishisher Visnshaftlekher Institut," *Di fraye yugnt,* no. 11 (1926).

40. Ibid.

41. *Kehilla* is the name of a traditional Jewish community governed by a board called the *Kahal.*

42. "Der Yidisher Visnshaftlekher Institut un di arbeter yugnt," *Di fraye yugnt,* no. 7 (1926); "Der Yidishisher Visnshaftlekher Institut," *Di fraye yugnt,* no. 11 (1926).

43. For the leftist attacks on the YIVO, see the protocols of the Second World Conference of the YIVO, August 14–19, 1935. Yidisher Visnshaftlekher Institut, *Der alveltlekher tsuzamenfor fun Yidishn Visnshaftlekhn Institut* (Vilna, 1936), esp. pp. 89–94; for Weinreich's conception of the mission of the YIVO, see pp. 62–68.

44. L. B. [Natan Buchsbaum], "Der Yivo un di yidishe arbetershaft," *Arbeter tsaytung,* no. 29 (1931).

45. Ibid.

46. For example, see Israel Sosis, "Di historishe 'visnshaft' fun yidishn visnshaftlekhn institut," *Tsaytshrift,* no. 4 (1930). This attack on the YIVO did not protect Sosis, perhaps the best of the Jewish historians in the USSR, from vicious attacks that questioned his own ideological orthodoxy.

47. Emanuel Ringelblum, "Der YIVO un di yidishe arbetershaft," *Arbeter tsyatung,* no. 32 (1931).

48. A few months later Buchsbaum asserted that the party should wait to see if the Left could take over the YIVO and change its orientation. But if that proved impossible, then the party should be prepared, "without any sentimentality" to break with the YIVO. See "Kultur Kongres," *Arbeter tsaytung,* no. 44 (1931).

49. As I argue elsewhere, the LPZ failed to develop a clear consensus on what it meant

by "proletarian culture." In the pages of the *Arbeter tsaytung,* the lack of support for Soviet Yiddish culture was striking. See Samuel Kassow, "The Left Poalei Zion in Interwar Poland," in *Yiddish and the Left: Papers of the Third Mendel Friedman International Conference on Yiddish,* ed. Gennady Estraikh and Mikhail Krutikov (Oxford, 2001), p. 117.

50. E. R. [Emanuel Ringelblum], "Tsum Kultur Kongres," *Arbeter tsaytung,* no. 29 (1931).

51. "Tsvey-Yorplan in kamf mitn analfabetizm," *Arbeter kultur* (1931).

52. Nakhman Mayzel, *Noente un eygene* (New York, 1957), p. 324.

53. Shakhne Zagan and Rafael Mahler were also members of the Polish delegation and did attend.

54. See *Ershter alveltlekher yidisher kultur kongres: Pariz 17–21 September, 1937* (Paris, 1937).

55. Natan Buchsbaum, "A PPSesher broshur gegn Bund un Bundizm," *Arbeter tsaytung,* no. 4 (1938).

56. Uriel [Rafael Mahler], "Di kultur badaytung far di yidishe masn in dem kamf farn territorialn arbeter tsenter," *Arbeter tsaytung,* no. 50 (1935). Mahler was perhaps purposely vague about whether the territory he had in mind was Palestine or Birobidzhan, the new Jewish autonomous region in the USSR.

57. For a succinct survey that analyzes the reasons for the Bund's surging popularity in the mid- and late 1930s, see Antony Polonsky, "The Bund in Polish Political Life, 1935–1939," *Jewish History: Essays in Honor of Chimen Abramsky,* ed. Ada Rapoport and Albert and Steven Zipperstein (London, 1988), pp. 547–581.

58. Viktor Alter, *Di Yidnfrage in Poyln* (Warsaw, 1937).

59. Jacob Zerubavel, "Tsu di problemen fun Poyle-Tsienizm," *Arbeter tsaytung,* no. 37/38 (1934).

60. Nakhum Nir-Rafalkes, "Eretsyisroeldige un khutsle'eretsdige likvidatsie in unzer bavegung," in *Tsu di shtraytfragn inm Poyle Tsiyenizm* (Jerusalem, 1934).

61. Betsalel Sherman, "Poyle Tsiyenizm kontra linkistishe umetumikayt," in ibid.

62. A good treatment of this is in Garncarska-Kadari, *Bihipusei dereh,* pp. 365–395.

63. For example, see Lev's important article "Problemen fun der yidisher virklikhkayt in der ibergangstkufe," *Arbeter tsaytung,* no. 48 (1934). This was the final article Lev would publish in the *Arbeter tsaytung* for a year and a half.

64. Here I have relied on Garncarska-Kadari, *Bihipusei dereh,* pp. 395–421.

65. "In tseykhn fun akhrayesdige oyfgabn," *Arbeter tsyatung,* no. 20 (1939).

66. Personal conversation with Jacob Waisbord, Queens, New York, July 1998.

67. Garncarska-Kadari, *Bihipusei dereh,* p. 416.

68. There are several snide references to this Bundist claim in the Ringelblum diaries. See, for example, *Ksovim fun geto,* 1:361.

69. Arnon Fishman-Tamir, "Mikhtav l'Arnon Fishman-Tamir," *Yalkut moreshet,* 1964.

3 HISTORY FOR THE PEOPLE

1. On the use of history by National Democratic publicists, see Artur Eisenbach, "Jewish Historiography in Interwar Poland," in *The Jews of Poland between the Two World Wars,* ed. Yisroel Gutman et al. (Hanover and London, 1989), p. 456.

2. Roman Rybarski, *Handel i polityka handlowa Polski w XVI stuleciu* (Poznań, 1928)

On the other hand it would be unfair to say that anti-Jewish themes were dominant in Polish historical scholarship. More accurate is the assertion, discussed below, that Polish scholars paid little attention to the history of Polish Jews and did not see it as an integral part of their country's history. See also, for an earlier period, Joanna Pisulińska, *Żydzi w polskiej myśli historycznej doby porozbiorowej* (Rzeszów, 2004).

3. S. M. Dubnow, "Ob izuchenii istorii ruskikh evreev i ob uchrezhdenii istoricheskogo obshchestva," *Voskhod* (April–September 1891): 1–91. A year later Dubnow also published a version of this appeal in Hebrew, aimed at the Jews who lived in the Pale of Settlement and who did not read Russian (Dubnow, *Nahpesa venahkora: kol kore el ha-nevonim ba-am, ha-mitnadvim le-esof homer le-binyan toldot bene yisrael be-polin ve-rusiya* [Odessa, 1892]). Thus the historian underscored that *zamling* could bring together Jews of different cultural and political backgrounds. Dubnow wrote in the Hebrew version:

> I appeal to all educated readers, regardless of their party: to the pious and to the enlightened, to the old and to the young, to traditional rabbis and to Crown Rabbis . [. . .] I call out to all of you: come and join the camp of the builders of history! Not every learned or literate person can be a great writer or historian. But every one of you can be a collector of material, and aid in the building of our history. [. . .] Let us work, gather our dispersed from their places of exile, arrange them, publish them, and build upon their foundation the temple of our history. Come let us search and inquire! (David Fishman, trans., *Embers Plucked from the Fire: The Rescue of Jewish Cultural Treasures in Vilna* [New York, 1996])

4. Later many historians, including Jacob Katz, would criticize Dubnow for not paying enough attention to sociology, despite the label he adopted.

5. Simon Dubnow, *Fun zhargon tsu Yidish* (Vilna, 1929).

6. Maxim Vinaver, "Kak my zanimalis' istoriei," *Evreiskaia starina,* no. 1 (1908). In a letter of March 21, 1923, to Dubnow, Vinaver told him that Dubnow had had as much impact on the Russian Jewish intelligentsia as Herzl (YA, Vinaver Collection, no. 77305, Letter).

7. The whole question of the regional differences in East European Jewish culture is a large and complicated topic, one beyond the scope of this book. Relevant factors included the presence or absence of Hasidism, the presence or absence of an attractive non-Jewish high culture, migration patterns, and specific forms of urbanization. As Isaac Bashevis Singer pointed out in a 1943 article on Yiddish literature in interwar Poland, the cultural modernization of Jewish Poland, especially Congress Poland, came late; unlike Jewish Lithuania, it had made relatively little headway before World War I. But when it did arrive, it took a sharper, more discordant form. See Y. Bashevis, "Arum der yidisher literatur in Poyln," *Di tsukunft* (August 1943).

8. Isaiah (Yeshie) Trunk, "Le-toldot ha-historiografiyah ha yehudit-polanit," *Gal ed,* no. 3 (1976): 252.

9. On this point, see Lucjan Dobroszycki, "YIVO in Interwar Poland: Work in the Historical Sciences," in Gutman et al., *The Jews of Poland between the Two World Wars,* pp. 496–497.

10. Ibid. This was Moses Schorr's dissertation titled "Organizational Structure of Jews in Poland from the Earliest Years until 1772." Although the *Kwartalnik historyczny* published this work, Schorr moved away from Polish-Jewish history in order to concentrate on the study of Assyriology.

11. N. M. Gelber, "Kishrei Galitsiya Dubnow," *He-avar,* no. 8 (1961): 73–80.

12. "Di yidishe arbetershaft un di geshikhtsvisnshaft," *Di fraye yugnt,* no. 1 (1924).

13. As Balaban wrote in the introduction to his history of the Jews of Lemberg (Lwów) at the turn of the sixteenth and seventeenth centuries, "the Jewish element was distinct and self-contained. It had its aims and aspirations, its institutions, authorities, courts, synagogues and schools; its sejms and diets; its own imposition of tax and its executive; its Weltanschauung; its upper and lower classes—yes its streets and towns, its ritual and its own law recognized by the Rzeczpospolita; its clothing, customs, guilds and brotherhoods, but above all its own original language." Quoted in Maria Dold, "'A Matter of National and Civic Honor': Majer Balaban and the Institute of Jewish Studies in Warsaw," *East European Jewish Affairs,* no. 2 (winter 2004): 58. It should be noted that although Balaban opposed assimilation, he certainly had nothing against acculturation. While corporate distinctiveness and linguistic distinctiveness may have had a positive national effect in the Commonwealth, by the mid-nineteenth century the acculturation of Galician Jewry, Balaban believed, deserved encouragement and support. See Natalia Aleksiun, "Polish Jewish Historians before 1918: Configuring the Liberal East European Jewish Intelligentsia," *East European Jewish Affairs,* no. 2 (winter 2004): 50.

14. On Balaban, see Israel Biderman, *Mayer Balaban: Historian of Polish Jewry* (New York, 1976); Aleksiun, "Polish Jewish Historians before 1918, pp. 40–53; Dold, "'A Matter of National and Civic Honor,'" pp. 55–72; Mahler, *Historiker un vegvayzer,* pp. 251–259; and Isaiah (Yeshie) Trunk, *Geshtaltn un gesheenishn* (Tel Aviv, 1983), pp. 19–32. On Schiper, see Jacob Litman, *The Economic Role of the Jews in Medieval Poland: The Contribution of Yitzhak Schiper* (Lanham, Md., 1984); Mahler, *Historiker un vegvayzer,* pp. 259–274; Shlomo Eidelberg, ed., *Yitzhak Schiper: Evaluation and Selected Writings* (New York, 1966); and Julien (Yekhil) Hirschhaut, "Dr. I Schiper-zayn lebn un shafn," *Fun noentn over* (New York, 1955).

15. Meyer Balaban, "Zagadnienia historjozofji żydowskiej w stosunku do historji Żydów w Polsce," *Miesięcznik Żydowski,* no. 2 (1932): 369. In November 1931, speaking to the students of the Institute of Judaic Studies in Warsaw, Balaban declared: "We must look at the Jews' development in connection with Poland's evolution. However, in doing so, time and again we will encounter phenomena which cannot be explained by Polish history alone, but are linked to Jewish history in general. We will therefore always look at what is beyond the borders of the Polish state." Quoted in Dold, "'A Matter of National and Civic Honor,'" pp. 55–56.

16. "Der fardinstfuler historiker fun di Poylishe Yidn," in Ringelblum, *Ksovim fun geto,* 2:159–164. On December 23, 1936, the group of younger historians that had been organized by Ringelblum (see below) voted not to send Balaban formal congratulations in honor of his sixtieth birthday, presumably because of what they perceived to be Balaban's hostility to Yiddish, expressed by the fact that Yiddish was not used in the Institute of Judaic Studies, which he headed. See YA, Cherikover Collection, no. 143067.

17. *Nasz przegląd,* October 9, 1932.

18. A good listing can be found in Israel Biderman, *Mayer Balaban: Historian of Polish Jewry* (New York, 1976).

19. Rafael Mahler and Isaiah Trunk made the same criticism of Balaban's work. See Mahler, *Historiker un vegvayzer,* p. 255; and Trunk, *Geshtaltn un gesheenishn,* pp. 23–24.

20. Rafael Mahler, "Ringelblum, the Historian of Polish Jewry," in *A Commemorative*

Symposium in Honor of Dr. Emanuel Ringelblum and His "Oyneg Shabbat" Underground Archives (Jerusalem, 1983), p. 31.

21. In a private conversation Shlomo Shvaitser, a party comrade and friend of Ringelblum's, told me that Ringelblum regarded Schiper as his "rebbe" (Holon, July 1998). In a 1927 letter to Eliyahu Cherikover, the editor of the YIVO's historical journal *Historishe shriftn*, Ringelblum asked permission to dedicate his forthcoming article in that journal to Schiper (Letter from Cherikover to Ringelblum, December 13, 1927, YA, Cherikover Collection, no. 135660). Cherikover responded that he did not think it appropriate to dedicate an article to Schiper in a scholarly journal but would do so if Ringelblum insisted.

22. Alexander Guterman, *Kehilat Varsha bein shtei milhamot ha'olam* (Tel Aviv, 1997), pp. 308–309.

23. Emanuel Ringelblum, "Dr. Y. Shiper un di virtshaftsgeshikhte fun di yidn in Poyln," *Vilner tog,* no. 295 (December 24 and 26, 1926).

24. Ringelblum quoted this passage both in his 1926 article and in his final essay on Schiper that he wrote in the bunker in 1943–44 (*Ksovim fun geto,* 2:152).

25. Mahler, *Historiker un vegvayzer,* p. 261.

26. Werner Sombart, *Die Juden und das Wirtschaftsleben* (Leipzig, 1911); for more on Sombart's views of the Jewish role in the development of capitalism, see Derek Penslar, *Shylock's Children; Economics and Jewish Identity in Modern Europe* (Berkeley, 2001), pp. 163–170. As Professor Moshe Rosman points out, "for all his acknowledged greatness, Schiper was perhaps the most controversial of Jewish historians. Some of his theories are considered far-fetched and his methodology has been called sloppy. He was accused of misquotation, quotation out of context, self-contradiction and lack of comprehensive bibliographic treatment. Even some of those closest to him, like Ringelblum and Mahler, subtly expressed reservations about parts of his work. . . . The judgment of others was that Schiper was more of a problem poser than a problem solver who brought to bear on Jewish history a new scientific approach. His writing was marred by a lack of restraint, a lack of scholarly meticulousness and a lack of precise use of sources." See Moshe Rosman's review of Jacob Litman's "The Economic Role of the Jews in Medieval Poland: The Contribution of Yitzhak Schiper," *Jewish Quarterly Review* 58, nos. 1–2 (July–October 1987): 152–153.

27. Ringelblum, *Ksovim fun geto,* 2:150–159.

28. A good summary of Ringelblum's position on this matter can be gained from the short history of the organs of Jewish self-government that he wrote for I. Bornstein, *Budżety gmin wyznaniowych żydowskich w Polsce* (Warsaw, 1929), pp. 1–11. Ringelblum did admit, however, that these organs played a vital role in the maintenance of Jewish religious culture.

29. Ringelblum, "Dr. Y. Shiper un di virtshaftsgeshikhte fun di yidn in Poyln"; idem, *Ksovim fun geto,* 2:150–159.

30. Jerzy Maternicki, *Historiografia Polska XX Wieku* (Wrocław, 1982), pp. 25–33; Eisenbach, "Jewish Historiography in Interwar Poland," p. 455.

31. A good short survey of Handelsman's life and work is Stefan Kieniewicz, "Marceli Handelsman," in *Historycy warszawscy ostatnich dwóch stuleci,* ed. Aleksander Gieysztor, Jerzy Maternicki, and Henryk Samsonowicz (Warsaw, 1986), pp. 257–273; see also Ringelblum, *Ksovim fun geto,* 2:173–175.

32. Marceli Handelsman, *Rozwój narodowości nowoczesnej* (Warsaw, 1924).

33. *Historyka: zasady metodologji i teorji poznania historycznego: podręcznik dla szkół wyższych* (Warsaw, 1928).

34. Mahler, "Ringelblum, the Historian of Polish Jewry," p. 30.

35. In an interview he gave to the *Krakowski kurjer wieczorny* on October 19, 1937, Handelsman stressed that national identity rested on psychological rather than racial factors and that Poland was historically "gente natione," where many different peoples found a common civic identity under the aegis of the Polish Republic. Handelsman also reaffirmed his conviction that democracy would inevitably triumph in Poland. The interview is reprinted in *Materiały do historii Klubów Demokratycznych i Stronnictwa Demokratycznego w latach 1937–1939,* ed. Leon Chajn (Warsaw, 1964), pp. 186–188.

36. Ringelblum, *Ksovim fun geto,* 2:174. Kieniewicz pointed out that Handelsman was known for helping his students, including facilitating the publication of their books. *Projekty i próby przewarstwowienia* was published under the aegis of the Institute for the Study of Nationality Problems, of which Handelsman was a leading member. See Andrzej Chojnowski, "The Jewish Question in the Work of the Instytut Badań Spraw Narodowościowych in Warsaw," *Polin* 4 (1989).

37. Anna Cienciala, "Tajne oblicze GL-AL i PPR: Dokumenty," *Sarmatian Review,* no. 2 (April 2001).

38. Eisenbach, "Jewish Historiography in Interwar Poland," p. 454.

39. Aryeh Tartakover, "Ha-makhon le'medayei yahadut b'varsha," in *Studies in Memory of Moses Schorr,* ed. Louis Ginzberg and Abraham Weiss (New York, 1944), pp. 163–176; Dold, "'A Matter of National and Civic Honor,'" pp. 55–72.

40. He had already held a professorship at the Wolna Wszechnica Polska since 1933. See Dold, "'A Matter of National and Civic Honor,'" p. 69.

41. Eisenbach, "Jewish Historiography in Interwar Poland," p. 468.

42. Rafael Mahler, "Der krayz 'Yunge Historiker' in Varshe," in idem, *Historiker un vegvayzer,* p. 303. Mahler mentions the correct attitude of the faculty. In the course of her research on Jewish historians in interwar Poland, Natalia Aleksiun discovered that Professor Roman Rybarski, who held marked anti-Jewish views, nonetheless stood ready to help Ber Mark, then a young Jewish student who was also a Communist (personal communication with author, January 20, 2006).

43. Besides money, a major problem was the opposition of Orthodox Jews, who protested the initial locale next to a synagogue on the grounds that the largely secular students would likely engage in immoral behavior and be an affront to the site. See "Był w Warszawie Żydowski Dom Akademicki," in Karol Morawski, *Kartki z dziejów Żydów warszawskich* (Warsaw, 1993), pp. 156–161. On the battle within the Jewish community, which led to an Orthodox riot that vandalized the main meeting room of the Warsaw Jewish Community Council, see Guterman, *Kehilat Varsha bein shtei milhamot ha'olam,* pp. 152–153. In the early 1920s the Academic House had provisional quarters in central Warsaw, on the Nowy Świat.

44. Another problem was Schiper's recent desertion of the Poalei Tsiyon, which had left hard feelings in the movement (conversation with Shlomo Shvaitser, Holon, Israel, July 1998).

45. Mahler stressed Ringelblum's central role in the organization of the circle. "Ringelblum's energetic initiative; his incredible determination; his unique organizational talent;

and above all, his devotion heart and soul to the mission of furthering Yiddish culture in general and scholarship in Yiddish in particular; all these rare qualities made [the Krayz] possible (*Historiker un vegvayzer,* p. 304).

46. Mahler, "Der krayz Yunger Historiker in Varshe," p. 305. In 1933 the Young Historians Circle changed its formal name to the "Historians Circle of the YIVO Society in Warsaw."

47. Emanuel Ringelblum, "A nayer tsushtayer," *Literarishe bleter,* no. 22 (1938).

48. Ibid.

49. Ibid.

50. Korzen, "Emanuel Ringelblum lifnei hamilhama u'biyameha harishonim," *Yediot Yad Va-shem,* nos. 21–22 (1959).

51. Emanuel Ringelblum, "Dray yor seminar," *Yunger historiker,* no. 10 (1926).

52. See Mahler's introduction to *Bleter far geshikhte,* no. 1 (1934): "The circle's purpose is not just to bring together young scholars of Jewish history. The circle consciously supports Yiddish mass culture and regards the basic mission of its members' scholarship to be the clarification of the dynamics of Jewish socioeconomic and cultural development, in order to better [help the Jewish masses] in their struggle for social and national liberation."

53. Emanuel Ringelblum, "Dray yor seminar," *Yunger historiker,* no. 10 (1926).

54. Emanuel Ringelblum, "Bleter far geshikhte," *Arbeter tsaytung,* no. 35 (1934).

55. Emanuel Ringelblum, "Farvos hot zikh dos yidishe folk nisht asimilirt?" *Der nayer dor,* no. 1 (1924). Reprinted in idem, *Kapitlen geshikhte,* pp. 459–467.

56. The transformation of the Jewish masses into workers and peasants, something the party expected and welcomed, would, of course, diminish the economic differences between Jews and their neighbors and, logically, increase the dangers of assimilation. This is one reason why the party attached so much importance to the "territorial base" in Palestine. The base would anchor the Jewish people culturally and psychologically, especially after the victorious revolution. For a cogent critique of Mahler and his defense of Borochovist theory on the interconnection of Jewish survival and economic abnormality, see Trunk, *Geshtaltn un gesheenishn,* pp. 36–37.

57. Emanuel Ringelblum, "Farvos hot zikh dos yidishe folk nisht asimilirt?" *Der nayer dor,* no. 1 (1924). Reprinted in idem, *Kapitlen geshikhte,* pp. 459–467.

58. Ringelblum, "Bleter far geshikhte."

59. Bela Mandelsberg-Schildkraut was murdered by the Nazis in 1943. In 1965 a collection of her writings was translated into Hebrew and published in Israel. See Hug mokire shemah shel Bela Mandelsberg-Schildkraut, *Mehkarim le-toldot yehudei Lublin* (Tel Aviv, 1965).

60. Ringelblum, "Bleter far geshikhte."

61. On Yiddish historical scholarship in the Soviet Union, see Alfred Abraham Greenbaum, *Jewish Scholarship and Scholarly Institutions in Soviet Russia: 1918–1953* (Jerusalem, 1978); Benjamin Nathans, "On Russian Jewish Historiography," in *The Historiography of Imperial Russia: The Profession and Writing of History in a Multinational State,* ed. Thomas Sanders (Armonk, N.Y., 1999) By the late 1920s, under the leadership of Israel Sosis, the Jewish department of the Institute for Belorussian Culture and its journal, *Tsaytshrift,* had become the leading center for the study of Jewish history in the USSR. Sosis, a former Bundist, also criticized Dubnow from the Left—but he still ran into political trouble for "Jewish nationalism." When his book, *Jewish Social Movements in Nineteenth-century*

Russia, was published in 1929, it appeared with an introduction that attacked him for alleged ideological mistakes. In 1931 Sosis was fired from the Institute, and he was arrested in 1936. Ringelblum's repeated calls for closer contacts with Soviet Jewish historians were, in light of the political situation, patently unrealistic. For example, the March–April 1930 issue of *Tsaytshrift* was largely given over to a vicious attack on the YIVO and its publications on history and economics.

62. Rafael Mahler, "Geshikhte un folk," *Yunger Historiker,* no. 1 (1926).

63. Rafael Mahler, "Tsi zenen di yidn geven a handlsfolk?" *Yivo bleter,* nos. 1–2 (1934).

64. These articles include "Di teories fun der Yidisher kultur geshikhte," *Yunger historiker,* no. 1 (1926); "Ahad Ha'am's teoriye fun der yidisher geshikhte un kultur," *Yunger historiker,* no. 2 (1929); "Teorje historiografji żydowskiej o rozwoju dziejowym kultury żydowskiej," *Miesięcznik Żydowski,* no. 12 (1933); and "A religiez-natsionalistishe teoriye fun der yidisher geshikhte," *Bleter far geshikhte,* no. 1 (1934). In 1933 the editor of *Miesięcznik Żydowski* declared that one of the most serious problems facing Jewish historians in Poland was the difficulty of getting their work published because of financial reasons. Therefore, he was ready to put the pages of his journal at their disposal. A good discussion of *Miesięcznik Żydowski* is in Natalia Aleksiun's unpublished talk at the 2003 annual meeting of the Association of Jewish Studies, "Configuring the Liberal Jewish Intelligentsia in Interwar Poland: *Miesięcznik Żydowski* and Its Audience."

65. Mahler, *Historiker un vegvayzer,* p. 277.

66. E. Ringelblum, *Żydzi w Warszawie, cz. I: Od czasów najdawnieszych do ostatniego wygnania w 1527* (Warsaw, 1932).

67. Ringelblum, *Ksovim fun geto,* 2:174–175.

68. For a more recent survey of the literature, see Paweł Fijałkowski, "Początki obecności Żydów na Mazowszu (do 1526r.)," *Kwartalnik historii Żydów* 198 (2001): 169–203.

69. Ringelblum, *Żydzi w Warszawie,* p. 129.

70. Isaac Schiper, "Di elste geshikhte fun Varshever yidn," *Haynt,* September 9, 1932.

71. Eleazar Feldman, "Dzieji Żydów w Warszawie," *Miesięcznik Żydowski* 3 (1933): 521–528; Isaiah (Yeshie) Trunk, review of Ringelblum's *Żydzi w Warszawie, Yivo bleter* 4 (1933): 61–66. Other historians also questioned Ringelblum's use of sources. Recently the Polish medievalist Hanna Węgrzynek argued that Ringelblum misread the evidence and mistakenly asserted that Mazowian Prince Bolesław V expelled the Jews from Warsaw in 1483. Węgrzynek showed that a document that introduced trading restrictions in an area of the city inhabited by Jews and clergy was not directed only against Jews but reflected a more general demand by the burghers to restrict trade by "outsiders" within the city. See Hanna Węgrzynek, "Czy w 1483 r. Książę Bolesław V wygnał Żydów z Warszawy? Możliwości interpretacji dokumentów miejskich" (Wrocław: Acta Universitatis Wratislaviensis, 2005), pp. 513–517. I am grateful to Professor Hanna Zaremska for pointing out this article to me.

72. *Nasz przegląd,* October 9, 1932.

73. *Kwartalnik historyczny* (1933), vol. 47, no. 1.

74. See the obituary published in *Kwartalnik historyczny* (1945), vol. 53, no. 3/4. In the preface to his book on the Warsaw Jews, Ringelblum thanked Siemieński for his help.

75. For a detailed listing of these articles in *Sotsiale meditsin,* as well as for an extensive but incomplete listing of Ringelblum's scholarly writings, see Ringelblum, *Kapitlen*

geshikhte, pp. 50–60; for another shorter listing of his major historical works, see Michał Szulkin, "Dr. Emanuel Ringelblum-historyk i organizator podziemnego archiwum getta warszawskiego," *BŻIH* 30 (1973): 124–125.

76. *Żydzi w powstaniu Kościuszkowskim* (Warsaw, 1938); "Żydzi w świetle prasy warszawskiej wieku XVIII," *Miesięcznik Żydowski*, vols. 6, 7/8, 9/10 (1932); *Projekty i próby przewarstwowienia Żydów w epoce Stanisławowskiej* (Warsaw, 1934).

77. *Tsu der geshikhte fun yidishn bukh un druk in Poiln in der tsveyter helft fun akhtsentn yorhundert* (Vilna, 1936).

78. Emanuel Ringelblum, "Dzieje zewnętrzne Żydów w dawnej Rzeczypospolitej," in *Żydzi w Polsce odrodzonej*, 2 vols. (Warsaw, 1932), 1:37–80.

79. "Shmuel Zbytkover," *Tsiyon*, no. 3 (1938).

80. Emanuel Ringelblum and Rafael Mahler, *Teksty źródłowe do nauki historii Żydów w Polsce i we wschodniej Europie* (Warsaw, 1930).

81. Ringelblum, *Żydzi w Warszawie*, p. 129.

82. Many of Ringelblum's articles on the history of Jewish medicine that first appeared in *Sotsiale meditsin* were reprinted in Ringelblum, *Kapitlen geshikhte*, pp. 183–389.

83. See Emanuel Ringelblum, "Apikorses un frumkayt tsvishn yidishe doktoyrim," in idem, *Kapitlen geshikhte*, p. 221.

84. Ringelblum prepared these guidelines for the 1936 World Congress of Jewish physicians in Tel Aviv. Jewish doctors, he stressed, should study the past in order to learn how their profession had once played a critical role in the modernization of the Jewish people. Unfortunately, he noted, in the recent past all too many Jewish doctors had opted for assimilation and material gain rather than social medicine and service to their people. In the present critical period of rising anti-Semitism, they once again had to step forward and lead. One way they could meet these obligations of national leadership would be to set up a project to create a world archive of the history of Jewish medicine. The archive would foster interest in studying the history of Jewish doctors and *feldshers* [medical practitioners without full medical qualifications]. It would also include folklore and a study of popular attitudes toward doctors and medicine. See Małgorzata Czeley-Wybieralska and Symcha Wajs, "Emanuel Ringelblum jako historyk medycyny żydowskiej," *Archiwum historii i filozofii medycyny*, bk. 2, 1988, pp. 207–212.

85. *Tsu der geshikhte fun yidishn bukh un druk in Poyln in der tsveyter helft fun akhtsentn yorhundert* (Vilna, 1936).

86. Emanuel Ringelbum, "Dray yor seminar," *Yunger historiker*, no. 1 (1926).

87. Emanuel Ringelblum, *Żydzi w Powstaniu Kościuszkowskiem* (Warsaw, 1938), p. 34.

88. Ringelblum commented that, in the next generation, the attitude of educated Warsaw Jews to Poland would change markedly. Polish education would transform the attitudes of middle-class Jewish youth and turn them into avid Polish patriots.

89. Shatzky, "Menakhem ben Fayvish Ringelblum," p. xxxi; Mahler, "Ringelblum, the Historian of Polish Jewry," p. 28.

90. In his article, "The Jews in Warsaw in the 18th Century," published in 1937, Ringelblum unearthed previously unused archival documents to reconstruct the communal institutions of a Jewish community which was legally not supposed to exist. He presented especially important material about the appointed heads of this community, the "syndics," who, in his view, were mostly unscrupulous and corrupt and shamelessly exploited their poorer breathren ("Yidn in Varshe in 18tn yorhundert," *Historishe shriftn*, vol. 2 (1937).

91. Ringelblum, "Bleter far geshikhte."

92. "Żydzi w świetle prasy warszawskiej w 18 stuleciu," *Miesięcznik Żydowski*, vol. 1 (1932), pp. 489–518; vol. 2 (1932), pp. 42–85, 219–377; "An opklang fun der frantsoyzisher revolutsie," *Yivo bleter*, no. 3 (1932): 223–227.

93. On this lack of realistic options, see, especially, Gershon Hundert, *Jews in Poland-Lithuania in the Eighteenth Century* (Berkeley, 2004), pp. 214–215.

94. Andrzej Chojnowski, "The Jewish Question in the Work of the Instytut Badań Spraw Narodowościowych in Warsaw," *Polin* 4 (1989).

95. Jacob Shatzky, "Menakhem ben Fayvish Ringelblum," p. xxxvi.

96. Emanuel Ringelblum, "Dos ineveynikste lebn fun varshever yidn fun der farkerter zayt," in idem, *Kapitlen geshikhte,* p. 101.

97. "A Prager galekh vegn yidishn familie lebn," reprinted in ibid., pp. 104–107.

98. "Dos ineveinikste lebn fun Varshever yidn fun der farkerter zayt," reprinted in ibid., pp. 94–96.

99. "A nay bukh mit alte ligns," in ibid., pp. 490–496.

100. Emanuel Ringelblum, "Dos lebn fun di yidishe gezeln un lernyinglekh inm altn Poyln," in ibid., p. 131

101. Emanuel Ringelblum, "Di gezelshaftlekh-medetsinishe tetigkayt fun di yidishe kehiles," in ibid., p. 381.

102. Shatsky's introduction to Ringelblum, *Kapitlen geshikhte,* p. xxxv.

103. Ibid., p. xxxvii.

104. Emanuel Ringelblum, "A Solide Geshikhte Arbet," *Literarishe bleter,* no. 39 (1929). Ringelblum strongly attacked Friedman in this review for referring to Yiddish as a "jargon."

105. A good work on the Folkspartei is Kalman Weiser's "The Politics of Yiddish: Noah Prilutski and the Folkspartey in Poland, 1920–1926," unpublished doctoral dissertation, Columbia University, 2001.

106. The best discussion of the memorandum and its ramifications is Cecile Kuznitz, "The Origins of Yiddish Scholarship and the YIVO Institute for Yiddish Research," unpublished doctoral dissertation, Stanford University, 2000.

107. Dan Miron, "Between Science and Faith," in *YIVO Annual of Jewish Social Science,* ed. Deborah Dash Moore, 23 vols. (Evanston and New York, 1946–96), vol. 19 (1990), p. 6.

108. This tendency on the part of Yiddishist scholars to see German-Jewish scholarship as desiccated, bloodless, and assimilationist was patently unfair. See Michael Brenner, *The Renaissance of Jewish Culture in Weimar Germany* (New Haven, 1996); Jacques Ehrenfreund, *Mémoire juive et nationalité allemande: les Juifs berlinois à la Belle Epoque* (Paris, 2000); and Kuznitz, "The Origins of Yiddish Scholarship and the YIVO Institute for Yiddish Research," p. 100. As Kuznitz notes, this straw man helped these scholars to construct and hone their own identity.

109. On Weinreich, besides Kuznitz, "The Origins of Yiddish Scholarship and the YIVO Institute for Yiddish Research," see David Fishman, "Bamerkungen vegn Vaynraykh's role in der antviklung fun der yiddisher visnshaft.," *Yivo bleter,* n.s. 3 (1997): 298–308; Barbara Kirshenblatt-Gimblett, "Coming of Age in the Thirties: Max Weinreich, Edward Sapir, and Jewish Social Science," in Moore, *YIVO Annual,* 23:1–103; David Roskies, "Maks Vaynraykh: oyf di shpurn fun a lebedikn over," *Yivo bleter* 3 (n.s.) (1997): 308–319.

110. Lucy Dawidowicz, *From That Time and Place* (New York, 1989), p. 79.

111. This paragraph closely follows the keynote address made by Dan Miron on March 24, 1985, to celebrate the YIVO's sixtieth anniversary. See Miron, "Between Science and Faith," in Moore, *YIVO Annual,* 19:1–17.

112. David Roskies, *The Jewish Search for a Usable Past* (Bloomington, 1999), p. 7. Roskies cites Raymond P. Scheindlin's translation which appears in *A Shtetl and other Yiddish Novellas,* ed. Ruth R. Wisse (Detroit, 1986), p. 272.

113. Max Weinreich, "Derkenen dem haynt," *YIVO bleter,* no. 1 (1931).

114. Ibid.

115. Letter from Weinreich to Cherikover, November 12, 1926, YA, Cherikover Collection, No. 138122.

116. YA, Cherikover Collection, no. 143123.

117. When Ringelblum proposed to Weinreich in 1927 that they issue the next edition of *Yunger historiker* as a Yivo publication, Weinreich demurred. He told Cherikover that he did not want the YIVO to lend its prestige to a journal of "beginners" (Letter from Weinreich to Cherikover, December 23, 1927, YA, Cherikover Collection, no. 138219). In his reply to Weinreich, Cherikover advised him not to be so hasty.

118. Indeed, in a letter that he and Shtif sent to the Yiddish literary and theater critic A. Mukdoni in January 1926, Cherikover stressed that younger historians [like Ringelblum] were already creating scholarship in Yiddish, even before the YIVO was started. But these young people needed to know that their work in Yiddish had a future. Therefore, it was all the more important to establish the YIVO on a sound footing. "It's not because of us that this scholarship has begun [among these young people]. Like Yiddishim in its earliest years, this scholarship is spontaneous, marked by enthusiasm and idealism. It proceeds in small *krayzn* (circles) with serious work, not empty talk" (Letter from Shtif and Cherikover to Mukdoni, January 28, 1926, YA, Cherikover Collection, no. 148128).

119. When Weinreich informed Cherikover that Ringelblum had set up a historical commission in Vilna, Cherikover sent back a furious reply. On November 30, 1926, Weinreich reassured Cherikover that no one had any intention of usurping his authority as the head of the historical section. But he was in Berlin. There were five or six people who wanted to study history in Vilna. Should the YIVO turn them down just because Cherikover was in Paris? (YA, Cherikover Collection, no. 138131).

120. Dobroszycki, "YIVO in Interwar Poland, p. 500.

121. Minutes of Warsaw Historical Commission Meeting, November 11, 1929, YA, Cherikover Collection, no. 143032.

122. Letter from Emanuel Ringelblum to Jacob Shatzky, November 23, 1932. Reprinted in Ringelblum, *Kapitlen geshikhte,* p. 515.

123. Emanuel Ringelblum, "Der internatsionaler kongres fun historisher visnshaft in Varshe un di yidishe visnshaft," reprinted in idem, *Kapitlen geshikhte,* p. 468.

124. Ibid.

125. YA, Cherikover Collection.

126. On Pankratova, see Reginald Zelnik, *The Perils of Pankratova* (Seattle, 2005).

127. Ringelblum, "Der internatsionaler kongres," p. 468.

128. See, for example, the article by Stefan Inglot on social and economic history, "Rozwój historii społecznej i gospodarczej," *Kwartalnik historyczny* (1937), 1:401. Professor Stefan Inglot devoted one short paragraph to Jewish history in which he singled out the work of non-Jewish scholars such as Bogdan Wasiutyński, Franciszek Bujak, Jan

Ptaśnik, and Stanisław Kutrzeba. Not one of these historians could read Hebrew or Yiddish! At the end of the paragraph Inglot added: "There is also a whole variety of works on local and general Jewish history written by Jews: Schorr, Schipper, Balaban, Friedman, and others." In a letter to Eliyahu Cherikover of May 27, 1939, Meyer Balaban hinted that the *Kwartalnik historyczny* had broken a promise to publish one of his articles. (It should be noted that the *Przegląd historyczny* maintained a slightly more forthcoming attitude to Jewish scholarship.) See YA, Cherikover Collection, no. 127048.

129. See Letter from Ringelblum to Cherikover, August 6, 1937, YA, Cherikover Collection, no. 135804.

130. See, for example, his remarks at the October 8, 1938, meeting of the YIVO Central Board, YA, RG.1.1, Box 1, Section III, Folder 15, Meeting of October 8, 1938.

131. Ringelblum, "Der ershter pruv."

132. Quoted in David G. Roskies, "*Landkentenish*: Yiddish Belles Lettres in the Warsaw Ghetto," in *Holocaust Chronicles: Individualizing the Holocaust through Diaries and Other Contemporaneous Accounts,* ed. Robert Moses Shapiro (New York, 1999), p. 11.

133. Emanuel Ringelblum, "Fun der reaktsiye," *Landkentenish,* no. 1 (1933).

134. Ibid.

135. G. Urinski, M. Volansky, N. Zuckerman, eds. *Pinkes fun der shot Pruzhene* (Pruzany, 1930); Emanuel Ringelblum, "An interesanter onheyb," *Literarishe bleter,* no. 27 (1931).

136. YA, Cherikover Collection, no. 142252. This interest in regional and local history was, of course, not confined to Jews. For good surveys of the burgeoning interest in local history among Poles, see Jacek Krawczyk and Jarosław Książek, eds., *Środowiska historyczne II Rzeczpospolitej. Część II* (Warsaw, 1987), pp. 119–233.

137. "Anvayzung far forshungen vegn der geshikhte fun yidishe yishuvim," *Yedies fun YIVO* (January–February 1938): 16–22. The guidelines, at Ringelblum's insistence, were written for the level of "young researchers with a secondary education." See "Report of the Activities of the Historical Commission, January–May 1937," YA, Cherikover Collection, no. 143149.

138. Protocol of November 17, 1934, meeting of Historical Commission for All Poland, YA, Cherikover Collection, no. 143062. Instead of using the names Schiper and Ringelblum, the protocol mentions a "first position" and a "second position," but the identities of the advocates are obvious.

139. A particularly good treatment of this large topic is Isaiah (Yeshie) Trunk, "YIVO un di yidishe historiografiye," in idem, *Geshtaltn un gesheenishn,* pp. 97–110.

140. Eliyahu Cherikover, ed., *Historishe shriftn,* 3 vols, 1:1.

141. Trunk, "YIVO un di yidishe historiografiye," pp. 248–253.

142. In a letter of May 26, 1934, to Cherikover, Jacob Shatzky in New York expressed his fear that, unless more money became available to publish scholarship in Yiddish, younger scholars would stop working in that language (YA, Cherikover Collection, no. 141603).

143. Kalmanovich and Reyzen, for example, found fault with the "*daytchmerizmen*" (Germanisms) that often characterized Galician speech but had no place in the refined Yiddish that the YIVO was trying to inculcate. For instance, for the term "questionnaire" Ringelblum used *frageboygn* instead of *fregboygn*.

144. Shatzky tried to make peace in separate letters he sent on March 18, 1938, to the Historical Commission in Warsaw and to Kalmanovich and Reyzen in Vilna. He told

the Warsaw historians that they should stop publishing materials without first securing approval from the historical section (that is, from Cherikover). Otherwise, he said, there would be anarchy. But he told Kalmanovich and Reyzen that their tone had been unacceptable. "I ask you to settle this matter. We cannot afford to lose such a key pillar [of our work] as Ringelblum, especially considering that all the young Warsaw historians are on his side" (YA, Cherikover Collection, no. 141667).

145. Kuznitz, *The Origins of Yiddish Scholarship*, p. 252.

146. Letter from Ringelblum to Cherikover, n.d., YA, Cherikover Collection, no. 135810. Although the letter is undated, Cherikover notes that it was received on March 27, 1938.

147. Kuznitz, *The Origins of Yiddish Scholarship*, p. 266.

148. AR II, no. 408.

149. It should be noted that many years after Ringelblum's death, Philip Friedman, in a review of Shatzky's 1953 selection of Ringelblum's writings, agreed with Shatzky's assertion that "Ringelblum, who opposed bourgeois apologetics, himself engaged in social apologetics." "Just as previous bourgeois historians," Friedman continued, "tried to prettify Jewish history with well-to-do Jews [*sheyne Yidn*], entrepreneurs, Polish patriots, and to glorify Jewish ethical norms and Jewish family life, so did Ringelblum rush to another extreme [*fargalopirt in an ander extrem*] and decorate Jewish history with ordinary workers [*horepashnikes*], proletarian masses, the hard-working Jewish poor, economic misery, the socially declassed." See Philip Friedman, "Dos Ringelblum Bukh," *Tsukunft* (October 1955). See also Shatzky, *Kapitlen geshikhte*, p. xxxii.

4 ORGANIZING THE COMMUNITY

1. "Ringelblum believed," Eck recalled, "that if history remembered him (and he was convinced that it would) then it would be because of his relief work and not necessarily because of his scholarly and documentation activities" (Eck, "Mit Emanuel Ringelblum in Varshever geto," p. 116.

2. An excellent history of the Joint Distribution Committee, including its activities in Poland before and during the Holocaust, is Yehuda Bauer's *My Brother's Keeper: A History of the American Joint Distribution Committee, 1929–1939* (Philadelphia, 1974).

3. The landsmanshaft was an association of immigrants from the same town.

4. Lucy Dawidowicz, *The War against the Jews* (New York, 1975), pp. 327–335. One should use this concept of a "countercommunity" with caution, as there was a wide array of differences between ghettos. Nonetheless it is relevant in describing the situation in the Warsaw Ghetto.

5. A useful study on the ghettos is Gustavo Corni, *Hitler's Ghettos: Voices from a Beleaguered Society, 1939–1944* (London, 2003).

6. There is a vast literature on the Lodz Ghetto. Especially good are Michal Unger, *Lodz: aharon ha-getaot b'polin* (Jerusalem, 2005); Isaiah Trunk, *Lodzher Geto* (New York, 1962); Lucjan Dobroszycki, ed., *The Chronicle of the Lodz Ghetto* (New Haven and London, 1984); Israel Gutman, "The Distinctiveness of the Lodz Ghetto," in *The Last Ghetto: Life in the Lodz Ghetto, 1940–44,* ed. Michal Unger (Jerusalem, 1995).

7. Of course, it should also be remembered that, for the most part, the Germans took relatively little interest in the internal life of the ghetto.

8. In this report to the inspector of the German Security Police, Auerswald noted:

Actually the Jew hates the Germans less than his "race brothers" who reign over him and of whom he would gladly be rid. In time, this attitude has changed to burning hatred against the governing Jewish circles without exception, and particularly against the Jewish Elder (Czerniakow). It is absolutely impossible to make a Jew kill another Jew; but in this case he would not stop short were he not afraid of the German authorities. (Isaiah Trunk, *Judenrat* [Lincoln, Nebr., 1972], p. 261)

9. "Sotsyale arbet in Poyln," June 1936, JDC Archives, Poland, General, no. 326a; Internal Memorandum, April 15, 1943, JDC Archives, Poland, Reconstruction, Gemiles Khesed Kases, no. 398.

10. Ringelblum, *Ksovim fun geto,* 2:130 Giterman, Ringelblum recalled, came to the office early, stayed late, and managed to get the most out of his subordinates. He listened to their ideas and inspired them to give their best.

11. Ibid.

12. "His Hasidic background gave Giterman the enthusiasm and inner fire that he passed on to those with whom he worked. His rebbe-like personality [*rebeshkayt*] shaped his dealings with the ordinary Jew, who would leave his office strengthened and inspired, just like a Hasid who leaves his rebbe" (ibid., 2:129).

13. Ibid., 2:130.

14. See Giterman's short autobiography in Moshe Shalit, ed., *Oyf di khurves fun milk-homes un mehumes: pinkes fun gegnt-komitet EKOPO* (Vilna, 1930), pp. 842–865. The following details on Giterman's life are taken from this source and from Ringelblum's essay, written in either late 1943 or early 1944, in *Ksovim fun geto,* vol. 2.

15. A worthwhile survey of the EKOPO is in Steven J. Zipperstein, "The Politics of Relief: The Transformation of Russian Jewish Communal Life during the First World War," in *Studies in Contemporary Jewry,* ed. Jonathan Frankel, vol. 4 (Oxford, 1988), pp. 22–40. On the political and social impact of relief in wartime Vilna, see Samuel Kassow, "Jewish Communal Politics in Transition: The Vilna Kehille, 1919–1920," in Moore, *YIVO Annual,* 20:61–93.

16. The well-known Yiddish writer S. Ansky left a vivid account of his experiences in war-torn Galicia in 1915. See S. Ansky, *Khurbm Galitsye,* in idem, Gezamlte shriftn, vols. 4–6 (Vilna, Warsaw, and New York, 1921).

17. Ringelblum, *Ksovim fun geto,* 2:129.

18. Korzen, "Emanuel Ringelblum lifnei ha-milhama u'biyameha harishonim." *Yediot Yad Va-shem,* nos. 21–22 (1959).

19. Yitzhak Giterman, "Gmiles khesed kases in der itstiger shverer tsayt," *Folkshilf* (April 1936).

20. See Edward D. Wynot, "'A Necessary Cruelty': The Emergence of Official Anti-Semitism in Poland," *American Historical Review* 76, no. 4 (October 1971); Emanuel Meltzer, *Maavak medini b'Malkodet: Yehudei Polin, 1935–1939* (Tel Aviv, 1982).

21. In a speech in the Sejm in June 1936, shortly after an anti-Jewish riot in Mińsk-Mazowiecki, Prime Minister Felicjan Sławoj-Składkowski declared: "Economic boycott, yes, by all means [*owszem!*]. But no violence!" (Paweł Korzec, "Antisemitism in Poland as an Intellectual, Social and Political Movement," in *Studies on Polish Jewry, 1919–1939,* ed. Joshua Fishman (New York, 1974), pp. 90–91.

22. Ringelblum, *Ksovim fun geto,* 2:127.

23. Yitzhak Giterman, "Di gmiles khesed kases in der itztiger shvere tsayt," *Folkshilf* (April 1936).

24. Bezalel Botchan, Report of Węgrów gemiles khesed kase, 1937, Jacob Lestschinsky Archives, Hebrew University, Jerusalem, File 258.

25. Among the naysayers was the most popular Jewish columnist in interwar Poland, Itchele (B. Yieshzon) of the *Haynt*.

26. Rafael Mahler, "Emanuel Ringelblum's briv fun Varshever geto," *Di goldene keyt*, no. 46 (1963): 11.

27. "Di Kases," *Folkshilf* (October 1935).

28. Samuel D. Kassow, "Community and Identity in the Interwar Shtetl," in Gutman et al., *The Jews of Poland between the Two World Wars*, p. 216.

29. Ringelblum, *Ksovim fun geto*, 2:127.

30. Ibid., 2:128.

31. Ibid., 2:124.

32. The best study of this episode is Jerzy Tomaszewski, *Preludium Zagłady: Wygnanie Żydów Polskich z Niemiec w 1938 r.* (Warsaw, 1998). See also Bauer, *My Brother's Keeper*, pp. 242–250.

33. Bauer, *My Brother's Keeper*, p. 245.

34. Michał Rudawski, *Mój obcy kraj?* (Warsaw, 1996), p. 57.

35. He wrote to Mahler that "the important thing is that here [in Zbąszyń] there is no division between 'givers' and 'takers.' The refugees see us as brothers who are rushing to their aid in a time of distress. Practically all the key posts in the camp are in their hands. . . . There are good relations between us, and we've avoided the taint of degrading philanthropy" (ibid.).

36. Rudawski recalled that "the group sent from Warsaw to help Ringelblum was full of the best intentions, but this was all a drop in the bucket compared to what had to be done. Ringelblum was ingenious and organized a large-scale system of self-help for the refugees. For the most part he recruited specialists from their ranks and set them to work; he organized doctors in a health service, tailors to repair clothing, [and] lawyers for a legal aid bureau to help refugees with questions pertaining to citizenship, property, and family members left behind in Germany. He organized a bureau to look for relatives. . . . There was also a special department to care for children. My father, along with other carpenters, worked at [putting the camp in order]" (ibid., p. 64).

37. Emanuel Ringelblum, "Zbąszyń," reprinted in idem, *Kapitlen geshikhte*, pp. 500–501.

38. Rafael Mahler, "Mikhtavei E. Ringelblum m' Zbąszyń v'al Zbąszyń," *Yalkut moreshet*, no. 2 (1964): 21.

39. Arnon Fishman-Tamir, "Mikhtav l'Arnon Fishman-Tamir," *Yalkut moreshet*, no. 2 (1964): 28–32. In a letter of May 5, 1939, to Fishman-Tamir, written in Yiddish, Ringelblum expressed how happy he was with his work for the Joint. His travels all over Poland showed him the immense determination of Polish Jewry to hold on and defend itself against economic anti-Semitism.

40. Letter from Ringelblum to Rafael Mahler, December 6, 1938, in Emanuel Ringelblum, *Ktavim ahronim* (Jerusalem, 1994), pp. 304–305.

41. Korzen, "Emanuel Ringelblum lifnei ha-milhama ubiyimeha harishonim," *Yediot Yad Va-shem*, no. 23–24 (1960): 19.

42. YA, Cherikover Collection, no. 135805.

43. Ringelblum, *Ksovim fun geto,* 1:26.

44. Daniel Leybl, "Mit Ringelblumen," *Kiyum* (January–April 1954).

45. Norman Rose, *Chaim Weizmann: A Biography* (New York, 1986), p. 354.

46. Korzen, "Emanuel Ringelblum lifnei ha-milhama ubiyimeha harishonim," *Yediot Yad Va-shem,* no. 23–24 (1960): 19.

47. Ibid., p. 29; and Fishman-Tamir, "Mikhtav l'Arnon Fishman-Tamir," pp. 28–32.

48. Jacob [Yankev] Zerubavel, *Geshtaltn* (Tel Aviv, 1967), pp. 159–160.

49. Ringelblum, *Ksovim fun geto,* 1:26–27.

50. Adolf Berman, *Vos der goyrl hot mir bashert* (Kibbutz Beit Lohamei Ha'Getaot, 1980), p. 53.

51. See Artur Eisenbach's introduction to Emanuel Ringelblum, *Kronika Getta Warszawkiego* (Warsaw, 1983), p. 11.

52. Jonas [Yanosh] Turkow, *Azoy iz es geven* (Buenos Aires, 1948), p. 71.

53. See M. M. Drozdowski, *Wspomnienia o Stefanie Starzyńskim* (Warsaw, 1982).

54. Auerbach, *Varshever tsvoes,* pp. 42–52.

55. Michał Weichert, *Zikhroynes: Milkhome,* vol. 3 (Tel Aviv, 1963), p. 30. According to Weichert, the woman was the wife of Natan Buchsbaum, a leader of the LPZ.

56. Auerbach, *Varshever tsvoes,* p. 63.

57. Ringelblum, *Ksovim fun geto,* 1:28.

58. Ibid., 2:255.

59. The best sources on the general history of Warsaw Jewry during the German occupation are Israel Gutman, *The Jews of Warsaw* (Bloomington, 1989); Barbara Engelking and Jacek Leociak, *Getto warszawskie: przewodnik po nieistniejącym mieście* (Warsaw, 2001).

60. Gutman, *The Jews of Warsaw,* p. 60.

61. Ibid., p. 64.

62. Just before the establishment of the ghetto the German-sanctioned Jewish newspaper *Gazeta Żydowska* had estimated that 75 percent of prewar Jewish businesses had been liquidated and that Jewish employment was only 12 percent of the prewar total in industry and 16 percent in commerce. See Ruta Sakowska, "Komitety domowe w getcie warszawskim," in *BŻIH,* no. 61 (1967): 60.

63. Gutman, *The Jews of Warsaw,* pp. 66–67. A questionnaire on food consumption in the Warsaw Ghetto showed that the average daily consumption was, in fact, 1,665 calories for Judenrat and Supply Authority officials, 1,395 for unemployed members of the intelligentsia, 1,407 for independent craftsmen, 1,229 for shop employees, 1,429 for wholesale merchants, 1,277 for street merchants, 1,544 for rickshaw drivers, 1,300 for doormen, 807 for refugees in hostels, and 784 for street beggars (ibid., p. 436). The accuracy of the questionnaire might be open to question but it does show the enormous importance of the smuggling that supplemented the officially allowed rations.

64. On November 28, 1939, General Governor Hans Frank issued an order that established the Judenräte in the General Government. A month earlier, on October 13, 1939, the Germans approved a list prepared by Czerniakow of proposed members of a Council of Elders that was to replace the prewar community board. This first Judenrat included leaders from across the political spectrum: Zionists Apolinary Hartglas and Senator Mojżesz Koerner; the Bundist Szmul Zygielbojm; Isaac Meir Lewin and Zisha Frydman

of the Orthdox Aguda; and others. Many members of this first Judenrat would leave Warsaw in 1939–40 and were replaced by other appointees. See Engelking and Leociak, *Getto warszawskie*, pp. 148–149.

65. Marian Fuks, "Adam Czerniakow i jego dziennik" in *Adama Czerniakowa dziennik Getta Warszawskiego*, ed. idem (Warsaw, 1983), p. 19.

66. Israel Gutman, "Adam Czerniakow: the Man and His Diary," in *The Catastrophe of European Jewry*, ed. Israel Gutman and Livia Rothkirchen (Jerusalem, 1976), pp. 451–490.

67. Raul Hilberg, Stanislaw Staron, Josef Kermisz, eds., *The Warsaw Diary of Adam Czerniakow* (New York, 1982), p. 93.

68. In a diary entry of January 7, 1942, Czerniakow wrote: "I read in Popioły by Żeromski: 'Don't I indeed have under my command all manner of thugs, cutthroats and murderers; and yet I spare them and prize them. For it is they that know best" (ibid., p. 313).

69. A useful though quite subjective survey of Judenrat members can be found in Stefan Ernest, *O wojnie wielkich Niemiec z Żydami Warszawy, 1939–1943* (Warsaw, 2003), pp. 150–162. Although first published in 2003, this account was actually written during the war. Adolf Berman gives a largely hostile account of the Judenrat membership. See his *Vos der goyrl hot mir bashert* (Kibbutz Beit Lohamei Ha'Getaot, 1980), pp. 81–87. A good general account is in Engelking and Leociak, *Getto warszawskie*, pp. 146–177.

70. Before the war the TOPOROL (Towarzystwo Popierania Rolnictwa) was a society that encouraged agricultural education among Jews; in the Warsaw Ghetto it organized the planting of vegetable gardens in vacant lots. ORT fostered occupational and handicraft training.

71. In his diary entry of May 29, 1942, Czerniakow wrote: "Considering the level of civilization in this community, the ghetto cannot be kept clean. People, unfortunately, behave like pigs. Centuries of slovenliness bear their fruit. And this is compounded by the utter misery and dire poverty" (Hilberg, Staron, and Kermisz, *The Warsaw Diary of Adam Czerniakow*, p. 360).

72. Diary entry of May 10, 1942, in ibid., p. 352.

73. See, for example, diary entry of May 26, 1942, in Ringelblum, *Ksovim fun geto*, 1:366–367.

74. Diary entry of December 12, 13, and 14, 1940, in ibid., 1:197.

75. Diary entry of March 23, 1941, in ibid., 1:232.

76. For more on the Jewish police, see Gutman, *The Jews of Warsaw*, pp. 86–91; and Engelking and Leociak, *Getto warszawskie*, pp. 194–219. A good survey of the police can be found in Aldona Podolska, *Służba Porządkowa w getcie warszawskim w latach 1940–43* (Warsaw, 1996). For an interesting insider's view see Stanislaw Adler, *In the Warsaw Ghetto, 1940–1943: The Memoirs of Stanislaw Adler* (Jerusalem, 1982); see also the excerpts from the notebooks of Samuel Puterman in *Pamiętniki z getta warszawskiego: fragmenty i regesty*, ed. Michał Grynberg (Warsaw, 1988).

77. Diary entry of November 29–December 2, 1940, in Ringelblum, *Ksovim fun geto*, 1:189.

78. See Engelking and Leociak, *Getto warszawskie*, p. 211. For proposals for police reform, see AR I, no. 100, "Wspomnienie o pracy w Służbie Porządkowej"; and AR I, no. 233, "Memoriał w sprawie reformy Służby Porządkowej w getcie warszawskim."

79. Ringelblum, *Ksovim fun geto*, 2:113; Gutman, *The Jews of Warsaw*, p. 84.

80. "During the meeting, Dr. Schiper again behaved foolishly. Since he contrasted those present with 'the true mentors of the people,' I asked him, where were those 'mentors'? Should we not look for them among those who have fled or among those who tried to leave but did not succeed?" (diary entry of October 5, 1941, in Hilberg, Staron, and Kermisz, *The Warsaw Diary of Adam Czerniakow,* p. 285).

81. Diary entry of July 21, 1940, in ibid. p. 176.

82. On the ORT, see Joseph Marcus, *Social and Political History of the Jews in Poland* (Berlin, New York, and Amsterdam, 1983), pp. 157–159.

83. Weichert, *Zikhroynes: Milkhome,* 3:23.

84. Ibid., 3:44–47.

85. According to Weichert, Giterman had no choice but to flee, since he had been a leader of an anti-Nazi committee before the war. See Michał Weichert, *Yidishe aleynhilf 1939–1945* (Tel Aviv, 1962), p. 328.

86. Meir Korzen, "Emanuel Ringelblum lifnei ha-milhama ubiyimeha harishonim," *Yediot Yad Va-shem,* no. 23–24 (1960): 19.

87. Berman, *Vos der goyrl hot mir bashert,* p. 93.

88. Ringelblum, *Ksovim fun geto,* 1:392. Compare this to the views expressed by Chaim Kaplan in his diary entry of March 14, 1941:

> As long as the Joint had the means, we continued to lay our burden on our rich uncle that he should support us. . . . It was our luck that the Joint was reduced to ruins and ended its assistance. When we saw that your problems grew, we had to say, 'If I am not for myself, who will be for me?' and the Jewish Self-Help society (Aleynhilf [SDK]) was created. In a short period of time, it became an organization with many branches and affiliates. It had a budget of a quarter million—besides sums which flowed in through other channels, especially through the house committees. The Aleynhilf offered equitable support for those in need. It can be said at this time that in you, the Jews in Poland, has been fulfilled their mission to the greatest heights . . . half a million zlotys in assistance to the needy within one month—who had dared even imagine that the Jews of Warsaw were capable of such giving? The Aleynhilf will certainly find a historian of documents and statistics who will tell generations to come of its scope, greatness and educational worth. (Cited by Israel Gutman, "Kiddush Hashem and Kiddush Hachayim," *Simon Wiesenthal Center Annual* 1 [1984]: 185)

89. For the most reliable guide to this array of titular and jurisdictional changes, see Engelking and Leociak, *Getto warszawskie,* pp. 289–325. In November 1941 the ŻTOS changed its name yet again to the Żydowska Opieka Społeczna (ŻOS). In March 1942 the ŻOS was formally incorporated into the ŻKOM and thus, formally at least, lost its previous autonomy.

90. The major Polish welfare organization was the RGO, the Rada Główna Opiekuńcza.

91. Weichert, *Zikhroynes: Milkhome,* 3:81.

92. Weichert, *Yidishe Aleynhilf 1939–1945,* p. 18.

93. Engelking and Leociak, *Getto warszawskie,* pp. 291–297.

94. Jonas (Yanosh) Turkow, one of Warsaw's leading Yiddish actors, worked with Ringelblum in the Aleynhilf. During the siege Ringelblum assigned him the task of tak-

ing a census of those who had lost their homes during the bombings. Turkow praised the decision to employ the Jewish intelligentsia:

> Time showed that this was a correct decision. Schoolteachers, public activists, writers, and artists proved themselves to be terrific organizers, The 3,000 [employees of the Aleynhilf] demonstrated that, unlike the Judenrat, they could organize and impose a sense of social discipline on a community of 600,000 Jews [*sic*]. For this reason it became possible to form, despite all the agents and informers, a Jewish underground movement in the Warsaw ghetto that later led to the heroic uprising. (Turkow, *Azoy iz es geven*, p. 65)

95. Auerbach, *Varshever tsvoes*, p. 63. At the same time Ringelblum told Auerbach that "a decision had been made to employ as many of the Jewish intelligentsia as possible in the institutions of the [Aleynhilf]—to save the cadres."

96. Eck, "Mit Emanuel Ringelblum in Varshever geto," pp. 107–108, Eck noted that "he looked well. His face was serene, serious, and he gave the impression of being a person who had been totally untouched by the war. But this was a false impression." Compare this to Meir Korzen's description of Ringelblum in Zbąszyń, in "Emanuel Ringelblum lifnei ha-milhama u'biyameha harishonim," *Yediot Yad Va-shem*, no. 21–22 (1959).

97. Just a partial listing of the Aleynhilf's key staff illustrates its political diversity and the talent the organization attracted. Rabbi Shimon Huberband, a refugee from Piotrków, headed the religious section; later he would become one of the key members of the Oyneg Shabes Archive. Lipe Bloch, another future Oyneg Shabes member who had been in charge of the Zionist Jewish National Fund (Keren Kayemet), ran the clothing section. Hersh Wasser, an economist from Lodz and secretary of the Oyneg Shabes Archive, helped run the landsmanshaft section based on the original hometowns of the refugees. Another important member of the Oyneg Shabes, the teacher Abraham Lewin, headed the youth committee. The leaders of the Finance Section included L. Starobinski, another key director of the Keren Kayemet, and Henryka Lazowert, a talented poet who wrote in Polish. The section for constructive help was run by the Bundist leaders Sonia Nowogrodzka and Etkin, a refugee from Lodz. Mordecai Maze, a former director of the famed Vilner Trupe, one of the finest Yiddish theater ensembles, headed the theater department. One of the YIVO's most talented scholars, Menakhem Linder, directed the Bureau of Statistics. A major Yiddish journalist, Elkhanon Tseitlin, helped run the press department.

98. Turkow, *Azoy iz es geven*, p. 66.

99. Hersh Wasser, "IKOR in Varshever Geto," *Dos naye lebn*, no. 57 (1947).

100. Turkow, *Azoy iz es geven*, p. 248.

101. Ibid., p. 249.

102. Ringelblum, *Ksovim fun geto*, 1:199, 235.

103. Gutman, *The Jews of Warsaw*, p. 176.

104. Emanuel Ringelblum, "Shie Broyde," in idem, *Ksovim fun geto*, 2:207–210.

105. For more on these soup kitchens, see Berman, *Vos der goyrl hot mir bashert*, pp. 189–193.

106. Eck, "Mit Emanuel Ringelblum in Varshever geto." Aside from Eck's recollections there is no other evidence to support this.

107. According to Berman, this committee included, besides the directors of the Joint, Maurycy Orzech of the Bund, Shakhne Zagan of the LPZ, Menakhem Kirshenbaum of

the General Zionists, and Alexander Zisha Frydman of the Agudas Yisroel. Two Judenrat members also sat on the committee: Abraham Gepner, representing the Provisioning Bureau and Stanisław Szereszewski representing the ŻKOM the official legal home of the Aleynhilf. See Berman, *Vos der goyrl hot mir bashert*, p. 95. Engelking and Leociak mention that Rabbi Isaac Nissenbaum of the Mizrachi and Joseph Lewartowski of the Communists also were part of the committee, the latter from the beginning of 1942 (*Getto warszawskie*, p. 326).

108. On the genesis of the house committees, see Sakowska, "Komitety domowe w getcie warszawskim"; see also Michael Mazor, "The House Committees in the Warsaw Ghetto," in *The Holocaust as Historical Experience*, ed. Yehuda Bauer and Nathan Rotenstreich (New York, 1981), pp. 95–109.

109. Peretz Opoczynski, "Di tragedye fun a hoyz komitet," AR I, no. 106.

110. For more on the governance patterns of the house committees, see "Struktury wewnętrzne Komitetów Domowych," AR I, no. 66.

111. Oyneg Shabes member and writer Yehuda Feld left a biting satire on the high-handed bosses of one of these house committees; see his "Kheykl, Feykl un Beykl: klal tuer fun a hoyz komitet, in AR I, no. 528.

112. Abraham Katsh, ed., *The Warsaw Diary of Chaim Kaplan* (New York, 1965), pp. 227–228.

113. AR I, no. 76. Also, Chaim Kaplan noted in his diary that,

A sort of vox populi came into existence which judged everyone according to his actions and his philanthropy. If they encountered a "stubborn pig" they softened his heart by various means, some ethical, some coercive. Whoever did not wish to give was considered an outcast in his neighbors' eyes and was publicly shamed. His name was listed on a blackboard which was hung on the gateway so that all who entered the courtyard would know that So-and-So had set himself apart from the community and would not come to the aid of the people. The courtyard committee assessed everyone's material resources and imposed a monthly payment upon each householder. (March 22, 1941, p. 259)

114. AR I, no. 68.

115. Peretz Opoczynski, "Di tragedye fun a hoyz komitet," in AR I, no. 106.

116. Reports of these women's circles can be found in AR II, nos. 19, 59.

117. The breakdown of these income sources varied depending on the inhabitants' economic position. In more economically stable houses, for example, income from theater and gambling constituted up to a quarter of the total, whereas in poorer houses they brought in very little income (Sakowska, "Komitety domowe w getcie warszawskim").

118. Jonas [Yanosh] Turkow, "Varshe vaylt zikh," AR I, no. 90.

119. See "Theses on the Theme of the House Committees," in AR I, no. 138. These theses were guidelines instructing writers on how to compose a study of the house committees. The checklist of questions and themes included the origins of the house committees; their functions and relations with the Judenrat, the Jewish police, and the Aleynhilf; their sources of income; and their historical and social roles. Under the rubric "negative aspects of house committee activity," the document mentioned "support of own tenants at the expense of the [general contributions] to the Aleynhilf."

120. AR I, no. 67.

121. Opoczynski's reportages on the house committees can be found in AR I, nos. 33,

106. Materials on Nalewki 23 can be found in AR I, nos. 67, 203. The report on Gęsia 19 is in AR I, no. 297.

122. Mazor, "The House Committees in the Warsaw Ghetto," in Bauer and Rotenstreich, *The Holocaust as Historical Experience,* p. 97. The term "social workers" would be better translated as "community workers."

123. Engelking and Leociak provide a table of organization of the Public Sector in their *Getto warszawskie,* p. 326.

124. The best single study of the house committees is Sakowska, "Komitety domowe w getcie warszawskim," p. 65.

125. AR I, no. 210. On the other hand, as Eleonora Bergman has pointed out to the author, another document, AR II, no. 39, stated that there were 1,108 committees in 1,124 buildings in January 1942.

126. "Aniyei irkha kodmim [The poor of your own town come first]," Babylonian Talmud, Tractate Bava Metzia, 33A.

127. Peretz Opoczynski, in a reportage on the house committee on Muranowska 6, noted that, in the early days of the occupation, "nobody thought of giving money to Jews who were not your immediate neighbors. . . . This was one of the great tragedies of Warsaw Jews, that they did not understand their national task, that their eyes focused not on the community as a whole [*dem klal*] but on their immediate neighbors. Each building was its own community, without close contact with [other] buildings" (AR I, no. 106).

128. Aaron Einhorn, the former editor of *Haynt,* Warsaw's largest Yiddish daily, and Natan Eck wrote a bulletin in an attempt to raise morale and encourage the house committees to accept the guidance of the Aleynhilf (Eck, "Mit Emanuel Ringelblum in Varshever geto," pp. 110–111). That this bulletin did not surface in the recovered parts of the Oyneg Shabes only reinforces the assumption that much of the archive was lost. It is inconceivable that Ringelblum would not have collected this bulletin.

129. "Like it or not, the Jewish people is one large family that is suffering the same tribulations and the same misfortunes and now has only one major task: to work together to hold out!" (AR I, no. 76).

130. Ibid.

131. According to Sakowska, the breakdown in house committee expenditures between "in-house" and "external" relief showed that, in January 1942, 71.5 percent of house committee money went "in house" and 28.5 percent went "outside." In the better-off third district of the ghetto, 39.7 percent went outside as opposed to only 14.2 percent in the impoverished first district. See Sakowska, "Komitety domowe w getcie warszawskim," p. 69.

132. Katsh, *The Warsaw Diary of Chaim Kaplan,* p.129; entry of March 9, 1940.

133. Eck, "Mit Emanuel Ringelblum in Varshever geto," p. 113.

134. Ringelblum, *Ksovim fun geto,* 1:391.

135. Rachel Auerbach, *Baym letstn veg* (Tel Aviv, 1977) p. 150.

136. Eck, "Mit Emanuel Ringelblum in Varshever geto," pp. 112–115.

137. Mazor, "The House Committees in the Warsaw Ghetto," p. 97. By the term "parliament" Mazor seems to mean the Central Commission.

138. Michael Mazor, *The Vanished City* (New York, 1993), p. 64.

139. Ibid., p. 101.

140. Ibid., p. 103.

141. "At the Central Commission of the house committees," Mazor recalled,

I made order reign and maintained strict rules of procedure with an insistence that bordered on pedantry. Meetings took place regularly every Tuesday at five o'clock in the afternoon; members prevented from coming had to supply an explanation. In general there were no absentees. Such details were perhaps trivial, but in the period of the Ghetto, when one had the impression that the world had gone mad and was rushing toward a precipice, such rules preserved the stability of moral values, and gave us the feeling that our activity was not in vain. ("The House Committees in the Warsaw Ghetto," p. 105)

142. AR I, no. 106.

143. AR I, no. 210.

144. Ibid.

145. Ibid.

146. Ringelblum, *Ksovim fun geto,* 1:100.

147. Ibid., 1:119.

148. Ibid., 1:315.

149. Ludwik Hirszfeld, *Historia jednego życia* (Warsaw, 1989), pp. 276–277.

150. AR I, no. 106.

151. Only five public bathhouses were within the terrain of the ghetto, and these could bathe seventeen thousand people a month (Engelking and Leociak, *Getto warszawskie,* p. 281). The soap the Jews received in these bathhouses was of a very poor quality.

152. A laconic Judenrat report on a disinfection that took place on Krochmalna Street on August 28 and 29 mentioned thousands of poor people forced out of their homes at 4:00 AM on August 28 and made to wait outside for their turn. One group returned from the baths at 7:30 PM and the rest had to wait all night. Distribution of soup was complicated by a lack of bowls, and many Jews took the soup in their caps or in their cupped hands (ibid., p. 285).

153. On August 29, 1941, Czerniakow tersely noted in his diary: "Today the German, Polish, and Jewish police sealed Krochmalna Street and escorted 8,000 people to public baths. Unfortunately the neighborhood scum used this opportunity to steal many articles from the residents."

154. See, for example, Tatiana Berenstein, "Praca przymusowa Żydów w Warszawie w czasie okupacji," *BŻIH,* no. 45–46 (1963); Christopher Browning, *The Origins of the Final Solution* (Lincoln, Nebr., and Jerusalem, 2004), pp. 141–151.

155. In a diary entry of September 6, 7, 8, and 9, 1940, Ringelblum wrote that "the terrible news from the camps has caused people who are called up not to report for service" (*Ksovim fun geto,* 1:137).

156. See, for example, Czerniakow's diary entries for May 7 and 10, 1941 (Hilberg, Staron, and Kermisz, *The Warsaw Diary of Adam Czerniakow,* pp. 232–235.

157. Browning, *The Origins of the Final Solution,* p. 151. According to Browning, 8,600 Warsaw Jews were sent to labor camps in the spring and summer of 1941, mainly to work on water regulation projects.

158. "One of the most important and serious descriptions is the comprehensive account of the labor camp in Kampinos, with its infamous hill of corpses, where more than

fifty young Jews were buried, after having been tortured or shot by the camp guards. The account, composed by Rabbi Huberband, is one of the most important documents on Hitlerite atrocities against the Jewish forced laborers" (Ringelblum, *Ksovim fun geto,* 2:91).

159. AR I, no. 379. Reprinted in Shimon Huberband, *Kiddush Hashem: Jewish Religious and Cultural Life during the Holocaust,* ed. Jeffrey Gurock and Robert Hirt, trans. David Fishman (New York, 1987), p. 72.

160. Ibid., p. 87.

161. Ibid., p. 101.

162. AR I, no. 106.

163. Ibid.

164. Sakowska, "Komitety domowe w getcie warszawskim," pp. 85–86.

165. AR I, no. 297.

166. Ringelblum, *Ksovim fun geto,* 1:335.

167. Ibid., 1:376.

168. Ibid., 1:316.

169. Rachel Auerbach, "Pgishot im Emanuel Ringelblum," *Davar,* March 20, 1964.

170. Auerbach, *Varshever tsvoes,* p. 275.

171. Auerbach's report on the soup kitchen is in AR I, no. 655; the rewritten and expanded version is in her *Varshever tsvoes.*

172. Auerbach, *Varshever tsvoes,* p. 109. Henie and the others would provide models for Auerbach's powerful elegy *Yizkor,* which she wrote in 1943.

173. Auerbach, *Varshever tsvoes,* p. 101.

174. AR I, no. 655.

175. AR I, no. 654.

176. Leyb Goldin, "Khronik fun eyn mes-les," in AR I, no. 1,167. Translation from Milton Teichman and Sharon Leder, eds., *Truth and Lamentation: Stories and Poems on the Holocaust* (Urbana and Chicago, 1994), pp. 52–66.

177. In his 1954 book on Jewish writing in the ghettos and concentration camps the Polish-Jewish communist historian and critic Ber Mark attacked this story for its "exaggerated expressionism." After all, real revolutionaries were thinking about resistance, not about their stomachs: "Goldin does not see the social aspect, he does not contrast this hungry individual with the well-fed elite, he does not think about the reasons for this, he does not embrace protest and revolt. Like his hungry hero—and perhaps he [Goldin] is indeed—he is the prisoner of his [animal hunger]" (Ber Mark, *Umgekumene shrayber fun di getos un lagern* [Warsaw, 1954], pp. 111–112).

178. As Sara Horowitz points out, "by writing, the chroniclers could establish the illusion of distance between themselves and those worse off, which mitigated their own sense of degeneration. The man who spoons spilled soup from a filthy staircase and the boys who grub for rancid potatoes stand in sharp relief—if only temporarily—to the person describing them. Even when this distance collapses, the act of writing reasserted one's dignity. As Goldin struggles to distinguish hungry humans from scavenging animals, his very ability to narrate—to assert, "We are not animals"—proves his humanity" (Horowitz, *Voicing the Void: Muteness and Memory in Holocaust Fiction* (Albany, 1997), pp. 59–60).

179. AR I, no. 654.

180. Ringelblum, *Ksovim fun geto,* 1:365.

5   A BAND OF COMRADES

1. Ringelblum, *Ksovim fun geto*, 2:101–102. Of course, the "brotherhood" included several women: Rachel Auerbach, Cecylia Słapakowa, Henryka Lazowert, Gustawa Jarecka, and Bluma Wasser.

2. Hersh Wasser, "Vi iz es geven?" *Unzer veg* (March 1954).

3. Ibid.

4. For an excellent study of the Bund in wartime Poland, see Daniel Blatman, *Lema'an heruteinu v'herutkhem: ha-Bund b'Polin 1939–1949* (Jerusalem, 1996).

5. On this possibility, see Ruta Sakowska, "Biuro Informacji i Propagandy KG Armii Krajowej a Archiwum Ringelbluma," *BŻIH,* nos. 162–163 (1992): 19–34.

6. AR I, no. 457. Reprinted in Yehuda Feld, *In di tsaytn fun Homen dem Tsveytn,* ed. Ber Mark (Warsaw, 1954). For biographical details on Feld, see Samuel Niger and Jacob Shatzky, eds., *Leksikon fun der nayer Yidisher literatur,* 8 vols. (New York, 1956–81), 7:413–414.

7. Hersh Wasser recalled that Ringelblum was always writing something down. As he rushed from meeting to meeting in the Aleynhilf or the IKOR, Ringelblum was always jotting down impressions on any handy scrap of paper. See Wasser, "A vort vegn Ringelblum Arkhiv."

8. Ringelblum, *Ksovim fun geto*, 2:77.

9. Ibid.

10. Ibid. This took place in his apartment on 18 Leszno Street.

11. A high percentage of the archive's inner circle consisted not of Warsaw Jews but of Jews from the provinces. It is possible that outsiders, who lacked extensive social networks in the big city, relied more on the alternate community based on membership in the Aleynhilf.

12. Personal conversation with Wasser's daughter, Leah Wasser, Givatayim Israel, June 7, 2004.

13. Hersh Wasser, "Untererdisher geto arkhiv," *Letste nayes,* April 16, 1954.

14. For one of the lists drawn up by Wasser, see AR I, no. 1152. It contains thirty-seven names of Oyneg Shabes collaborators. Many were people who did not write for the archive; one can assume they were copiers.

15. See, for example, AR I, nos. 1147 and 1176. These lists are not complete and were partially damaged.

16. Personal conversation with Leah Wasser, Givatayim, Israel, June 7, 2004.

17. *Dray: [ondenkbukh] / Pola Elster, Hersh Berlinski, Eliyahu 'Erlikh* (Tel Aviv, 1966), p. 169. At one key meeting on the organization of the ŻOB, which took place at the end of October 1942, the LPZ delegates (including Hersh Berlinski and Wasser) had a tense confrontation with Mordecai Anielewicz, who represented the Hashomer Hatzair, and Yitzhak Zuckerman, who represented Dror. The standoff essentially concerned the relationship between the youth movements and the political parties in the ŻOB. The LPZ wanted a two-tiered organization of the ŻOB that would guarantee a role for the political parties. Anielewicz and Zuckerman thought this was a bad idea. They did not want to take orders from the parties, believing that it was the youth movements that had taken the lead in organizing the resistance. They also spoke contemptuously about the adult political parties in the ghetto, which angered the LPZ. This sparked an angry tirade from LPZ representatives who reminded Anielewicz and Zuckerman that a few broken-down

revolvers did not give them the right to decide the fate of the ghetto. The parties, not the youth movements, had represented the Jewish masses before the war, and, whatever happened to the ghetto, they insisted, it would be the parties that would shape Jewish life in the postwar world. Finally, Anielewicz and Zuckerman, at least according to Berlinski's account, agreed to the LPZ's proposal. See *Dray*, pp. 169–170.

18. Personal conversation with Leah Wasser, Givatayim Israel, June 7, 2004.

19. See Hersh Wasser, "Pola Elster," in *Dray*, pp. 32–37.

20. See Melekh Nayshtat, *Khurbm un oyfshtand fun di yidn in Varshe: Eydes bleter un azkores* (Tel Aviv, 1948), pp. 394–396.

21. Before the war Dror-Frayhayt had established a loose union with the Right Poalei Tsiyon.

22. Yitzhak Zuckerman did not particularly like Ringelblum and did not offer to give him information. He also considered him to be a boring lecturer. See Zuckerman, *A Surplus of Memory* (Berkeley, 1993), p. 116.

23. Ibid., p. 53. Despite the large difference in age between the two, they addressed each other using the familiar Yiddish "du."

24. A copy was preserved in the Ringelblum Archive, AR I. no. 751.

25. Joseph Kermish, ed., *Itonut ha-Mahteret ha-Yehudit b'Varsha*, vol. 1 (Tel Aviv, 1979), pp. 46–47.

26. "It was a source of educational inspiration," Zuckerman recalled,

> and it gives an idea of what we could learn and couldn't learn from previous generations. It was still impossible to learn of Treblinka from history or literature. . . . Nowhere and never had there been pogroms, persecutions, and tribulations everywhere at the same time. Sometimes Jews fled from east to west as in the days of Chmielnicki or from west to east as during the Crusades. But [mass murder everywhere] was unprecedented in Jewish history. (Zuckerman, *A Surplus of Memory*, p. 72)

27. On the other hand, Zuckerman refused to share the top-secret Dror archive. It was destroyed during the war.

28. See chapter 7.

29. Mazor, who survived the war, described their conversation as the train slowly took them to Treblinka:

> Our convoy crossed the Vistula, we could make out the Poniatowski bridge, the trolley cars that circled on it, the beautiful city of Warsaw with all its splendors, a whole world where people could still breathe, live, love. While this picture unfolded before our eyes, we spoke of the fate that awaited us with terrifying objectivity. "Tomorrow," we said, "there will still be trolley cars and people wearing bright clothes on Poniatowski bridge, but we won't exist any longer."
>
> Only Asz, a young, very dynamic man, could not accept the idea of his vanishing. He was plunged into a gloom of despair and kept saying: "We've got to find a way out of this." I started to speak to him about an old book I admired very much, Boethius's *The Consolation of Philosophy*, but he cut me off harshly: "What am I supposed to do with your philosophy at a time like this!"—"What value would philosophy have," I answered, "if it didn't console at a moment like

this?" And the train kept rolling through the night, toward the gas chambers of Treblinka. It was then that they noticed the loose wire over the window. (Mazor, *The Vanished City*, pp. 173–174)

30. "Daily entries of Hersh Wasser," introduction and notes by Joseph Kermish, *Yad Vashem Studies*, vol. 15 (1983): 276.

31. AR I, no. 174. "Der tsveyter ofener briv tsu di askonim 'zitsers.'"

32. Jonas [Yanosh] Turkow mentions that in early 1943, when he, Ringelblum, and others were discussing a scheme to raise money to send Jewish children to Polish monasteries and convents, it was Kon who reported back that he had spoken with wealthy Hasidim and that they had rejected the idea. The archive also contains a friendly letter from the Piaseczner Rebbe, Kalonymous Shapiro, asking Kon to visit him (AR I, no. 593).

33. See Kon's diary, entry for August 18, 1942, AR II, no. 208.

34. AR I, no. 175. Reprinted in Kermish, *To Live with Honor*, p. 24.

35. AR II, no. 208. Reprinted in ibid., pp. 80–81. Kon's account is puzzling because other memoirs speak of the Landau shop as a refuge. For example, Mazor recalled that the "shop had become a haven for [Aleynhilf] workers. . . . [P]eople from quite varied circumstances begged the Landau brothers to be let in there. They were rarely refused and the premises became jam-packed" (*The Vanished City*, p. 157).

36. There are two useful sources on Winter. The first is Meir Kuczynski, "Shmuel Winter," in *Wloclawek v'ha-Svivah: Sefer Zikaron*, ed. Katriel Tkhursh and Meir Korzen (Tel Aviv, 1967), pp. 459–468; See also Auerbach, *Varshever tsvoes*, pp. 272–284.

37. Auerbach, *Varshever tsvoes*, p. 272.

38. See Weinreich's obituary for Winter, *YIVO bleter*, no. 1 (1945).

39. The best discussion of the Zakład Zaopatrywania can be found in Engelking and Leociak, *Getto warszawskie*, pp. 410–421. Gepner himself may very well have taken the lead in recruiting Winter.

40. Auerbach recalls that "the publicly minded leaders, grouped around the Aleynhilf, needed a trusted liaison to the other place (the Judenrat). Winter became this liaison" (*Varshever tsvoes*, p. 273), Thanks to Winter and Joseph Jaszunski, another Judenrat member, the Judenrat began to issue its proclamations in Yiddish as well as Polish.

41. Israel Gutman, *Mered ha-Netzurim: Mordecai Anielewicz u-milhemet geto Varshah* (Merhaviyah, 1963), p. 237.

42. Ibid.

43. Unpublished essay by Rachel Auerbach on the Oyneg Shabes Archive, Yad Vashem Archive, P16–27.

44. Most of his diary entries had no date, and many words were missing. But in one entry he mentioned an acquaintance who had just heard from his daughter on the Aryan side. "Such a simple Jew did everything he could to save his loved ones, and I failed." The original diary seems to have disappeared from the ŻIH, and there are no copies. Excerpts were published after the war by Ber Mark. Yitzhak Zuckerman also published short excerpts from a diary that he says was Winter's. Both Mark and Zuckerman agree that the remains of the diary were found at Świętojerska 34. Ber Mark, "Shmuel Winter's togbukh: A vogiker tsushtayer tsu der erev khurbm oyfshtand dokumentatsie," *Bleter far geshikhte*, vols. 1–2 (1950): 33.

45. Without access to the original document it is hard to verify Mark's assertion.

Mark was notorious for "editing" texts, especially to make them fit the party line. But it is perfectly plausible that in early 1943 Winter, like many other Warsaw Jews, were obsessed with the good news coming from Stalingrad and other major battles.

46. Yitzhak Zuckerman, quoting from what he asserts is Winter's diary in 1947, wrote that on the first day of the January action, Winter wrote, "I heard rumors that Jews were fighting on Niska and Zamenhofa streets—members of Hashomer and Halutzim. What kind of ideas do they have, these idealists? What will the consequences be? I think that from a historical point of view and also with regard to the future, the work of the [Oyneg Shabes] is more important than the fighting of the Jews." But three days later Winter wrote: "On the second day of the uprising the Germans received orders to withdraw from the ghetto. . . . The Germans withdrew and left the ghetto. I think that the fighting of the young men has forced them to do this." Cited by Philip Friedman, in idem, ed., *Martyrs and Fighters: The Epic of the Warsaw Ghetto* (New York, 1954), pp. 220–221. See also Gutman, *Mered netzurim,* p. 311.

47. "I told Emanuel that I am not happy that I have to receive thousands without a receipt and that I give away thousands without a receipt. Of the 5,000 that I got from Shtibl, I gave [Menakhem] Kon 4,120. Rotbalt's 3,000 I gave to Ringelblum, and Mlawski's 5,000 went to Mordecai (Anielewicz)" (Ber Mark, "Shmuel Winter's togbukh," p. 47).

48. Auerbach, *Varshever tsvoes,* p. 280.

49. Nonetheless a notation in a fragment of his diary shows that he, too, cared about helping Jewish intellectuals and writers escape. He asked Shie Perle's son, Lutek, to convince Polish writers to help rescue some of their Jewish counterparts. See Ber Mark, "Shmuel Winter's togbukh," p. 46. And, according to Auerbach, toward the end Winter asked her to contact a Polish friend of his in order to try to save his daughter and son (*Varshever tsvoes,* p. 281).

50. Ber Mark, "Shmuel Winter's togbukh," p. 41.

51. Gutman, *Mered netzurim,* p. 375.

52. Auerbach, *Varshever tsvoes,* pp. 282–283.

53. Berman, *Vos der goyrl hot mir bashert,* pp. 296–297.

54. Natan Eck, *Ha'toim b'darkhei ha-mavet* (Tel Aviv, 1960), pp. 46–48.

55. Ibid.

56. See Nayshtat, *Khurbm un oyfshtand fun di yidn in varshe,* p. 138.

57. Gutman, *Mered ha-Netzurim,* p. 308.

58. He was a son of the Bialer rebbe and a direct descendent of "The Jew of Przysucha," Yakov Yitzhak Rabinowitz. His wife was a great granddaughter of Menakhem Mendel, the famous Kotsker rebbe.

59. There is a long and entertaining discussion of Rabinowitz's colorful youth in Yekhil Yeshaye Trunk, *Poyln,* 7 vols. (New York, 1953), 7:201–217.

60. A Bundist obituary that appeared after the war called Rabinowitz "the tsadik of the Warsaw Ghetto." The same source also states that he "headed the archive commission" of the underground Bund but totally ignored his key position in the Oyneg Shabes. See Jacob Sholem Hertz, ed., *Doyres Bundistn,* 3 vols. (New York, 1956), 2:284–286.

61. "In his political persuasion, this man, a well-to-do merchant from an Orthodox family, was a staunch Bundist. Sincerity, moral integrity and devotion to social work—these were characteristic traits that earned him the respect and veneration of all who had dealings with him" (Mazor, *The Vanished City,* p. 75).

62. According to Natan Eck, Bloch was surprised by Ringelblum's intelligence and capabilities and continually praised him. See Eck, *Ha'toim b'darkhei ha-mavet,* p. 35.

63. For more on Lipe Bloch, see Nayshtat, *Khurbm un oyfshtand fun di yidn in varshe,* pp. 367–369.

64. On this camp, see ibid., p. 193. The "Jewish Elder" of the Budzyn camp was a decent man who tried to save the rabbis and former community leaders by assigning them easy work. There were lectures and secret religious services, with a concealed Torah scroll and phylacteries.

65. Raya Cohen, "'Against the Current': Hashomer Hatzair in the Warsaw Ghetto," *Jewish Social Studies* 7, no. 1 (2000): 63–81.

66. Gutman, *The Jews of Warsaw,* pp. 132–144; idem, *Mered ha-Netzurim,* p. 172.

67. See Ringelblum's essay on Mordecai Anielewicz in his *Ksovim fun geto,* 2:141–143.

68. See Cohen, "'Against the Current,'" pp. 63–81; also see idem, "Ha-emnam derekh ahat? Od al mikoma shel hitnagdut ha-mizuyenet b'getaot," *Ha-shoah: historiyah vezikaron: kovetz maamarim shai le-Yisrael Gutman* (Jerusalem, 2001); Gutman, *Mered ha-Netzurim,* p. 14.

69. Cohen, "'Against the Current,'" pp. 63–81.

70. As early as the spring of 1940 Ringelblum praised an article he had read in *Neged ha-zerem,* the Hashomer's main newspaper. See the entry for April 20–May 1, 1940, in *Ksovim fun geto,* 1:120. In his essay on Anielewicz he noted that "one of my strongest experiences was lecturing to such young people who proudly carried the banner of idealism in a sea of barbarism. When I looked at the rapt faces of that youth, so hungry for knowledge, then I was able to forget that a war was raging in the world" (ibid., 2:143). For their part the audience did not remember Ringelblum's lectures on the history of the Jewish labor movement as particularly dynamic or engaging, see Gutman, *Mered ha-Netzurim,* p. 180.

71. Ringelblum, *Ksovim fun geto,* 1:320.

72. Ibid., 2:147.

73. See Joseph Shamir, *Shmuel Breslav: ha-maavak v'ha-tikvah* (Tel Aviv, 1994).

74. Zuckerman, *A Surplus of Memory,* p. 202.

75. Zuckerman considered Breslav and Mordecai Anielewicz extreme leftists who, had they survived, may well have ended up in the Communist Party. (We should take this with a grain of salt, however.) On the other hand, he remembered Kaplan as "one of us. He was a carpenter by trade, a common man, with a sense of humor; he also spoke Polish but Yiddish and Hebrew were his languages" (ibid., p. 258).

76. See Abraham Lewin, *A Cup of Tears: A Diary of the Warsaw Ghetto* (Oxford, 1988), p. 164; diary entry for August 24, 1942. Hereafter all Lewin's quotes are from this source, unless noted otherwise, and page numbers are given in the text.

77. Ringelblum, *Ksovim fun geto,* 2:58.

78. AR II, no. 282. Reprinted in Kermish, *To Live with Honor,* pp. 55–57.

79. On this point, see Natan Cohen, *Sefer, sofer v'iton: merkaz ha-tarbut ha'yehudit b'varsha, 1918–1942* (Jerusalem, 2003), pp. 178–187.

80. The term "Responsa Literature" refers to written rulings made by rabbis under *halakha,* Jewish law, in response to questions submitted to them in writing, throughout the post-Talmudic period (from the fifth or sixth century to the present).

81. Nachman Blumenthal and Joseph Kermish, "On Rabbi Shimon Huberband," in Gurock and Hirt, *Kiddush Hashem*, pp. xxi–xxix. This collection of Rabbi Huberband's writings was found in the Oyneg Shabes.

82. Ringelblum, *Ksovim fun geto*, 1:217.

83. These reports for the Oyneg Shabes, "The Destruction of Synagogues, Houses of Study, and Cemeteries" and "Concerning the Rescue of Jewish Cultural Treasures in Occupied Poland," have been reprinted in S. Huberband, *Kiddush Hashem*, pp. 274–334, 454–459, respectively.

84. For example, see AR II, no. 370. Among the many issues Shapiro addressed in these weekly sermons, at which Huberband no doubt was present, was the question of why the Jews were undergoing such suffering. On July 11, 1942, less than two weeks before the beginning of the Great Deportation, Shapiro asked: "How can we tell if the sufferings are only on account of our sins, or whether they are to sanctify his Name? By noticing whether the enemies torment only us or whether their hatred is basically for the Torah, and, as a consequence they torment us as well." Then Rabbi Shapiro explained the difference between Purim and Hanukkah: "Regarding Haman's decree the Talmud asks, 'What did the Jews of that generation do to deserve destruction?' whereas regarding (Hanukah) the Talmud does not raise that question, despite the fact that thousands of Jews were killed, nearly all the land of Israel was conquered and the Temple was invaded. The difference is that Haman's decree was directed only against the Jews [not their religion]; it follows then that the decree against them . . . was on account of some sin. But in the story of Hanukah, the Jews suffered not because they committed a sin, but because they were defending the Torah." Reprinted in David Roskies, *The Literature of Destruction* (Philadelphia and New York, 1988), p. 509. See also Nehemia Polen, *The Holy Fire: The Teachings of Rabbi Kalonymus Kalman Shapira, the Rebbe of the Warsaw Ghetto* (Northvale, 1994).

85. Huberband, *Kiddush Hashem*, p. 136.

86. Ibid., p. 247.

87. Ibid., p. 254.

88. Ibid., p. 157.

89. Ringelblum, *Ksovim fun geto*, 2:59.

90. A memorial volume put out by alumnae of the school is filled with glowing references to Lewin. Typical is the following memoir by Nina Danzig-Weltser:

> He was not only a teacher; to us he was a rich personality and a thinker of some depth. His appearance reinforced this impression. He was tall and thin, with fair hair and a pale complexion. He spoke softly and in a restrained manner, although in interpreting the Prophets he was enthusiastic to the point of ecstasy. Lewin was blessed with a deep appreciation of the beauties of nature. In class outings he used to talk with a small group of the girls about the beauty of the landscape. He spoke not as a teacher but as a friend talking to equals. (Quoted in Lewin, *A Cup of Tears*, p. 10)

91. In Ringelblum's words;

> The diary of A. L-n, the author of the book *Kantonistn*, is a valuable document. The author has been keeping it for a year and a half and has poured all his literary talent into it. Every sentence in it is measured. L. has packed the diary

not only with everything he has managed to learn about Warsaw, but also with the terrible suffering of the provincial Jews. During the deportation, even as bitter misfortune struck him when his wife Luba was taken away, he continued to record in his diary under the most impossible conditions. The clean and compressed style of the diary, its accuracy and precision in relating facts, and its grave contents qualify it as an important literary document which must be published as soon as possible after the war. (*Ksovim fun geto*, 2:100–101)

92. In September 1941, in a talk commemorating the anniversary of the death of the Yiddish writer I. M. Weissenberg, Lewin stressed that although life in the ghetto was dominated by death and despair, "we wish to live on, to continue as free and creative men. This shall be our test. If, under the thick layer of ashes our life is not extinguished, this will prove the triumph of the human over the inhuman and that our will to live is mightier than the will to destruction; that we are capable of overcoming all evil forces which attempt to engulf us" (AR II, no. 369; translation from Lewin, *A Cup of Tears*, p. 54).

93. Abraham Lewin, *Kantonistn* (Warsaw, 1934). In the preface he thanked his friend Emanuel Ringelblum for his encouragement and support (p. iv).

94. Herzen came across a Russian sergeant who was escorting a group of Jewish children in Vyatka in 1835. The young boys had just been drafted into the army. The sergeant complained that one-third of his charges had already died on the road. "The little ones were assembled and arrayed in a military line. This was one of the most frightening things that I saw in my life. Such unlucky children! The twelve year olds were somehow hanging on, but the younger ones, the eight year olds and the ten year olds—no pen will be able to describe this. Pale, tired, tortured they stood in their soldiers uniforms with upturned collars and looked with imploring glances at the rough soldiers who were arranging them in the ranks" (Alexander Herzen, *Sochineniia*, Vol. 4 [Moscow, 1956], p. 233).

95. Lewin, *Kantonistn*, p. iii.

96. Later historians would take a more nuanced view of the *rekrutchina*. Isaiah (Yeshie) Trunk emphasized that the Jewish leadership was given little choice in the matter. Michael Stanislawski pointed out that Jews were not the only group to suffer this fate. The sons of Polish nobles were also subject to the draft after the failed uprising of 1830–31. Later historians have also pointed out that many Maskilim (Jewish enlighteners) collaborated—albeit reluctantly—with the Russian government, because they saw the traditional elites as a greater long-term danger. See Trunk, *Geshtaltn un gesheenishn*, p. 41; and Michael Stanislawski, *Tsar Nicholas I and the Jews* (Philadelphia and New York, 1983), p. 48.

97. On this point, see also Jacek Leociak, *Tekst wobec zagłady* (Wrocław, 1997), pp. 141–142.

98. See Roskies, *The Jewish Search for a Usable Past*, p. 33.

99. Ringelblum, *Ksovim fun geto*, 2:224–225.

100. Tadeusz Epsztein believes that Natan Koninski, not Aaron Koninski, wrote this essay. There was indeed a Natan Koninski who wrote for the archive, and it is impossible to determine precisely who wrote this essay about the children. However, Ruta Sakowska believes that the author is Aaron, whom she calls Aron Nusn. Two points support her guess. First the essay concerns the subject of children on which Aron Koninski was an expert; and, second, Wasser himself asserted that the author was Aaron Koninski. See Tadeusz Epsztein, "Introduction to the Catalog of the Warsaw Ghetto's Underground Archive," unpublished manuscript, p. 39.

101. Ringelblum, *Ksovim fun geto*, 2:86. Ringelblum recalled that Kampelmacher was deeply grateful for the chance to work in the archive.

102. *Yivo bleter* 20 (1942): 286–287.

103. Both Ringelblum and Auerbach wrote short biographies of Linder. See, respectively, *Ksovim fun geto*, 2:164–168; and *Varshever tsvoes*, pp. 244–251.

104. Auerbach, *Varshever tsvoes*, p. 248.

105. For example, Linder coined the word *golim* (exiles), since he believed that the word for refugees (*pleytim*) did not really apply to people who had not left their homes but were brutally expelled from them.

106. Zuckerman, *A Surplus of Memory*, p. 116.

107. Ringelblum, *Ksovim fun geto*, 2:68.

108. What few sketchy biographical details there are on Winkler can be found in the short introduction by M. Solarska to his Oyneg Shabes essay, "Getto walczy z niewolą gospodarczą," which was reprinted in *BŻIH*, no. 3–4 (1950): 3–4.

109. AR I, no. 62.

110. AR I, no. 83; "Vegn gezunt tsushtand fun der yiddisher bafelkerung in Varshe (sof 1939 un 1940)."

111. AR I, no. 667.

112. Ringelblum, *Ksovim fun geto*, 2:166.

113. M. Solarska, introduction to "The Ghetto Struggles against Economic Enslavement," *BŻIH*, no. 3–4 (1950): 3–4. Ruta Sakowska believes that Winkler helped compile the statistical section of the report on the mass extermination that the Oyneg Shabes sent abroad in November 1942. This seems unlikely since Ringelblum recalled that Winkler perished during the Great Deportation. Wasser does not mention Winkler's participation in his terse memoir of the report. See Hersh Wasser, "Ha'du"akh ha-rishon al shoat yehudei Varsha," *Yediot beit lohamei ha-getaot* 16–17 (April 1956).

114. He entitled one essay on a shtetl, "Bagatelles pour un Massacre," the same title as the book by the anti-Semitic French writer Paul Celine. A study of Jewish prisoners of war, highly praised by Ringelblum, bore the title, "Die waren in Deutschland Gefangen."

115. AR I, no. 871; see also Ruta Sakowska, "Relacje Daniela Fligelmana—Członka 'Oyneg Szabat,'" *BŻIH*, no. 1–2 (1986): 171.

116. There are hardly any sources about his life, aside from a few traces in the Oyneg Shabes Archive: his many essays, disbursements recorded in Menakhem Kon's account book, and a short remark of Ringelblum's. Ruta Sakowska makes good use of these in her introduction to an autobiographical essay by Fligelman, published in *BŻIH*, describing his family's flight from Alexandrow to the Warsaw Ghetto. My remarks on Fligelman closely follow Sakowska's. See her, "Relacje Daniela Fligelmana," pp. 167–174.

117. Ringelblum, *Ksovim fun geto*, 2:102.

118. AR II, no. 212; Sakowska, "Relacje Daniela Fligelmana," p. 168.

119. See Ringelblum's account in *Ksovim fun geto*, 2:93.

120. In Polish the female [married] form of the last name Słapak would be Słapakowa.

121. Auerbach, *Varshever tsvoes*, pp. 53–60.

122. Turkow, *Azoy iz es geven*, pp. 27–28; *Leksikon fun der nayer yiddisher literatur*, ed. Shmuel Niger and Jacob Shatzky, 8 vols. (New York, 1961), 4:68–69.

123. AR I, no. 192.

124. Kermish, *To Live with Honor*, p. 669.

125. AR II, no. 237. The quotes by Gorny that follow are all from this source.

126. Furst was killed by the Jewish Fighting Organization. At this point either Gorny was not yet a member of the ŻOB or was not privy to all its secrets

127. Kener, *Kvershnit*, p. 260.

128. Ibid.

129. Ringelblum, *Ksovim fun geto*, 2:186–187. It does not appear in either cache of the archive and was probably lost.

130. Turkow, *Azoy iz es geven*, p. 128.

131. Ringelblum, *Ksovim fun geto*, 2:56.

132. Marcel Reich-Ranicki, *Moje Życie* (Warsaw, 2000), pp. 136–137.

133. Ibid., p. 152.

134. Ibid., p. 150.

135. AR II, no. 197. Reprinted in Kermish, *To Live with Honor*, p. 704.

136. Hillel Seidman, *Togbukh fun Varshever geto* (Buenos Aires, 1947), p. 173. Seidman's diary, however, is not entirely reliable.

137. Reich-Ranicki, *Moje Życie,* p. 170.

138. Ringelblum, *Ksovim fun geto*, 2:82.

139. On details of Opoczynski's prewar life, see Rina-Opper Opochinsky, "Mayn bruder Peretz Opoczynski," in Peretz Opoczynski, *Gezamlte shriftn* (New York, 1951), pp. 5–60.

140. An obituary in Melekh Nayshtat's book on the Warsaw Ghetto stressed that Opoczynski was a militant Zionist who loved Hebrew literature and especially admired the iconoclastic novels of Joseph Khayim Brenner. On the other hand, the Communist Jewish historian Ber Mark played down Opoczynski's Zionism. See his introduction in Peretz Opoczynski, *Reportazhn fun Varshever geto* (Warsaw, 1954). The best essay on Opoczynski is Tsvi Shner's "Ha-reshimot u'mehabran," in Peretz Opoczynski, *Reshimot* (Tel Aviv, 1970).

141. Zuckerman, on the other hand, strongly implies that it was the Right Poalei Tsiyon who got him the job (*A Surplus of Memory*, p. 100).

142. This entire collection of letters and postcards from the Ringelblum Archive has been collected and published by Ruta Sakowska in *Archiwum Ringelbluma: Listy o zagładzie* (Warsaw, 1997).

143. The extensive reportage that he wrote for the Oyneg Shabes, besides "The Ghetto Mailman," included two sketches of the house committees on Muranowska 6 and Wołyńska 21; a description of how the Jews of his building, Wołyńska 21, dealt with the early days of the war; a vivid sketch of the milieu of the smugglers and how they operated; an angry article about starving children in the street; a reportage on Poles who slipped into the ghetto to trade; the Parówka; and, after the Great Deportation, a description of life in the shops. Two editions of his reports have appeared though neither is complete. The first was Peretz Opoczynski, *Reportazhn fun Varshever geto* (Warsaw, 1954). Edited and with an introduction by Ber Mark, this edition should be used with caution. A fuller though incomplete edition, edited by Tzvi Shner, appeared in Israel in 1970. See *Reshimot: Peretz Opotśinski* (Tel Aviv, 1970).

144. See AR I, no. 455. See also "Der Yidisher Brivntreger," in Opoczynski, *Reportazhn fun Varshever geto*, pp. 75–93.

145. In Opoczynski's reportage, the packages from the Soviet Union conveyed the impression, ironically, that it was not only a land of hope but also of abundance.

146. Peretz Opoczynski, "Kinder oyfn bruk," in idem, *Reportazhn fun Varshever geto*, p. 49. See also AR I, no. 430.

147. Ibid., p. 52.

148. Ibid., p. 61.

149. Opoczynski, "Megiles Parowke," in ibid., p. 26.

150. "Goyim in geto," in AR I, no. 323.

151. Ibid.

152. AR II, no. 289. Opoczynski's brief diary entries that follow are all from this source.

153. On the suicide of Perle's wife, see Melekh Ravitch, *Mayn leksikon*, 3 vols. (Montreal, 1945), 1:170. Sara had belonged to the drama circle organized by Y. L. Peretz, and it was Peretz who had introduced her to Perle. Ravitch was with Perle when they entered the apartment to see Sara's hanging body. For months, Ravitch recalled, Perle would keep asking himself "Why?" In his essay titled "4580," Perle confided that Sara had wanted his letters to her placed in her coffin.

154. See Sh. Hertz, *Doyres Bundistn*, Volume 2 (New York, 1956), pp. 256–257.

155. See Leo Finkelshteyn, "Yehoshue Perle," in Yehoshua Perle, *Yidn fun a gants yor* (Tel Aviv, 1990), p. xiii.

156. Nakhman Mayzel, *Geven amol a lebn* (Buenos Aires, 1951), p. 367.

157. No other sources corroborate this, however.

158. Ringelblum, *Ksovim fun geto*, 2:180.

159. The report was never found in either cache of the archive.

160. AR I, no. 88. All quotes by Perle in this particular section of the text are from this source.

161. Ringelblum, *Ksovim fun geto*, 2:57.

162. AR II, no. 199.

163. Auerbach, *Varshever tsvoes*, p. 195.

164. Perle imputed to the Judenrat much more power than it actually had.

165. This is implicit in the text although Perle does not state the connection clearly.

166. AR II, no. 245. All quotations from the essay are from Elinor Robinson's translation of "4580," in Roskies, *The Literature of Destruction*, pp. 450–454.

167. Auerbach recalls that after Sara's suicide in 1926 Perle developed an obsessive attachment to his son. He wouldn't let him out of his sight and constantly worried about his welfare. Even after Lolek married, Perle insisted that the couple live with him (*Varshever tsvoes*, p. 333).

168. For more on this convoluted and murky story, see Abraham Shulman, *The Case of the Hotel Polski* (New York, 1982); and Agnieszka Haska, *Jestem Żydem, Chcę wejść: Hotel Polski w Warszawie, 1943* (Warsaw, 2006).

169. On Perle's time in Bergen-Belsen, see the memoirs of Ester Boyman, a survivor who got to know him there, titled "Di letste khodoshim fun Yehoshue Perle in Bergen Belsen," in *Dos naye lebn*, no. 16 (1948).

170. Finkelshteyn, "Yehoshue Perle," p. xv.

171. A survivor of the Sonderkommando recalled that the Germans deceived the transport until the bitter end. In the yard of the crematorium an SS man, standing in front of signs with letters in alphabetical order, posed as a representative of the German

Foreign Office. He explained to those in the transport that the Swiss were demanding a certificate acknowledging that those in the transport had undergone a delousing process. He reminded them that, after the procedure, they were to line up in front of the proper letter to facilitate the processing of their travel documents. One Jewish woman, in the room where they were undressing for the process, played out a provocative striptease at the last moment. When she saw that she had caught the attention of SS officer Schillinger, she lunged for his pistol and shot him. See Filip Muller, *Eyewitness Auschwitz* (New York, 1979), pp. 85–87.

172. "[In the essay] the entire 300,000-strong community of Warsaw Jews is portrayed as a herd of cattle or sheep that is beaten, tortured, robbed, and killed not so much [by the Germans] as by [degenerate Jews]" (H. Leyvik, "Tsvey dokumentn," *Der tog,* March 17, 1952). For Mark's reply, see Ber Mark, "Yudenratishe ahavas yisroel: an entfer oyfn bilbul fun H. Leyvik," in *Bleter far geshikhte,* no. 3 (1952). On this issue I also benefited from a conversation with David Roskies.

173. AR I, no. 655.

174. Rachel Auerbach, *Bi'hutsot Varsha* (Tel Aviv, 1954), p. 7.

175. Ravitch, *Mayn Leksikon,* 2:101.

176. Auerbach, *Varshever tsvoes,* pp. 139–140.

177. The full story is found in Rachel Auerbach, "Nisht oysgeshpunene fedem," *Di goldene keyt,* no. 50 (1964): 131–143.

178. The original diary is in AR I, no. 641. There are also copies in the Auerbach collection in the Yad Vashem Archive.

179. Yad Vashem Archive, Rachel Auerbach Collection, P-16–1, diary entry for March 6, 1942.

180. Auerbach's gripping story of that summer is contained in *Varshever tsvoes,* pp. 116–130.

181. Auerbach describes her experiences on the Aryan side in *Baym letstn veg,* especially pp. 213–305.

182. On this issue, see Rachel Auerbach, "Arkhiv 'Hemshekh' oyf der Arisher zayt" in Yad Vashem Archives, Rachel Auerbach Collection, P-16–32.

183. Auerbach, *Baym letstn veg,* pp. 300–302.

184. Rachel Auerbach, "Yidn fun a gants yor," *Literarishe bleter,* December 13, 1935.

185. From "Yizkor," as translated by Leonard Wolf in Roskies, *The Literature of Destruction,* p. 461.

186. Ibid., pp. 459–460.

187. Yizkor is the Jewish prayer for the dead said on Yom Kippur, Shemini Atzeret, Passover, and Shavuot.

188. "Yizkor," as translated by Leonard Wolf in Roskies, *The Literature of Destruction,* pp. 459–460.

189. Roskies, "Landkentenish: Yiddish Belles Lettres in the Warsaw Ghetto," in Shapiro, *Holocaust Chronicles,* p. 26. I have benefited from several conversations on this subject with David Roskies.

190. Mendel Mann, "Rokhl Auerbach tsu ir bazukh in Pariz," *Unzer vort,* August 6, 1966.

191. Yad Vashem Archives, Rachel Auerbach Collection, "Poylishe shrayber vegn yidishn umkum," P-16–23.

192. For more on the Commission, see Natalia Aleksiun, "The Central Jewish His-

torical Commission in Poland, 1944–47," which will appear in a forthcoming issue of *Polin.*

193. Personal conversation with Esther Rochman, Jerusalem, March, 1990.

194. On this issue, see, for example, Rachel Auerbach, "Dr. Philip Friedman—Dermonung un Gezegenung," in the Yad Vashem Archives, Rachel Auerbach Collection, P-16-32. She wrote here that "Dr. Friedman was one of the first who publicized the problem of 'learning from the Shoah' [*lekah ha-shoah*]. This meant learning a lesson from our terrible experiences that might serve the Jewish people in the present and in the future, in Israel as well as in the Diaspora."

195. This controversy is discussed in the unpublished doctoral dissertation of Dr. Boaz Cohen and in his "The Birth Pangs of Holocaust Research in Israel," *Yad Vashem Studies,* no. 33 (2005).

196. See, for example, her rebuttal of Dinur in Rachel Auerbach, "Al ma natush ha-vikuah b"Yad Va-shem, teshuva l'teshuvto shel Profesor Ben Tziyon Dinur," in the Yad Vashem Archives, Rachel Auerbach Collection, P-16-24. See also Joseph Kermish, "Rachel Auerbach, Di grinderin funm eydes verk 'Yad Vashem,'" in Auerbach, *Baym letstn veg,* pp. 305–318.

197. Rachel Auerbach, "Dr. Philip Friedman—Dermonung un Gezegenung," in the Yad Vashem Archives, Rachel Auerbach Collection, P-16-32.

198. Personal conversation with Esther Rochman, Jerusalem, March, 1990.

199. This correspondence is contained in the Yad Vashem Archives, Rachel Auerbach Collection, P-16-36. See the illuminating study of Samuel Moyn, *A Holocaust Controversy: The Treblinka Affair in Postwar France* (Hanover and London, 2005), pp. 127–137.

6 THE DIFFERENT VOICES OF POLISH JEWRY

1. There are many references to the German film crews in the Warsaw Ghetto in the spring of 1942. See Auerbach, *Bi'khuvot Varsha,* pp. 91-303 and Lewin, *A Cup of Tears,* pp. 71, 75.

2. In Peretz's words:

We must become the historians of our part in the process. We and you who are living through this now must put away for the near and distant future each sign that the historical process inscribes upon our people. Otherwise our account will be empty, and neither people nor history will owe us anything, and our name will be erased from the page on which the world records its terrible and painful process as entitlement for better times.

And that is not all.

Worse is that others—total strangers—will write for us and in our names! And among these strangers we have so few friends. And our enemies will stop at nothing: no means that won't justify the end of blackening the Jewish name. And not merely will our entitlement to rights and to righteousness be obliterated for a long, long time to come, but the factory of lies and fabrications and the wildest accusations will be working overtime. . . .

And when a friend appears who will want to defend us, who will want to reveal the truth, he will lack for material with which to flesh out the truth.

(Quoted in Roskies, *The Literature of Destruction,* pp. 209–210)

3. Alexander Donat, *The Holocaust Kingdom* (New York: Holt Rinehart and Winston, 1965), p. 211; quoted in Alvin Rosenfeld, *A Double Dying* (Bloomington and London: Indiana University Press, 1980), pp. 37–38.

4. On archives in the Vilna Ghetto Archive, see Kruk, *The Last Days of the Jerusalem of Lithuania*; Avrom Sutzkever, *Vilner geto* (Buenos Aires, 1947), pp. 112–117; Yitzhak Arad, "Ha-arkhiyon ha-mehtarti shel geto Vilna," in *Mi'gniza,* ed. Israel Gutman (Jerusalem, 1997), pp. 151–161; and David Fishman, *Embers Plucked from the Fire: The Rescue of Jewish Cultural Treasures in Vilna* (New York, 1996).

5. The best short treatment of the secret archive in the Białystok Ghetto is Sarah Bender, "Arkhiyon hamahteret bi'Bialystok," in Gutman, *Mi'gniza,* pp. 121–133. See also Bronka Klebanski, "Al Mordecai v'al arkhiyono," in Mordecai Tenenbaum-Tamaroff, *Dapim min ha'dleka: pirkei yoman, mikhtavim, maamarim* (Jerusalem, 1984), pp. 205–215. On Tenenbaum's elliptical reference to the Oyneg Shabes, see his "Mikhtav l'haverim," in *Dapim min ha'dleka,* p. 99.

6. The Lodz Ghetto Archive was part of the official ghetto administration. Its stated task was to collect statistical and demographic data about the ghetto, but, as in so many other matters, Chaim Rumkowski had complicated agendas. Not a man to encourage open criticism of his methods and policies, he nonetheless wanted the Lodz Ghetto Archive to become a real historical resource and not just a repository of statistics and official reports. Whatever his motives Rumkowski chose no stooge to direct the archive. Henryk Neftalin was a highly regarded lawyer who managed to gain the respect of both Rumkowski and the wider ghetto community. Rumkowski told the ghetto administration to help Neftalin, and in time the archive began to produce important studies of various aspects of ghetto life.

Neftalin assembled a talented staff that included Czech and German Jews who arrived in the ghetto as deportees. One of the archive's major projects was the enormous Chronicle of the Lodz Ghetto, which ran to thousands of pages and was a collective project documenting the life of the ghetto from 1940 until a few weeks before the final liquidation in August 1944. Another major project was the ambitious Encyclopedia of the Lodz Ghetto, which included many entries on ghetto officials, ghetto folklore, and even the particular language of ghetto life. The archive also included thousands of other documents including invaluable reportage by Joseph Zelkowicz, whose wartime writings were quite similar to those of fellow Lodzer Peretz Opoczynski in the Oyneg Shabes.

Although Rumkowski clearly knew about the archive and encouraged its work, it is impossible to say just how much the staff hid from him.

After the war two caches of the Lodz Ghetto Archive surfaced. Nachman Zonabend, an inmate of the ghetto, had avoided deportation to Auschwitz and stayed in a hideout in the former ghetto grounds until the city's liberation by the Red Army in 1945. Zonabend had hidden a large number of documents from the Lodz Ghetto Archive and managed to take them along when he left Poland in 1946. Another cache of documents was buried underneath the building that housed the former ghetto fire department. In October 1946, just one month after the discovery of the Oyneg Shabes, a team led by Joseph Kermish of the Central Jewish Historical Commission found that cache. Unfortunately the Germans succeeded in discovering and destroying a third major cache that had been buried in the Jewish cemetery. The best overview of the Lodz Ghetto Archive can be found in Dobroszycki, *The Chronicle of the Lodz Ghetto,* pp. ix–lxviii.

7. On Kruk, see idem, *The Last Days of the Jerusalem of Lithuania*; see also Samuel

David Kassow, "Vilna and Warsaw, Two Ghetto Diaries: Herman Kruk and Emanuel Ringelblum," in Shapiro, *Holocaust Chronicles*, pp. 171–217.

8. Klebanski, "Al Mordecai v'al arkhiyono," pp. 205–215.

9. See Dobroszycki, *The Chronicle of the Lodz Ghetto*, pp. xxvi–xxviii.

10. Sarah Bender, "Arkhiyon hamahteret bi'Bialystok," in Gutman, *Mi'gniza*, pp. 122–123. Barash gave Tenenbaum a special room for the archive as well as protocols of Judenrat meetings and other official documents. He passed on to Tenenbaum crucial information about Treblinka, including documents and photographs found in articles of clothing that had been sent from Treblinka to the Białystok ghetto.

11. For example, in October 1942, Gens had sent Jewish police from the Vilna Ghetto to help conduct a "selection" in the small town of Oszmiana. Many Jews were critical of Gens's action, but Gens called a meeting of the ghetto intelligentsia and reminded them that when he had refused a similar order in another small town, the Germans had done the job themselves and had liquidated everybody. He also called in Kruk for a private conversation and tried to explain himself. Kruk wrote in his diary in an entry of November 9, 1942:

> [Gens] tries to justify himself. Through me he wants to get to the so-called Vilna society . . . He is sure, he says, that if he had taken it in hand, [in the other town] he would have saved many Jews . . . Obviously the chief is nervous. He feels that things really aren't all right. He is looking for people with social understanding to settle accounts with. You feel the influence of strangers moving him and persuading him to all those actions. Our chief is torn apart and is seeking support. (Kruk, *The Last Days of the Jerusalem of Lithuania*, p. 406)

12. See AR I, no. 1222. They included street scenes of the ghetto, starving children, the Jewish police, the building of walls, smugglers throwing sacks of flour across the ghetto walls, people listening to loudspeakers on the street, and so on.

13. The idea of the Oyneg Shabes as a center of civil resistance has been discussed by Ruta Sakowska in her "Opór cywilny getta warszawskiego," *BŻIH*, nos. 86–87 (1973): 79–81.

14. There are several good treatments of the Jewish underground press in the Warsaw ghetto. See Kermish, *Itonut ha-Mahteret ha-Yehudit b'Varsha*, pp. xxvii–lxxxi; Daniel Blatman, "Itonut mahteret v'hevra," in idem, ed., *Geto varsha, sipur itonai* (Jerusalem, 2002), pp. 7–87; Gutman, *The Jews of Warsaw*, pp. 146–154.

15. According to Tadeusz Epsztein, who has prepared the most comprehensive catalogue of the archive, the first cache contained 25,540 pages of material and the second held 9,829 pages. The latter covered August 1942 until February 1943. Epsztein also pointed out other marked differences between the caches: "In [the first cache] Yiddish and Polish predominate. Yiddish appears in ca. 930 documents, while Polish appears in ca. 900. German appears in ca. 230 places, while Hebrew appears in ca. 45. In [the second cache], about 570 documents are in Polish, about 190 are in Yiddish, ca. 140 in German and over 35 in Hebrew" (Epsztein, "Introduction to the Catalog of the Warsaw Ghetto's Underground Archive," pp. 3–4).

16. Rachel Auerbach wrote that a special cellar had been prepared for that part of the archive. See Yad Vashem Archives, Rachel Auerbach Collection, P-16–82, p. 15.

17. Epsztein quotes Michał Borwicz, who was present when the first cache of the archive was found:

The organizers did not manage to solder the containers shut before burial. The faithful soil defended the collections against German fury, but in the course of four years of underground lethargy—water filled the interior of the boxes, saturating the materials concealed in them. Dangerous fungus repeatedly arose. Bundles of valuable papers increased in volume—due to moisture and swelling. Moreover, they were lying tightly packed and adhering very precisely to the metal walls. As a result—it was apparent at the first glance that a wet and elastic mass filled the box. In order not to damage it during removal, the metal was taken apart. (*Pieśń ujdzie cało. Antologia wierszy o Żydach pod okupacją niemiecką*, ed. M. Borwicz [Warsaw–Lodz–Kraków, 1947], p. 43; quoted in Epsztein, "Introduction to the Catalog of the Warsaw Ghetto's Underground Archive," p. 4)

18. Epsztein, "Introduction to the Catalog of the Warsaw Ghetto's Underground Archive," p. 5.

19. Zuckerman, *A Surplus of Memory*, p. 112.

20. In an unpublished memoir contained in her archive in the Yad Vashem, Rachel Auerbach recalled that when the ten boxes of the first cache were found Hersh Wasser told Pleszczyński, the engineer who was supervising the excavations, that much more had been buried. At that time Wasser was sure that there had been a third cellar, in addition to the two they had already found (Yad Vashem Archives, Rachel Auerbach Collection, P-16–82, p. 15).

21. Examples are essays by Henryka Lazowert on a Jewish family, and by Shie Perle on Lwów.

22. AR I, no. 1152.

23. Copies of these lists can be found in AR I, nos. 1147 and 1176.

24. See, for example, Lewin's diary entry of May 30, 1942: "Today a group of community officials were sitting together and for two hours a lawyer from Lwow recited to us the Book of Lamentations of Lwow and the whole of eastern Galicia. And what he said was so horrific and gruesome that words can not convey what happened." The "group of community officials" is certainly the Oyneg Shabes. See Lewin, *A Cup of Tears*, p. 107.

25. See Lewin's diary entry for July 29, 1942: "A meeting of Oyneg Shabes. Its tragic character. They discuss the question of ownership and the transfer of the archive to America to the YIVO if we all die" (Lewin, *A Cup of Tears*, p. 141). The archive remained in Warsaw, however, at the Jewish Historical Institute.

26. Wasser, "A vort vegn Ringelblum Arkhiv."

27. Named after its headquarters on Leszno 13, the "Thirteen" was headed by the talented and smooth-talking Abraham Gancwajch, who furnished information to the Gestapo. This organization emerged as a rival to the Judenrat and the Jewish police. See Gutman, *The Jews of Warsaw*, pp. 90–94.

28. The major activity of some members was copying and transcribing, whereas others performed several functions at once, for example, writing diaries, interviewing, copying, and transcribing.

29. For example, Oyneg Shabes members that worked in the Aleynhilf, of whom there were many, might have been tempted to "censor" interviews of refugees who criticized mutual aid in the ghetto. Tadeusz Epsztein believes that there was no censorship as a rule. One exception he found was Bluma Wasser's copy of an essay about Góra Kalwaria

(AR I, no. 809) that "omitted fragments from the original which critically discussed the posture of several social activists in the Warsaw Ghetto (among others, of the Joint) in regard to refugees from Góra Kalwaria." See Epsztein, "Introduction to the Catalog of the Warsaw Ghetto's Underground Archive," p. 13.

30. On the complex difficulties of sorting out copies from originals, see Epsztein, "Introduction to the Catalog of the Warsaw Ghetto's Underground Archive," pp. 7–15.

31. Ibid.

32. AR I, no. 432.

33. Epsztein, "Introduction to the Catalog of the Warsaw Ghetto's Underground Archive," p. 13. When the first cache was discovered in 1946, the staff of the Jewish Historical Institute numbered the tin boxes and noted the contents of each.

34. "Few people really knew the actual purpose of the conversations. Quite often, especially in the few months just before the Great Deportation, our people would transcribe the conversation only after they had left the interviewee. That diminished the value of the material but our need for secrecy left us no other choice" (Ringelblum, *Ksovim fun geto*, 2:87).

35. AR I, no. 134. Reprinted in Kermish, *To Live with Honor*, pp. 27–28.

36. Ibid.

37. AR II, 210. The way in which the account book was kept made it difficult to decipher. Kon, whose handwriting was illegible to begin with, used abbreviations, codes, and initials. Nonetheless the account book does afford an approximate sense of the finances of the Oyneg Shabes.

38. Ringelblum, *Ksovim fun geto*, 1:353; diary entry of May 12, 1942.

39. Auerbach, *Varshever tsvoes*, p. 185.

40. Ringelblum, *Ksovim fun geto*, 2:102.

41. According to Epsztein, the latest date found on material in the second cache was February 1, 1943.

42. Rachel Auerbach, *Varshever tsvoes* p. 166.

43. Ibid., p. 344.

44. Ringelblum, *Ksovim fun geto*, 2:98.

45. On Lehman, see Auerbach, *Varshever tsvoes*, pp. 133–162; and Itzik Nakhmen Gottesman, *Defining the Yiddish Nation: The Jewish Folklorists of Poland* (Detroit, 2003), pp. 24–28, 127–128.

46. Auerbach, *Varshever tsvoes*, pp. 159–161.

7   TRACES OF LIFE AND DEATH

1. Wasser, "A vort vegn Ringelblum Arkhiv," pp. 15–16.

2. Ringelblum, *Ksovim fun geto*, 2:81. Ringelblum used the term "100 *drukboygn*" or 100 printed sheets. Assuming standard octavo format, then each "sheet" would have included 16 pages. I am grateful to Zachary Baker, the Judaica librarian of Stanford University, for his explanations regarding this matter.

3. Ibid., 2:417.

4. Ibid., 2:81.

5. AR I, no. 339. Four names appeared either on top of the theses or in the margin: Hersh Wasser, Alexander Landau, Nahum Remba, and Israel Milejkowski. It is not possible to determine why these names were there.

6. AR I, no. 141. Many of the twenty-eight topics were in turn divided into subtopics. The questions began with the reactions of Polish Jewry to the prewar persecution of German Jews and covered a wide range of issues: the "relatively decent" attitude of the Wehrmacht; the attitude of the SS and the Gestapo (with seven subheadings); the inciting of the Polish rabble by the Germans to take part in pogroms; German policies aimed at worsening Polish-Jewish relations; the use of legal edicts to confiscate Jewish property; the outright theft of Jewish property; and the mass expulsions of Jews. It was clear that these theses were compiled sometime in the spring of 1942. Topic 26 bore the stark title "mass murders." The topics of the last section, no. 28, included "the extermination of Jews in accordance with Hitler's statements; the clearing of the Warthegau of Jews— Chełmno; the extermination of Jews in the Lublin region; the extermination of Jews in eastern and western Galicia."

7. "Tezn tsu der teme koruptsie un ganeyves," in AR I, no. 136.

8. Zelig Kalmanovich, "Togbukh fun Vilner geto," *YIVO bleter* 3, n.s. (1997): 77; diary entry of July 19, 1942. For Kalmanovich, who had devoted his life to the YIVO, this was a bitter pill that reinforced the growing doubts he had had long before the war about the ultimate staying power of Yiddish secular culture.

9. Cited by Andrzej Żbikowski, "Polish Jews under Soviet Occupation," in *Contested Memories: Poles and Jews during the Holocaust and Its Aftermath,* ed. Joshua D. Zimmerman (New Brunswick, N.J., and London, 2003), pp. 59–60.

10. AR I, no. 142.

11. AR I, no. 474.

12. Ringelblum, *Ksovim fun geto,* 2:85.

13. AR I, no. 456.

14. AR I, no. 23.

15. AR I, no. 75.

16. AR I, no. 459.

17. See Eliyahu Cherikover, "Di tragediye fun a shvakhn dor," and Zelig Kalmanovich, "Untern hamer fun geshikhte," both in *Oyfn sheydveg,* ed. Eliyahu Cherikover (Paris, 1939).

18. Simon Dubnow, *Nationalism and History: Essays on Old and New Judaism,* ed. Koppel Pinson (New York, 1958), pp. 357–358.

19. See Ringelblum's diary entry of March 1941 in *Ksovim fun geto,* 1:239. In noting Einhorn's views, Ringelblum commented that "the analogy with the [medieval ghetto] is not correct because that ghetto had been an outgrowth of historical circumstances whereas this ghetto is like a concentration camp, where the inhabitants have to find a way to survive."

20. An essay for the archive entitled "Polish-Jewish Relations," probably written by Stanisław Różycki, described this inferiority complex:

But what strikes a jarring note is a feeling of absolute inferiority, the inferiority complex. This inferiority complex makes every Jew proud to look like a Pole, and boast of contacts and acquaintances with Poles, as if this fact alone could be a claim to pride. Most of the Jews humble themselves in the presence of Poles, fawning on them and serving them, just as if they felt inferior. A Jewess is proud of an occasional flirtation with a tram driver or a repair man; a Jew bows humbly, like a Jewish leaseholder to a nobleman in the old days. Obviously this must be in their blood and cannot be uprooted. (AR I, no. 92. Reprinted in Kermish, *To Live with Honor*, p. 621)

Although he did not express it explicitly, Różycki's comments clearly applied to acculturated Jews, not to the Yiddish-speaking masses or to Orthodox Jews. Whether they were exaggerated is less relevant than the fact that they show that many intellectuals were deeply concerned over what they saw as the demoralization and self-abasement of large sectors of Jewish society.

21. These notes appear in Artur Eisenbach, "Visnshaftlekhe forshungen in Varshever getto" in *Bleter far geshikhte* 1 (1948). The documents made available to me were of poor quality, and the notes were illegible. On the survey of intellectuals, see also Joseph Kermish, "Anshei ha-ruah b'geto Varsha," *Yediot Yad Vashem*, no. 8–9 (1955).

22. Eisenbach, "Visnshaftlekhe forshungen in Varshever getto."

23. All the responses were contained in AR I, no. 88. A sample is reprinted and translated in Kermish, *To Live with Honor*, pp. 734–760.

24. These fears were indeed based on fact. The correspondence between the Polish Underground and the London Government-in-Exile made it quite clear that most Poles would not tolerate letting the Jews regain their businesses and their properties. Most of the major political parties in the underground favored emigration as a solution to the Jewish problem. See David Engel, *In the Shadow of Auschwitz: The Polish Government-in-Exile and the Jews, 1939–1942* (Chapel Hill and London, 1987).

25. For an important study of this medical research in the Warsaw Ghetto, see Charles Roland, *Courage under Siege* (New York, 1992). The manuscript of this research was smuggled out of the ghetto, entrusted to the care of Professor Witold Orłowski and published after the war. The book included research on the effects of hunger conducted by twenty-five Jewish doctors in the ghetto. In the introduction Dr. Milejkowski wrote:

The pain of the word . . . I have never felt this as deeply as now, when I begin to write this introduction. I hold the pen in my hand, and death looks into my room from the vacant, sad houses and from the empty streets. Our language is too weak to convey the depths of the catastrophe. I am looking for the right words, I am living through the pain of the word. (Quoted in Berman, *Vos der goyrl hot mir bashert*, p. 168)

26. Ber Mark, *Khurves dertseyln* (Lodz, 1947), p. 140.

27. Berman, *Vos der goyrl hot mir bashert*, p. 168.

28. Ringelblum, *Ksovim fun geto*, 1:357.

29. Natan Eck, "B'shulei mishal Ringelblum, *Yediot Yad Vashem*, no. 12 (1957).

30. Ringelblum, *Ksovim fun geto*, 1:375.

31. Cited by Paula Hyman, *Gender and Assimilation in Modern Jewish History* (Seattle, 1995), p. 12.

32. On the problems that Zionist parties and pioneering movements had in addressing women's concerns, see Ezra Mendelsohn, *Zionism in Poland: The Formative Years, 1915–1926* (New Haven, 1981), pp. 339–341.

33. Daniel Blatman, "Women in the Jewish Labor Bund," in *Women in the Holocaust*, ed. Dalia Ofer and Lenore J. Weitzman (New Haven, 1998), p. 82.

34. "Walking the streets I observe this sickly elegance and am ashamed in my own eyes. These women look as if their silk garments are pulled over shrouds. It seems that a

hunger for jewelry and fine clothes is a national weakness of ours. It is not for nothing that we can find regulations and decrees against women's silk dresses and jewelry in the records of the Council of the Four Lands. . . . It pains me that Jewish women have so little sense of modesty and moderation" (Lewin, *A Cup of Tears*, p. 85).

35. On this matter, see an illuminating article by Gershon Bacon, "Woman?—Youth?—Jew? The Search for Identity of Jewish Young Women in Interwar Poland," in *Gender, Place and Memory in the Modern Jewish Experience*, ed., Judith Tydor Baumel and Tova Cohen (London, 2003), pp. 3–29. A selection of these autobiographies may be found in Jeffrey Shandler, ed., *Awakening Lives: Autobiographies of Jewish Youth in Poland before the Holocaust* (New Haven, 2002).

36. See Dalia Ofer, "Gender Issues in Diaries and Testimonies of the Ghetto: The Case of Warsaw," in Ofer and Weitzman, *Women in the Holocaust*, p. 145. See also AR II, no. 212.

37. *Ksovim fun geto*, 1:61.

38. On this point, see Sara Horowitz, "Gender, Genocide and Jewish Memory," *Prooftexts* (January 2000): 158–190.

39. A copy of the study plan, titled "The Jewish Woman in Warsaw from September 1939 until the End of 1941," is in AR I, no. 128. The various categories of women to be studied included "ordinary women [*folks froy*]," members of the intelligentsia, working-class women, middle-class women, and "women as a group [*di froyen tsuzamen*]." Another section added additional subcategories: religious women, women in the political under-ground, teachers, and women who had survived German massacres in the East, for ex-ample, in Wilno and Slonim. The subsections were quite detailed. To guide the study of Jewish women during the siege of Warsaw, queries were included about their role in dig-ging trenches, fighting fires, helping the wounded, and feeding hungry children. Another section called for a comparison of the behavior of women whose husbands had left War-saw and those whose husbands had remained. Part 4 concerned the role of Jewish women in the period between the start of the German occupation and the establishment of the ghetto. Points of inquiry included the German treatment of Jewish women, physical and sexual abuse, and how women supported their families when their husbands found it too dangerous to leave home. A special section concerned women who smuggled goods to the Soviet zone or had tried to rejoin their husbands there. The section on the ghetto included questions about refugees, the ghetto's impact on various social classes, the problem of loss of social status, the effect of the ghetto on family life, the role of women in ghetto insti-tutions, women as caregivers for children and refugees, and, finally, the role of women in the economic life of the ghetto.

40. Huberband, *Kiddush Hashem*, p. 240.

41. Reprinted and translated in Huberband, *Kiddush Hashem*, p. 243. The ellipses in-dicate where the original text was illegible. Sarah Horowitz has asked "whether Huber-band is suggesting that women generally behaved worse—that is, more selfishly or less ethically—than men in the face of the dire privations of the Holocaust, or whether men and women behaved similarly badly, but that one expects better of women than of men, even (or especially) under extraordinarily trying circumstances. If so, would similar be-havior be adjudged worse for the one than for the other?" ("Gender, Genocide and Jewish Memory," p. 172). In fact, Huberband answers Horowitz's question. He indeed expected a higher standard of behavior from women. He prefaced his essay by noting that, "if Jews in general have been called 'the compassionate children of compassionate ones,' then the

Jewish woman should be called by that appellation even more so. The Jewish woman had always exhibited great compassion, both in individual situations and in public campaigns for the needy" (*Kiddush Hashem*, p. 240). Although Huberband's essay is indeed harsh, it is, we should recall, only a fragment of a larger composition. The lost chapters—"The Moral Suffering of the Jewish Women during the War" (chapter 1), "The Agunahs" (chapter 2), and the "Addendum to Chapter One" (chapter 4)—might have produced a more balanced and nuanced impression had they survived.

42. See, for example, AR I, no. 158, "A Conversation with Ms. G." This is most likely another of Słapakowa's interviews, but it is a separate file. The interviewer writes that, "women [during the siege] acted better than men. Some went out for bread at three in the morning, during the heaviest bombardments. When Ms. G was standing in the bread line, a shell exploded [closeby]. . . . As their building was being bombed and people wanted to flee, Ms. G calmed them and pointed out that the whole city was being bombed and that it made no sense to run from one place to another. She was composed the whole time, went around with [medicinal] drops to give to men who fainted. Meantime men were afraid or were ashamed. Men sat home and women did everything."

43. Dalia Ofer has written two helpful articles on Słapakowa's study: "Gender Issues in Diaries and Testimonies of the Ghetto," in Ofer and Weitzman, *Women in the Holocaust;* and "Her View through My Lens: Cecilia Slepak Studies Women in the Warsaw Ghetto," in Baumel and Cohen, *Gender, Place and Memory in the Modern Jewish Experience.* On Słapakowa herself, see chapter 5.

44. AR I, no. 49, notebook 1.

45. Ibid.

46. Ibid., notebook 4. Dalia Ofer believes, in fact, that Ms. C and Ms. G are the same person. I believe they are two different people.

47. On Ms. F, see AR I, no. 49, notebook 1.

48. "She reacts toward the changes and zigzags in her life with a fatalistic resignation. She has adopted the same kind of philosophy that characterizes many Jewish women now. What she says is, 'everything I have to bear is a necessary evil. The main thing is to survive. After the war, I'll make it all up.'"

49. AR I, no. 49, notebook 2.

50. A good source on Temkin-Berman is her wartime diary. See Basia Temkin-Bermanowa, *Dziennik z podziemia,* edited and with an introduction by Anka Grupińska and Paweł Szapiro (Warsaw, 2000).

51. AR I, no. 49, notebook 5.

52. Reprinted in Ringelblum, *Ksovim fun geto,* 2:417.

53. Ibid, 2:338.

54. In the collection of ghetto folklore and stories that he collected for the archive, Rabbi Huberband cited several stories told by Orthodox Jews that saw the ghetto as "gam zu l'tovah [this is all for the best]." These stories, probably popular in the period just after the creation of the ghetto in November 1940, recounted how the ghetto saved the Jews from German repressions aimed at the Poles. One such story concerned the German reprisals carried out after the Polish underground murdered the well-known Polish film director Igo Sym, who began to collaborate with the Germans. Just before Sym was killed, a group of religious Jewish women had gone a Hasidic rebbe to wail that the closing of the ghetto threatened them with starvation. "Dear women," the rebbe replied. "You must know that the Lord our God will not forsake us. Whatever the Almighty does is for the

best. Before long, everyone will see that even the sealing of the ghetto is for the best." After Sym's murder and the German reprisals, Huberband's account continued, "everyone recognized the great holiness of Rabbi Yehoshua's words, that whatever the Lord does is for the best; even the sealing of the ghetto." See Huberband, *Kiddush Hashem,* p. 128.

55. Ringelblum, *Ksovim fun geto,* 2:44–45.

56. Ringelblum avidly collected rumors that constantly flooded the ghetto streets. On the positive side, jokes and rumors were another weapon of psychological resistance, a barometer that measured the determination of the ordinary Jew to keep his spirits up and hold out. On the other hand, as he noted on May 18, 1941, they could also serve as a narcotic, an echo of the mass delusion and mass psychosis that had characterized Jewish society during the Sabbatai Tsvi episode of 1665–66, when many Jews pinned their hopes on a false Messiah. The worse the news was, the more fantastic the rumors. Right after the street massacres of April 17–18, 1942, the mood in the ghetto had turned somber. But then spirits rose again, buoyed by rumors. On May 8, 1942, Ringelblum noted rumors that 60,000 paratroopers had landed west of Smolensk, that 160 ships had discharged a large army near Murmansk, that a revolution had overthrown Mussolini, and that Hitler had collapsed of fright. This was in connection with a rumor that swept through the streets concerning the alleged death of Hermann Goering. Jews told each other that after a vicious argument at a high level Nazi meeting, Goering tried to escape but died of his wounds. Jews were so ecstatic, Ringelblum reported, that many were ready to cross over to the Aryan side, confident that no one would try to stop them.

57. AR I, no. 135.

58. AR I, nos. 154, 428, 429, and 50, respectively.

59. The candle seller is also punning on the well-known Yiddish curse, "May you burn like a candle [Zolstu brenen vi a likht]." Reprinted in Ber Mark, ed., *Tsvishn lebn un toyt* (Warsaw, 1955), pp. 98–99; and in Kermish, *To Live with Honor,* pp. 667–668. Also, although Ber Mark and Joseph Kermish both cite "In the Streets" as coming from the first part of the Ringelblum archive, the ŻIH-USMHM catalogue does not list it. It actually appeared in the December 17, 1940, issue of *Bafrayung,* the underground newspaper of the Right Poalei Tsiyon. See AR I, no. 1019; and Kermish, *Itonut ha-Mahteret ha-Yehudit b'Varsha,* 1:202–204.

60. Mark, *Tsvishn lebn un toyt,* p. 98.

61. Tytelman wrote that, in trying to collect street songs for the archives, one of his best informants and guides was a boy around thirteen or fourteen years of age, Yankev Leyb Solnitzki. Yankev Leyb had lost both his parents and wandered around the streets in rags. His voice was so sweet that crowds threw him small coins. He also stayed alive by rooting around for garbage and leftovers. Tytelman invited him to his home so he could write the words to the boy's songs. "The boy gives the impression that he has not become completely dulled. He talks intelligently and pays attention to how I write down the songs. A few times he pointed out that I was not writing it down correctly, that I was forgetting to insert the refrain. Maybe we can help this boy?" Tytelman's report, dated June 1942, is in AR I, no. 172.

62. Ibid. The refrain in the verse below is "Money, money, money is it!"

Mrs Czerniakow is always getting her hair done,
Poor children go to bed without dinner. [refrain]
The Judenrat squeezes you for taxes

And gives you cabbage and saccharine to eat. [refrain]
The Jewish jail is full of prisoners
But the Jewish factory owners like this war. [refrain]
Each Jewish policeman is a hoodlum;
If you don't pay him you go to a camp [refrain]
All trades are lousy
Except for the bakers, they are riding high.
There are house committees everywhere,
They make you clean the stairs and they inspect your beds. [refrain]
If you're already selling your pants and your shirt
You are just about ready to climb into the coffin.

63. Oy di bone / Ja nie chcę oddać bonę . . . yingl halt zikh / halt zikh dos gantse lebn
/ ze du zolst di bone nisht avekgebn / chłopcze trzymaj się / trzymaj się fest / trzymają się
wszyscy póki bona jest . . . kh'bin nokh ying / yakh vil nisht avekgebn di bone / yakh vil
nokh epes gits derlebn (ibid.).

64. AR I, no. 111.

65. AR I, no. 1017. Reprinted in Kermish, *To Live with Honor,* p. 78.

66. Feld, *In di tsaytn fun Homen dem Tsveytn,* p. 38. Original is in AR I, no. 527.

67. Ringelblum, *Ksovim fun geto,* 1:281.

68. A good description of the activities of the CENTOS can be found in Berman,
Vos der goyrl hot mir bashert, pp. 99–155. For a description of "Month of the Child," see
p. 140.

69. Ruta Sakowska, *Ludzie z dzielnicy zamkniętej* (Warsaw, 1993), p. 97.

70. Ringelblum, *Ksovim fun geto,* 1:316. While Berman praised Czerniakow for his
participation in "The Month of the Child" campaign, Ringelblum criticized the "fawning" attitude toward him. He also expressed deep disappointment that the house committees had contributed only fifty thousand zlotys. It should be noted that Czerniakow
keenly felt the tragedy of the Jewish child in the ghetto. In his diary entry of June 14,
1942, he wrote about his meeting with street children who had been collected by the Jewish police. "They are living skeletons from the ranks of the street beggars. Some of them
came into my office. They talked to me like grown-ups—these eight-year-old citizens. I
am ashamed to admit it, but I wept as I have not wept for a long time. I gave a chocolate
bar to each of them. They all received soup as well. Damn those of us who have enough to
eat and drink and forget about these children" (Hilberg, Staron, and Kermisz, *The Warsaw Diary of Adam Czerniakow,* p. 166).

71. AR I, no. 125. Reprinted in Ruta Sakowska, *Archiwum Ringelbluma: Dzieci-tajne
nauczanie w getcie Warszawskim* (Warsaw, 2001), pp. 147–148. Sukowska's book is an extremely valuable collection of documents from the Ringelblum archive concerning children and clandestine education, with excellent explanatory notes by Sakowska.

72. "The Face of the Jewish Child," written by Koninski in November 1941, is in AR
I, no. 47. Reprinted in Sakowska, *Archiwum Ringelbluma: Dzieci-tajne nauczanie w getcie
Warszawskim,* pp. 358–377.

73. AR I, no. 39. Reprinted, with annotations by Sakowska, in idem, *Archiwum Ringelbluma: Dzieci-tajne nauczanie w getcie Warszawskim,* pp. 3–46.

74. A representative essay was that of Rywka Zelcer:

Before the war I was happy. I lived on Ostrowska 13. My father worked and I went to school on 21 Stawki Street. In 1939 the war started and I stopped going to school. We began to go hungry. We started to sell our things from home, but we quickly ran out of things to sell. My father could not hold on and died of hunger. I thought that my mother would survive the war but she could not hold on and died. So I became an orphan. I found out from friends that there was this day care center. I tried to get in. When they admitted me I was very happy. (AR I, no. 39)

75. The Oyneg Shabes published a detailed report of the liquidation of the hospital in its journal *Wiadomości*, no. 2 (December 5, 1942). See Israel Shaham, ed., *Itonut ha-mahteret*, vol. 6 (Jerusalem, 1997), pp. 556–557. As Szwajger recalled in her memoirs, "I took the morphine upstairs. Dr. Margolis was there, and I told her what I wanted to do. So we took a spoon and went to the infants' room. And just as during those two years of real work in the hospital, I bent down over the tiny little mouths. Only Dr. Margolis was with me. And downstairs there was screaming because the Szauls and the Germans were already there, taking the sick from the wards to the cattle trucks. After that we went to the older children and told them that this medicine was going to make their pain disappear. They believed me and drank the required amount from the glass." See Adina Blady-Szwajger, *I Remember Nothing More* (New York, 1990), p. 57.

76. "Scenes from the Children's Hospital," AR I, no. 989. Reprinted in Sakowska, *Archiwum Ringelbluma: Dzieci-tajne nauczanie w getcie Warszawskim*, pp. 132–133.

77. This story, "On a heym" (Homeless) was part of a cycle of stories written by Feld entitled *In di tsaytn fun Homen dem Tsveytn* (In the time of Haman the Second), in AR I, no. 527. These stories are in Feld, *In di tsaytn fun Homen dem Tsveytn*, pp. 44–53.

78. AR II, no. 110. Reprinted in Sakowska, *Archiwum Ringelbluma: Dzieci-tajne nauczanie w getcie Warszawskim*, pp. 183–234. Although these reports all date from 1941, they were found in the second part of the Ringelblum Archive,

79. Ibid., Reprinted in Sakowska, *Archiwum Ringelbluma: Dzieci-tajne nauczanie w getcie Warszawskim*, p. 185.

80. Sakowska, *Archiwum Ringelbluma: Dzieci-tajne nauczanie w getcie Warszawskim*, p. 207.

81. Władysław Szlengel, "Rozmowa z Dzieckiem" (A talk with a child), trans. Halina Berenbaum, ed. Ada Holtzman. Available at www.zchor.org/szlengel/child.

82. AR II, no. 110. Reprinted in Sakowska, *Archiwum Ringelbluma: Dzieci-tajne nauczanie w getcie Warszawskim*, p. 197. Other caregivers supervised projects about wildlife and flowers.

83. Betty Jean Lifton, *King of the Children: The Life and Death of Janusz Korczak* (New York, 1988), p. 320.

84. Emanuel Ringelblum, *Ksovim fun geto*, 2:88. The theses are in AR I, no. 155.

85. Ibid., p. 84.

86. AR I, no. 1146. Skalov's report was entitled "A Shpatsir iber a punktn" (Visits to the refugee centers). It is reprinted in Mark, *Tsvishn lebn un toyt*, pp. 73–96.

87. AR I, no. 906.

88. AR I, no. 838.

89. "By the shores of the waters of the Vistula, in woods of tall pine trees a bit off the Radom Lublin railway line, lies the historic Jewish town of Kozienice. All know the say-

ing: Why is Kozienice called Kozienice? Because of the Kozhenitser Magid. And even though he lived a hundred years ago, even today when you come into the shtetl, you can feel his presence, both in the historic buildings and in the everyday lives of the Jews. When a Kozhenits Jew is in trouble, he goes to pray at the Magid's tomb. Women go to the Magid's ritual bath. Merchants will swear on his name, and even Christians will accept such an oath. And the Christians also tell legends about the holiness of the Magid. And you should know this: the well-known Polish prince Jozef Poniatowski followed the popular custom and wrote his name on the wall of the Magid's house the day that he visited it" (AR I, no. 846).

90. AR I, no. 869.

91. AR I, no. 447.

92. AR I, no. 922; Reprinted in Kermish, *To Live with Honor,* pp. 201–208.

93. Ibid.

94. AR I, no. 875.

95. Ringelblum, *Ksovim fun geto,* 2:86.

96. Eva Hoffman, *Shtetl: The Life and Death of a Small Town and the World of Polish Jews* (Boston, 1997), pp. 12–13.

97. AR I, no. 921.

98. AR I, no. 818.

99. AR I, no. 915.

100. AR I, no. 924.

101. This point was made not only in shtetl monographs but also in other Oyneg Shabes memoirs. For example, a young Bundist who fled to the East in September 1939 mentioned the friendly and helpful attitude of the Polish soldiers he encountered on his journey. They shared their food with him and provided directions, "without the slightest hint of anti-Semitism." See AR I, no. 456.

102. AR I, no. 826.

103. AR I, no. 789.

104. AR I, no. 905.

105. AR I, no. 942.

106. AR I, no. 846.

107. AR I, no. 901.

108. It should be noted that this was an extreme reaction, not duplicated in other shtetl accounts.

109. Cited by Feliks Tych, *Długi Cień Zagłady: szkice historyczne* (Warsaw, 1999), p. 43.

110. AR II, no. 306.

111. Reprinted in Kermish, *To Live with Honor,* p. 213.

112. In her well-researched doctoral dissertation on Jewish perceptions of Poles during the war, Havi Ben-Sasson argues that, until 1942, the Jewish perception of Poles was, on the whole, positive. See Havi Ben-Sasson, *Polin u'polanim b'eyney yehudei Polin b'tkufat milhemet ha-olam ha-shniya* (Jewish perceptions of Poland and Poles during the Second World War), Ph.D. dissertation, Hebrew University, Jerusalem, 2005.

113. Ruta Sakowska, "Wiadomości, ARG i raport o zagładzie. Status Archiwum Ringelbluma w getcie szczątkowym Warszawy," *Kwartalnik historii Żydów* I, no. 213 (2005): 42.

114. Hilberg, Staron, and Kermisz, *The Warsaw Diary of Adam Czerniakow,* p. 305.

115. As reprinted in Artur Eisenbach, "Visnshaftlekhe forshungen in Varshever getto," in *Bleter far geshikhte* 1 (1948): 61.

116. "We worked out good guidelines on various economic topics, but we achieved little because we did not have the right collaborators. Economic studies demand a stable environment. They demand that one has enough time, proper source materials based on comprehensive research; we had neither the time nor the proper working conditions. And yet we did manage to get several worthwhile results, especially the essay of our comrade V-r [Jerzy Winkler]" (Ringelblum, *Ksovim fun geto*, 2:94).

117. Some of the more important of these studies included David Berliner's "New Trades in Wartime" (AR I, no. 216); Moyshe Zak's essay on Jewish barbers in the ghetto (AR I, no. 58); an anonymous essay, "Processes of the Adaptation of the Jewish Artisan to Wartime Conditions" (AR I, no. 59); an anonymous study of wealthy Jewish brushmaking entrepreneurs Emil Weitz and Krygier (AR I, no. 101); Eliyahu Gutkowski's study of price changes in foodstuffs and various basic commodities (AR I, no. 238); an anonymous study of ghetto exports (AR I, no. 371); a study of the Transferstelle (AR I, no. 256); Sz. Shainkinder's study of the trade in used articles (AR I, no. 55); T. Tykocinski's study of the same subject, which focused on the 'Gęsiówka', the gigantic flea market on the corner of Gęsia and Lubecka Streets (AR I, no. 57); an anonymous study, "Jewish Economic Life in Poland during the War and Occupation" (AR I, no. 64); Eliyahu Gutkowski's study of the black market in foreign currency (AR I, no. 61); and Peretz Opoczyski's reportage on smuggling in the ghetto (AR I, no. 52) and on the shops (AR II, no. 244).

118. AR I, no. 62, Reprinted in *Bleter far geshikhte,* 1, nos. 3–4 (1948).

119. Gutman, *The Jews of Warsaw,* p. 75; Opoczynski, "The Shops," AR II, no. 244.

120. AR I, no. 428.

121. Gutman, *The Jews of Warsaw,* p. 65.

8   THE TIDINGS OF JOB

1. Blatman, *Geto varsha, sipur itonai,* p. 69.

2. One Polish scout, Irena Adamowicz, had frequently visited Hashomer and Dror in the Warsaw Ghetto and was a close friend of Aleksander Kamiński (code-named Hubert). Kamiński edited the major publication of the Polish Home Army, *Biuletyn informacyjny,* and headed its Bureau of Information and Propaganda. In August 1941 Adamowicz dispatched another Polish scout, Henryk Grabowski, to Vilna. There Grabowski met with the leaders of the Hashomer Hatzair and learned of the massacres that had decimated the Jewish population. He returned to Warsaw in October 1941 and reported what he had learned—including his own eyewitness account of the German massacre of the Jews of Troki (Yitzhak Arad, *Ghetto in Flames* [New York, 1982], p. 223).

3. Ibid., p. 372.

4. On September 4, 1941, Herman Kruk first recorded the reports of mass executions in Ponar. Six Jews, including two young Jewish girls whom Kruk had interviewed, eleven-year-old Yudis Trojak and sixteen-year-old Pesye Schloss, who had survived the shootings and, not having been wounded, made their way back to the Vilna Ghetto. In his first diary entry after talking to these survivors, Kruk made no effort to hide his horror and fear: "I don't know if I'll ever live to see these lines but if anyone anywhere comes upon them I want him to know this is my last wish: let the words someday reach the living world and let people know about it from eyewitness accounts. Can the world not

scream? Can history never take revenge? If the heavens can open up, when should that happen if not today?" (*The Last Days of the Jerusalem of Lithuania*, pp. 90–93).

5. AR I, no. 487. Fligelman entitled Wilner's account "Mon retour de l'URSS."

6. AR I, no. 935. Reprinted in Gurock and Hirt, *Kiddush Hashem*, p. 334; and in Andrzej Żbikowski, ed., *Archiwum Ringelbluma: Relacje z Kresów* (Warsaw, 2000), p. 326.

7. The January 1, 1942, proclamation, issued by all the pioneering Zionist youth movements in the Vilna Ghetto, warned "those who waver [to] put aside all illusion. Your children, your wives and husbands are no more. Ponar is no concentration camp. All were shot dead there. Hitler conspires to kill all the Jews of Europe, and the Jews of Lithuania have been picked at the first line. Let us not be led as sheep to the slaughter!" (Arad, *Ghetto in Flames*, p. 232).

8. Ibid., p. 227.

9. Zuckerman, *A Surplus of Memory*, pp. 156–158.

10. Diary entry of November 22, 1941, in Ringelblum, *Ksovim fun geto*, 1:317. The executions also showed that Jews had deluded themselves into thinking that ghetto commissar Heinz Auerswald was a "moderate" and they augured a tougher time for Warsaw Jewry. See also Shimon Huberband's account in Jeffrey Gurock, *Kiddush hashem*, pp. 150–167.

11. Chaim Lazar, *Metsada shel Varsha: Ha-irgun ha-Tzvai ha-Yehudi be-Mered Getto Varsha* (Tel Aviv, 1963), p. 84. Reprinted in Gutman, *The Jews of Warsaw*, p. 163. Even as late as April 1942 Isaac Schiper chided a revisionist leader, David Wdowinski, who brought the news of the mass deportations from Lublin. When Wdowinski urged that Warsaw Jewry prepare for self-defense, Schiper retorted that Revisionists were always hot-headed. The Germans, he said, would not dare to wipe out the largest Jewish community in Europe. See David Wdowinski, *And We Are Not Saved* (London, 1964), pp. 55–56.

12. To conceal the identity of "Szlamek," Hersh Wasser called him Jacob Grojanowski, and this is the name some scholars have used. His real name, however, was either Szlomo Fajner or Szlomo Bajler. Another escapee from Chełmno, Mechl Podchlebnik, testified in 1945 that Szlamek's real name was Shlomo Fajner. Since his sister-in-law in Zamość was named Bajler, his name might also be Shlomo Bajler. Indeed, in the latest catalogue of the first part of the Ringelblum archive compiled by the Jewish Historical Institute for the USHMM, the note describing Szlamek's testimony lists his last name as Bajler. See Sakowska, *Archiwum Ringelbluma: Listy o zagładzie*, p. 113. See also idem, "Szlamek-ucieknier z ośrodka zagłady w Chełmnie nad Nerem," *BŻIH*, nos. 131–132 (1984).

13. AR I, no. 412. Ruta Sakowska translated the original Oyneg Shabes testimony from Yiddish into Polish. See her *Dwa Etapy: hitlerowska polityka eksterminacji Żydów w oczach ofiar: szkic historyczny i dokumenty* (Wroclaw, 1986), pp. 112–133. I have used a copy of the original Yiddish document found in the Hersh Wasser Collection in the YIVO Archive, 4/1. Sakowska omitted small sections of the original testimony in her Polish translation.

14. Although the note on his testimony (AR I, no. 412) indicates that Hersh Wasser was the interviewer, Bluma Wasser recalls that she also wrote down an account of Chełmno that could only have been Szlamek's. See Bluma Wasser, "Likht in der nakht," in *Pinkes Hrubieszow*, ed. Borukh Kaplinski (Tel Aviv, 1962), p. 706.

15. Szlamek could not have seen this himself. He told Wasser that a Jew in one of the transports had managed to hide in a side room during the rush from the reception floor

to the gas vans. The Germans found him and sent him to the Sonderkommando in the cellar, where he told Szlamek his story. The Germans shot him the next day.

16. Sakowska, "Szlamek-ucieknier z ośrodka zagłady w Chełmnie nad Nerem," p. 131.

17. Sakowska, *Archiwum Ringelbluma: Listy o zagładzie,* pp. 3–7.

18. On this issue, see ibid., pp. 112–134. These are copies of the correspondence between Szlamek, Hersh Wasser, and others. A copy of Szlamek's photograph can be found on page xix.

19. Zuckerman, *A Surplus of Memory,* pp. 156–157.

20. See Sakowska's notes in *Archiwum Ringelblum: Listy o zagładzie,* p. 116.

21. Ibid., p. 130. German postal regulations required that all letters be in Latin characters.

22. "Ehr macht kalt of aza ofn vi in Chełmno, es halt bei unz! Das Beysojlem ist in Belzyc kalt hot men szojn gemacht die sztetlekh was zenen geszriben in brif [they make cold in the same way that they did in Chełmno. The cemetery is in Belzyc. The towns mentioned in the letter have already been made cold]" (ibid. p. 131).

23. Ibid., p. 134.

24. Ibid., pp 152–153.

25. AR I, no. 811.

26. In his postwar memoirs Zuckerman wrote that years later he realized there was no contradiction between cultural activities and resistance. Without the seminars and educational training, resistance would have been impossible to organize. See *A Surplus of Memory,* p. 159.

27. Ibid., p. 159.

28. A protocol of the meeting is in AR I, no. 1207.

29. On the Anti-Fascist Bloc, see Gutman, *The Jews of Warsaw,* pp. 169–175; Zuckerman, *A Surplus of Memory,* pp. 181–184; and Berman, *Vos der goyrl hot mir bashert,* pp. 248–271. Berman asserted that the LPZ took the lead in organizing the Bloc, whereas Zuckerman insisted that it was the PPR.

30. See Letter from Emanuel Ringelblum to Adolf Berman, March 1, 1944, in the Adolf Berman Collection, Archive of Kibbutz Lohamei Ha'Getaot, File 358.

31. In the report "The Jewish Fighting Organization," composed on the Aryan side in 1944 and sent to London in May 1944, Ringelblum, Gutkowski, and Wasser were mentioned as comprising the archive section of the Jewish National Committee. See Nayshtat, *Khurbm un oyfshtand fun di yidn in Varshe,* p. 147. See also Ruta Sakowska, "Wiadomości, ARG i raport o zagładzie. Status Archiwum Ringelbluma w getcie szczątkowym Warszawy," *Kwartalnik historii Żydów* 1, no. 213 (2005): 33.

32. On this general topic, see Ruta Sakowska, "Archiwum Ringelbluma—Ogniwem Konspiracji Warszawskiego Getta," *BŻIH,* no. 152 (1989), no. 153 (1990), and nos. 155–156 (1990); "Two Forms of Resistance in the Warsaw Ghetto," *Yad Vashem Studies* 21 (1991); and Walter Laqueur, *The Terrible Secret* (London, 1980).

33. In terse and hurried notes written sometime in late 1942, Ringelblum outlined his essay on the Oyneg Shabes. Toward the end of these notes he wrote: "The last period— a time of describing mass murder, not possible to write monographs [for the "Two and a Half Years" project] because of the shadows of Ponary, the nine thousand [victims] of Slonim—the deportations . . . Chełmno–gas–Treblinka, therefore forgot about schools, communities. Period of persecutions succeeded by period of atrocities" (Ringelblum, *Ksovim fun geto,* 2:422).

34. AR I, no. 259.

35. Wasser, "A vort vegn Ringelblum Arkhiv."

36. AR I, nos. 259, 262, and 473; AR I, no. 665, a description of Chełmno written by Hersh Wasser; AR I, no. 469, "Drugi Etap" (The second stage); Other bulletins include AR I, nos. 1217, 1062, 813, 261, 317, 472, 1220, 167, and 144. The last bulletin in the first part of the archive was, according to Tadeusz Epsztein, dated July 8, 1942.

37. AR I, no. 144.

38. In the report, written in Polish, "Ausrottung" appeared in the original German spelling. In German it means extermination. Also see Ruta Sakowska, *Dwa Etapy* (Warsaw, 1986).

39. For information on the Slonim massacre, the Oyneg Shabes had Daniel Fligelman conduct a detailed interview with an eyewitness, a refugee from Radom. See AR I, no. 938; reprinted in Żbikowski, *Archiwum Ringelbluma*, pp. 169–182. Many details of this report were included in the Oyneg Shabes dispatch abroad. The eyewitness to the massacre noted that several Germans had refused to participate in the killings and were forced, as a punishment, to groom and clean horses for two weeks. The report also mentioned that some Germans helped Jews to escape. See also the report given by another eyewitness, Abram Gliklikh, to the Oyneg Shabes, in AR I, no. 465.

40. See Ruta Sakowska, "Biuro Informacji i Propagandy KG Armii Krajowej a Archiwum Ringelbluma (luty-lipiec 1942)," *BŻIH*, nos. 162–163 (1992).

41. Ibid.

42. A possible hint of Oyneg Shabes collaboration with the Bund can be found in a letter from Ringelblum to Adolf Berman written on December 20, 1943, when Ringelblum was in hiding. In that letter, Ringelblum asked Berman to procure materials on the Jewish Fighting Organization. Ringelblum said that he wanted to ask Antek (presumably Yitzhak Zuckerman) and then speculated that "Marek will probably not give [the materials]. I ask you to discuss this with him. Remind him that I once gave them everything [Maurycy and the others]." "Marek" here probably refers to Marek Edelman, a surviving Bundist commander of the Jewish Fighting Organization, and "Maurycy" could well refer to Maurycy Orzech, the Bundist leader in the Warsaw Ghetto. See the Adolf Berman Collection, Archive of Kibbutz Lohamei Ha'Getaot, File 358. In his notes for the preparation of his essay on the Oyneg Shabes, Ringelblum added the cryptic comment: "The attitude of the Bund."

43. Laqueur, *The Terrible Secret*, pp. 103–105.

44. Ringelblum, *Ksovim fun geto*, 1:376–377.

45. See, for example, Auerbach, *Bi'hutsot Varsha*, p. 70.

46. Lewin, *A Cup of Tears*, diary entry of June 6, 1942. The "group of activists in the Jewish community" was, of course, the executive committee of the Oyneg Shabes.

47. Ringelblum, *Ksovim fun geto*, 2:411–412.

48. AR I, no. 1189. Reprinted in Sakowska, *Archiwum Ringelbluma: Dzieci-tajne nauczanie w getcie Warszawskim*, p. 295.

49. AR I, no. 657. Reprinted in ibid., p. 297.

50. On this issue, see Israel Gutman, "Adam Czerniakow: The Man and His Diary," in *The Catastrophe of European Jewry*, ed. Israel Gutman and Livia Rothkirchen (Jerusalem, 1976), 451–489.

51. AR II, no. 201. Reprinted in Ruta Sakowska, *Archiwum Ringelbluma, Getto Warszawskie: lipiec 1942–styczeń 1943* (Warsaw, 1980), p. 137.

52. Umschlagplatz (literally, "transshipment square" was the former railway siding by Dzika Street where the Jews were assembled to board the freight cars for "resettlement to the East" but, in fact, were transported to the death camps at Treblinka.

53. Many sources describe the particular nightmare of the "cauldron," which went on from September 6 until September 10. A good survey is in Gutman, *The Jews of Warsaw*, p. 211; and Engelking and Leociak, *Getto warszawskie*, pp. 687–689. The second part of the archive contained several eyewitness accounts, including in AR II, no. 206.

54. Lewin, *A Cup of Tears*, p. 141, diary entry of July 29, 1942.

55. Israel Lichtenstein, "Un es iz geshen" (And it happened), in AR I, no. 1190.

56. Lewin, *A Cup of Tears*, p. 232.

57. AR II, no. 190. Reprinted in Sakowska, *Archiwum Ringelbluma, Getto Warszawskie: lipiec 1942–styczeń 1943*, pp. 33–37.

58. AR II, no. 187. Reprinted in ibid., p. 39.

59. AR II, no. 187. Reprinted in ibid., p. 42.

60. AR II, no. 191. Reprinted in ibid., pp. 67–79.

61. AR II, no. 219. Reprinted in ibid., p. 161. Kirman wrote several poems and essays that were preserved in the archive, including "After the Blockade" (AR II, no. 351). Kirman was deeply attached to his wife and two young children and sent them out of the ghetto to a small provincial town, where he thought they would get better nourishment. Auerbach recalled how desperately he missed his children; he sublimated his feelings by helping starving beggar children in the ghetto. He would roam the streets of the ghetto and hand out his last coins to them. He also wrote a vivid vignette, titled "The Mercy of a Quiet Death." It was about a dying street child, covered in sores and lice, whose animal screams at the entrance to the Jewish hospital forced doctors to admit him so that he could die in a bed instead of in the street. Kirman did not see his wife and children again. They were murdered outside of Warsaw. Kirman himself was killed during the mass executions of the Jews in the Lublin camps on November 3, 1943. On Kirman in the ghetto, see, especially, Auerbach, *Varshever tsvoes*, pp. 287–307. See also Auerbach's diary entry of spring 1942 in the Yad Vashem Archives, Auerbach Collection, P-16–1, p. 20.

62. AR II, no. 273. Reprinted in Sakowska, *Archiwum Ringelbluma, Getto Warszawskie: lipiec 1942–styczeń 1943*, p. 179.

63. The Oyneg Shabes probably got the figures from sources in the Judenrat, perhaps, from Reich-Ranicki or Jarecka. Another possibility is Shmuel Winter.

64. The German sources used by the Oyneg Shabes recorded 498 Jews shot in the streets or at the Umschlagplatz between July 22 and July 31, 1942. In August 1942, 2,445 were shot, 155 committed suicide, and 2,037 died a "natural death." During the "cauldron" period, between September 6 and September 12, there were 2,648 shootings and 60 suicides; 339 had died a "natural death."

65. This number included those seized during the one-day roundup on Yom Kippur, September 21.

66. "The Liquidation of Jewish Warsaw," in AR II, no. 192. This report was prepared by the Oyneg Shabes for the Polish Government-in-Exile in London. Why those in the Oyneg Shabes thought that the Germans wanted to minimize the numbers is not explained.

67. AR II, no. 193.

68. AR II, no. 197.

69. Wasser, "Ha'du"akh ha-rishon al shoat yehudei Varsha," p. 73.

70. All these statistics come from *Wiadomości,* December 22, 1942. Reprinted in Shaham, *Itonut ha-mahteret,* 6:562–564. See also AR II, no. 338. As these figures would not count the "wild Jews," those who were not registered and who did not have shop numbers, the percentages of those deported were probably somewhat inflated.

71. On the guidelines for these studies, both prepared by Ringelblum, see AR II, no. 242 (Werkschutz) and AR II, no. 243 (The Shops). Reprinted in Sakowska, *Archiwum Ringelbluma, Getto Warszawskie: lipiec 1942–styczeń 1943,* pp. 237–240.

72. For example, in addition to the diaries of Lewin, Opoczynski, and Gorny, the archive collected other important materials: the memoirs of an anonymous woman worker in a woodworking company (Ostdeutsche Bautischlerei-Werkstätte [OBW]) about the selection (AR II, no. 206); Natan Smolar's description of the selection (AR II, no. 201); Leizer Czarnobroda's diary (AR II, no. 205); and Ana Grasberg's diary (AR II, no. 209).

73. For Nowodworski, see AR II, no. 296; and for Rabinowitz, AR II, no. 298.

74. On these details, see Auerbach's memoir, Yad Vashem Archives, Rachel Auerbach Collection, P-16–82.

75. "A mensh iz antlofn fun Treblinke," in AR II, no. 299. This was Krzepicki's account with a short introduction written by Auerbach. "After the door closed," Krzepicki told Auerbach, "some of the people said, 'Jews, we're finished!' But I and some others did not want to believe that. 'It can't be,' we argued, 'they won't kill so many people! Maybe the old people and the children but not us. We're young. They're taking us to work.'" One should note that Krzepicki, as a member of a Zionist youth organization, would have had ample opportunity to have read the underground press and its reports of mass murder.

76. These translations from Krzepicki's account come from Alexander Donat, ed., *Death Camp Treblinka: A Documentary* (New York, 1979), p. 11.

77. Ibid., p. 112. The Oyneg Shabes used this exact phrase in its November report to the Polish Government-in-Exile in London.

78. Hersh Wasser, "Ha'du"akh ha-rishon al shoat yehudei Varsha," *Yediot beit lohamei ha-getaot,* no. 16–17 (April 1956): 73.

79. Ibid.

80. "The Liquidation of Jewish Warsaw," in AR II, no. 192. Reprinted in Sakowska, *Archiwum Ringelbluma, Getto Warszawskie: lipiec 1942–styczeń 1943,* pp. 275–320.

81. This journal is reprinted in Szymon Datner, "*Wiadomości,* podziemny organ prasowy w Getcie Warszawskim z okresu po wielkim 'wysiedleniu,'" *BŻIH,* no. 76 (1970); and Shaham, *Itonut ha-mahteret,* vol. 6. Volume 4 of "*Wiadomości* is reprinted, with an explanatory article, in Ruta Sakowska, "Wiadomości, ARG i raport o zagładzie. Status Archiwum Ringelbluma w getcie szczątkowym Warszawy," *Kwartalnik historii Żydów* 1, no. 213 (2005). The original is in AR II, no. 338.

82. *Wiadomości,* no. 6 (January 9–15, 1943).

83. AR II, no. 370. On the Piaseczno rebbe, see Nehemiah Polen, *The Holy Fire: The Teachings of Rabbi Kalonymus Kalman Shapira, the Rebbe of the Warsaw Ghetto* (New York, 1994); see also Henry Abramson, "Deciphering the Ancestral Paradigm: A Hasidic Court in the Warsaw Ghetto," unpublished Paper, United States Holocaust Memorial Museum Symposium: The Ghettos of the Holocaust, New Research and Perspectives on Definition, Daily Life, and Survival.

84. In a Hanukkah sermon he gave in December 1941, the rebbe had emphasized that

previous ordeals suffered by the Jewish people had been as bad as those they were now experiencing. But in December 1942 he added the following note:

> Only persecutions such as those inflicted until the end of 5702 [fall 1941]
> had earlier precedent. The grotesque persecutions, however, and the terrible,
> grotesque deaths that the unnatural wicked murderers created for us, the House
> of Israel, since the end of 5702—according to my knowledge of the word of our
> Sages of blessed memory and the histories of Jews in general, there has never
> been anything like this. May God have mercy on us and rescue us from their
> hands in the blink of an eye.

For this quote, see Abramson, "Deciphering the Ancestral Paradigm," p. 22. As Abramson also points out, the rebbe "had ample opportunity to express fundamental doubts of faith, yet he refused to do so."

85. AR II, no. 348.

86. AR II, no. 359.

87. Lichtenstein, "And it Happened," in AR I, no. 1190.

88. Ibid.

89. Ber Mark, "Shmuel Winter's Togbukh: A vogiker tsushtayer tsu der erev khurbm oyfshtand dokumentatsie," *Bleter far geshikhte,* nos. 1–2 (1950): 33.

90. AR II, 201.

91. Halina Birenbaum, a survivor of the Warsaw ghetto, recalled that "the poems of Władysław Szlengel were read in the houses of the ghetto and outside, in the evenings, and were passed from hand to hand and from mouth to mouth. The poems were written in burning passion as the events, which seemed to last for centuries, occurred. They were a living reflection of our feelings, thoughts, needs, pain, and merciless fight for every moment of life" ("Słowo które nie ginie nigdy," *Nowiny kurier,* October 21, 1983).

92. I have slightly modified Halina Birenbaum's translation as published online at http://www.zchor.org/szlengel/monument.htm.

93. AR II, no. 354. The original Polish reads: "I kiedy kat Cię popędzi i zmusi / zagna i wepchnie w komorę parową / zamknie za Tobą hermetyczne wieka / gorąca para zacznie dusić, dusić / i będziesz krzyczał, będziesz chciał uciekać- / kiedy się skończą już konania męki / Zawloką, wrzucą tam potwornym dołem / wyrwą ci gwiazdy—złote zęby z szczęki— / a potem spalą / i będziesz popiołem." Reprinted in Irena Maciejewska, ed., *Władysław Szlengel: Co czytałem umarłym* (Warsaw, 1977), pp. 129–130. In late 1942 the Oyneg Shabes still believed, based on erroneous reports from escapees from Treblinka, that Jews were killed by hot steam chambers rather than by carbon monoxide gas.

94. See "Wladyslaw Szlengel: The Poet of the Ghetto" in Ringelblum, *Ksovim fun geto,* 2:189–193. The first part of the archive contained several satirical poems that Szlengel wrote before the beginning of the Great Deportation. These included "Raz kupiłem sobie tak," a satire of the forced requisitioning of furs at the beginning of 1942 (AR I, no. 525); several poems that lampooned a house committee (Komitet Domowy przy Świętojerskiej 16); poems about the armbands (*opaski*), as well as other subjects (AR I, no. 526). The second part of the archive contained additional poems including "Rzeczy" (Things) "Mała Stacja Treblinka" (The small station Treblinka). "Paszport" (The passport), "Za pięć dwunasta" (Five minutes to twelve), and "Telefon" (The telephone) (AR II, nos. 353 and 354). Many of the poems that Ringelblum cited in his essay on Szlengel were not found in the archive. It is possible that many more poems were in the third part of the archive that

disappeared. Ringelblum probably had copies in his hideout on Grójecka, sent to him by Adolf Berman. Less likely, but possible, is that he cited the passages from memory.

95. "The poems conveyed the moods of the ghetto. They were declaimed and recited. . . . They were passed from hand to hand in typed and hectographed copies. Although the poems were artistically mediocre, they became very popular and moved those who heard them to tears because they were topical, about problems the Jews lived with and felt" (Ringelblum, *Ksovim fun geto,* 2:189).

96. According to Natan Gross, Szlengel was born in Warsaw in 1914. His father, who painted cinema advertisements, sent him to the Warsaw Commercial Institute. In the 1930s he published light, satirical poetry in *Szpilki* and more serious, pessimistic poems—such as "Don't Buy the New Year Calendar" and "A Frightened Generation" in *Nasz przegląd.* See Natan Gross, "Władysław Szlengel: The Ghetto Poet, Alive, Dying, Fighting," available at http://www.zachor.org/szlengel/szlengel.htm.

97. Szlengel marked his resignation from the Jewish police in his poem, "Good-bye to My Hat." Other copies of the poem bore the title "The Three Hats." This poem is reprinted in Irena Maciejewska, ed., *Władysław Szlengel: co czytałem umarłym* (Warsaw, 1977), pp. 151–154. Before the war, we learn from the poem, he had worn a student's hat. When the war started, he had fought in the Polish army and had worn a soldier's hat. Then he joined the Jewish police and donned a policeman's hat.

> Who you are depends on the hat you wear,
> It's more important than an Aryan grandmother.
> Before they check your papers or look into your trousers,
> Your hat will announce how much you are worth.

Szlengel knew that by quitting the Jewish police he was taking a big risk. As he ended his poem, saying farewell to his policeman's hat, he wrote:

> Good-bye, my policeman's hat,
> I'm starting a new life,
> Farewell, my hat,
> You won't protect me any more.
> The world waits for me everywhere,
> The world that is a giant trap,
> I don't know for better or for worse,
> Good-bye, my hat.

98. Ibid., pp. 37–51. I have also used, with my own modifications, an English translation by Andrew Kobos, available at www.zchor.org/szlengel/prose.htm.

99. See Irena Maciejewska's introduction to *Władysław Szlengel: co czytałem umarłym,* p. 28.

100. Ibid., p. 24.

101. A copy of "Rzeczy" (Things) is in AR II, no. 353.

102. As translated in Frieda Aaron, *Bearing the Unbearable: Yiddish and Polish Poetry in the Ghettos and Concentration Camps* (Albany, 1990), pp. 43–45. This important book also contains enlightening insights into Szlengel's poetry.

103. Rachel Scharf, "Literature in the Ghetto in the Polish Language: *Z otchłani*— From the Abyss," in Shapiro, *Holocaust Chronicles,* p. 37.

104. See Maciejewska, *Władysław Szlengel: co czytałem umarłym,* p. 165. These poems,

along with the Oyneg Shabes manuscripts, are now in the archive of the ŻIH in Warsaw. Szlengel also gave many of his poems to a Polish friend, Julian Kudasiewicz on October 8, 1942. This collection survived the war and was used by Michał Borwicz in *Pieśń ujdzie cało. Antolgia wierszy o Żydach pod okupacją niemiecką,* which appeared in 1947. See also Maciejewska, *Władysław Szlengel: co czytałem umarłym,* p. 164.

105. "Wladyslaw Szlengel: The Poet of the Ghetto," in Ringelblum, *Ksovim fun geto,* 2:193.

106. Ibid., 2:190.

107. Maciejewska, *Władysław Szlengel: Co czytałem umarłym,* p. 70.

108. Ibid., p. 63.

109. Ibid., p. 105.

110. In the original Polish, the final line of the poem reads: "Abyśmy mieli także swe Westerplatte [so that we, too, could have our Westerplatte]." Westerplatte, a fort near Danzig, was the scene of a fierce battle in September 1939, where a Polish garrison held off numerically superior German troops for several days. It became a symbol of Polish heroism and courage.

111. "Do polskiego czytelnika," in Maciejewska, *Władysław Szlengel: co czytałem umarłym,* p. 55.

112. "The Janitor has the Key" describes how he, the Jewish poet, and the Polish janitor Wiśniewski had once been comrades. They had gone off together to fight for Poland in 1939, but then the war started. And one day Szlengel saw Wiśniewski, drunk and happy, wearing the poet's fur coat.

> You have won the war, my Wiśniewski,
> You don't even think about tomorrow.
> You scum, how do you enjoy
> The coat you acquired so easily?

In "A Note to Pedants," Szlengel stressed that he would not include this poem in a collection of his published works for Polish readers until "the day comes when the nationalist passions inflamed by the [Nazis] will fade and then we will be able to calmly consider the sins of our neighbors." See "Notatka dla pedantów," in Maciejewska, *Władysław Szlengel: co czytałem umarłym,* p. 53.

113. Halina Birenbaum recalled hearing her twenty-year brother, Chilek, declaiming this poem on April 18, 1943, the day before the outbreak of the ghetto uprising.

114. This translation is by Michael Steinlauf in Milton Teichman and Sharon Leder, eds., *Truth and Lamentation: Stories and Poems on the Holocaust* (Urbana and Chicago, 1994), pp. 252–257.

115. On this point, see also Rut Shenfeld, "Wladyslaw Szlengel v'shirato b'geto Varsha," *Gal-ed* 10 (1987): 277.

116. Maciejewska, *Władysław Szlengel: Co czytałem umarłym,* p. 50.

117. Shenfeld, "Wladyslaw Szlengel v'shirato b'geto Varsha," 279.

118. Mark, *Umgekumene shrayber fun di getos un lagern,* p. 149.

119. Ziva Shavitsky, "Yitzhak Katzenelson," in S. Lillian Kremer, ed., *Holocaust Literature: An Encyclopedia of Writers and Their Work,* vol. 1 (New York and London, 2003), p. 617.

120. Natan Eck, "Mitn dikhter in di yorn fun khurbm," *Di goldene keyt,* no. 49 (1964).

121. See Yitzhak Zuckerman, "Zikhronotav v divrav shel Yitzhak Zuckerman," and Chava Folman, "Tora b'khoninut matmedet," both in Yudka Helman, ed., *Edut* 11 (1994).

122. In his diary entry of December 31, 1940–January 5, 1941, Ringelblum noted that, "[Katzenelson's poem] 'Yizkor' makes a powerful impression, although artistically it is nothing special [*nisht gehoybn*]. The poet demands revenge for the troubles and sufferings, he describes the kidnappings, the deadly fear in the streets, the labor camps from which no one returns, the terrible deeds of the Judenrat types who are often worse than them [the Germans]" (*Ksovim fun geto*, 1:209).

123. Mordecai Tenenbaum-Tamaroff, *Dapim min Hadleka* (Jerusalem, 1984), p. 92.

124. Yitzhak Katzenelson, *Yidishe geto ksovim,* ed. Yekhiel Shaintukh (Tel Aviv, 1984), p. 63.

125. Although Katzenelson did not mention Ringelblum in his writings, he had absolutely no use for Bundists, the Left Poalei Zion, and ideological Yiddishists. One can surmise, therefore, that the two were not close. For his part, Ringelblum was critical of Katzenelson's willingness, along with other ghetto intellectuals, to accept invitations from the notorious Gestapo agent Abraham Gancwajch. Although Ringelblum did not accuse him of collaboration with the Germans, he regretted what he considered to be naïveté and poor judgment. See, for example, Ringelblum's diary entry of May 2, 1942, in *Ksovim fun geto,* 1:355. Yitzhak Zuckerman also warned Katzenelson about Gancwajch and gave him an ultimatum: either us (Dror) or him. See Zuckerman, "Zikhronotav v dvorav shel Yitzhak Zuckerman," p. 40.

126. Yitzhak Katzenelson, *Vitel Diary* (Tel Aviv, 1964), p. 133.

127. Zuckerman, *A Surplus of Memory,* pp. 215–217.

128. "Now in the cellar we have become dumb, silent. Guzik has turned his face sidewards, while Giterman has buried his head in his hands, and dug his elbows into his knees. The two gentlemen of the Joint who are here are embarrassed, just as I am" (Katzenelson, *Vitel Diary,* p. 239).

129. Tuvia Borzykowski, *Tsvishn falndike vent* (Warsaw, 1949), p. 19.

130. Shavitsky, "Yitzhak Katzenelson," in Kremer, *Holocaust Literature,* 1:617.

131. Yekhiel Shaintukh, "Yitzhak Katzenelson v'ha-korei ha-ivri," *Edut* 11 (1994): 63.

132. Eck, *Ha'toim b'darkhei ha-mavet,* pp. 218.

133. Translation by Jacob Sonntag, in Teichman and Leder, *Truth and Lamentation,* p. 422.

134. On this poem, see Yekhiel Shaintukh's informative introduction in Yitzhak Katzenelson, *Yidishe geto ksovim,* pp. 640–642. Shaintukh had the opportunity to talk to Zhelichowski's sister.

135. Ibid., p. 662.

136. Leiner's grandfather, Gershon Henoch Leiner, became famous for restoring the use of the special blue dye (*tchelet*) on a fringe of the prayer shawl. The blue prayer shawls became a hallmark of the Radzyner Hasidim. In the interwar years Shmuel Shlomo founded a yeshiva in Radzyn called Sod Hayesharim (The secret of the righteous). See "Radzyn," in Abraham Weiss, ed., *Pinkas Ha-kehillot. Polin. entsiḳlopedyah shel ha-yishuvim ha-Yehudiyim le-min hiyasdam ye-ad le-aḥar Sho'at Milḥemet ha-olam ha-sheniyah,* vol. 7 (Jerusalem, 1999), pp. 543–546.

137. Ringelblum, *Ksovim fun geto,* 1:349.

138. Shaham, *Itonut ha-mahteret,* 6:345.

139. Ibid. See also Lewin, *A Cup of Tears,* p. 121. According to Nachman Blumenthal, the person who tried to impersonate the rabbi was actually his sexton. See Blumenthal, "Ha shir al ha-Radzynai shel Yitzhak Katzenelson," *Yediot beit lohamei ha-getaot,* no. 8 (January 1955): 4–7.

140. See Motl Raykhman, "Der umkum fun Radzyner Rebbn," in *Vlodava v'Hasviva: Sefer Zikaron* (Tel Aviv, 1974).

141. Even as Jews in Lublin and the provincial ghettos were being massacred, Warsaw was perceived as a haven for Polish Jewry, protected by its sheer size. That the Germans were able to uproot Warsaw Jewry reinforced, in Katzenelson's mind, the unprecedented scope of the catastrophe.

142. Something like this actually happened but in 1940, not 1942. A survivor of the Włodawa Ghetto recalled that many Jews had died in labor camps near Sobibór. Leiner spearheaded a campaign to find their bodies and give them a Jewish burial. See Raykhman, "Der umkum fun Radzyner Rebbn." The story about the rebbe paying peasants to bring in both live and dead Jews was similar to a popular legend about the wealthy Praga Jew Shmuel Zbytkover, about whom Ringelblum wrote in *Zion* in 1938. During the Russian attack on Praga in 1794, Zbytkover supposedly offered the Russian Cossacks a bounty for living and dead Jews.

143. In Genesis 47:29 Jacob asks his son Joseph to "deal kindly and truthfully with me [v'asita imadi hesed v'emet]" He asks his son not to bury him in Egypt. The great biblical commentator Rashi noted in his comment on this verse that "hesed v'emet" (kindness and truth) was the kindness shown to the dead since in that case one cannot hope for any reward.

144. Katzenelson, *Yidishe geto ksovim,* p. 704.

145. Rabbi Akiba supported the anti-Roman revolt of Bar Kochba, but he is mainly remembered for his legal and moral teachings and for his martyrdom.

146. As modern Jewish secular culture developed in Eastern Europe, Hasidism had evoked a mixed response from historians and Jewish writers. The historian Simon Dubnow contrasted the early, creative period of the Hasidim with what he saw as its later decline. For Y. L. Peretz, Hasidism had been a vital national movement that was now doomed to decay unless its positive values could be redeemed and enhanced through a new Jewish secular, humanist culture.

147. For an illuminating discussion of "Di Goldene Keyt," see Ruth Wisse, *I. L. Peretz and the Making of Modern Jewish Culture* (Seattle, 1991), pp. 63–67. I have also benefited from a conversation with David Roskies on this topic.

148. Yitzhak Katzenelson, *Yidishe geto ksovim,* p. 45.

149. Katzenelson, *Vitel Diary,* p. 124.

150. Translation by Jacob Sonntag, in Teichman and Leder, *Truth and Lamentation,* p. 127.

9 A HISTORIAN'S FINAL MISSION

1. See Auerbach, "Arkhiv 'Hemshekh' oyf der Arisher zayt."

2. Ringelblum, *Ksovim fun geto,* 2:392. Perhaps these were notes for a more coherent narrative once the pressure let up. The sentences cited above were probably written at different times, not in one sitting.

3. Ibid., 2:395.

4. This was a common view among the youth movement leaders and activists of the left-wing parties. See, for example, Marek Edelman, *Strażnik* (Warsaw, 1999), p. 204.

5. This was not the only example where Ringelblum made questionable judgments about individuals. In his diary entry of June 10, 1941, he called famed pedagogue and children's writer Janusz Korczak "senile [*oyver botlnik*]" (*Ksovim fun geto*, 1:277). In his essay on the Oyneg Shabes, he spoke in a patronizing tone about Chaim Kaplan's important ghetto diary. "Kaplan," he wrote, "did not have wide horizons. But everything that an average Warsaw Jew lived through, his pain and his feelings, his thirst for revenge—all this was faithfully reflected in Kaplan's diary. In fact, it is Kaplan's very ordinariness that gives the diary its value" (ibid., 2:98). In March 1940 he complained about the physician Israel Milejkowski's "inferiority complex," since Milejkowski, who headed the Judenrat's health department, had asked the convert Dr. Ludwik Hirszfeld to lecture to Jewish doctors. Ringelblum loathed Hirszfeld because the latter, before the war, according to Ringelblum, had fired all the Jews who worked in his institute (ibid., 1:236).

6. Mazor, *The Vanished City*, p. 133.

7. Quoted in Gutman, *The Jews of Warsaw*, p. 229.

8. Ibid.

9. Ringelblum, *Ksovim fun geto*, 2:10.

10. Ibid., 2:11; emphasis added. This was probably written in September or October 1942.

11. Ibid., 2:121.

12. Ibid., 2:122.

13. Zuckerman, *A Surplus of Memory*, p. 220.

14. Personal conversation with Wanda Rotenberg, Tel Aviv, July 1999.

15. On Berlinski, see *Dray: [ondenkbukh] / Pola Elster, Hersh Berlinski, Eliyahu 'Erlikh* (Tel Aviv, 1966). This volume includes the fragmentary diary and notes that Berlinski kept during the war.

16. In notes written after the ghetto uprising, Berlinski refers to the Finance Committee of the Jewish National Committee, indicating that it was composed of Yitzhak Giterman, Emanuel Ringelblum, Lipe Bloch, Menkakhem Kon, Alexander Landau, Menakhem Kirshenbaum, and Yohanan Morgenstern. This committee was charged with buying arms for the ŻOB. A few pages later he remarks that this was a committee of "old has-beens [*opgeklapte hoshannes*]" that failed to get wealthy Jews in the ghetto to cough up money for weapons. See ibid., p. 188.

17. Berlinski escaped through the sewers on May 10, 1943. On September 26, 1944, the Germans surrounded the bunker in Żoliborz where Berlinski, Pola Elster, Eliyahu Erlich, and Hersh and Bluma Wasser were hiding. Only the Wassers survived the shootout that followed.

18. Vladka Meed recalled that, during the first week of the Great Deportation, she saw Ringelblum working without letup to hand out Aleynhilf ID cards (personal communication to author, July 2000).

19. Eck, "Mit Emanuel Ringelblum in Varshever geto," p. 117.

20. Mazor, *The Vanished City*, pp. 146–147.

21. Ringelblum, *Ksovim fun geto*, 2:10.

22. For more on Shur, see Auerbach, *Varshever tsvoes*, pp. 261–267.

23. *Ksovim fun geto*, 2:72.

24. Ibid., 2:67–68.

25. Ibid., 2:11.

26. Genie Silkes, "Tsvey bagegenishn mit Emanuel Ringelblum," YA, Hersh Wasser Collection (HWC), 44.1, p. 2.

27. For a lengthy discussion of this word and the whole practice of combing the ghetto for abandoned property, see Peretz Opoczynski's ghetto diary, entry for December 27, 1942, in AR II, no. 289.

28. On October 19, 1942, Peretz Opoczynski, who worked in the OBW shop, made the following entry in his diary:

> In the morning the mood of the workers . . . was so depressed that no one
> wanted to work. At any time they can come and take us to the slaughter. In
> the afternoon, when we learned that we might live at least until December 31,
> the mood got a little better. But later on someone came with the news that the
> Germans will deport fifty-five hundred more people. And everyone once again
> lapsed into despair. And so we bounce back and forth ten times a day, our moods
> change every hour and fear gnaws at our souls. (AR II, no. 289)

29. See ibid., diary entry for December 10, 1942. See also Borzykowski, *Tsvishn faln-dike vent*, p. 11.

30. Ringelblum, *Ksovim fun geto*, 2:18.

31. AR II, no. 284.

32. In this essay, written in late 1942 and titled "The Marks of the Modern Slaves," Ringelblum wrote that the shop workers wore numbers; lived in barracks; had lost their wives and children ("slaves do not need families"); could only move in groups; were beaten and terrorized at work; suffered exploitation reminiscent of the conditions of Chinese coolies; were forbidden to protest or organize; and were totally dependent on the whims of the German bosses and the bosses' Jewish associates. At any moment the shop worker could be sent to the Umschlagplatz. The shop workers, Ringelblum pointed out, had to work even when sick with a high fever. After work they were not allowed to walk the streets. In other ways they were even worse off than slaves: at least slaves knew they were not facing an automatic death sentence and could rely on their masters for food. The Jews, however, knew they would die and even had to somehow provide their own food. See Ringelblum, *Ksovim fun geto*, 2:20–21.

33. AR II, no. 240. Reprinted in Sakowska, *Archiwum Ringelbluma, Getto Warszawskie: lipiec 1942–styczeń 1943*, pp. 329–331.

34. See *Dray*, p. 179.

35. The protocols of several meetings of the mutual aid group held in Hallman's shop are in AR II, no. 235. These meetings spanned a period from December 12, 1942, to January 27, 1943, and apparently Ringelblum played a very active role (Ringelblum, *Ksovim fun geto*, 2:138).

36. Ringelblum, *Ksovim fun geto*, 2:138.

37. Ibid., 2:151–152.

38. AR II, no. 284. This essay, which was probably written in November or December 1942, had not been completed.

39. Ibid., p. 32.

40. Auerbach, *Varshever tsvoes*, p. 191.

41. Ringelblum, *Ksovim fun geto*, 1:108, diary entry of March 30, 1940.

42. Ibid., 1:102, diary entry of March 28, 1940.

43. Ibid., 1:351, diary entry of May 2, 1942.

44. Ibid., 1:379.

45. Shaham, *Itonut ha-mahteret*, 6:530. See also AR II, no. 338.

46. Shaham, *Itonut ha-mahteret,* 6:560. See also AR II, no. 338. On the other hand, Peretz Opoczynski still clung to the view that the Wehrmacht was more humane than the SS. On October 25, 1942, he wrote: "It is believed that the Wehrmacht has no contact with the SS and does not support its Jew-hating policies" (AR II, no. 289).

47. Reprinted in Datner, "*Wiadomości,* podziemny organ prasowy w Getcie Warszawskim."

48. Emanuel Ringelblum, "Straty i odszkodowania ludności żydowskiej w czasie drugiej wojny światowej," Archive of Kibbutz Lohamei Hageta'ot, Adolf Berman Collection. The next page of this document was missing, and so whatever modifiers Ringelblum attached to this statement can only be surmised. It should be noted that Ringelblum expressed these thoughts, written in extreme circumstances, in a private letter to a trusted friend. Probably he would not have vented them in a publication written for a wider audience.

49. Ibid.

50. Ringelblum, *Ksovim fun geto,* 2:140. One might note that Giterman, like Ringelblum, became less moderate toward the Germans after having witnessed the Great Deportation. The poet Yitzhak Katzenelson had written an emotional poem, "Vey dir" (Woe to you) that cursed the German people and called them a nation of murderers. In his *Vitel Diary,* Katzenelson recalled that Giterman praised the poem. About a week before the Germans killed Giterman, the Joint director told the poet: "Those curses that we read when we came up from the cellar, preserve them and keep them—not a single word will go astray as far as I am concerned . . . I therefore want to read it again . . . but when, Katzenelson, when?" (Katzenelson, *Vitel Diary,* p. 247). It is most unlikely that Ringelblum would not have known about Giterman's feelings; but what he chose to include in the essay on Giterman were the latter's warnings against revenge, and not the anger he expressed in late 1942 and early 1943.

51. Ringelblum, *Ksovim fun geto,* 1:100.

52. Ibid., 1:132.

53. Ibid., 1:346.

54. Ibid., 1:381.

55. Ibid., 1:382.

56. A good, general discussion of the entire problem of Kiddush Hashem in the Holocaust can be found in Gutman, "Kiddush Hashem and Kiddush Hachayim," pp. 185–201. See also Roskies, *Against the Apocalypse,* p. 29.

57. In BT Brachot, 5A, if a person cannot find that he is suffering because of any actions he committed, then he should assume that he is suffering because of God's love. Rashi, commenting on this, explained that God afflicts those in this world who are without sin in order to increase their share of the world to come.

58. It would be wrong to infer that Kiddush Hashem was the only Jewish response, that Jews never fought back against their enemies or that Kiddush Hashem met with unquestioning acceptance in the past. See, for example, the work of Israel Yuval, "Ha nakam v'haklalah, ha-dam v'ha-alilah: me-alilot-kedoshim l'alilot dam," *Zion* 55, no. 1 (1993), as well as the responses to Yuval's argument in *Zion* 59, no. 2–3 (1994); see also David Biale, "Blood Libels and Blood Vengeance," *Tikkun* (July–August 1994).

59. On this issue, see Roskies, *Against the Apocalypse,* pp. 89–91.

60. In his diaries Ringelblum noted more than once that this war had produced few instances of Kiddush Hashem—a point contradicted by his colleague Rabbi Huberband, who had gathered for the archive many examples of sublime courage shown by both religious and secular Jews.

61. Ringelblum, *Ksovim fun geto,* 1:234.

62. Natan Eck, who worked closely with Ringelblum in the Aleynhilf, wrote that "the topic of the speeches and discussions that infused the occupants of the ghetto at that time was the concept of Kiddush ha-Shem. One sensed that something was about to happen. . . . News of slaughter [in other cities] reached the ghetto. At that point the oft-repeated statement of Rabbi Yitzhak Nissenbaum reverberated in the ghetto: 'This is a time for Kiddush Hahayim and not for death through Kiddush Hashem. In the past, our enemies demanded the Jewish soul and the Jew sacrificed himself through Kiddush Hashem. Now the enemy demands the Jewish body and the Jew must defend himself and his life!' Indeed, at that point the occupants of the ghetto were suffused with a strong desire to live; they revealed a hidden power whose like is not found in normal life." Quoted in Gutman, "Kiddush Hashem and Kiddush Hachayim," 185–186.

63. Ringelblum, *Ksovim fun geto,* 2:41.

64. AR I, no. 811.

65. Ringelblum, *Ksovim fun geto,* 2:409.

66. One popular rumor that swept through the ghetto concerned an alleged Jewish revolt in the town of Nowogródek . Although some resistance did take place there, wildly exaggerated accounts of the revolt reached the Warsaw Ghetto. On March 28, 1942, Hashomer's *Jutrznia* published an article titled "Nowogródek" that recounted an alleged revolt of two hundred young Jews in that town who refused to be led to the slaughter and who all died fighting. Reprinted in Blatman, *Geto varsha, sipur itonai,* pp. 443–444.

67. Ringelblum, *Ksovim fun geto,* 2:410–411.

68. Ibid., 2:15–16.

69. "Military Strategy of the Germans against the Jews," in ibid., 2:29–30. See also *Wiadomości,* no. 5 (January 1–8, 1943).

70. Ringelblum, *Ksovim fun geto,* 2:55.

71. Ibid., 2:28, diary entry of December 5, 1942.

72. But, he admitted, some Jews hung on to false hopes. His essay, "The Ten Tribes," examined Jews who tried to shield themselves from the full consciousness of the ongoing annihilation by clinging to rumors about loved ones who were alive somewhere "in the East." Ringelblum compared this willful denial to how the Jews in biblical Palestine reacted to the exile of the ten tribes of Israel. Rather than admit the final disappearance of a majority of the nation, the Jewish collective memory repeated tales of the "Red Jews," the descendants of the Ten Lost Tribes who lived in distant and remote places beyond the "dark mountains." See *Ksovim fun geto,* 2:42–44.

73. In an unpublished essay Rachel Auerbach wrote that the mass movement to build bunkers merited a special historical study. "The psychological basis for this entire enterprise was the conviction that the war would end very soon, especially in light of the [German defeat at] Stalingrad." See Yad Vashem Archives, Rachel Auerbach Collection, P-16–27.

74. In his letters to Adolf Berman between September 1943 and March 1944 Ringelblum made several references to this project. For example, on December 20, 1943, he

asked Berman to supply him with materials on the ŻOB (Adolf Berman Collection, Archive of Kibbutz Lohamei Ha'Getaot, File 358, Letter from Ringelblum to Berman, December 20, 1943).

75. Ringelblum, *Ksovim fun geto,* 2:137.

76. Winter complained that too much money was changing hands without receipts or proper accounting. "I told Emanuel that I was not happy that I handle thousands without a receipt and give away thousands without a receipt." See Mark, "Shmuel Winter's Togbukh," p. 47.

77. On the ŻZW, see Moshe Arens, "The Jewish Military Organization (ŻZW) in the Warsaw Ghetto," *Holocaust and Genocide Studies* 19, no. 2 (2005).

78. On these organizations, see Gutman, *The Jews of Warsaw,* esp. pp. 228–249.

79. Ringelblum, *Ksovim fun geto,* 2:333.

80. Adolf Berman Collection, Archive of Kibbutz Lohamei Ha'Getaot, File 358, Letter from Emanuel Ringelblum to Adolf Berman, December 28, 1943.

81. See Zuckerman, *A Surplus of Memory,* pp. 273–274.

82. See *Dray,* p. 168.

83. Ringelblum, *Ksovim fun geto,* 2:336.

84. Ibid., 2:144; Gutman, *Mered ha-Netzurim,* pp. 299–300.

85. Borzykowski, *Tsvishn falndike vent,* p. 19.

86. AR II, no. 288.

87. Gutman, *The Jews of Warsaw,* pp. 307–316. Gutman believed that the German caught five thousand Jews and not the sixty-five hundred that they reported.

88. Other factors were at work here. First, in Vilna and Białystok Jacob Gens and Efroym Barash provided leadership and even hope for survival. In Warsaw, on the other hand, after Czerniakow's suicide, the authority of the Judenrat quickly faded, and later it became easier for the ŻOB to establish its authority in the ghetto, especially after eliminating collaborators. Another factor affecting Warsaw Jewry was the moral and psychological torment of seeing their fellow Jews—the Jewish police—aid in the slaughter of their own people over a six-week period. This ordeal, together with the taunts of Poles that Jews lacked courage and honor, also helped to tip the psychological scales toward support of armed resistance. See also Daniel Blatman and Israel Gutman, "Youth and Resistance Movements in Historical Perspective," *Yad Vashem Studies,* no. 23 (1993).

89. Ringelblum, *Ksovim fun geto,* 2:76.

90. Basia Berman, "Rydzewski: Ringelblum oyf der Arisher zayt," in *Linke Poalei Tsiyon,* April 19, 1948.

91. Ringelblum, *Ksovim fun geto,* 2:314–315. Uri soon joined his mother in the Grójecka hideout.

92. Ber Mark, "Der letster baal pinkes fun Varshever geto," in Archives of ŻIH, Ber Mark Collection, no. 14. Ringelblum wrote that Hormuszko rescued many Jews: "He took money from the rich and rescued the poor gratis, and even helped them with his own funds. He is known in Grodno and in Warsaw. [The Jews] trust him without limit and entrust him with large sums of money and, more important, human lives. Mister Pawel is a very modest man, and does this because he is a humanitarian and a patriot" (*Ksovim fun geto,* 2:374–375).

93. Berman, "Rydzewski: Ringelblum oyf der Arisher zayt."

94. Yad Vashem Archives, Rachel Auerbach Collection, P16–82.

95. Winter wrote: "Unfortunately the Oyneg Shabes is barely functioning. Every-

body cares only about fleeing to the Aryan side. This is a wrong which one should not commit in such terrible times" (Mark, "Shmuel Winter's Togbukh," p. 41).

96. Turkow, *Azoy iz es geven*, pp. 370–371.

97. Ringelblum, *Ksovim fun geto*, 2:40–41.

98. AR II, no. 283. Reprinted in Kermish, *To Live with Honor*, pp. 407–409. I have altered the translation.

99. Ringelblum, *Ksovim fun geto*, 2:41.

100. Turkow, *Azoy is es geven*, pp. 491–492.

101. Ringelblum, *Ksovim fun geto*, 2:222.

102. Hersh Wasser, "Fun fraytik biz fraytik," *Arbeter tsaytung*, April 15, 1948.

103. The information that Kon was at Brauer's came from Turkow. See Turkow, *Azoy iz es geven*, p. 431.

104. Ringelblum, *Ksovim fun geto*, 2:176.

105. Berman, "Rydzewski: Ringelblum oyf der Arisher zayt." Unfortunately there are virtually no sources that describe Ringelblum's time in Trawniki.

106. On the details of this escape, see Anna Grupińska's interview with Kossower, "Ja myślałam że wszyscy są razem," available at http://www.tygodnik.com.pl/numer/2703/grupinska.html. See also Kossower's memoirs in the Yad Vashem Archive, no. 0-33-50.

107. Ibid.

108. Auerbach, *Varshever tsvoes*, pp. 206–207.

109. Adolf Berman Collection, Archive of Kibbutz Lohamei Ha'Getaot, File 358, Letters of Emanuel and Judyta (Yehudis) Ringelblum to Adolf Berman, March 3, 1944.

110. Berman, "Rydzewski: Ringelblum oyf der Arisher zayt."

111. Adolf Berman Collection, Archive of Kibbutz Lohamei Ha'Getaot, File 358, Letter from Emanuel Ringelblum to Adolf Berman, November 25, 1943. "The idea of duty," Ringelblum wrote to Berman, "no longer means what it once did." Also cited by Steven Paulsson, *Secret City: The Hidden Jews of Warsaw, 1940–1945* (New Haven, 2002), p. 88.

112. Basia Temkin-Bermanowa, *Dziennik z podziemia* (Warsaw, 2000), p. 245; Adolf Berman, "Yehudim be'Tzad ha-Ari," in *Entsyklopediya shel ha-Geluyot*, ed. Yitzhak Greenbaum, vol. 6, pt. B (Jerusalem, 1953), pp. 723–725.

113. Berman cited a letter that Wacław (Henryk Woliński) sent to the Home Army sometime in March or April 1944. Wacław, who was in charge of the department of Jewish Affairs in the Home Army, reported that because Gestapo pressure had paralyzed the activities of Zuckerman and Berman, Ringelblum was supposed to take over some of their responsibilities. But, as Wacław reported, before this could happen, Ringelblum was caught by the Gestapo. See Berman, "Yehudim be'Tsad ha-Ari," p. 724.

114. Berman, "Rydzewski: Ringelblum oyf der Arisher zayt."

115. Ringelblum, "Straty i odszkodowania ludności żydowskiej w czasie drugiej wojny światowej."

116. As Christopher Browning has noted, the Operation Harvest Festival was "the single largest German killing operation against the Jews in the entire war." See Browning, *Ordinary Men: Reserve Police Battalion 101 and the Final Solution in Poland* (New York, 1998), p. 135.

117. Two of the Jews left the Krysia before it was discovered, and one teenaged girl, as will be seen, died.

118. See the protocol, signed by Małgorzata Szadurska and Halina Michałecka (Wolski's sisters), describing the building and the functioning of the Krysia. The protocol was

signed on July 29, 1988. I thank Mordechai Paldiel of Yad Vashem for making this information available to me.

119. Ringelblum also mentions this. See *Ksovim fun geto,* 2:364.

120. See the note by Joseph Kermish, in ibid.

121. Yankev Celemenski, *Mitn farshnitenem folk* (New York, 1963), pp. 279–280.

122. Ringelblum also encouraged Passenstein to write while in the Krysia. The latter wrote two essays about social conditions in the Warsaw Ghetto and about smuggling. Both were sent out to Berman. See Marek Passenstein, "Szmugiel w getcie warszawskim," *BŻIH,* no. 26 (1958).

123. Berman, "Rydzewski: Ringelblum oyf der Arisher zayt."

124. Ringelblum thought that the space was twenty-eight square meters. On January 6, 1944, shortly after Berman was blackmailed and had to change his living quarters, Ringelblum suggested that he and Basia might think of moving to the Krysia:

> As far as Ms. Krysia is concerned, thirty-eight people live in twenty-eight square meters. There are fourteen bed boards where thirty-four people sleep, some three to a board, including Jurek [Uri, Ringelblum's son] and me. Jurek sleeps at my feet. The other four sleep on cots. If you came here you would have to find a place to sleep and you would, except that it would not be very comfortable. One of you would have to sleep on the table and another with either Passenstein or Melman. The food is not bad, but the crowding is indescribable. And then there are the fleas and the bedbugs. I'm telling you this because the "chief" wants a lot of money up front, twenty to thirty thousand, and there's no chance of getting it back. But a big plus is that [at night] you can go up and get fresh air.

See Adolf Berman Collection, Archive of Kibbutz Lohamei Ha'Getaot, File 358, Letter from Emanuel Ringelblum to Adolf Berman, January 6, 1944.

125. Orna Jagur, *The Hiding Place* (Lodz, 1997), p. 26. Jagur and her husband, Joseph, left the Krysia shortly before its location was betrayed. Today Joseph Jagur is a professor at the Weizman Institute in Israel, and Orna Jagur is a retired librarian.

126. Ibid., pp. 47–48.

127. Ibid., p. 28.

128. Ibid., pp. 34–37.

129. Ibid., p. 40. "Borowski" was a false name the Jagurs used to conceal his true identity.

130. Ibid., pp. 53–59. Ringelblum and Yehudis also refer to this incident in their letters to Berman.

131. Ringelblum, *Ksovim fun geto,* 2:366.

132. Jagur, *The Hiding Place,* p. 50.

133. Ibid., p. 44.

134. Personal conversation with Wanda Rotenberg, Tel Aviv, July 1999. Wanda Rotenberg's maiden name had been Wanda Elster. In a letter of January 20, 1944, to Berman, Ringelblum expressed great worry that Wanda had not appeared that week.

135. See, for example, Ringelblum's letter of November 25, 1943, Adolf Berman Collection, File 358.

136. Ringelblum, *Ksovim fun geto,* 2:366.

137. Ibid., 2:368.

138. Ringelblum to Berman, letter of February 3, 1944: "E [Ringelblum] is going through a serious mental depression caused by the hopelessness of the situation. Jozia [Ringelblum's wife] is totally against the idea of leaving, as she feels that given E's present state he cannot perform the functions that have been proposed." On the offer made by the Polish underground to smuggle some prominent surviving Jews, including Ringelblum, out of Poland, see Adolf Berman, "Yehudim be'Tsad ha-Ari," p. 723.

139. Ringelblum, *Ksovim fun geto*, 2:150–159 and 173–175, respectively.

140. Ibid., 2:159–164.

141. Ibid., 2:76.

142. Ibid., 2:164–172, 176–178, 217–221, and 207–210, respectively.

143. Cited in Sidra DeKoven Ezrahi, *By Words Alone: The Holocaust in Literature* (Chicago, 1980), p. 112.

144. Adolf Berman Collection, Archive of Kibbutz Lohamei Ha'Getaot, File 358, Letter from Emanuel Ringelblum to Adolf Berman, November 25, 1943.

145. Emanuel Ringelblum, "Straty i odszkodowania ludności żydowskiej w czasie drugiej wojny światowej."

146. Ringelblum, *Ksovim fun geto*, 2:137.

147. In a note written sometime after the beginning of the Great Deportation, Ringelblum wrote; "The crime of the Judenrat: did not create trustworthy documents [*ayzerne briv*] for the elite and for intellectuals. Criminal indifference of Dr. Wielikowski, impotence of Czerniakow" (ibid., 2:24).

148. Ibid., 2:61.

149. A careful reading of the essay also explains why Bundists wrote about Ringelblum with such hostility after the war and why scholars like Nachman Blumenthal erred when they believed that Ringelblum's writings were free of political partisanship. To quote Ringelblum, Zagan became "the recognized leader of public life in the Warsaw Ghetto [Khaver Zagan vert itzt der anerkenter firer fun der varshever gezelshaftlekhkayt]." There is no doubt that Zagan became an important leader in the ghetto. To call him *the* recognized leader of the community sheds more light on Ringelblum's politics than it does on his objectivity. See Ringelblum, *Ksovim fun geto*, 2:106.

150. In the ghetto the Party [*partey*] also referred to the ŻOB. But the context of this quote makes it clear that Ringelblum was referring to political parties like his own. Or perhaps by this time he had subconsciously conflated the real differences between the political parties and the ŻOB (ibid., 2:114).

151. Ibid., 2:106.

152. Ibid., 2:118–119. Ringelblum was thinking of Jesus' words in Matthew 18:20: "For where two or three are gathered together in my name, there am I in the midst of them."

153. Ringelblum, *Ksovim fun geto*, 2:111.

154. In a diary entry of May 1942 he wrote, "The news that comes from there [the USSR] shows galloping assimilation. The Jewish schools in Kiev and Minsk—which were Jewish cities—have been closed and the only support for Jewish culture is the theater. There is no Jewish scholarship" (Ringelblum, *Ksovim fun geto*, 1:371).

155. Adolf Berman Collection, Archive of Kibbutz Lohamei Ha'Getaot, File 358, Letter from Emanuel Ringelblum to Adolf Berman, December 28, 1943.

156. Hillel Seidman writes that he was present at a discussion that took place on December 6, 1942, which included a number of Jewish cultural figures, among them Emanuel Ringelblum and Isaac Schiper. When the discussion turned to the present catastro-

phe and the future of the Jewish people, Seidman recalled that the historians emphasized just how enormous a blow the destruction of East European Jewry would be for the entire Jewish people: "Never before in Jewish history—and both Ringelblum and Schiper agree on this—have so many national resources been concentrated in one place. [Poland] was the center of all that was living and creative in the Jewish people" (Seidman, *Togbukh fun Varshever geto*, p. 173).

157. Adolf Berman Collection, Archive of Kibbutz Lohamei Ha'Getaot, File 358, Letter from Emanuel Ringelblum to Adolf Berman, March 1, 1944. "Chodzi o to by móc uwydatnić rolę i stanowisko p. Stolarskiego. Niewątpliwie p. Chal. odegrał przodujące stanowisko w tym wszystkim, ale o ile p. Stolarski nie przypomni swego wkladu w tym wszystkim obraz rzeczywistości będzie zniekształcony. Proszę Was przeto, abyście wpłynęli na Jeleńskiego by fotograficznie oddał konferencję Sagańskiego z Paprockim i wogóle wszelkie próby(?) a potym (naszą rolę?) w ob." "Stolarski" probably refers to the Left Poalei Zion, "Chal." to the Zionist youth movements, "Paprocki" to the PPR, and "Saganski" to Shakhne Zagan. Jelenski was the code name of Hersh Berlinski, who was in hiding on the Aryan side. Ringelblum was saying, in effect, that, although the Zionist youth movements played the leading role in the uprising, history should not forget the contribution of the LPZ and especially its role in the formation of the antifascist bloc in early 1942. In another letter to Berman, Ringelblum would express his irritation that the Bund would try to claim an inordinate amount of credit for the uprising.

158. Ringelblum, *Ksovim fun geto*, 2:145.

159. Ibid., 2:142 The Oyneg Shabes commissioned several reports and studies about youth in the ghetto. See, for example, the guidelines for a study of youth in the ghetto as part of the "Two and a Half Years" project (AR I, no. 45); the fragment of a report on the situation of youth in the ghetto (AR I, no. 46); Young People in the House Committees: The Case of Ewa Gurfinkel (AR I, no. 40); Marian Małowist's essay on the interests and conduct of Jewish and Polish youth during the war and the occupation (AR I, no. 38); and guidelines for a youth essay competition (AR I, no. 640) .

160. After the war certain writers attacked the cultural activities in the ghettos—theaters, lectures, songs, poetry recitals, and so on—labeling them a narcotic that deluded the Jews and diverted them from the need to prepare to fight back. As the Vilna writer Shlome Belis wrote: "Culture linked to resistance—that's real power. Culture without resistance—that's passivity, inertia, helplessness. Culture in lieu of resistance—that's a betrayal of the basic interests of the people" (Belis, *Portretn un Problemen* [Warsaw, 1964], p. 315). Yitzhak Zuckerman wrote in his memoirs that, once the main youth movements learned of the genocide, they quickly lost interest in cultural work. After the war, however, Zuckerman realized that cultural work and armed resistance had not been mutually exclusive. Without the seminars and study of Jewish history and literature, the youth movements could not have maintained the idealistic commitment to plan a hopeless battle. Others, like Mark Dvorzhetzky who survived the Vilna Ghetto, stressed how important theater and cultural activities were in warding off depression and apathy. See Mark Dvorzhetsky, *Yerushalayim d'Lite in Kamf un Umkum* (Paris, 1948), p. 248. See also Cohen, "Ha-emnam derekh ahat? Od al mikoma shel hitnagdut ha-mizuyenet b'getaot."

161. Ringelblum, *Ksovim fun geto*, 2:148–149. When he mentioned "a thousand well-reasoned arguments against fighting the occupier," he was certainly correct—if one was

determined to think logically in July and August 1942. Unfortunately, as Zygmunt Bauman has noted, the Nazis succeeded in creating a calculus where rational choices and calculations served to make their own job easier. As Bauman wrote,

> By and large the rulers can count on rationality being on their side. The Nazi rulers twisted the stakes of the game so that the rationality of survival would render all other motives of human action irrational. Inside the Nazi-made unreal and inhuman world, reason was the enemy of morality. Logic required consent to crime. Rational defense of one's survival called for nonresistance to the other's destruction.

See Zygmunt Bauman, "On Immoral Reason and Illogical Morality," in *POLIN: A Journal of Polish Jewish Studies,* no. 3 (1988): 296–297. Quoted in Antony Polonsky, "Jews, Poles, and the Problems of Divided Memory," unpublished manuscript, p. 11.

162. Ringelblum, 2:330.

163. Lawrence Langer, *Admitting the Holocaust: Collected Essays* (Oxford, 1995), p. 46.

164. Ibid., 2:150.

165. Ibid., 2:238.

166. Ringelblum to Berman, Letter of November 25, 1943.

167. In his essay on Yitzhak Giterman, written in the Krysia, Ringelblum recalled a conversation they had had shortly after Giterman's return from a German internment camp in April 1940. At first Giterman's Polish fellow prisoners had treated him coldly, but soon they all became fast friends and even arranged a farewell party when he left the camp. Ringelblum quoted his friend as saying that "Polish-Jewish relations have been bad because a wall of prejudice and misunderstanding separated the two peoples. The major reason for hostility between Poles and Jews is that, although Jews have been the Poles' neighbors, the Poles knew nothing about their lives, their culture, and so on" (Ringelblum, *Ksovim fun geto,* 2:139). The experience of most Jewish POWs with their Polish brothers-in-arms was, on the whole, less friendly than Giterman described.

168. Ringelblum, *Ksovim fun geto,* 2:267.

169. Ibid. "The Jews," Ringelblum wrote, "were able to overcome all the economic barriers . . . and continued their prewar production for the needs of the Aryan market. They had overcome the [prewar boycott of the Polish anti-Semites] . . . and also the current invaders who wanted the Jews to starve en masse in the ghetto. *Economic life knows no differences of nationality and race.*" See ibid., 2:279; emphasis added.

170. In his summary of the problem of smuggling, written in late 1943, Ringelblum concluded that smuggling was one of the "finest pages in the mutual relations of both peoples during the present war" (ibid., 2:278).

171. Ibid., 1:364.

172. AR I, no. 130. Reprinted in Kermish, *To Live with Honor,* p. 157.

173. AR I, no. 492. These guidelines, presented in Appendix A of this volume, include dozens of different questions and reflect Ringelblum's determination to avoid hastiness and oversimplification in the study of Polish-Jewish relations. The last set of questions concerns the Polish reaction to the news of Chełmno and Wilno. Mass murder had already begun, but Ringelblum was only beginning to guess its true scope.

174. Ringelblum, *Ksovim fun geto,* 2:250.

175. Ibid., 2:252. In his diary entry of December 7–10, 1940, Ringelblum, after citing

various examples of Jewish courage on the battlefield, wrote that "the Jews were an exemplar of endurance and heroism" (1:194).

176. See Lewin, *A Cup of Tears*, p. 124.

177. As reprinted in Emanuel Ringelblum, *Polish-Jewish Relations during the Second World War,* ed. Joseph Kermish and Shmuel Krakowski (Evanston, 1974), p. 308.

178. Ringelblum, *Ksovim fun geto,* 2:408.

179. For a recent study of this pogrom, see Tomasz Szarota, *U progu zagłady: zajścia antyżydowskie i pogromy w okupowanej Europie* (Warsaw, 2000), pp. 25–82.

180. Ringelblum, *Ksovim fun geto,* 2:262–263.

181. Ibid., 1:180.

182. AR I, no. 92. Reprinted in Kermish, *To Live with Honor,* p. 616.

183. AR I, no. 25. The interviewee may very well have been Irena Adamowicz, who had helped Hashomer and the Dror a great deal.

184. The question of alleged Jewish collaboration remains a controversial issue that has attracted the attention of scholars and has had a major impact on the discussion of Polish-Jewish relations during the Holocaust. The recent controversy over Jan Gross's book, *Neighbors,* has reopened the debate. Broadly speaking, not only Polish right-wing circles but also respectable scholars like Tomasz Strzembosz and Marek Wierzbicki have stressed that Jews indeed welcomed the Soviet occupation of the territories east of the Bug. Strzembosz and Wierzbicki, citing Polish memoir literature and testimonies, asserted that in many instances Jews attacked the retreating Polish army. In any case, these scholars stress that the Poles' *perception* that the Jews "were dancing on Poland's grave" had a disastrous impact on Polish attitudes toward the Jews and explained much of the support, both tacit and active, that the Germans received from the local population east of the Bug as they exterminated the Jews. Rejecting this viewpoint is a large group of scholars who make several basic arguments. First, most Jews were not pro-Communist, although certainly they saw Soviet occupation as a lesser evil than Nazi occupation. Second, accusations of Jewish collaboration in the Soviet persecution of Poles lose their force when one remembers that the proportion of Jews among the deportees to Siberia was no less than the proportion of Poles. The Soviets deported not only political opponents like Zionists and Bundists but also members of the Jewish middle classes and many refugees from central and western Poland who had refused to accept Soviet passports. Third, the notion that Jews rushed to fill the ranks of the local Soviet administration and the secret police should be weighed against the fact that the Soviets were quite happy, after the initial period, to employ Poles in these jobs, and that many Poles were happy to volunteer. Moreover, for many poorer Jews in the small towns of eastern Poland, the Soviets provided employment opportunities denied them by the Poles. Fourth, many of the higher-level jobs in the Soviet administration were not filled by locals but by cadres brought in from the Soviet Union. Fifth, the evidence that "most" Jews welcomed the Soviets was impressionistic and superficial. To judge Jewish attitudes on the basis of who attended a parade ignored the fact that such spectators may have constituted only a small part of the Jewish population. That many Jewish refugees in Soviet-occupied Poland refused to accept Soviet citizenship also tempers the view of wholesale Jewish acceptance of the USSR. The retreating Polish units included many Jewish soldiers, and Jewish officers in the Polish army died along with the Poles during the Soviet executions of Polish officers in the spring of 1940. Finally, if Jews had a choice only between Nazi and Soviet rule, then un-

doubtedly they would prefer the latter. The literature on the issue of Polish-Jewish relations during the Soviet occupation of 1939–41 is enormous. See Ben Cion Pinchuk, "Facing Hitler and Stalin: On the Subject of Jewish Collaboration in Soviet-occupied Eastern Poland," in Zimmerman, *Contested Memories;* Ben Cion Pinchuk, *Shtetl Jews under Soviet Rule* (Cambridge, 1990); Andrzej Żbikowski, "Polish Jews under Soviet Occupation," in Zimmerman, *Contested Memories;* Jan Gross, *Neighbors: The Destruction of the Jewish Community of Jedwabne, Poland* (Princeton, N.J., 2001); and Krzysztof Jasiewicz, *Tygiel narodów: stosunki społeczne i etniczne na ziemiach wschodnich dawnej Rzeczypospolitej* (Warsaw, 2002). For a different perspective, see Marek Wierzbicki, *Polacy i Żydzi w zaborze sowieckim* (Warsaw, 2001).

185. An extreme example of this kind of testimony was the account of a twenty-two-year-old Jewish refugee, who had fled to Vilna in 1939 and had returned to Warsaw in late 1941, a testimony that could have been furnished by any rabid Polish anti-Semite. "Under the Bolshevik occupation Polish anti-Semitism increased markedly. In large part the Jews themselves are responsible for this. They used every occasion to jeer the Poles and to yell, 'Your Poland is gone' . . . Jewish Communists denounced Poles, Jews disarmed Polish soldiers and spit in their face" (AR I, no. 932). A twenty-year-old Jewish woman who had fled to Grodno told Yekhiel Gorny that "the Jews received the Bolsheviks with great joy. They [Jews] had a feeling of arrogance and pride, they treated the Poles with condescension, taunted them for their weakness" (AR I, no. 934). On the other hand, many accounts described the arrests of Jews by the Soviets as well as the widespread reluctance of Jewish refugees from the German-occupied zone of Poland to accept Soviet citizenship.

186. Ringelblum, *Ksovim fun geto,* 2:444–445.

187. Ibid., 2:261.

188. Ibid., 2:256 Ringelblum noted that there were many Jewish names in the lists of Polish officers who were murdered.

189. Translation from Kermish and Krakowski's edited volume of Ringelblum's *Polish Jewish Relations during the Second World War*, pp. 1–2.

190. See, for example, Edward D. Wynot, "A Necessary Cruelty: The Emergence of Official Anti-Semitism in Poland, 1936–1939," *American Historical Review* 76 (1971): 1035–1058; Emanuel Melzer, *No Way Out: The Politics of Polish Jewry, 1935–1939* (Cincinnati, 1997).

191. See, for example, Feliks Tych, *Długi cień zagłady* (Warsaw, 1999), p. 50.

192. Gunnar S. Paulsson, "Ringelblum Revisited: Polish-Jewish Relations in Occupied Warsaw," in Zimmerman, *Contested Memories*, pp. 179–181. In comparing the survival rates of Jews in Nazi-occupied Warsaw and the Netherlands, Paulsson takes as his starting point for both cases the Jewish population in September 1942, that is, after the first stage of the Great Deportation had ended in Warsaw. It was around that time, he argues, that both Warsaw Jews and Dutch Jews began to go into hiding. Using 60,000 as his starting point for Warsaw Jewry, the number of Jews in the ghetto in September 1942, he asserts that 11,000 survived, about 18 percent. Of the 140,000 Dutch Jews, about 20,000 to 25,000 went into hiding, and 16,000 survived. If one takes the Jewish population in 1939 as a starting point, rather than September 1942, then Ringelblum's assertions stand up much better.

193. Emanuel Ringelblum, *Ksovim fun geto,* 2:382. Paulsson estimated that on the eve

of the August 1944 Polish Uprising, about eight months after Ringelblum wrote this, there were 17,000 Jews in hiding in Warsaw.

194. As reprinted in Kermish and Krakowski's edited volume of Ringelblum's *Polish Jewish Relations during the Second World War*, p. 226.

195. Ibid., p. 305.

196. As Michael Steinlauf notes in his important study *Bondage to the Dead,* Polish passivity toward Jews "was reinforced by three factors: the difficulty of daily life under German occupation, especially the extreme terror; the imposition of the death sentence against those accused of aiding Jews; and the widespread perception that Jews were beyond the Polish universe of obligation, that they were not, in other words, 'ours.'" See Steinlauf, *Bondage to the Dead: Poland and the Memory of the Holocaust* (Syracuse, 1997), p. 41. On the term "universe of obligation," see Helen Fein, *Accounting for Genocide: National Responses and Jewish Victimization during the Holocaust* (Chicago, 1979), p. 33.

197. Translation from Kermish and Krakowski's edited volume of Ringelblum's *Polish Jewish Relations during the Second World War*, p. 7.

198. Some death sentences were meted out at the urging of Żegota and the Jewish National Committee, but Jewish leaders believed that the underground could have done more. See Berman, "Yehudim be'Tsad ha-Ari," pp. 717–723.

199. Ringelblum, *Ksovim fun geto,* 2:213. A good source on Żegota is Teresa Prekerowa, *Konspiracyjna Rada Pomocy Żydom w Warszawie 1942–1945* (Warsaw, 1982). Żegota included representatives from the Polish Peasant Party (SL), the Polish Socialist Party (PPS), the Polish Democratic Party (SD), and, for a time, members of the Catholic Front for the Rebirth of Poland (FOP). It also included Jewish representatives from the Jewish National Committee (Adolf Berman) and from the Bund (Leon Feiner). Although its resources were limited, Żegota did, in fact, do a lot of important work. Its very existence reminded Jews that they were not *completely* alone and that at least some parts of Polish society wanted to help them. It distributed small monthly grants to Jews in hiding and helped many find apartments. One of its more important services was to provide forged identity documents. See also Israel Gutman and Shmuel Krakowski, *Unequal Victims: Poles and Jews during World War Two* (New York, 1986), pp. 252–300.

200. Ibid., p. 247. Ringelblum, as we have seen, had a tendency to label as "fascist" anyone he viewed as an opponent of the progressive Left. In 1934 he also called the Jewish bourgeoisie "fascist."

201. The three sources are a personal conversation with Wanda Rotenberg, Tel Aviv, July 1999; Rachel Auerbach, *Varshever tsvoes,* p. 210; and Yankev Tselemenski, *Mitn farshnitenem folk* (New York, 1963), p. 281.

202. These accounts may not contradict each other. Wolski's disgruntled lover might have divulged the secret to Łakiński, who then informed the Gestapo. Prekerowa also states that it was Łakiński who betrayed the hideout

203. Yad Vashem Archives, Protocol of Małgorzata Szadurska and Halina Michałecka (Wolski's sisters), July 29, 1988.

204. Ibid.

205. His exact words, according to Hirschaut, were "I'd rather go to Kiddush Hashem together with them" (Yekhiel Hirschaut, *Finstere nekht in Paviak* [Buenos Aires, 1948], p. 199). It is impossible, of course, to corroborate this.

206. Ibid.

207. The text of the letter is in Emanuel Ringelblum, *Kapitlen geshikhte fun amolikn yidishn lebn in Poyln,* ed. Jacob Shatzky (Buenos Aires, 1953), p. 545.

208. Mark Dvorzhetsky, "Farshvaygn-oder dertseyln dem gantsn emes?" *Yidisher kemfer,* July 20, 1945.

209. Wasser, "A vort vegn Ringelblum Arkhiv," pp. 15–16. Wasser wrote these words in Stalinist Poland, and he may have embellished their tone to fit the prevailing party line. Their general tenor, however, indeed comports with Ringelbum's known views.

210. AR I, no. 1190. Translation from Kermish, *To Live with Honor,* pp. 58–59.

SELECTED BIBLIOGRAPHY

INTRODUCTION

Archive of ŻIH (Jewish Historical Institute), Warsaw
    Ber Mark Collection
    Ringelblum Archive
Archive of Kibbutz Lohamei Ha'Getaot
    Collection 358, Adolf Berman Papers
Archive of United States Holocaust Memorial Museum
    RG-15.079M Clandestine Archives of the Warsaw Ghetto, Ringelblum Archives
Jacob Lestschinsky Archives, Hebrew University, Jerusalem, File 258
Joint Distribution Committee Archives
Yad Vashem Archives
    AR I (Ringelblum Archives)
    AR II (Ringelblum Archives)
    Rachel Auerbach Collection
    Individual Testimonies
Yivo Archives
    Cherikover Collection
    Hersh Wasser Collection
    YIVO Collection

UNPUBLISHED MATERIAL

Abramson, Henry. "Deciphering the Ancestral Paradigm: A Hasidic Court in the Warsaw Ghetto." Unpublished paper, United States Holocaust Memorial Museum Symposium: The Ghettos of the Holocaust, New Research and Perspectives on Definition, Daily Life, and Survival.

Ben-Sasson, Havi. "Polin u'polanim b'einei yehudei Polin b'tkufat milhemet ha-olam ha-shniya." Ph.D. dissertation, Hebrew University, Jerusalem, Israel, 2005.

Epsztein, Tadeusz. "Introduction to the Catalog of the Warsaw Ghetto's Underground

Archive." Jewish Historical Institute, Warsaw / United States Memorial Holocaust Museum, 2005.

Kuznitz, Cecile. "The Origins of Yiddish Scholarship and the YIVO Institute for Yiddish Research." Ph.D. dissertation, Stanford University, 2000.

Polonsky, Antony. "Jews, Poles, and the Problems of Divided Memory." Unpublished manuscript.

DOCUMENT COLLECTIONS

Congress for Jewish Culture. *Ershter alveltlekher yidisher kultur kongres: Pariz 17–21 September 1937.* Paris, 1937.

Kermish, Joseph, ed. *To Live with Honor and Die with Honor: Selected Documents from the Warsaw Ghetto Underground Archives Oyneg Shabbath.* Jerusalem, 1986.

Sakowska, Ruta, ed. *Archiwum Ringelbluma: Listy o zagładzie.* Warsaw, 1997.

———. *Archiwum Ringelbluma: Dzieci-tajne nauczanie w getcie Warszawskim.* Warsaw, 2001.

———. *Archiwum Ringelbluma, getto warszawskie: lipiec 1942–styczeń 1943.* Warsaw, 1980.

Żbikowski, Andrzej, ed. *Archiwum Ringelbluma: Relacje z Kresów.* Warsaw, 2000.

INTERVIEWS

Vladka Meed, Beit lohamei ha'getaot, July 2000.

Anna Olcanetzka, New York, June 1999.

Esther Rochman, June 1990.

Wanda Rotenberg, Tel Aviv, July 1999.

Shlomo Shvaitser, Holon, Israel, July 1998.

Jacob Waisbord, Queens, New York, July 1998.

Leah Wasser, Givatayim, Israel, June 2004.

MEMOIRS

Adler, Stanislaw. *In the Warsaw Ghetto, 1940–1943: The Memoirs of Stanislaw Adler.* Jerusalem, 1982.

Agnon, Shmuel Yosef. "B'tokh iri:perek ehad shel sipur ehad." In *Sefer Buczacz,* ed. Yisroel Cahan. Tel Aviv, 1955.

Auerbach, Rachel. *Baym letstn veg.* Tel Aviv, 1977.

———. *Bi'hutsot Varsha.* Tel Aviv, 1954.

———. *Varshever tsvoes.* Tel Aviv, 1974.

———. "Vi azoy iz oysgegrobn gevorn der Ringelblum Arkhiv." *Arbeter vort,* June 27, 1947.

Berman, Adolf. *Vos der goyrl hot mir bashert.* Kibbutz Beit Lohamei Ha'Getaot, 1980.

———. "Yehudim be'Tzad ha-Ari." In *Entsyklopediya shel ha-Geluyot,* ed. Yitzhak Greenbaum. Varsha, vol. 6, pt. B. Jerusalem, 1953.

Berman, Basia. *Dziennik z Podziemia.* Warsaw, 2000.

———. "Rydzewski: Ringelblum oyf der Arisher zayt." *Linke Poalei Tsiyon,* April 19, 1948.

Borzykowski, Tuvia. *Tsvishn falndike vent.* Warsaw, 1949.

Brand, Khaim. "Emanuel Ringelblum." *Zhurnal tsum tsenyorikn yoyvl fun Dr. Emanuel Ringelblum Arbeter Ring Tsvayg 612.* New York, 1957.

Celemenski, Yankev. *Mitn farshnitenem folk.* New York, 1963.

Cherikover, Eliyahu. "Ber Borochov, vi ikh ken im." *Literarishe bleter,* no. 51 (1927).

Donat, Alexander. *The Holocaust Kingdom.* New York, 1965.

Draenger, Gusta Davidson. *Justyna's Narrative.* Amherst, Mass., 1996.

Drozdowski, Marek Marian. *Wspomnienia o Stefanie Starzyńskim.* Warsaw, 1982.

Dubnow, Semen Markovich. *Kniga zhizni.* Jerusalem and Moscow, 2004.

Dvorzhetsky, Mark. *Yerushalayim d'Lite in Kamf un Umkum.* Paris, 1948.

Eck, Natan. *Ha'toim b'darkhei ha-mavet.* Tel Aviv, 1960.

———. "In baginen fun yorhundert." In *Galitsianer Yidn: yoyvl bukh,* ed. Tsentral Farband fun Galitsianer Yidn in Argentine. Buenos Aires, 1966.

———. "Mit Emanuel Ringelblum in Varshever Geto." *Di goldene keyt,* no. 24 (1955).

———. "Mitn dikhter in di yorn fun khurbm." *Di goldene keyt,* no. 49 (1964).

Edelman, Marek. *Strażnik.* Warsaw, 1999.

Ernest, Stefan. *O wojnie wielkich Niemiec z Żydami Warszawy 1939–1943.* Warsaw, 2003.

Finkelshteyn, Leo. "Yehoshue Perle." In *Yidn fun a gants yor,* ed. Yehoshua Perle. Tel Aviv, 1990.

Folman, Chava. "Tora b'khoninut matmedet." In Yudka Helman, ed., *Edut* 11 (1994).

Fuks, Marian, ed. *Adama Czerniakowa dziennik getta warszawskiego.* Warsaw, 1983.

Grynberg, Michał, ed. *Pamiętniki z getta warszawskiego: fragmenty i regesty.* Warsaw, 1988.

Gutman, Israel. *Mered ha-Netzurim: Mordecai Anielewicz u-milhemet geto Varshah.* Merhaviyah, Israel, 1963.

Heller, Tzvi. "Mi-zikhronotai." In *Sefer Buczacz,* ed. Yisroel Cahan. Tel Aviv, 1955.

Herzen, Alexander. *Sochineniia v deviati tomakh.* Moscow, 1954.

Hilberg, Raul, Stanislaw Staron, and Josef Kermisz, eds. *The Warsaw Diary of Adam Czerniakow.* New York, 1982.

Hirschaut, Hanka Warhaftig. "Emanuel Ringelblum: Hero as Teacher." *The Forward,* January 4, 1985.

Hirszfeld, Ludwik. *Historia jednego życia.* Warsaw, 1989.

Jagur, Orna. *The Hiding Place.* Lodz, 1997.

Katsh, Abraham, ed. *The Warsaw Diary of Chaim Kaplan.* New York, 1965.

Katzenelson, Yitzhak. *Vitel Diary.* Tel Aviv, 1964.

Kazdan, Khaim-Shloyme, ed. *Lerer yizkor bukh.* New York, 1954.

Kener, Yakov. *Emanuel Ringelblum: a held in legion fun di giburei Yisroel in geto.* Munich, 1948.

———. *Kvershnit.* New York, 1947.

Korzen, Meir. "Emanuel Ringelblum lifnei ha-milhama u'biyameha harishonim." *Yediot Yad Va-shem,* no. 21–22 (1959); no. 23–24 (1960).

Kruk, Herman. *The Last Days of the Jerusalem of Lithuania.* Edited and with an introduction by Benjamin Harshav. Translated by Barbara Harshav. New Haven and London, 2002.

Lewin, Abraham. *A Cup of Tears.* Antony Polonsky, ed. Oxford, 1988.

Leybel, Daniel. "Mit Ringelblumen." *Nayvelt* (April 1954).

Mahler, Rafael. "Doktor Emanuel Ringelblum, historiker fun poylishe yidn un fun zeyer umkum un gvure." In *Sefer Sanz,* ed. Rafael Mahler. Tel Aviv, 1970.

———. "Shaul Amsterdam." In *Sefer Sanz,* ed. Rafael Mahler. Tel Aviv, 1970.

Mark, Ber. "Shmuel Winter's Togbukh: A vogiker tsushtayer tsu der erev khurbm oyf-shtand dokumentatsie." *Bleter far geshikhte* 1–2 (1950).

Mazor, Michael. "The House Committees in the Warsaw Ghetto." In *The Holocaust as Historical Experience,* ed. Yehuda Bauer and Nathan Rotenstreich. New York, 1981.

———. *The Vanished City.* New York, 1993.

Mozner, Yehuda. "Mayne yugnt yorn in Buczacz." In *Pinkas Galitsie,* ed. Nehemia Tsu-ker (Buenos Aires, 1945).

Naygroshl, Mendl. "Vegn E. Ringelblum's yugnt yorn," In *Zhurnal tsum tsen yorikn yoyvl fun Dr. Emanuel Ringelblum. Arbeter Ring Tsvayg 612.* New York, 1957.

Pohorila, David. "Pirkei Hayai." In *Sefer Buczacz,* ed. Yisroel Cahan. Tel Aviv, 1955.

Ravitch, Melekh. *Mayn leksikon.* 3 vols. Montreal, 1945/1947/1958.

Reich-Ranicki, Marcel. *Moje Życie.* Warsaw, 2000.

Ringelblum, Emanuel. *Kronika getta warszawskiego.* Warsaw, 1983.

———. *Ksovim fun geto.* 2 vols. Tel Aviv, 1985.

———. *Ktavim ahronim.* Jerusalem, 1994.

Rudawski, Michał. *Mój obcy kraj?* Warsaw, 1996.

Seidman, Hillel. *Togbukh fun Varshever geto.* Buenos Aires, 1947.

Silkes, Genie. "Tsvey bagegenishn mit Emanuel Ringelblum." YIVO Archives, Hersh Wasser Collection (HWC), 44.1.

Sutzkever, Avrom. *Vilner geto.* Buenos Aires, 1947.

Tenenbaum-Tamaroff, Mordecai. *Dapim min ha'dleka: pirkei yoman, mikhtavim, maama-rim.* Jerusalem, 1984.

Trunk, Yekhil Yeshaye. *Poyln.* 7 vols. New York, 1953.

Turkow, Jonas [Yanosh]. *Azoy iz es geven.* Buenos Aires, 1948.

Vinaver, Maxim. "Kak my zanimalis' istoriei." *Evreiskaia starina,* no. 1 (1908).

Wasser, Hersh. "Fun fraytik biz fraytik." *Arbeter tsaytung,* April 15, 1948.

———. "Arkhiyon Ha-geto: mifalo shel Dr. E. Ringelblum." *Yediot beit lohamei hagetaot* 9–10 (1955).

———. "A vort vegn Ringelblum Arkhiv." Unpublished manuscript, YIVO Archives, New York.

Wdowinski, David. *And We Are Not Saved.* London, 1964.

Weichert, Michal. *Zikhroynes: Milkhome.* Vol. 3. Tel Aviv, 1963.

Winkler, Jerzy. "Getto walczy z niewolą gospodarczą." *BŻIH,* no. 3–4 (1950).

Zerubavel, Jacob [Yankev]. *Geshtaltn.* Tel Aviv, 1967.

Zuckerman, Yitzhak. *A Surplus of Memory.* Berkeley, 1993.

———. "Zikhronotav v dvorav shel Yitzhak Zuckerman." *Edut* 11 (1994).

NEWSPAPERS

Arbeter kultur	*Di fraye yugnt*	*Haint*	*Tsaytshrift*
Arbeter tsaytung	*Folkshilf*	*Nasz przegląd*	*Yunger historiker*
Bleter far geshikhte	*Forverts*	*Tog*	

PRIMARY SOURCES

Borochov, Ber. *Nationalism and the Class Struggle: A Marxist Approach to the Jewish Problem.* Westport, Conn., 1972.

———. *Shprakh-forshung un literatur geshikhte.* Tel Aviv, 1966.

Borwicz, Michał, ed. *Pieśń ujdzie cało. Antologia wierszy o Żydach pod okupacją niemiecką.* Warsaw, Lodz, and Kraków, 1947.

Dobroszycki, Lucjan, ed. *The Chronicle of the Lodz Ghetto.* New Haven and London, 1984.

Donat, Alexander, ed. *Death Camp Treblinka: A Documentary.* New York, 1979.

Friedman, Philip, ed. *Martyrs and Fighters: The Epic of the Warsaw Ghetto.* New York, 1954.

Huberband, Shimon. *Kiddush Hashem: Jewish Religious and Cultural Life during the Holocaust.* Edited by Jeffrey Gurock and Robert Hirt. New York, 1987.

Kalmanovich, Zelig. "Togbukh fun Vilner geto." *YIVO bleter* 3 (n.s.) (1997).

Katzenelson, Yitzhak. *Yidishe geto ksovim.* Edited by Yehiel Shaintukh. Tel Aviv, 1984.

Kermish, Joseph, ed. "Daily Entries of Hersh Wasser." Introduction and notes by Joseph Kermish. *Yad Vashem Studies* 15 (1983).

———. *Itonut ha-Mahteret ha-Yehudit b'Varsha.* 6 vols. Tel Aviv and Jerusalem, 1979–97.

Maciejewska, Irena, ed. *Władysław Szlengel: Co czytałem umarłym.* Warsaw, 1977.

Opoczynski, Peretz. *Gezamlte shriftn.* New York, 1951.

Reportazhn fun Varshever geto. Edited and with an introduction by Ber Mark. Warsaw, 1954.

Reshimot. Edited by Tzvi Shner. Tel Aviv, 1970.

Reyzen, Zalmen, ed. *Pinkes fun der geshikhte fun Vilne in di yorn fun milkhome un okupatsiye.* Vilna, 1922.

Ringelblum, Emanuel [Heler, Munie]. "Bleter far geshikhte." *Arbeter tsaytung,* no. 35 (1934).

———. [Heler, Munie]. "A blutige vorenung." *Di fraye yugnt,* no. 3 (1925).

———. "Dr. Y. Shiper un di virtshaftsgeshikhte fun di yidn in Poyln." *Vilner tog,* no. 295 (1926).

———. "Dray yor seminar." *Yunger historiker,* no. 1 (1926).

———. "Dzieje zewnętrzne Żydów w dawnej Rzeczypospolitej," *Żydzi w Polsce odrodzonej.* Vol. 1. Warsaw, 1932.

———. "Der Ershter Pruv." *Literarishe bleter,* no. 15 (1929).

———. "An interesanter onheyb." *Literarishe bleter,* no. 27 (1931).

———. *Kapitlen geshikhte fun amolikn yidishn lebn in Poyln.* Edited and with an introduction by Jacob Shatzky. Buenos Aires, 1953.

———. "A nayer tsushtayer." *Literarishe bleter,* no. 22 (1938).

———. "An opklang fun der frantsoyzisher revolutsie." *Yivo bleter,* no. 3 (1932).

———. *Polish-Jewish Relations during the Second World War.* Edited by Joseph Kermish and Shmuel Krakowski. Evanston, 1974.

———. *Projekty i próby przewarstwowienia Żydów w epoce Stanisławowskiej.* Warsaw, 1934.

———. "Shmuel Zbytkover." *Tsiyon,* no. 3 (1938).

———. "A Solide Geshikhte Arbet." *Literarishe bleter,* no. 39 (1929).

———. *Tsu der geshikhte fun yidishn bukh un druk in Poyln in der tsveyter helft fun akhtsentn yorhundert.* Vilna, 1936.

———. "Tsum Kultur Kongres." *Arbeter tsaytung,* no. 29 (1931).

———. "Yidishe Kultur Konferents." *Vilner tog,* no. 235 (1926).

———[Heler, Munie]. "Der Yidishisher Visnshaftlekher Institut." *Di fraye yugnt,* no. 11 (1926).

——— [Heler, Munie]. "Der Yidisher Visnshaftlekher Institut un di arbeter yugnt." *Di fraye yugnt,* no. 7 (1926).

——— [Heler, Munie]. "Di yidishe arbetershaft un di geshikhtsvisnshaft." *Di fraye yugnt,* no. 1 (1924).

———. "Yidn in Varshe in 18tn yorhundert." *Historishe shriftn* 2 (1937).

———. *Żydzi w powstaniu Kościuszkowskim.* Warsaw, 1938.

———. "Żydzi w świetle prasy warszawskiej wieku XVIII." *Miesięcznik Żydowski* 6, 7/8, 9/10 (1932).

———. *Żydzi w Warszawie, cz. I: Od czasów najdawnieszych do ostatniego wygnania w 1527.* Warsaw, 1932.

Ringelblum, Emanuel, and Rafael Mahler. *Teksty źródłowe do nauki historii Żydów w Polsce i we wschodniej Europie.* Warsaw, 1930.

Roskies, David. *The Literature of Destruction.* Philadelphia and New York, 1988.

Shabad, Tsemakh, and Moshe Shalit, eds. *Vilner zamlbukh.* 2 vols. Vilna, 1916/1918.

Yidisher Visnshaftlekher Institut. *Der alveltlekher tsuzamenfor fun Yidishn Visnshaftlekhn Institut.* Vilna, 1936.

SECONDARY SOURCES

Aaron, Frieda. *Bearing the Unbearable: Yiddish and Polish Poetry in the Ghettos and Concentration Camps.* Albany, 1990.

Aleksiun, Natalia. "Polish Jewish Historians before 1918: Configuring the Liberal East European Jewish Intelligentsia." *East European Jewish Affairs,* no. 2 (winter 2004).

Alter, Viktor. *Di Yidnfrage in Poyln.* Warsaw, 1937.

Arad, Yitzhak. *Ghetto in Flames.* New York, 1982.

Arens, Moshe. "The Jewish Military Organization (ŻZW) in the Warsaw Ghetto." *Holocaust and Genocide Studies* 19, no. 2 (2005).

Avineri, Shlomo. *The Making of Modern Zionism.* New York, 1981.

Bacon, Gershon. "Woman?–Youth?–Jew? The Search for Identity of Jewish Young Women in Interwar Poland." In *Gender, Place, and Memory in the Modern Jewish Experience,* ed. Judith Tydor Baumel and Tova Cohen. London, 2003.

Balaban, Meyer. "Buczacz." *Evreiskaia entsyklopediia.* Edited by L. Katsnelson and Baron David Ginzburg. Vol. 5. Saint Petersburg, n.d.

———. "Zagadnienia historjozofji żydowskiej w stosunku do historji Żydów w Polsce." *Miesięcznik Żydowski,* no. 2 (1932).

Bauer, Yehuda. *My Brother's Keeper: A History of the American Joint Distribution Committee, 1929–1939.* Philadelphia, 1974.

Bauer, Yehuda, and Nathan Rotenstreich, eds. *The Holocaust as Historical Experience.* New York, 1981.

Bauman, Zygmunt. "On Immoral Reason and Illogical Morality." In *POLIN: A Journal of Polish Jewish Studies,* no. 3 (1988): 296–297.

Baumel, Judith Tydor, and Tova Cohen, eds. *Gender, Place, and Memory in the Modern Jewish Experience.* London, 2003.

Belis, Shloyme. *Portretn un problemen.* Warsaw, 1964.

Bender, Sarah. "Arkhiyon hamahteret bi'Bialystok." In *Mi'gniza,* ed. Israel Gutman. Jerusalem, 1997.

Berenstein, Tatiana. "Praca przymusowa Żydów w Warszawie w czasie okupacji." *BŻIH* 45–46 (1963).

Biderman, Israel. *Mayer Balaban: Historian of Polish Jewry.* New York, 1976.

Blatman, Daniel, ed. *Geto varsha, sipur itonai.* Jerusalem, 2002.

———. *Lema'an heruteinu v'herutkhem: ha-Bund b'Polin 1939–1949.* Jerusalem, 1996.

———. "Women in the Jewish Labor Bund." In *Women in the Holocaust,* ed. Dalia Ofer and Lenore J. Weitzman. New Haven, 1998.

Blumenthal, Nachman. "Der historiker—tsu der ferter yortsayt." *Arbeter tsaytung,* no. 3 (1948).

———. "Ha shir al ha-Radzynai shel Yitzhak Katzenelson." *Yediot beit lohamei ha-getaot,* no. 8 (January 1955).

Bornstein, I. *Budżety gmin wyznaniowych żydowskich w Polsce.* Warsaw, 1929.

Brenner, Michael. *The Renaissance of Jewish Culture in Weimar Germany.* New Haven, 1996.

Browning, Christopher. *Ordinary Men: Reserve Police Battalion 101 and the Final Solution in Poland.* Lincoln, Nebr., and Jerusalem, 2004.

Buchsbaum, Natan. "A PPSesher broshur gegn Bund un Bundizm." *Arbeter tsaytung,* no. 4 (1938).

———. "Kultur Kongres." *Arbeter tsaytung,* no. 44 (1931).

———. [L. B.]. "Der Yivo un di yidishe arbetershaft." *Arbeter tsaytung,* no. 29 (1931).

Chajn, Leon, ed. *Materiały do historii Klubów Demokratycznych i Stronnictwa Demokratycznego w latach 1937–1939.* Warsaw, 1964.

Cherikover, Eliyahu, ed. *Oyfn Sheydveg.* Paris, 1939.

Chojnowski, Andrzej. "The Jewish Question in the Work of the Instytut Badań Spraw Narodowościowych in Warsaw." *Polin* 4. Oxford, 1989.

Cienciala, Anna. "Tajne oblicze GL-AL i PPR: Dokumenty." *Sarmatian Review,* no. 2 (April 2001).

Cohen, Boaz. "The Birthpangs of Holocaust Research in Israel." *Yad Vashem Studies,* no. 33 (2005).

Cohen, Mitchell, ed. *Class Struggle and the Jewish Nation.* New Brunswick, 1984.

Cohen, Natan. *Sefer, sofer v'iton: merkaz ha-tarbut ha'yehudit b'varsha, 1918–1942.* Jerusalem, 2003.

Cohen, Raya. "'Against the Current': Hashomer Hatzair in the Warsaw Ghetto," *Jewish Social Studies* 7, no. 1 (2000).

———. "Emanuel Ringelblum: Between Historiographical Tradition and Unprecedented History." *Gal-ed* 15–16 (1997).

———. "Ha-emnam derekh ahat? Od al mikoma shel hitnagdut ha-mizuyenet b'getaot." In *Ha-shoah: historiyah vezikaron: kovetz maamarim shai le-Yisrael Gutman.* Jerusalem, 2001.

Corni, Gustavo. *Hitler's Ghettos: Voices from a Beleaguered Society, 1939–1944*. London, 2003.

Czeley-Wybieralska, Małgorzata, and Symcha Wajs. "Emanuel Ringelblum jako historyk medycyny żydowskiej." In *Archiwum Historii i Filozofii Medycyny*, bk. 2, 1988.

Datner, Szymon. "*Wiadomości*, podziemny organ prasowy w Getcie Warszawskim z Okresu po Wielkim 'Wysiedleniu.'" *BŻIH*, no. 76 (1970).

Dawidowicz, Lucy. *From That Time and Place*. New York. 1989.

———. *The War against the Jews*. New York, 1975.

Dobroszycki, Lucjan. "YIVO in Interwar Poland: Work in the Historical Sciences." In *The Jews of Poland between the Two World Wars*, ed. Israel Gutman et al. Hanover and London, 1989.

Dold, Maria. "'A Matter of National and Civic Honor': Majer Balaban and the Institute of Jewish Studies in Warsaw." *East European Jewish Affairs* (winter 2004).

Dray: [ondenkbukh] / Pola Elster, Hersh Berlinski, Eliyahu Erlikh. Tel Aviv, 1966.

Dubnow, Semen Markovich. *Fun zhargon tsu Yidish*. Vilna, 1929.

———. *Nahpesa venahkora: kol kore el ha-nevonim ba-am, ha-mitnadvim le-esof homer le-binyan toldot bene yisrael be-polin ve-rusiya*. Odessa, 1892.

———. "Ob izuchenii istorii russkikh evreev i ob uchrezhdenii istoricheskogo obshchest-va." *Voskhod* (April–September 1891).

Eck, Natan. "B'shulei mishal Ringelblum." *Yediot Yad Vashem*, no. 12 (1957).

Edelman, Marek. "Kwestia moralności." *Midrasz* (November 1999).

Ehrenfreund, Jacques. *Mémoire juive et nationalité allemande: les Juifs berlinois à la Belle Epoque*. Paris, 2000.

Eidelberg, Shlomo, ed. *Yitzhak Schiper: Evaluation and Selected Writings*. New York, 1966.

Eisenbach, Artur. "Jewish Historiography in Interwar Poland." In *The Jews of Poland between the Two World Wars*, ed. Israel Gutman et al. (Hanover and London, 1989).

Engel, David. *In the Shadow of Auschwitz: The Polish Government-in-Exile and the Jews, 1939–1942*. Chapel Hill, N.C., and London, 1987.

Engelking, Barbara, and Jacek Leociak. *Getto warszawskie: przewodnik po nieistniejącym mieście*. Warsaw, 2001.

Ezrahi, Sidra DeKoven. *By Words Alone: The Holocaust in Literature*. Chicago, 1980.

Fein, Helen. *Accounting for Genocide: National Responses and Jewish Victimization during the Holocaust*. Chicago, 1979.

Fishman, David. "Bamerkungen vegn Vaynraykh's role in der antviklung fun der yiddisher visnshaft." *Yivo bleter* 3 (1997).

———. *Embers Plucked from the Fire: The Rescue of Jewish Cultural Treasures in Vilna*. New York, 1996.

Fishman-Tamir, Arnon. "Mikhtav l'Arnon Fishman-Tamir." *Yalkut moreshet* (1964).

Frankel, Jonathan. *Prophecy and Politics*. Cambridge, 1981.

Garncarska-Kadari, Bina. *Bihipusei derekh: Poalei Tsiyon Smol b'Polin ad milhemet ha'olam ha'shniya*. Tel Aviv, 1995.

Gelber, Nahum. "Kishrei Galitsiya Dubnow." *He-avar* (1961).

Gieysztor, Aleksander, Jerzy Maternicki, and Henryk Samsonowicz, eds. *Historycy warszawscy ostatnich dwóch stuleci*. Warsaw, 1986.

Giterman, Yitzhak. "Gmiles khesed kasses in der itstiger shverer tsayt." *Folkshilf* (April 1936).

Gottesman, Itzik Nakhmen. *Defining the Yiddish Nation: The Jewish Folklorists of Poland.* Detroit, 2003.

Greenbaum, Alfred Abraham. *Jewish Scholarship and Scholarly Institutions in Soviet Russia: 1918–1953.* Jerusalem, 1978.

Grupińska, Anka. *Ciągle po kole.* Warsaw, 2000.

———. "Ja myślałam że wszyscy są razem." *Tygodnik Powszechny Online* (December 2000).

Guterman, Alexander. *Kehilat Varsha bein shtei milhamot ha'olam.* Tel Aviv, 1997.

Gutman, Israel. "Adam Czerniakow: The Man and His Diary." In *The Catastrophe of European Jewry,* ed. Israel Gutman and Livia Rothkirchen. Jerusalem, 1976.

———. "The Distinctiveness of the Lodz Ghetto." In *The Last Ghetto: Life in the Lodz Ghetto, 1940–44,* ed. Michal Unger. Jerusalem, 1995.

———. *The Jews of Warsaw.* Bloomington, 1989.

———. "Kiddush Hashem and Kiddush Hachayim." *Simon Wiesenthal Center Annual* 1 (1984).

———, ed. *Mi'gniza.* Jerusalem, 1997.

Gutman, Israel, and Shmuel Krakowski. *Unequal Victims: Poles and Jews during World War Two.* New York, 1986.

Handelsman, Marceli. *Historyka: zasady metodologji i teorji poznania historycznego: podręcznik dla szkół wyższych.* Warsaw, 1928.

———. *Rozwój narodowości nowoczesnej.* Warsaw, 1924.

Hersey, John. *The Wall.* New York, 1950.

Hertz Jacob, Sholem [Hart, Y.]. *Doyres Bundistn.* Vol. 2. New York, 1956.

———. "Nisht di khronik fun di tragishe Varshever yidn." *Unzer tsayt,* no. 9 (1953).

———. "Vegn Ringelblum's notitsn fun Varshever geto." *Unzer tsayt,* no. 7–8 (1953).

Hirschaut, Julien. "Dr. I Schiper-zayn lebn un shafn." *Fun noentn over.* New York, 1955.

———. *In gang fun der geshikhte.* Tel Aviv, 1984.

Hoffman, Eva. *Shtetl: The Life and Death of a Small Town and the World of Polish Jews.* Boston, 1997.

Horowitz, Sara. "Gender, Genocide and Jewish Memory." *Prooftexts* (January 2000).

———. *Voicing the Void: Muteness and Memory in Holocaust Fiction.* Albany, 1997.

Hundert, Gershon. *Jews in Poland-Lithuania in the Eighteenth Century.* Berkeley, 2004.

Hyman, Paula. *Gender and Assimilation in Modern Jewish History.* Seattle, 1995.

Inglot, Stefan. "Rozwój historii społecznej i gospodarczej." *Kwartalnik Historyczny* 1 (1937).

Kassow, Samuel. "Community and Identity in the Interwar Shtetl." In *The Jews of Poland between the Two World Wars,* ed. Israel Gutman et al. Hanover and London, 1989.

———. "Jewish Communal Politics in Transition: The Vilna Kehille, 1919–1920." In *YIVO Annual,* vol. 20, ed. Deborah Dash Moore. Evanston, 1991.

———. "The Left Poalei Zion in Interwar Poland." In *Yiddish and the Left: Papers of the Third Mendel Friedman International Conference on Yiddish,* ed. Gennady Estraikh and Mikhail Krutikov. Oxford, 2001.

Kirshenblatt-Gimblett, Barbara. "Coming of Age in the Thirties: Max Weinreich, Edward Sapir and Jewish Social Science." In *YIVO Annual,* vol. 23, ed. Deborah Dash Moore. New York, 1996.

Kligsberg, Moshe. "Di yidishe yugnt bavegung in Poyln tsvishn beyde velt milkhomes." In *Studies on Polish Jewry, 1919–1939,* ed. Joshua A. Fishman. New York, 1974.

Korzec, Paweł. "Antisemitism in Poland as an Intellectual, Social, and Political Movement." In *Studies on Polish Jewry, 1919–1939*, ed. Joshua Fishman. New York, 1974.

Kuczynski, Meir. "Shmuel Winter." In W*loclawek v'ha-Svivah: Sefer Zikaron*, ed. Katriel Tkhursh and Meir Korzen. Tel Aviv, 1967.

Laor, Dan. *Hayei Agnon*. Tel Aviv, 1998.

Laqueur, Walter. *The Terrible Secret*. London, 1980.

Leociak, Jacek. *Tekst wobec zagłady*. Wrocław, 1997.

Lestschinsky, Jacob. "Emanuel Ringelblum." *Forverts*, December 20, 1953.

Lev, Yitzhak. "Problemen fun der yidisher virklekhkayt in der ibergangstkufe." *Arbeter tsaytung*, no. 48 (1934).

Leyvik, H. "Tsvey dokumentn." *Der tog*, March 17, 1952.

Litman, Jacob. *The Economic Role of the Jews in Medieval Poland: The Contribution of Yitzhak Schiper*. Lanham, Md., 1984.

Mahler, Rafael. "Emanuel Ringelblum's briv fun Varshever Geto," *Di goldene keyt*, no. 46 (1963).

———. "Geshikhte un folk," *Yunger historiker*, no. 1 (1926).

———. *Historiker un Vegvayzer*. Tel Aviv, 1967.

——— [Uriel]. "Di kultur badaytung far di yidishe masn in dem kamf farn territorialn arbeter tsenter." *Arbeter tsaytung*, no. 50 (1935).

———. "Mikhtavei E. Ringelblum m' Zbąszyń v'al Zbąszyń." *Yalkut moreshet*, no. 2 (1964).

———. "A religiez-natsionalistishe teoriye fun der yiddisher geshikhte." *Bleter far geshikhte*, no. 1 (1934).

———. "Ringelblum, the Historian of Polish Jewry." In *A Commemorative Symposium in Honor of Dr. Emanuel Ringelblum and his "Oyneg Shabbat" Underground Archives*. Jerusalem, 1983.

———. "Di teories fun der Yidisher kultur geshikhte." *Yunger historiker*, no. 1 (1926).

———. "Teorje historiografji żydowskiej o rozwoju dziejowym kultury żydowskiej." *Miesięcznik Żydowski*, no. 12 (1933).

———. "Tsi zenen di yidn geven a handlsfolk?" *Yivo bleter*, nos. 1–2 (1934).

———. "Yugnt-tnuat ha'noar shel poalei tsiyon smol b'Polin." *Ha-tsionut*, no. 6 (1973).

Marcus, Joseph. *Social and Political History of the Jews in Poland*. Berlin, New York, and Amsterdam, 1983.

Mark, Ber. *Khurves dertseyln*. Lodz, 1947.

———. "Der letster baal pinkes fun Varshever geto." In Archives of ŻIH, Ber Mark Collection, no. 14.

———. *Megiles 'Oyshvits*. Tel Aviv, 1977.

———. *Umgekumene Shrayber fun di getos un lagern*. Warsaw, 1954.

———. "Yudenratishe ahavas yisroel: an entfer oyfn bilbul fun H. Leyvik." *Bleter far geshikhte*, no. 3 (1952).

Maternicki, Jerzy. *Historiografia Polska XX Wieku*. Wrocław, 1982.

Meltzer, Emanuel. *Maavak medini b'Malkodet: Yehudei Polin, 1935–1939*. Tel Aviv, 1982.

Mendelsohn, Ezra. *Zionism in Poland: The Formative Years, 1915–1926*. New Haven and London, 1981.

Mayzel, Nakhman. *Geven amol a lebn*. Buenos Aires, 1951.

———. *Noente un eygene*. New York, 1957.

Mintz, Matityahu. *Ber Borochov: Ha-ma'agal ha-rishon.* Tel Aviv, 1978.

———. *Naye tsaytn, naye lider.* Tel Aviv, 1993.

Miron, Dan. "Between Science and Faith." In *YIVO Annual,* vol. 19, ed. Deborah Dash Moore. Evanston and New York, 1990.

Morawski, Karol. *Kartki z dziejów Żydów warszawskich.* Warsaw, 1993.

Moyn, Samuel. *A Holocaust Controversy: The Treblinka Affair in Postwar France.* Hanover, N.H., and London, 2005.

Nathans, Benjamin. "On Russian Jewish Historiography." In *The Historiography of Imperial Russia: The Profession and Writing of History in a Multinational State,* ed. Thomas Sanders. Armonk, N.Y., 1999.

Nayshtat, Melekh. *Khurbm un oyfshtand fun di Yidn in Varshe: eydes bleter un azkores.* Tel Aviv, 1948.

Niger, Samuel, and Jacob Shatzky, eds. *Leksikon fun der nayer Yidisher Literatur.* 8 vols. New York, 1956–1981.

Nir-Rafalkes, Nahum. "Eretsyisroeldige un khutsle'eretsdige likvidatsie in unzer bavegung." *Tsu di shtraytfragn inm Poyle Tsiyenizm.* Jerusalem, 1934.

Ofer, Dalia, and Lenore J. Weitzman. "Gender Issues in Diaries and Testimonies of the Ghetto: The Case of Warsaw." In *Women in the Holocaust,* ed. Dalia Ofer. New Haven, 1998.

———. "Her View through My Lens: Cecilia Slepak Studies Women in the Warsaw Ghetto." In *Gender, Place, and Memory in the Modern Jewish Experience,* ed. Judith Tydor Baumel and Tova Cohen. London, 2003.

———, eds. *Women in the Holocaust.* New Haven, 1998.

Oppenheim, Israel Oppenheim. "Yahas 'Poalei Tsiyon Smol' b'Polin l'rayon ha-halutsi u li'he-haluts: ha-reka ha'rayoni." *Gal-ed,* no. 6 (1982).

Paulsson, Steven. *Secret City: The Hidden Jews of Warsaw, 1940–1945.* New Haven, 2002.

Penslar, Derek. *Shylock's Children: Economics and Jewish Identity in Modern Europe.* Berkeley, 2001.

Pisulińska, Joanna. *Żydzi w polskiej myśli historycznej doby porozbiorowej.* Rzeszów, 2004.

Podolska, Aldona. *Służba Porządkowa w getcie warszawskim w latach 1940–1943.* Warsaw, 1996.

Polen, Nehemiah. *The Holy Fire: The Teachings of Rabbi Kalonymous Kalman Shapira, the Rebbe of the Warsaw Ghetto.* New York, 1994.

Polonsky, Antony. "The Bund in Polish Political Life, 1935–1939." In *Jewish History: Essays in Honor of Chimen Abramsky,* ed. Ada Rapoport-Albert and Steven Zipperstein. London, 1988.

Prekerowa, Teresa. *Konspiracyjna Rada Pomocy Żydom w Warszawie 1942–1945.* Warsaw, 1982.

Raykhman, Motl. "Der umkum fun Radzyner Rebbn." In *Vlodava v'Hasviva: Sefer Zikaron,* ed. Shimon Kantz. Tel Aviv, 1974.

Reyzen, Zalmen. "In rekhtn oyfbli." *Literarishe bleter,* no. 51 (1927).

Rose, Norman. *Chaim Weizmann: A Biography.* New York, 1986.

Rosenfeld, Alvin. *A Double Dying.* Bloomington and London, 1980.

Roskies, David G. *Against the Apocalypse: Responses to Catastrophe in Modern Jewish Culture.* Cambridge, Mass., 1984.

———. "*Landkentenish*: Yiddish Belles Lettres in the Warsaw Ghetto." In *Holocaust Chronicles: Individualizing the Holocaust through Diaries and Other Contemporaneous Personal Accounts,* ed. Robert Moses Shapiro. New York, 1999.

———. "Maks Vaynraykh: oyf di shpurn fun a lebedikn over." *Yivo bleter* 3 (1997).

Roland, Charles. *Courage under Siege.* New York, 1992.

Rybarski, Roman. *Handel i polityka handlowa Polski w XVI stuleciu.* Poznań, 1928.

Sakowska, Ruta. "Archiwum Ringelbluma-Ogniwem Konspiracji Warszawskiego Getta." *BŻIH,* no. 152 (1989); nos. 153, 155–156 (1990).

———. "Biuro Informacji i Propagandy KG Armii Krajowej a Archiwum Ringelbluma." *BŻIH,* nos. 162–163 (1992).

———. *Dwa Etapy: hitlerowska polityka eksterminacji Żydów w oczach ofiar: szkic historyczny i dokumenty.* Wrocław, 1986.

———. "Komitety domowe w getcie warszawskim." *BŻIH,* no. 61 (1967).

———. "Opór cywilny getta warszawskiego." *Biuletyn Żydowskiego Instytutu Historycznego,* nos. 86–87 (1973).

———. "Relacje Daniela Fligelmana—członka "Oyneg Szabat." *BŻIH,* no. 1–2 (1986).

———. "Szlamek-ucieknier z ośrodka zagłady w Chełmnie nad Nerem." *BŻIH,* nos. 131–132 (1984).

———. "Two Forms of Resistance in the Warsaw Ghetto." *Yad Vashem Studies* 21 (1991).

———. "Wiadomości, ARG i raport o zagładzie. Status Archiwum Ringelbluma w getcie szczątkowym Warszawy." *Kwartalnik historii Żydów* 1, no. 213 (2005).

Scharf, Rafael. "Literature in the Ghetto in the Polish Language: *Z otchłani*—From the Abyss." In *Holocaust Chronicles: Individualizing the Holocaust through Diaries and Other Contemporaneous Personal Accounts,* ed. Robert Moses Shapiro. New York, 1999.

Schiper, *Yitzhak.* "Di elste geshikhte fun Varshever Yidn." *Haynt,* September 9, 1932.

Shaintukh, Yehiel. "Yitzhak Katzenelson v'ha-korei ha-ivri." *Edut* 11 (1994).

Shalit, Moshe, ed. *Oyf di khurves fun milkhomes un mehumes: pinkes fun gegent-komitet EKOPO.* Vilna, 1930.

Shamir, Joseph. *Shmuel Breslav: ha-maavak v'hatikvah.* Tel Aviv, 1994.

Shandler, Jeffrey, ed. *Awakening Lives: Autobiographies of Jewish Youth in Poland before the Holocaust.* Introduction by Barbara Kirshenblatt-Gimblett, Marcus Moseley, and Michael Stanislawski. New Haven, 2002.

Shapiro, Robert Moses, ed. *Holocaust Chronicles: Individualizing the Holocaust through Diaries and Other Contemporaneous Personal Accounts.* New York, 1999.

Shatzky, Jacob. "Emanuel Ringelblum der historiker." *Zhurnal tsum tsenyorikn yoyvl fun Dr. Emanuel Ringelblum Arbeter Ring Tsvayg 612.* New York, 1957

———. "Finf un tzvantig yor YIVO." In Jacob Shatzky, *Shatzky bukh.* New York, 1958.

Shavitsky, Ziva. "Yitzhak Katzenelson." In *Holocaust Literature: An Encyclopedia of Writers and Their Work,* vol. 1, ed. S. Lillian Kremer. New York and London, 2003.

Shenfeld, Rut. "Wladyslaw Szlengel v'shirato b'geto Varsha." *Gal-ed* 10 (1987).

Sherman, Betsalel. "Poyle Tsiyenizm kontra linkistishe umetumikayt." *Tsu di shtraytfragn inm Poyle Tsiyenizm.* Jerusalem, 1934.

Singer, Isaac Bashevis [Y. Bashevis]. "Arum der yidisher literatur in Poyln." *Di tsukunft* (August 1943).

Sosis, Israel. "Di historishe 'visnshaft' fun yidishn visnshaftlekhn institut." *Tsaytshrift,* no. 4 (1930).

Stanislawski, Michael. *Tsar Nicholas I and the Jews.* Philadelphia and New York, 1983.

Steinlauf, Michael. *Bondage to the Dead: Poland and the Memory of the Holocaust.* Syracuse, 1997.

Szarota, Tomasz. *U progu zagłady: zajścia antyżydowskie i pogromy w okupowanej Europie.* Warsaw, 2000.

Szulkin, Michał. "Dr. Emanuel Ringelblum-historyk i organizator podziemnego archiwum getta warszawskiego." *BŻIH* 30 (1973).

Tartakover, Aryeh. "Ha-makhon le'medayei yahadut b'varsha." In *Studies in Memory of Moses Schorr,* ed. Louis Ginzberg and Abraham Weiss. New York, 1944.

Tomaszewski, Jerzy. *Preludium Zagłady: Wygnanie Żydów Polskich z Niemiec w 1938 r.* Warsaw, 1998.

Trunk, Isaiah. *Geshtaltn un gesheenishn.* Tel Aviv, 1983.

———. *Judenrat.* Lincoln, 1972.

———. "Le-toldot ha-historiografiyah ha-yehudit-polanit." *Gal ed,* no. 3 (1976).

———. *Lodzher geto.* New York, 1962.

Tsuker, Nehemia, ed. *Pinkes Galitsie.* Buenos Aires, 1945.

Tych, Feliks. *Długi Cień Zagłady: szkice historyczne.* Warsaw, 1999.

Unger, Michal, ed. *The Last Ghetto: Life in the Lodz Ghetto, 1940–44.* Jerusalem, 1995.

———. *Lodz: aharon ha-getaot b'polin.* Jerusalem, 2005.

Urinski, G., M. Volansky, and N. Tsukerman, eds. *Pinkes fun der shot Pruzhene.* Pruzany, 1930.

Wasser, Hersh. "IKOR in Varshever geto." *Dos naye lebn,* no. 57 (1947).

———. "Vi iz es geven?" *Unzer veg* (March 1954).

Weichert, Michal. *Yidishe aleynhtlf 1939–1945.* Tel Aviv, 1962.

Weinreich, Max. "Derkenen dem haynt." *YIVO bleter,* no. 1 (1931).

Wisse, Ruth. *I. L. Peretz and the Making of Modern Jewish Culture.* Seattle, 1991.

Wynot, Edward D. "'A Necessary Cruelty': The Emergence of Official Anti-Semitism in Poland." *American Historical Review* 76, no. 4 (October 1971).

Yerushalmi, Yosef. *Zakhor: Jewish History and Jewish Memory.* New York, 1989.

Żbikowski, Andrzej, ed. *Archiwum Ringelbluma: Relacje z Kresów.* Warsaw, 2000.

———. "Polish Jews under Soviet Occupation." In *Contested Memories: Poles and Jews during the Holocaust and Its Aftermath,* ed. Joshua D. Zimmerman. New Brunswick, N.J., and London, 2003.

Zelnik, Reginald. *The Perils of Pankratova.* Seattle, 2005.

Zerubavel, Jacob. "Tsu di problemen fun Polyle-Tsienizm." *Arbeter tsaytung,* nos. 37, 38 (1934).

Zimmerman, Joshua D., ed. *Contested Memories: Poles and Jews during the Holocaust and Its Aftermath.* New Brunswick, N.J., and London, 2003.

Zipperstein, Steven J. "The Politics of Relief: The Transformation of Russian Jewish Communal Life during the First World War." In *Studies in Contemporary Jewry* 4, ed. Jonathan Frankel. Oxford, 1988.

INDEX

Abramovich, Sholem, 80
Abramovich, Ze'ev, 45–46
acculturation, 20, 23, 232, 236
Adamowicz, Irena, 298
adolescents, 122
AGAD (Archiwum Główne Akt
  Dawnych), 67
Agnon, Shmuel Yosef, 17, 18
agriculture, 71–72, 380
Akiva, 348
Al Ha-mishmar, 55
alcohol, 340
Aleikhem, Sholom, 117, 366
Aleynhilf ("self help"), 91–92, 112–19;
  and Auerbach, 207, 208; budget, 221;
  and children, 260; and communal
  responsibility, 142; cooperation in,
  166; corruption in, 125–26, 127;
  cultural organizations, 116–18;
  Czerniakow on, 111; and deportation, 301, 306; documentation of,
  216; efficacy of, 237, 348; and food
  supplies, 173; and human dignity,
  207; and Judenrat, 94–95, 112, 115,
  133, 135, 136, 338; leadership of,
  426n97; legal status, 114–15; moral
  pretensions, 142; and Oyneg Shabes,
  14, 208; and philanthropy, 110;

propaganda, 181; Public Sector, 106,
  119, 123, 124, 127, 135 (see also house
  committees); and Rabinowitz, 161;
  refusing help, 248; relief funds, 114,
  115, 124–26; and resistance, 335; and
  Ringelblum, 90, 91–92, 94, 95;
  statistical section, 175; and Winter,
  156; and work certificates, 303, 337–
  38; youth in, 370
Allies, Western, 157, 180, 311, 353, 360
alltagsgeschichte (the history of everyday
  life), 11, 13
Alter, Victor, 44
Alterman, Nathan, 366
Amalek, 196–97
American Red Cross, 115
Amsterdam, Saul (later: Gustaw
  Henrykowski), 23–24
Anielewicz, Mordecai: death of, 371–72;
  and LPZ, 431–32n17; Oyneg Shabes
  material on, 366, 370–72; resistance
  efforts of, 160, 164, 355, 359; Zuckerman on, 435n75
Anti-Fascist Bloc, 164, 294–95, 474n157
anti-Semitism: and Bolshevik Revolution, 24; decline in, 376; and economic issues, 31; effect on nation,
  71–72; and fascism, 76, 380, 383; and

anti-Semitism (continued)
ghetto life, 93; and immigration, 32; increases in, 83–84, 98; and Jewish historians, 50; and Jewish survival, 61; of Nazis, 296, 345; perspectives on, 235; and Polish-Jewish relations, 20, 375; Ringelblum on, 70, 274, 373; and self-help, 90

Apel, Cecylia, 267

apprentices, 74–75, 342

Arabs, 34, 103

Arbeter Heym, 35

Arbeter kultur, 42

Arbeter tsaytung: and difficulties of LPZ, 47; on interconnectedness of Jews, 43; and LPZ finances, 47; Ringelblum's articles in, 37–38, 41, 76; on territorialization, 44, 45–46; on Yiddishism, 40

Arbeter vort, 47

architecture, Jewish, 84–85

archives: archives from other ghettos, 210–12; destruction of archives, 211, 443n6; and Siemieński, 67. See also Oyneg Shabes

armbands, 107, 251, 256

art, Jewish, 5, 84, 167

artifacts, 167, 213, 218

artisans, 280–81

Artstein, Zecharia, 326

Arukh, Shulkhan, 167

Asch, Sholem, 51, 272, 385

Asher b. Jehiel, 167

assimilation: attempts to reverse, 12; and emancipation, 231; Heller on, 63; and Jewish historical scholarship, 53, 60; and the Jewish Question, 31; and Landkentenish movement, 85; Ringelblum on, 83; and Soviet Union, 229, 235; support for, 20, 21, 22; threat of, 414n56; and women, 240

Asz, Nathan, 153

Attempts to reform the Jewish occupational structure in the reign of Stanislaw August (Ringelblum), 57, 71–72

Auerbach, Rachel: collection of archive materials, 220; diary, 200–201, 218; employment, 157; on Final Solution reports, 311; on German film crews, 209; on Jewish police, 313; and Krzepicki, 309–10; and Opoczynski, 218; as Oyneg Shabes collaborator, 185, 198–208, 217; postwar essays, 218; retrieval of archives, 1–2, 150, 205–206, 216, 445n20; and Ringelblum, 200, 360; and Słapak, 178; and soup kitchens, 116, 125; survival of, 146, 205; and Winter, 155, 158, 159; and YIVO, 147

Auerswald, Heinz, 94, 420–21n8

Auschwitz, 160, 161, 198

Austria, 71

authors. See writers of the Oyneg Shabes Archive

autonomy, Jewish, 52, 54, 75

Avreml (Rabbi), 120

Babylonia, 52

Balaban, Meyer: on acculturation, 411n13; autobiography, 223; death of, 372; Galician origins, 17; and Institute of Jewish Studies, 58; Oyneg Shabes material on, 366; publications, 51; and Ringelblum, 54–55, 66, 411n16; scholarship of, 9, 49, 53–55, 85; and schools offering Jewish history, 58

Balfour Declaration (1917), 24, 33, 47, 48, 103

Balicki, Zygmunt, 50

bank accounts, 279

Baranowski, Ryszard, 319

Barash, Ephraim, 212, 470n88

Baron, Salo, 17

baths, ritual, 209, 429n151

Bauer, Yehuda, 14, 100–103

Baym letstn veg (Auerbach), 198

BBC, 298–99, 345

begging: avoidance of, 250; beggars' chants, 257; of children, 251, 256–57, 258, 259, 264; reactions to, 254–55; of refugees, 270

behavior of Jews: documentation of,

154–55, 387; personal vs. civic behavior, 376–77; perspectives on, 231–32, 234, 235–38; Różycki on, 255; self-centeredness, 189, 236, 242; of youth, 370. *See also* passivity of Jews

Beiler, Abram, 292–93

Belorussia (Ostland), 297

Bełżec, 292, 295, 299, 300

Berenhholtz, Esther, 268

Berenson, Leon, 374

Bergelson, David, 24, 96

Bergen Belsen, 161, 197

Berliner, Meir, 310

Berlinski, Hersh, 150–51, 180, 337, 357, 466n17

Berman, Adolf: in Aryan Warsaw, 337, 357; and Bloch, 162; on children, 260, 261; and essays of Ringelblum, 365, 372; and Hashomer Hatzair, 164; and Jewish National Committee, 334; letter to New York YIVO, 2, 385–86; and Ovnt kursn, 36; relief work, 105; and resistance, 383; and Ringelblum's escape, 27, 157, 360; on soup kitchens, 119; underground work of, 360–61

Berman, Basia: in Aryan Warsaw, 337, 357; and library, 261; and Ringelblum's escape, 27, 360; and Shur, 338; and Słapakowa's essay, 244, 248; underground work of, 360–61

Berman, Jacob, 62

Bernhard Hallman, 4–5

Bernstein, Yitzhak, 147

Berson and Bauman Hospital for Jewish Children, 264–66

beys din (religious court), 122

B'hutsot varshe (Auerbach), 198

Biała Podlaska, 350

Bialer Hasidim, 161

Bialik, Chaim Nachman, 301

Bialik, H. N., 349

Białystok Ghetto: archive of, 210, 211, 212; leadership of, 470n88; Oyneg Shabes material on, 378; resistance in, 356, 385–86; synagogue massacre, 285

Biłgoraj, 292

binyan haaretz, 48

biographies of contributors, 146

Birenbaum, Halina, 461n91

Birobidzhan territory, 45, 46

Biuletyn Informacyjny, 298

Black Monday, 106

Blatman, Daniel, 240

Bleter far geshikhte, 59, 64, 76

Bloch, Eliezer Lipe: and Kon, 155; as Oyneg Shabes collaborator, 147, 161–62; relief work, 341; and resistance, 353; and Ringelblum, 435n62; and "Two and a Half Years," 226

Blumenfeld, Diana, 182, 359

Blumenthal, Nachman, 8, 15, 206

Bolek, 246–47

Bolshevik Revolution (1917), 24

book trade, 69

"Boots" (Ringelblum), 251–52

Borochov, Ber: economic theory, 44–45; influence of, 29–33, 406n8; on interconnectedness of Jews, 43; and Jewish historical scholarship, 63; and LPZ, 28; and Poalei Tsiyon movement, 21; proponents of, 47; and Ringelblum, 29; and territorialization, 44; and Yiddishism, 22, 28, 29–30, 39, 78, 406n9; and Zionism, 32

Borochov School, 146

Borochovism, 33, 60, 61

Borowski, 364

"bottom Jews," 288, 289

bourgeoisie: and Borochov, 32; and fascism, 76; and the Jewish Question, 31; and Judenrat, 135–36; moral failings of, 12, 348; and *rekrutchina,* 170–71; and Yiddish, 39

boycotts on Jewish businesses, 98, 191, 275–76, 374

Brajtman, Chil, 263–64

Brandt, Karl Georg, 341

Braude, Shie, 125

Braude-Heller, Anna, 265

Breslav, Shmuel: death of, 191, 336; on massacres, 286; as Oyneg Shabes collaborator, 162–65; on Polish-

Breslav, Shmuel (*continued*)
Jewish relations, 377–78; and
resistance, 164–65; underground
press, 215; Zuckerman on, 435n75
Brest pogrom, 98
bribery, 227
Brocksmeier, Abraham, 139
Broyde, Shie, 118, 366
Buchsbaum, Natan, 21–22, 40–42, 44,
47, 408n48
Buczacz, 17–18
Budzyn labor camp, 162
Bund: and CYSHO, 34; *doikayt*
emphasis of, 28; and gender roles,
240; and humanism, 230; ideology,
44; and Jewish National Committee
(ŻKN), 354; and the Jewish
Question, 31; and Marxism, 77; and
news of Final Solution, 298; and
Oyneg Shabes, 148, 292, 458n42;
perceptions of, 21; platform, 44–45;
and Rabinowitz, 161; reactions to,
327; and resistance, 294, 474n157;
and Ringelblum, 8, 48, 473n149;
significance of, 35; and Winter, 155;
and Yiddish culture congress, 43;
and YIVO, 40
Bureau of Information and Propaganda
of the Polish Home Army (Armia
Krajowa), 298
burial of archives: authorization for, 333;
burial of Auerbach's writing, 201–
202; burial of first cache, 388; burial
of second cache, 5, 223, 357–58; and
condition of caches, 215–16; and
deportation, 303; of Lodz archive,
443n6; responsibility for, 2–4, 146,
219
burial of dead, 122, 129, 139, 265, 329,
465n142
business owners, 156, 279

cafes, 213, 259, 316
"Cafes" (Różycki), 253
candor in Oyneg Shabes, 171
cannibalism, 213
Capistrano, Juan de, 66

capitalism, 56, 63, 369
Case White campaign, 103
caste, Jews as, 63, 64
Catholic Church, 98, 110, 358–59, 433n32
CEKABE (Centrala Kas Bezprocentowych), 91, 100, 112, 175
Celemenski, Jacob, 362
cemeteries, 167
censors, 292
census fight of 1910, 21
CENTOS (Central Organization for
the Care of Orphans): and Aleyn-
hilf, 116; autonomy of, 115; criticism
of, 261; efforts of, 112, 260, 262; and
food supplies, 173; and IKOR, 117–
18; leadership of, 119; and Oyneg
Shabes project, 148; support from,
267
Central Commission of House
Committees, 126, 127, 134, 161
Central Committee to Support Work in
the Shops (CKPPwS), 341–42
Central Council for Social Welfare
(NRO), 115
Central Yiddish School Organization
(CYSHO), 26, 34, 40, 41–42
Chagall, Bella, 178
charity *(tsedaka)*, 120, 124
Charny, Daniel, 178
Chełm, 275
Chełmno death camp: news of, 128, 293,
302; Oyneg Shabes reports on, 296,
298, 299; reactions to, 219; Szlamek's
account of, 287–92
Cherikover, Eliyahu: on future of Jews,
230; and *Historishe shriftn,* 87; and
Ringelblum, 83, 412n21; and
Ukrainian pogroms, 213; and YIVO,
81, 82, 88, 418n118; and Zbąszyń
refugee crisis, 102
children, 259–68; begging of, 251, 256–
57, 258, 259, 264; and Catholic
Church, 358–59, 433n32; and
Czerniakow, 452n70; day care
centers, 260; deaths of, 260, 261,
265–66, 303, 453n75; and deportation, 216, 268, 303, 306, 308, 309,

367; emotional states of, 266–67; and Final Solution, 288, 289; food for, 118–19, 138–39, 260, 262, 266; and German officials, 341; hospital for, 264–66; and house committees, 122, 260, 261, 262; interviews, 263; and Koninski, 173–74; Opoczynski on, 189–90; Oyneg Shabes material on, 169, 189–90, 217, 261–63; programs for, 300–301; refugees, 189–90, 260, 262, 263, 266, 267; and relief efforts, 260–61; Ringelblum's efforts for, 358–59; of shtetlekh, 269; theatrical productions, 123; at Treblinka, 309–10; and "Two and a Half Years," 227; and women's roles, 240; Yiddish activities for, 117–18. *See also* CENTOS; orphans and orphanages

"Children on the Pavement" (Opoczynski), 189, 261

Chitowski (Rabbi), 132–33

Cholodenko, David, 148

Christian population, 68

"Chronicle of a Single Day" (Goldin), 140, 315–16

Chwila, 51

"City of Slaughter" (Bialik), 349

civil defense organization (LOPP), 105

civil society, 94, 254, 268

clothing, 122, 235–36, 260–61, 277

Cohen, Raya, 164

collective memory of Jews, 11

Commission for Polish Relief, 115

communes, 163

communication, 157

Communists, 475n167; and Amsterdam, 23; and Anti-Fascist Bloc, 164; and assimilation of Jews, 234; and Birobidzhan, 45, 47; and CYSHO schools, 41–42; leadership of, 23; and LPZ, 28, 35, 43, 46; and Oyneg Shabes, 148; platform, 44; and Poalei Tsiyon movement, 24; and resistance, 294; and territory for Jews, 28; and youth, 35; and Żydokummuna (Jewish-Communist cabal), 379

community and self-help, 90

community chronicles *(pinkesim)*, 84, 87–88

concentration camps, 132, 133, 361

Congress Poland, 269

converts, 110, 349, 358–59

Coordinating Committee, 112–13, 114. *See also* Aleynhilf ("self help")

correspondence: from deportees, 213; of Germans, 216, 306; left by individuals, 211; in Oyneg Shabes, 186; warnings in, 292, 293

corruption: archive material on, 227, 239; and deportation, 302; Opoczynski on, 190; Różycki on, 255; scope of, 187, 232

Council of the Four Lands (Vaad Arba Aratsot), 56

"Counterattack" (Szlengel), 321–23

credit societies. *See* free loan societies *(gmiles hesed kases)*

crimes of Nazis, 213

cultural organizations, 36–37

Cultural Revolution of USSR, 41

culture: attempts to eradicate, 167, 297, 366–67; congresses on, 42, 43; cultural organizations, 116–17 *(see also specific organizations)*; cultural resistance, 170; and Jewish historical scholarship, 64; and language, 42–43; leadership of, 366; loyalty to Jewish culture, 110; and Oyneg Shabes collaborators, 147; party influence on, 42–43; proletarian culture, 38; role of women in, 243; and territorialization, 43–44; and youth, 240

curfews, 259

Czerniakow, Adam: and Aleynhilf, 92, 94; on children, 452n70; criticism of, 94, 111, 420–21n8; and deportation, 183, 301; on house committees, 135; on illegal trade, 279; and Jewish masses, 110; and labor camps, 132; leadership of, 108, 133–34; and Lehman, 224; and Ringelblum, 8, 134, 212, 452n70; and Sekstein, 5;

Czerniakow, Adam *(continued)*
suicide of, 195, 301, 335; and Yiddish,
117
Czuma, 105

Danzig Jewish museum, 97
Dawidowicz, Lucy, 79, 92
death camps, 287–92. *See also specific
camps*
death tolls: burial of dead, 122, 129, 139,
265, 329; of children, 260, 261, 265–
66, 303, 453n75; from disease, 92,
107; German sources on, 459n64; in
labor camps, 131, 133, 429–30n158;
stabilization of, 283; from starvation,
92, 107, 108, 137, 139. *See also* Final
Solution
Delegate's Office, 372
denial of Holocaust, 206
Department of Provisioning and Supply
(ZZ), 156, 157
deportation, 299–311; of children, 216,
268; and contents of archives, 216;
and correspondence, 213; effect on
archive activities, 222; and employment, 301, 302, 303–304, 337–38; and
families, 303; and Final Solution,
286, 299–300; and German film
crews, 209; hiding from, 154–55, 159–
60, 303, 304, 355, 381; and intelligentsia, 306, 308, 367; and Jewish police,
302; and Judenrat, 183; Oyneg
Shabes material on, 154–55, 194–95,
201, 213, 216, 222–23, 295, 297, 306–
309, 311; Perle on, 194–95; reactions
to, 325; resettlement announcement,
301–302; and restrictions on movement, 305–306; rumors about, 302;
by Soviets, 228; statistics on, 307–
309; voluntary reporting for, 306–
307. *See also* resistance
Der Ruf, 294
Der Untergang des Judentums (Heller),
63
Der Yidisher Arbeter, 22
"The destruction of Warsaw" (Perle),
195, 196, 343

Deutsche Allgemeine Zeitung, 345
"Di Bone" (The ration card), 257
Di fraye yugnt, 34, 37
"Di Goldene Keyt" (Peretz), 330
diaries: of archive collaborators, 218,
304 (*see also specific individuals*);
collection of, 206, 223; left behind,
211; on secrecy, 218
Diaspora: and autonomy, 52; and
Borochov, 32; Dubnow on, 64;
economies of, 29, 31, 32; and Israel,
199; and Palestine, 44; and political
parties, 28, 44; and scholars, 50–51
Dickstein, Halina, 338
dietary laws, 250
Dinur, Ben Zion, 200, 207
disease: deaths from, 92, 107; decline
in, 283; and disinfections, 129; and
house committees, 122; and poverty,
254; in refugee centers, 219–20. *See
also* typhus
disinfections (*parówki*), 111, 129–31, 227,
289, 429n152
district commissions, 124
Dobroszycki, Lucjan, 52
do-dortn (here-there), 28, 45, 46, 48,
163
doikayt (hereness), 28, 193
Dos vort, 151, 185
Draenger, Gusta Davidson, 7
Dror-Frayhayt: and Anti-Fascist Bloc,
164; and Bloch, 162; and Gutkowski,
151; and Katzenelson, 152, 324, 325,
326; and LPZ, 431–32n17; and news
of massacres, 285; and resistance, 163,
294, 336, 356; and Ringelblum,
354–55
Dubnow, Simon: Abramovich portrayal
of, 80; on collection of Jewish
history, 9, 386, 410n3; on future of
Jews, 231; Mahler on, 64; and *Oyfn
sheydveg,* 230; scholarship of, 38,
51–52; translation of work, 178; and
Yunger Historiker Krayz, 62
Dukus (Katsyzne), 51
Dutch Jewry, 381
Dvorzhetsky, Mark, 387

Dzieje robotnikow przemyslowych w Polsce (Wóycicki), 74

Eastern Europe, 10, 52
Eck, Natan: on Bloch, 435n62; and Katzenelson, 326, 332; and Landau, 159–60; on Opoczynski, 186; on outlooks of Jews, 239; on Ringelblum, 18, 90, 116, 119, 125, 126, 426n96
Economic History of the Jews in Poland during the Middle Ages (Schiper), 25, 56
economics: and anti-Semitism, 66; Borochovian economics, 44–45; and businesses of Jews, 279, 423n62; of Diaspora, 31, 32; and family life, 240–41; fragility of, 249; in ghettos, 107, 108, 176; and Jewish historical scholarship, 63; and Jewish survival, 61–62; in Nazi strategies, 374; Oyneg Shabes reports on, 176, 280, 297, 455n116; and Polish-Jewish relations, 374, 376, 377, 378; Ringelblum on, 72; trade, 190, 191, 279, 374; and "Two and a Half Years," 227, 279–83; underground economy, 279
Edelman, Marek, 159, 336, 458n42
education: in Buczacz, 19; and house committees, 122; IKOR lectures, 118; Ringelblum on, 416n88; secular education, 68; Shul Kult (school movement), 173; and teachers, 266, 306; of women, 244; women's roles in, 240; of workers, 36–37, 39; and youth, 241
Eighth International Congress, 84
Einhorn, Aaron, 231, 234
Eisenbach, Arthur, 17, 24, 62, 105
Eisenberg, Shayne, 179
Eizenshtat, Borukh, 36–37
Eizenshtat, Marysia, 208
Ejszyszki, 286
EKOPO (Jewish Committee to Help War Victims), 96–97
El Alamein, German defeats at, 5
election law of 1907, 21

Elster, Pola, 119, 150–51, 360
Elster, Wanda, 365
emancipation, 231
employment: and deportation, 301, 302, 303–304, 337–38; occupations, Jewish, 45, 71–72, 93, 147, 280–81; opportunities for, 157, 283, 423n62; wages, 227, 281, 282; of women, 241–42, 243–50, 309; work numbers, 303, 309, 340
Engelking, Barbara, 129
Enlightenment, 230–31, 255
entrepreneurship, 72
Epsztein, Tadeusz, 444n15, 445–46n29
equal rights, 44
Erlich, Eliyahu, 150–51
"Erntefest" (Operation Harvest Festival), 361
esn teg tradition, 121–22
"The Eternal Jew" (film), 209
Evreiskaia starina, 52, 53
expulsions of Jews, 107, 270–78, 297
extermination program. *See* Final Solution
extortion, 190

"The Face of the Jewish Child" (Koninski), 262–63
families: and deportation, 182, 303; and economy of ghetto, 282; loss of, 313, 314–15, 325, 339; and poverty, 240–41, 250; and social collapse, 340; women's role in, 243–50
fascism, 76, 345, 348, 380, 383
fashion, 251–52
Feld, Yehuda: and CENTOS, 261; on children, 266; on ghetto life, 258–59; as Oyneg Shabes collaborator, 148, 185; on role of women, 240
Feldman, Eleazar, 66
Femina Theater, 301
feminism, 240
film crews, German, 209
Final Solution: accounts of, 215, 217, 285–87, 455n2; Chełmno death camp, 287–92; and disbelief of Jews, 184, 301–302; documentation of, 295;

Final Solution *(continued)*
  gas chambers, 287, 315, 456–57n15;
  massacres, 285–86; motivations
  behind, 296; Oyneg Shabes reports
  on, 148, 150, 152, 295–97, 311–13, 335,
  355; psychological effects of, 216;
  scope of, 351; "second stage," 296. *See
  also* deportation; resistance
Finekind, Moshe, 81
Finkelstein, 277–78
First, Israel, 339
Fishman-Tamir, Arnon, 102
"Five Minutes to Twelve" (Szlengel), 323
Fligelman, Daniel: as Oyneg Shabes
  collaborator, 147, 176–77, 229; on
  Polish-Jewish relations, 276;
  Ringelblum on, 177; and Vilna
  refugees, 286; and Wilner, 286
Fogel, Dvora, 200
folk song archive, 223
folklore, 60–61, 223, 361
Folkshilf (journal): and Giterman, 95,
  97; language of, 98; Ringelblum's
  role in, 91, 95, 100, 342; scope of, 99,
  100
Folkspartei, 77
Folman, Chava, 293, 350
food: for children, 260, 262, 266; and
  closure of ghetto, 107–108; and
  corruption, 227; and deportation,
  307; and disinfections, 130; and
  economy of ghetto, 282; and film
  crews, 209; German food policies,
  115; in German shops, 340; and labor
  camps, 131, 132; money for, 220–21;
  prices, 302–303; shops offering, 254;
  smuggling, 423n63; from Soviet
  Union, 187. *See also* hunger and
  starvation; soup kitchens
"Four Sons" (Szlengel), 319
France, 71
Franciszkańska 30, 157, 158
Frankel, Jonathan, 32
free loan societies (*gmiles hesed kases*),
  88, 95, 98–99
Frenk, Ezriel, 65
Freud, Jacob, 18

Freud, Sigmund, 202
Friedman, Philip: Galician origins, 17;
  in hiding, 372–73; and Jewish
  Historical Institute, 206, 207; on
  Ringelblum, 420n149; scholarship
  of, 49, 76
From That Time and Place (Dawidow-
  icz), 79
Frydman, Zisha, 109, 127, 335
Furst, Israel, 180

Galicia, 14–15, 17–22, 97, 269, 297
Gancwajch, Abraham, 218, 464n125
gas chambers, 287, 315, 456–57n15
"The Gehenna of Polish Jewry," 296
Gelber, Natan, 17
Gelblum, Halina, 137–38
Gelernter, Joseph, 271
gender ratios in ghetto, 241
General Zionists, 170
Generalgouvernement (General
  Government): and craftsmen and
  artisans, 280; and deportations, 297;
  and labor camps, 131; and relief
  organizations, 114, 115; and Warsaw
  Ghetto, 93
genocide, 387. *See also* Final Solution
Gens, Jacob, 92, 212, 444n11, 470n88
"Gentiles in the Ghetto" (Opoczynski),
  190
Gepner, Abraham: and Central
  Committee to Support Work in the
  Shops, 341, 342; Judenrat membership, 109; and uprising, 158; values,
  110–11; and Winter, 156
German Encyclopedia Judaica, 67
German Social Democratic Party, 369
Germany: army, 106; brutality of, 271,
  272–73, 276, 345–46; collaboration
  with, 232; cynical humor of, 341; and
  deportation, 302; and Final Solution,
  296; German Jews, 110; invasion of
  Poland, 91; Jewish-German relations,
  207, 227, 458n39; and Jewish
  prostitution, 242; Opoczynski on,
  190, 192; Oyneg Shabes material on,
  344; and Polish-Jewish relations, 375;

and revenge of Jews, 347; and "Two and a Half Years," 227; and United States, 114. *See also specific events and people*

Gęsia 19, 123, 135
Gęsia 30, 154, 157
Gęsia Street jail, 374
Gestapo, 308
"The Ghetto Fights Back against Economic Enslavement" (Winkler), 280–81
"The Ghetto Mailman" (Opoczynski), 186–87
"The Ghetto Struggles against Economic Enslavement" (Winkler), 176
ghettos: differences in, 92–93; establishment of, 107–108, 214; illegal entries and exits, 245, 276, 287; medieval ghettos, 231–32; memories of, 13–14; in Nazi strategies, 374; pathologies of, 231–32; Różycki on, 253–56; social order in, 92–95; suffering in, 92; and underground political movements, 118, 119. *See also specific ghettos*
Gilbert, Shlomo, 185
Ginzberg, Asher, 64
Ginzburg, Shlomo, 100–102
Giterman, Yitzhak: and condemned prisoners, 127–28; death of, 342, 356–57; on Germans, 344; hiding from deportation, 325; and IKOR lectures, 118; and Joint Distribution Committee (JDC), 90, 91, 95–100; and Lehman, 224; and Oyneg Shabes, 114, 217, 221, 366; on Polish-Jewish relations, 475n167; relief work, 103, 113–14, 116–17, 341; rescue of Kirman, 307; and resistance, 353; and Ringelblum, 97, 346–47, 421n10; and YIVO, 88, 147, 156
Glatshteyn, Yankel, 208
Główno, 272
Gola v'Nekhar (Kaufman), 64, 76
Goldheimer, 126–27
Goldin, Leyb, 139–42, 148, 185, 315–16
Goldstein, Bernard, 336
Gordonia, 326

Gorny, Yekhiel: diary, 304; as Oyneg Shabes collaborator, 179, 180, 229; on resistance, 313, 356
Graber, David: burial of archives, 3, 4, 146; hiding from deportation, 155, 304; review of archive materials, 219
Grabów, 291
Gradowski, Zalman, 7
Graetz, Heinrich, 38, 51
grass-root mobilization of Jewry, 106, 242
Great Britain: and news of Final Solution, 298–99; perceptions of, 163–64; relationship to Zionists, 237; and White Paper, 47, 48, 103, 163
Great Depression, 45, 72
grief, 202
Grojanowski, Jacob, 291, 456n12
Grójecka 81 bunker, 357, 360, 362–65, 383–85, 472n124
Gruenbaum, Yitzhak, 55
Grzywacz, Nahum, 3, 4, 146, 155, 304
Gurion, David Ben, 32
Gustafsson, Carl, 298
Gutchke (cook), 138
Gutkowski, Eliyahu: and Auerbach, 136; collection of archive materials, 6; and Dror, 354–55; and Final Solution, 293, 295–97; hiding from deportation, 304; and Katzenelson, 325; and resistance, 294; as secretary of Oyneg Shabes, 2, 149, 151–53; and soup kitchens, 221; on stability of ghetto, 283; Treblinka report, 311; and "Two and a Half Years," 226, 229, 281; underground press, 214; and Vilna refugees, 286; and Winter, 157; and YIVO, 147
Gutkowski, Gabriel-Ze'ev, 153
Gutkowski, Jacob, 151
Gutkowski, Luba, 153
Gutman, Hanoch, 326
Gutman, Israel, 156, 157, 158–59, 162
Guzik, Daniel: on Grójecka 81 bunker, 362; hiding from deportation, 325; and Oyneg Shabes Archive, 114;

Guzik, Daniel (*continued*)
  relief work, 113–14, 116; and Ringelblum, 372; underground work of, 361

Ha'am, Ahad, 64
Ha-Hoar Ha-Tsiyoni, 309
haircuts, 130
Hallman, Bernhard, 157, 304, 341
Handelsman, Marceli: criticism of, 65;
  as mentor, 82; on national identity,
  413n35; and 1933 Congress, 83; Oyneg
  Shabes material on, 366; Ringelblum
  on, 57–58; scholarship of, 57–58, 347
Hanukkah, 120
Habsburg Empire, 22, 24
Hashomer Hatzair: German knowledge
  of, 222; leadership of, 34, 162–65;
  and LPZ, 431–32n17; and news of
  massacres, 285; and resistance, 157,
  294, 336; and Ringelblum, 102, 152;
  and Winter, 157
Hasidim and Hasidism, 19, 21, 51, 187,
  329–30, 465n146
Haskala, 19
Haynt, Moment, Nasz przegląd, 51, 66
Hebraist Tekuma, 324
Hebrew culture, 116
Hebrew language: and Bloch, 161; and
  Borochov, 28, 29; censorship of, 293;
  and Hashomer Hatzair, 163; and
  Jewish suffering, 172; and Oyneg
  Shabes collaborators, 147; poetry,
  316, 324; reactions of Jews to, 231;
  and youth movements, 34
he-Haluts, 24, 102
Heinkel, 162
Heler, Munie (pen name), 37
Heller, Otto, 63, 64
Heller, Zvi, 18
Herman, Yehudis. *See* Ringelblum,
  Yehudis (Judyta)
heroism, 327–28
Hershele, 208
Herslow, Carl Wilhelm, 298
Hertzlich, Feige, 119
Herzlich-Blit, Fela, 359
hideouts, 353, 356, 362–65

Himmler, Heinrich, 355, 356
Hirschaut, Hanna, 26
Hirschaut, Yekhiel, 385
Hirszfeld, Ludwik, 129, 205
Histadrut, 28, 47
Historical Commission for All of
  Poland, 82, 84–85, 86–88
Historical Commission of the Central
  Committee of Polish Jews, 206, 207
Historishe shriftn (Cherikover, ed.), 87,
  88
history and historians, 8–14; alienation
  of, 84; and anti-Semitism, 50;
  "counter-professions," 49–50;
  documentation of, 209–10; of
  Galicia, 17; and identity of Jews, 236;
  importance of, 53–54, 63; interest in,
  52, 58; missions of, 49; and non-
  Jewish history, 56; partisan involve-
  ment, 50; perception of, 60; and
  political parties, 29; role in secular
  culture, 77–78; schools offering
  Jewish history, 58; sources, 38, 51–52,
  65, 73, 74, 84; in Warsaw, 51
History of the Jews of Lodz (Friedman),
  89
"History of Warsaw Jewry" (Ringelblum), 216
Hitler, Adolf, 45, 103, 234–35, 348
Höffle, Hermann, 301, 306
Hoffman, Eva, 274–75
holocaust (*khurbm*), 199
Hormuszko, Paweł, 357, 470n92
Horowitz, Sara, 243, 430n178,
  449–50n41
hospital, children's, 264–66
Hospital of St. Sophia, 376
house committees, 91–92, 119–28;
  Central Commission, 126, 127, 134,
  161; and children, 122, 260, 261, 262;
  and collective responsibility, 121–22;
  and compassion of Jews, 238; and
  condemned prisoners, 127–28;
  decline, 128–29; and deportation,
  216, 306; and disinfections, 129–31;
  and district commissions, 124;
  emergence of, 106; and Judenrat, 92,

115, 135; and labor camps, 134; leadership of, 134–35; Opoczynski on, 120, 123, 127, 134, 428n127; Oyneg Shabes material on, 121, 123, 127, 128–29, 134–35, 227, 427n119; raising relief funds, 122–23, 124–26; residences described, 119–20; and Ringelblum, 119, 123, 124–26; role played by, 93; tenant disputes, 122; types of, 120–21; and women, 122, 239–40, 242–43; and Yiddish language, 175

"How the War Changed Our Lives" essays, 263

hoyf (courtyards), 119–20

Huberband, Shimon: and authorship questions, 219; and Chitowski memoirs, 132, 133; death of, 337; on *gam zu l'tovah* stories, 450–51n54; and Kon, 154, 155; as Oyneg Shabes collaborator, 165–69; and Ringelblum, 166; and Soviet Union, 228; typhus infection, 153, 219–20; and Vilna refugees, 286; on women, 240, 242, 449–50n41; and YIVO, 147

humanism, 230

humor in ghetto, 256

hunger and starvation: caloric allotments, 108, 423n63; of children, 263–64; deaths from, 92, 107, 108, 137, 139; and deportation, 303; and dietary laws, 250; and house committees, 122, 127; and Jewish women, 242; medical research on, 238; in Nazi strategies, 374; Oyneg Shabes material on, 136–43, 182; and passivity of Jews, 279; and Polish-Jewish relations, 190–91; reactions to, 231; of refugees, 118, 263–64, 279; scope of problem, 92, 237; and smugglers, 281, 423n63. *See also* food; soup kitchens

hygiene, 251, 340, 341, 424n72, 429n151

identity, Jewish, 52, 231, 236

"If Not Higher" (Peretz), 330

IKOR (Yiddish Cultural Organization), 116–18; and Katzenelson, 324; and Linder, 175; and Rabinowitz, 161; and Winter, 156

immigration: Borochov on, 31–32; to Palestine, 33, 45, 46; restrictions on, 45, 103; and territorialization, 44

impressment of Jewish boys, 170–71, 437nn94,96

In Poylishe Velder (Opatoshu), 51

In the days of Haman the Second (Feld), 148

"In the Streets" (Shaynkinder), 256

inferiority complex of Jews, 110, 232–33, 330, 447–48n20

informers, Jewish: Opoczynski on, 189; as pathology of ghettos, 231; reactions to, 168; Ringelblum on, 351; as topic of Oyneg Shabes, 227

Inglot, Stefan, 418–19n128

Institute for the Study of Nationality Problems, 72

Institute of Judaic Studies, 58, 59

Instytut Nauk Jadaistycznych, 83

intelligentsia, Jewish: archive materials from, 201, 217; attempts to save, 348, 355, 359, 367; cultural background, 19; and deportation, 306, 308, 367; emergence of, 22; employment of, 116, 183; in Grójecka 81 bunker, 362; and house committees, 124; and Jewish masses, 202; as leaders of Aleynhilf, 138; loss of, 172; and Oyneg Shabes collaborators, 147; Ringelblum's essays on, 365–67; in Sanz, 23; and soup kitchens, 136, 143; and "Two and a Half Years," 227; and Yiddishism, 21

intermediate organizations, 14

Israel, 199

Israeli Holocaust Archive and Museum, 206

"It Is Time" (Szlengel), 315

Itsik, Meyer, 205

Izabelin, 357

Jabotinsky, Vladimir, 28
Jagiellonian University, 57
Jagur family, 364, 383–84
Jan Kazimierz University, 56–57
"The Janitor Has the Key" (Szlengel), 321
Jarecka, Gustawa: on deportation, 308; on Final Solution, 6–7, 302; and Judenrat documentation, 306; as Oyneg Shabes collaborator, 147, 181, 182–84
Jaszunski, Joseph, 109
JEAS (Jewish Emigration Society), 173
Jerusalem, 366
Jewish Academic House in Praga, 58
Jewish Academic House in Warsaw, 55
Jewish City Aid Committee (ZKOM), 114, 115, 425n89
Jewish Committee to Help War Victims (EKOPO), 96–97
Jewish Community Council, 66, 105
Jewish Coordinating Committee (ŻKK), 353
Jewish Councils (kahals), 56
Jewish Day of Atonement, 107
Jewish Emigration Society (JEAS), 173
Jewish Fighting Organization (ŻOB): accounts of resistance, 216; and Anti-Fascist Bloc, 295; arms, 158, 325, 356, 466n16; founding of, 165; and Krzepicki, 310; leadership of, 164; and LPZ, 150, 431–32n17; Oyneg Shabes material on, 358, 458n42; preparations for resistance, 192, 294–95; 353–54; ranks of, 342; and Ringelblum, 342, 353, 354, 355; support of, 114, 158, 162, 311
Jewish Historical Institute (ZIH): building, 116, 175; publication of "Khurbm Varshe," 198; retrieval of archives, 2, 150; and survivors' testimonies, 206
Jewish Labor Committee, 206
Jewish Merchants Union (Yidisher Soykhrim Fareyn), 155
Jewish National Committee (ŻKN): and Auerbach, 199, 201; and

Bermans, 360–61; and Oyneg Shabes, 334, 355; report on Great Deportation, 311; and ŻOB, 466n16
Jewish police: boots, 252; brutality, 343–44; and children, 260; cooperation with Germans, 351; corruption, 129–31; and Czerniakow, 94–95; and deportation, 302, 308; and disinfections, 129–31; and food supplies, 115; and house committees, 91–92; and inferiority complex of Jews, 232–33; and labor camps, 189; and Oyneg Shabes, 216, 218; as pathology of ghettos, 231; Perle on, 195; power of, 254; reactions to, 93, 111, 180, 313, 327, 343–44; retaliation against, 355; satire directed at, 257; and Szlengel, 316; and "Two and a Half Years," 227
Jewish Question: and Borochov, 30–31; Heller on, 63, 64; and LPZ, 29; and Polish-Jewish relations, 71
Jewish Social Self-Help, Coordinating Committee (ŻSS), 114
Jewish Society for Knowledge of the Land, 85
Jewish Society for Public Welfare (ŻTOS), 114
Joint Distribution Committee (JDC): criticism of, 367; free loan societies (gmiles hesed kases), 88, 95, 98–99; and intelligentsia, 116; investment scheme, 113–14; and Oyneg Shabes Archive, 221; relief operations, 112–13, 114; and Ringelblum, 15, 90–91, 97–102, 422n39; and siege of Warsaw, 106; and Zbąszyń refugee crisis, 91, 100–102
Joselewicz, Berek, 70
Joseph II, 71
Jot, Isaac Markus, 38
journals, 52. See also specific journal titles
Judaic Library, 116
Judenrat: and Aleynhilf, 94–95, 112, 115, 133, 135, 136, 338; and children, 260, 261, 262; control exercised by, 93, 108–11; corruption in, 131–34; and deportation, 183, 301, 306, 307;

documentation of, 216; and economics of ghetto, 281–82; establishment of, 423–24n64; and food supplies, 115, 130; and forced labor, 107, 189; and house committees, 92, 115, 135; and Jarecka, 6; and labor camps, 131–34; leadership of, 5; moral failings of, 348; and Oyneg Shabes, 212, 216, 218, 297, 306, 308; Perle on, 195; reactions to, 14, 128, 257; and social welfare, 92; tax policies, 237; and Winter, 156, 212, 433n40; and Yiddish, 117

justice: desire for, 157; for Jewish police, 180; as motive for archives, 6–7, 155, 213–14; for refugees, 270

Kaczerginski, Shmerke, 210, 211–12

Kaganovich, Pinchas (pseudonym: Der Nister), 96

kahals (Jewish Councils), 56

Kalisz, 276

Kalmanovich, Zelig: on future of Jews, 230–31; and Ringelblum, 88, 419n143, 419–20n144; on secularism, 231; on Soviet Union, 228; and YIVO, 40, 88

Kaminer, Meshulam, 109

Kamiński, Aleksander, 298

Kampelmacher, Bernard, 169–70, 220

Kantonistn (Lewin), 170–71

Kaplan, Chaim, 121, 125–26, 425n88, 427n113, 466n5

Kaplan, Joseph, 162–65, 223

Kapote, Yossele, 336

Karasiówna, Esther, 267, 268

kases. See free loan societies (*gmiles hesed kases*)

Katsyzne, Alter, 51

Katyn massacre, 379

Katz, Szymon, 323

Katzenelson, Benjamin, 325

Katzenelson, Bentzion, 325

Katzenelson, Chana, 314

Katzenelson, Hannah, 325

Katzenelson, Tzvi, 325, 326

Katzenelson, Yitzhak: death of, 326; and

Gutkowski, 152; as Oyneg Shabes collaborator, 185; poetry, 213, 312, 314, 315, 316, 324–32, 464n122, 468n50; and Ringelblum, 325, 464n125; and Vittel internment camp, 160

Kaufman, Yehezkiel, 64, 70, 76

kedoyshim (martyrs): Auerbach on, 201; Huberband on, 168; Lewin on, 172; Leyvik on, 198; Ringelblum on, 349, 367; of Zduńska Wola, 300

kehilla kedosha (holy community), 100, 109, 271

Kener, Jacob, 29, 35, 37, 75

Kener, Yakov, 23

Keren Kayemet (Jewish National Fund), 161, 162

Kermish, Joseph, 62, 206, 443n6

Khazars, 56

"Khurbm Varshe" (Perle), 195, 196, 198, 343

Kiddush Hashem, 168, 201, 300, 348–49, 358

Kiddush Hashem (Asch), 51

Kiddush Hashem (Huberband), 168

Kipnis, Menakhem, 223

Kirman, Joseph, 185, 208, 213, 307, 459n61

Kirshenbaum, Menakhem, 337–38

Kishinev pogrom, 349

klal yisroel (the collective), 202

Klein, David, 362

Kochanowski, Jan, 57

Kon, Menakhem Mendel: accounting for archive, 217, 220–21; on children, 266, 433n32; hiding from deportation, 304, 433n35; on Huberband, 166, 167; and Opoczynski, 186; as Oyneg Shabes collaborator, 153–55, 217; and resistance, 353; and Ringelblum, 155, 222, 359; and Szlamek, 221, 291–92

Koninski, Aaron: on children, 262–64; death of, 268, 367; as Oyneg Shabes collaborator, 169, 261; and YIVO, 147

Koninski, Natan, 437n100

Korczak, Janusz, 268, 301, 321, 323, 367

Korzen, Meir, 97, 102, 104, 113

Kościuszko, Tadeusz, 38

Kościuszko Uprising, 67, 69–70

Kossower, Emilka, 162, 360

Kovner, Abba, 286

Kovno Ghetto, 211

Kozienice, 272, 453–54n89

Krakow, 300

Kraushar, Alexander, 38–39, 53

Krayz (Young Historians Circle), 58–63, 81, 82

Krinka, 278

Kristallnacht pogrom, 102

Kruk, Herman, 7, 210, 211, 212, 455–56n4

Krysia, 357, 360, 362–65, 383–85, 472n124

Krzepicki, Abraham, 201, 309–10, 460n75

Kujawy, 275

Kultur Lige, 97

Kutno, 272

Kwartalnik historyczny, 66–67, 83–84

Kwartalnik poswiecony badaniom przeszlosci Zydow w Polsce, 52

labor camps, 94, 131–34, 296, 429–30n158

laborers and labor movements: Borochov on, 32; emergence of, 21, 31; influence of, 22; marginalization of, 45; unions, 34, 99

Lajner, Shlomo Velvel, 293

Łakiński, Jan, 384

land ownership, 71–72

Landau, Alexander: archive materials from, 217; financial support of archives, 221; and resistance, 353; shop of, 152, 154, 159–60, 433n35

Landau, Margalit (Emilka), 160

Landkentenish/Krajoznawstwo, 85

Landkentenish movement, 85–86, 88

landsmanshaft, 91, 99–100, 150, 293, 306

Landwarów, 286

Langer, Lawrence, 371

Lanzmann, Claude, 290

"The Last Stage of Resettlement Is Death" (Jarecka), 6–7, 183

Latin American Jews, 326

Lazar-Melman, Itke, 362

Lazowert, Henryka, 147, 181–82

leadership, Jewish, 14, 211, 212, 250

League for Anti-Aircraft and Anti-Gas Defense, 105

Lederman, Israel, 264

Left Poalei Zion (LPZ), 27–29; and Anti-Fascist Bloc, 295, 474n157; arms, 355; and Birobidzhan territory, 45; and Borochov, 28; and Bund, 148; and Communist Party, 43, 46; criticism of, 45–46; evening schools, 25; and Hashomer Hatzair, 163; on immigration, 31–32; influence of, 407n21; leadership of, 105; and Marxism, 77; and outbreak of war, 104; and Oyneg Shabes collaborators, 179; Oyneg Shabes material on, 367–70; and Palestine, 45; platform, 44, 45; press, 43, 47; and prognostic Zionism, 32; and resistance, 294, 474n157; and Revisionists, 354; and Ringelblum, 8, 15, 26, 29, 34, 47–48, 119, 125, 359, 367–70; significance of, 35; and soup kitchens, 118; and Soviet Union, 164, 369; split with Poalei Tsiyon, 32, 33; and Stern, 34; Twenty-first Zionist Congress, 103–104; and Wasser, 150; and YIVO, 40; and Yugnt, 34–36, 37, 44, 46, 62–63; Yungbor, 35–36; and Zionism, 28, 47

Lehman, Shmuel, 200, 223–24, 366

Leiner, Shmuel Shlomo, 328–30, 464n136, 465n142

Lemberg, 298

Lenin, Vladimir Ilyich, 31, 64

Lepak, Hersch, 307

Lestschinsky, Jacob, 29

Lestschinsky Archives, 98–99

Leszno 2, 134

Leszno 24, 121–22, 123

Leszno 40, 136–39

letters, 186, 211

Lev, Yitzhak, 46–47, 48

Lewin, Abraham: Danzig-Weltser on, 436n90; and deportation, 306; diary, 218, 300, 304, 436–37n91; family of, 315; on food prices, 302–303; and Hashomer Hatzair, 165; as Oyneg Shabes collaborator, 169, 170–73; on Polish-Jewish relations, 375; and Ringelblum, 25, 170; and Soviet Union, 228; on survival, 437n92; and "Two and a Half Years," 228; on women, 240; and YIVO, 147

Lewin, Celina, 123
Lewin, Luba, 170, 171–72
Lewin, Ora, 170, 172
Leybel, Daniel, 25, 405n25
Leyvik, H., 43, 198, 385
libraries, 42, 248, 338
Lichtenstein, Israel: attempts to save, 359; and Borochov School, 119; burial of archives, 2–4, 5, 146, 216, 219, 388; death of, 313; and ghetto schools, 261; and IKOR, 117; and Kon, 155; and leadership of archives, 219, 304, 313, 337; as Oyneg Shabes collaborator, 169; and Wasser, 149

Lichtenstein, Margalit, 3, 359
Lifton, Betty, 268
Liga Obrony Powietrznej i Przeciwgazowej (LOPP), 105
Linder, Menakhem: death of, 118, 280; diary, 223; and IKOR, 116; Oyneg Shabes material on, 366; and risks associated with archives, 222; role in Oyneg Shabes, 174–76; and "Two and a Half Years," 226, 280; and Yiddishism, 117; and YIVO, 88, 147

Lipowski, Yitzhak, 338
Lis, Kalman, 185, 208, 213
Literarishe bleter, 76, 200
literature, 42–43, 60, 166
Lithuania, 286–87, 297
Litvaks, 25
"Living Newspaper" (Szlengel), 316
Lodz Ghetto, 92–93, 210, 211, 212, 443n6
LOPP (*Liga Obrony Powietrznej i Przeciwgazowej*), 105
"Love Looks for an Apartment," 213

lower and lower-middle classes, 34. *See also* social class
LPZ. *See* Left Poalei Zion
Lubelski, Shimon, 366
Lubetkin, Zivia, 165
Lublin, 62, 292, 295–97, 328, 465n141
Luftwaffe, 105
Łuków, 277, 278
Lwów, 17, 84, 297, 378

Maciejewska, Irena, 317
Mahler, Rafael: on Amsterdam, 24; on Balaban, 55; on Borochov, 63; and final Oyneg Shabes letter, 385; Galician origins, 17; on Handelsman, 57; historical scholarship of, 12, 49, 63–64; on Kaufman's research, 76; and 1933 Congress, 83; in Ovnt kursn, 36; on Ringelblum, 23, 99, 413–14n45; and territorialization, 44; on uprising, 70; and Yugnt, 62; and Yunger Historiker Krayz, 58, 59, 62–64; and Zbąszyń refugee crisis, 101–102

mailmen, 186–87, 217, 303
The Main Archive of Old Documents (AGAD), 67
Mandelsberg, Bela, 36, 49, 62
Manger, Itzik, 200, 223
Mann, Mendel, 205
Manteuffel, Tadeusz, 83
Marek, Pavel, 75
Mark, Ber, 157, 198, 430n177, 433–34n45
Maroco, Avrom Mordkhe, 168
Marranodom, 349, 359
marriage, 240
martyrs (*kedoyshim*): Auerbach on, 201; Huberband on, 168; Lewin on, 172; Leyvik on, 198; Ringelblum on, 349, 367; of Zduńska Wola, 300
Marxism: and Borochov, 29, 30–31; and Jewish historical scholarship, 60, 61; on Jewish Question, 64; and Poalei Tsiyon movement, 21; and Ringelblum, 75–77, 346; and Yunger Historiker Krayz, 62
mass graves, 286, 288

Mauthausen camp, 162
May Day demonstrations, 35
Mayzel, Nakhman, 43, 96
Mazor, Michael, 123, 126–27, 153, 161, 335, 429n141, 432–33n29
Mazowsze, 65–66, 275
medical care and research: on effects of hunger, 238, 448n25; and historical scholarship, 416n84; hospitals, 264–66, 376, 453n75; and house committees, 122; and labor camps, 132, 133; and Oyneg Shabes financing, 220–21; physicians, 68–69, 112; women's roles in, 240
Medzinski, Meir, 270
Meisels, Maurycy, 108
memoirs, 205–206, 207, 229
memories, recording of, 13–14
Mende, Gerhardt, 341
Metropolitan Committee of Social Welfare (SKSS), 112
Mickiewicz, Adam, 323
middle class, 32, 34. See also social class
Miesięcznik Żydowski, 64, 66
Mila Street house committee, 128–29
Milejkowski, Israel, 109, 212, 234, 238
milk cans, 5
Mińsk-Mazowiecki pogrom, 98
Mintz, Matityahu, 32
Miron, Dan, 78, 193
Miteylungen, 295
modernization, 44
Modlin, 345
"Moes" (Money), 257
"Month of the Child" campaign, 260, 261
"The Moral Decline of the Jewish Woman during the War" (Huberband), 242
morale: attempts to sustain, 98–99; of children, 267; decline, 128–29, 180; and disinfections, 129–31; and house committees, 127, 135; perspectives on, 238–39; and Słapak's salons, 178; volatility of, 257–58, 467n28
morality, 242, 251–52, 347–48
Morawski, Marjan, 50

motivations for the archive creation: of Auerbach, 199; of Jarecka, 6–7, 183; justice, 6–7, 155, 213–14; Kon on, 155; prevention, 183; revenge, 198; of Ringelblum, 12
mourning, 202
Mundlak, Regina, 338
Muranowska 6, 122, 123, 131, 134
music: musical productions, 122–23, 375–76; music archive, 223; street songs, 257, 451n61; symphony orchestra, 375–76
Mussolini, Benito, 360
mutual aid organizations, 339–40, 341–42, 366, 368, 385–86
Mylna 18, 173

Nachbush, Noah, 101–102
Naczelna Rada Opiekuńcza (Central Council for Social Welfare), 115
Neftalin, Henryk, 211, 443n6
Naiberg, Leon, 323–24
Nalewki 23, 123
Nasz przegląd, 25, 54, 66, 178, 200
Nasze hasła, 34, 37
National Democratic party, 50
National Radical Camp (ONR), 381
nationalism: and acculturation of Jews, 232; and assimilationists, 83; of historians, 17; and Holocaust, 206; and intelligentsia, 22; and Jewish historical scholarship, 53; national identity, 7, 9, 10, 57, 103, 413n35; rejection of, 60; and Sosis, 414–15n61; and Zionism, 20–21, 32
Naygroshl, Mendl, 22, 23, 24, 30
Nazis: anti-Semitism of, 296, 345; and capitalism, 369; strategies of, 374; and typhus, 190; values of, 252
Nazi-Soviet non-aggression pact, 103
Neged Hazerem, 285–86
Netherlands, 381
Neuman, Y. M., 85
"A New Book with Old Lies" (Ringelblum), 74
New Yishuv, 44
Niemenczyn, 286

Niger, Shmuel, 178
Nir-Rafalkes, Nahum, 46
Nomberg, Dovid, 193
Normann, Sven, 298
Novich, Miriam, 326
Nowodworski, David, 309
Nowogródek, 469n66
Nowogrodzka, Sonia, 117, 234
Nowolipki 59, 157
Nowolipki 68, 1, 5, 146, 155, 357
Nowo-Wilejka, 286
NRO (Central Council for Social
    Welfare), 115
number assignments, 196–97
Nussbaum, Hilary, 38–39, 53

occupations, Jewish, 45, 71–72, 93, 147,
    280–81
occupied nations, 232
October Revolution, 28
Olcanetzka, Anna, 35–36
"one Jewish People" (*klal yisroel*), 10
ONR (National Radical Camp), 381
Opatoshu, Joseph, 43, 51, 385
Opoczynski, Daniel, 186, 193
Opoczynski, Miriam, 185, 193
Opoczynski, Peretz: and Auerbach, 218;
    on children, 261; diary, 304, 467n28;
    on disinfections, 129, 130, 131; and
    Gutkowski, 151; on house commit-
    tees, 120, 123, 127, 134, 428n127; as
    Oyneg Shabes collaborator, 13, 185–
    96, 216, 439n143; on resistance, 313;
    on smuggling, 281; typhus infection,
    153, 219–20; Zionism of, 439n140
optimism: and future of Jews, 234–35,
    237; and humor, 258; of Jewish
    population, 184, 202; of Ringelblum,
    15–16, 210, 300, 347, 348
orchestra, 375–76
Order Service. *See* Jewish police
Orlean, J. L., 234
Orleska, Miriam, 208
orphans and orphanages: artistic
    programs, 301; and CENTOS, 112,
    260; deportation of, 216, 268, 321,
    367; and house committees, 122;

hunger of, 262; Oyneg Shabes
    material on, 213, 262; plights of, 260;
    and soup kitchens, 138–39
ORT (The Society for the Promotion of
    Vocational and Agricultural Work
    among Jews), 109
Orthodox Agudas Israel Party, 109–10
Orthodox Jews, 251, 271, 413n43
Orzech, Maurycy, 113, 234
Ostdeutsche Bautischlerei Werkstätte,
    159
Ostrowska, Salomea, 146, 286
"Our Platform" (Borochov), 31, 32–33
Ovnt kursn far arbeter, 36–37
Oyfbroyz, 164
Oyfn sheydveg (Cherikover, ed.), 230, 231
Oyneg Shabes (Note: Given the
    archive's central role in the text,
    additional references regarding
    topics of the archive can be found
    throughout the index): and Aleyn-
    hilf, 92; authorship questions, 219;
    censorship of, 445–46n29; collection
    of documents, 6; collective character
    of, 208; condition of caches, 215–16,
    444–45n17; contents of, 213, 216,
    218–19; copies and copiers of
    archives, 217, 218–19; and deporta-
    tions, 300–301, 305–309; and
    Giterman, 114; guidelines, 344, 389–
    92, 393–95, 396–99; honoraria for
    authors, 136, 217, 220; inclusivity of,
    147–48; interviews, 220, 226, 233–34,
    243–50, 263; and Jewish National
    Committee, 334, 355; and Judenrat,
    212; leadership of, 7, 158, 206, 304,
    313, 358, 431n11; letter to New York
    YIVO, 385–86; name, 401n1; number
    of caches, 215–16; organization of,
    149; and other archives, 210–12;
    personal nature of, 311–13; priorities,
    11, 12, 13, 213, 214, 226, 239, 295;
    proposed destination of, 218, 303,
    333, 385–86; questionnaires, 149, 217,
    226, 227; and resistance, 295;
    restoration of, 216; retrieval of
    archives, 1–2, 150, 151, 205–206,

Oyneg Shabes *(continued)*
  215–17, 401n3, 402n16; risks associated with, 219–20, 221–22; secrecy
  of, 146–47, 184, 211; time constraints,
  229–30; uniqueness of, 210–12;
  weekly meetings, 300; and YIVO,
  81, 303. *See also* burial of archives

Pain and heroism (Gutkowski and
  Zuckerman), 151–52
Pajewski, Tadeusz, 162, 360
Palestine: and Balfour Declaration, 24;
  and *binyan haaretz,* 48; and
  Borochov, 32; and Diaspora, 44;
  emigration to, 33, 45, 46; and future
  of Jews, 235, 369, 370, 414n56; and
  Hashomer Hatzair, 163; and land
  sales to Jews, 103; and LPZ, 28,
  45–46, 48; and New Yishuv, 44;
  and Peel Commission, 47; and
  Ringelblum, 48; settlements, 34;
  and Zionism, 20, 33
Pankratova, Anna, 83
Parnas, Josef, 168
parówki (disinfections), 111, 129–31, 227,
  289, 429n152
Passenstein, Marek, 362
passivity of Jews: explanations for, 279,
  350, 478n196; reactions to, 343, 349,
  352, 383
Passover relief, 114
passports, 197, 326
Paulsson, Gunnar S., 381
Pawiak Prison, 384–85
Pearl Harbor, 187
Peel Commission, 47
people of Oyneg Shabes, 145–208; about
  the collective, 145–49, 208; deportation of, 303–304; economists, 174–
  76; executive committee, 146–47,
  148, 149, 153–69, 217, 292, 333; party
  representatives, 179–81; Polish
  language writers, 181–84; recruitment of collaborators, 217, 218;
  refugees, 176–77; secretaries, 149–53;
  stipends, 150; teachers, 169–74;

translators, 178; Yiddish writers and
  journalists, 184–208
Peretz, Yitzhak Leybush, 30, 117, 209,
  235, 330, 442n2
Perezhitoe, 52
Perle, Lolek, 197, 440n167
Perle, Shie: employment, 157; "Khurbm
  Varshe," 195, 196, 343; as Oyneg
  Shabes collaborator, 185; review of
  novel, 202; and Ringelblum, 194;
  and Soviet Union, 235; "Two and a
  Half Years" interview, 234; wife's
  suicide, 440nn153,167
Petlura, Semyon, 213
Peykus, Yosef, 169
philanthropy, 90, 110, 368
photographs, 213, 218, 219
physicians, Jewish, 68–69, 112
Piłsudski, Józef, 57, 83, 98, 108, 380
pinkesim, 172
Piotrków, 291
Piotrkowski, Josef, 272
Plekhanov, Georgi, 64
Plotnicka, Frumka, 293, 350
Poalei Tsiyon: and Borochov, 33;
  difficulties experienced by, 47;
  emergence of, 21; membership of,
  24; and Ringelblum, 23, 271; split
  of, 32
Podchlebnik, Mechl, 290
poetry: of Katzenelson, 213, 312, 314,
  316, 324–32; of Kirman, 213; of Lis,
  213; of Szlengel, 213, 314–15, 316–24
pogroms, 98, 102, 213, 285, 349
Poland: anti-Jewish violence in, 98;
  anti-Semitism, 20, 21; army, 104,
  372, 383; census fight of 1910, 21;
  cooperative movements, 18; eastern
  Poland, 269; election law of 1907, 21;
  as independent state, 24, 25; invasion
  of, 91; Jews of (see Polish Jewry);
  language of (see Polish language);
  loyalty to, 12, 20, 110, 378; murders,
  311, 346; outbreak of war in, 103–106;
  Polish Uprising (1830–31), 323; and
  resistance, 320–21; Ringelblum on,

373; underground, 384. *See also* Polish-Jewish relations

police, German, 251, 278

police, Jewish. *See* Jewish police

police, Polish, 35

Polish Communist Party (KPP), 23, 28, 35, 47

Polish Home Army, 372, 383

Polish Jewry: economic issues, 175; emergence of, 25; exodus of, 104–105; fate of, 146, 172; interest in history, 52, 84; and outbreak of war, 104–105; and Oyneg Shabes, 208; reactions of, 198; self-centeredness, 189, 236, 242 (*see also* behavior of Jews); status of, 232

Polish language: and culture congresses, 42–43; in ghettos, 231; and Judenrat, 111; and Oyneg Shabes collaborators, 147, 181–84; poetry, 316; Ringelblum's use of, 334; theater productions in, 123; in Warsaw Ghetto, 117, 236

Polish Socialist Party, 57, 298, 362

Polish Workers Party (PPR), 294–95

Polish-Jewish Committee to Help Jews (Zegota), 372, 383, 478n199

Polish-Jewish relations: and accultura-tion of Jews, 19, 232; assistance from Poles, 245–46, 247, 381; and census fight of 1910, 21; cooperation between, 108, 190–91; deterioration of, 20, 24, 277–78, 376–77; econom-ic component of, 374, 376, 377, 378; and election law of 1907, 21; friendships between, 320; and Giterman, 475n167; indifference in, 377; and labor camps, 132; personal vs. civic behavior, 376–77; and postwar culture, 234, 237, 239, 448n24; risks for Poles, 381–82; romantic relationships, 245–47; scholarship on, 8–9, 65, 69–71, 334, 361, 362, 365, 372–83, 389–92; and *shabreven,* 340; in towns and provinces, 274–78; and "Two and a Half Years," 227–28

"Polish-Jewish Relations" (Różycki), 377

Polish-Jewish Relations during the Second World War (Ringelblum), 334, 361, 362, 365, 372–83

political parties: and Aleynhilf, 118–19; and Final Solution, 293; and free loan societies, 99; presses, 214; and resistance, 294; and soup kitchens, 118. *See also specific parties*

political underground, 118, 119, 149

"Pomnik" (Szlengel), 314–15

Ponar, 285, 286, 297, 455–56n4, 456n7

populism, 77

possessions and property, 189, 288, 317–19, 377, 378

postal service, 186–87, 217, 303

postcards, 186, 213, 217, 293, 307

posters, 218

"The Postman" (Tagore), 268

Potockis family, 18

poverty: and disease, 254; and family life, 240–41, 250; and forced labor, 94, 107; and house committees, 121–22; and postal service, 187–88; Ringelblum's interest in, 71–73

Powsinoga, Mates-Borukh, 274

Powsinoga, Sara, 273–74

Powsinoga, Simon, 273–74

pride, national, 110, 235–36, 327, 329, 356

printing, Jewish, 69

Projekty i próby przewarstwowienia Żydów w epoce Stanisławowskiej (Ringelblum), 57, 71–72

proletariat: and Borochov, 32; and culture congresses, 42; culture of, 38; education for, 36–37, 39; and the Jewish Question, 31; and Marxism, 77; origins of, 81; Perle on, 194, 197; Ringelblum's interest in, 72–73; and youth organizations, 35

propaganda, 129, 209, 375, 379

property rights, 71–72

prostitution, 242, 244

Provisioning Agency, 305

Prussia, 71

Pruzhany project, 80, 86
Przegląd historyczny, 57
Przytyk pogrom, 98
psychological effects of ghettos, 225, 266–67, 352
psychological weapons, 202
Ptaśnik, Jan, 50
Public Sector of Aleynhilf: development of, 106; and district commissions, 124; and morale, 135; and Ringelblum, 119, 123; role of, 91–92, 127. *See also* house committees
punktn (refugee centers), 94, 249

quarantines, 111

Rabinowitz, Jacob, 309
Rabinowitz, Shie, 147, 148, 160–61, 221
raids of Jewish homes, 148–49
Rajfeld-Pechnik, Czesława, 126
Ravitch, Melekh, 15, 194, 199
Rawa Ruska, 292
reb yisroel (the individual), 202
"Reckoning with God" (Szlengel), 319
Red Army, 294
"Reduta Ordona" (Szlengel), 323
refugees: archive materials from, 217; arms, 295; begging of, 270; children, 189–90, 260, 262, 263, 266, 267; disease, 219–20; expulsions from homes, 94, 107, 270–78, 297; and house committees, 120, 122; hunger and starvation of, 118, 263–64, 279; and Jewish leadership, 105; and Kampelmacher, 174; and Koninski, 173; and labor camps, 132; and Mylna 18, 173; punktn (refugee centers), 94, 249; and siege of Warsaw, 106; social relief, 92, 422n35; theft, 227; treatment of, 343; women, 243, 249; Zbąszyń crisis, 91, 100–102
Regesty i nadpisi, 52
registration and selection, 191–92
Reich-Ranicki, Marcel, 182–83, 184, 306
rekrutchina, 170–71, 437nn94,96
religion and religious life: and anti-Semitism, 66; and coping strategies, 312; debates on, 290; Dubnow on, 64; effect of ghetto on, 237–38; and future of Jews, 61, 231, 235, 236–37; and gender roles, 240; under Nazis, 167; poetic references to, 319, 329, 331–32; rejection of, 60; religious observance, 65, 168, 236, 272; and Soviet Union, 228; and survival of Jews, 64, 76; and "Two and a Half Years," 227
resettlement, 301. *See also* deportation
resilience of Jews, 12, 152, 256, 347–48, 352, 374
resistance, 353–61; absence of, 183–84, 195, 196, 204, 216, 236, 310, 313; accounts of, 216; and acculturation of Jews, 232; and Aleynhilf, 335; and Anielewicz, 370–72; arms, 294, 325, 353, 354, 355, 359, 383; battles, 356, 385–86; calls for, 286, 294–95, 309, 311, 313, 320–21, 352; and Czerniakow, 335; decisions to not resist, 290–91, 350–51; expectations for, 355; forms of, 235, 326, 349, 352; individual resistance, 307; and Katzenelson, 330; and LPZ, 294, 474n157; Opoczynski on, 191, 192; opponents of, 335–36, 356; and Oyneg Shabes, 12, 213, 214, 295; and passivity of Jews, 279, 343, 349–50, 352, 383, 478n196; poetic references to, 321–23, 327; reactions to, 157–58; and Ringelblum, 336, 342, 350–51, 353, 354, 365, 366; and solidarity, 356; support for, 159, 164–65, 336, 356; in Trawniki, 361; and Winter, 157; of youth groups, 163, 385
restaurants, 259
restrictions, 106–107, 157, 305–306
retaliation, 73–74, 157, 312, 440–41n171
Revisionists (Żydowski Związek Wojskowy), 28, 342, 353–54, 358, 456n11
Revolution of 1905, 161
Reyzen, Zalmen, 40, 88, 419n143, 419–20n144

Right Poalei Tsiyon: and Anti-Fascist Bloc, 164; and Gutkowski, 151; and Histadrut, 28; and Koninski, 173; and Opoczynski, 186; and outbreak of war, 103; and resistance, 294; split with Poalei Tsiyon, 32, 33; and Zionism, 44

Ringelblum, Emanuel (Note: Given Ringelblum's central role in the text, additional references about him can be found throughout the index): about, 14–16; on children, 261; criticisms of, 304, 337, 403n25, 405–406n27; death of, 385; dedication of, 99, 113, 413–14n45; diary, 15, 148, 238–39, 304, 334–35, 348; early employment, 25–26; on economics of ghetto, 279, 280; as educator, 36–37; on executions, 287; on Final Solution, 295–97; freedom of movement, 305; in Galicia, 14–15; in hiding, 304, 357, 360–61, 364–65, 383–85; and house committees, 119, 123, 124–26; and IKOR, 118; and intelligentsia, 116, 158, 359, 365–67; and Jewish Fighting Organization, 342, 353, 354, 355; on Jewish Question, 71; and Joint Distribution Committee, 15, 90–91, 97–102, 422n39; on Judenrat, 135–36; on Kiddush Hashem, 348–49; on labor camps, 134; and Landkentenish movement, 85–86; and LPZ, 8, 15, 26, 29, 34, 47–48, 119, 125, 359, 367–70; as Marxist, 75–77, 346; optimism of, 15–16, 210, 300, 347, 348; and outbreak of war, 104–105; relief work, 91, 100–103, 339–40, 341–42, 420n1, 422n36 (see also specific organizations); and resistance, 336, 342, 350–51, 353, 354, 365, 366; and shops, 339–42; on shtetlekh, 269, 274; and soup kitchens, 221; on starvation, 142–43; and Trawniki labor camp, 27, 360, 361, 365, 372; and Umschlagplatz, 338–39, 342, 344; on women, 250–51; and YIVO, 15, 39–

42, 81–89, 156, 342; youth, 17–18, 22–23; and Yugnt, 35, 37, 62–63. See also Oyneg Shabes; scholarship of Ringelblum

Ringelblum, Fayvish, 18, 22

Ringelblum, Munie (née Heler), 18

Ringelblum, Uri: attempts to protect, 158, 304, 336, 357, 365; birth and early years, 388; death of, 385; in Grójecka 81 bunker, 383–85; information about, 15

Ringelblum, Yehudis (Judyta): attempts to protect, 304, 336; and CENTOS, 261; death of, 385; departure from ghetto, 158; in Grójecka 81 bunker, 357, 360, 362, 365, 383–85; information about, 15; marriage and motherhood, 26

Rogazhytsky, H. B., 127

Rosen, Joseph, 36

Rosenblum, 357

Roskies, David, 193, 204

Rovno, 335

Roy, Abram, 291

Rozen, Henryk: and condemned prisoners, 127; on future of Jews, 237; interview of, 212, 234, 235; and labor camps, 134; on national pride, 235

Różycki, Stanisław, 146, 229, 253–56, 282, 377, 447–48n20

Rudawski, Michał, 101

Rumkowski, Chaim, 92–93, 210–11, 212

Russian Jews, 52, 96–97

Russian Revolution, 28, 32, 33

Rybarski, Roman, 50

Rydyger, Sima, 266

Rydzewski, Pan, 360

Rzeczpospolita, 54, 69, 71–72

Sabbath, observance of, 236, 272

Sącz, Nowy, 17

Sakowska, Ruta, 177, 298

Sanz, 22–25

Sborow, Sara, 264

"Scenes from the Children's Hospital" (Wajnerman), 265

Schiper, Isaac: and archives, 29, 218,

Schiper, Isaac *(continued)*
223, 366; criticism of, 412n26; death
of, 372, 383; Galician origins, 17; and
Huberband, 166; and IKOR lectures,
118; on local histories, 87; and Poalei
Tsiyon movement, 21, 22, 23, 406n5,
413n44; publications, 25, 51, 66; on
resistance, 335–36; and Ringelblum,
9, 54, 55–57, 342, 347, 412n21;
scholarship of, 12, 49, 53–54, 347;
and schools offering Jewish history,
58; on writing of history, 210
Schmidt, Andrzej, 294, 295
scholarship of Ringelblum: descriptive
emphasis, 55, 75; dissertation, 65–67;
education, 24–25, 50; goals of, 7–10,
49, 77–78 (*see also* Oyneg Shabes);
influences on, 9, 29, 51–58, 75–77;
objectivity in scholarship, 8, 347;
publications, 57, 64–73; sources, 73,
415n71; study of Polish-Jewish
relations, 69–73, 334, 361, 362, 372–
83; while in hiding, 365–67, 372–83
schools, 216, 261, 262, 306, 341
Schorr, Moses, 58
Schulz, Bruno, 200
Schwartzbard, Daniel, 181
Schwartzbard, Miriam, 181
Schwartzbard, Mordecai, 179, 180–81
Schwarzbard, Shalom, 213
Scott, Joan, 240
"Scream, Jews, Scream: Scenes from the
Street" (Feld), 258–59
Second Action, 160
secularism: and Giterman, 96; and
historical scholarship, 12, 60, 78; and
Orthodox Jews, 166; and postwar
culture, 230; and Winter, 155–56; and
YIVO, 78
Seidman, Hillel, 184, 473–74n156
Sejm of Poland, 71
Sekstein, Gele, 3, 4–5, 261, 359, 402n9
serfdom, 71–72
settlements, 33, 34
Seventh International Congress of the
Historical Sciences, 82–84
sexual promiscuity, 340

Sforim, Mendele Moykher, 30, 80, 117,
235
shabreven, 340
Shapiro, Kolonymous, 162, 167, 312,
433n32, 436n84
Shatzky, Jacob: and LPZ, 29; and
Ringelblum, 73, 75–76, 88, 419–
20n144; on uprising, 70; and YIVO,
40, 82
Shaynkinder, Sh., 256
Shenfeld, Rut, 323
Sherman, Betsalel, 46
Shloyme (Rabbi), 120
Shloyme reb Khayim's (Sforim), 80
Shoah (film), 290
shops, German: and CKPPwS, 341–42;
conditions, 340, 341, 467n32; and
deportation, 280, 301, 302, 303–304,
308; exploitation in, 281–82, 340;
Oyneg Shabes material on, 223; and
Ringelblum, 339–42; Werkschutz
(Jewish shop police), 309, 339, 355
Shor, Lev, 208
"Should We Hide the Truth?" (Dvor-
zhetsky), 387
Shtatman, Dvora, 292
Shtern, Berish, 20, 21
shtetl, 12, 99–100, 268–78, 396–99,
454n101
Shtif, Nahum, 78
Shul Kult (school movement), 173
Sylman, Jacob, 291
Shur, Leyb, 338
Siemieński, Józef, 66–67
Sieradz, 270
Silkes, Genia, 263, 339
Six Day War, 206
Skalov, Leyb, 271
Skalov, Moshe, 185
Skalov, Zalmen, 270
Skempa, 271
"Sketches from the Ghetto," 258
SKSS (Metropolitan Committee of
Social Welfare), 112
SŁapakowa, Cecylia, 13, 147, 178, 217,
243–50, 450n42
slaughter, ritual, 232, 272

Slonim, 285, 297, 298, 458n39

Smocza Street, 129

Smolar, Natan: attempts to save, 359; and Borochov School, 119; and ghetto schools, 261; on loss of daughter, 313; and uprising, 5; on Warsaw Jews, 301

Smolar, Ninkele, 313

smuggling: of children, 264; and deportation, 302; and fate of the ghetto, 257; importance of, 108, 280, 281, 423n63; and Jewish police, 111; Opoczynski on, 190–91; Oyneg Shabes material on, 108, 281; and Polish-Jewish relations, 190–91, 374; by women, 244, 245

"Smuggling in the Warsaw Ghetto" (Opoczynski), 190–91

Sobibór, 293, 300, 350

Sobieszczański, Franciszek, 65

Sochaczew, 275

social class: class struggles, 32, 67–68, 69; effect of ghetto on, 254–55; gaps in, 242; Oyneg Shabes' study of, 241; and youth movements, 34. See also bourgeoisie; proletariat

social history, 9, 227. See also history and historians

social psychology, 202

socialism, 30, 37

Society for the Promotion of Vocational and Agricultural Work among Jews (ORT), 109

Society for the Protection of Health (TOZ), 112

Society of Friends for the Study of History, 57

Society of the Friends of History, 65

Sokolow, Nahum, 65

solidarity: decline in, 183–84, 254; and deportation, 183–84; and Enlightenment, 231; and "Month of the Child" campaign, 260; Opoczynski on, 188, 189; perceptions of, 256; and Polish-Jewish relations, 383; reliance on, 239; and resistance efforts, 356; and underground press, 215

Soloveitchik, Aharon, 300

Sombart, Werner, 56

"The Song of Shlomo Zhelichowski" (Katzenelson), 327

"The Song of the Murdered Jewish People" (Katzenelson), 326, 327, 331, 332

"The Song of the Radzyner" (Katzenelson), 327, 330, 331

Sosis, Israel, 414–15n61

Sotsiale meditsin, 67, 166

soup kitchens, 118–19; Auerbach's account, 136–39, 142, 207; and children, 260; and compassion of Jews, 238; establishment of, 118–19; Goldin's account, 139–42; and house committees, 120, 122; and Judenrat, 115; and labor camps, 132; leadership of, 116; Oyneg Shabes material on, 136–43, 220; and Schwartzbard, 181; and starvation, 128; and "Two and a Half Years," 227; and Winter, 156; and Zagan, 368

Soviet Union: and Birobidzhan territory, 45, 46, 47; and Communists, 294; and Cultural Revolution, 41; and culture congresses, 42; faith of Jews in, 157, 163, 164, 194, 235, 370; invasion of, 187; Jewish collaboration with, 378–79, 476–77n184, 477n185; Jewish culture in, 44; and LPZ, 33, 164, 369; and Marxism, 77; and Nazi-Soviet non-aggression pact, 103; Różycki on, 253; scholarship in, 414–15n61; and "Two and a Half Years," 227–29

Spain, 52

Stalin, Joseph, 31, 47, 64

Stalingrad, German defeats at, 5, 359

Starzyński, Stefan, 105, 108

Stawki 9, 179

Stein, Edmund, 234

Steiner, Jacques, 200

Steiner, Jean, 207

Stern, 34

St. Petersburg, 51

"The Street" (Ringelblum), 252–53

"The Street" (Różycki), 253
"Street Scenes" (Różycki), 253
street songs, 257, 451n61
Stronnictwo Demokratyczne (SD), 57
student organizations, 88
Stupnicki, Shaul, 237
suicides, 238, 290, 326, 352, 384, 459n64
Supply Department, 109
survival: anticipation of, 230, 388;
    diminished hopes for, 306; and
    historical scholarship, 61–62;
    Paulsson on, 381; and role of religion,
    64, 76; survivor identity, 14, 343;
    testimonies, 206. *See also* Rachel
    Auerbach; Bluma Wasser; Hersh
    Wasser
Sutzkever, Avrom, 210, 211–12
Święciany, 286
Świętojerska 34, 5, 215
symphony orchestra, 375–76
synagogues, 113, 167, 271, 285
Szereszewska, Stefania, 123, 134–35
Szereszewski, Stanisław, 109
Szeryński, Józef, 111
szlachta, 71–72
Szlamek, 221, 287–92, 296, 456nn12,14
Szlengel, Władysław: and Jewish police,
    181; Oyneg Shabes material on, 181,
    316–24; poetry, 213, 267, 314–15,
    462nn96,97, 463n112; and Ringel-
    blum, 316
Szmerling, MieczysŁaw, 338
Szpilman, Władysław, 205, 316
Szwajger, Adina (Inka), 26, 265

Tagore, Rabindranath, 268
"A Talk with a Child" (Szlengel), 267
Tamir-Fishman, Arnon, 104
Tarbut, 161
Tarnów, 17
"The Tasks of Yiddish Philology"
    (Borochov), 22, 30
tax policies, 237, 279
teachers, 266, 306
Tekuma, 116
"The Telephone" (Szlengel), 320
telephones, 157, 254, 357

Tenenbaum, Mordecai, 210, 211, 212,
    324–25, 444n10
territorialization, 43–44, 46, 237
testimonies, 211, 213, 229
Theater Commission, 123
theaters of the ghetto: archive materials,
    213, 223; and house committees, 122–
    23; Ringelblum on, 42, 43
theft, 227, 259, 260, 429n153
"Things" (Szlengel), 317–19, 321
"Thirteen," 218
"This Is the Ghetto" (Różycki), 253, 282
Tłomackie 5, 127, 175
Tłomackie Synagogue, 113
tlushim (uprooted misfits), 163
Tłuszcz, 272
"To the Child Smuggler" (Lazowert),
    182
"To the Polish Reader" (Szlengel), 321
A Tog in Regensberg (Opatoshu), 51
"Together with the people" (Auerbach),
    202
Tokarz, Wacław, 57
Torah, 271
torture, 271
tourism, 85–86
Towarzystwo Miłośników Historii
    (Society of the Friends of History),
    65
TOZ (Society for the Protection of
    Health), 112
trade, 190, 191, 279, 374
transcribers, 218–19
Transferstelle, 279, 281
Trawniki, 27, 360, 361, 365, 372
Treblinka: accounts of, 293, 300, 309–
    10; children, 268, 309–10, 367;
    documentation of, 216, 309–10, 311;
    escapees from, 157, 173, 201, 222,
    277–78, 309–10; fictionalized
    account of, 207; mass deportations
    to, 2; poetic references to, 318;
    postcards from, 307; rumors about,
    192
Troki, 286
Trunk, Isaiah (Shie), 49, 62, 66
Trunk, Y. Y., 272

tsedaka (charity), 120, 124
Tseirei Tsiyon, 21
Tseitlin, Hillel, 168, 234, 235, 236–37
Tsukunft, 34
Tsushtayer, 200
"Tsuzamen mitn folk" (Auerbach), 202
Turkow, Jonas (Yanosh): on Aleynhilf staff, 116, 117, 425–26n94; archive materials from, 223; on Catholic assistance, 358, 433n32; and Ringelblum, 359; on theaters, 123
Turobin, 276
Twenty-first Zionist Congress, 103–104
Twenty-second Zionist World Congress, 48
Twerski, R. Mordecai Ber, 96
"Two and a Half Years" of Oyneg Shabes, 226–30; on children, 259–68; on economics of ghetto, 175, 176, 279–83; on future of Jews, 230–39; on ghetto life, 251–59; guidelines, 344, 374; interviews, 233–34; leadership of, 161–62; priority of, 295, 305, 306; questionnaires, 217; the shtetl, 268–78; time constraints, 215; on women, 239–51
"Two Deaths" (Szlengel), 320–21
"Two Men in the Snow" (Szlengel), 320
typhus: and archive collaborators, 219–20; and Nazis, 190; in refugee centers, 174; threat of, 129, 249–50, 251; treatment of, 177
Tytelman, Nehemia, 179–80, 257, 281, 451n61

Ukrainians and the Ukraine, 18, 20–21, 213, 229, 308
Umschlagplatz: and Landau, 160; Oyneg Shabes material on, 213, 308; purpose, 459n52; rescues from, 176, 367; and resistance, 356; Ringelblum's efforts in, 338–39, 342, 344
underground press: on Final Solution, 293–94, 295; German knowledge of, 222; on massacres, 285–86; in Oyneg Shabes archive, 213, 214–15
United States: and Allies, 164; emigra-
tion to, 32; entry into war, 114, 135; financial support from, 114; Jewish culture in, 44; perceived indifference of, 319; pressure on Germany, 115; relatives of Jews in, 99, 114
United States Memorial Holocaust Museum, 216
uprising: and Anielewicz, 370–72; importance of, 385–86; and LPZ, 369; and Ringelblum, 359–60; support for, 70; women's role in, 251

Varshever tsvoes (Auerbach), 198
Vashem, Yad, 200, 206, 207
Vayskof, Avrom, 168
"Vey dir" (Katzenelson), 312, 468n50
Vienna, Austria, 42
Vilna: pogroms, 378; Ringelblum in, 25; and Yiddish culture congress, 43
Vilna Ghetto: archives, 210, 212; and Final Solution, 298, 299, 302; and Judenrat, 92; language of, 117; leadership of, 470n88; massacres, 177, 285–86, 455–56n4; and resistance, 356
Vilna War Chronicle, 10
Vilna Zamlbikher (almanacs), 10–11
Vilner, Aryeh, 177
Vilner tog, 156
Vinaver, Maxim, 52
Vitel, France, 326, 331–32
Vitel Diary (Katzenelson), 326
Vittel, 160
volunteerism, 248

wages, 227, 281, 282
Wailing Wall, 366
Wajnerman, Dora, 265
Wajzer (house committee leader), 135
war, 103–11, 114
War and Peace (Tolstoy), 348
Warsaw: districts of, 124; early migration to, 19, 25; exodus of, 104–105; German occupation, 106–107; history of Jewish population, 65–66; and Jewish historical scholarship, 51, 53, 58, 82; Jewish leadership in, 104,

Warsaw *(continued)*
109; and Polish Jewry, 172; Ringelblum in, 25–26, 91, 104–105; siege on, 105–106, 120. *See also* Warsaw Ghetto

Warsaw Ghetto: Aryan side, 93, 201, 245–46, 253, 276, 279, 287, 337, 357; conditions, 187–88; creation of, 92, 377; day-by-day accounts of, 180, 304; described in Oyneg Shabes, 251–59, 393–95; gender ratios, 241; illegal entries and exits, 245, 276, 287; pathologies of, 231–32; postal service, 186–87, 217, 303; social order in, 92–95; suffering in, 92; and "Two and a Half Years," 226; uprising, 70, 251, 359–60, 369, 370–72, 385–86

Warsaw Historical Commission (later: Historical Commission for All of Poland), 82, 84–85, 86–88

Warsaw Shtern, 179

Warsaw University, 57, 58

Warthegau, 269, 293, 297

Wasser, Bluma: in Aryan Warsaw, 358; deportation of, 304; retrieval of archive, 1; role in Oyneg Shabes, 150; survival of, 146, 205, 466n17; and Szlamek, 287, 289, 290, 456n14

Wasser, Hersh: archive materials from, 218; in Aryan Warsaw, 358; and authorship questions, 219; collection of archive materials, 6, 13, 220; on deportation statistics, 308; diary, 218; on Final Solution, 295–97, 311; on Fligelman, 177; on IKOR, 117; on inclusivity of Oyneg Shabes, 147, 148; and Jewish National Committee, 334; on Kon, 153–54; on Lehman, 223–24; on Opoczynski, 186; retrieval of archives, 1–2, 3, 206, 216, 445n20; on Ringelblum, 431n7; as secretary of Oyneg Shabes, 149–51, 217; and soup kitchens, 221; survival of, 146, 205, 466n17; and Szlamek, 221, 287–88, 289, 290, 291, 456n12; transfer of archives, 219; and

"Two and a Half Years," 229; and underground press, 164, 214, 295; and Winter, 157; and YIVO, 147

Wasser, Leah, 150

Węgrów, 98–99

Wegrzynek, Hanna, 415n71

Weichert, MichaŁ, 112, 114, 115, 216

Weinreich, Max: on Linder, 174; and social psychology, 202; on Winter, 156; and YIVO, 40, 78–81, 88–89, 418n117

Weitz, Emil, 155, 169

Weizmann, Chaim, 104

Werfel, Franz, 299

Werkschutz (Jewish shop police), 309, 339, 355

Werterfassung, 340

"What I Read to the Dead" (Szlengel), 316–17, 323

"Where Is God?" (author unknown), 312

White Paper of May (1939), 47, 48, 103, 163

"Why Did the Jewish People Not Assimilate?" (Ringelblum), 61

Wiadomości, 223, 278, 311, 345, 355

Wieliczker, Leon, 206

Wielikowski, Gustaw, 341, 342

Wilcznska, Stefania, 268

Wilczynski, Yehezkiel, 147, 148

"Will We Stay?" (Ringelblum), 352

William Tell Festival in Interlaken, 103

Wilner, Aryeh, 285, 286

"The Window Facing the Other Side" (Szlengel), 320, 321

Winkler, Jerzy, 147, 176, 280–81, 438n113

Winter, Heniek, 157

Winter, Julek, 157

Winter, Marysia, 157

Winter, Shmuel: and Auerbach, 201; diary, 5, 223, 433n44, 434n46; financial support of archives, 221; and Judenrat, 156, 212, 433n40; on leadership of Oyneg Shabes, 358, 434n49; as Oyneg Shabes collaborator, 217, 305; and Perle, 195; and resistance, 313, 353, 355, 434n46; and

Ringelblum, 158, 342, 359; telephone, 357; and YIVO, 147
Winter, Tobke, 157
Wiskitki, 276
Wissenschaft des Judentums, 78
Włodawa, 293, 328
Wolski family, 362–65, 383–85
Wołyńska 23, 123
women: adaptation of, 242–44; courage of, 242–43, 251; and deportation, 308–309; employment of, 241–42, 243–50; feminism, 240; gender ratios, 241; and house committees, 122, 239–40, 242–43; Oyneg Shabes study of, 122, 178, 239–51, 449n39; Słapakowa's interviews, 243–50, 450n42; at Treblinka, 309–10; and "Two and a Half Years," 226
Workmen's Circle, 28
World History of the Jewish People (Dubnow), 178
World War I, 10, 119–20, 124
World Zionist Organization, 32, 33, 47
Wóycicki, Aleksander, 74
writers of the Oyneg Shabes Archive, 184–208; amateur writers, 184; Rachel Auerbach, 198–208; Peretz Opoczynski, 185–93; organization of Oyneg Shabes, 217; Shie (Yehoshua) Perle, 193–98
writing contests, 220, 226
Wysocki, Janusz, 362–63, 364, 384

Yedies, 293–94, 328
Yediot, 375
Yehudia, 25–26
Yerushalmi, Yosef Khaim, 11
Yiddish and Yiddishism: and Borochov, 22, 28, 29–30; in business, 156; and culture congresses, 42–43; in ghettos, 93, 95; and Hashomer Hatzair, 163; and IKOR, 116–18; and intelligentsia, 21; leadership of, 366; and libraries, 42; and Linder, 175; and LPZ, 28; and 1910 census, 21; and Opoczynski, 188; and Poalei

Tsiyon movement, 21; poetry, 316, 324; and political parties, 31, 44; and Rabinowitz, 161; reactions of Jews to, 194, 231; Ringelblum's devotion to, 39, 408n38; in Sanz, 23; and Schiper, 56; and scholars, 50–51; and Soviet Union, 229; and survival of Jews, 334; and territorialization, 44; theater productions in, 123; in Warsaw, 25; and Winter, 155; and YIVO, 39–42, 78 (*see also main entry for* YIVO); and Zbąszyń refugee crisis, 101–102
Yiddish Humanistic Gymnasium, 81
Yiddish PEN Club, 385
Yidishe Arbeter Froy (YAF), 240
Yidishe Folksbibliotek, 366
Yidisher Soykhrim Fareyn (Jewish Merchants Union), 155
Yidn fun a gants yor (Perle), 193
yishuv (Jewish Palestine), 28
YIVO (Yiddish Scientific Institute), 78–89; administration, 88; building, 79; conferences, 193–94; founding of, 49–50, 78; graduate program, 87, 88, 174–75; historical section, 81–82, 84–85, 86–88; as home for archive, 2, 218, 303, 333, 385–86; and Joint Distribution Committee, 90–91; journal, 64, 66, 156; and Landkentenish movement, 85–86; and Lewin, 170; and Linder, 174–75; and 1933 Congress, 82–84; and Orthodox Jews, 166; and Oyneg Shabes project, 147; and Rabinowitz, 161; and Ringelblum, 15, 39–42, 81–89, 156, 342; scholarship of, 9, 39–42, 79–81, 87, 418n118; and Weinreich, 78–81; and Winter, 156; and youth study, 240–41; and Yunger Historiker Krayz, 59
YIVO bleter, 64, 66, 156
yizker bikher (memorial books), 270
"Yizkor (Remember)" (Auerbach), 202–203
Young Historians Circle, 58–63, 81, 82

youth and youth movements: growth in, 240; and Jewish Fighting Organization, 295; and Oyneg Shabes, 151, 292; and *Payn un gvure* anthology, 152; presses, 214; response to Final Solution, 286, 293–94; role of, 162–65; of shtetlekh, 269, 270; and soup kitchens, 118; and "Two and a Half Years," 226. *See also specific groups*
Yugnt, 34–36, 37, 44, 46, 62–63
Yung Vilne, 212
Yungbor, 35–36
Yunger historiker, 52, 59–60, 63, 64, 69, 418n117
Yunger Historiker Krayz, 58–63, 81, 82

Zagan, Shakhne: and Aleynhilf, 119; and Anti-Fascist Bloc, 295; death of, 95, 336–37; and deportation, 335; on future of Jews, 232; and LPZ, 48; Oyneg Shabes material on, 366, 367–70; and Palestine, 47; and Perle, 194; relief work, 105, 117; and Ringelblum, 337, 356, 367–70, 473n149
Zaitchik, Sh., 85
Zakhor (Yerushalmi), 11
zamling and zamlers: Dubnow on, 51, 410n3; groups of, 41; and Landkentenish movement, 85; and research agendas and questionnaires, 149; and Ringelblum, 73; role in Oyneg Shabes, 9–10, 208; and YIVO, 9–10, 40, 156
Zamość, 292, 378
Zandman, Avraham, 355
Zbąszyń refugee crisis, 91, 100–102
Zbytkover, Shmuel, 67
Zduńska Wola, 300, 327
Żegota (Polish-Jewish Committee to Help Jews), 372, 383, 478n199
Zerubavel, Jacob, 33, 45, 46, 47, 104
Zhelichowski, Gerer Hasid Shlomo, 327, 330, 331
Zhitlovsky, Chaim, 43
ZIH (Jewish Historical Institute):

building, 116, 175; publication of "Khurbm Varshe," 198; retrieval of archives, 2, 150; and survivors' testimonies, 206
Zionism, 20–21; and Borochov, 29, 32; in Buczacz, 19; and Bund, 148; determinist (prognostic) Zionism, 32, 33; and future of Jews, 231; and gender roles, 240; and humanism, 230; and LPZ, 28, 47; and Oyneg Shabes, 292; and political parties, 44; voluntarist Zionism, 32, 33
Zionist youth movement, 34, 294, 295, 336
ŻKK (Jewish Coordinating Committee), 353
ŻKN (Jewish National Committee): and Auerbach, 199, 201; and Bermans, 360–61; and Oyneg Shabes, 334, 355; report on Great Deportation, 311; and ŻOB, 466n16
ZKOM (Jewish City Aid Committee), 114, 115, 425n89
ŻOB (Jewish Fighting Organization): accounts of resistance, 216; and Anti-Fascist Bloc, 295; arms, 158, 325, 356, 466n16; founding of, 165; and Krzepicki, 310; leadership of, 164; and LPZ, 150; Oyneg Shabes material on, 358, 458n42; preparations for resistance, 192, 294–95, 353–54; ranks of, 342; and Ringelblum, 342, 353, 354, 355; support of, 114, 158, 162, 311
Zonabend, Nachman, 443n6
ŻSS (Jewish Social Self-Help, Coordinating Committee), 114
ŻTOS (Jewish Society for Public Welfare), 114
Zuckerman, Yitzhak: on Anielewicz, 435n75; archive documents of, 216; on Breslav, 435n75; and Final Solution, 287, 292; and Gutkowski, 151, 153; and Jewish Fighting Organization, 165, 325; and Katzenelson, 330; and LPZ, 431–32n17; and resistance, 152, 336, 354, 356, 383,

474n160; and Ringelblum, 354, 432n22; and risks associated with archives, 222; underground work of, 361

Żydokummuna (Jewish-Communist cabal), 379

Żydzi w Polsce Odrodzonej, 67

ZZ (Department of Provisioning and Supply), 156, 157

ŻZW (Żydowski Związek Wojskowy), 28, 342, 353–54, 358, 456n11

HITLER'S WILLING EXECUTIONERS
by Daniel Jonah Goldhagen

Daniel Jonah Goldhagen reconstructs the climate of "eliminationist antisemitism" that made Hitler's pursuit of his genocidal goals possible and the radical persecution of the Jews during the 1930s popular. Drawing on a wealth of unused archival materials, principally the testimony of the killers themselves, he takes us into the killing fields where Germans voluntarily hunted Jews like animals, tortured them wantonly, and then posed cheerfully for snapshots with their victims. From mobile killing units, to camps, to the death marches, Goldhagen shows how ordinary Germans, nurtured in a society where Jews were seen as unalterably evil and dangerous, willingly followed their beliefs to their logical conclusion.

History/978-0-679-77268-2

IN MY HANDS
by Irene Gut Opdyke

In the fall of 1939 the Nazis invaded Irene Gut's beloved Poland, ending her training as a nurse and thrusting the sixteen-year-old Catholic girl into a world of horrors that somehow gave her the strength to accomplish what amounted to miracles. Brutally abused and left for dead by Russian soldiers, Irene escaped into German-occupied territory, where she was forced to work for the German army. Her Aryan features landed her a job in the relative safety of an officers' dining room. With access to food and supplies, as well as the dinner conversation of SS officials, Irene was able to smuggle nourishment and information to the Jews in the ghetto, transport work camp prisoners to a forest enclave, and ultimately hide a dozen Jews in the home of the Nazi major for whom she was housekeeper. A harrowing and deeply affecting story of resistance and an extraordinary memoir of one young woman's belief in humanity, *In My Hands* stakes an impressive claim as a contemporary classic.

History/978-0-385-72032-8

THE LAST SURVIVOR
by Timothy Ryback

In *The Last Survivor*, journalist Timothy Ryback explores the surprising—and often disturbing—ways the citizens of Dachau go about their lives in a city the rest of us associate with gas chambers and mass graves. A grandmother recalls the echo of wooden shoes on cobblestone, the clip-clop of inmates marched from boxcars to barracks under the cover of night. A mother-to-be opts to deliver in a neighboring town, so that her child's birth certificate will not be stamped DACHAU. An "SS baby," now middle-aged, wonders about the father he never knew. And should you visit Dachau, you will meet Martin Zaidenstadt, an 87-year-old who accosts tourists with a firsthand account of the camp before its liberation in 1945. Beautifully written, compassionate, and wise, *The Last Survivor* takes us to a place that bears the mark of Cain—and a people unwilling to be defined by the past, yet painfully unable to forget.

History/978-0-679-75826-6

MASTERS OF DEATH
by Richard Rhodes

In *Masters of Death*, Rhodes gives full weight, for the first time, to the Einsatzgruppen's role in the Holocaust. These "special task forces," organized by Heinrich Himmler to follow the German army as it advanced into eastern Poland and Russia, were the agents of the first phase of the Final Solution. They murdered more than 1.5 million men, women, and children between 1941 and 1943, often by shooting them into killing pits, as at Babi Yar. These massive crimes have been generally overlooked or underestimated by Holocaust historians, who have focused on the gas chambers. In this painstaking account, Pulitzer Prize–winning author Richard Rhodes profiles the eastern campaign's architects as well as its "ordinary"soldiers and policemen, and helps us understand how such men were conditioned to carry out mass murder.

History/978-0-375-70822-0

THE NUREMBERG INTERVIEWS
by Leon Goldensohn

During the Nuremberg trials, Dr. Leon Goldensohn—a psychiatrist for the U.S. Army—monitored the mental health of two dozen German leaders charged with carrying out genocide. These recorded conversations have gone largely unexamined for more than fifty years, until Robert Gellately—one of the premier historians of Nazi Germany—made them available to the public in this remarkable collection. Here are the interviews with the likes of Hans Frank, Hermann Goering, Ernst Kaltenbrunner, and Joachim von Ribbentrop—the highest ranking Nazi officials in the Nuremberg jails. Here too are interviews with lesser-known officials essential to the inner workings of the Third Reich. Candid and often shockingly truthful, *The Nuremberg Interviews* is a profound addition to our understanding of the Nazi mind and mission.

World War II/Holocaust Studies/978-1-4000-3043-9

VINTAGE AND ANCHOR BOOKS
Available at your local bookstore, or visit
www.randomhouse.com